B1xy/12

Jm

LUCIA JOYCE

LUCIA JOYCE

TO DANCE IN THE WAKE

CAROL LOEB SHLOSS

BLOOMSBURY

First published in Great Britain 2004
This paperback edition published 2005

Copyright © 2003 by Carol Loeb Shloss

Published by arrangement with Farrar Straus & Giroux LLC,
19 Union Square West, New York, NY 10003, USA

Owing to limitations of space, all acknowledgements for
permission to reprint previously published and unpublished
material can be found on page 561

The moral right of the author has been asserted

A CIP catalogue record for this book
is available from the British Library

Bloomsbury Publishing plc, 38 Soho Square, London W1D 3HB

ISBN 0 7475 7413 8
9780747574132

10 9 8 7 6 5 4 3 2 1

All papers used by Bloomsbury Publishing are natural,
recyclable products made from wood grown in well-managed forests.
The manufacturing processes conform to the
environmental regulations of the country of origin.

Printed by Clays Ltd, St Ives plc

Frontispiece: Lucia Joyce dancing in a costume she made herself for a
competition at the Bal Bullier in Paris, May 1929. Photographer unknown.

www.bloomsbury.com/carolloebshloss

TO ROB

But I, am I not a reminder of what you buried
in oblivion to build your world?

—LUCE IRIGARAY, *Elemental Passions*

CONTENTS

LUCIA JOYCE

INTRODUCTION
WHAT HAPPENED TO LUCIA JOYCE?

I. A FATHER, A DAUGHTER, AND THE WHOLE WIDE WORLD

Imagine a cacophony of voices. First came those who knew Lucia: I think that Lucia's mind is "deranged."[1] I ran into her on the Champs-Elysées and "had never seen her so pretty, so gay, so strangely tranquil."[2] "That anyone could call her insane seems to me . . . absurd."[3] "Evidently one is inclined to think that she is more confused than she actually is."[4] She was "the most normal of the family, tactful, with humor and good sense. A wonderful girl."[5] "It seems that L[ucia], by playing her part so well, has come to be dominated by it and is, in some respects, genuinely out of her wits."[6] "I did not at the time know that she liked to pose as having been insane, as your sister told me later she did."[7] "She walked . . . as if she owned the whole bloody world. . . . Her voice was lovely. It bubbled up as if from a deep country well. She had great scope to her."[8] "Nothing serious happened in Ireland. Everyone who saw Lucia there agreed that she was stronger and less unhappy. But she lived like a gypsy in squalor."[9] "Lucia . . . went completely mad, and had to be taken out in a straitjacket."[10] She should be "shut in and left there to sink or swim."[11]

Next came the voices of the doctors who examined her: "There is nothing mentally wrong with her now."[12] She's "not lunatic but markedly neurotic."[13] "There [is] not much the matter with the girl, and . . . whatever it [is], she [will] soon get over it."[14] Lucia is "schizophrenic with pithiatic elements."[15] "Forel said that after seven months he does not feel that he can write a diagnosis; he would not sign his name to a conclusive statement about her."[16] "He thinks she has made a steady improvement."[17] She's "catatonic."[18] She's neurotic. She has cyclothymia. "There's [emphatically] something to be saved."[19]

A generation later, the voices of the biographers chimed in: She was "a tortured and blocked replica of genius";[20] she was the "shadow of her father's mind."[21] Poor Nora. She had to care for a rude, violent daughter.[22] Everyone had a different opinion about what was wrong with Lucia Joyce. The label that stuck most often was "schizophrenia." But in one way or another she has sifted down through the years as the mad daughter of a man of genius.

But she was not mad in the eyes of her father. James Joyce disagreed with everybody, and in this disagreement lies the heart of the story told in this book. No matter what happened to Lucia, Joyce did not lose sight of the beauty and talent of his child; he saw the pathos and desperation of her life; he learned from her, and he refused to abandon her. To him she retained the qualities that he had seen in her at birth when he had associated her with Dante's Beatrice: "Once arrived at the place of its desiring, [the soul] sees a lady held in reverence, splendid in light; and through her radiance, the pilgrim spirit looks upon her being."[23] To him she was Lucia the light-giver, the "wonder wild." Thus whatever else we can say about Lucia Joyce now, so many long years after her death, we know that she was dearly loved. We know that she was greatly talented and that the story of her struggles, amid all its bitter contention, is one of the great love stories of the twentieth century.

It is also a story that will arouse debate. Reading this book is more akin to entering a labyrinth than to undertaking a windswept journey to a safe and easy harbor. Something was the matter with her, and in trying to identify the problem, Joyce and Lucia sometimes got lost; they took wrong turns; they wandered around, and then they would find the thread again and go on. They had helping figures; the help failed. They listened to advice; the advice proved futile. They went on, alone, and in the mind of the daughter their journey proved that she and her extraordinary father were stronger than all the doctors of Europe combined.[24] In the mind of the father, when he was near the end of his life, the lesson to be learned was that it's better to rely on your own wits. In 1937 Joyce wrote to Carola Giedion-Welcker, an old and trusted family friend, "keep clear of all the so-called mental and moral physicians."[25]

Neither father nor daughter knew that they were close to the truth. "Madness" isn't understood now; it was just as perplexing in Lucia's lifetime, and love can be a strong medicine in the face of uncertainty. In the 1930s, psychiatry was as newly and awkwardly modern as the ungainly books that made James Joyce famous. There were no uniform diagnostic categories, and as Eugen Bleuler, the teacher of several of Lucia's doctors, acknowledged, "with many patients, the number of diagnoses made equals the number of institutions they have been to."[26] In 1956, looking back on a life lived among many of the men and women most concerned to understand schizophrenia, Carl Gustav Jung was certain that "[w]e know far too little about the contents and the meaning of pathological mental products, and the little we do know is prejudiced by theoretical assumptions. This is particularly true of the psychology of schizophrenia."[27] The most honest of Lucia's doctors threw up their hands. Oscar Forel would not sign his name to a conclusive diagnosis.[28] Jung agreed that she was a most singular case.[29] Of what, then, did Lucia's "madness" consist?

In the meantime, amid all the turmoil about what happened to her in later life, an important part of Lucia's story got lost. People tended to forget that she, too, had been an artist, a dancer, who worked with a fervor and vision comparable to Joyce's own. From a young age, she had shown a marked aptitude for sport, for physical culture, for dance. She studied modern dance; she studied for the classical ballet; she joined a performing troupe; she toured Europe; she danced in a Jean Renoir movie; she entered competitions and claimed the attention of one of Paris's leading dance critics. In judging a contest in 1928, Charles de Saint-Cyr spoke of Lucia as a "very remarkable artist [with] totally subtle and barbaric" powers.[30]

By the time she was twenty-one, she was blazing with the same kind of discovery that had fueled the talents of performers like Mary Wigman and had convinced other young women of her generation that they were creating a new religion through the movement of their dancing bodies. The *Paris Times*, interviewing Lucia in 1928, noticed the Irish lilt in her voice and described her as "tall, slender, remarkably graceful, with brown bobbed hair, blue eyes and very clear skin." "She dances all day long, if

not with Les Six de rythme et couleur, studying under Lois Hutton and
Hélène Vanel then by herself. She never tires. . . . When she is not dancing, she is planning costumes, working out color schemes, designing
color effects." In the interviewer's judgment, Lucia had "Joyce's enthusiasm, energy, and a not-yet-determined amount of his genius." He predicted that "when she reaches her full capacity for rhythmic dancing,
James Joyce may yet be known as his daughter's father."[31]

But the attention that people later paid to Lucia's mysterious illness
came to eclipse the nature of her own desires and achievements, making
it seem as if her periodic outbursts of rage sprang up out of a blighted
spirit for no discernible reason. Joyce knew differently. Eventually he
came to see his daughter's talent, to recognize her calling, and to understand the fury that she directed at the world. Lucia faulted her mother
for discouraging her, her brother Giorgio for abandoning her, and, once
Ulysses was acknowledged to be one of the masterpieces of world literature, her father for overshadowing her. Kay Boyle, who befriended Lucia in Paris during the height of Joyce's fame, could also see that Lucia's
anger was specific and clearly directed. She remembered resentment as a
constant theme of her friend's youth: "Giorgio and Lucia were bitter
about their father, and agreed on the question of the crippling effect his
fame had on their lives," she wrote to Jane Lidderdale in early 1983.
"What a book could be written about their anguish!"[32] And then Boyle
wrote another letter to Richard Ellmann. "And now Lucia is dead . . . I
cannot help grieving for the beautiful, vibrant girl she was when we
studied dance together in Paris with Elizabeth Duncan, so many years
ago."[33]

What happened to that lively radiance? Joyce watched the growing
turbulence of his daughter's personal relationships in Paris. Lucia became the lover of Samuel Beckett, Alexander Calder, and other young
men of the expatriate community, the lesbian lover of Myrsine Moschos,
Sylvia Beach's assistant at Shakespeare and Company, and friend of
George Antheil, Darius Milhaud, and Kay Boyle. All of them commemorated her in their music and writing, but none of them re-created the
complexity of her character more eloquently than her father did.

To him she served as a dark muse, whose life he saw in tandem with
his own. Joyce considered Lucia to be wild, beautiful, and unsparingly
truthful. As he strove to understand the passions that seemed to rule her

conduct, he came eventually to see her as an unexpected but true heir to genius. In 1934 he wrote, "Whatever spark or gift I possess has been transmitted to Lucia and it has kindled a fire in her brain."[34] His friend Paul Léon, looking over Joyce's emotional shoulders, would soon repeat this claim, writing that Joyce had finally understood that it was "not to his son but to his daughter" that his "sparkle of gift" had been given. "Hence the feeling of responsibility, the remorse, the desire to still that spiritual thirst which he considers he set afire within her."[35]

A year later, in 1935, writing to Harriet Weaver, Joyce said that Lucia had a mind "as clear and as unsparing as the lightning. She is a fantastic being, speaking a curious abbreviated language of her own. I understand it or most of it."[36] His absorption in her fate colored the final years of his life, drawing him into the worlds of mime, dance, and surrealism and into reconsidering the performative nature of language as well as the fictional aspects of everyday life. Eventually, with her nervous breakdown in the 1930s, Lucia pulled him into the dark circles of psychiatric medicine in its early modern years. With the outbreak of World War II, he found himself engaged in a desperate struggle to outwit the bureaucracies of Vichy, German-occupied France, and Switzerland in a valiant but futile effort to save her from permanent institutionalization behind enemy lines.

To others—her mother Nora, her brother Giorgio, and many of the women who stood arrayed around her father—it was appropriate for Lucia to sacrifice her life for her father's art. They believed that Joyce was the sole genius in their midst whose talent had at all times to be protected and nourished. Paul Léon wrote letter after letter to Harriet Weaver in England, insisting that Mr. Joyce could not work unless he knew that his daughter was well taken care of. They arranged to get her out of Paris. They worried increasingly that Joyce, in his preoccupation first with Lucia's career and later with her mental illness, would not finish the fabulous, unwieldy, and often unfathomable *Work in Progress*— the book later called *Finnegans Wake*, which, even more than *Ulysses*, changed the face of modern literature in the West. In 1935 Paul Léon wrote to Harriet Weaver that "the illness of his child has acquired the dimensions of some enormous unfathomable moral or more correctly spiritual problem for him which he considers he must solve cost it what it may. Whatever the motives, affections, remorse, responsibility or anything else, this problem has overshadowed everything else and there is not a moment, a gesture, a thought during the day or the night which is not devoted some way or other to the solution of this problem."[37] As they understood it, it was their duty to keep this fabulous, unwieldy, and often unfathomable young woman quiet so that her father could have the peace of mind to write.

To Lucia's own friends, whose loyalties spanned seventy years, she was a victim. She was the price that had been paid for a book, the sacrifice made to male egocentrism, an expropriation exacted by a writer's drive for fame. They were angry that she was forced to live out the majority of her years imprisoned in institutions. When phenothiazine drugs were used to sedate her, they saw her as a medicated shadow of her former self. In 1980 Dominique Maroger, a friend of Lucia's Parisian youth, a fellow dancer who remembered her as a graceful performer and comical Charlie Chaplin impersonator, went to visit Lucia in England. It was clear to her that Lucia was only "killing time" in the genteel asylums that for thirty years had substituted for a home. "As in the legends of central Europe," she observed, "a woman was put into a bridge during its construction in order to ensure its preservation, her life was a supporting sacrifice for a novel."[38]

To Lucia herself, fused in a dark creative bond with her father, forging an identity from the habits of performance and from the silent kinetic communication that marked their mutual regard, Lucia was at first not so much a captive as a willing partner. Some, for want of a better word, labeled their relationship incestuous. Others, wanting to protect "genius" from "madness," strove to separate them, but Joyce and Lucia understood that their bond defied facile categories. Cary F. Baynes, Lucia's companion in Zurich in 1934, watched in amazement as Lucia dramatized her life in anticipation of its transfiguration into fiction. "Do you want new material for *Work in Progress*?" she would ask her father. "Maybe I can provide you with something new." At other times she would send him messages: "Tell him I am a crossword puzzle, and if he does not mind seeing a crossword puzzle, he is to come out [to see me]."[39]

Such scenes were part of an obscure channeling of creative energy and communicative behavior that few within the small circle of the Joyces' acquaintance could see or appreciate but that eventually found issue in *Finnegans Wake*. Toward the end of his life, when he spoke about

Lucia, Joyce used the language of mystery, as if pure intellection could puncture the darkness of circumstance. His daughter's illness presented him with life's greatest enigma. He struggled to understand not only the effect of his own character on Lucia but also the "wounding" influence of his work. That Lucia held sway over him was undeniable. For many years she had given both form and substance to his writing. But his own "waking" depended upon understanding something quite different: he had to see how his writing was implicated in her fate. As Jacques Mercanton, with whom Joyce often talked in Lausanne in 1938, observed, "In that night wherein his spirit struggled, that 'bewildering of the nicht,' lay hidden the poignant reality of a face dearly loved." Joyce hid nothing. He recounted the various diagnoses that she had been given; he was able to speak dispassionately about her wild escapades. With the *Finnegans Wake* manuscript in hand, he said, "Sometimes I tell myself that when I leave this dark night, she too will be cured."[40]

In some ways, you could say that this book also originated with "the poignant reality of a face," although in my case I was keeping faith only with a photograph. I had read about a certain image of Lucia but had never seen it, and I thought it likely that, like so many other documents of Lucia's life, it had been lost or thrown away. But Stuart Gilbert had saved a print, and some years ago I found it stashed in the back of one of the folders at the Harry Ransom Humanities Research Center in Austin, Texas.

Sometime around 1928, Berenice Abbott photographed Lucia doing her "will o' the wisp" dance. She was arrayed in a costume she had devised for herself, adorned head to toe in silver moiré "scales" like some phantasmagoric creature newly arrived from the deep. The woman in the photograph was inwardly focused, intense, and almost savagely beautiful. She had made her living body into a poetic image, and I could see why Charles de Saint-Cyr had described the power of her movement as "subtle and barbaric." I could see why Joyce had insisted that she was "a fantastic being." She reminded me of Nijinksy, of Pavlova, of Makarova. Here was energy and originality that could tear your heart out. Here was the legendary pearl of great price whose father, of all fathers on earth, was exquisitely equipped to recognize its value. And

I believed that James and Nora Joyce's biographers had got her story wrong.

By reconstructing the allure and complexity of Lucia Joyce's life, I hope to restore her, in our imaginations, to the place she held in her father's heart. I hope to see her life as it once was, whole and filled with promise. Hopes for oneself, especially in youth, die hard, and I am convinced that Lucia did not sink down inevitably or easily or with a bias that was fixed from birth. Hers is the story of a great struggle, and we are the ones who reap the comfortable rewards of her brutally honest conduct of life. She had what we can only imagine: a creative partnership with James Joyce.

This book is the story of that silent partnership, the tracing of affinities and lines of intensity, a meditation on the roles that fathers and daughters play in each other's lives, inciting flows of desire, excessive, singular, bordering on danger, but capable too of regenerating entire cultures. It is also the story of art's transposition into life and a study of the processes of making art. For those in his family, Joyce's writing was both a way of life, exacting in its demands in human attention, dedication, and energy, and an assertion of values that challenged bourgeois orthodoxy. Within the family, recognized as the one reader of Joyce's work, Lucia was sired as much by the realms of her father's imagination as by the habits of his workday. And if she incited her father to creativity, finding herself inscribed in his fiction as Milly, Issy, Isolde, Anna Livia Plurabelle, and the other avatars of the female adolescent, she also found reciprocal relationship with those characters. She used them to examine the mores of those around her and to mount her own challenge to the status quo. In this respect, she resembled Pearl, the errant daughter in Nathaniel Hawthorne's *The Scarlet Letter*: she refused to let anyone forget the extraordinary circumstances that created her. We can imagine her to be a kind of living writing, a Wakean "letter" that replicated in her very person Joyce's measured disregard for authority, his defiance of expectations, and his insistent drive to discover new modes of expression. Through her we watch the birth of modernism, not just as a series of texts but as a mode of daring, troubled, and troubling life.

In the end, Lucia's story poses several very simple but profound questions: What is the price of a child's life? What is the worth of a book? What is the relation between genius and "madness"? Joyce and Lucia lived out that relationship in ways that are poignant, original, and chillingly complex. Together they have a lot to teach us about resisting that exile that is often imposed on people who live in the wake of traumatic experiences or unruly emotions. Both of them dealt with homelessness by living in art. They met each other however they could: in Latin grammar books, in poems, in dances, and in songs they both knew in Italian, French, German, and English. But their lives and their abiding mutual loyalty tell us in a moving and compelling way that they found a common language.

II. THE REALM OF DECORUM: DISAPPEARING LETTERS

This is a story that was not supposed to be told. For all its inherent interest as a tale about the fate of talent in the world, for all its relevance to understanding Joyce's writing and its relation to the love he bore for his daughter, for all it has to tell us about the relationship between the arts of writing and dance, for all it forces upon us in the weighing of moral issues, Lucia's story has remained hidden away in trunks or kept locked in library archives for many years. Like Lucia herself, the evidence of what happened to her seemed to some people to be shameful or dangerous. It was something better left under lock and key, erased from records, and expunged from memory. This attitude developed even before the death of Joyce in 1941 and certainly well before the death of Lucia in 1982.

According to Maria Jolas, who knew the Joyces when they lived in Paris, Joyce and Nora were their own first censors. At the onset of war between Germany and Poland in September 1939, they began to pore over their own papers with a mind to saving some and destroying others. Joyce was at that time frantically reading proof for *Finnegans Wake*, trying to relocate Lucia in a clinic outside of Paris, and trying to plan for the safety of the rest of the family as well. With the threat of war, he didn't want to renew the lease on his flat on the rue Edmond Valentin; and in anticipation of moving, he "burned" many letters. Jolas observed that Joyce had sent hundreds of letters to Lucia in hospitals and "gave me a trunk-full [*sic*], asking me to dispose of them."[41] The fate of this trunk—what was in it and who could see it—has been contested almost since its existence came to light, as it did, for example, when Richard Ellmann began to write his monumental biography of James Joyce in 1952.[42]

When Ellmann first approached Maria Jolas to ask for her assistance in writing the biography, she was, it seems, immediately cooperative. She showed him the documents in her possession, but at the same time she swore him to secrecy. In September 1953 she cautioned him to "tell *nobody* that you have seen these papers, as knowledge of this act spread about might easily compromise their later availability. In *langage clair*, it is in my opinion very much to your advantage to 'let sleeping dogs lie.' "[43] Ellmann, in turn, assured Maria Jolas of his discretion and later reassured her when the subject of ownership of the trunk came to bother her. She had no intention of claiming the letters, she explained, but she worried about what would happen to them should either Giorgio or Nora rise out of their "prolonged apathy in connection with this material."[44] Stephen Joyce's increasing curiosity about his grandfather's estate also worried her. Four months later, she repeated her injunction to Ellmann: "be sure and keep really quite mum on the subject of the papers. Many would love to see them and I have no doubt that eventually they will be asked for by their logical owner even though his Mother gave them to me."[45]

Eventually, Maria Jolas admitted, "the trunkfull [*sic*] of documents rather burns my closet." Patricia Hutchins, preparing a book on *James Joyce's World*, went to visit Jolas and asked point-blank if she knew where Harriet Weaver's letters to Joyce were.[46] Jolas equivocated. Knowing that Giorgio and Stuart Gilbert, who was at work on the first collection of Joyce's letters, knew she had the trunk, she reasoned that the secret would soon be out. She wanted to get the trunk out of her life; what was Ellmann's opinion? "Do write," she asked, "for I am getting rather weary of the whole affair and the fact is that if Georgio [*sic*] were to die before it is settled (Stevie told me he almost did die last summer) it would be an awful mess. . . . No use to keep this letter. In fact, I suggest not."[47]

Ellmann sympathized but also worried about the trunk's contents. He advised Maria Jolas to microfilm the letters before handing them over, and he even offered to have Northwestern University reimburse her for the expense. If she wanted money for the collection, he also thought he could quietly engineer a private buyer for one of the American universities that took an interest in Joyceana. "Do please have them microfilmed first—George is sure to destroy or lose some of the stuff."[48] But Maria Jolas did no such thing. By the end of the year, she had persuaded Giorgio to take possession of the letters and had traveled to Zurich to give them to him.

At the time, Ellmann and Jolas's intrigue primarily concerned the publication of certain letters about Joyce and Nora's sex lives. The papers that seemed most controversial to them were apparently Joyce's letters to his would-be lover in Zurich, Marthe Fleischmann. Should they be made public? Should they be suppressed? What would their publication do to Joyce's image? The "hundreds of letters to Lucia" (and presumably from Lucia) that the Joyces had given into Jolas's keeping did not even come under discussion. Had Jolas already destroyed them? Or were they still intact but now in the hands of Giorgio Joyce? There is no way to answer this question, for when Giorgio took possession of the trunk, its contents were never again seen by anyone outside the Joyce family. We can notice, however, that the issue of destroying letters was very much on Maria Jolas's mind as early as 1939; for seemingly in preparation for writing a memoir of Joyce, she took notes on his final days at Saint-Gérand-le-Puy. Here, in abbreviated form, she listed under a "destroy immediately" category, "letter about Georgio" [*sic*] and, twice, "letters about Lucia."[49]

Along with Maria Jolas's decision to share documents with Richard Ellmann came a quite direct offer to assist him in any way she could. Over the years, this help was invaluable to Ellmann. In 1981, looking back over his groundbreaking work, he wrote in gratitude, "I want also to tell you again how deeply grateful I shall always be for your wonderful kindness to me over so many years. If it hadn't been for the famous trunk, and your decision that I should see its contents with or without other authorization, I should hardly have had the courage to press on with my biography. It enabled me to speak to Stanislaus and others from a position of strength."[50]

But Ellmann was not at a similar advantage with regard to Maria Jolas herself, and with her cooperation came a more subtle kind of influence, which she called "silent help": "I am very eager that you should write the best possible book and am more than ready to bring all the silent help I can towards its realization."[51] As Ellmann proceeded with his work, he learned that Maria Jolas was annoyed at Stuart Gilbert for not including her in the assembly of Joyce's letters. "I imagine he is determined that, if possible, I shall be excluded from preparation of the collection," she admitted in 1955.[52] Gradually, apparently hoping for more influence in other quarters, she revealed the critical assumptions she thought Ellmann should espouse. They were, of course, her own assumptions. She claimed, for example, that the most reliable version of history had to come from eyewitness accounts, and in this way she implied that she understood events better than he, a distant scholar, ever could: "in general I find that persons who were not there, and must reconstruct from documents, are sometimes tempted to lay the accent in the wrong place, as I felt you did in the chapter on friendship."[53] In 1959 she was even blunter. In January she wrote:

> I have asked myself if you haven't lived too intimately with James Joyce for several years now, for you seem not to like or even admire him any more. The old story in other words, of the forest and the trees. I must ask you, therefore, to bear patiently with me if, many times, in my notes, I have called you on this particular subject. In my opinion you should never let your reader forget that
>
> a. Here is undoubtedly the greatest literary genius of the xx Century
> b. Writing a completely original, much-combated book, after having already written two others that were much combated.
> c. Struggling against poverty, half-blind, and the increasing madness of his daughter, the increasing futility of his son.[54]

Having called the young Ellmann to task, she warned him to be cautious of other eyewitnesses. "But don't forget that you've talked to a lot of people, some of them rather little people, and that they seem to have tended to occasionally give themselves more importance than they had. It's only human too, that before the other's stature, which reduces their own, they should be inclined to *chercher la petite bête*."[55]

Maria Jolas seemed to discredit the testimony of other members of Joyce's Paris circle. When she learned, for example, that Sylvia Beach intended to publish her own account of the controversy surrounding the payment of royalties for *Ulysses*, she not only enlisted Ellmann's help in suppressing the "ugly story" but summed up the "birdlike Sylvia" as someone "incapable of generalizing about anything or—*osons dire?*—of consecutive thought."[56] When she heard that Ellmann had had dinner with Helen Kastor Joyce, Giorgio's ex-wife, in New York, she dismissed her: "Poor Helen! What a tragic thing to happen to so childish, so untragic a person!"[57] She did not hesitate to tell Ellmann that Sylvia Beach and Lucie Léon were "skeptical of your motives."[58] Even Nora did not escape her disparagement. She considered that Nora was "jealous of her because of what she fancied to be her [Jolas's] ascendancy over Joyce," and she asserted that "during the war Mrs. Joyce lost her precision of memory—her reports of the past are undependable."[59] When Frances Steloff, founder of the James Joyce Society at the Gotham Book Mart in New York, came up with the idea of giving Lucia a useful life outside an asylum, she too was labeled: "Borderline, I fear she is mixed up on many things."[60]

Maria Jolas also seemed skeptical about Ellmann's seeing Lucia herself. In October 1961, having just visited Frances Steloff in New York, Ellmann wrote a defensive letter to Jolas, saying "she [Steloff] disturbed me by saying you were upset at my having 'interviewed' Lucia. The word 'interview' is meaningless in connection with her, and if she chose to consider me as an interviewer, I would hope you would take the idea with some skepticism. . . . I encouraged her to talk so as to liven up the afternoon, but I expected no information, sought none, got none. Her situation inspired disinterested sympathy, and that is what I felt."[61] Maria Jolas insisted that Frances Steloff had misunderstood her: she "felt it [the visit] could only have given pleasure to Lucia."

In any event, Ellmann apparently encouraged Lucia to write a small essay about herself. She did so and entitled it "My Life," dating it 24 October 1961. This joined another essay, "The Real Life of James Joyce," as one of the two primary sources of Lucia's understanding of the salient features of her own life. She had prepared "The Real Life of James Joyce" in installments between November 1958 and July 1959, at the request of Sylvia Beach "to send to Professor Ellmann as he asked for it," and with the encouragement of Harriet Weaver, who translated it from Lucia's Italian and typed it.[62]

Maria Jolas's desire to shape Ellmann's portrait of Lucia ended neither with the interviews she granted Ellmann in 1953 and 1954 nor with the letters she wrote to him during that time, but with notes that she assembled in January 1959 about the completed draft of his manuscript. Her long series of comments and corrections were almost entirely about Lucia and her doctors. Some of her remarks were made to correct errors of fact. On page 815 of the typescript, for example, she told Ellmann that Lucia's "fit" on Joyce's fiftieth birthday had occurred "[n]o, not during

the party. This had happened at home." On page 864, she told him that
Dr. Macdonald, in England, "was not head of St. Andrews. He only sent
her there." But she also questioned Ellmann's personal conclusions about
Lucia. About page 818, she asked, "Are you sure that Beckett had 'more
than a casual interest' in Lucia?" On page 857, she asked again, "Are you
sure that Joyce said Lucia was a genius?" And she was apparently concerned to call attention to the strange implications of Lucia's conduct. On
page 852, for example, she commented, "This footnote is inaccurate. It
was much spookier than that. She [Lucia] sent a letter to Lucie Léon
with, on the back of the envelope, a note telling her to look under the
stamp. This was done. She had drawn a minute skeleton and a crutch,
crossed like a knife and fork. Then, around the rectangle, written so
tinily that it all fitted under the stamp, were the words: *'attention au
squelette et à la béquille'* if I recall rightly, in French. Alex Poniszowski's
[*sic*] twin brother died very suddenly shortly after this incident, and Alex
himself fell in a metro and broke his leg so that he had to walk on a
crutch." She ended by telling Ellmann that she thought that he had too
many "medical details of Lucia's illness" in his book.[63]

This denigration of other possible versions of Joyce and Lucia's past
had particular repercussions for later generations of people who wanted
to know what happened to Lucia Joyce. Simply by following the notes in
Richard Ellmann's biography, we can see that Maria Jolas's "silent help"
heavily influenced the image he painted of Lucia. In the same way that
Stanislaus Joyce became a secret sharer in shaping what we learn from
Ellmann of Joyce's Dublin youth and his years in Trieste, so Ellmann's
decision to trust Maria Jolas—as opposed to, say, Joyce himself, or Joyce's
sister, Eileen Schaurek, or Lucia's own friends, or all of them together—
has colored the historical record.[64] Ellmann, it seems, was well aware of
the possible pitfalls of his method of working. In 1946, long before he began to write the biography, he told Ellsworth Mason, "You can't work on
a man so recently dead without being a constant prey of his friends' mis-
conceptions."[65] But we can still see that a book with claims to using an
impartial method of narrating relies quite heavily on what we can instead call "personal-acquaintance criticism."[66]

As a result, for almost a half-century, we have lived with the image of
Lucia Joyce as a scapegoat. Her madness is portrayed as a kind of autonomous, self-evident state of being that was separated from the cir-

cumstances that might have generated disequilibrium. Lucia, in this perspective, was too disruptive; she got in the way; her father couldn't write with her around and her mother couldn't think. How sad, but violent people often have to be put away. Because Lucia was mad, Nora became a victim, whose impatience and anxieties were justified, and Joyce himself was a kind of loving and indulgent dupe—"fond and foolish," like King Lear raging upon the heath. His thoughts are devoted "frantically and impotently to his daughter."[67] In Ellmann's hands, Joyce becomes similar to what he was in Maria Jolas's hands: someone who needs to be rescued from his own lack of insight into the dynamics of his immediate family.

During the same years when Ellmann was preparing his biography, Stuart Gilbert was working on the first collection of Joyce's letters.[68] His book, which came out in 1957, presented him with a slightly different set of problems, but they too required him to make choices in regard to letters to, from, or about Lucia. As he explained in the introduction, "The letters on this subject published in the present volume represent only a tithe of those in which, writing to members of his family or trusted friends, he [Joyce] records his hopes and fears."[69]

Gilbert's first challenge was simply to assemble what letters he could. Eileen Schaurek, Lucia's aunt, was at first reluctant to contribute anything, but according to Harriet Weaver, she was eventually persuaded by Patricia Hutchins to loan Gilbert Joyce's letters. She had two sets of letters in her possession: letters from Joyce to her about Lucia's fateful stay in Ireland in 1935, and letters Joyce wrote to Lucia during the same time period. She sent both to Harriet Weaver, and as they were all written in Italian, Miss Weaver translated them into English. "I deciphered and translated the Italian original so far as I could (which wasn't so very far), then called in the help of a young man, now in Oxford who had been for three and a half years with the British consul in Italy. . . . I finally appealed again to the professor of Italian in Oxford, Professor d'Entreves, who quickly elucidated them. He said he *must* see the proofs when ready."[70] Miss Weaver left Gilbert to decide which ones to include. Of the eleven letters addressed to Lucia in the published volume, six are from Eileen Schaurek's loan. Gilbert let Professor d'Entreves's translations stand, but he cautioned his readers: "The letters to Lucia Joyce, especially, are written in an allusive, familiar, often playful style; there was in fact a sort of 'little language' (in the Swiftian sense) which Lucia and her father used between themselves."[71]

Gilbert then learned from Patricia Hutchins, on whom he relied for locating other letters, that a collection of letters about Lucia's brief visit to London in 1935 had already been destroyed. On 8 August 1949, she reported, "When I called about Mrs. Charles Joyce's letters—after two previous attempts to find the family in—I had a great shock on being told that her son had recently burnt all—letters, first editions of *Ulysses, Finnegans Wake* and other books." When she mentioned to the son that the letters and papers had historical value, he (Lucia's cousin) replied, " 'oh I am satisfied in my mind about what I have done.' "[72] And that was that.

Gilbert's last primary resource for letters connected with Lucia was Harriet Weaver herself. Although she left some matters of selection to Gilbert, she did not grant him that license with her own correspondence. She sent him no originals, but only typed copies with numerous ellipses to indicate where she had made abridgements. She also went through sixteen photostats of letters to Giorgio that had been sent to her by Robert Kastor (Giorgio's brother-in-law). "I stumbled through them my-self to select the three that seemed to be of the most general interest, dis-carding the ones . . . that had intimate details about Lucia or about family matters."[73] In November 1949, she apparently had second thoughts about what she had done and wrote to Gilbert "about deletions I made, or suggested making, in some of the letters to me. . . . And per-haps some of the passages about Lucia that I had deleted or suggested deleting, might also be retained as the fact of her illness seems to be widely known now and they throw light on Mr. Joyce's very great affec-tion and solicitude for her."[74] Since Miss Weaver was Joyce's literary ex-ecutor, Gilbert had no choice but to acquiesce in heeding her decorum, but judging from his introductory note, we can imagine that he shared many of her scruples. "It has been a difficult task," he wrote, "deciding which of the more intimate letters should be published. Undoubtedly there is something slightly repellent in the modern habit of probing into the private lives of great creative artists and interpreting the facts un-earthed in terms of the now fashionable psychology."[75] In his notes about his editing, the first thing he explained was the dots that indicated omis-sions. "Some of these omissions have been made at the request, always for valid reasons, of those to whom the letters were addressed. Others have been made by the editor . . . for the most part these affect passages relating to personal and private matters, of no general interest."[76] Of the many letters from Joyce to Lucia that Harriet Weaver sent him, Gilbert chose only three from July and September 1935. Thus he too became a gatekeeper of Lucia's story.

By far the most monumental task of selecting what information about Lucia became part of the public record belonged to Harriet Weaver. Not only was she the literary executor of Joyce's estate, but she was also Lucia Joyce's legal guardian. As Joyce's publisher, patron, and friend of long standing, she had been corresponding with the Joyces from 1914 until Joyce's death, sometimes directly with family members and sometimes through Paul Léon, who came to be Joyce's amanuensis in Paris around 1930. Sometime in the late 1940s, even before Gilbert agreed to edit a volume of Joyce's letters, she had begun the arduous task of sorting out Joyce's correspondence with her. She decided which of the letters she was prepared to see published in whole or in part and began to type them in triplicate.[77] Once he received the letters that Miss Weaver agreed to include in his collection, Gilbert immediately saw that she had given him one of the book's two most valuable resources about Joyce's life. (The other was Frank Budgen's collection.) In October 1950 he met with her in Paris and asked her whether the omissions were necessary. "Yes," Miss Weaver replied. She had two principles: to avoid hurting anyone's feelings, and to protect the Joyce family's privacy.[78]

Gilbert of course respected Harriet Weaver's wishes, but the same issue remained with regard to her collection of Joyce letters as a whole, especially when she began to consider which library should receive her bequest. Her own first choice was the National Library of Ireland in Dublin. In her mind, Joyce would always belong to the Irish, and she thought that Ireland would be the appropriate repository of her many *Finnegans Wake* manuscripts as well. She reckoned, however, without the very decided opinions of Joyce's widow. Nora did not want the country that had denied her husband's body a final resting place to claim his intellectual remains. Miss Weaver let the matter rest until she heard from Giorgio that Nora was on her deathbed. Being the kind, scrupulous, and thoughtful person she was, she could not refuse the wish of a dying woman; and so it was that the British Museum in London became home to the Harriet Weaver papers. Miss Weaver died on 14 October 1961, leaving an injunction that the letters could not be opened until ten years after her death. Until 1971, then, the only available images of Joyce and Lucia's lives were filtered through Harriet Weaver's deletions.

Since the Weaver papers were still closed when Richard Ellmann edited the second and third volumes of Joyce's letters, published in 1966, he could not expand our knowledge of Lucia with information from the British Museum any more than Stuart Gilbert could in 1957. But in the subsequent 1,136 letters he included, a slight picture of Lucia as a girl with a restless talent and a troubled heart does emerge. The curiosity of Ellmann's impressive collection concerns the issue of privacy—not about Lucia but about the letters Joyce wrote to Marthe Fleischmann in Zurich and to Nora during his trips to Ireland in 1909 and 1912.

The question of how to deal with some of these "obscene" letters, so explicit in their sexual detail, had arisen when Ellmann was preparing his biography, and he and Maria Jolas had discussed the matter quite explicitly. But now the question of the letters' legal status arose as well. Harriet Weaver had understood that the decision about whether to publish them rested in her hands, and she had sought clarification about her prerogatives from her lawyers even back when Gilbert had been editing the first volume of letters. In 1954 she had told Gilbert, "Two or three weeks ago I heard from Mr. Monteith, writing on behalf of Mr. Eliot, that Mr. Monro (who had reported to the firm that the right of veto conferred on Mrs. Joyce in the contract was a purely personal one, not passing on to her son), had told them he expected to be paying a visit to Switzerland towards the end of the year and would try to see George Joyce and have a good talk with him." Although she had been left Joyce's custodian "in all matters relating to his writing (in which apparently letters are included)," and although she had been informed that Joyce's son had no legal rights in publishing decisions, she told Gilbert that she would be reluctant, on moral grounds, to overrule Giorgio's wishes about what should be printed.[79]

Her own position was clear, however. According to her goddaughter, Jane Lidderdale, Harriet Weaver "would have favored publication because she was opposed to censorship and to inviting piracy by suppression."[80] Ellmann was of a similar mind. He wanted to publish the whole lot. "The editor has sought to publish all the letters in their entirety," he said in the preface to volume two, "for a new generation does not con-firm the privacy of a dead author's conjugal life." Despite these bold stances, we can presume that some compromise had to be struck, for the book went to press with two letters omitted and lines deleted from eight letters in the remaining sequence.[81]

It is curious that Ellmann claimed in the same preface that "most of Joyce's letters have evidently been saved,"[82] for he knew that Maria Jolas had disposed of "hundreds of letters to Lucia." His two volumes of ed-ited letters, while seeming to uphold the principle of publishing all let-ters in their entirety, were in fact based upon a knowing exclusion of documents about Lucia and Joyce's relationship. In 1975, on the eve of Giorgio's death on 12 June 1976, Ellmann finally got his wish to print all of Joyce's naughty letters to Nora in a new one-volume *Selected Letters*, but nothing was said about the continued censorship of Lucia.

Miss Weaver's attitude was also notable. Having justified the publica-tion of letters to Nora, comprising highly charged sexual fantasies, on the grounds that all censorship was bad, she nonetheless continued to censor Lucia's letters. Jane Lidderdale understood this seeming paradox to be founded upon another principle: "The letters about Joyce's relationship to his wife were germane to Joyce's work; letters about Lucia's behavior were not."[83]

Harriet Weaver presumed a difference that needed to be proved. As we shall see, the figure of the daughter assumed more and more weight in Joyce's writing. It carried such an intensity of interest for the creator of *Finnegans Wake* that the Rainbow girl character became united in imagi-nation with Lewis Carroll's Alice, with Daddy Browning's "Peaches," and with Wagner's Isolde, all of them bearing the cultural burdens that late Victorians and early Moderns placed upon the figure of the younger woman, the "it" girl, the flapper, the young ingenue and her cross-generation relation with older men. In retrospect it becomes clear that Miss Weaver, acting in all good faith, based her decisions about censor-ing Lucia on what she did not know.

The subject of missing letters about Lucia continued to haunt the various projects of publishing Joyce. Donagh MacDonagh, in reviewing volumes two and three of *James Joyce's Letters*, remembers the mysterious disappearance of other letters at still earlier times: "There are many, many distressing letters from Joyce about Lucia, but some of the most distressing of all appear to have disappeared forever. These were letters which John Dulanty, who had been our High Commissioner in London, showed to me, in which Joyce bitterly reproached himself for her condition. I can't remember how many letters there were, perhaps half a dozen, but shortly afterwards there was a burglary at Dulanty's house and among the property stolen were Joyce's letters—surely a very odd choice for a thief."[84]

Given Harriet Weaver's stance against the suppression of documents, the opening of her archive in 1971 brought its own series of surprises. As Mary Reynolds, who did an excellent early survey of what was in the British Museum, learned, "the amount of material in his [Joyce's] letters that was withheld by Miss Weaver is about equal in bulk (especially when the count includes the letters destroyed) to the amount of correspondence she released."[85] We can imagine the struggle that this amazing "50 percent withheld" figure represents. It suggests a conflict in the many and complicated roles Miss Weaver played in the lives of the Joyce family. It suggests a woman's bold intellectual principles clashing with her desire to protect the family's privacy, her duties as literary executor conflicting with the obligations of friendship. Perhaps this censorship also shows us that Miss Weaver's goodness did not lift her above the realm of ordinary human emotions and that she lived with guilt and a need to hide it. Jane Lidderdale was convinced that her godmother suffered from a lingering sense that somehow, in the matter of Lucia, she had failed the people and the creativity she had most vowed to serve.[86]

The eight volumes of letters donated to the British Museum are punctuated with Miss Weaver's notes indicating that she had destroyed "many letters" written at various times.[87] One envelope says, for example, "I destroyed on July 5, 1946 this long letter of 6 February 1932." Another note, headed May 1933–December 1933, says, "Many written by Mr. Léon on Mr. Joyce's behalf largely about Lucia. I destroyed most of these in 1945. I was in Paris in February 1933 for 10–12 days, Lucia then to be sent to Switzerland. And in Paris again for a short while at the end of April or May" (vol. 8, folio 8). As Mary Reynolds notes, the last of Miss Weaver's own notes says, "I was in Paris for a fortnight from late in November to December 12, 1936. I never saw Mr. Joyce again" (vol. 8, folio 110).[88]

The one exception to this pattern seems to have come about from the valiant efforts of Joyce's friend Paul Léon. A Russian Jew living in Paris, he quite literally risked his life to save the papers, books, and documents that the Joyces had been forced to leave behind in May 1939 when they fled the Nazi occupation of Paris and went to Saint-Gérand-le-Puy. At the beginning of the German invasion, Léon and his wife, Lucie, had also gone to Saint-Gérand-le-Puy; but with their money diminishing and all of their own belongings still in their flat on the rue Casimir Périer, they sought and eventually received travel permits to return to Paris. They could not have foreseen that this move would cost Léon his life. Yet before he was found out and interned, Léon succeeded in rescuing the most valuable items of Joyce's literary estate.

Léon arrived back in Paris on 4 September 1940 and immediately turned his attention to Joyce's affairs. The first thing he did was to gather the important papers and documents in his own possession and put them in a brown suitcase. He separated out his own correspondence with Joyce and put these letters in nineteen large envelopes with instructions that, should he die, the letters were bequeathed to the National Library of Ireland. Lucie Léon (later calling herself Lucie Noël) remembered that he took the envelopes personally to Count O'Kelly, then head of the Irish Legation in Paris, and asked him to transfer them to Dublin. His plan was to get the letters out of the country while the French government remained in the hands of the Nazis, but the letters apparently stayed safely in Paris until they were transferred to Ireland in 1946.[89]

Léon's efforts on behalf of the Joyces did not stop there. The owner of the Joyces' flat in the rue des Vignes in Passy decided in their absence to auction off all of the family's possessions in lieu of the rent that was owed to him. Learning of this intention, Léon braved discovery by the landlord and by the Gestapo to rescue what he could. Paying off the concierge, he and a handyman made two trips to the rue des Vignes, filling a pushcart with first editions and papers. Then on 7 March 1941, when the auction was held at the Salle Drouot, he bid for the other books that had remained behind. Alec Ponisovsky, an old flame of Lucia's from the early 1930s, was, in an odd twist of fate, the only person in the Joyce circle with enough money to bid at the Salle Drouot auction. He gave Léon twenty or twenty-five thousand francs for the bidding, and Léon came away satisfied that he had once more intervened in time. He had bought all of what he considered the most valuable items, with the exception of the first book that Lucia ever illustrated: a deluxe edition of her father's poems, *Pomes Penyeach*.

The Léons catalogued everything carefully and divided their new acquisitions for safekeeping between a lawyer and a personal friend. By 1942 only one item of Joyce's, another suitcase similar to the one in the care of Maria Jolas, remained, and the Léons, already subjected to three Nazi raids of their home, were increasingly worried about keeping anything themselves. Lucie Léon finally persuaded another lawyer, Maître Gervais, to store everything else in their possession.[90]

Paul Léon was subsequently interned at the Gestapo's prison camp in Drancy. He was killed sometime in early April 1942. In 1946 Count O'Kelly sent Léon's nineteen envelopes of correspondence to Ireland. Léon had dealt with the issue of sensitive material, particularly about Lucia, not by destroying the historical record but by imposing a waiting period on it, one sufficiently long to ensure that those discussed would no longer be living. He stipulated that the letters should not be opened for fifty years (1990).

By 1949 Maria Jolas had retrieved the letters, books, and manuscripts given into the keeping of Maître Gervais for storage. Together with Patricia Hutchins, she planned to organize an exhibition and sale of these items for the financial benefit of Nora Joyce. The exhibition took place at the La Hune Gallery in Paris from 8 to 25 October 1949.[91] When no firm bidder for the material, which Nora Joyce wanted to sell as a single collection, came forward, Patricia Hutchins, with Harriet Weaver's help, organized a second exhibition, held at the Institute of Contemporary Arts in Dover Street, London, in June 1950. Finally the State University of New York at Buffalo came forward with a $10,000 bid. Thus the remainder of Paul Léon's heroic salvaging efforts came to rest in an American university in upstate New York.[92]

Among the papers saved at Buffalo, at the risk of life, was a meager collection of Lucia's dance programs, copies of newspaper interviews of her, copies of the magazine published by her dance teachers, Lois Hutton and Hélène Vanel, photographs of Lucia dancing, a postcard collection of dancers whom Lucia admired, original artwork with the comments of her teachers on the back, and a music notebook, the record of voice lessons, with scores by Pergolesi and Brahms. Here at last was the first glimpse of the second generation of creativity in the Joyce family.

When the James Joyce–Paul Léon papers were opened to the public in 1992, it seemed finally as if another door to the secrets of the past might be opened. But here again, in another generation, the old problems recurred. Lucia's nephew, Stephen Joyce, decided that his aunt's story was a private one, of no interest to the reading public, and prevailed upon the National Library of Ireland to give him access to the collection before it was opened. There are two assessments of his right to do this, one offered by Lucie Léon and the other by Patricia Donlon, director of the library. According to Lucie Léon, her husband stipulated that the nineteen envelopes consisted of "private correspondence between James Joyce and Paul Léon. In the event of my death I bequeath these letters to the Dublin Library. They are not to be opened before fifty years from now (1990). Only the immediate family of James Joyce and his literary executors may have access to these letters, when necessary."[93] The catalogue to the Léon papers claims also to quote from the statement accompanying Léon's envelopes, but it is a slightly different statement. "This is the property of Paul Léon, 27 rue Casimir, Paris. To be returned to him at his request. In case of death to be handed to Mr. James Joyce. In case of both being dead to be deposited with the Public Library of Ireland or the British Museum to be made accessible for literary use fifty years after Mr. Joyce's death; directions to be sought at present from Mr. C. Curran and at any time agreement of Mr. Joyce's family."[94] In one case, Joyce's descendants could look at Léon's papers but not alter them; in the other they presumably had the right to withhold their presentation to the public. Whatever the wording of Léon's bequest, the director of the library chose to abide by Stephen Joyce's wishes and allowed him to take certain items from the collection.

In some cases, it is possible to identify what was taken. There seem to have been two rounds of activity: one before the catalogue was printed—in which case there is no record of letters or documents unless they were mentioned or described elsewhere. We can, for example, use a list that Harriet Weaver compiled for Richard Ellmann on 20 February 1958 to infer such a loss. In her list, she itemized seventeen letters written to her by Paul Léon between 1934 and 1939 and asked Ellmann if he wanted to use them for his biography.[95] In checking for copies of the seventeen letters in the Léon archive (Léon was in the habit of typing carbon copies of his correspondence), we find that thirteen of them are missing.[96] The second round must have occurred later, for in these cases the catalogue itself describes the library's holdings, but the items are not on the microfiche. For example, letters written on 12 July 1934; 25 October 1935, [?5 September 1936]; 31 July 1933; 11 August 1933; 26 February 1935; 21 February 1936 and 23 February 1936 are gone.

As important as these omissions from the archives are, in one way the deletions are beside the point. They take our attention away from the fact that an archive of some one thousand items contains no letters by Lucia, even though they were clearly the ones that Joyce most valued. "I am grateful for your letters," he wrote to Harriet Weaver in 1935, "but the only ones which enlighten me, even if they are wild, are Lucia's own."[97] Ten years after Lucia's death in 1982, the story that "enlightened" her father still remained buried.

There were signs along the way that this might happen. In a long letter of December 1954, Maria Jolas told Ellmann that Stephen Joyce (whom she called Stevie) had been to see her and that he was "anxious to get his hands on the famous trunk, not to mention, eventually, the management of the literary executorship. I was a little taken aback when I realized this and could only be grateful that not only Miss Weaver but Georgio himself are still there to stand between any such arrangement."[98]

After Harriet Weaver and Giorgio Joyce had died, after they were no longer there "to stand between any such arrangement," and shortly before Lucia's death, Peter du Sautoy, then a trustee of the James Joyce estate, wrote a lengthy letter to Stephen Joyce explaining his legal and financial situation with regard to the estates of James Joyce, his father Giorgio, and his aunt Lucia. Du Sautoy explained how the trustees had arrived at their decision to grant publication rights, and he explained that Maria Jolas's trunk—or as he preferred to call it, "the box"—belonged legally to the trustees of Giorgio Joyce's estate. This signaled the beginning of a lengthy negotiation for possession of the "famous trunk" and the beginning of Stephen Joyce's public animosity toward Richard Ellmann and anyone connected with publishing Nora's love letters. At a 1984 Joyce symposium in Frankfurt, he stared at Ellmann and said, "Intimate very personal private letters, which were never meant for the public eye, have been sold, pirated and published. I condemn and deplore this intolerable shameless invasion of privacy, as would my grandparents, were they standing beside me here today."[99] By December of that year, he had won a settlement with the estates of James and Giorgio Joyce, and the "famous trunk" was finally given to him.[100] And the trunk brought in its wake, as if history were some inexorable circle, the issue of Lucia.

There the competing claims of privacy and access to historical records stood until the summer of 1988, when to my own surprise I became part of the story. In that year, Brenda Maddox, whom I had met in Frankfurt in 1984, was about to publish her excellent biography of Nora Joyce. In anticipation of this event, I had invited her to join me in speaking about biographies of the Joyces at a symposium in Venice in June 1988. I also invited Stephen Joyce to speak and was looking forward to discussing how Brenda's new book might change our view of James Joyce. The idea of reversing roles and looking at a famous man through the eyes of his wife seemed a shrewd, interesting, and important one. The only puzzling aspect of this panel discussion was the secrecy Stephen Joyce imposed upon it. In my correspondence with him, he instructed me to tell no one that he was coming. He was not, he said, certain that he could attend, but come or no, he didn't want his name on the program. I rather assumed that he would not show up, but as a young scholar, I was grateful to him for considering my invitation. Then a few days before my own departure, he telephoned to confirm the time and place of the panel discussion. He had something to say.

When I arrived in the Venice airport, a friend who had come to Venice by way of London greeted me. "Hey, Carol, what do you think of this?" he asked, thrusting the headlines of a London newspaper under my nose. I looked and was informed that Stephen Joyce had just announced to the literary world that he had destroyed his aunt Lucia's letters to him and had also persuaded Samuel Beckett to do the same. That evening the little drama continued to unfold. Participants at the symposium were buzzing with the gossip that concerned our small focused world. I learned that there had been some kind of problem with the publication of Brenda Maddox's Nora Joyce biography. In return for gaining permission to quote from Joyce material in the main body of the text, she had been required to delete an epilogue she had written about Lucia. The book was already in galley proofs. There was some kind of private settlement. She wasn't allowed to talk. She wasn't coming to the conference. Stephen Joyce wasn't coming.

I felt as if I had walked into a small disaster zone; and even at this early point I could see that Lucia was once again the sacrifice for an approved image of Joyce and Nora. The anticipated pleasures of our panel discussion were ruined. But as I continued to speak to people, I slowly came to sense that I could guess at Stephen Joyce's intentions more than they could. "He's coming," I finally told the president of the Joyce Foundation. And come he did, using my panel as a platform to inform the Joyce world that he had taken things into his own hands. Later in a newspaper interview granted to the *New York Times*, he explained, "I didn't want to have greedy little eyes and greedy little fingers going over them. . . . My aunt may have been many things, but to my knowledge she was not a writer."[101] As I was later to discover, Lucia had been a writer of both poems and a novel of her own.

In the audience that day in Venice sat Mary de Rachewiltz, the daughter of the American poet Ezra Pound. At the question-and-answer period, she arose, identified herself, and pleaded, "Please, Mr. Joyce, don't destroy anything"; and she told a moving story about going to St. Elizabeth's Hospital, the asylum where her father had been interned for thirteen years. In all that time she had been plagued by doubts. What was going on? Was he a political prisoner? Had his mind been deranged? Only the truth could console her, and when she found it settled quietly in the loops and curves of the doctors' handwritten reports, she had breathed in relief. Her father had not been considered "mad."

Sitting not far from Rachewiltz was a slender, quietly dressed man who asked to be acknowledged. He too went to the microphone and began to speak. "My name," he told the assembled company, "is Michael Yeats. I am the son of the Irish poet William Butler Yeats." To me it seemed as if poetic justice had just flown in through the windows and spread its wings. Knowing the anger that Stephen Joyce harbored against the publishers of his grandmother's letters, I anticipated that he would find it difficult to listen to any argument about censorship posed by a scholar. But here, seemingly provided by fate, were two of the only people in the world who might intercede out of compassionate knowledge of his position as a descendant of a famous modernist writer. And both of them urged him to delete nothing from the historical record. Their parents were part of the world's heritage, said Michael Yeats. By virtue of their extraordinary talent, they no longer belonged, in a simple way, only to their children.

Stephen Joyce seemed to remain unconvinced, and the following week, when I visited him and his wife, Solange, in their Paris apartment, they served me afternoon tea, in the best tradition of Nora Joyce. He continued to uphold his position; he was both fervent and adamant. "Where do you draw the line?" he had asked in his *New York Times* interview.

III. AN EXPERIMENT IN BIOGRAPHY

The destruction of so much evidence in Lucia's story made me think at first that it would be impossible to write a continuous narrative about her life. I had come to Paris in 1988 with a much more modest goal: I wanted to find out more about Lucia and the dance. Equipped with a simple list of Lucia's dance teachers that Richard Ellmann had once assembled, I went first to the Bibliothèque de l'Opéra and then to the Rondelle Collection at the Bibliothèque de l'Arsenal. I found records of Lucia's ensemble group and their performances at each place; I found records of Lucia herself; I found folders about the artists she had studied with. The wan image I had of her began to shift. She was no longer simply the appendage of a famous father but someone whose own pursuit of art had left a shadowy record. I wrote about Lucia; I wrote about the dance and its relation to the writing of Joyce; and still she remained like the will-o'-the-wisp of her own choreography: someone just beyond reach. But she haunted me all the same, the way Nietzsche seemed haunted by the figure of the dancer in *Thus Spoke Zarathustra*, when he wrote: "One thirsts for her and is not satisfied, one looks at her through veils, one snatches at her through nets."[102] Murray Beja, the president of the James Joyce Foundation, read the manuscript I had compiled about Lucia's creative life and asked if I might write a full biography. I decided to try. It meant, I knew, writing against the grain of received and indeed almost canonized images and around the problems posed by several generations of censorship.

The Achilles' heel in this suppression was money or at any rate the traces money leaves. Many of the opinions of Lucia's doctors had been suppressed, but a trail had been left in medical bills that Paul Léon had saved. Somehow these financial records had escaped the "editing" of his Dublin papers. These bills, along with the copious notes that Richard Ellmann took about the material in the "famous trunk," have provided the scaffolding for the second part of my book. Without them I doubt that the second half of Lucia's life could have been reconstructed at all. These records gave me exact dates and names of doctors; and the amazing collection at the National Library of Medicine at Bethesda, Maryland, let me discover who these doctors were and how they looked at the practice of psychiatric medicine in the 1930s. Because we no longer have all the diagnoses of Lucia, we are sometimes left to infer that she was treated as patients were supposed to be treated according to these doctors' own clinical manuals. I have not tried to reanalyze Lucia in light of later or presumably better psychoanalytic theories. I have tried instead to place her in her own time, to recontextualize her life in the history of medicine, in the sexual ethics of her own generation, in the world of the performing arts in Paris, and in the ideologies of the physical culture movement that were so decisive to her and in the rise of the National Socialist youth movement.

At a certain point, doubts arose. Should I stop writing? Were there any ethical issues that I was conveniently not heeding? Lucia was not around to ask, but I did write to Jane Lidderdale, Lucia's former guardian, who, sadly, was on her own deathbed. Did she think that Lucia wanted her story to be told? Yes, but not in a silly or prurient way, Lidderdale replied via her niece, Hester Hawkes.[103] And so I persisted.

At a later point, I began to realize that, even among the people most instrumental in generating the images of Lucia as a mad woman, lingering doubts remained. After his biography of Joyce had been published, Richard Ellmann, for example, continued to write to various people in the Joyce circle, asking them quite explicitly if there had been any signs of madness when they knew Lucia. Kay Boyle said no; William Bird said no; Myron Nutting said no; George Anthiel said no. As friends from Lucia's youth gradually emerged—initiating contact with and identifying themselves to Ellmann after they read his book—the picture became even more complicated. Dominique Maroger (Dominique Gillet when Lucia knew her) said no, Lucia had been a bright, eager young woman, and then she wrote a kind of counternarrative about Lucia as she remembered her: dancer, mime, published poet, writer of her own novel; it appeared in Editions de l'Herne's book about Joyce in 1985. Hélène Vanel, one of Lucia's dance teachers, did the same thing. Margaret Morris, another dance teacher, remembered Lucia in her autobiography and in her letters to Mary Sykes; Albert Hubbell wrote to Ellmann about being Lucia's friend and lover; Jeanne Wertenberg recalled their childhood together in Zurich when Lucia was a happy and talented child. Adèle Fernandez remembered Lucia as a slightly older teenager who dated her brother and who appeared to her to be beautiful and glamorous. Ximena de Angulo Roelli, the daughter of Cary F. Baynes, who had been Lucia's companion during her treatment with Jung in Zurich, came forward with a book of notes her mother had taken about the experience. Stella Steyn, a young Irish artist who studied in Paris, wrote a memoir that included her friendship with Lucia. Helen Kastor Joyce, it turned out, had written an autobiographical narrative that mentioned her, which Ellmann had chosen not to use. Eventually the evidence seemed compelling: Joyce's daughter may have had problems, but she was no lunatic.

My own desire to answer a few basic questions pushed me forward. Why was Joyce's own sense of the beauty and talent of his child so at odds with the opinions of other people in his circle? Why should Joyce's primary biographer have judged Joyce to be a man of extraordinary discernment in some matters but foolish in judging Lucia? Why was Joyce upbraided for trying to save Lucia instead of admired for the steadfastness of his love?

My own book is, in some ways, built on a few simple reversals of other narratives. I take as a major premise the conviction that Joyce did know Lucia much better than anyone else, including well-meaning family friends. I use as another principle the idea that Lucia's self-understanding deserves a place in the historical record, as does Helen Kastor Joyce's sense of the importance of her life in the Joyce family.

I imposed several rules designed, I hoped, to reclaim the inherent dignity of Lucia's experience: I would describe behavior and attempt to explain it rather than judge it; I would write about her experience going forward from the beginning without presuming the end. In this way, I hoped to avoid a "bias toward madness" and the consequent need to look for symptoms foreshadowing an inevitable breakdown. I determined to use what letters about her did remain in scrupulous chronological order and in reference to specific life events. I had noticed, in my research, that previous biographers sometimes grouped letters, say, from 1932, 1933, and 1935 in single paragraphs in order to prove a point that could not honestly be made except in such an ahistorical way.

As I worked, I began to see patterns emerging. Joyce had once written to his brother Stanislaus that his wife's character was resolutely proof against any attempt of his to influence it. But the same was not true for Lucia. She was alternately supple clay and resistant reed, but rarely did she live without expressing her responses to her father. And rarely did she live without registering his responses to her. Too much scrutiny, I saw, can turn into too much self-scrutiny. Something creative, compelling, and possibly dangerous had been going on between two extraordinary people, and it was important to see that the merest strand separated one from the other. Sanity is not in one place and insanity in another. A pane of glass crossing the road, a moment's indecision, and things might have been different for either one of them. I think that Joyce and Lucia understood this, and that such knowledge underlay their love for each other.

Because of the circumstances in which I wrote, because I was writing in the wake of earlier suppressions of material, and because of the meagerness of the undestroyed resources, I have had to construct the contexts of Lucia's experiences and then put her into them. A salient example would be her experiences as a dancer. None of her diaries or letters survive; her parents and brother didn't know what she was studying; but I found out who her teachers were, what kind of dance they taught, when they offered classes, and what philosophies guided their work. Another example would be Lucia's seven-month stay at Les Rives de Prangins, on the outskirts of Geneva, in 1934. Swiss cantonese hospitals were a certain type of institution in the 1930s with identifiable philosophies and medical practices. We can infer that Lucia received certain types of treatment, and we can speculate about how someone of her temperament might have responded to such experiences. "Lucia" is woven in and around the circumstances that shaped her.

Another consequence of writing when most of the material about Lucia Joyce was destroyed is that the Lucia who is presented here is almost totally refracted through the eyes of others. I would have preferred to let her speak for herself and to illustrate her character with her own words from her letters, poems, and novel. But she can't and I can't, and so we must live with what is so manifestly true: that she was a person of great seriousness and intensity, and that others who lived in her presence drew light from her being.

PART ONE

THE DANCE OF LIFE

Lucia with Eva Joyce, Trieste, 1910. Photographer unknown. (Courtesy of the Rare Book and Manuscript Collection, Carl A. Kroch Library, Cornell University)

1

THE CURTAIN OPENS

TRIESTE 1907-15

1. A BEAUTIFUL LITTLE GIRL WHO WAS NAMED LUCIA

The story begins with the birth of a girl child in a pauper's hospital. She was the daughter of a beautiful, imperious woman and a famous man in his undiscovered youth. Scolded by her mother (Lucia you have dropped the doll and broken it. You have butter hands), she loved the father even more (Tell Lucia I am bringing her a new doll from Ireland, but the maker hasn't finished with its head yet. Love to Lucia.) Her father read to her and made up songs in Italian, which was the language spoken in Trieste, where they lived far from her parents' home in the island country of Ireland. "C'era una volta, una bella bambina / Che is chiamava Lucia / Dormiva durante il giorno / Dormiva durante la notte / Perché non sapeva comminare."[1] "Once upon a time there was a beautiful little girl / who was named Lucia / she slept during the day / she slept during the night / because she didn't know how to walk." His name was James Joyce; her name was Lucia. She was the light-giver, the patron saint of eyesight, and the guide through dark places. Their story was to involve light and shadow, blindness and insight, and it changed the course of modern literature.

II. A MOTHER, A FATHER, A BROTHER

Lucia Anna Joyce was born in the Ospedale Civico di Trieste on 26 July 1907. She was placed in a pauper's ward, which she shared not only with her mother, Nora Barnacle, but also with her father, James Joyce, who had been struck down with rheumatic fever earlier in the summer.[2] Joyce, then an itinerant schoolteacher, an erstwhile bank clerk, a gay Irish adventurer, and an as-yet-undiscovered literary genius, gave her a name that he had chosen several years earlier while he awaited the birth of his first child.[3] Giorgio, two years her senior, had been named in memory of Joyce's much-loved younger brother, but his daughter's name resonated with myth and legend. Back in Dublin, Joyce's oldest sister, Poppie, thought he was daft. "What on earth made you call her that?" she asked, adding, "Pappie wanted to know were you quite mad when you selected that?"[4] But Joyce knew what he was doing. Lucia was the patron saint of light and an imagined guide to Dante's trip through the Inferno; she blessed eyes and helped to lead the way for uninitiated pilgrims who found themselves in dark and treacherous places. Her father associated her with a most gracious lady "splendid in sight and radiance,"[5] but he had not failed to notice that "Lucia" was also the mad heroine of Donizetti's famous opera *Lucia di Lammermoor* and the more traditional spouse in Alessandro Manzoni's *The Betrothed*. Thus, like the books that would eventually make her young errant father into the most celebrated and scandalous writer in modern Europe, Lucia's entry into the world was grounded in difficult fact and tinged with imagined glories.

For her no-nonsense, west-of-Ireland mother, the birth of a daughter held no such portentous associations. In 1907 Nora Barnacle was one of the displaced poor of Europe. Far from her home in Ireland, unschooled in Italian, and at the mercy of her husband's mercurial ways, she told her Triestine friends, the Francini Brunis, that Lucia had been born "almost in the street."[6] She neglected to mention that both her children had been born out of wedlock, but everyone knew that there was little beside the street to shelter the young Joyces. When Nora took her daughter home on 5 August, she was given a pauper's share of twenty crowns. Then she headed back to the flat paid for by Joyce's brother, Stanislaus, to wait out the damp, enervating heat of the Triestine summer and the recovery of the "husband" who still languished in the hospital.

Preoccupied by her own struggle to survive with a new baby, a two-year-old, and an unemployed partner, Nora's thoughts remained focused on her own family, but many of her own dissatisfactions were mirrored in the larger world. The year 1907 was an unsettled one, a year that heralded many of the upheavals in Europe that were to shape her daughter's youth and ensure, as much as James Joyce's penchant for exile did, that her life would be disrupted. Acts of rebellion against the state were common, both in Europe—where workers struggled for votes, parliamentary representation, and better working hours—and in northern Africa, where French, German, and British assertions of their colonial power frequently aroused Muslim resistance. In England more and more women were demanding the right to vote; on 9 February, thousands of ladies of title and distinction joined in a procession through the streets that, because of the horrible weather, would be remembered as the Mud March. In Russia revolutionary excesses had been met by force, and Lenin, to avoid arrest, left Russia for exile in Europe. In the Balkans the promise of greater local autonomy led various factions to kill or expel rival groups.[7] Even in Trieste, the Adriatic port that was now part of the Austro-Hungarian Empire, the streets were covered with posters and graffiti, as socialists and irredentists competed with Austrian authorities for the loyalty of its citizens.[8] The Joyces could not anticipate that European politics would magnify their displacement, driving them twice more from an adopted city, a new language, and their network of friends.

For the time being, Lucia was simply a gentle child who was born with the fine bone structure of her father's family, her mother's blue eyes and dark coloring, and a slight cast in her left eye. Joyce's aunt Josephine Murray, putting aside her misgivings about Nora's second pregnancy, greeted the girl warmly from Dublin: "A thousand welcomes to the little lady who has opened her eyes in Trieste."[9]

By 1907, three years after their arrival in continental Europe, her parents' ways of coping, and not coping, with emigrant life were fairly well established. Lucia entered into a life that was rich in counterpoint, woven from the strands of rebellion, optimism, volatile high spirits, and sheer, brazen talent that had brought her parents from Ireland to Europe. It was a loquacious, opinionated life that was filled with music, books, potatoes, cabbages, Irish bacon, polenta, colorful conversation, and a lackadaisical attention to custom. Poverty competed with extravagance in the household of her parents, sober realities with lavish drink, and father and mother both called upon luck to soften the blows of fate.

Giorgio's birth had at least gotten them past their initial ignorance about childbearing. In 1904 it had taken the young couple (he twenty-two, she just twenty) three months to recognize that Nora was pregnant. And though Joyce wrote to Stanislaus at the end of December announcing this fact, all he could say at the time was that, although he would claim paternity, no child of his would ever be baptized. "I do not like talking of this subject yet," he admitted.[10] By February 1905, having apparently decided that Aunt Josephine Murray would be a better female confidante than Nora's own mother, Annie Barnacle, Joyce was fretting at her continued silence and wondering why she didn't write to him.[11] He sent Stanislaus to the medical library in Dublin to do research on midwifery and used the time of Nora's confinement to rethink his reasons for eloping with her in the first place.

Remembering the moment in 1904 when a twenty-year-old country girl from Galway, with little more experience than serving as a maid in Finn's Hotel, had slipped unnoticed onto a steamship in Dublin Harbor, he admired his wife for her honesty, her courage, and her trustworthy nature. He especially liked her willingness to cast her lot with the risky prospects of an unknown artist bent on leaving his homeland. She had also acquiesced in his singular beliefs about private life, agreeing not to marry him, even though he suspected that her unmarried status embarrassed her. Years later her niece, Bozena Berta, remembered Nora as acutely self-conscious about being "spliced by the blacksmith of Gretna Green,"[12] but Joyce countered her discomfort with his own more libertine views. He didn't see why he and Nora should have to swear their lives to each other in front of a priest or a lawyer, he told Stanislaus in May 1905. And he certainly didn't want to "superimpose on my child the very troublesome burden of belief which my father and mother superimposed on me."[13] In his judgment, Nora's love for him was greater than his own for her, and he could see that her dependence on him, in a land whose language was initially beyond her mastery, was almost absolute. She found Triestine women incredibly rude to her, and she grew afraid to walk the streets alone with her awkward Irish clothing and her linguistic ineptness; Joyce found himself obliged to help with the marketing as well as doing his work as a teacher at the Berlitz School each day.[14]

By the final month of her first pregnancy, Nora was in bad shape. She complained; she cried every day, had trouble eating, refused to cook, and felt enervated by the humid heat of the Mediterranean summer. Even after Aunt Josephine sent patterns and Joyce bought cloth, she could not make herself sew clothes in anticipation of the baby's arrival. Joyce told his ever-receptive brother that his wife seemed not to have a "robust constitution" and he feared that she was like a fragile plant "which cannot be safely transplanted." While never doubting the principles that had guided him into exile from Ireland (he had left Ireland not only to write but also to live "in conformity with [his] moral nature"), he could see that the success of the pregnancy and Nora's health stood in the balance. The still unborn child was, he wrote, "an unforgettable part of the problem."[15]

As Joyce weighed possibilities for the future (Should he and Nora remain in Europe? Should he take her back to Ireland, perhaps to share a cottage with Stanislaus outside Dublin?), more immediate problems presented themselves. Trieste, for all its cosmopolitan vigor and robust sea trade, was not a place where babies were welcomed in rented houses. As one landlady after another sent eviction notices or refused to consider the young parents-to-be, Joyce's spirits lagged, and he blamed Nora for destroying, or at any rate weakening, "a great part of my natural cheerfulness and irresponsibility," he reported to his brother.[16] Life in exile began to seem unsatisfactory, and he found himself more and more in opposition to his young vulnerable wife. Nora called their disputes "lovers' quarrels," and Joyce reported some of them to Stannie after they had obviously been resolved; but they remain as evidence that the idea of paternity, which he wholeheartedly embraced, was in conflict with its real challenges in care and money and time. These tensions, though offset by Giorgio's placid, though unexpected, arrival on 27 July 1905 (they had miscalculated his birth date by a month), were not resolved when Lucia appeared on the scene two years later.

Nora breast-fed Giorgio (the child had no official name until after he was two months old), and both parents settled into discovering the pleasures and concerns of parenting.[17] Joyce described the birth to Stanislaus by dramatizing the moment of its announcement to him. The midwife

had come to the door of their flat, saying " 'Xe un bel maschio, Signore.'
('It's a fine boy, Sir.') So then I knew an heir was born."[18] By the return
post, Stanislaus admitted that he was happy the child was a son, and
wrote that the boy would inherit the "dignity, nobility and amiability" of
his father's character. He added his appreciation of Joyce's decision to
rear the child outside of the Catholic faith and the British Empire. "The
fact remains," he said, "that few sons are born as free as yours because
the priest and the king are so seldom tied in a tether."[19]

This simple exchange, with only a passing mention of Nora and her
"melancholy," lets us glimpse the symbolic importance of Giorgio's birth
and the assumptions that tied him to the life of his family. For at the
same time that the Joyce brothers congratulated themselves on the child's
freedom from the ordinary restrictions of church and state, they bound
him immediately into a private dynasty: he was the firstborn son of a
firstborn son. Just as James Joyce (1882–1941) was the eldest son of his father, John Stanislaus Joyce (1849–1931), so had John Stanislaus been the
oldest (and only) son of James Augustine Joyce (1827–1866). He, in turn,
had been the oldest son of an earlier James Joyce.[20] In the minds of these
men, families were perpetuated through male progeny. This circumstance seemed so natural to Joyce that twenty-six years later, when he
and Nora legalized their union in 1931, he left his family portraits (the
faces of these male ancestors), his books, and all his real property only to
Giorgio.[21]

Lucia was to spend her life trying to change this perspective. The
story of Lucia Joyce is in large part the story of a simple but powerful
truth that was grasped too late: that daughters may and can prefer to create rather than to provide inspiration for someone else's creativity. As the
family came to realize slowly, painfully, and often with heated resistance,
the somber, gentlemanly faces of the Joyce family portraits were remarkable as much for what they obscured as for what they so manifestly portrayed. Exclusion was but one of their sinister truths.

As it happened, Lucia was also a child who lived without a strong
bond with her mother. From the start and throughout his life, Giorgio
was Nora's favorite. Joyce, "married" less than ten months when his son
was born (he and Nora celebrated their "wedding" anniversary on 8 October every year), sensed the shift in Nora's affections and experienced
his baby son as an unexpected rival. Still, both parents seem to have

taken genuine pleasure in their child's development. Joyce peppered his letters to Stanislaus with news of Giorgio's health. And when they moved to Rome a year later for Joyce to take up a banking position there, he kept Stannie abreast of the newest words, the latest skills, and the intimate scenes of everyday affection and humor. Giorgio beat time to music in the Piazza Colonna and greeted the arrival of restaurant dishes with "Ettaro, ettaro." ("Here it is.")[22] His appetite for language seemed voracious. He mimicked every sound he heard—a clock chiming, a vendor calling, a song coming in through the window. The Roman love of children, manifested by signs of affection given to the boy by total strangers on the street, encouraged them in their new enterprise as parents. Joyce, looking back on his life in January 1907, thinking of his writing, his marriage, and his professional status, summed it all up: "Certainly Georgie is the most successful thing connected with me."[23]

But this narrative of young married life told only part of the story. Nora, left alone to manage with the boy day after day, was the first to feel the stress of her husband's irresponsibility with money; and saddled with the boy at night, she was faced with the misery of Joyce's drinking. The child was not only her primary accomplishment but also her silent witness to isolation and frustration. Their bond, established in these lonely times, sustained them throughout Nora's life. At her death in 1951, he was still at her side.

When Stanislaus left Ireland on 20 October 1905 to join his brother in Trieste, he found the young family hungry, broke, and cranky. It wasn't simply that his brother periodically drank himself under the table but that Nora couldn't cope with motherhood. In June 1906, Aunt Josephine wrote to Stanislaus, "I can't understand Nora. Surely it is a monstrous thing to expect Jim to cook or mind the baby when he is doing his utmost to support both of them surely she can make as good an attempt as Jim it seems very soon for her to be so disappointed I wonder does she know what it is to be with a person with a scurrilous tongue from which you are never safe there is some excuse for Jim drinking it is the old story of finding forgetfulness." She wrote as an aunt whose primary loyalty was to her side of the family, but she paused to wonder what would happen to Nora if she carried out her repeated threats to take Giorgio and return to her people in Galway. And she worried that Nora might become pregnant again.[24]

She had reason to be worried. She had gotten an even darker glimpse of her nephew's situation the previous December, when Joyce himself had written to say that he was "simply waiting for a little financial change," before making alterations in his life plan. He expected this would happen within two years, "but even if it does not come I shall do the best I can. I have hesitated before telling you that I imagine the present relations between Nora and myself are about to suffer some alteration."[25] Another, unwanted child, as Aunt Josephine could see, would have made a difficult human relationship, threatened at least in part by the tensions of caring for one child, into a disaster.

But in February 1906, their old friends the Francini Brunis invited all the Joyces, Stanislaus included, to share a house on the Via Giovanni Boccaccio. Collective life offered everyone ways of deflecting their irritations. Their pooled money went farther; Nora once again had the company of Clothilde, who was herself the mother of young children, and Stanislaus had Alessandro Francini Bruni as an ally in the fight against Joyce's evening wanderings among the cafés and bars in the old quarter of the city. Francini Bruni regretted his friend's drinking but attributed its worst excesses to writing setbacks. "His artistic reversals had a disastrous effect on his animal spirits. His self-destruction was cold and premeditated. He would plunge recklessly when the world treated him badly." In the evenings, Francini Bruni would set out to find Joyce in some bistro, singing "high-pitched, out of tune" choruses about the need for more wine: "Ancora un litro di quel bon / Che no go la chiave del porto."[26] Throwing Joyce's limp body over his shoulder, he would stagger home, where the pattern of escape and rescue would repeat itself.

Joyce was not the only culprit. Francini Bruni remembered the house on the Via Giovanni Boccaccio as a bohemian household. They were all young, poor, aware of the absurdities of teaching foreign languages according to the Berlitz method, and full of animal vigor. One of Joyce's biographers, Herbert Gorman, says, "There were evenings in the house . . . when Francini Bruni would get into the infant Giorgio's carriage, suck at a milk bottle and cry, squeal and regurgitate like a baby while Joyce trundled him about the place. This would be at midnight. And after the clowning was over Joyce would sing Gregorian chants and the excitable Francini Bruni, who had a high shrill laugh like a goat, would kiss the singer in an ecstasy of joy."[27]

   The problem, aside from difficulties in his work at the Berlitz School, was that Joyce couldn't, or at least didn't, write in this high-spirited and boisterous environment. With the poems of *Chamber Music* completed, most of the stories of *Dubliners* in hand, and close to a thousand pages of his autobiographical novel finished, he still had had no book accepted for publication. By the end of July 1906, he'd had as much as he could stand, and with Nora and the year-old Giorgio in tow, he headed for a new position in Rome.

   The move was a mistake. Joyce wrote to the Francini Brunis that he thought of the ancient part of the city as an "exquisite panorama" composed of "flowers of death, ruins, piles of bones and skeletons."[28] He discovered that, although he qualified for the job he had wanted, he had underestimated the number of hours he would have to spend at the bank. Nastkolb and Schumacher required him to work from eight-thirty in the morning until seven-thirty at night. Nora was once again left alone with Giorgio with long, empty hours to fill; and when tensions over money arose, as they inevitably did, Joyce once again took up tutoring private students. These extra hours of work exacerbated the alienation that the young husband and wife were both feeling not only from the city but also from the life they could offer each other. They needed each other, but they were not soul mates. Through all these early years of marriage, Joyce would write to Stanislaus, telling him some version of the same story: that Nora didn't "care a rambling damn about art."[29] Brenda Maddox, Nora's biographer, claimed that this period in the Joyces' lives cemented their union: "cut off from everybody but one another, each learned to tolerate the other's alien temperament, to delight in their child, and to live as Italians."[30] But Joyce's letters to Stanislaus paint a different picture of cramped rented rooms, serial evictions, and traipsing around the city "accompanied by a plaintive woman with infant (also plaintive)." In December he lamented his situation with "no pen, no ink, no table, no room, no time, no quiet, no inclination. Never mind." He feared that his imagination was weakening, that "all the things I was going to write about have become uncapturable images."[31]

   It was in these circumstances that Lucia Anna was conceived. On 10 January 1907, when Joyce let Stanislaus know that Nora was expecting again, he wrote with pride about Giorgio but added a strange addendum: "he's only a small part mine."[32] Perhaps this was a way of responding to the intensity of the relationship between mother and child that he watched evolve during those months in Rome. In another letter to his brother, he acknowledged that while he might be considered cynical, he nonetheless felt that "a lot of this talk about love is nonsense. A woman's love is always maternal and egoistic. A man, on the contrary . . . possesses a fund of genuine affection for the 'beloved' or 'once beloved' object."[33] These sound like the words of a man who, though constant in his own love for his wife, is aware of being superseded in her regard.

We have no record of what Nora thought about her second pregnancy, but we can notice that she didn't stop nursing Giorgio. Nora must have conceived Lucia in the later part of November 1906. Although Aunt Josephine had cautioned her to wean the boy in the event of another pregnancy, Nora continued to breast-feed her son until February 1907.[34] Giorgio claimed to remember this experience. When he married in 1930, he told his wife that his mother had nursed him for two years; and Helen wrongly imagined that, after Lucia was born, Nora had suckled both children together, one at each breast.[35] Any one of the Joyces could have corrected her, for they knew Lucia had not been breast-fed at all. In later years, Joyce told Padraic and Mary Colum how much he regretted Nora's decision on this score, but he apparently couldn't dissuade her at the time.[36]

His own response to the imminence of a second baby must have been complicated. In theory he was clear. In later years he told his sister Eva that "the most important thing that can happen to a man is the birth of a child,"[37] but it was also a fearful prospect. Still, the anticipation of a larger family did little to alter Joyce's vision of his future life. In early March, he wrote sharply to Stanislaus, as if in response to some criticism, "You seem to imagine that I should settle down to make myself a *carriera* here, beginning at 250 Frs. a month and ending 20 years hence at 450 Frs. a month, with all the accompaniments of such a *carriera*, a quarter, a servant, children at school, a small bank a/c and a great fear of everything in me. This is what I *should* do but I doubt very much if I *will* ever do it."[38] In the end, whatever it was—intellectual and artistic loneliness, financial worries, the need for Stanislaus's proximity, concern for his equally lonely wife—he took Giorgio and the pregnant Nora back to Trieste in March 1907. Here he resumed work at the Berlitz School, began once again to build up a roster of private clients, and then was struck down with rheumatic fever. Even before he recovered, he had a small daughter at home, and a new chapter in the life of the Triestine Joyces began.

III. CHILDREN EVERYWHERE

After her days in the hospital, Nora brought Lucia back to a household even more destitute than usual. To pay for her confinement and for Joyce's stay in the hospital, Stanislaus had taken out loans from Mr. Artifoni, his employer at the Berlitz School, who assured him that the debts would be forgiven. But Artifoni soon leased the school, turning over Stanislaus's promissory notes to the new directors. The result, for Nora, was a summer of anxiety; for Stanislaus, in his own words, it was "a hell."[39] Whether Nora actually lived in Stanislaus's apartment is uncertain, for three biographical authorities on Joyce disagree on this point.[40] My own guess is that she did share living quarters with him until Joyce had recovered enough to look for a new flat in September. Later Joyce claimed that Nora took in laundry to carry them through, but Stanislaus's memory was that the financial care of mother and children fell entirely into his lap.[41] In the months after Lucia's birth, we can imagine Nora like a welfare mother without the welfare. She was relying on a relative's charity for the very roof over her head, and she had the daily responsibility of an infant and a toddler whose boisterous interest in life had not abated just because he had a baby sister.

For Joyce Lucia's birth seemed, oddly, more propitious. With his return to Trieste came his first taste of recognition as a journalist and public lecturer. Between March and September he wrote three articles for *Il Piccolo della Sera*: "Il Fenianismo" (Fenianism) was published on 22 March; "Home Rule Maggiorenne" (Home Rule Comes of Age) on 19 May, and "L'Irlanda alla Sbarra" (Ireland at the Bar) on 16 September. These successes led Francini Bruni to propose that Joyce lecture at the Università Popolare. In April he had spoken about "Ireland, Island of Saints and Sages"[42] for which he had received twenty crowns (the same amount as Nora's pauper's gift for Lucia's birth). And despite his misgivings about Joyce's earlier writing, the London publisher Elkins Mathews finally published *Chamber Music* in May. Joyce was also busy reading the plays of J. M. Synge and was brushing up on how to get rich quick by studying Edward Mott Woolley's *The Art of Selling Goods*. He had the idea he could sell Donegal tweeds in Europe.

To his amazement, the birth of his second child seemed to bring a rebirth of his own creativity. The fascination with gestation and infant development that was already manifest in his delight in Giorgio seemed to intensify, turning into one of the most powerful metaphors of his writing career. The idea of the artist as a "mother" and the art itself as a kind of progeny controlled the reshaping of *Stephen Hero*, provided a structuring device for *Ulysses*, and led him to fashion *Finnegans Wake* as the great epic story of the regeneration of the earth. The time of Lucia's early childhood was, Ellmann claimed, the most inventive, forward-looking period of Joyce's three-year struggle to find creative direction and the means to pursue it.[43] The next seven years of Joyce's writing life emerged from the plans laid in sickbed, the vision of literature as "the phenomenon of artistic conception, artistic gestation and artistic reproduction," his newly honed sense that "in the virgin womb of the [artist's] imagination the word is made flesh,"[44] and the model of his young daughter's literal emergence into the world.

The consequences of her father's way of perceiving his life as an artist were, for Lucia, manifold and profound. That she had a parent who was secure in his vocation was all to the good, but a parent preoccupied with his art and figuring his preoccupation in terms of another "child" had a more dubious effect. It meant that Lucia's life was accompanied by spectral children—Stephen Dedalus, Leopold, Molly, and Milly Bloom, Anna Livia Plurabelle, H. C. Earwicker—whose presence was ubiquitous. In the Joyce household, real children and invented ones lived, competed, wrestled with one another for places of ascendancy, and fell asleep to similar lullabies. Lucia grew up with her father's eyes always upon her—not just as a doting father but as an artist looking for material. From his earliest days, he believed himself to be someone who "takes into the vital center of his life the life that surrounds it, flinging it abroad again amid planetary music."[45] Joyce's art surrounded her, haunted her from birth; and she in turn was part of the life that surrounded the maker of that art. She gave him the means to fling it amid planetary music.

Lucia's first several years of life were quiet ones punctuated by sporadic childhood illnesses. She got the mumps, which somehow left her with a small scar on her chin. Once she got boils.[46] She was a more fretful baby than Giorgio, but then she was not an only child, not a firstborn and most beloved child, not a boy, not breast-fed, and her mother was in trouble. Nora nagged at her, establishing a persisting pattern of favoritism and impatience. One of Lucia's earliest memories was of being taunted for breaking a doll.[47]

In 1909, when she was two, she stayed in her mother's arms when Joyce made two trips back to Ireland. On the first trip, undertaken between 29 July and mid-September, he took Giorgio with him in the hope that his beautiful young son would reconcile his family and erstwhile friends to his five-year absence in Europe and to his having sneaked off with Nora. The second trip was a business venture, suggested to him by his sister Eva, who wondered why a city the size of Dublin had no movie theaters. With the financial backing of some Triestine businessmen, Joyce returned to Dublin in October intent on becoming a movie mogul. He also wanted to further his plans for selling Irish tweeds in Europe.[48]

These trips, the first separation of Lucia's parents since their elopement together in 1904, profoundly affected their relationship to each other and consequently their relationship to their children. Back in Trieste, Nora received news of her husband's adventures until, in a letter dated 6 August, Joyce dropped a bombshell on her. His old friend Vincent Cosgrave had claimed that he, as well as Joyce, had been Nora's lover in the summer of 1904. Joyce now accused her of infidelity. The next morning, in anguish, he wrote to ask if Giorgio was his son.

What does a young girl sense about her mother's life? Certainly she cannot yet understand the erotic dimension of it. In 1909 Lucia could not have known of her father's accusation or that Nora never answered Joyce's letter. Instead her mother waited; she sought sympathy from Stanislaus, and eventually, after Joyce withdrew his insanely jealous allegations, she told him something that she hoped would please him: she'd been reading the poems in *Chamber Music*. As her parents tentatively and then fervently tried to heal the wound inflicted by Cosgrave's insidious suggestion, could the child have intuitively recognized a shifting emotional landscape, or felt in some subterranean way that her parents were adjusting the priority they had previously given to her and her brother?

For the crisis had brought her father face to face with the abyss. In the panic of losing his wife, as he thought, Joyce had thrown his kids into the bargain. "If I could forget my books and my children and forget that the girl I loved was false to me and remember her only as I saw her with the eyes of my boyish love I would go out of life content,"[49] he wrote, and continued to send letters in the same vein: "Our children (much as I love them) <u>must not</u> come between us. If they are good and noble-natured it is because of *us*, dear."[50]

Everyone says things in the heat of the moment; you can cut off your own fingers in a peak of jealous rage. But what was distinctive about Joyce's attachment to Nora—what he required of her, what he demanded—was expressed in the language of a child to his mother who was imagined as both virgin and whore. That August, and then again later in the fall and winter, as one letter after another crossed from Ireland to Trieste, he discovered that it was not enough to use correspondence to create masturbatory fantasies with his wife, to imagine torsos arched in pleasure and all the possibilities of the marriage bed. Joyce needed to imagine his relation to Nora in terms of fetal intimacy. "My little mother," he wrote to her on Christmas Eve 1909, "take me into the dark sanctuary of your womb. Shelter me, dear, from harm! I am too childish and impulsive to live alone. . . . I am so helpless tonight, helpless, helpless!"[51]

No one knows exactly what Nora thought about Joyce's way of imagining their relationship. Her letters have been lost or destroyed, but if she entered into this exchange of naughty letters, she also retained her skepticism about her long-absent husband. By December she'd had enough. She threatened to take Lucia and Giorgio back to her people in Galway because she couldn't endure any more of Joyce's profligacy about money. There'd been another eviction notice. Her real children needed a roof over their heads and food in their stomachs.

Although Nora did not take them away—Stanislaus rescued them once more—it must have been clear to her that the partnership she had entered into with her husband was a peculiarly needy one. If Joyce imagined his books to be children, he also imagined himself as an infant in relation to his wife. Thus there was a full house of Joyces, a house swimming with children and their requirements, even before Joyce imported his own sisters, Eva and Eileen, to their flat on the Via Scussa in Trieste.

Eva came in September 1909, Eileen in January 1910—one with each of Joyce's return trips from Dublin.

Joyce had written to both Stanislaus and Nora from Dublin, sending them advice about readying the house for its new members. Apart from proposing new physical arrangements, Joyce was careful to remind Nora that it was she who had initially suggested that his sisters come, since she wanted help with housekeeping and child care. Initially Eva slept in a camp bed in Giorgio's room and Eileen joined her there, but by August they had all moved to a bigger apartment on the Via della Barriera Vecchia 32.[52] Eileen described their initial response to Joyce's proposal as "overjoyed."[53] For both of them, their brother offered a chance to escape from their father's drinking, his niggardly house in Dublin, and their own lack of education or prospects.

But Eva lasted for less than two years in Trieste; she immediately became homesick. Whatever she had lacked in Dublin, it was at least a familiar lack. In Trieste she had trouble with the language, with the cosmopolitan racial mix of the city, with loneliness, and with the bohemian nature of Joyce and Nora's ménage. She thought their flat was as chaotic and poorly managed as the house that her father refused to keep; the couple practiced no religion, and Nora's natural indolence, opinionated ways, and lax, oddball approach to housekeeping left her feeling that her would-be sister-in-law was common. Nora did things like putting "pee pot[s]" on top of her living-room furniture.[54] And Eva could never forget, it seems, that her brother refused to marry the mother of his children.

Eileen, on the other hand, flourished in her new communal home. Joyce was her favorite brother. He bought her clothes for the journey, promised to pay for voice lessons so that she could train for the opera, and eventually, through his wealthy students, was instrumental in placing her in the home of Ettore Schmitz (Italo Svevo) as a governess for his daughter, Letizia.[55] Frantisek Schaurek, a Czech bank cashier in Trieste whom she was to marry in 1915, was also one of Joyce's private students. "Looking back on it now," she told Alice Curtayne in 1963, "I see that those were the happiest years of my life. You see, I was twenty when I went out and that's a lovely age to travel for the first time."[56] Lucia was two when Eva arrived, two and a half when she met her aunt Eileen.

Thus it was that Joyce's daughter met the first two of the surrogate

mothers who, in a long chain until the end of her life, replaced the real
mother who preferred Giorgio. Eva admitted to Stanislaus, a year after
her return to Dublin in July 1911, "I never took such a fancy to any child
as I did to her."[57] Amid all of Eva's negative responses to her new environment, Lucia was the single bright spot. In 1910 she had a studio portrait made of herself with her three-year-old niece. Dressed in white
ruffles with an enormous hat, the delicate Lucia stands companionably
on a chair, holding Eva's hand as if she were indeed her mother. Eileen
too seemed curiously unbothered that her role in the Triestine household
was as a housewife and mother in Nora's place. In her own words, she
"did most of the housekeeping and . . . took care of Jim's two children,
Giorgio and Lucia."[58] When in 1915 she married Frantisek Schaurek,
whom she dearly loved, she described herself as "brokenhearted" about
leaving the children. "You see," she continued, "I had really reared Giorgio and Lucia. I used to do everything for them and we were always
together."[59]

   Although the Joyces lived on the constant, wearing edge of poverty,
none of them let it get them down. If their home was squalid, it was also
high-spirited; if it was financially insecure, it was filled with the gusto
and optimism and vociferous opinions of youth. Francini Bruni summed
it up: "So it went in Trieste before the war, when one made less money
and laughed more. In Austria everyone laughed. Harlequin could pay
the bills."[60] Amid this general gaiety Lucia laughed and cried, too. On
his Dublin trips Joyce sent messages to his comical daughter: he would
send her a doll, but not yet, for "l'uomo non ha mess la testa ancora."
("The man hasn't put the head on yet.")[61] The doll was to replace one
whose head had broken when it fell from a chair, an occasion Lucia
never forgot.[62] Her father had chased away her tears with a song. In 1958
she could still remember its lyrics: "we sang 'Bambola chinina etc.
Quando era Babbi nella ancor di bambole un tesori essa dice mamma
pappa essa diceva mamma pappa etc.' "[63]

   Music was as abundant in the Joyce home as laughter. However
much he might have been in debt, Joyce always rented a piano, so music
was his family's daily fare. Eileen remembered grand parties when
everyone, including the children, sang. Joyce and Eileen played the key-
board; Nora was learning. Their sheet music included works by Debussy, Beethoven, Wagner, and Verdi but also collections of Irish music:

Butler's *Seven Original Irish Melodies* and Cecil Sharp's *A Book of British Song for Home and School*.[64] Eileen had a flair for dramatic parlor songs like "The Last Rose of Summer" or "Una Furtiva Lacrima" (A Furtive Tear),[65] while her father had a particular fondness for Renaissance music both sacred and secular. He owned Dodge's *Twelve Elizabethan Songs* and used to return from Mass humming Gregorian chants like *Vidae Acquam*.[66] But as she grew, the lyrics for the lullaby he composed were changed: "Era una piccola bambina che rideva durante il giorno e non dormiva durante la notte."[67] ("There was a little girl who laughed during the day and did not sleep at night.")

As Lucia grew, she became aware of her mother as "the prettiest girl in Galway" and of a skinny, nearsighted, and foppishly well-dressed father. Francini Bruni said Joyce described himself as belonging to the giraffe family and wrote that he was "agile, lean, his rigid legs like the poles of a compass, he went about with an abstracted look. In summer, he wore a Panama hat of indescribable color and old shoes; in winter a shabby overcoat with a raised fur collar."[68] His niece, Bozena Berta Schaurek, remembered that "his clothes were dramatic and careless."[69] Always he wore outlandish ties, which Lucia got to choose for him in the morning: "What a lot of ties he had."[70]

Though she had no way to measure it, idiosyncrasy was the norm in her household. Her father was terrified of thunderstorms, somehow associating them with the wrath of God, and flew about the house closing windows when one threatened. His love of Ibsen drew him to a love for anything Danish, so when there was money enough for furniture, he had a local carpenter copy modern Danish chairs pictured in a magazine. He liked them so much that he had more and more of them made, like the pot that never stopped boiling, until the living room was awash with chairs. This was, of course, so that her father could rest his arms and legs on them as well as his torso when he was writing.[71]

Unlike the fathers of other children, her own father was usually around the house, for Joyce had given up teaching at the Berlitz School in favor of giving private lessons in his home. In the afternoons when his students came, she and Giorgio had to make themselves scarce. Nora could keep them out of the living room but couldn't keep them quiet any more than she could keep her husband and his brother quiet when they disagreed. Lucia grew up watching the discrepancies of emigrant life when her Irish father and uncle fumed and sputtered at one another in Italian inflected with a brogue.[72] Their mornings were interrupted by the arrival of the Triestine milkwoman with her tin and zinc vessels and a small measure for pouring milk. Sometimes a blind piano tuner came.[73] Eventually, despite her father's inordinate fear of beasts, the family acquired a dog, Fido, which, as Lucia thought, "ran away after he had eaten all the pudding, which was in the kitchen."[74] (Her parents had actually given the little dog into the keeping of the Schmitz family, who discovered the dog's sex only when its puppies arrived.[75]) The Joyces' lives were punctuated by the Triestine celebrations of Christmas and Easter and by the decidedly un-Triestine celebration of Saint Patrick's Day.

Years later Lucia remembered "going with my mother for bathing." They went to the Barcola, the cliffs along the shore of the Adriatic, on an open tram. She loved the warmth, the sunshine; she remembered her mother's pleasure in sunbathing. Her father took her to Venice, only an hour from Trieste, to see St. Mark's Church and the beautiful piazza that adjoined it.[76] Her aunt Eileen taught her English. Giorgio, whom she adored, entered school; then it was her turn.

Here was a jolt in their family life, the first intimation that the Joyces' implicit expectations about their children's places in the world would prove wrong. Lucia was good at everything in the Scuola Elementari on the Via Parini, while Giorgio, although well behaved, was marked unsatisfactory across the board.[77] And he didn't seem to mind. One child was bright, charming, insecure, eager to please, edgy about criticism; the other, secure in his mother's affections and sure of inheriting his father's position in the family, was also, it seems, heir to a complacent disposition.

Lucia remembered going to school with pleasure, but the best times for her were still in the evenings at home when her parents were there. Her aunt Eileen understood this. "Jim," she could see, "was a wonderful father. . . . He used to play by the hour with Giorgio and Lucia. He adored them."[78] Later, in 1919, when her own family had joined in living with the Joyces, Lucia's cousin Bozena Berta Schaurek remembered her uncle Jim sitting on the carpet to play "Forfeits" where everyone had to pay fines.[79]

But it is even more moving, more interesting, to imagine Joyce reading to his children, as his father before him had read to him. Envision him introducing them to the world conjured by fancy, teaching them, as does any parent who reads to a child, the pleasures and sonorities of hearing and imagining. Think of them experiencing those rare and remarkable moments when fantasy seems to invade and even merge with reality. While Joyce was raising Lucia, he was representing the memory of being read to in his own fiction. "Once upon a time and a very good time it was there was a moocow" who met a little boy. "His father told him that story." Here, in the opening page of *A Portrait of the Artist as a Young Man*, the book that Joyce began to revise in the months following Lucia's birth, the child understands himself to be part and parcel of the story: "He was baby tuckoo."[80] He sees that fiction encompasses him and that his future identity is built not only upon participation in the story but also upon his relation to the reading parent. In this book, Joyce invented a simple, beautiful way to represent the formative power of imagination. His sister remembered that he often read to the whole family at night, and many of the six hundred or so books in his Triestine library were tales beloved by children.[81]

And so though Joyce and Nora frequently took the children to eat in cafés in the evening, and though Joyce himself rambled around in bars alone, we can imagine that on many a night the children were attentive and secure, listening to a voice that was at once melodious and precise, a voice trained in the beauties and subtleties of meter and diction, reading from *The Arabian Nights*, *Peter Pan*, *The High History of the Holy Grail*, *The Tales of Poe*, *Gulliver's Travels*, *Hansel and Gretel*, and even *Aquila: The Adventures of Prince Aga*.[82]

If Joyce read to his daughter from his copy of *The Fisher Lassie*, a book by Bjørnstjerne Bjørnson, we can imagine it as an event with great consequences. *The Fisher Lassie* may have interested her father because of his more general enthusiasm for Ibsen and Nordic culture, but for Lucia it would have remained memorable for what it manifestly is, a saga about a young provincial girl, a girl not unlike herself, awakening to a vocation as an artist. The story begins in a lovely valley on the west coast of Norway where a rough and untutored child, Petra, daughter of Gunlaug, is caught stealing a neighbor's apples. One consequence of her delinquency is the attention of a well-to-do gentleman of the town, Hans Oedegaard, who decides to take her education in hand. "Day by day" Hans would read to her and "bring before her eyes characters from the

Bible or from history, in such a way as to point out to her the call that God had given them. He would tell her of Saul leading his wild life, or of the young David tending his father's flocks, till Samuel came and laid on him the hands of the Lord. But the greatest of all was the Call when the Lord walked upon earth, tarried among the fisher-folk, and called them to His work." When the child asks her mentor about her own "Call," Oedegaard, taking her lowly origins and gender into account, tells her that the "Call" might be "insignificant and unimportant, but that it existed for everyone." The girl, who longs to be a boy and who has "strange longings for adventure," gradually represses her own desires and grows "fond of her long tresses, and for their sake sacrifice[s] her chance of a heroine's fame."[83]

In other words, Petra seems to succumb to her biological and cultural destiny, as these were understood in the 1860s when Bjørnson wrote his tale. Were this the end of the story, we might conclude that the Joyces were reading a Nordic version of Snow White, who learns to dwarf her own talents until, at the height of her passivity, a prince takes her to wife. But Petra's love life takes her into one romantic fiasco after another. Her studies are similarly ineffective. Oedegaard notices "there was something remarkable in the girl [that] he had never doubted since the time when she was a child, and he had been used to seeing her march about singing at the head of the town's street boys. But the longer he taught her, the less he understood the natural bent of her talents and powers."[84] In words that seem eerily to foreshadow the perceptions Joyce came to have about Lucia in the 1920s, Oedegaard sees that Petra's talents are not conventionally academic. "There was evidence of them in every movement: whatever she happened to be thinking, to be wanting, that her whole body and spirit portrayed, with the fullness of her strength and the glory of her beauty. Yet in words—still more in writing—her thoughts were mere childishness. She seemed to be nothing but wayward imagination."[85]

Many experiences have to pass before this young woman comes to see that her talent is for the theater, and many new people have to be befriended before she meets God-fearing folk who do not regard a woman's pursuit of a stage career as sacrilege. But the novella brings Petra to the point where Oedegaard revises his earlier opinion: "forth from these letters rose Petra's artist's nature before him. The key to her being."[86] Eventually he argues that "the man [sic] who does not follow the calling his powers fit him for becomes irresolute, restless, and unfitted for any other, and therefore falls a far easier prey to temptation than if he had followed his natural bent."[87] The novella ends with a priest's blessing: "for the bridegroom is Art, the actor's mighty Art, and his betrothed my foster daughter, my dear Petra. May you be happy together! I tremble to think of it; but those whom God hath joined together, let no man put asunder. God be with you, my daughter!"[88] "And the curtain rose."[89]

For the young Triestine Lucia, no debut was in sight, but for the Joyces, father and daughter, reading and writing would remain a private way to communicate. In later years, the gift of a book would be the gift of a sentiment, a particular text would be understood as an invitation to consider the world from the vantage point suggested by the author. Though we cannot know that Joyce read this particular book to Lucia, we can notice that Lucia loved to read. One of the earliest photographs of her is of a handsome young girl, somberly dressed, who sits with downcast eyes, immersed in a book.[90] And we can reflect upon the lingering power of images encountered early in life. Can it be entirely a coincidence that one of Lucia's most beautiful and evocative dance costumes, the outfit designed for the Bal Bullier in 1929 and known to her contemporaries as the *poisson d'or* (goldfish), was a dress that turned her into a "fisher lass"?

Whatever the pleasures of having a musical, punning, limerick-writing, banister-sliding, extravagant, and indulgent father, Lucia and Giorgio's childhood also had a dark side. Hunger was a constant theme in these years, a serious one. Stanislaus remembered his five-year-old nephew snapping out at him one day, "We had no dinner today. Keep that in your head."[91] Giorgio remembered later that his family had been so poor that he had been taught to sing for their supper. Beginning when he was two, he later confided to his wife, he had sung in a café whose proprietor would then give the Joyces free meals. Lucia would toddle after him, "blindly obedient to his slightest command." Before long he was entrusted with her on the evenings when Nora and James "went out carousing."[92] By the time the Joyces moved to Zurich in 1914, this habit of leaving their children unattended while they went out in the evening was met by their children's equally insistent response—Giorgio and Lucia would yell out the window, "You are locking us up like pigs in a sty!"[93]

Her parents argued, particularly about money. Nora, according to
Eileen, was always after her husband to stop "the silly writing" and to
take in more language students. Once in a fit of anger Joyce met these
reproaches by throwing his manuscript of *Stephen Hero* into the woodstove. Eileen burned her hands in rescuing the pages and had to wear
mittens until they healed.[94] And then there was the incessant moving,
which started a kind of cumulative insecurity. By the time she was seven
in 1914, Lucia was a pro at the evade-the-landlord game. She'd lived at
five different addresses and dodged as many threats of eviction.

In 1912, at a time just short of her fifth birthday, Nora took Lucia to
Ireland, where she met her Dublin relatives and her mother's people in
Galway for the first time. Lucia was too young to understand the network of grudges, rejections, and aspirations that had led her parents to
choose exile, and she spoke only Italian, but she evidently impressed her
relatives. John Joyce, his heart softened by meeting young Giorgio in
1909, wept openly when he saw his little granddaughter.[95] On an outing
to the Hill of Howth, the ocean headlands to the north of Dublin, she
sang for the family at tea.[96]

Then Nora swept her away to the west of Ireland, to Galway, the
town where she had been raised and that still sheltered her mother, Annie Barnacle; her uncle, Michael Healy; and two of her five sisters, Kathleen and Delia. Annie Barnacle, long separated from her bottle-toting
baker of a husband, lived by herself in an artisan's cottage in Bowling
Green, a narrow backstreet. (The simplicity of the small house—one
room with a fireplace downstairs and a single bedroom above—led Lucia's parents and brother—yes, Joyce had borrowed money from Ettore
Schmitz to bring Giorgio and follow his wife and daughter to Ireland—
to accept hospitality at the home of Michael Healy.) Here too Lucia won
the heart of her grandparent. Nora described it all in a letter to Eileen
back in Trieste: "We usually go to the beach in the morning the air is
splendid here and the food Jim Georgie and myself are sleeping in my
Uncle's Lucia sleeps with mother you'd be surprised at how homely she
has got every night about ten or so when we are leaving Mother's we say
good night to Lucia and she goes up to bed singing she is wonderful she
is as rosey the two children love the place they are out all day they dont
give themselves time to eat."[97] In later years Lucia was to think of these
truncated glimpses of Irish life as an essential part of her identity, as if

she had somehow been robbed of an imagined wholeness by her parents' rejection of their native land. And their alienation was about to magnify.

Though Lucia could not know it, trouble was brewing even as her family enjoyed their leisure in the bracing sea air of Galway. The backdrop to their holiday featured the eventually familiar blend of treachery and betrayal. As well as walking with his family along the strand, going to the Galway Races with Nora, and traveling to the Aran Islands, Joyce took time away from them to bicycle out to the nearby town of Oughterard. He wanted to see the grave of Michael Bodkin, one of Nora's adolescent lovers who had supposedly died for love of her. Jealousy and a brooding preoccupation with his wife's sexuality apart from his life with her undercut the simple pleasures to be had with his family. Supposed personal injury was then joined by professional insult. During this time, Joyce also learned that he had not received the certificate that would allow him to teach in the Triestine public schools. And George Roberts in Dublin, the supposed publisher of *Dubliners*, Joyce's collection of short stories, decided not to bring the book out. Fear of lawsuits led him to destroy the already printed sheets and to pie the type. From Dublin, where he had gone to try to salvage his writing, Joyce wrote to Nora of the fate of his book as if he were the anguished mother of a stillborn baby. He spoke of "the book I have written, the child which I have carried for years and years in the womb of the imagination as you carried in your womb the children you love, and of how I had fed it day after day out of my brain and my memory."[98] In September Lucia returned to Trieste with her mother and father, her brother, and an unborn book.

IV. COMPLEXITIES; SIMPLICITY

Unknown to Lucia, as she made friends, learned languages, and went about the life of a young Irish girl growing up in a seaport in a distant corner of the Austro-Hungarian Empire, the erotic dimension of her parents' lives once again erupted with troubling intensity. There was no overt crisis; instead a kind of watchfulness settled over her parents as each of them flirted with the affections, attentions, and evasions of lovers. These disturbances had their origins, in one way or another, in the private English lessons Joyce gave to various Triestine students either in their homes or in the living room of his own flat. For Nora the student was Roberto Prezioso, editor of the local newspaper *Il Piccolo della Sera*; for Joyce it was probably a young woman named Amalia Popper. In both cases, the flirtations were teasing and ambiguous, partly revealed and partly hidden, and interesting for their psychological revelations rather than their realized passion. But in Joyce's case, these entanglements indirectly affected the prism through which he viewed his young daughter.

Sometime around 1913, Nora got embroiled with a dashing aristocratic man. Prezioso was the married father of two children, from a prosperous Venetian family, and rumored to be bisexual.[99] She had known him since 1905, when he had given Joyce a character reference to take with him to Rome, and his visits with Nora in the Joyces' flat were initially clouded with ambiguity. Nora's biographer, Brenda Maddox, claims that Joyce himself had encouraged Prezioso's attentions to his wife, motivated by "the thrill of imagining Nora in the embrace of another man." Maddox writes of Prezioso as the Joyces' "first victim," as if they had schemed together to create a sexual scenario for their own mutual amusement.[100] We can imagine other emotional complications that are more common to affairs: lessening passion between marriage partners; approaching middle age and the need for reassurance about one's attractiveness; loneliness; and yes, the allure of sex itself. We know more about how the affair ended than we will ever know about its motives, for it came to an abrupt and humiliating conclusion when flirtation turned to seduction. Joyce confronted his erstwhile friend in the street. Whatever he said to Prezioso caused him to weep, and his visits to Nora ceased.[101]

Yet Joyce must have recognized that his own adoration of Nora was not sufficient to keep him from similar sexual longings. It is doubtful that there was any kind of kiss-and-tell dynamic to Joyce's infatuation. If he flirted to see what illicit sex was like so that he could write about it, it is hard to imagine him sharing the needs and directions of his errant heart with his wife. Instead, probably between the years 1911 and 1914, he kept a kind of secret journal of impressions, which he eventually copied in his best calligraphy onto eight oversize sheets of sketching paper.[102]

In this sketchbook, which we have come to call *Giacomo Joyce*, Joyce's ladylove is a young woman of many fine and interesting qualities. Her pale face is surrounded with furs; she is shy; she wears "quizzing glasses"; she writes with a delicate script. He catches a glimpse of a white undergarment when he watches her tobogganing with her father and another glimpse when a sudden movement catches her skirt. In helping her to button a dress, he touches her back. The impressions continue: she is Jewish; she is pale, chill, thin. "Her flesh recalls the thrill of that raw mist-veiled morning." Among the signs of her leisure-class origins—expensive clothing, cultured activities, protected upbringing, good education (after all, Joyce is her teacher)—what titillates the keeper of this secret diary seems to be a kind of innocent anticipation. The mystery lady is a virgin—unripe, but on the edge of discovering her own sensuality. Amid these glimpses of lust and of lust resisted by virtue, the writer pauses to notice that his beloved student has given a flower to Lucia; and in reverie, he unites the gift, the giver, and his daughter: "Frail are her hands that gave / whose soul is sere . . . Frail gift, frail giver, frail blue-veined child."[103]

In 1913 Joyce would use this observation, about a flower, a lover, and a child, as the basis for a poem, "A Flower Given to My Daughter," in a little book of verse he eventually called *Pomes Penyeach*. To a tormented and undecided father, situating himself between the heavy sensuality of his wife and the green, budding eroticism of a would-be lover, the daughter seemed in these years akin more to his lover than his wife. The poem, which speaks of a beauty symbolically passed from one generation to another, places the daughter in the unorthodox company of a cultured woman who is not her mother but whom the father nonetheless perceives to be a kindred spirit. In all of Joyce's writing there would never be a Madonna-and-child image for Nora and Lucia. Instead, he takes pleasure in comparing one delicate creature with another and he pauses, with heart-wrenching tenderness, to look at his own little girl as she must look to the "gentle eyes" of the more mature woman. She is a "wonder wild."[104]

He paused once more in these early years of Lucia's childhood to linger over the meaning of his daughter's life, and he implicitly contrasted her to the complications of his own erotic life with Nora and with the mystery lady of his secret journal. In 1915 he wrote her another poem entitled "Simples." It begins with a quotation from an Italian popular song—*"ella bionda, ei come l'onda!"*[105] The father watches a child gathering salad greens in moonlight and speaks of the haunting beauty of the child, of her talent, and of the innocence of the moment.[106] The girl sings but is unaware that she is being watched. Be mine, the father prays, and asks for a "waxen ear" to shield him from her "childish croon." Part of the allure of her as-yet-unselfconscious relation to life lies in her implicit contrast to the dark, complicated sexuality of her mother and the erotic obsessions of *Giacomo Joyce*. The poem marks a kind of return to an earlier sensibility, a going backward in time to retrieve that which has been lost in the intervening years of adulthood. In *A Portrait of the Artist as a Young Man* the young Stephen Dedalus is represented as being sated by sexual drive and concerned to find new relations with women. "Are you not weary of ardent ways?" the developing artist asks himself,[107] and this sentiment is curiously akin to the voice of the father observing his daughter in "Simples." He has faith in the child; he finds her piercingly beautiful, and in her singing moonlit self he glimpses a world complete and completely self-contained. Her concentration on the simple task of gathering greenery both excludes him and rends his heart; and because of this, his poem is akin to a prayer.

Lucia is the first of Joyce's sirens. Nora and the mystery lady represent to him love that beckons and that invites completion. Lucia represents a love that is too intense to follow. Give me waxen ears so that I cannot hear her song, he prays. Shield my heart from all that I see here. And if this poem represents the child as siren, it implicitly represents the father as Odysseus. He is a man who needs his friends to cover his ears and tie him to a figurative mast so that he can complete his journey back to a wife, who is, at least in a lazy, half-flirtatious way, already busy with other suitors on the Via della Barriera Vecchia.

This vision of Lucia is a vision that Joyce never relinquished. Twenty years later, when she was in the midst of emotional entanglements that seemed incapable of resolution, he was sustained by its simple clarity. In 1935, writing to his old friend Constantine Curran, he said that "gaiety and gentleness" were the essential qualities of Lucia's nature.[108] In 1935 his singular and intense purpose was to return his daughter to her childhood self.

2

THE THEATER OF WAR
ZURICH 1915-19

I. NEW LANGUAGES

When Lucia was five, her aunt Eva returned to Dublin; when she was eight, her aunt Eileen married Frantisek Schaurek and moved to Prague. The six years the niece had enjoyed in the company of maiden ladies who adored her had ended. But even greater disruptions were about to intrude on the life of the Joyce family, signaled in January 1914 by the arrest of her uncle Stanislaus for his outspoken opposition to Austrian rule of Trieste. Stripped of his job and his students, he was to sit out the Great War in detention camps in Austria. At first it may have seemed that the life of the rest of her family could continue as usual, for the Joyces, carrying British passports, were not citizens of an enemy nation at the onset of hostilities in July 1914. But England quickly joined the war effort; and when Italy entered the war in May 1915, Trieste, with its long history of Italian and Austrian antagonisms, became a dangerous place to live.

Left to his own devices, Joyce might have stayed put. Encouraged by Grant Richards's publication of *Dubliners* in June 1914 and by the serial publication of *A Portrait of the Artist as a Young Man* in *The Egoist* between February 1914 and September 1915, he was deeply immersed in writing his play *Exiles*. He was also starting *Ulysses*, which he thought of as the sequel to *A Portrait of the Artist as a Young Man*. For him the

Lucia with Nora and Giorgio Joyce, Zurich, circa 1916. (Courtesy of the Poetry–Rare Books Collection, State University of New York at Buffalo)

worlds he invented took precedence over the worlds that nation-states tore apart, but personal preferences soon became irrelevant. Trieste was bombed four times, and soon the Austrian military authorities ordered a partial evacuation.[1] Even had the Joyces evaded the evacuation order, they had no source of income, for the Scuola Superiore di Commercio where Joyce had worked closed after most of its Austrian staff had been conscripted. Joyce turned his eyes back to the sad wreck of the actual world. With the help of well-placed former students, he secured visas and exit permits, bought train tickets to the border of Switzerland, and leaving books and furniture behind, took his young family away from the only home his children had ever known.

With the resilience of youth Lucia took what fortune offered next. For a few weeks in June 1915, she and her family moved into the Gasthaus Hoffnung in Zurich—the pension where her parents had stayed when they first came to Europe in 1904. Felix Béran, a Viennese writer living in Zurich, remembered looking up from his writing in the small pension garden and seeing the Joyces arrive: "The unknown lanky man with the eyeglasses came directly to me. He was leading a little girl by the hand. Close behind him came a lady, apparently his wife, young, with lovely dark eyes. A lusty little youngster was dragging at her right hand."[2] But then the family moved three times in quick succession as rented room followed rented room.[3] Lucia's memories of life in Switzerland were memories of damp and crowded poverty, of being a schoolgirl, and of a dawning assessment of change as she began to recognize that her father was at work on a project of stunning proportions. "When *Ulysses* was finished," she recalled in "My Life," "they said it was a masterpiece and I was very excited about it."[4]

While her father worked, she and Giorgio were placed in a public school where her teacher was Heinrich Gallmann. Lucia's judgment was that "Herr Gallmann seemed to like me and he always asked me to sing. I was good at arithmetic geography and gymnastic. *Rundlauf* was wonderful. You had to run and then you sort of fly in the air."[5] Already adept at two languages, she now tackled German, which she found "very interesting as a language."[6] Soon she and Giorgio were chattering away in *Schwyzertutsch*, the Swiss German dialect. Tucked away from the killing fields of the war, the Zurich schools were filled with other refugees like herself who bought a relatively normal childhood for the small price of learning an unfamiliar tongue. Lucia remembered her mother having to make her own butter and the struggle to get enough food; she remembered their poverty, but in other ways, Switzerland seems to have shielded her from the horrors of a war-torn continent.[7]

In a remarkably short time, Lucia was leading a life with its full share of childish pleasures. She went on school outings, taking sandwiches, fruit, and chocolate that Nora provided; she made friends; she played outside after school. Her especial friend was Jeanne Wertenberg, whose family had come to Zurich from Neuchâtel. Many years later, Jeanne, now Frau Gisiger, remembered Lucia as "a very happy and talented child." The two girls had played at each other's houses and slept overnight with each other; their friendship had endured, sustained by letters, long past their schooldays and on into the 1930s. Frau Gisiger remembered that Lucia's parents were rarely at home during the day, that they left their children largely to fend for themselves, but she had explained this to herself as the eccentricity to be expected in an artist's household. The two girls' more immediate concerns were playing ball, skating, and sliding on the ice on Bolleystrasse, where the Jarnachs, Lucia's former neighbors, lived.[8] When Frank Budgen became her father's close friend and confidant, he taught Giorgio and Lucia to swim, and Lucia remembered that he—like Giorgio and still later Ottocaro Weiss—called her with a secret whistle. After school, she began to study the piano with Fräulein Stuhlmuller, from Vienna, who lived in the Stampfenbadstrasse. Lucia remembered her as a strict person who was an excellent musician and fine teacher.[9]

In time, financial help and the first glimmerings of fame came from unexpected places. In 1916, Joyce was, for the first time, included in *Who's Who*, but he was helped more by hard currency than he was by honor. Nora's uncle Michael Healy, anticipating that the young couple would need money to tide them over in their second, war-induced exile, sent them fifteen pounds.[10] From another corner of the world, Ezra Pound and W. B. Yeats took up Joyce's cause, writing letters and arranging contacts until the Royal Literary Fund in London awarded him a grant of seventy-five pounds, payable in nine installments.[11] "I believe him to be a man of genius," Yeats wrote on his behalf, and he followed that letter with another one in 1916, this time to ask the prime minister to make Joyce a hundred-pound grant from England's Civil List. Joyce's work, he said, "has a curious brooding intensity"; he was "just such a man as it is well to help."[12] If these bequests made a meager life possible, the two anonymous donations that followed in 1917 allowed the Joyces their first taste of middle-class comfort. Both gifts were provided by "admirers" who chose to keep their identities secret, but Joyce was eventually to discover that Harriet Weaver, publisher of *The Egoist* in London, had provided four fifty-pound checks. The remainder of his good fortune he owed to Mrs. Edith McCormick, the daughter of John D. Rockefeller, who patronized the arts in Zurich during the war.[13]

For the first time in his adult life, Joyce was able to devote himself to writing full-time. In a letter to the American poet Ezra Pound, he explained his preoccupation: "As regards *Ulysses* I write and think and write and think all day and part of the night."[14] Lucia could see that her father was absorbed in his book. By the end of 1917 he had written the first three sections about Stephen Dedalus, the hero of *A Portrait of the Artist as a Young Man*, whose life continued over into *Ulysses*. In March 1918, he wrote a chapter called "Calypso"; in April "The Lotus Eaters"; in May "Hades"; in August "Aeolus." Several years later in Paris, when Pound had been enlisted to help find Lucia and Giorgio beds, he had entreated Jenny Serruys to "get [Joyce] a bed for his too large son to sleep on."[15] But in those wartime years in Zurich, it was really *Ulysses* that was growing rapidly into a gigantic and demanding progeny. It took up more and more psychic and literal space. Lucia remembered that her father often spread out his papers on the floor of the house and that he developed a system for marking the manuscript with red pencil.[16] But mostly *Ulysses* drew her father farther and farther into a realm where none of them could follow.

For Nora, as her husband could see, nothing had changed since their early married years in Trieste and Rome. She took no more interest in his writing now than she had in the days when the manuscript of *Stephen Hero* had been thrown into the woodstove. She preferred sentimental women's magazines that you could pick up in the railway station.[17] For Giorgio, Wild West stories provided better reading.[18]

When their father was not at home writing, he tended to disappear into a kind of café life. Some of it was familiar—he had always been adept at evening binges—but some of it was new and involved an elaborate kind of storytelling with friends like Frank Budgen, Paul Suter, Ot-

tocaro Weiss, Claud Sykes, and Paul Ruggiero. To them Joyce would
talk about the development of his imaginary creation. In early August
1917, Georges Borach, one of his language students, recorded his
teacher's thoughts about using a modern version of Ulysses as his hero.
"Now, in *mezzo del cammin*," Joyce told him, "I find the subject of
Ulysses the most human in world literature. Ulysses didn't want to go off
to Troy; he knew that the official reason for the war, the dissemination of
the culture of the Hellas, was only a pretext for the Greek merchants,
who were seeking new markets. When the recruiting officers arrived, he
happened to be plowing. He pretended to be mad. Thereupon they
placed his little two-year-old son in the furrow. Observe the beauty of the
motifs: the only man in Hellas who is against the war, and the father."[19]

But if the mythic Ulysses was admired because of the scope of his realistic experiences (he was not only a son, as Joyce's character Stephen
Dedalus had been, but also a husband and father), the real husband and
father to a flesh-and-blood family was becoming more and more of a
mythic, spectral being. He remained closeted in his own imagination, interested in aspects of his wife and children's lives partly for what they
contributed to his work, and interested in his work above all else. There
were to be real consequences to his emotional absence.

In the late summer of 1917, when Lucia was ten, Nora suffered some
kind of nervous breakdown. A few weeks were left before the beginning
of the new school year, so using money from Joyce's benefactors, she took
Lucia and Giorgio to Locarno, where she hoped to quiet her nerves and
give her husband the peace and quiet he needed to write. "I hope you're
writing Ulisses without us to bother you," she wrote in mid-August.[20]
She and the children lived a leisurely tourists' life: they ate well, took
walks, and rowed on Lake Maggiore. Lucia remembered the lake outing
to visit an elderly lady, the Baronessa Saint Leger, when a thunderstorm
came up while they were in the little boat. Nora, praying for their safety,
was terrified that they would not get to the Isola Saint Leger safely, but
fate was kind. They got there, bought jam made of figs and apricots for
their father, and returned unharmed to Locarno.[21] In some ways they felt
more at home here than in Zurich, for the Italian language as well as the
noise, dirt, and general commotion in the outdoor markets reminded
them of Trieste.[22]

But it was an aimless life, and Nora's letters are full of reminders to her husband that the two children would return to Zurich for the start of the school year. In the interim, Giorgio and Lucia played the gramophone incessantly and wrestled with each other in bed. "I havent any trouble with them," Nora reported, "except in the morning before they get up its a regular game with them they have a boxing match in the bed and of course I have to pull the two of them out on the floor Georgie is very shy he is afraid of his life I might see his prick so that he rolls himself up in the quilt."[23] Nora finds her twelve-year-old son's sexual self-consciousness amusing, but her letter gives us a glimpse of the emotional, and possibly the sexual, dynamics between a brother and sister who were accustomed to being locked up together "like pigs in a sty" when their parents went out. They were frequently unsupervised; they had only each other, and we can imagine them enclosed in a private world drawn from the loneliness of their life circumstances.

Later in August, Nora, Giorgio, and Lucia were precipitously called back to Zurich, for in their absence Joyce had suffered a debilitating attack of glaucoma. The severity of the pain led his ophthalmologist to perform an iridectomy at the Augenklinik, but his eyes continued to hurt, and Lucia remembered her father actually crying from the pain. No matter what the meaning of her name, no matter what symbolic role she played in the life of the parent with troubled eyesight, she remembered that she had no idea, when it came down to it, how to console him.[24]

In October her parents took her and Giorgio out of school and moved, cat and all, to Locarno. Herr Gallmann, Fräulein Stuhlmuller, and Jeanne Wertenberg were left behind, and she and Giorgio were enrolled in the Italian-speaking school there. Once again they lived in the Pension Daheim, as they had in the summer; once again she presumably slept with Giorgio, and once again Joyce's papers and pencils and manuscript leaves were spread around the living room. Apart from its good climate and being a place to work, Locarno must have had something of a carnival about it, for at different times both her parents seem to have carried on flirtations there. In Joyce's absence during August, Nora had sought other dancing partners[25] and had reported her experiences in a letter addressed to her husband, with intentions that are difficult for us to discern, as "Dear Cuckold."[26] Joyce's infatuation with a young German doctor recovering from tuberculosis is no less difficult to under-

Lucia Joyce, Zurich, circa
1917. Photographer
unknown. (Courtesy of Frau
Gisiger and Marilyn Reizbaum)

James Joyce, Zurich, circa 1917.
(Courtesy of the Croessmann Collection,
Morris Library, Southern Illinois University
at Carbondale)

stand, for he seems to have pursued her even in the company of his entire family, both in Locarno and later in Zurich. According to the woman herself, whose name was Gertrude Kaempffer, Joyce shared intimacies that she found unwelcome, and he persisted in claiming that he loved her even after she made it clear that his feelings would not be reciprocated. Like the previous "mystery lady" of Joyce's Triestine infatuation, she rebuffed Joyce's advances.[27]

Lucia's reminiscences about living in Locarno (she was ten years old at the time) were also erotic memories. Locarno was, she claimed in 1961, a place of romance for herself as well: "When we went to Locarno I met a young man from the South of America. I think he spoke Spanish. I fell in love with him but he had tuberculosis. We went in the park by moonlight. It was rather romantic."[28] Almost twenty years later, in chatting with her girlhood friend Dominique Maroger, Lucia continued to remember this young man, whom she now called "Sempo," and to associate him with the possibility of becoming pregnant. "In order for me to grow up, he wanted me to have a baby."[29]

Memory can deceive, it can distort, and it can serve unacknowledged motives, but even granting such truths, Lucia's are remarkable statements. What has happened to the virginal simplicity of the young Triestine girl who won the heart of her watchful father in 1915? Lucia also remembered their former neighbor in Zurich, Charlotte Sauermann, who lived with them at 73 Seefeldstrasse. She was not simply a performer in the city opera but also a woman who was "living in sin." "On the same floor," Lucia told Richard Ellmann, "Fräulein Sauermann and her lover Philip . . . lived together. She was learning the part of Madame Butterfly for the Stadtheater in Zurich." Slipping into French, she continued, "Elle ne me croyait pas dans sa candeur naïve que l'amour innocent qui germait dans son coeur puisse changer un jour en une ardeur piu vive." ("She would not have me believe, in her naïve candor, that love that grows innocently in one's heart can one day change into a more passionate ardor.")[30] Was Lucia remembering Madame Butterfly's erotic awakening, Charlotte Sauermann's, or her own? Her question lets us glimpse a young girl whose gawky long legs, little velvet dresses, and schoolgirl demeanor hide an intelligence attuned to the nuances and possible treacheries of adult sexual conduct. Nora's assumption that her children were behaving innocently in the absence of their parents seems too complacent. Why was the ten-year-old Lucia free to meet anybody at all in a moonlit field? Why was she sleeping in the same bed with her sexually self-conscious brother?

Lucia's memories also suggest that Nora's sense of being erotically invisible to her children was similarly mistaken, for Lucia understood that one of her father's friends, Ottocaro Weiss, took more than a casual interest in her mother. Weiss was a young Triestine Jew who was studying political science at Zurich University. He had been introduced to the family through one of Joyce's students in Trieste, Oscar Schwarz. Lucia remembered the two young men in the manner of her father: as a pair of odd, coincidental puns on *black* and *white*. Weiss had dark hair while Schwarz was fair. During the war, Weiss had served in the military, but he had returned to Zurich in January 1919 and had become a frequent companion to the family at restaurants and concerts. He shared Nora's particular passion for the music of Wagner. Lucia remembered that she and her mother would promenade with Weiss along the Universität-strasse and that her mother and Weiss would sometimes travel alone. She noticed that he took Nora by boat to Schaffhausen and that her parents had eventually quarreled over him. Claud Sykes, watching from the sidelines, had also noticed Weiss's attentions to Nora and in later years diffidently told Herbert Gorman, Joyce's first biographer, that he believed Weiss had been in love with her.[31]

We don't know how many of these erotic entanglements were on Lucia's mind in the fall and winter of 1917, but numerous other complications may in some way explain the need that both her parents eventually felt for other partners. During the three months in Locarno, Nora had frequently been ill with what Joyce described to Claud Sykes as "bad nervous breakdowns."[32] She cried; she was anxious and depressed and seemed in general to have lost her normal equilibrium. We can imagine Lucia perceiving her mother's distress and her parents' estrangement from each other. We can also picture her as a silent witness to another kind of brooding stillness: the profound quietness in which her father pursued his intense and focused art. "Telemachus" was written then; "Nestor" was written; "Proteus" was written. *Ulysses* was launched—the son was sent in search of his missing father, while the mother handled the stress of his absence as best she could. In this respect, Nora was like that long-ago Penelope of fable, but it was a book rather than a journey that claimed the talents of her man. When they moved from Locarno back to Zurich in January 1918, Nora told her best friend, Daisy Sykes, that her husband "never spoke a word to [her] at the Pension Daheim."[33] For Lucia the implicit lesson in her parents' marriage at this stage in their lives had to do with the power of art and the lure of an invented world. She also noticed the silence that can ensue when the creative passion of one person remains beyond the ken of the other, no matter how well loved and needed that mate may be. Joyce read parts of *Ulysses* aloud to Nora, but as Lucia could see, her mother turned away.

In January 1918, when the Joyces came back to Zurich, they moved into a different neighborhood on the Universitätstrasse, first at number 38 and later at number 29, where they would remain until the end of their sojourn in Switzerland a year and a half later. Lucia and Giorgio gamely trotted back to the German-speaking public school, although their new address meant that it had to be an unfamiliar branch of it. In March 1918, Joyce wrote "Calypso" and headed into his contemporary rendering of Ulysses in his guise as husband and father. An Irish Jew, Leopold Bloom, plays the role of Joyce's modern-day Ulysses, wandering about Dublin on 16 June 1904, weaving thoughts of his wife, his daughter, and his dead infant son into the fabric of his everyday musings.

II. MILLY BLOOM

And so the young Lucia entered into a less simple place in her father's fiction. In June 1918, when Joyce was setting up the imaginative home life of Leopold and Molly Bloom and their daughter, Milly, Lucia was eleven. When he wrote "Nausicaa" between 1919 and March 1920, about the seductive nymph who holds Ulysses in thrall on her island kingdom, she was between twelve and thirteen. As she grew, so did *Ulysses*. As one child emerged into the light, so did the other, rivalrous offspring for a father's affection, competitors for his brooding attention. The portraits of young girls in Joyce's writing of these years project them slightly further into pubescence. Milly is just about to turn fifteen; Gerty MacDowell is somewhat older. They are interesting not only for what they reveal about adolescence as Joyce saw it but also for what they tell us about his idea of parents watching their children emerge into young adulthood. Joyce chooses to present Milly almost entirely through the eyes of her parents.

When "Calypso" opens, it is early morning. Bloom is busy buying food, making breakfast, feeding the cat, and looking at the mail. We learn that Milly, his daughter, has been sent to Mullingar, a Dublin suburb, to become an assistant in a photographer's shop. She writes to her parents. To her mother she sends a simple thank-you note for birthday presents and to Bloom a more extended letter. Then, having written her only original lines—to "Dearest Papli" . . . from "Your fond daughter" (U 4.397–411)—she disappears from sight. From this point, she will appear only as an image refracted through the minds of others.

But she is an interesting case, even in her name. Milly reminds us of Joyce's description of his student lover in his secret diary from Trieste. There the young girl, a "filly," was also someone pursued with hungry eyes, thought about and imagined in places where the writer/lover cannot follow: "Twilight. Crossing the piazza. Grey eve lowering on wide sagegreen pasturelands, shedding silently dusk and dew. She follows her mother with ungainly grace, the mare leading her filly foal. Grey twilight moulds softly the slim and shapely haunches, the meek supple tendonous neck, the fine-boned skull."[34] Joyce borrowed this language almost exactly for a later episode of Ulysses, "Oxen of the Sun." Once again, Joyce imagines his fictional daughter as the spiritual heir not of Molly/Nora, her own mother, but of that once coveted but impossible-to-possess student lover from days gone by. To herself she is "silly Milly" (U 4.409), but to her father she is "Millicent the young the dear the radiant" who "follows her mother with ungainly steps, a mare leading her filly-foal. Twilight phantoms are they yet moulded in prophetic grace of structure, slim shapely haunches, a supple tendonous neck, the meek apprehensive skull" (U 14.1082–85). From the mother Molly to the daughter Milly, from the mother mare to the daughter filly, the girl child in Ulysses is perceived to be a smaller, newer version of the older woman. This is so whether that woman is considered to be her actual mother or her more spiritually similar progenitor, the mystery lady from Trieste who gave her a flower. She is "the same thing [as her precursor] watered down" (U 6.87), as if all women, in time, shared the same biological fate. "Destiny," thinks Bloom (U 4.229–30).

Molly Bloom imagines her daughter in a similar light, seeing her destiny in the simple fact of her maturing sex: "they all look at her like me when I was her age of course" (*U* 18.1036). At the end of the novel, as she drifts into sleep at the close of day, Molly remembers Milly primarily for the trouble she has caused, thinking of her daughter's childhood with more annoyance than affection: "what I went through with Milly nobody would believe cutting her teeth" (*U* 18.158–59). "I had a great breast of milk with Milly . . . hurt me they used to weaning her" (*U* 18.570–75); "when she was a child . . . she had worms" (*U* 18.1167–68). And while Molly recognizes her life as circumscribed by domestic chores, her mind sees only those characteristics in her daughter that remind her of her own sexuality: "Like Milly's little ones now when she runs up the stairs" (*U* 18.150–51). "Shes restless knowing shes pretty . . . I was too" (*U* 18.1065–66). In this maternal view, the only heritage that counts is beauty, which is, however, a short-lived asset.

From these perceptions of a growing girl arise some of the major themes of Joyce's epic: the mother's jealousy of her own daughter; the father's libidinous interest in his own child; the mother's clandestine affair with her lover, Blazes Boylan; the mother's annoyance at having a curious and prepubescent child poking around the house; and the daughter's subliminal knowledge of her mother's adulterous relationship.

Joyce's fictional pubescent daughter is a delinquent; she refuses to stay in place. Molly concludes that "its as well he sent her where she is she was just getting out of bounds" (*U* 18.1027) and remembers one transgression after another: "I had to tell her not to cock her legs up like that on show on the windowsill before all the people passing" (*U* 18.1034–36). She broke a small "statue with her roughness and carelessness before she left" (*U* 18.1012–15). She was sly; she flirted (*U* 18.1023); she smoked cigarettes in secret (*U* 18.1028); she helped herself to her mother's face powder (*U* 18.1064). She received secret letters from Conny Connolly (*U* 18.1052–53). An obstreperous child. A "saucebox" (*U* 4.423). These are not the signs of the younger generation's smooth transition into a readily accepted female "destiny."

Gerty MacDowell, the other adolescent girl in *Ulysses*, lures the attentive, masturbatory fantasies of Leopold Bloom as he stares at her in the mild Dublin twilight. This character was probably a composite creature. Joyce gave her Gertrude Kaempffer's first name and many of the characteristics of Marthe Fleischmann, another of his own erotic interests in Zurich. He composed the episode in a sickly sweet style influenced by

novelettes sent to him from Dublin by his aunt Josephine Murray.[35] By
the time he was writing "Nausicaa," he had hauled his family back to
Trieste and into the apartment shared by Stanislaus and by Eileen's family, now expanded by the births of two daughters, Bozena Berta and
Eleanora. Frank Budgen was not at hand in a café, and Joyce had to describe his writing in letters to him. The style was, he wrote, "a namby-
pamby jammy marmalady drawersy (alto la!) style with effects of
incense, mariolatry, masturbation, stewed cockles, painter's palette,
chitchat, circumlocutions, etc etc."[36] But if Lucia could claim little real
kinship with these characters, they were, nonetheless, the young women
who populated her father's imagination between the years 1918 and
1921.

Among the many things that we can observe from juxtaposing Joyce's
inner and outer worlds is an extraordinary discordance between his image of female adolescence and the testimony of his daughter's young life.
Whatever sexual stirring she did feel in these years, whatever "wildness"
she expressed in her character, she was no namby-pamby smarmy young
airhead. She was a serious child; she could be droll and witty; she was an
excellent linguist and a budding mathematician who loved physical culture and sport. She was also a talented singer and pianist, even though
Joyce was in the habit of showing off the musical abilities of his son
while Lucia had to resort to the attentions of a primary schoolteacher
who recognized a pretty voice when he heard one. She and Giorgio were
given theater experience when they took bit parts in the English Players'
performance of Synge's Riders to the Sea. During their years in Zurich,
both children had become accustomed to adult society and to the café
life of a major European city. They had a wild father who made up
songs about "Mr. Dooley-ooley-ooley-oo" and naughty lyrics about his
friends—"Oh! Budgen, boozer, bard, and canvas dauber." They had a
father who broke into spontaneous "spider dances" in the street, drank
himself under the table if he felt like it, and always sobered up to begin
the serious work of creating a great comic novel about the extraordinary dimensions of everyday life. If Lucia was shy in the presence of
strangers, if she was accustomed to keeping serious thoughts to herself,
she was also a cosmopolitan child with experiences that had demanded
far more of her than children raised in more consistent, protected
environments.

In a quiet way, the Joyces' life in Zurich was already a world askew. Joyce, the father, had a kind of poetic blindness to the nature of the very real young and modern female existence unfolding before him. He seemed to miss, at first, what became so painfully evident in later years: that his daughter received her heritage from him not as a text but as a mandate for living. If Nora's personality was proof against any of Joyce's influence, Lucia's was not. The evidence was all there in the opening image of their arrival in Zurich, with the little girl's trust in her father's protection and her preference for his company. He is the person from whom she springs; her mother is otherwise occupied. Felix Béran had seen it: "The unknown lanky man with the eyeglasses came directly to me. He was leading a little girl by the hand. Close behind him came a lady, apparently his wife, young, with lovely dark eyes. A lusty little youngster was dragging at her right hand." The evidence was there in Lucia's excellent report cards, in her interest in modern languages, and in her keen assessments of what was important in life. "She was a very happy and talented child." It was a simple but profound truth that Joyce seemed to miss in the years between 1915 and 1919. Lucia was a father-identified child; she took after him.

LUCIA
JOYCE

Lucia Joyce, Paris, 1923. Pencil sketch by Myron Nutting. (Courtesy of the Library of Special Collections, Northwestern University)

3

MOVING INTO ADOLESCENCE

PARIS 1920–24

In 1920, when Lucia arrived in Paris, she was a thirteen-year-old whom her father described as a "saucebox." She spoke back to him, calling him "l'Esclamadore." "You're always exclaiming!" she teased. She surrounded herself and Joyce in a realm whose walls were a private language.[2] It didn't matter what country they were in—Italy, Switzerland, France, or England—she continued to speak Italian with her father, for it was the language of her birth. To others who met her in the early days in Paris, no matter what language she spoke, she was a "wonderfully sweet girl"; but she was quiet in front of strangers, and they couldn't see everything.[3]

Within her immediate family, Lucia was mordant, especially for a child. Eager, critical, outspoken, curious about the new world she inhabited, frustrated by the need to learn yet another language, resentful of all she had lost in moving from Trieste, uncomfortable in her isolation, she covered her awkwardness by talking to Giorgio in German and by rarely talking to anyone at all outside of the family. Sitting down to tea with Helen Nutting in 1921, once a school had finally been chosen for her daughter, Nora sighed with relief. "I cannot tell you what it is like to have that child out of the way!" she admitted. "I was nearly mad with her about all day."[4]

Lucia had been "about" for lack of anything better to do. At first she had had no idea that Paris would be anything more than a stopover on the family's way to London or to some other place where her father could continue to write his novel. The whole family stayed in the Latin Quarter at 9 rue de l'Université, making do in a small hotel that her father's friend Ezra Pound had booked for them. Brenda Maddox claims that this was a place favored by the literati, but to Myron Nutting, who was then a family friend, it was simply, and probably more accurately, "this old hotel down by the river."[5] Then when Pound, whom Lucia called "Signor Sterlina,"[6] found them a place to stay for the summer, the several weeks turned into several months and there they were. Even the servant's flat on the rue de l'Assomption that had been loaned to them by a stranger, Ludmila Bloch-Savitsky, was crowded. With only two rooms, the place had beds for neither Lucia nor her brother, and even after these were borrowed, there were no sheets, no blankets, no bathtub, and only broken teacups.[7]

In these cramped circumstances, Lucia resumed her familiar life on the margins of someone else's creativity. It was already a life that alternately seduced and repelled her, and both its allure and its repugnance would grow as Joyce emerged in these years from the obscurity that had marked the early reception of his work to become the most famous modernist writer of his generation. She had to remain quiet while her father worked—this time on the phantasmagoric chapter of *Ulysses* called "Circe."

Few thirteen-year-olds can imagine the license displayed by their own father's imagination, but it is difficult to suppose that a young girl would not recognize the emotional investment bestowed upon her by a creative parent. Indeed it is likely that Lucia as a child sensed not only her parent's attention but also the shades of that attention. While she chafed under the regime imposed by Joyce's writing, seeing only the intensity and withdrawal of his mind, he was pushing at the very contours of representation in Western literature. He was writing about the "indecencies" of adult libidinal life, changing men into the modern equivalent of swine, picturing them as they walked around the red-light district of Dublin and surrounding them with the wild voices of children like herself. In Joyce's imagination, the young lived in the darkness of unconscious desire just as much as fully grown men. There they were in

Nighttown. He wrote, *"[a] chain of children's hands imprisons him"* (*U* 15.15–16).

As Lucia hovered aimlessly around him in overcrowded spaces, Joyce brought her figuratively with him into the palace of Circe. He repeated his earlier portrayal of her as Milly who was, from the beginning, a "wild piece of goods" and who had borne the weight of her father's incestuous longings. "Milly too. Young kisses: the first . . . A soft qualm of regret, flowed down his backbone, increasing. Will happen, yes. Prevent. Useless" (*U* 4.66–67). While her father turned bed and suitcase into a writing chamber, we can imagine Lucia grasping at the edges of adult sexual knowledge, finding eloquence in unspoken intensities and in the cramped spaces of hotel rooms and servants' closets. Here, just as in her father's mind, no doors marked the symbolic distinction between adults and children. The forbidden territories of unconscious life were not unknown in the Joyces' life together.

It was from the self-absorbed Joyce and from the priority accorded to him in their household that Lucia learned the power that accrued from dedication to the arts. In the rudimentary way that children begin to forge an image of their own possible destiny, she turned and weighed options, evaluating the repertoire of possible choices represented to her by her parents. She could formulate a vision of her own potential place within that world. She saw more life-giving possibilities in her father's existence. Lucia's adolescent life cannot be described simply as a Freudian triangle, where a daughter, like Elektra, turns from the mother to embrace the parent of the opposite sex. It is better to think of it as an improvisation upon a theme, a sorting out of a dense, complicated background according to private necessity. She was a sort of *bricoleur*, someone dancing with emotional and cultural structures, swindling authority, violating boundaries, reworking and transgressing an identification at the very moment that it was being constituted. She was a young girl who, amid the collective judgment that she was "wonderfully sweet," was privately engaged in stealing fire.

During that first summer in Paris, her conscious thoughts were far from any such intentions. She liked kids' stuff. She discovered the comic strip *Gasoline Alley* and put it on the mantelpiece. Frank Budgen, who had taught her to swim in Zurich, arrived for a visit and took her swimming in the pool at the Pont de Grenelle; and like many ordinary French

kids, she became consumed by a craze for Napoleon. Many years later
Myron Nutting still remembered, "I don't know how long the Napoleon
interest lasted, but there was a period when any memento in the way of a
figurine, post-card, clipping, or historical print was sure of being a welcome present."[8]

But whatever her fervor—the pin-ups, the soldiers, the maps of conquest—it was soon eclipsed by more immediate and more serious problems that had grown from a lifetime of haphazard attention on the part
of both of her parents. If the Joyces were going to settle in Paris, Lucia
needed to go to school. She had had two years of education at the Scuola
Elementare in Trieste and four and a half years more at a Volksschule in
Zurich, and that was it. She had already been held back in school because
she had needed to learn German in Switzerland. Now a single further
step in her education required her to learn still another language and to
face the fact that, no matter how proficient a linguist she became, she
would never have an unambivalent home in any spoken words. As summer moved into autumn and the family was forced to retreat to hotel
rooms on the rue de l'Université, Joyce paused from his writing to look
at his children. To John Quinn he admitted, "I do not know what to do
about my daughter."[9]

As an immediate measure, Joyce and Nora placed her in a private
school to learn French. Lucia would have to know how to conduct her
life in Paris, and she would have to master the language in order eventually to enter a lycée. Giorgio chose a different path. Even though both
children understood that part of Harriet Weaver's bequest to their father
was to be used for their education, Lucia watched while her brother
tabled his plans for medical school and, at fifteen, accepted a position in a
bank. Several months later, Joyce reported to Stanislaus that Giorgio had
assumed a new position with an American Trust Agency that promised
that he could become a secretary and eventually travel for them.[10] By the
following summer, Giorgio was allowed to take his holidays in Zurich in
the company of his friends "Hummel and Magli" (Daniel Hummel and
Rudolf Maeglin). He was beginning to have an autonomous life, but Lucia remained bound to her parents and to whatever haphazard nuclear
family they cared to establish.[11]

In December 1920, the Joyces finally succeeded in locating a flat of
their own at 5 boulevard Raspail. Joyce justified its expense to Ezra

Pound and to John Rodker by claiming that his eye attacks had been brought on by freezing temperatures in their hotel room.[12] In August Joyce's benefactor, whom Lucia now called "Saint Harriet," had made him the beneficiary of a second, more liberal and accessible bequest, and with this and with anticipated royalties from *Ulysses*, he felt able to meet a sizable rent. As Christmas approached, Lucia experienced her first privacy and warmth in Paris, and she once again had a piano to practice on. She had missed having lessons as she had had in Zurich and Trieste. Soon she found herself the recipient of another unexpected tribute. Where her own father had been too poor to buy her a present or even to take her to dinner on her birthday in July, December was different. The Joyces opened the door one day to find two young American men, Richard Wallace and Myron Nutting, standing there with Christmas gifts for both herself and Giorgio.[13]

No one could have foreseen the chain of connections that brought all these people together in such a happy way. Many years later, Nutting explained that their life with the Joyces in Paris had its roots in experiences long before the start of the Great War, in Capri, where he and his young wife, Helen, had met another young couple named Richard and Lillian Wallace. When the war started, he and Richard had signed up for duty with the Red Cross and had gone into service under Joseph Collins. Then Collins had written to Wallace in 1920 asking him if he had read *A Portrait of the Artist as a Young Man*. The author of this remarkable book, he wrote, now lived in Paris and was reported to be blind and living in poverty. Nutting, who was now a painter, and Wallace, who became a book, magazine, and advertising illustrator for firms like *Century Magazine* and Hachette, were calling on the Joyces simply to deliver Collins's holiday gift to the Joyce children, but they turned into the proverbial man who came to dinner. As Nutting later said of Wallace, "I don't think I ever knew a man who, with no special education, talent, or wit, so quickly won friends."[14] A three-hour lunch with Joyce turned into other lunches and then finally into family friendships that lasted until the Nuttings left Paris to return to the United States in 1929.

For Lucia, the visit had many further ramifications, for the Nuttings were looking after their niece, Helen Kieffer, who was exactly Lucia's age. Helen spoke English and, like Lucia, was at loose ends. Neither of them had any way to become part of the inner circle of teenage Parisian social life, and so they made do with each other. Helen became Lucia's first new friend. On 2 February 1922, Helen Nutting was able to look with satisfaction at the two girls sitting companionably at the dinner arranged to celebrate Joyce's birthday and, after all this time, the publication of *Ulysses*. While the eyes of literary Paris were fixed on the genius of the father, Helen Nutting alone remembered that *Ulysses* was also an event in the life of two children: "Dinner at the Italian restaurant, Ferrari's, with all the Joyces, two Wallaces, two Nuttings, and Helen Kieffer. Joyce at the head of the table, sitting sideways, melancholy, eating nothing. . . . Giorgio sat at the further end of the table from his father, eating nothing and saying nothing. The two girls were happy but quiet."[15]

Soon the girls' friendship took a further turn, for young Helen was studying dance at the Jaques-Dalcroze Institute at 28 rue de l'Annonciation. In addition to attending the Lycée Victor Duray, Lucia began to dance with Helen and found a comfortable companionship with Mrs. Nutting. She took the two girls frequently to tea and, of all the adults in the senior Joyce circle, seemed genuinely to value Lucia's company. Lucia was, she decided after several years of friendship with the Joyces, "the most normal of the family, tactful, with humor and good sense. A wonderful girl."[16] All the Joyces soon began to join in the Nuttings' *vie bohème* and to visit their studio at 9 rue Falguière in Montparnasse, a place that Myron described as "a typical Paris studio with a wide balcony at one end that served as our bedroom."[17]

But the great benefit for Lucia was the Jaques-Dalcroze Institute, which taught her a way to channel her energy and to translate music, at which she was already adept, into the language of movement. Emile Jaques-Dalcroze had first developed his system of what he called eurhythmics at the Geneva Conservatory as a way to enhance his music students' sense of rhythm by making them not just listen but walk, run, and move about according to various rhythmic patterns. By 1921 he had been invited to run a permanent institute in the new garden city of Hellerau, where he became famous for his large public spectacles and festival plays. Eventually he founded an institute in Geneva, and eurhythmics as a discipline became well established in Paris as well. In addition to the two Paris schools devoted solely to this method, its techniques were incorporated into the curriculum of the Opéra and the Schola Cantorum, where both Lucia and Giorgio were later to study.

With Helen and with the daughters of Joyce's literary friends Valery Larbaud and William Bird,[18] Lucia embarked on a program that would show her how to make her body into an instrument capable of articulating the subtlest of musical rhythms. Jaques-Dalcroze had invented a series of physical exercises that translated musical rhythms and tempi into bodily motions in space. He began by explaining the nature of the body's equilibrium in terms of not just its musculature but its need for even breathing. In time his students learned the rapport between musical harmony and rhythm and between voice, gesture, and walking or running. When they had mastered these skills, they also learned how to sight-read music, using solfège techniques so that they could listen to, recognize, and produce the different tones and half tones of the Western music scales.

André Levinson, the foremost dance critic of Paris in the 1920s, disparaged these exercises, claiming that "an adept of Dalcroze eurhythmics is as much a dancer as a metronome is a musical instrument,"[19] but for Lucia eurhythmics was perfect. On the piano, she was learning to play the Prelude to Wagner's *Tristan und Isolde*; with her friends she was pulled into a world where she could express herself directly with her body without needing French or German or Italian or English. For any child, the Jaques-Dalcroze Institute would have been beneficial; for Lucia Joyce, it was a brilliant choice. At the institute she found, seemingly by some profound intuition, a way to circumvent her verbal disadvantages and to express her psychological displacement. Dance was, in the mid-1920s, a universal language, and it was in dance that Lucia found the brief but eloquent speech that lets us know that she was not simply a "tortured and blocked replica of genius."[20] Without secure resources in the French language, she communicated nonetheless, and she let her body—so trammeled by displacement, so cramped by the poor and often slovenly places where the Joyces lived out their poverty—speak out its pain, its desire, its independence, and its collapse. Myron Nutting remembered his young friend in those years as someone who "seemed to take up any project or study with enthusiasm" and noticed the joy that dancing brought to Lucia from the very beginning of her efforts.[21]

The Nuttings' diaries are full of glimpses of Lucia's unselfconscious adolescent enthusiasms. They knew about her dancing, of course, for she and young Helen used to practice together at the studio on the rue Falguière, but they were equally astonished by her singing. "One afternoon at our place," Myron recalled, "we asked her to sing, thinking that with her parents' love of music she too would be in the habit of singing. She demurred, said she never sang, had no voice, etc. However she finally consented to try some simple thing we had on the piano. Her first note about lifted us off our chairs. Her voice was strong, but she seemed at first a sort of Trilby, assuming she really had something. We decided that she had, but Giorgio got the encouragement and help."[22] Later years would prove the Nuttings right, for even at this young age Lucia was moving in the direction of an art form that she could call distinctively her own, swerving out of the path of writing, out of the path of singing, never entirely relinquishing either, but moving nonetheless toward the singularity of her own fate.

During these first years in Paris, Lucia also extended her love of the cinema into the small pantomimes that everyone who knew the Joyces intimately would always remember her performing. Father and daughter went to see Lillian Gish in *Orphans of the Storm* (1921); they saw *Mater Dolorosa*, based on the book by Maria Shkapskaia (1921), *La Mélodie du Monde*, by Robert Chauvelot (1930), and most memorably, Charlie Chaplin and Jackie Coogan in *The Kid* (1921).[23] Lucia went home to raid the wardrobes of both father and brother, and the Nuttings remembered that she assembled a creditable Chaplin getup and "loved to appear at the height of things . . . going through her repertoire of mimicry."[24] With baggy trousers, a cane, a bowler hat, and boots too large for her feet ("her father's, big for her though small for the part"[25]), Lucia bowed and shuffled and poked and peeped. Even before dance gave her the vocabulary of trained and expressive gesture, she was the pantomime artist, the silent actor whose movements were guaranteed, like Chaplin's, to bring a "smile and perhaps a tear."[26]

Lucia became so absorbed with her impersonations of Charlie Chaplin that by 1924 Valery Larbaud had noticed her, and when the French journal *Le Disque vert* requested an essay on the French response to "Charlot," which he could not provide, he suggested that Lucia write one instead. In February Joyce wrote Larbaud to announce that she had completed her "articolossa" and to warn him that the essay ran about the same length as a Chaplin short.[27] Written in French, the article was in fact only four hundred words long; and at seventeen Lucia found herself in the printed company of many of the major surrealists of her time: Blaise Cendrars, René Crevel, Henri Michaux, Jean Cocteau, and her father's friend and translator Philippe Soupault had also contributed to the special edition.

Larbaud, in his introduction to the piece, pictured Lucia at fourteen as both an artist and an accomplished linguist. At his desk, he told his French audience, he faced a portrait of Chaplin that Lucia had drawn and given to him as a gift, and he noted that Lucia now wrote in French as well as she did in Italian and English. In her essay, which she entitled "Charlie et les gosses" (Charlie and the Kids), Lucia in turn sat facing a photograph of Chaplin, whose "intelligent and sad" eyes, she wrote, regarded her as she strove to express her appreciation of his great gift for comedy. She described the growth of Chaplin's career in the noteworthy terms of a dumb show. First he had been a mere puppet; then he had learned more animation and had transformed himself into a marionette; next he became a "buffoon"; and finally, in his current apotheosis, he had grown into "a big kid."

It was a natural metaphor to choose, for three years earlier, in 1921, Chaplin had come to Paris to promote *The Kid*, the six-reel movie that everyone agreed was his best work to date. After they had seen it, Joyce and the fourteen-year-old Lucia had ventured out again, hoping for a glimpse of the actual man who was visiting their city. It was a long shot by anyone's calculations. In the 1920s, Europe was collectively in love with the Tramp. The American writer Waldo Frank, who was introduced to Chaplin at the time and who spent the greater part of his days in Paris with him, later described the experience of going to the circus in a *New Yorker* profile. Once Chaplin was recognized, the audience became "a high-tiered human monster, suddenly shouting *Charlot!* with a thousand throats, avalanched down upon a single spot of the arena rail, where a little man in a dapper dining coat sat blinking. . . . A score of gendarmes broke into the delirious maze of men and women, pressing on Chaplin as if they were hungry to devour him. The police . . . formed a phalanx about him and he shuffled out into the Place Pigalle."[28] Fortunately Frank and Chaplin had quieter times together, and Frank remembered that they were especially fond of sitting out on the Champs-Elysées in the early mornings.

It was there too that the Joyces encountered their idol, in a quiet and unexpected moment that Lucia described beautifully: "He was worth seeing at any price," she admitted, and luck had been with her. "He had neither his cane nor his droll walk, [so] I didn't recognize him until he stopped at the Petit Guignol to watch the spectacle that had captured the lively interest of the children." There, she explained, "his gestures and his attitudes finally unmasked him to me. Those little kids, screaming with joy at the puppets, what would they have done if they had known that the real, the living puppet was behind them?"[29]

One of the small happinesses of Lucia's essay was that it showed she understood that life presents itself as a spectacle for people who create in any genre. She was watching the artist watching, and at fourteen she already had a lifetime of experience to tell her how to do it. Although Larbaud's introduction to her essay emphasized her youth—she was a young girl, he said, whose opinion might be valued because of Chaplin's immense influence on a whole generation of children—Lucia herself revealed a double identity. She saw herself both as a judge of artistry who "unmasked" the actor—and as an artist herself. Like scores of her contemporaries, male and female, she took pleasure in imitating Chaplin's ragged costume, droll walk, buffoonery, and impertinence. "I dressed myself up in 'Charlie,' we had a lot of fun and I had a great succes [sic]. We danced and played, sang and I don't know what else," she wrote at Christmas in 1922.[30]

During these years, as Joyce found himself increasingly in the position of having to explain the innovations of his own writing style in *Ulysses*, he frequently spoke of what was required to represent the concurrent nature of experience. "In *Ulysses*," he said to Djuna Barnes, "I have recorded simultaneously what a man says, sees, thinks and what such seeing, thinking, saying does to what you Freudians call the unconscious."[31] Of these functions, the ceaseless process of seeing and transposing the bounty of the performed world into art was the one that shaped the life and the sensibility of his young daughter. It was as if she lived in the presence of a private movie camera, waiting for the "intelligent and sad" eyes of her father to find her and read her. Her essay on Chaplin shows that her early choices, her improvisations for a life of fullness, unwittingly contained destructive seeds. As if the vocation of artist were not difficult enough, Lucia internalized both the need to be an artist and the continued need to perform for one.

Lucia Joyce with Helen Kieffer, Paris, circa 1921. (Courtesy of the Myron Chester and Muriel Leone [Tyler] Nutting Collection, Archives of American Art, Smithsonian Institution)

Sandwiched between Lucia's Chaplinesque drolleries were events that made her father's eyes both intelligent and sad, events whose importance none could then judge. No longer was Joyce's attention focused solely on the need to finish writing *Ulysses*; now he needed to attend to its publication and its reception. Even before it was finished, *Ulysses* was an international sensation. When, in December 1921, Larbaud gave an introductory "séance" about *Ulysses* at Sylvia Beach's Shakespeare and Company bookstore, he began by remarking that among literary people, Joyce's name was now as common as the names of Freud and Einstein among those of a scientific bent.

Initially Joyce's reputation in Paris did not directly affect the lives of his children. He spent afternoons in Sylvia Beach's bookstore and attended literary dinners with adults whose lives and conversations did not reach down into the world of adolescence. But it became impossible to remain aloof from or indifferent to *Ulysses*'s reception. Even before the novel was under contract in book form, its contents had aroused contro-

versies that came to a head earlier in 1921 when the New York Society
for the Suppression of Vice sued Jane Heap and Margaret Anderson
for publishing "Nausicaa" in *The Little Review*. John Quinn, in rebut-
ting the obscenity charges, had had to argue that the adolescent Gerty
MacDowell's exhibitionism and Bloom's masturbatory fantasies were
disgusting rather than indecent, that the work evoked anger rather than
lascivious thoughts.[32] But one of the issues in the lawsuit involved the
concept of the mind and consciousness of young girls perceived as readers. Could the book corrupt them? Quinn also had to address Joyce's representation of a young girl imagined as a sexual actor. What did it mean
to portray Gerty not simply as the object of male desire but as its provo-
cateur?

As it happened, Quinn's defense coincided in time almost exactly
with the Joyces' move back to the overcrowded two rooms of the hotel
on the rue de l'Université. This was the place that Joyce ruefully described as "the damned brothel"[33] where he shared his bedroom with
both his wife and his daughter for the sake of economy. In those days,
August Suter remembered Nora's spirited defense of Wagner to her husband in the face of his penchant for obscenities: "Es gibt viele Schweine-
rien auch in deinen Buch." ("There's a lot of shit in your book too.")[34]
This little snippet of memory lets us glimpse a family accustomed to
voicing opinions about obscenity, boundaries, and the requirements of
human decency. Did Nora's defense of Wagner and derision of her husband's writing conceal a more uncomfortable awareness of a shifting,
unspoken dynamic at work in their home?

As Joyce's work faced public scrutiny, so it seems did his emotional
proclivities. One way to understand Nora's frequent irritation with
Joyce—which in later years was more and more often displaced onto her
daughter—is to posit her tacit anxiety about a man who could thus
imagine a pubescent child. Nora had first expressed this kind of distress
several years earlier, in a dream about the performance of a play. Shakespeare had figured in it as well as two ghosts, and Nora had told Joyce
that in her dream she had feared that Lucia would be frightened by the
play. Joyce had responded by interpreting the dream. He said that the
child was "herself [Nora] in little" and suggested that the fear was perhaps "that either subsequent honors or the future development of my
mind or art with its extravagant excursions into forbidden territory may

bring unrest into her life."[35] Casting himself as the playwright, the hidden choreographer of a dynamic fiction, Joyce passed over the manifest content of the dream—where it was the child who had been frightened—but understood immediately that his mind's "extravagant excursions into forbidden territory" could bring disruption into the lives of actual people. What neither dreamer nor interpreter had considered in parsing the dream was the importance of Lucia's presence in it. In the eyes of her parents, her gifts were still unformulated.

The *Little Review* trial was just the beginning of public furor over the new psychic territory explored in Joyce's novel. When Jane Heap and Margaret Anderson lost their case, B. W. Huebsch, Joyce's American publisher, qualified its offer to publish *Ulysses*, holding forth for changes that Joyce refused to make; another firm, Boni and Liveright, similarly withdrew their interest in the book. The ruin of all hope was dispelled close to home by Sylvia Beach's offer to bring out *Ulysses* in Paris and to pay for its publication by an aggressive plan of subscriptions. Amid flurries of typing and constant revisions, comments about the nature of the writing as it had appeared in serial form continued to come in. These ranged from Valery Larbaud's contention that Joyce's writing had the greatness and scope of Rabelais to George Bernard Shaw's judgment that the book was "a revolting record of a disgusting phase of civilization."[36]

With each triumph and each setback, Joyce's mood would swing, he would drink, and Nora would castigate him and threaten to take the children back to Ireland, until finally he became bedridden for five weeks with one of his increasingly frequent bouts of iritis. Only cocaine seemed to relieve its agony. The Joyce family must have been hard put to find coherent reasons for the difficulties of this Parisian middle passage. As much as she recalled the fame and the infamy that followed Joyce, Lucia also remembered the inner edge of anxiety in the discord between her parents. She also recalled her own ineptitude in handling her father's incapacitating eye diseases, their treatment with leeches or operations or stays in clinics: "My father was crying once with the pain he had in his eyes but I was awkward and could not console him."[37]

In June Valery Larbaud offered them a respite from rented lodgings by loaning them his elegant flat at 71 rue du Cardinal Lemoine, in the fifth arrondissement. For the first time since their arrival in Paris, the Joyces spread out in adequate space, where they could read and work in privacy and comfort. Giorgio left for Zurich for a month, and the Wallaces helped pass the tedium of an urban summer by inviting Nora, Joyce, and Lucia to their country house in Châtillon. Here, according to Joyce and as later remembered by Myron Nutting, Joyce decided upon the final word of *Ulysses* when he overheard Lillian Wallace negotiating endlessly with a house painter. As time passed, Mrs. Wallace kept responding with the word *yes* "over and over again in different tones of voice" until "*La voilà*: yes," as Joyce wrote to Larbaud later that summer.[38] Though life had inspired art, his book soon offered a prophetic reversal, serving as an uncanny anticipation of another assignation not unlike Blazes Boylan's tryst with Molly Bloom: Giorgio was just about to embark on his own first experience with adultery.

As summer turned into fall, the Joyces returned to the dreary rue de l'Université rooms. Nora grumbled, but her discomfort was mitigated by new acquaintances that included a young American couple. Sometime in early 1922 the Joyces met Leon and Helen Kastor Fleischman while dining at a café, Chez Francis, at the Place de l'Alma. Joyce and Leon Fleischman had met previously in Paris, and the two men had known of each other since Fleischman's days as a director of Boni and Liveright. Helen remembered what she wore on that evening; she remembered talking to Nora about children, life in Paris, clothing, and the kinds of subjects that "women from time immemorial have discussed," while the two men talked of politics and literature, food and wine.[39] None of them knew that the friendships formed in this pleasant evening coincidence would change the course of their lives.

Helen and Leon Fleischman's decision to move to Paris had been inspired by their friend Peggy Guggenheim. They had met Peggy several years previously in New York City at the Sunwise Turn bookshop, which was owned by Peggy's cousin Harold Loeb. For Peggy, whose private inheritance gave her the freedom to escape from the bourgeois world of her wealthy Jewish parents, hanging around this bookstore had been an amateurish way of trying to become an intellectual. Restless and without a sense of inner direction, she sought purpose in her life by socializing with artists and writers in Greenwich Village. At the bookshop she met Laurence Vail, who in 1922 was to become her first husband, and Leon Fleischman, already married to Helen and, at Boni and Liveright, immersed in the world of publishing. Peggy's three enthusiasms—for art, for the friendship of original and distinguished people, and for sexual dalliance—were all well established before she first went to Europe. These young people customarily tinged their friendships with eroticism. Far in advance of any ideas they might have gleaned from reading Joyce's shockingly candid picture of marital infidelity in *Ulysses*, they were keen to explore a world of sexual license, and family money let them have a go at it.

In F. Scott Fitzgerald's novel of the 1920s, *Tender Is the Night*, the mother of a young actress, Rosemary Hoyt, tells her daughter that she may do as she likes in sexual matters because economically she is a boy. Neither Helen nor Peggy had to earn a living, but money's effects on them were similar. Independent incomes took both women out of the world in which virginity was considered to be an asset to unmarried women. Money placed them soundly in "certain circles" where, as Ira S. Wile courageously contended in 1934, "popular thinking has swung to the other extreme and women compelled to endure a temporary period of continence claim to be gravely concerned about the wholesomeness of their lives."[40] The "certain circle" assembled around the Sunwise Turn bookshop took things a step further. Peggy remembered falling in love with Leon, "who to me looked like a Greek God, but Helen didn't mind. They were so free."[41] She also remembered that part of Helen's "not minding" arose from Helen's own affair with Laurence Vail, who in Guggenheim's 1946 memoir was renamed "Florenz Dale." Leon, she claimed, not only knew of but also pushed Helen into the relationship because "it excited him."[42]

Soon they were all in Paris. Peggy had made a quick trip there by herself, and then, returning to New York for her sister Hazel's wedding to Sigmund Kempner, had persuaded the Fleischmans, who were also wedding guests, to abandon their American life for whatever adventures lay ahead of them in Europe. In effect they imported an intricate and emotionally incestuous lifestyle to the streets and boulevards of a new city where they hoped to be shielded with more anonymity than their native land could grant them. Peggy took Laurence Vail away from Helen, supposedly making Leon "furious." Leon was in turn prevailed upon to send money to Djuna Barnes who, along with another of Vail's former mistresses, also joined the Guggenheim ménage in Paris. They all made a café life for themselves, meeting first at the Café de la Rotonde in

Montparnasse and later at the Dôme. Guggenheim thought of Vail as "the King of Bohemia," and she intended to marry him.[43]

Of course none of these intricacies was visible to the Joyces when they met the Fleischmans for the first time. In consequence, when Peggy Guggenheim and Laurence Vail asked the whole family to their wedding breakfast in March 1922, they were baffled. They did not immediately recognize that the Fleischmans were behind the invitation. Yet this new circle of friends expanded in subsequent years to include Helen's friend Alec Ponisovsky; Alec's sister Lucie and her husband, Paul Léon; and finally, though indirectly, Hazel Guggenheim and Elsa Schiaparelli. It was a powerful network of affiliations, and the group gradually, with various personal motives, surrounded the Joyce family. Their views came to color the Joyces' expectations of the possibilities that life afforded them in Paris. They gave them, especially Giorgio and Lucia, a set of attitudes, a sense of material expectations, and a sexual ethic that seemed to promise delight and then turned delight into jealousy, unmet desire, and discord. But in 1922, puzzled though he may have been by the unexpected wedding invitation, Joyce was more worried about his family's imminent departure for Ireland.

II. UNDER FIRE

It was a trip Nora had insisted upon. By April she had become fed up with Joyce's evening drunkenness, his dependence, and his literary preoccupations. She wanted to see her mother, and with financial resources that now seemed sufficient, she wanted to gain some perspective on her marriage. It is likely, since she and Joyce discussed a monthly allowance for herself and the children, that she anticipated staying away for a long time.[44] Lucia and Giorgio, now fifteen and seventeen, were to go with her. Almost certainly they did not consider the political dangers that their father, with more insight into the ways history can intervene in private destiny, worried about on their behalf. Thinking not just of her mother's family but also of her father's, Lucia memorized the addresses of her father's Dublin relatives and set out for a place she had not seen since she was five. But first their mother took them to London for a week.

From the first, Joyce was filled with anxiety about his family's safety in Ireland. He bombarded them with letters and telegrams asking them to reconsider crossing the Irish Sea, but to no avail. Nora was intent on going and was more persuaded by the nonchalance of her Galway friends than by the worry of her husband. Accustomed to the ferocious antagonisms of a nation struggling for independence, they had down-played the effects of political animosities and convinced Nora that her journey would be without incident. As it turned out, they were wrong, and whatever perspective Nora had hoped to gain from her time in Ire-land was eclipsed by the immediate need to shield her children from physical harm.

From London they crossed to Dublin, where Nora's uncle, Michael Healy, met them and took them to dinner with their paternal grandfa-ther, John Stanislaus Joyce, and one of his friends, Tom Devlin. They did not linger in Dublin but went straight on to Galway, where they quickly found themselves embroiled in conflicts between the Regular Irish Re-publican Army, which supported the proposed treaty for an Irish Free State, and the Irregulars, who felt that the Free State was a compromise and favored holding out for an independent and united Ireland.

Lucia was probably too young to understand the political ramifica-tions of the fighting that surrounded her, and in consequence her re-sponses to Galway ranged from boredom with her grandmother's habitual way of life to terror at its interruption by gunfire. In the ten years since her last visit, she and Giorgio had grown accustomed to the densities of life in Paris and Zurich, and they looked at Galway through critical eyes. They liked neither their grandmother's cooking nor the closeness of her small cottage. Nora booked rooms for them at a board-inghouse on Nun's Island off the coast, fed them in a café, and nattered at them for lolling about on the window ledge of Mrs. Barnacle's house.[45] A photograph taken at the time by Kathleen Griffen shows Lucia as a gangly, disaffected teenager—skinny, long-legged, and curly-headed—dressed in an outfit better suited to a much younger child. She is wearing a short white dress, ankle socks, and maryjanes. Whatever interest the place had for her came from seeing the Presentation Convent, where their mother had worked as a girl, and from the lively gossip of her two aunts, Delia and Kathleen.

Richard Ellmann and Brenda Maddox have both stressed the trauma that the IRA's local hostility inflicted on the visitors: soldiers jeered at Giorgio's cosmopolitan style, borrowed the Joyces' bedroom window for mounting machine guns, and opened fire on their train to Dublin. But these overt and public antagonisms cloaked more pernicious and private divisions within the Joyce household. Nora's presence in Galway meant that she might "divorce" her "husband." For her children, it meant that a boring visit to little-known relatives might turn into a diminished life away from their father and away from their plans for their futures in Paris, however meager. When Nora had had enough of terrorism, she packed them all off to Dublin and then back to the continent. On reflection it had occurred to her that what she really wanted was a life alone with her husband. He had obliged her by agreeing that he "would go anywhere in the world if I could be sure that I could be alone with your dear self without family and without friends."[46] What lay in store for the children of parents who preferred life without them was not immediately clear.

Finally, and it was a very long time in coming, Lucia was allowed to do something on her own. After all of her father's herculean efforts to finish writing *Ulysses* and see it into print, after his preoccupation with publicity for it, after his lawsuits, his illnesses, his drinking bouts, and her mother's exasperated response to it all, she was allowed to go to camp. In the summer of 1922, Joyce and Nora acted upon their desire to be alone without children. The entire family separated. Joyce and Nora intended to go to London; Giorgio would return to the Swiss Tyrol; and Lucia, with Helen Kieffer as her companion, was allowed to go to Deauville on the coast of Brittany, where a gentleman named George Hebert ran a summer program for adolescents. Helen Nutting was responsible for finding the program. In Nora's absence she had looked for a place where the two girls might experience something of the French countryside and had persuaded the Joyces to let their daughter share a tent with Helen.

George Hebert was a retired marine officer who had quit life on the sea in order to promote a method of physical training that was natural and relaxed, as opposed to the rigid Swedish gymnastics that were then in favor both within and without the armed forces. He thought that different sports should have special techniques that depended on their distinctive goals, and he thought that health did not end at the edge of the playing field.[47] He was, in short, an early avatar of holistic living, a man who promoted oneness with nature by dressing his young charges in bright tunics and sending them running through the grass in bare feet. He fed them a vegetarian diet, let them conduct all their summer projects outdoors, and at night tucked them into tents by the side of the sea. As a treat, the teenagers were introduced to King Alfonso of Spain. Lucia and Helen went regularly to church in the village. Lucia bathed in the ocean, ate healthy food, learned to play a version of Wagner's "O Du Mein Holden Abendstern" (from *Tannhäuser*) on the harp, and discovered not only that she loved Hebert's regimes but that she excelled in them.

Lucia remained there for four months, from May through August. When she returned, Joyce took one look at her blossoming complexion, the light in her eyes, and the enthusiasm of her manner and decided that his daughter should continue her gymnastics. He told his aunt Josephine in Ireland that after her summer, Lucia "could go on a circus trapeze."[48] But as happened often in her family, abstract resolution did not mean commitment in fact. There was no way to duplicate Lucia's summer experiences in Paris. Over the summer, moreover, Joyce had decided that Parisian life was too dear and depressing, and its climate too harsh for his eyes. He had had another frightening round of problems with his vision, and rather than face immediate surgery, he decided that he must winter in a mild climate. On 9 October, Nora went to tell the Nuttings that they were leaving for Nice and would perhaps remain there.

Good friends that they were, the Nuttings dropped everything and arranged to take the Joyces to dinner that evening. They waited for Joyce and Lucia to return from the oculist's, and when they came in, he was "very tired, nervous, with red eyes behind the thick glasses." His sadness alarmed Nora, and Helen recorded her friends' efforts at coping with a world that, in spite of Joyce's fame, offered them neither cooperation nor solace. Nora "kept saying, 'What's the matter, Jim? Did the doctor say you were worse? For God's sake what's the matter?' He turned it off, saying the doctor said it was no worse. 'Wouldn't a man be tired who had sat waiting from three o'clock till seven?' He and Lucia had gone out about five for a cup of tea, to a miserable room full of lights; and they had ordered one tea and then asked for another cup. 'And,' said Lucia fiercely, 'they were so mean. They said, "Another cup is another order and you will pay for it in full. I must tell the Padrone." And she went and talked to the Padrone.' And Joyce said, 'Six francs for one cup of tea. And the room full of lights.' "[49]

Nice did not relieve their gloom. Leaving Giorgio behind in Paris to study voice at the Schola Cantorum, the Joyces settled directly on the water's edge at the Hôtel Suisse, considered putting Lucia in school, decided against it, and began a life directed only by impulse. By mid-November, they had tired of teas on the promenade punctuated by shopping and sightseeing. Since they had already taken a six-month lease on a furnished flat on the avenue Charles Floquet, they did not have to procrastinate. Back they went to Paris where, to his amazement, Joyce's young daughter showed him that he did not have to know "what to do about" her. She knew what she would do about herself. She would dance.

4

THE ART OF DANCING

PARIS 1924–28

I. ULYSSES IN PARIS

Lucia's first teacher in Paris was the brother of Isadora Duncan. By almost any standard, Raymond Duncan was a man of extraordinary, even ludicrous eccentricity, but for a fifteen-year-old girl eager to do something with herself besides listen to the world praise her father, he fit the bill.[1] In contrast to the chic world of Parisian fashion, Duncan's followers wore tunics and sandals, lived simply together in a commune, and ate a vegetarian diet. To her pragmatic mother's horror, Lucia, in joining Duncan's entourage, was about to opt for goat cheese and pine nuts. Which was part of the point. Duncan may have been an almost comically narcissistic character, but he gave Lucia a place to go where she could discover who she was and what she was capable of achieving.

According to Helen Fleischman, Lucia needed to get away from her mother as well as her father, for Nora made a point of saying to both children that people weren't interested in her or them but "only interested in 'Himself.' "[2] But if Lucia chose to leave a father who threatened to overwhelm her and a mother bent on making her into a smaller version of "Herself," she did so in a way that had curious resonance with her own family. It was as if she were transposing a familiar song into an offbeat key.

In 1904, inspired by his love of Homer, Raymond Duncan had gone

Lucia Joyce in profile as from a Greek vase painting, Paris, circa 1925.

to Greece. By the time he landed on Ithaca with his mother, his sister Isadora, and two other siblings, he had cast aside Western clothing and made an intellectual loop that made Greek culture of the time of Odysseus into a blueprint for living in the present. From this point, his life's mission would be to restore a "classical" lifestyle to anyone who was willing to listen to him. Literally instructing the fishermen who rowed his family from Venice to Brindisi to Santa Maura and then on to Ithaca to re-create "as much as possible" the journey of Odysseus traveling back to his homeland, Raymond Duncan never doubted that Odysseus had navigated the waters described in the *Odyssey* "from cape to cape; from isle to isle."[3]

There is, consequently, a quirky appropriateness to the fact that those who saw him years later in Paris thought of him as "the man . . . who looked like an unbearded Ulysses."[4] Until his death in 1955, Duncan never again wore trousers. The toga and sandals of ancient civilization became his standard dress, and he could be seen in all seasons and in most of the capitals of Europe and America dressed in this garb. He was tremendously charismatic to the young and the dissatisfied, and particularly to Lucia. Not only did she study with him, but she also discovered that the values and techniques of her other teachers—Margaret Morris, Lois Hutton, and Hélène Vanel—had their origin in his beliefs and commitments.

For all the Duncans, the journey to Greece had been important. Isadora had responded to it by dancing in the tunics and veils that later became her trademark, but to Raymond Athens was not simply an appropriate setting for dancing; it was fate itself. At the Acropolis he met the then-nineteen-year-old Greek poet Angelos Sikelianos, and through him his sister Penelope. They too wore ancient Greek chitons and sandals, and as in his own family their lives were dedicated to art. Penelope read classical Greek texts, played ancient Greek and Byzantine music, practiced choral movement and chanting, and knew how to weave by hand.[5] Together Raymond and Penelope bought land near the Acropolis and established the prototype of the many schools or "Akademias" that became Duncan's life mission. They called their retreat "the Palace of Agamemnon" and managed to ignore the fact that its rocky base prohibited modern plumbing and held no water for drinking or hygiene. Their primary concern lay elsewhere: in learning to farm, to weave, to batik, and to make pottery. During this time Duncan studied the science of movement and Greek music, finding a rationale and a method that distinguished him from Isadora, whose dance he considered authentically Greek but too feminine for him to emulate.

In a year the young couple followed Isadora back to Paris, where Gertrude Stein remembered them as utterly destitute. She gave them coal and a chair for Penelope, now pregnant, to sit on during the day.[6] Their first and only child was named Raymond, but everyone knew him as Menalkas, the shepherd boy in Theocritus. (Had he been named Telemachus, the Homeric pattern would have been complete.) How could Lucia Joyce have failed to notice the oddly appropriate nature of her choice of teacher? It was as if the figures of her father's imagination had suddenly taken corporeal form and walked the earth. Joyce himself seems to have been captivated by this coincidence, for Kay Boyle, who lived in Duncan's Neuilly commune in the late 1920s, remembers Joyce haunting the store where she was clerking to learn more about sandals and homespun cloth.[7]

Long before the Joyces met them in the 1920s, the Duncans were controversial figures whose combination of nonconformity and audacious health offended anyone with a well-developed sense of propriety. In 1909, when Duncan took his family and a band of Greek thespians to the United States for a series of lectures and performances of Sophoclean tragedy, Penelope's sister and a friend, walking around with Menalkas dressed only in a tunic, were arrested and locked up by an agent of the New York Children's Society. They were charged with being "improperly clothed and causing a minor to be improperly and cruelly clothed."[8] The case was thrown out, but in every city on the tour its effect was re-created. Newspaper headlines told the story. In Pittsburgh: "Duncan Bares His Shins to Women"; in Chicago: "Duncan in Bath Towel Does Rhythmic Stunt"; in Boston: "Dressed as Greeks, Indians and Assyrians, They Follow Arts and Crafts of Ancients"; "Duncans Sail, Shiver like Hellenists." Whatever his beliefs—and he told a fairly predictable story about the value of health foods and self-reliance—Raymond Duncan was good copy. His lecture topics in New York included "The War of Art against Nature," "The Value of Failure," "Love in Spite of Tradition," and "Freud, Smoke and Sex."[9] The same sense of outrage greeted his return to Paris, where in 1912 his neighbors in the avenue Charles

Floquet (the Joyces' own street between November 1922 and June 1923) succeeded in ousting him for "excessive nudity" and for playing Doric music on the lyre at night.[10]

Nonetheless Duncan settled in Paris, teaching and selling homespun cloth to such advantage that he eventually acquired the nickname "the Executive." He made the brown robes and sandals that Gertrude and Leo Stein wore to such idiosyncratic effect at their salon; even Myron Nutting broke down and bought a toga for himself.[11] His school was initially situated on the rue Mouffetard; soon he moved it to the rue des Ursulines, and finally in 1929 he settled in the rue des Beaux-Arts, a small street that, at the approach to the courtyard of l'Ecole des Beaux-Arts, connects the rue Bonaparte with the rue de Seine.[12] In his nomadic urban existence, he rivaled the Joyces, and like theirs his peripatetic habits had early roots. Isadora remembered the constant, enervating removal from house to house during their childhood in San Francisco. "When I was five we had a cottage on 23rd Street. Failing to pay the rent, we could not remain there but moved to 17th Street, and in a short time, as funds were low, the landlord objected, so we moved to 22nd Street, where we were not allowed to live peacefully but were moved to 10th Street."[13] They might have been the Dedalus family from Joyce's *A Portrait of the Artist as a Young Man*, so closely did their youthful experience parallel the nomadic life that John Stanislaus Joyce had provided for his luckless brood in Dublin.

By the time Lucia and Kay Boyle met him, Raymond was in his fifties, living with another companion named Aia Bertrand and still going strong. He had established a printing press at which he published his own newspaper, *Exangelos*, and was teaching a philosophy course at the Ecole des hautes études sociales in addition to his classes in movement and dance. Kay Boyle could not reconcile his alternative lifestyle with his decision to buy a DeSoto motorcar; nor could she see anything funny in his long gray hair flying behind him as he careened down the road to Nice during the summers. Being an unabashed child of the bourgeoisie, she was revolted by the debris surrounding him. In *My Next Bride* she described his commune in Neuilly: "There were pieces of board and box and discarded pottery cast out on the winter stubble in the garden, and in the windows of the porch the blocked and painted stuffs were hanging as if nailed over provisionally against the weather. Standing in cold and vacant confusion [it was] a dismantled, disreputable caricature of what it once had been."[14]

When Lucia Joyce walked through the doors of the Akademia Raymond Duncan, she walked into far more than a dance class. To anyone who came of age in the 1960s, the nature of her experience is immediately clear, for what she was drawn to was a counterculture. In 1968 when she revised *Being Geniuses Together*, Kay Boyle wrote, "Only now do I recognize that the costume I wore and the tumult of my spirit were a moment in the same history of protest that is being acted out by the tormented young today."[15] She and Lucia had spent their time together being Parisian hippies.

At the heart of their studies was, as Duncan put it, a philosophy of action. "Our cult," he said, "is that of human companionship, and we commit moral suicide—we kill old-fashioned habits which have been carried on merely in imitation. We live originally."[16] He was not interested in introspection; instead he taught his students to use their bodies daemonically in the worship of Dionysos. In this he was like Rudolf Laban and the "barefoot prophets" who had founded the Monte Verità Art of Life School in Ascona, Switzerland, in the early 1900s. The great dance pioneer Mary Wigman, one of Laban's most articulate students, spoke of this experience as a "change and interchange of soul-states," saying that in dancing we "become alive in the person as a rhythmic moving to and fro. . . . Grief, joy, fear, are terms too fixed and static to describe the sources of my work. My dances flow rather from certain states of being, different stages of vitality which release in me a varying play of the emotions."[17] Where the social order tried to repress energy, Duncan tried to harness it, taunting his audiences to follow suit and cast off their inhibitions along with their socks.

Duncan began by teaching his students how to dress and move as if they were figures from Greek vase paintings. His movement system, with its counterbalancing of forms and tensions within the body of the dancer, was strenuous and more akin to gymnastics than to the expressive dance being developed by his sister Isadora. Students who remembered studying with him recalled his vigor and his emphasis on health more than his gracefulness.[18] In performance he tended to move in profile in order to accentuate the resemblance between his silhouette and the flattened perspective of the body in vase painting. In his own practice,

Duncan usually, like his sister, danced alone, but as a teacher, he emphasized the efforts of groups.[19] Boyle remembered that even in the midst of other dancers, Duncan retained a private inward focus:

> Wearing a white tunic that came to his knees, Sorrel [i.e., Duncan] leapt agilely from one movement to the next. His hands and feet were small and finely made, certain and clean, and his pure hair was turned up from the neck and bound with a white cord across his brow. The sinew ran thin and knotted under his skin as he danced alive and separate from the others, as a farmer might leap human and lean through rows of man-high corn. "One, two, and—three!" cried the voice of Sorrel in the voice of a farmer starved strident and wild in the west, leaping bewitched through his wind-crazed, monstrous crops. . . . Only in Sorrel's body was there a frenzy and delight, a knowing, scribe-like set of face and neck unshaken as he led the others down the room.[20]

As many as two hundred students at a time were following his frenzied lead when Lucia joined the throng.

And so was instituted in the Joyce household a secret world with its own language and rules of combination. Raymond Duncan's aim in teaching dance had never been to establish a troupe of performers but instead to make his students into whole, self-sufficient human beings. Did Nora fuss about fashions? Did her father agonize over the exact wording of a sentence in his new book? Lucia's mind was filled with the grammar of vitality, prizing the dynamic over the static order. She imagined herself in terms of tension and its release; she felt the anxieties of opposing muscle to muscle and the heady mastery of resistances, knew the peace of working with gravity and not against it. To drop, to rebound, to lift, to suspend oneself. To fall and recover, to know the experience of grounding oneself and then arising to circle to the edge of ecstasy. Priests danced, children danced, philosophers' thoughts rose and fell in rhythmic sequence; lovers danced, and so did Lucia. "She dances through it all," Joyce wrote to Harriet Weaver about his young daughter's new devotion.[21]

But she took in some weird ideas along with her dance steps. Duncan thought that the conventional world was utterly lunatic. He insisted that institutions should exist to enhance the quality of life for each person and that labor existed for the worker: "Do not specialize. The value of labor and occupation is not monetary gain but the development and bettering of yourself," he wrote. "The best preparation for the future is the acquired energy and talent from the day's work."[22] During the 1930s, his pronouncements became more strident, and his newspaper, *Exangelos (New–Paris–York)*, became the platform for views on far more than dance and gymnastics. Like Harold Loeb's *Broom* (to sweep away the debris of the past), *Exangelos* seemed unable to find anything in contemporary civilization worth saving. "So great had become this striving and mania for the durable that the present distruction [*sic*] of the world as it is takes on a pleasing aspect. The clearing off of all the encumbering rubbish to give place to a new order where the small hourly treasures are not forced by the push of the general mess, of past barbarism, opens up the promise of a fresh life."[23]

In these years, Duncan vacillated between advocating a simple, honest, and vigorous life and denouncing the public policies of all modern nation-states. He called approving attention to Gandhi, to the activities of pacifists, to the Women's International League for Peace and Freedom. He praised the work of Jane Addams, who had recently won the Nobel Peace Prize. He noticed with horror that Hitler had received eleven million votes, that Japan manipulated the world of European diplomacy through finances, and that the "genial people of Spain" faced a painful cure in trying to rid themselves of monarchy. When other European newspapers decried the kidnapping of the Lindberghs' ten-month-old baby, Duncan pointed out that "the nations take the sons of millions at the military age." He claimed that the Irish could be understood only in the context of "siècles d'injustice et martyr."[24]

While her mother concerned herself with modern dress design, Lucia could read in *Exangelos* that "the Women of Fashion can be at last freed from dressmakers and gowned in works of art." While Nora worried about Lucia's extreme unworldliness, her daughter was reading about birth control techniques. If Joyce was anxious about the effect that impending war might have on his art, Lucia was reading Schopenhauer as quoted by Duncan: "Thought without action is a disease." "Human culture," Duncan told her, "is the result of close contacts between men. The more this contact takes place between many men, and the more intimate it becomes of so much better quality . . . The city is the school above all. . . . Therefore I have thought it would be a good thing to join together

Paris and New York. . . . And to throw a bridge across the Atlantic. . . .
War is declared against isolation and the distance that separates men."[25]

Duncan's generally pacifist political ideas were neither original nor
sensible. He asserted them without support, posted them as leads of articles without argumentation, wrote them as if debate had no place in
the midst of such self-evident truth. But they influenced Lucia Joyce
nonetheless. Like her young American counterparts in the 1960s, she
didn't care if Duncan's ideas were reasonable; she responded to their idealism and to their vision of a personally more coherent world.

In a few years Lucia would let Duncan's quirky pacifism guide her
own political agenda with Ireland and its relation to her father. But
in the middle and late 1920s, her goals were more self-contained. She
wanted to pursue the self-actualization of dancing and, through this
training, to acquire a vocation, a means of support, and the company of
other young people who pursued art as ardently as she did. For a brief
span of years, she joined those who believed, with Rudolf Laban, that
"the art of dance could be the only completely full expression of this
life."[26] On stage she embodied the deepest meaning of her experience as
a daughter of genius: in order to live artistically, she had to swerve. Raymond Duncan may have been a strange teacher, but he helped her calculate her own genius and measure the degree of transgression that would
be needed to fulfill it.

This is what we can imagine Lucia doing, year after year, when
friends of the Joyce family noticed a teenage girl slipping away to her
dance classes. Helen Fleischman remembered the Joyces' flat at 2 square
Robiac as "my new magic country," where she went to work with Joyce
as his "self-appointed volunteer secretary." Nora would greet her when
she arrived and then disappear into her room. "Lucia would wave to me
on her way to a dancing class."[27] Helen wanted to be in the circle; she
wanted to be close to the creator of *Ulysses*. Lucia needed to figure out
how to slip past the normal intensities. She was on the way out.

II. SURREALISM AND "HARD-BOILED EGGS"

Things stood this way for several years. A photograph of Lucia taken
during her years of work with Raymond Duncan shows her clad in a

simple vest and briefs, standing in profile, arms bent at extreme angles, one extended up behind her head, the other down and parallel to the torso. She is balanced on one foot; the other leg is lifted and bent backward at the knee. We see her in the midst of transformation. Instead of a disgruntled teenager at loose ends in Ireland, we see a young woman with an intense, directed expression making her body into shapes similar to those found in Greek vase painting. A door had opened for her, a way of life had been seen, steps had been taken.

During this time, Helen Nutting remembered Lucia as a cut-up, lively at parties, and an increasingly good linguist. Sylvia Beach had the impression that Lucia made all the family's arrangements with domestic help because her French was the most fluent.[28] She remained immersed in the dance world. She began to design her own costumes and showed a quirky flair for the performative qualities of everyday life. Like her father, who imagined a bar of soap dancing around and singing in *Ulysses*, Lucia animated the inanimate, creating a costume that looked like a walking gramophone.[29] She had photographs made of herself in "fancy costume" which she, as well as her parents, gave out to her friends.

In May 1922, she went to see the Ballet suédois with her parents, and she went again in October 1923 and in March 1924. She accompanied them to performances of Wagner, seeing first *Tristan und Isolde* and later *Die Meistersinger*. By herself in 1924, she went to see L'Argentina, the stage name used by Antonia Merce, who almost single-handedly created a renascence of Spanish dancing in Paris.[30] André Levinson, who adored L'Argentina's work, described her as "slender, sinuous, sheathed in a long, tight, triple-flounced gown that, in a foam of black spangled tulle, lengthens into a train, the dancer . . . like some heraldic serpent undulating on its tail." Her movement he characterized in terms that Joyce reserved for describing the interlacing strapwork of the illuminations in the Book of Kells: it was a series of "curves, spirals, and ellipses, those interlaced ornaments and sinuous calligrams." And he tried to make sense of her appeal in terms of "barbarism" and "subtlety," using exactly the same words that Charles de Saint-Cyr later used to describe the distinctive quality of Lucia's dancing.[31]

Life assumed a familiar and interesting pattern. Lucia was good with her hands—knitting and embroidering came easily. She skated with her friends or rowed on the lake of the Bois de Boulogne. She noticed the swans and the little cygnets that followed them and considered that "it was extremely interesting and picturesque to watch them sliding along the surface of the water."[32] Joyce often "held court" at Shakespeare and Company, spending whole afternoons in Sylvia Beach's company. But the Joyces were also notorious for using the shop as a post office, a bank, and a lending library, and Lucia and Giorgio had often been sent there by themselves when something was needed at home. When Miss Beach decided to move her bookshop from the rue Dupuytren to the rue de l'Odéon, Lucia helped carry books from one location to the other, in this way meeting Myrsine and Helene Moschos, the young Greek women who served as Miss Beach's assistants.[33]

It was probably here too that Lucia met the members of the Fernandez family—Adèle, Yva, Yolande, and Emile—who all became important personal friends. Almost immediately Yva Fernandez was drawn to Joyce's writing and began translating "A Painful Case"—one of the stories of *Dubliners*—into French. She worked on it alone in her apartment; years later her sister Adèle remembered that Yva was considered something of a scandal because she was unmarried and living independently from her parents.[34] Adèle thought she was simply in advance of the ideas of a very bourgeois epoch. In 1922 the first fruit of Yva's translation work was published in the *Revue de genève,* and she persisted until the entire collection of stories was published in French in 1926.

Emile, her younger brother, although primarily interested in music, also had a literary bent. In 1921 he had become involved with a small group of students who decided, as a lark, to publish a literary journal. At twenty-one he was one of the oldest of the crowd—most of them were between seventeen and eighteen—and sympathetic to their surrealistic inclinations. Gérald Rosenthal, Pierre Villoteau, and Georges Duvau were all reading philosophy together at the Sorbonne; Jean Albert-Weil was studying medicine; and Mathias Lubeck was still at the Lycée Carnot, where he too studied philosophy.[35]

Early in their venture these young men were encouraged by André Salmon, already a well-published writer, who offered to start them out with a poem he had originally written for *La Nouvelle revue française* entitled "L'Age de l'humanité." Salmon also advised them to distinguish themselves from already existing symbolist and traditional literary journals by choosing a unique name for themselves. Lubeck came up with

L'Oeuf dur (*The Hard[-boiled] Egg*) and contributed a poem, using the pseudonym Lesle Flint, to explain it. Hard Eggs were "eggs whose shells are red, impregnated with Eosine . . . eggs displayed sterilely in the window of the milkman . . . eggs formerly laid on some obscene dungheap . . . eggs indigestible as a novel by Mr. Proust . . . eggs insipid, banal, repugnant, amorphous." From this title came other features of the periodical. A column called "the Egg Vendor" kept track of other magazines and interesting literary events around the city. The editors wrote a manifesto that spoofed the idea of manifestos (we're beautiful, love us; praise us), signed their work "Les Cinq" (The Five), and in their first issue held a contest to choose the Prince of Pomposity. They filled the pages with their own writing, disguised by an array of noms de plume.[36] By the fifth issue, they had formed an explicit alliance with Jean Cocteau, who redesigned the magazine's cover. Cocteau's presence as a kind of cultural father had already been surmised since the eggs of *L'Oeuf dur* were hatched from Cocteau's *Le Coq et l'arlequin* (*The Hen and the Harlequin*). They (Les Cinq) formed an implicit brotherhood with the six musicians whom Cocteau had called upon to create a new and distinctively French music (Les Six).

Heady with the stellar array of writers whom they eventually attracted—Francis Carco, Pierre Drieu La Rochelle, Blaise Cendrars, François Mauriac, Joseph Delteil, Louis Aragon, Pierre Mac Orlan, Pierre Reverdy—they conducted an outrageous flirtation in print with Tristan Tzara. They published headlines in *La Revue européenne* urging him to join them. Valery Larbaud contributed to the magazine, as did Philippe Soupault, famous for his *Les Champs magnétiques*, a piece of automatic writing that had grown out of his collaboration with André Breton. Sylvia Beach did not stock *L'Oeuf dur* because it was not an English-language journal, but Adrienne Monnier did, as well as other galleries on the rue de l'Odéon.[37]

Emile Fernandez's first poem, "The Taxi of Shackleton," appeared in *L'Oeuf dur* in March 1922. The three sections of the poem are represented as stops that a taxi makes in its journey around Paris. "First stop: Concorde"; "Second stop: Caumartin"; "Third stop: Montmartre." Each section locates a distinctive experience and mood. The speaker visits a hurly-gurly but remembers the water in the gutter that splashed his gray trousers. He goes from a wild and disturbing fog into a bar where he

Raymond Duncan's students dancing in Nathalie Barney's garden, Paris, circa 1925.
(Courtesy of Doree Duncan Seligmann)

Raymond Duncan (in black cloak) in "The Death of Agisthos" from Sophocles' *Electra*, Théâtre de Châtelet, Paris, 1912. (Courtesy of Doree Duncan Seligmann)

salutes Negroes and Latinos with his cocktail; he notices old walls that support vice, and he thinks once again of a "beautiful Negro" who is imprisoned within them.

His second poem, "Epithélium" (Epithalamium), which appeared in the ninth issue (April 1922), was meant to shock. It opened with the epigraph "Your mother, your aunt, even your father take pleasure in discussing adultery"—and it is a meditation on the speaker's father, who is attracted to another man's wife. The "other woman" is identified as distinctively modern. She goes to movies alone, she buys "stuff" (drugs); she is sexually experienced (her "flounces are rumpled"). Modernity is also evoked by machines (the telephone, the typewriter), vice by banjos and "the syncopated" (the latest dance craze). Sex is alluded to metaphorically as "planting seeds in your garden" and as occurring outside of language, in its "ellipses" and "parabolas," while "the little husband is hidden in back."[38]

Both poems are slight, and they follow a familiar aesthetic. Surrealism was meant to break taboos and to explore prohibitions. It was meant to ignore order, to be indifferent, to be absentminded, to exploit the resources of the unconscious. Emile Fernandez's work cannot be called automatic writing, for it does not rely on the productive power of the mind at the edge of consciousness. But it does work by free association and by allowing forbidden subjects to be explored. In one poem this is represented by a child's open knowledge of a parent's illicit sexual exploits and in another by a young man's view of Paris as a city of corruption. Fernandez was openly playing with the disappearance of rational controls, working in a style that André Breton called "that lyricism of the uncontrollable, which still had no name."[39]

In 1922 the surrealist manifestos by which we remember this age were still a few years in the future, but the writers of L'Oeuf dur cultivated outrage, sought the scandal of hysteria, opened themselves to the power of primitive instincts, and through all these commitments assaulted the idea of genius.[40] As Louis Aragon declared, "The moral arising out of this exploration is the bluff of genius; what will strike one is indignation at this sleight of hand . . . this method is within everyone's reach."[41]

Anyone who could rid him- or herself of inhibitions would find latent talent, these young writers believed, and for this reason they were committed to challenging received ideas about institutionalized insanity.

They read with interest Dr. Walter Morgenthaler's book *Un Aliène artiste* (*An Alien Artist*) (1921) about the "mad" artist Adolf Woelfli (1864–1930). They read Dr. Hans Prinzhorn's *Bildnerei der Geisteskranken* (*Artistry of the Mentally Ill*) (1922) about the resources of the unconscious, which were admired because they were "beyond the frame, unrelated to the norm." When Antonin Artaud guest-edited a special issue of *La Révolution surréaliste* on 3 April 1925, he asked Robert Desnos to write a "Letter to the Medical Directors of Insane Asylums" calling attention to their belief that the insane were simply people who didn't fit into established codes of behavior. Three years later, in 1928, Aragon and Breton celebrated the fiftieth anniversary of "hysteria" by calling it "a supreme mode of expression."[42]

All this was heady stuff for a fifteen-year-old girl, especially one who was suffering from daily reminders of her father's fame. Boyle remembered that Lucia's "rage against being the child of a famous man was an obsession. Both she and Giorgio used to argue with me about this, and when I suggested that Joyce was, after all, not *that* famous (which he actually wasn't at that time), Lucia would become very angry and insist her father was as famous as Rabelais. . . . This resentment, however senseless and unjustified, was paramount in their lives in the period that I knew them."[43] Lucia's friendship with Emile Fernandez brought her into further contact with a movement that not only scandalized the bourgeoisie but also challenged the very foundations of the Western concept of genius.

She took from these loose affiliations with surrealist youth a confirmation of her own legitimacy as an artist: one didn't have to be a genius to be a dancer; one had only to give oneself up to the project of expression. She took from them the idea of social license: bourgeois life was boring; to grow artistically, one needed to confront and outrage the commonplace. And she gained a specific commitment to writing poems herself. It was this poetry that Dominique Maroger remembered reading in the 1930s,[44] that Carl Gustav Jung read in 1934 and used to judge Lucia's "language disorder," and that Joyce defended to Jung as a language experiment of the new generation. In Joyce's eyes, it was the wordplay of a teenager whose high spirits had equaled the outrageousness of everyone around her, especially the spirited young people who produced *L'Oeuf dur*.

On a more intimate level the Fernandezes furnished Lucia and Gior-

gio Joyce with personal friendship and an entry into a financially prosperous and culturally vibrant family life. They were Jews of Sephardic
origin, once members of the large Jewish community in Salonika, in
northwestern Greece,[45] who could trace their ancestry back to Spain and
then to Constantinople, where, Rafaella Benini claimed, Emile and Yva's
great-grandfather had been an Italian consul. The family had made their
money in rice and rubber; they had owned mines in Greece and Yugoslavia; and they had founded the Banque d'Indochine in Marseille. By
the 1920s they lived in a big flat on the Champ de Mars near the Eiffel
Tower, a place that, in Lucia's memory, was filled with the comings and
goings of cousins, aunts, uncles, and many friends. One might find any
number of the avant-garde at their dinner table. According to Emile's
daughter, Jean Cocteau, Erik Satie, Max Jacob, Francis Poulenc, Raymond Radiguet, Maurice Sack, Henri Michaux, Paul Morand, and Jean
Renoir were all to be found at the Fernandezes on one evening or another. Playing hostess to all these artists, Mrs. Fernandez nonetheless
took a special interest in Lucia, showing her the family's heirlooms—real
diamonds, rubies, emeralds, and pearls—and invited her often for
lunches, teas, and dinners.[46]

Lucia remembered the people according to which language she spoke
with each one: with Tante Helene, who was Viennese, German; with
Tante Noemi and Tante Corrine and Tante Rita, Italian and French;
with Emile himself, Italian, French, and English. After lunch they
would often go directly to the piano, where Emile indulged in his love of
American jazz. Through Emile Lucia learned about "Negroes and Negro music," and he taught her to sing "God Send You Back to Me,"
"Way Down South," and "Limehouse Blues." Through him she met his
cousin Yolande who, at least at the beginning, was Lucia's best friend.
Adèle Fernandez remembered the household as a series of pairs: Joyce
and the Fernandez grandmother, Pauline; Emile and Giorgio; and
Yolande and Lucia. As the years passed, the configuration changed.
Eventually Emile and Lucia were expected to go out together; and Lucia, being slightly older than Adèle and Yolande, would tell them about
her evenings with him. He took her driving on Sundays in "a little red
car" often to the Bois de Boulogne and once to Saint-Germain-en-Laye.
They went to nightclubs and to Prunier's, where they would have cocktails and caviar. One of their favorite pastimes was social dancing and

evening soirées.[47] Adèle remembered Lucia's misery when she thought she would have to decline an invitation because she had no formal evening wear, and then her joy when Nora relented and took her to "un grande maison de couture."[48] At one of these balls on the rue George V, Lucia met Emile's cousins by marriage, Darius and Madeleine Milhaud. In 1930, when Milhaud decided to write a musical setting (for voice and piano) for some of Joyce's work, he chose the poem written to the infant Lucia, "A Flower Given to My Daughter."[49]

Emile's other cousins eventually offered Lucia other kinds of companionship. Joella Lloyd, who worked in Mina Loy and Peggy Guggenheim's lampshade shop on the rue Saint-Honoré, went with her to the Eiffel Tower. Another of her beaus, Roger Bickart, was a Fernandez cousin. He too took Lucia driving in the Bois de Boulogne, to good restaurants, to the cinema, and to the cabaret.[50] Adèle, a friend through all the years, remembered Lucia at this time as her favorite Joyce. Giorgio's taciturn manner left her cold: "Je trouvait le fils idiot." ("I found the son idiotic.") Mrs. Joyce was "très gentille" ("very nice") although plainspoken at evening gatherings. Mr. Joyce was someone with whom she felt uncomfortable, as if she didn't understand him. Despite her anxiety she had given him a small reddish kitten, bringing it to him from Marseille in an eight-hour train ride and carrying it over to their flat through the streets of Paris. In later years Samuel Beckett would remember Joyce's continued fondness for the little creature: "It's nice to have a cat around the place—it furnishes a room, a cat."[51] But for Lucia, Adèle reserved her fondest words. She was "très amie avec Lucia qui était joie, charmante, jolie, pleine de gentillesse." Lucia was "joyful, charming, pretty, and very nice."[52]

In June 1923, the lease on the Joyces' flat was up, and Joyce, rather than find a new one, decided to pack up his books and take a holiday in England. It was decided that Lucia would go with her parents for the first part of the trip and then return to France, where she would once again spend the summer at Deauville. Helen Kieffer would return, and this year the daughter of William Bird would join them.[53] With the prospect of further dancing and a chance to see her friends ahead of her, Lucia set out knowing that her father was starting a new book, and this time she was old enough to take an active interest in it.[54]

Indeed, it would have been hard to ignore the new book since their family vacations from this point on would in some way be connected to Joyce's research. The town of Bognor in Cornwall had been chosen because of a certain "Giant's Grave" that Harriet Weaver had mentioned to him, and he referred to the goal of the trip as the "interview with the 'Giant.' "[55] Joyce swore his family to secrecy, not about the book but about its title. To the world they were to refer to it as *Work in Progress*. Joyce would work on this new project for the next seventeen years. Its composition would provide Lucia with a certain kind of imaginative companionship throughout her adolescence and into her young adulthood. In fact, as Giorgio moved away from her, we could say that *Finnegans Wake* became a kind of rival sibling and then a kind of fantastic child whose birth would more and more preoccupy her. Was she in competition with the requirements of this book, or was she in some ghostly way its precursor? Did its creation take love, attention, resources away from her? Or did she act as its inspiration, becoming more and more the daughter-wife whose flowing movements carried her father's imagination from "swerve of shore and bend of bay" out into an imaginative ocean whose depths had not yet been explored in fiction?

It is safe to imagine that in mid-1923 none of these questions had been formulated in her mind. Lucia saw Joyce's writing, at least in part, as a weird, funny transposition of familiar things. In July and August, as she danced by the sea, Joyce began writing about *Tristan und Isolde*, which they had seen at the Théâtre des Champs-Elysées the previous season. Then in September he started another section that he referred to as "Mamalujo" after Matthew, Mark, Luke, and John, the four evangelists of the New Testament. Joyce referred to his work as making "jigsaw puzzle sketches" and as a "Mah Jongg puzzle."[56] Lucia, who learned part of the manuscript word for word when she made a fair copy of it for Harriet Weaver, called it "cinese" (Chinese).[57]

For Joyce personally, 1923 was a time of rather acute suffering. Giorgio, whom he had appointed housing agent during the summer in Paris, had failed to find them a suitable flat. So the Joyces once again moved into a family hotel, this time at a slightly better address: the Victoria Palace on the rue Blaise Desgoff. It was a makeshift arrangement at best. Joyce wrote on a green suitcase from his summer holidays, struggled with diminishing sight, and conluded that "this noisy, dark hotel must be laden with germs."[58] He needed to have his teeth extracted in preparation for further eye surgery, and then Nora decided that she would have similar extractions. At Christmas he observed that "we seem to be sinking deeper into the morass." Looking back in April, he admitted to Harriet Weaver that it had been a "dreadful winter."[59]

For Lucia it was a time of waiting and of giving way to the prerogatives of others. Giorgio took up a position in the Banque nationale du crédit and began to study voice at the Schola Cantorum. His coach, Arthur Laubenstein, who was organist and choirmaster at St. Luke's Church, invited him to sing with the chapel choir. Lucia was enrolled at the Schola Cantorum too and had inherited a voice that was as fine as Giorgio's. But in singing, as her friend Dominique Gillet noticed, she felt overshadowed by her brother, by her father, and by earlier generations of male Joyces.[60] She dropped out of the Schola, choosing instead to continue the piano and to sing informally for other patrons of the Victoria Palace Hotel.[61]

The year passed. Even after Helen Kieffer returned to the United States, Helen Nutting continued to invite Lucia to her studio and take her to tea. Myron did a pencil sketch of her reading a book, then decided in early spring to do a formal portrait. She began her sittings on 5 May and continued them throughout the month. She made the decision to eat by herself in the hotel instead of traipsing with her parents to their lengthy evening fetes.[62] She worked on more dance costumes. She continued working with Raymond Duncan.

By this time, Giorgio and Emile Fernandez had become fast friends, and the Nuttings rarely visited without finding Emile and, increasingly, Lillian Wallace with the Joyce family. The dismal side of Lucia's home life was visible even to such optimistic and generous people as the Nuttings. They could see that the hotel was dark and crowded and that it offered no privacy either to Joyce for his writing or to Lucia for her practicing. To Helen the Joyces seemed dour, turned in upon themselves, their rooms swarming with unspoken intensities. Some of this darkness was unavoidable, especially when Joyce was in physical pain. Her diary for 1925 mentions "misery at the Joyces, he with one eye blind, and the other looking atrophied. He thin from fretting and pain, not eating, and taking no exercise." The clinic where he went on the rue du Regard seemed to her like "a Caligari interior," but not all the family's heaviness could be explained by illness. On another day Helen confided to her diary that she felt, "as I do at times, the restlessness of that family, devoted to each other as they are."[63] Given the opportunity to visit Robert McAlmon in the south of France, Giorgio refused, curiously, to leave his mother and sister.[64]

In this claustrophobic setting, Joyce pressed forward, beginning now to worry about how other people looked at his new work. To Harriet Weaver he confided that he sometimes began to see "stupefaction freezing them into silence. For instance Shaun, after a long absurd and rather incestuous Lenten lecture to Izzy, his sister, takes leave of her 'with a half a glance of Irish frisky from under the shag of his parallel brows.' "[65] The brother was not the only one who was taking leave. In May the Joyces all paused to notice that Leon and Helen Fleischman were returning to America in a last-ditch effort to save their crumbling marriage.

III. THE LARGER STAGE

No matter what was happening at home, Lucia undoubtedly noticed the verve, the style, the dazzling variety of dancers who surrounded her in Paris. She began to keep a pin-up collection. Following this vast spectacle gave her a focus beyond her immediate family and a vision of what was possible for herself in the future. Through her affiliation with Raymond Duncan she knew about his sister Isadora, who had swept through Paris like a force of nature, casting aside costumes and slippers in favor of gauze and bare feet, trading formal artistic unity and learned steps for a more natural grace. Along with four of her young pupils, whom the world knew as "the Isadorables," she had opened a year-long Festival of Music and Dance that first played at the Trocadéro on 27 November 1920.[66] Even within the world of ballet, tradition battled with innovation. The Paris Opéra Ballet continued to appeal to those who took comfort in traditional performance techniques, but Sergei Diaghilev's Ballets russes was committed to the extraordinary choreography of Léonide Massine, Bronislawa Nijinska, and George Balanchine, to modernist musical scores, to extravagant costumes by Léon Bakst, and to sets designed by the Ecole de Paris. During the early 1920s its repertoire included *Petrouchka*, *L'Après-midi d'un faune*, *Soleil de nuit*, *Parade*, *Zéphire et Flore*, *The Gods Go A-Begging*, and *La Pastorale*. The Ballet suédois followed with its own modernist permutations. The Comte de Beaumont sponsored the Soirées de Paris, asking Massine to devise dances for him as well as Diaghilev, and commissioned music from Darius Milhaud and Arthur Honegger. Anna Pavlova, whom Lucia idolized (as her pin-up collection attests) the way young girls often adore movie stars, came to the Théâtre des Champs-Elysées to perform "The Dying Swan."[67]

Outside ballet the dance scene was just as vibrant and varied. It was the age of the music hall, acrobatics, and girl acts. The Hoffmann Girls, who specialized in precision dances done in unison like the later Rockettes of Radio City Music Hall, did their shows at the Moulin Rouge, lining up like "a caterpillar with thirty-two feet." Their number, uniformity, and impersonal beauty led André Levinson to call them "the serial-soul" girls. Lucia despised them because they had nothing original to express but seemed to have been multiplied to order.[68]

Josephine Baker, who first came to La Revue nègre when she was just nineteen, roused passions with her dazzling and uninhibited ragtime rhythms. Emile Fernandez was wild about her. His sister Adèle said he was "in love" with Baker, not making it clear whether this was the adoration of a fan or the aspiration of a suitor. Many years later, after the collapse of his marriage in the 1950s, Emile went to the Ivory Coast, where he acted out his fantasy by fathering a child with a fifteen-year-old black girl.[69] The primitive rhythms of black dancers were interspersed with the greatest of the Spanish dancers—L'Argentina, whom Lucia first saw perform in 1924, and Vicente Escudero—and with dancers who brought the arts of Cambodia, India, North Africa, and Tibet with them to the stage.

It was a world not simply of abundance but of conflict, struggling, like Yeats's Byzantium, to bring forth a new aesthetic. With all these innovations and investments of creative energy in the meaning and procedures of dance, even those who were predisposed to value dance found themselves confused and unable to "read" the performing body. To them the dance world of Paris seemed to be divided within itself. Some dancers defended the beauty of the classical tradition—the vocabulary of ballet that had already been codified and accepted—while others saw new forms of expressive movement as the herald of the future. To them classical ballet was bankrupt, reduced to drawing from a repertoire of ornaments whose original significance had long been lost. Even the glorious spectacles of Diaghilev's Ballets russes were sometimes seen as a last, desperate search for an authentic or persuasive style that could never be sustained within the bounds of the balletic tradition.[70]

Among Joyce's contemporaries, the reviewer who gave himself with the most fervor and insight to the task of reading the performing body was André Levinson. As Paris's foremost dance critic in the 1920s, he often lectured about the artistic quarrels that were unfolding before Parisian eyes, taking upon himself the defense of classical ballet. He saw clearly the nature of the problem he faced in writing anything intelligible about movement. "We are exceedingly ill-equipped for the study of things in flux," he wrote in "The Spirit of Classical Dance." And he identified his dilemma as part of a much more far-reaching historical circumstance: "It is because the art of the dance is so peculiarly inarticulate that it has never possessed a proper aesthetic philosophy."[71] Like the poet Stéphane Mallarmé, he valued the artifice, the training, and the subordination of individual sensibility to aesthetic purpose that characterized traditional ballet. And like Mallarmé, he considered ballet to be "the interpreter of the emotions and their symbolic equivalent."[72]

According to Levinson, a dancer could reveal more than she could understand but at a decided cost to herself. "To discipline the body to this ideal function, to make a dancer of a graceful child, it is necessary to begin by dehumanizing . . . [her] or rather by overcoming the habits of ordinary life." Levinson set himself the task of becoming the ideal reader of movement. He wanted to be able to understand and to describe the "writing of the body," or as Mallarmé put it, the "hieroglyph of a mysterious writing."[73] More than any other critic of his time and place, he mastered what he called "the alphabet of the inexpressible." But even as he wrote, he understood his beleaguered position. He knew that the ballet that he so ardently defended was threatened by "cures by antiquity, painting, music, rationalism, psychology, naturalness."[74] His passion was singular in the sense of being both unique and solitary. Despite the enormous popularity of the Ballets russes, by the time Levinson began his defense of classicism, the modern dance movement was strong enough to sweep past his criticisms.

Levinson's anxieties were as well founded as they were futile. On the one hand, many of the new tendencies that he hated would lead to the eclipse not only of ballet but also of civilization as he knew it. By the late

1920s, the National Socialists in Germany were usurping many of the characteristics of modern dance—the frenzies of mass movements, the unthinking uniformities of line dance, the collective and fervent worship of vitality and brute health—and amending them to serve as part of the ideological underpinning of what would become the Hitler Youth movement. Levinson anticipated this development. When he watched the Hoffmann Girls, he called them "the army of the modern Eve, the anonymous sportswoman, the impersonal beauty, the serial-soul."[75] Phalanxes of nude legs, he thought, could turn into phalanxes of war and industry. "There is in these girls something suggestive of a parade step, something reminiscent of those military ballets . . . a return to the barracks, drum beating, flares flaming."[76] In 1923 the German youth magazine *Junge Menschen* devoted a whole issue to the dance, and in 1928 a huge *Ausdruckstanz* conference was held in Essen. These activities served as forerunners of Hitler's later worship of physical vigor in the service of Aryan nationalism. The Deutsche Tanzbühne would eventually be incorporated into the Ministry of Propaganda under Josef Goebbels.[77]

The obverse side of this movement was another group of young dancers who refused to let state ideologies dictate behavior or subject the body to discipline. They saw entirely new possibilities in the ability of modern dance to organize the body into new systems of meaning. They understood the passion that dance was capable of evoking, the freedom it envisioned, the forbidden ground it dared to walk. The daemonic was as much a part of its territory as the holy, and these poles of existence were both approached by the moving body. Mary Wigman considered a dancer to be entering "the most fascinating expedition existing . . . to discover [her] own body and its metamorphosis from body into instrument."[78]

In 1920, the year the Joyces moved to Paris, Rudolf Laban had written about the wider social significance of the dance. In *Die Welt des Tänzers* he claimed that "the dance can and must help in the shaping of the general culture. For me," he continued, "dancer means that new man who does not create his consciousness out of the brutality of [mere] thinking, feeling, or willing. . . . All these things must be harmonized and must live in interchange. We want . . . to fill the world with the dance of the reharmonized body-soul-spirit."[79] Lucia's teacher Emile Jaques-Dalcroze concurred. The eurhythmist, he claimed, has "a special profession, which employs the methods of art for ethical ends. . . . Eu-rhythmics does not want to establish a church or a state. It awakens a nonreligious and nonlegal conscience, and that will create the new social forms for itself."[80] Suzanne Perrottet, who began her dance career with Jaques-Dalcroze and then became a student of Laban, explained that dance was "a religion for me . . . this new thing that did not yet exist, I lived entirely for it."[81]

It was at this moment in cultural history that Lucia decided to make her move. Her training so far had been a part of the physical culture movement. She had learned rhythm as an aspect of sport, rhythm as an aspect of health, movement as a kind of renewed classicism asserted against the damages of modern urban life. She was restless and ready for change. When the English dancer Margaret Morris set up a modern dance school in Paris in the fall of 1925, Lucia decided to throw her talent and energy in with the new dancers of the age.

Her choices placed her in the midst of some of the most vital modernist enterprises in Paris and in the cross-currents of an artistic debate whose ramifications were as far-reaching as those aroused by her father's writing. While Stephen Dedalus thinks of his flight to Europe as a step toward creating the conscience of his race, Rudolf Laban saw the same redemptive task in the communicative work of the body. "The fate of our race," Laban wrote, "is the awakening to dance. We dancers are the pioneers of a new dawn of art."[82] According to his system of values, it was Joyce's real child, and not the children of his imagination, who would usher in the future of Western civilization.

5

LEAPING WITH
THE RAINBOW GIRLS

NICE 1928

I. LEARNING THE SAVAGE ELEMENT

When Lucia met Margaret Morris, she met a woman who was everything that Nora, her mother, had not been in her life. Gone was the nattering criticism, the unwanted attention alternating with neglect, and the unthinking assumption that a girl's life would follow an age-old pattern of domestic companionship. Like her aunts Eva and Eileen, Morris became Lucia's surrogate mother, but she was also an artistic mother whose encouragement was like manna.

As the principal dancer of her own troupe and the founder of many schools, Morris performed in Paris regularly, but it was probably on 23 June 1924 that Lucia first saw her dance at the Comédie of the Théâtre des Champs-Elysées.[1] She went to the performance with her father. Aside from Lucia's urging, Joyce had the added incentive of knowing that Margaret Morris had married the fauve painter John Duncan Ferguson, an old acquaintance from Dublin.[2] After the performance they spoke to Morris backstage. Listening to Lucia speak of her work with Raymond Duncan and John d'Auban, a dance teacher with whom she had also started to take lessons, Morris sensed the girl's passion and encouraged her to think of dance as a vocation. But she wanted her to stop working with her current masters. Morris had plans to return to Paris the following fall and saw Lucia as precisely the kind of young

Margaret Morris, Juan-les-Pins, circa 1928. Photograph by Fred Daniels.

woman who could benefit from her training. As she told John Galsworthy, she wanted to work with Lucia before Duncan had altered "the savage element which modern civilization causes us to stifle."[3] In November 1925, Lucia got her chance. Morris established her school in a studio at 10 avenue de la Bourdonnais, taught there herself until she was called back to England, and then left the girls in the care of Mary Sykes, who wrote Morris often to tell her of Lucia's rapid progress.[4] Lucia worked as an apprentice until April 1926 and then, with Morris's help and encouragement, joined a group of young women who were intent upon establishing their own careers as performers.

Lucia could not have found a better teacher, for Morris's movement strategies had grown out of the system that Raymond Duncan had advocated when he had toured through England as a young man. At a formative time in her own career as an expressive dancer, Morris had attended one of Duncan's lecture-demonstrations and had come away inspired by his love of classicism, the beauty of his poses, and the logic of the physical system he advocated. Like him, she began to explore the highly articulated postures found in Greek art, and like him she saw immediately the health and freedom of movement fostered by exercise in nonbinding clothing. She was by all accounts a passionate and graceful dancer, but since she led a conventional personal life, she encountered none of the amusement that Duncan's untrousered existence aroused.

To the contrary, Margaret Morris intuitively inspired the trust of the medical profession, who looked to her for guidance in creating therapies for physically handicapped children, for war veterans, and for pregnant women. She became one of the great innovators of the physical culture curriculum in English and European schools, advocating a combination of rhythmic music and movement to develop the aesthetic sensibilities of ordinary people. Where Raymond Duncan trumpeted the advent of a new age, Margaret Morris helped to usher it in.

In her native England, Morris based her work in a studio and a club in Chelsea where those in the neighborhood could congregate, take classes, and watch small local performances. As the granddaughter of William Morris, she had a high visibility in the arts; but as doctors in England discovered the attractiveness of her exercise regimes to those in need of physical rehabilitation, her talents were increasingly drawn away from the stage. Eventually she acquired a degree in physical therapy, adding knowledge of physiology to her innate sense of aesthetics. She saw the importance of beauty as a motivation for physical improvement of whatever kind. She appraised her own historic moment as deeply divided between those with an aesthetic sensibility and those interested in physical culture, and she thought her own contribution could be one of synthesis: "First of all, pupils should be made to realize that every movement and position they make must be good to look at. Not by an effort to be 'graceful'; striving after grace is fatal to good movement; real grace and good looking easy movements can only be the outcome of health and strength. An obvious illustration is the panther or the tiger."[5]

"The first step in the creative appeal," she continued, "is that the pupils should feel themselves to be part of a rhythmic whole." Anyone at all could be a Margaret Morris dancer. She saw benefits in her method for typists and accountants and the "various sedentary, and for the most part uninteresting, occupations of the majority of people."[6] Her method included "everything that is necessary for the development of healthy, intelligent human beings . . . it requires no special conditions . . . it is absorbingly interesting . . . [and] suitable for . . . all ages from two years as the exercises can be graduated to suit any age, or state of physical fitness or weakness."[7]

She believed that rhythmic movement was the foundation of health, and she saw her work in relation to the discoveries of Freud and the nascent psychiatric sciences. In her judgment, the body itself could offer the greatest responsiveness to its own unconscious illness. "One reason why so many people are discontented and repressed," she claimed, "is to a great extent because they have never had any outlet for their emotions in their youth. . . . By discovering a means of expression, the repressions that are the cause of so many disorders in later life can for the most part be avoided. . . . So I begin first by helping the child balance itself."[8]

Like her contemporary Maria Montessori, whose work she knew intimately, Morris educated children through their senses. Babies were taught to improvise to music, to compose steps, to work in groups, and to make cooperative compositions. They were taught about forms, color, sound, movement, and the fundamentals of design. Each element of Morris's program was created to foster self-esteem; each child's artistic efforts were taken seriously: "Everything that children put their hearts into is a serious business to them. . . . The copying or even looking at

painting and drawings I entirely disapprove of for young children. All
art is an impression of something as seen by the artist. As far as possible
first impressions should be obtained first-hand, and not through the eyes
of another—even a great artist."[9] Even a great father.

We can imagine the appeal of these tenets to a young girl educated as
haphazardly as Lucia had been. That the development of children could
be fostered by simple carefulness must have come as a surprise to her.
Four years later, in 1929, Lucia decided to become a Margaret Morris
teacher in Paris, and in the interim she discovered a world for herself.
Morris not only offered her the prospect of a career but also acted as a
feminine role model—a woman who was beautiful, gifted, happy in her
personal life, and purposefully employed. She also offered Lucia the
companionship of other talented young women. Chief among these were
two of her older students, Lois Hutton and Hélène Vanel.

II. LEARNING RHYTHM AND COLOR

In 1921 Morris had hit upon the idea of moving her annual summer
school to Juan-les-Pins, in the south of France. Eventually she arranged
to house the girls who studied with her in the Hôtel Beau Site, which
fronted directly on the sea. She taught the girls to dance in the fresh air,
to dress for comfort and freedom of movement, and to bathe in the sea.
By 1924 she had made the project so attractive that *Vogue*, *Tattler*, and
The Graphic all carried lead articles about her, with photographs of the
girls at Eden Rock diving into the Mediterranean and dancing in the
woods. The principal teacher was Lois Hutton, a young Scottish woman
who had come to Morris already trained as a gymnast and with experience as a teacher of physical education and games at the Roedean School.
Hutton was, in Morris's estimation, the finest teacher she ever employed,
and she credited her with planning and systematizing the teacher-
training program and with introducing the study of anatomy and physiology into the curriculum.[10]

For her own part, Lois Hutton fell in love with the Riviera, and after
returning there for four years with Margaret Morris, she decided, along
with one of Morris's French students, Hélène Vanel, to settle in France
rather than return to London. "Together," Morris recalled in 1969, "they

started a tiny theatre right inside the little hill town of Saint-Paul, near Vence, and called themselves Les Danseuses de Saint-Paul."[11] The room they danced in held seats for only forty people, it was lit solely with oil lamps, and the performances were so well attended that the girls often had to repeat them after midnight.[12] Later, when Hutton and Vanel moved their troupe to Paris for the winter months, their success was often attributed to the distinctive cast of their sylvan retreat. "Their great originality comes from their private life," wrote one reviewer. "They are eight or ten young girls—perhaps sixteen and over—who retreat for many months to a remote corner of the Alpes Maritimes to consecrate their lives to Dance."[13]

Indeed the landscape itself seems to have inspired their creativity. Isadora and Raymond Duncan summered in nearby Nice; Margaret Morris continued her school in Juan-les-Pins; but so great was the beauty of Saint-Paul that those who visited Les Danseuses sensed that they had entered the portals of another world.

It is likely that Lucia spent the summer of 1926 with them here and occasionally returned to visit at least until 1932,[14] not taking holidays in Nice and environs, as Ellmann assumed, but returning to those who had taught her, encouraged her, and danced with her. Henri Bidou, a journalist who went to the area in 1931, described the blocks of red schist and violet-colored porphyry that ended at Cannes, and then asked his readers to continue imaginatively toward the east, where the mountains folded up from the sea and opened valleys into the interior.

> One such valley is the Valley of the Wolf some kilometers from Antibes. A river framed by large trees, an air of coolness in a shadowy country, luxuriant and verdant. . . . If we go from there towards the interior we arrive in a region of light gray hills very different from what we are accustomed to seeing in Provence. The foliage of the olive trees harmonizes with this tone of dried soil. In the expanse of vineyards, the long low rows of vine stocks extend, now in violet-purple color. In the gardens everywhere peach and orange trees abound.

Bidou followed the landscape to the house of Lois Hutton and Hélène Vanel, where

> at this moment a manuscript is being finished. From a vestibule a small flight of wooden stairs ascends. A room with a very beautiful fireplace, a ceiling

Margaret Morris's students dancing at the Riviera, circa 1928. Photograph by Fred Daniels.

Lois Hutton, Paris, circa 1926. Photograph by Fred Daniels.

"Etincelles." Dance and costumes by Lois Hutton to music by Ravel, Paris, circa 1926. Photograph by Fred Daniels.

supported by projecting joists, brown and cracked. The windows open onto
an abyss of gold, clear green and sky.[15]

These people and this landscape were to provide Lucia with an artistic home for the formative years of her young adulthood. When she had
come to this part of France with her parents in 1922 and again in 1925,
she had been a member of the Joyce entourage. She had acted as a copy-
ist for manuscripts and as a slightly burdensome companion. But Lois
Hutton, Hélène Vanel, and another friend, Kathleen Dillon, three girls
hardly older than she, were to kindle her dormant and undirected energy and bring the abstract and errant teachings of Raymond Duncan
into personal focus.

These young women were extraordinarily idealistic about their work
together, but they also knew what they needed to survive. On the one
hand, they wrote poems and essays about dedication to art that they published twice a year as *Cahiers rythme et couleur*; on the other, they assembled the financial resources that would allow them to pursue their
aesthetic goals. By 1925, one year after they decided to establish a studio
independent of Margaret Morris, they had attracted close to seventy subscribers from places as diverse as London, Paris, Geneva, Tunis, Chicago,
and Louth, Scotland. And though the girls spoke exultantly about conse-
crating their lives to Art, they also saw clearly that teaching was part of
their social mission that would also generate money.

The history of their collaboration, documented impeccably in *Cahiers*,
reveals a constant alternation between teaching and performance.
Demonstrations to interest new students were interlaced with auditions
to create new performance opportunities. In April and May 1925, they
lived in Vence, teaching dance-painting and organizing their summer
courses; in June and July they went to Paris, where they immediately
arranged lecture-demonstrations in "danse pour amateurs" at the Théâtre des Champs-Elysées. Within a week they had inaugurated two dance
groups that met at the Pré catalan (Théâtre de Verdure), a performance
space in the Bois de Boulogne named after a court minstrel from Provence who was murdered in the fourteenth century.

On 6 July they auditioned for the Agences théâtrales at the Théâtre
des Champs-Elysées. On 14 July they spoke with the writer Constant
Lounsbery about creating a new dance piece with his poems. On 20 July

they met with Carlos Lavin to discuss combining their dances with his music. By 1 August they were back in Vence, opening their dance class for amateurs on the beach at Juan-les-Pins as well as another class for children in the pine forest at Juan-les-Pins. Then they retreated briefly to Vitry-le-François to prepare the first issue of *Cahiers*. On 9 September they celebrated the first anniversary of the Studio rythme et couleur in the south of France.

One senses their excitement merely by following their itinerary, and this zest is apparent in their writing as well. Their gift was energy rather than originality. Their greater gift was stagecraft. Their best was in a style of being-in-the-world: at a young age, they found a way to live out their alternative to careless bourgeois existence, helping to make the south of France more than a resort for the leisured classes. A photograph taken of Lucia in Vence with the other girls who eventually became Les Six de rythme et couleur shows her embraced by two friends, flanked by three others, all of them smiling. They are standing in front of a rough shed in bare feet and tunics, wholeheartedly and unselfconsciously bringing in the new age.

Cahiers rythme et couleur was designed as a way of making a community. In it the young women defined their mission, invited the comments of readers, and created a format for demonstrating their students' achievements. Each issue contained prose, poems, croquis, photographs, and a calendar of events and accomplishments. They kept track of new dances choreographed each year and remembered those that would be worth repeating. In a column on "The Dancer as Artist and Educator," Hélène Vanel, the most eloquent of the group, worked out their creed.

Like Havelock Ellis, Vanel claimed that rhythm was the pulse of all the arts: the movement of an artist's drawing hand was dance; the fingers of a pianist danced. "Does the firmness and daring of a line not come from the rhythmic impulse of the hand which guides the pencil?"[16] The cinema followed the same logic of meaningful gesture; so did driving an automobile or flying an airplane. But movement was not something that the ignorant public was trained to see. Women noticed details of clothes without recognizing the quality of the moving body within them; sports spectators kept score but did not see the "movement, sure, rhythmic, precise which guaranteed . . . winning." Predictably, the dancer was a savior whose interior harmony connected her to the universe. Her work was poignant for the same reason that musical performance was: "being 'life' that is ephemeral, movement dies as soon as it is born; it escapes us once executed."[17]

Their lifestyle was that of well-organized post-Victorian hippies. Lois Hutton, Hélène Vanel, and Kathleen Dillon lived together in Vence in a place they called the Ramparts, giving glimpses of their domestic arrangements in vignettes published as "the Three Dancers." Identifying themselves as "the Darkest One," "the Smallest One," and "the Youngest One," they represented themselves with a combination of sincerity and irony, which admitted that dedication to purity in art could have a trou-bled interface with the pedestrian world. Their cats they named "Fa-ther" and "Wife," in one slight gesture subordinating patriarchy to their own idiosyncratic rule. The peasant on whom they relied for transporta-tion down the mountain they dubbed "Stravinsky," presumably for his subversion of universal harmony: "He produced as usual, an original concatenation of rhythmic percussion as he bore the Three Dancers downhill that morning, and up again in the evening—flashing green lightning, smelling strongly of good, healthy, garlic and singing still stranger songs as he groaned and shrieked uphill to the aloof serenity of the Ramparts."[18]

Lucia could have done far worse for herself. Not only were these girls dreamers of an alternative world built on the truth, humility, and sincer-ity of their efforts, but they were also level-headed, the first to laugh at themselves when their high-mindedness failed. "The *chef d'orchestre*, groping in the air with his violin-bow, impressed on the drummer: '*UN-deux-ET-trois*,' hoping to conciliate the Three Dancers who, harnessing their gnashing teeth with brave, pathetic smiles, explained that the time signature was four-four, and that C sharp was not E flat when they were young." "On that fateful night the Darkest One sat sewing a costume that only her optimism could have held together, while curtain-rings, hammers, pins, and other implements indispensable to a régisseur fell like manna around. . . . The Smallest One stood below, drawing con-vincing diagrams to demonstrate her theory that a single cord should be capable of pulling two separate curtains either together or apart as re-quired."[19] Their robust good humor rested on a solid foundation, for they were convinced of the importance of their work. "The artist is man in all his excellence. The artist is the pure man and a strong man. It is he who understands the vanity of ambition and of money," Hélène Vanel wrote, the resources of her culture giving her the concept of the serious woman artist though not the syntax to inscribe it.[20] And they rejected the concept of the unbalanced artist, "half-mad, possessed by an inspiring demon, which drags him equally into folly and into immortal works of art,"[21] a romantic concept they considered irresponsible. They thought the goal of art to be normality, not as experienced by ordinary people (who were "stupefied, brutalized, debilitated and irritable"), but in the sense of being attuned to "the most delicate strings of [one's] vibrant sensibility."[22]

Together they taught Lucia that the artist was a complete being, not someone who redeemed the faults, weaknesses, and ugliness of his daily life with a few hours of inspiration. They cautioned her to seek perfection larger than herself and to let the amplitude of her vision carry her beyond "competency, talent, exploitation of a trick."[23] The "halo" of an artistic career, measured by others, might still "unfortunately be glory," but she was to hone herself to a more rigorous standard: "The real artist can only be pure. If he considers for a single moment, while creating or performing, his chances of success, he ceases to be pure. Money and vanity consume him and make him a despicable being who calls himself by a name he doesn't merit."[24] And they were extreme: they counseled artists to take the risk of scorn and a hungry death.

To them dance was not merely a technique—it was a spiritual event: "They should be improving their spirit before starting to perform. There is so much to do, simply to adjust to the world, so much to look at, to astonish one, so much to look for, so many essential problems to consider, so much to bring into harmony, to combine, until the spirit draws its own conclusions."[25] They envisioned the artist as having an aura, a "radiance," that little by little, through words, suggestions, and revelations, would penetrate the subconscious, bringing the student to a realization of her own truth.[26]

Lois Hutton and Hélène Vanel went periodically to Paris, where they taught more classes and established performing careers for themselves. They were not simply bohemians with a mission; they were talented. The first performance of which we have a record was given on 20 November 1926, at the Théâtre des Champs-Elysées.[27] From the first, Lucia danced with them, and from the first the group received favorable notice in the press. In Paris they changed their name to the more cosmopolitan Les Six de rythme et couleur, calling attention to their spiritual affinity with Les Six (the Group of Six), the young composers whose work was ushering in a new age of French music. Milhaud identified the musical climate of the times by saying that young musicians were "reacting against the impressionism of the post-Debussy composers" and asking for "a clearer, sturdier, more precise type of art which should yet not have lost its qualities of human sympathy and sensitivity."[28]

Like Les Six who gave concerts together, met every Friday night, and "gave free rein to their high spirits,"[29] Lucia's group was recognized in Paris as a group with a vocation. A "curtain-opener" in the French press spoke of them as "a group of young artists from a class formed in Provence. For two years, they have worked furiously on the hills around the 'city' of Saint-Paul, well known to painters, and their efforts were much appreciated by the artistic elite of the Midi in France and of Switzerland. . . . [They] will give several performances next month at the Vieux-Colombier."[30] They repeated their performance at the Théâtre des Champs-Elysées on 18 December and held a third recital at the Ancien Théâtre du Marais on 21 December.

Their first program was ambitious, consisting of twelve dances marked by the combination of dance, mime, and parody that was to become their artistic trademark. They danced to music by Brahms, Ravel, Scarlatti, Stravinsky, Debussy, and to music Hélène Vanel had composed herself. Dances such as *Panthère verte*, *Faunesque*, *Jardins sous la pluie*, and *Les Vignes sauvages* expressed their concern for the vitality of nature. Others were designed more specifically to reveal the basic premise of their collaboration: that rhythm and color are manifest in all aspects of life (*Rythme et couleur*: *Ashnur*, *Primavera*, *Burlesques*). Several were created with the elaborate sense of play that characterized their living as well as their art (*Un deux et trois bouffons*, *Burlesques*, *Carnavalesque*). They mimed poetry, taking pleasure in transposing from one art form to another (*Poème mime*, *Extract from the Diary of a Young Female Egoist*, *Poème de Hester Sainsbury*); they mimed types of people they knew (*Deux bergères deux bergers*). Jack Nicholson might be astonished to learn that "Five Easy Pieces" originated with these young women's *Cinq pièces*

Playbill, Théâtre du Vieux-Colombier, 1927. (Courtesy of the Rondelle Collection, Bibliothèque de l'Arsenal, Paris)

Samedi 9 Avril à 17 heures

MATINÉE DE DANSE

donnée par

RYTHME ET COULEUR

LOÏS HUTTON ET HÉLÈNE VANEL

Zdenka Podhajska,
Kathleen Neel, Julia Tcherniz, Lucia Joyce,
Jacqueline Albert-Lambert

AU PROGRAMME :

Panthère Verte (H. Vanel) ; Danse sur la "Pavane pour une
Infante défunte" (Ravel) ; Burlesques (Stravinsky) ; "Un, Deux
et Trois Bouffons" (Grieg-Schumann),
Etc. etc...
En première audition
Prêtresse Primitive (H. Vanel) ; Tristesses d'Idole ;
Effets de Rythme

ORCHESTRE
sous la direction de
Mʀ LÉON KAITUN

Prix des places : 3ᵉ série 6 fr., 2ᵉ série 10 fr., 1ʳᵉ série 15 fr.

LA LOCATION EST OUVERTE
tous les jours de 11 h. à 18 h. 30 sans augmentation de prix
(Téléphone : Fleurus 5. 87)

Lucia Joyce with Les Six de rythme et couleur, Vence, circa 1927. (Courtesy of the Eugene and Maria Jolas Collection, Beinecke Rare Book and Manuscript Library, Yale University)

faciles. Lucia's part was usually to dance in "natural" roles like those provided by *Ballet faunesque*, *Les Vignes sauvages*, and *Prêtresse primitive*.

The review of their Vieux-Colombier performance in 1927 spoke of
the program as both "comprehensive and lofty" and noticed that the
young women were well received, "in spite of their inexperience," by a
"public attentive to their efforts and realizations." The reviewer spoke of
the group's "great originality" and predicted that they would soon be
performing in larger music halls in Paris.[31]

By 1930 André Levinson, the greatest dance critic in Paris, had noticed them. He was struck by the differences between Hutton and Vanel.
In February of that year, a critic in the south of France had described
them as "complement[ing] each other perfectly: this one posturing, that
one more a dancer, both sensitive to the slightest variations in the music
and embroidering the melody with fine and spontaneous arabesques,
which did not detract from either the profound meaning or inner resonance" of the piece.[32]

Levinson too was interested in the contrast between the two women:
"The blond and the brunette, the dancer and the mime, the young
girl with hair of flax and the Sulamite, or more exactly, David." Since
he associated them with dancing in the open air at Juan-les-Pins, he
wondered what had made them choose the intimacy of the stage at
the Cinéma des Ursulines, which he thought too restrictive a space.
But he answered his own question when he remarked that having
experienced "the approbation of the mob" at the Empire Théâtre, they
had retreated to the smaller quarters precisely for their warmth and
closeness.

From this point, he separated the two dancers, for he thought Hélène
Vanel's performance wholly lacking in the "radiance" or "magnetism"
that he considered indispensable for any mimetic art. When he watched
her posturing (she apparently was the mime in this performance), he was
not convinced by "her expression of mystic exaltation or warlike power."
He found her to have a "sensuous charm," but the images Vanel desired
to convey of sanctity, heroism, or luxury did not come to fruition. The
draperies that enveloped her "cold simulacrums of ecstasy" he found "in-
sufficiently varied." In fact, he said she had the flexibility of a "trunk."[33]

Lois Hutton fared better, for she had an exquisite sense of timing and
a highly developed comic flair. In addition to being a good gymnast, she

shared one of Levinson's pet peeves: an aversion to "girl shows" like the Hoffmann Girls that were then coming into vogue.[34] She parodied them as well as "the exercises of the school dancer," to his great amusement. (He did not like Jaques-Dalcroze's eurhythmics either.) "She changes her feet, tries to escape from 'on [ballet] point,' and finishes the dance, assisted by a chair. She stretches, crosses her legs languorously and with mechanical dexterity, and is "entirely entertaining."[35]

One wonders what the dancers made of this mottled bundle of praise and blame and remembers their account of the aftermath of a performance in Saint-Paul that was an unmitigated disaster: "At six o'clock in the morning, the Three Dancers said to the dawn: 'Sic itur ad astra . . .' And immediately fell into a sound sleep."[36]

For Lucia, Les Six de rythme et couleur was far more than a performing group. It gave her a life apart from her family. In May 1925, her home life, while in some ways more emotionally entangled, was at least more comfortable than it had been. Her parents had decided to find a regular flat and to buy their own furniture. At 2 square Robiac, where they lived until 1931, she finally had her own room and her first taste of privacy. But her father's life was never quiet. In 1926 Joyce was fretting because Samuel Roth had pirated *Ulysses* in America. While the obscenity trials that had marred their early years in Paris threatened to turn into another round of trials about intellectual property rights, Lucia withdrew into her own community of friends and into the interesting consequences of a life on the stage.

Her exact peers were Zdenka Podhajsky, Barbara Mole, and Olga Hargreaves, dancers who all participated in the first performance of the group in November 1926.[37] In April 1927, Kathleen Neel, Julia Tcherniz, and Jacqueline Albert-Lambert joined the ensemble. Kathleen, whom her friends called Kitten, and Lucia were inseparable, and like Hutton and Vanel, they were remembered as opposites. Vanel wrote that she was "accustomed to seeing Lucia in the company of her great friend, Kathleen Neel, pretty, statuesque, large, blond with the appearance of a pretty American child, perfectly rosy and smooth. [Their friendship] resembled some kind of ethereal drama. One might say that Kathleen was a body and that Lucia was a spirit, so strong was the contrast, bound to a complementarity that made the two friends inseparable. But in a certain sense, the dazzling clarity of Kathleen prevented one from immediately seizing the finesse and all of the mystery that lay within the personality of Lucia."[38] To her, Lucia's character was "gold" that, like the alchemist's gold, was capable of extraordinary fluidity and change. In it, one could find "inquietude" but also extraordinary richness.

By this time, Lucia's "guise" was superficially that of a young "it" girl. Thomas Wolfe, who met the Joyce family on a bus trip to Waterloo in 1926, remarked that "the girl was rather pretty. I thought at first she was a little American flapper."[39] Hélène Vanel remembered that dark sunglasses were then de rigueur and that Lucia never appeared without them. Her stride was "not hesitant but gentle and measured according to an interior cadence." This inner certainty gave Lucia's dancing "a kind of impalpable presence that could not be rendered perceptible except through the movements of a body which was thrillingly fragile and fluid." Her great gift was revealed in disguise and in her self-created transformations. Covered by costume and gesture, she was capable of impersonating not just Charlie Chaplin, for which she was already famous, but Pierrot or Petrouchka or any "multiply tragic soul, the naked soul of the absolute scoffer." "With her, symbols became living actions." If one paused to notice, Lucia's subtlety surpassed the more obvious, beautifully modeled presence of Kitten Neel. Lucia was eager; she was "full of fervor and exultation," and she could carry an audience "to the limit of hallucination" in her ability to interpret the obsessive rhythms and the abrupt movements of music like that of *Prêtresse primitive*.[40]

While Lucia was dancing on the stages of Paris in *Prêtresse primitive*, *Le Jardin enchanté*, and as a "savage vine" of the forest, Joyce proceeded with his *Work in Progress*, describing the young Isabel/Isolde with lyrics from William Bird's *Woods so Wild*. "Shall I go walk in the woods so wild, Wand'ring, wand'ring here and there, As I was once full sore beguiled, Alas! for love! I die with woe, Wand'ring, wand'ring here and there . . . "[41] In March 1926, father and daughter were both preoccupied with nature personified as the body of a young dancing girl and with the forest as the location of disappointed erotic life. In the fourth chapter of the book of Shaun (*FW* 556), written during the month of Lucia's debut, Isabel, with her "wildwood's eyes and primarose hair," lies sleeping in her "april cot." She is finally still and quiet, but it is a sad stillness that follows having "growed up one Sunday"—not from sexual experience but seemingly from its lack. She is, in her current incarnation, "sister Iso-bel, beautiful and still in her teens," and she is a "nurse," "a nun," "a widow." The "child of tree, like some losthappy leaf, like blowing flower stilled," is as full of woe as William Bird's song. And the sequence that transmutes the woodland body of the dancing child into the emotional landscape of the sleeping young woman is spoken by a voice that con-nects the savagery of the staged performance with an underlying grief. "Win me, woo me, wed me"—the sequence of a young woman's de-sire—ends here not with consummation but with "ah weary me!" Both the father and the teacher, watching Lucia bring the insistent cadences of the wilderness to symbolic life, suspected that suffering found expression in the savage beauty of her dance.

Joyce was not the only artist who took an interest in the vitality of Lucia's performance that spring. Less than two weeks after his *Woods so Wild* letter, Joyce wrote to tell Miss Weaver that an Irish sculptor, John Knox, who had also watched Lucia dance, had asked if he could do a full figure of her.[42] These poses were followed by a session with the young American photographer Berenice Abbott, friend of Peggy Guggenheim, who was working in Paris as the assistant of Man Ray. The photographs, taken in Abbott's Paris apartment, show a young woman who is solemn, graceful, and self-possessed. The camera catches her sitting at a three-quarter angle, looking slightly to the side. She has cropped her hair: on the sides and back, it is sculpted to her head; the severity of the effect is mitigated by the marcelled waves that cascade down her forehead almost to the level of her eyes. She is tastefully dressed in a soft dark suit. For the moment the camera seems to say she has used rhythm and color to good effect. The gangly child in maryjanes has disappeared. The ea-ger brightness of the young gymnast has been transposed. The still-adolescent Lucia Joyce sits before the lens with a distinctive style of her own.

In the spring of 1927, Lucia left Paris to make a tour of Italy with Les Six de rythme et couleur. The girls were heading toward an inter-national dance competition, but Lois Hutton and Hélène Vanel had arranged for them to perform en route, bringing, as Dominique Maroger claimed, "the first representation of modern dance to Italy." In Genoa, Rome, Bergamo, and Trieste, they danced *Le Jardin enchanté* to the music of Ravel and *Le Combat d'un faune et d'une faunesse* to the music of Joaquin Turina.[43] In May the ten dancers returned to the garret and improvised stage at Saint-Paul. Lucia went with them but then decided to return to Paris, for she had learned that Jean Borlin, lead dancer of the famous Ballet suédois, had opened a private studio at 36 rue Singer.

6

CHOOSING PARTNERS
PARIS AND SALZBURG 1928

I. LUCIA AND HARLEQUIN

Jean Borlin was a breathtaking dancer. He was a legend in his own time, a master who offered Lucia an unprecedented dance vocabulary. She and her family had been going to see Borlin perform to new music ever since 5 October 1923,[1] when the Ballet suédois had given the world premiere of *La Création du monde*. Their interest had been spurred in part by a new friend, George Antheil, whose *Airplane Sonata* and *Mechanism* had created the kind of scandal that was also associated with the high antics of Borlin on stage.

For five seasons in Paris, Borlin and the Ballet suédois claimed the attention of the avant-garde dance world and eventually came to challenge the artistic hegemony of Diaghilev's Ballets russes. Rolf de Mare, its director, was passionately interested in folk culture and in the ways the elements of such traditional dancing could be combined with the visionary achievements of new young artists. He did not hesitate to call upon the "bad boys" of Paris and to make his productions a center for the combined talents of the musicians and visual artists of the French avantgarde.

In 1919 he had come from Sweden to Paris with his lead dancer, Jean Borlin, and when he considered the success of this young performer assured, he rented the city's largest theater and brought his company to

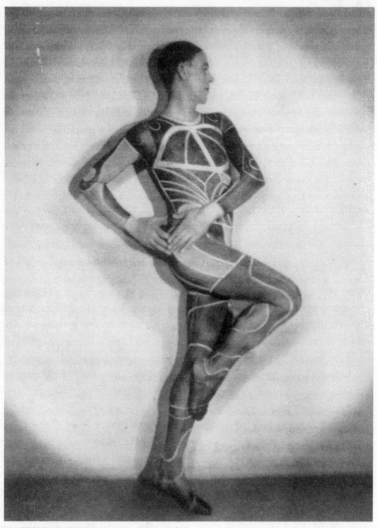

Jean Borlin as Harlequin, Paris, circa 1922.

France. Between 24 October 1920 and 4 December 1924, they performed a repertoire of twenty-four dances at the Théâtre des Champs-Elysées, dancing to the music of Ravel, Scriabin, Saint-Saëns, Debussy, and Liszt as well as Darius Milhaud and Les Six.[2]

The troupe was then disbanded, but Borlin continued dancing by himself at the opera-music hall of the Théâtre des Champs-Elysées. This was in all likelihood where he met Lois Hutton, Hélène Vanel, and probably Lucia herself, for by 1925 this was their artistic home as well. By February 1927 Hutton and Vanel were using some of Borlin's repertoire, having choreographed Ravel's *Pavane pour un infante défunte*.[3]

Borlin's signature was his almost contagious vitality. In one context after another—in the memories of his teachers, in the mouths of dance critics, and in the pages of the press—he was known to be the child of Dionysos. Mikhail Fokine, who left the Ballets russes in protest when Diaghilev invited Vaslav Nijinsky to choreograph as well as dance, taught Borlin parts for *Cléopâtre*, *Shéhérazade*, and *Le Dieu bleu* and recalled him with these words:

> He skimmed the stage with immense jumps, dropped with all his weight, and glided over the floor, among the groups of bacchantes. What a nature! What ecstasy! The fanatical sacrifice of a bruised body in order to create the maximum choreographic expression. It was a revelation for me. . . . These Scandinavians . . . a northern people, cold and stony. Where did this fervor come from? From where did this ardent flame burst forth?[4]

And Pierre Tugal, who watched him work with Fokine, was if anything more explicit about his friend's exuberance:

> The technique of Jean Borlin was already very assured; he was flexible, elegant and gracious. Nevertheless, the vivacity and nervous elasticity of the dancers born under the midday sun and the completely oriental frenzy of the Russians were still foreign to us. At this time Borlin, to [use] the image of Nietzsche, was solely under the influence of Apollo. But in the studio of Fokine, the impetuous god [Dionysos] was awakened in him. The art of Borlin—sober, intellectual, purebred—came from audacious pursuit and at times attained sublime stylizations that delighted Fokine.[5]

What Borlin had to offer Lucia was both a more classical vocabulary of movements than she could have learned from Raymond Duncan or her young teachers, and a more shocking, exhilarating extreme of execution. Although Paris, blazing with debate, cast modern dance and traditional ballet as antagonists, Lucia herself did not take sides. She pursued both classical and modernist training, and we can imagine that Borlin was attractive to her because he was a master of both styles. Trained by the school attached to the Royal Theater in Stockholm, he had learned both the Danish Bournonville technique and the Italian academic method of ballet.[6] Unlike her other ballet teacher, Madame Lubov Egorova, he had the breadth of imagination to integrate the old and the new. Where Egorova, who had danced with the Imperial Ballet of Petrograd, was of the "plus haute école d'un classicisme pur, d'un très noble style," Borlin had the attraction of youth and the gift of vivacious friendship.[7]

Of the twenty-four ballets that Borlin composed in Paris, three especially distinguished him: *L'Homme et son désir* (1921), *La Création du monde* (1923), and *Relâche* (1924). Joyce seems to have taken notice of two of his other solo roles: "Harlequin"[8] and the ecstatic, whirling skirt dances of the Mevlevi dervishes.[9] Aside from Joyce, the French were especially impressed by the company's willingness to work on "the frontiers between the arts, the ages and the nationalities."[10] By 1923 the troupe had acquired the reputation of being "interesting and weird."[11] It offered, said the *New York American*, "an orgy of weird impressionism."[12]

L'Homme et son désir was inspired by Nijinsky of the Ballets russes and was originally choreographed for him. Paul Claudel (the scenarist), Darius Milhaud (the composer), and André Parr (the costumer and set designer) had seen Nijinsky perform in Rio de Janeiro in 1917 and had thought him "lyricism incarnate." "He walked as tigers walk," said Claudel. "[I]t was not the shifting of a dead weight from one foot to the other, but all the complex of muscles and nerves moving buoyantly, as a wing moves in the air, in a body which was not a mere trunk or a statue, but the perfect organ of power and movement."[13] By the 1920s when the three had completed their work, Nijinsky was no longer well enough to perform, so they approached the Ballet suédois. It was a more appropriate move than they could have anticipated, for Borlin, already trying to find ways of "translating forms in painting into dynamism," was immediately receptive to Claudel's attempts to relate gesture to rhythmic speech and to find forms of plastic expression for the poetic image.[14] For the journal *La Danse* Claudel wrote a long but apt description of *L'Homme et son désir*:

This little drama in movement had its birth in the atmosphere of the Brazilian forest which, in its vast uniformity, seemed like an element in which we were immersed. It is most strange at night, when it begins to be filled with movement, cries, and gleams of light; and it is one such night that we are trying to show in our poem. . . . Th[e] stage appears vertical to the eye, like a picture or a book being read. It is, if you like, a page of music in which each action is written on a different stave. The Hours of Night, all in black with gilded headdresses, move one by one along the topmost ridge. Below, the Moon led across the sky by a cloud, like a servant walking before a great lady. At the very bottom, in the waters of the vast primeval swamp, the Reflection of the Moon and her Servant follows the measured walk of the celestial pair. The drama proper takes place on the platform halfway between heaven and earth. And the principal character is the Man in the grip of primeval powers, robbed by Night and Sleep of both face and name. He enters led by two women, identical in their veils, who confuse him by turning him round and round like a child blindfolded for a game. One is Image and the other Desire, one is Memory and the other Illusion. Both mock him for a while, then disappear.

He remains there, standing with outstretched arms, sleeping in the brilliance of the tropical moon, like a man drowned in deep waters. And all the animals, all the noises of the eternal forest come out of the orchestra to watch him and din in his ears: the Bells and the Panpipes, the Strings and the Cymbals.

The Man begins to move in his dream, and to dance. And his dance is the age-old dance of nostalgia, desire and exile, the dance of captives and deserted lovers, of those insomniacs who pace in a fever from one end to the other of their verandah, of caged beasts that fling themselves and fling themselves again—and again, and again—upon the impassable bars. Sometimes a hand from behind pulls him back, sometimes a fragrance, which saps all vitality. The theme of obsession becomes more and more violent and frenzied, and then, at the darkest of the dark hours before the dawn, one of the women returns, and circles round the man as though fascinated. Is this a dead woman or a live one? The sleeper grasps the corner of her veil; she whirls round him and her veil unwinds until he is wrapped around like a chrysalis, and she is almost naked—and then, joined by the last wisp of stuff, very like that of our dreams, the woman puts her hand on his face and both move away to the side of the stage.

Of the Moon and her attendant all we see is the reflection, down below.

The black Hours have ceased to file past, and the first white Hours appear.[15]

"In the bugginning is the woid, in the muddle is the sounddance and thereinofter you're in the unbewised again," Joyce wrote in *Finnegans Wake* (378.29–30). The sleeping body of the man, the representation of the world of the night, as if in dream, the circular passage of time; the stage a "dantellising" dark text, to be read on four levels at once. Lucia's father was not alone in his search for ways to represent the unconscious. For Claudel, Borlin, and the participants of this drama, dance was also a kind of "nat language" that writes itself directly on the audience's experience; it took place in a kind of "noughttime" where death and sleep were twin brothers, the sons of night. We can imagine Lucia watching and listening, learning from Borlin as much as from her father how the somnolent music of the body expresses itself. We can picture her practicing the rhythms that precede spoken and written language, already at twenty familiar with the book of the dark.

From Borlin Lucia also learned that Africa could have a symbolic power similar to the power that ancient Greece held for Raymond Duncan. *La Création du monde*, the Ballet suédois's "ballet nègre," followed *L'Homme et son désir* in 1923. The troupe was hardly alone in its obsession with primitive tribal ritual. It was as if all of Paris were preoccupied with the construction of an elsewhere of culture, searching for alternatives on which to base its hopes of social renewal. Where Raymond Duncan had returned periodically to Greece, Rolf de Mare maintained a second home in Africa during the 1920s.[16] Blaise Cendrars had just finished editing an *Anthologie nègre* in 1921, and Kay Boyle remembered that "his ambition of the moment seemed to become as African Negroid as possible."[17] Lucien Lévy-Bruel had just published *La Mentalité primitive* (1922). Philippe Soupault was researching the short story collection that he would call *Le Nègre* (1927) and anticipating the essay "Terpsichore," which would exhort Parisians to approach sexual liberation by means of black dancing. In 1928 he described Saturday nights at a Caribbean dance hall as full of "joy so miraculous and mad and spontaneous that you could smell it in the air. And love, the presence of sex."[18]

Whatever their individual motivations, all these artists were working variations on what they would have known as the *bamboula*. For them African dance was marked by "a powerful magic rhythm, a frenzy of sound and movement, of hysterical dancing, bacchanals, where all art is lost to fury, to delirium, to rampant obscenity. . . . The *bamboula*, as it has been described in colonial literature, is simply license, totally unfettered animal sensuality, eroticism without shame, brutal and bestial; it is the fury of the libido whipped up collectively by the sorcery of the tom-tom."[19]

This, at least, is what Blaise Cendrars saw in Berlin on stage. His dancing was like that of "sailors, mulattos, Negroes, savages—and that's what I admire about it most. . . . With your Swedish peasant's feet, you are the exact opposite of the Ballets russes, you've thrown a monkey-wrench into the French balletic tradition as it has come down to us from the *ancien régime* and Italianism via St. Petersburg. . . . Billboards and loudspeakers have made you forget the pedagogy of the Académies de Danse. . . . [You have] rhythm, which opens five new continents to us: Discipline, balance, health, strength, speed."[20]

In *La Création du monde* the curtain opened on a scene before the creation of the world, where Nzame, Medere, and K'kva, the three masters of creation, circled a central pile of dancers, who gradually came to life, becoming trees, monkeys, crabs, and turtles until, in Act III, a man and a woman emerged from the disorder. Their mating dance ended the spectacle. Milhaud's score for the ballet was experienced as "cacophonous, dissonant, and pounding." Leger's costumes and set were considered exotic, with an artificial elephant hanging in the air, and replicas of monkeys clamoring along the ceiling.[21]

For Lucia this dance presented still another lesson in using energy.[22] She was learning to read Berlin's creation story, his story of human desire, and his message about the inadequacy of bourgeois aesthetic, ethical, and social values. For this is what she would have gleaned from studying *Relâche*. The repertoire of the troupe offered a heady diet for someone whose home life revolved around the silence of a creative father. A young woman of her silently rebellious temperament would have taken this ballet's absurdity and excess immediately to heart.

Relâche, the final creation of the Ballet suédois in its 1924 season, presented Lucia with the wild machinations of Dada. Subtitled *An Instantaneous Ballet in Two Acts and a Cinematographic Entr'acte, and a Dog's Tail*, it was conceived by Francis Picabia; it included film made by René Clair, music composed by Erik Satie, and choreography by Berlin. *Relâche* means "no performance," and though people wandered on and off the stage during the piece, it made no attempt to sustain the appearance of

Relâche: An Instantaneous Ballet in Two Acts and a Cinematographic Entr'acte, and a Dog's Tail, Paris, 1924. This was the possible source for Lucia's using record disks as curtains in her cottage at Bray.

an active performance. René Dumesnil remembered that "a fireman entered, smoking. A woman in evening dress walked onto the stage from the auditorium and smoked a cigarette. She danced, without music; and when her dance ended, the music resumed. Several men from the audience went up on the stage and danced with the woman, and one of them carried her off the stage."[23]

For someone intent on stage and costume design, as well as choreography, the event was of equal interest. The inner curtain for Act I was covered with graffiti, which, when backlit, looked like neon signs. A screen with discordant cinematic images projected on it replaced the backdrop. Round disks, like hundreds of gramophone records hung from a window, superseded this screen. A funeral procession came on stage, and a coffin fell from the hearse. The corpse arose, smiled, and made everyone else disappear. *Relâche* was someone else's *Work in Progress*.

Whether she wanted it or not, Lucia was once again living in a

Joycean world. Here was *Finnegans Wake* transposed into living images. Here was another version of Tim Finnegan waking up to carouse at his own wake. Joyce was not alone in imagining a sleeping giant who comes to life in dreams. In avant-garde Paris her father was not the only artist trying to represent the "great part of every human existence [which] is passed in a state which cannot be rendered sensible by the use of wideawake language, cutanddry grammar and goahead plot," as Joyce put it.[24]

Lucia interrupted her training with Jean Borlin to dance in various shows with Les Six de rythme et couleur, and in 1927 they all interrupted their performance schedules to participate in the filming of a new movie by Jean Renoir. *La Petite marchande d'allumettes* (*The Little Match Girl*) was based on Hans Christian Andersen's story. In the match girl's delirium, at the point of death, she imagines a world of satisfied desire, which in the movie is represented by the animation of a toy-store window. Hutton and Vanel's troupe were to create the dance of the toy soldiers, and Lucia and Kitten Neel were to have a small duet. "Lucia and Kitten became charming automatons and comics," Hélène Vanel said. She used one particular moment during the rehearsal schedule when the girls came into the music hall at the Empire Théâtre to focus her insight into the meaning of dance to Lucia. The hall where they practiced was extraordinarily large, so that it was often hard to restrain the girls' "illimitable desire to leap and to run." "There I saw Lucia absolutely joyous—it was a rare thing for everything with her was serious. . . . I should like to recapture the picture of Lucia who threw herself without restraint through the empty side of the great chamber. It was evident that dance was for her a guarantee of equilibrium and of energy. That is, she was perhaps never fully conscious of it, but she felt that her efforts were salutary; they gave her a taste of life and a beautiful way to express her dreams with all of her being, both body and soul."[25]

Vanel believed that Joyce's creative spark had been passed to Lucia and that she searched "for access to a universe of plenitude in the act of creation." "Yes," she continued, "she was really the spiritual daughter of James Joyce; she was his extension. She was the single element on earth that prolonged his existence, both inside and outside of his work."[26] But Vanel did not end her memoir on a wholly positive note. She thought there was "reason [Lucia] dreamed her life away. She lived through many strange adventures, which she would tell us about, and I believe that they were often with her brother."[27] Noticing the shadow side of Lucia's creativity, she was hinting at some kind of darkness, which was disturbing enough to be mentioned and disturbing enough to remain shrouded in mystery. Vanel knew something that she felt she must refrain from saying, and her unspoken words were reserved for Giorgio.

If it is true that some uncomfortable secret troubled Lucia, it was not universally noticed. In the fall of 1927, Joyce was preoccupied with his own work, wanting to get away from Paris but reluctant to go to the south of France until the summer tourists left. While he struggled to revise the Anna Livia Plurabelle section of *Work in Progress*, he sent "the children"—now twenty and twenty-two—for a ten-day holiday on the Channel coast by themselves.[28] In early October, he estimated that he had spent at least twelve hundred hours of work on seventeen pages of manuscript, and though he could boast that 350 names of rivers were woven into the text, he also admitted, "I am utterly 'moidered' by Anna Livia." "Moidered," he explained to Miss Weaver, was Irish for confused in the head.[29]

By February 1928, Joyce was more sanguine. Helen Nutting remembered his birthday party at square Robiac as an awkward, formal affair that mellowed as the evening wore on. As she looked out over the room, she noticed that "Lucia, Mrs. Antheil, and Kitten sat on the sofa. Lucia's face is fine and thoughtful this winter, Kitten handsome and plump and Mrs. Antheil small and dark, in a *robe de style*, elegant and discreet. Joyce stayed in the background and Nora the same, until Adrienne [Monnier] began to tell of table tapping and a long story of messages she and her friends had received from the spirits. Joyce remarked that *le seul esprit* he believed in was *l'esprit de l'escalier*. Then Antheil was asked to play old English music, and Joyce and [Robert] MacAlmon [*sic*] danced quietly in the back parlor, improvising rhythmic movements, MacAlmon on Negro themes and Joyce Greek, so that Adrienne exclaimed, 'Mais regardez donc ce Joyce; Il est tout à fait Grecque. C'est le satyre sur un vase grecque!' (Look at Joyce; he's totally Greek. He's a satyr on a Greek vase!) And it was so, skipping, delicate with a clean line. After three songs he stopped [singing ballads] and we had champagne, dancing and singing, and everything was gay, stiffness melted."[30]

While McAlmon did his version of the *bamboula* and Joyce imitated

Lucia's dancing à la Raymond Duncan, she herself was busy choreographing a comic opera. *Le Pont d'or: un operette-bouffe franco-américaine* had a libretto by Edward Comingman and a score composed by Emile Fernandez, with whom Lucia was working professionally for the first time.[31] The piece was coming together, but the rehearsals with Kitten and Julia Tcherniz since the previous December had often been trying. Helen Nutting came into the Joyces' kitchen on 31 December to hear Lucia telling about one "which broke up because the principal actor left when Emile told him he had had enough and to *fiche le camp* [get out]. It was because this young man came an hour and a quarter late, and then was so silly that nothing could go on. Emile, after great patience, broke out and made a scene, or as Lucia put it reproachfully, 'Emile forgot himself.' Giorgio upheld Emile, saying if he had begun by being stern and exacting all would go well now. But Lucia repeated mournfully, 'No, Giorgio, Emile forgot himself. The play . . . is very "futuristic." A lady is in love with the Alexander Bridge, something like that. I really don't understand it and I don't want to. You will perhaps be shocked. It is acted by rich young men who have nothing to do but spend money. They are rather good, but foolish.' "[32]

The young people got their act together, and *Le Pont d'or* was performed on 18 February 1928. It appeared in a program that included Darius Milhaud's music for *La Création du monde*—the jazz ballet score that used African folk mythology to depict "prehistoric monsters freeing themselves from chaos and evolving toward the light"[33]—and Elsie Lynn and her Special Trio, a group that sang American Negro spirituals.

The following month, Lucia was interviewed by the *Paris Times*. "Lucia Joyce is her father's daughter," the article began. "She has James Joyce's enthusiasm, energy, and a not-yet-determined amount of his genius." Raymond Duncan and Margaret Morris had been only a beginning. In 1928, she was blazing with the kind of discovery that fueled the talents of performers like Mary Wigman and convinced other young women they were creating a new religion. "She dances all day long, if not with Les Six de rythme et couleur, studying under Lois Hutton and Hélène Vanel then by herself. She never tires . . . When she is not dancing, she is planning costumes, working out color schemes, designing color effects." After noting her choreography for *Le Pont d'or*, her performances with Les Six, her skill as a linguist, and her Irish good looks ("tall, slender, remarkably graceful, with brown bobbed hair, blue eyes and very clear skin"), the article concluded with a noteworthy reversal: "When she reaches her full capacity for rhythmic dancing, James Joyce may yet be known as his daughter's father."[34]

II. LUCIA AND THE DEVIL HIMSELF

In the first week of March 1928 Lucia's aunt Eileen Schaurek and her three children visited the Joyces in Paris on their way to Ireland. Bozena Berta, the eldest daughter, had vivid memories of the occasion even fifty years later. While he worked or on the occasions when he sang, "Lucia danced silently in the background."[35] There are two artists in this room, and both of them are working. Joyce is watching and learning. The two communicate with a secret, unarticulated voice. The writing of the pen, the writing of the body become a dialogue of artists, performing and counterperforming, the pen, the limbs writing away.

The father notices the dance's autonomous eloquence. He understands the body to be the hieroglyphic of a mysterious writing, the dancer's steps to be an alphabet of the inexpressible. Like André Levinson, he is learning that "we are exceedingly ill-equipped for the study of things in flux, even for considering motion in itself as such."[36] Watching the silent eloquence of his daughter's moving body, he begins to describe the meaning of his own language experiment in *Work in Progress* in analogous terms. Arthur Power remembers Joyce speaking about the risks the writer must take in the process of writing. "In other words, we must write dangerously: everything is inclined to flux and change nowadays and modern literature, to be valid, must express that flux."[37] To another friend who complained it was just Dada, he said, "It is an attempt to subordinate words to the rhythm of water."[38]

Rivers, like the bodies of young dancers, slip away, flow onward, out, away. What was characteristic of the "language of the night" was not its obscurity, as if words were stones in shadow, but the illegibility of the movement in which they participated. The world in sleep was a world that failed to stay in place. In dream images are fleeting, meanings are transient; they fade, slip, recede, fail to be grasped. Like "pure dance," as Samuel Beckett was shortly to recognize, *Finnegans Wake* was "not about something; it is that something itself."[39] Like Diaghilev's Ballets russes, here was an art form about to jettison the story line, a narrative on the verge of becoming its own performance. Consequently here was a brace of words, unstable, unfixable, which would pose one of the deepest mysteries of dance and indeed of life itself: that the body is always passing from presence to absence. Displacement and disappearance are the most powerful aspects of our existence.

The daughter, who is carrying around the libretto of *Lucia di Lammermoor*,[40] is also a student. She is a young girl for whom art is as serious as life itself. Her father teaches her that it is to be learned from, taken to heart, emulated. The place where she meets her father is not in consciousness but in some more primitive place before consciousness. They understand each other, for they speak the same language, a language not yet arrived into words and concepts but a language nonetheless, founded on the communicative body. In the room are flows, intensities, unexpressed longings. They heed desires that are unfettered by social convention, before they are made presentable to the commonplace world.

III. DANCING WITH NATIONAL SOCIALISM

Nineteen twenty-eight was the year in which Lucia told her father that she would have her name "on top of the first page of the papers before you"[41] and began lobbying for an apartment of her own, like her friends Yva Fernandez and Zdenka Podhajsky. Yva had long been an independent single woman, but Lucia was even more influenced by Zdenka, a young Czech woman and fellow dancer who was her exact peer. Zdenka had come to Paris in 1925 and set up an apartment with two Greek girls, all of them around twenty. Kitten Neel still lived with her parents (Boyd Neel, a banker in Paris on the boulevard des Capucines, and his American wife)[42] but Zdenka had the freedom to invent her own life. She danced, taught ballet, and lived in a garret where she was free to come and go and to invite over anyone she pleased—and she knew many interesting artists. One of her roommates eventually married Nikos Kazantzakis, the Greek writer who was to become famous for *Zorba the Greek*. She spent her time with Les Six and with another dance troupe known as La Pantomime futuriste. They were riding the crest of the

Futurist movement, founded by the Italian poet Filippo Marinetti in 1909, and their work was intended to shock. "We will destroy museums, libraries and fight against moralism, feminism and all utilitarian cowardice," their manifesto had shouted. "We will glorify war, the only true hygiene of the world."[43]

After the Great War, Zdenka's Futurist friends had tempered their pronouncements about war but continued to make abrasive art and to live in shocking ways. Zdenka danced with the painter Raoul Dufy at Le Bœuf sur le toit, the Parisian meeting place for artists; Leoš Janáček sketched her as Kata Kabanova, the heroine of one of his operas. The architect Le Corbusier made sketches for her on napkins. She kept company with Max Brod. She went to hear the music of the Czech composer Bohuslav Martinu and became his intimate friend. Martinu played the piano when she gave ballet lessons; and because he was so tall, he helped her to paper the walls of her garret. She did his mending.[44]

To Lucia, who was shoved to the side at home, Zdenka's lifestyle must have seemed heavenly, but Lucia's appeal to have her own apartment fell on deaf ears until March, when her aunt Eileen Schaurek visited the family. Eileen was on her way back to Dublin, but Joyce tried to persuade her to remain in Paris and to take a flat with Lucia. In return he offered to pay the expenses of putting her three children in boarding school. Eileen was on the verge of agreeing when letters from her Dublin sisters arrived asking if she'd lost her mind. Her duty, they pointed out, was to her own children. In the end, she returned to her job in Dublin, and Lucia's desire was stifled.[45] She was not to get away from home so easily.

In fact Lucia had to wait until the summer to get her way about anything that was important to her. She wanted to go to Salzburg, Austria, where Elizabeth Duncan, sister of Raymond and Isadora, held a summer school each year, but she had to fight even to get Joyce and Nora to listen to her. Joyce asked Kay Boyle if she thought it would be harmful for a young girl to go off alone to a foreign country. "Lucia and you are maybe within a year or two of each other," he reportedly said. "But surely close enough for you to know what her tribulations and misgivings could be. Ah well, who in the world can decide for another? It would be asking too much to think that one young woman could take the responsibility of entering into another young woman's hopes and fears. As far as my children are concerned, I am always asking the impossible. A father feels at a loss."[46]

Boyle remembered the two elder Joyces as being constantly anxious that year. For one thing, they worried about the inward cast of Lucia's left eye. Should she undergo corrective surgery, or would it right itself in time? Joyce also wanted Lucia to retreat from dancing and to take up drawing and bookbinding with more persistence. But Robert McAlmon (whose first essay about *Finnegans Wake* would use ballet as a way to understand Joyce's writing) thought that dancing could "release . . . her tensions" much more effectively. Joyce rallied to McAlmon's vision of his daughter's vocation. "Yes, yes, she was born to dance," he repeated.[47] But he was tense, as if he didn't really understand or support what she was doing.

Boyle remembered Lucia as skittish and tentative: "as she sat in the sunlight that came hot through the plate-glass window, I felt her tragically reaching, seeking for what could probably never be found, and for a fearful moment I believed I was looking at my own reflection in a glass. She was like the high, perishable, wishful tendril of a vine moving blindly up a wall, and the vine from which she sought escape was rooted in a territory that had for her no recognizable name."[48]

Joyce and Nora solved their misgivings about sending Lucia to a foreign country alone by deciding themselves to vacation in Salzburg with Stuart and Moune Gilbert. While her parents and their friends settled into the Hotel Mirabelle, Lucia went out to Schloss Klessheim, where she got to know the other women in her course.[49] She had no way of knowing that in following the dictates of her own heart, she was about to become embroiled in ideological debates that contributed to the beginning of the Second World War.

The Elizabeth Duncan School, which met more regularly in Darmstadt, Germany, was the project of Isadora's sister. She too had chosen dance as a vocation and, more than twenty years earlier, had worked with Isadora to establish the first Duncan School of Dance in Grünewald, Germany. It was run on a shoestring, so Isadora would periodically schedule fund-raising tours, leaving Elizabeth behind to run the school.

The more pedestrian of the sisters, Elizabeth was also the more proficient. From the account of Irma Duncan, one of the original "Isadorables," she was a capable administrator and a stern disciplinar-

Elizabeth Duncan School. (Courtesy of the San Francisco Performing Arts Library and Museum)

Elizabeth Duncan, circa 1928. (Courtesy of the San Francisco Performing Arts Library and Museum)

Students at the Elizabeth Duncan School, Salzburg, 1928. (Courtesy of Doree Duncan Seligmann)

ian.[50] Nonetheless, in the minds of her young charges, she was an ogre. Irma called her Tante Miss and came to see her as "the bad cop." No matter how long Isadora was away from the school, she always played the "good" roles of savior, lover of children, and artistic inspiration. The girls associated Elizabeth with the cares of everyday existence, and eventually they blamed her for devoting the school more to *Körperkultur* (physical culture) than to dance.

But the school was shortly in real danger. In 1908 the number of students had dwindled to about a dozen, and neither sister could muster the financial resources to continue it. Rather than close down entirely, they sent the girls to stay at the Château Villegenis in the suburbs of Paris while Isadora again raised money by touring. To her utter amazement, she returned to an empty cradle.

In the interim, Elizabeth and her companion, Max Merz, Grünewald's former pianist, had decided to establish their own school. Capitalizing on the fact that most of the original students were German, they persuaded their parents that it would be far better to let their daughters remain in Germany than to follow Isadora to France: "Merz wasted no time in transforming the school according to his own precepts and . . . his ideas were forerunners of what almost a quarter of a century later were to be the themes of Adolf Hitler's *Kraft durch Freude* (strength through joy) movement and the Hitler *Jugend*."[51]

Merz identified the school's primary raison d'être as "Veredlung der Rasse" (ennobling of the race). He also spoke of the self-evident importance of educating future teachers as part of this national "striving."[52] The five points in the Duncan school's educational philosophy were designed to encourage the health and discipline of the entire organism. Merz pictured the libido as a vast store of restless energy that was waiting to be directed, and he claimed that examinations and facts were futile until one had given each child discipline and physical harmony. Accordingly, the school would offer each child the opportunity to (1) strengthen her vitality, (2) cultivate her instincts and develop her will, (3) learn necessary life skills in the arts and sciences, (4) build character and ethical judgment, and (5) bring talents to aesthetic fruition through their natural expression.[53]

Two kinds of students could come to the Elizabeth Duncan School: those without any particular vocation who wanted simply to increase their well-being, and those who wanted to be teachers. For both groups, the day-to-day program included mornings of mathematics, composition, languages, botany, zoology, chemistry, physics, physiology, literature, art history, or ethics, followed by afternoons devoted to physical training, music, or the practical skills of household management.[54] Some people might think of the Duncan school as a dance academy, Merz observed, but it was in fact far more than that. And indeed in 1911 its directors included an impressive list of professors from Frankfurt, Stuttgart, Munich, Wiesbaden, Berlin, Düsseldorf, and Leipzig, as well as artists, sculptors, and writers.

In an essay published along with Merz's credo, which was meant to place the school in a larger social context, Dr. A. Mallwitz contended that the goals of the school could be most appreciated through a historical perspective that started in the Middle Ages. Citing various attitudes toward the female body that had their origin in the "gray" teachings of that time, he argued that contemporary German women were crippled by corseted bodies, pointed shoes, mincing steps, and a general decorum that insisted on their fragility. Looking farther back in time, he called his audience's attention to the Spartans of ancient Greece who valued human strength above all else and indeed abandoned weak children on the mountainsides. Having created the poles of his genealogy, he went on to say that "the opening of the Elizabeth Duncan School signifies a decided turning point in our culture."[55] Through it young women could reclaim their bodies as the "*heiligen Tempel*" (holy temples) that they were.

As he continued in this vein, Mallwitz began to sound like a "come-to-Jesus" evangelist: "A piercing stream of light points the way to the future: finally someone has hit upon the ideal of restoring the woman's body to its rightful place in nature."[56] "Give your daughters these opportunities," he importuned. After creating images of healthy girls enjoying sun, wind, water, and movement, he asked his audience to agree that "you want to have purposeful, healthy, beautiful women who are capable of being family helpmates and of withstanding difficult circumstances." He closed by reminding everyone that "the German fatherland needs well-grown examples of women educated not in the Spartan manner but according to the influence of progress and our own era's understanding of hygiene."[57]

Max Merz was successful in marketing his ideas in a way that Isadora

Duncan never was. Recognizing the drawing power of the Duncan name, he called the institute the Elizabeth Duncan School of Dance, but its benefactors knew they were supporting the perfect image of German womanhood and not some abstract dedication to Art. Merz's principal patron, Ernest Louis, grand duke of Hesse, donated a large property for the school in Darmstadt, but the help of many others was enlisted, and by 1911 his roster of patrons read like a Who's Who of German royalty. Prince Wilhelm and Princess Gerta von Sachsen-Weimar, Princess Olga von Isenburg, and Princess Hermann zu Solms-Braunfels were a few of the aristocrats who supported Merz. He maintained their enthusiasm by periodic tours that presented the girls, the former Isadorables, as specimens of what any farmer's daughter might become by studying at Darmstadt.[58]

Although she had returned voluntarily to the custody of Merz, Irma Duncan would forever regard herself as kidnapped, and at the least we can say that she was lured back under false pretenses. She wanted to continue to dance as she had with Isadora and thought that she could keep that hope alive by remaining affiliated with a school that carried the Duncan name. As she learned the school's new regimen of classes, she grew contemptuous of Merz's vision. Instead of silk tunics, the girls wore gray woolen uniforms. Instead of dance, they learned Swedish gymnastic exercises. Instead of cultivating grace or imagination, they were taught strength and endurance. By 1911 Merz had arranged not only for the publication of his book (*Elizabeth Duncan-Schule*) but also to have plaster casts made of the different body parts of the girls, displaying them, along with an artificial pumping heart, at the Hygienic Exhibition in Dresden that year. Together these casts of arms and legs, hands and feet, individually mounted, supposedly composed the Ideal Body of German Womanhood, and they supported Merz's belief in the need for racial purity, especially among the women who would be the future mothers of the German race.

Even Victor Seroff, who later came to know Merz and Elizabeth quite well during the time he spent summering in one of the palaces of Schloss Klessheim, "failed to recognize the true reasons for Merz's racial discrimination toward the girls of the . . . third generation of pupils."[59] Irma Duncan careened between discouragement and contempt: She detested the strenuous exercise regime in which exercise was an end in itself, and she found Merz's fanaticism impossible to believe in. She represented his false ideas of grandeur with a scene in which he supposedly evoked the Teutonic gods: " 'Baldur! O mighty sun god! I implore thee to cast thy golden rays upon our work! Oh, Irma, shut up!' "[60]

How much of the inflated and conflicted ideology behind Merz's efforts would have been recognized by a twenty-one-year-old who came to Austria, in all innocence, to enlarge her knowledge of dance is hard to say. When Elizabeth Duncan came to Paris to teach for a while in October 1928, Kay Boyle observed none of it. She regarded Elizabeth as a kind elderly lady who won her confidence by alerting her to the possibility that Raymond Duncan and Aia Bertrand were capable of stealing her child, Sharon.[61] She represented herself and Elizabeth, in bedraggled clothing, being driven each morning from Raymond's ramshackle commune to Elizabeth's studio in Harry and Caresse Crosby's chauffeured limousine. Photographs of the young dancers taken during the summer when Lucia was in Salzburg look no different from myriad others of that era that depict nubile girls dressed in tunics dancing on a lawn. Looking back on it in 1961, Lucia remembered nothing about ideology but considered that she had had excellent dance instruction. "We used to dance with a young woman called Dora Koeritz. She was a wonderful dancer—better than Isadora Duncan herself."[62] And she remembered the repertory used in her private voice lessons: some Lieder by Brahms ("Es Steht ein' Lind' in jenem Tal" and "Du Stille Nacht!") and "Fac, ut ardeat cor meum" from Pergolesi's *Stabat Mater*. Lucia liked what she had done in Salzburg enough to continue dancing with Elizabeth (and Kay Boyle) when she returned to Paris in the fall.[63]

But only in asking questions about Merz's ideology can we begin to understand the constellation of historical circumstances that might explain a seemingly fateful comment that Joyce made in a letter to Harriet Weaver on 19 October 1929: "Lucia turned down the Darmstadt offer and seems to have come to the conclusion that she has not the physique for a strenuous dancing career the result of which has been a month of tears as she thinks that she has thrown away three or four years of hard work and is sacrificing a talent."[64]

This letter has always been controversial. Even to people who thought erroneously that Lucia was just taking dancing lessons, in the manner of a well-bred daughter of leisured parents, this moment carried tremendous weight. For it seemed to mark the end of Lucia's productive life and to signal the troubled road that lay ahead of her. Brenda Maddox, to give one example, translates Joyce's letter into a statement of fact: "Upon their return [from London] Lucia had decided to give up dancing."[65] But we do not know that. We know only that Lucia did exactly what Joyce said: She "turned down the Darmstadt offer." This decision may not have been painless, but Darmstadt, as young dancers like Irma Duncan knew from harsh experience, was not an uncomplicated place to be in the late 1920s.

Placed into the context of Max Merz, Elizabeth Duncan, and their school, the information in Joyce's letter takes on a previously unnoticed set of historical nuances. For one thing it represents a level of achievement of which Joyce seemed to be unaware. The "Darmstadt offer" was unlikely to have been an offer to study, for the curriculum was designed for German girls from prosperous families who were much younger than Lucia was. It was more likely an offer of a teaching position, which must have originated with Elizabeth Duncan, who had watched Lucia's development since July 1928.

To Max Merz, Lucia would have been an attractive teacher. She was not German, but she spoke German fluently. Irma and the other "Isadorables" had forsaken him, preferring to perform and teach in other European cities and in America. Why did Lucia decide not to get involved? Had she understood that Merz's worship of the Aryan body had little or nothing to do with the spirit of friends such as Lois Hutton and Hélène Vanel? Had Merz's influence that summer contributed to her own anxiety about her appearance? Had he found some subtle way to increase her fixation on her imperfect eye so that she disqualified herself without understanding exactly why she felt at a loss? Had he invited her while at the same time undermining her self-confidence? Was Lucia's self-assessment connected not just to mirrors? Was she responding in some way to Merz's "racial discrimination toward the girls of the . . . third generation of pupils"?

There is no way to know exactly. At around this time, Lucia did become more obsessed with the cast in her left eye. But young women are frequently preoccupied with their appearance, and performers are trained to imagine the effect of their physical presentation. Whatever the case, in August 1928 no big decisions lay immediately before her. Lucia was preparing to go back to a rehearsal schedule with Les Six de rythme et couleur, which was planning to enter a dance competition in Brussels. She was also preparing a solo number for another competition in Paris. She wanted to think about its music, choreography, and costume. As it turned out, these projects were interrupted not by proto-Nazi ideologies but by her parents' ill health and by their ways of coping with it.

7

STUMBLING AND RECOVERY

PARIS 1928-31

I. LUCIA, SHAUN, AND THE "DANCEKERL"

In September 1928, Joyce suffered another bout of eye disease. As he wrote to Harriet Weaver, he had episcleritus, conjunctivitis, blepharitus, and a general nervous fatigue. He couldn't see print and was preoccupied with the Samuel Roth piracy case in America. His own miseries did not prevent him from understanding that his wife was unwell too, but Nora tried to ignore her own symptoms, claiming that one invalid was enough in the family. By November, she could no longer neglect herself. Dr. Thérèse Bertrand-Fontaine, a new family doctor recommended by Sylvia Beach, feared that Nora had uterine cancer.[1]

All the Joyces and their circle of friends handled this crisis by withholding the serious nature of her condition from Nora herself. Consequently no one could persuade her to undergo surgery. Joyce went to Helen Fleischman at this time and asked if she could assist him in changing Nora's mind. It was, he said, a matter of life and death. She took Nora to her own gynecologist for a second opinion and was distressed to learn that he too suspected cancer.[2] Finally Nora consented to minor surgery to be followed by radium treatments, and she entered the hospital on 8 November. She recovered, only to relapse and to face a hysterectomy in February 1929.

For Lucia this illness brought a double displacement. Joyce decided

Lucia Joyce dancing to Schubert's
"Marche militaire," 1929.
Photographs by Berenice Abbott.
(Courtesy of Commerce Graphics Ltd.)

that he would not part with his wife, and despite Nora's grumbling, he moved into her clinic with books, notebooks, and all his writing paraphernalia. Their apartment on square Robiac was closed (Helen claimed for five months, from November to March 1929), and Lucia, along with Giorgio, went to stay with Helen at Helen's apartment in the rue Huysmans.[3] Not only was Lucia afraid that her mother would die, but these circumstances forced her to confront the complicated nature of her feelings for her brother, his lover, and the sexual ethics they had chosen to live by. She was, we can imagine, lonely, jealous, resentful, full of rage, full of outrage, full of longing, and her feelings were explicitly sexual. Helen later wrote about this period of time as one in which she was taking care of "the children" while Nora was in the hospital.[4] But Lucia knew that Helen's presence in their lives marked the end of their childhood and of the special relationship she had shared with her brother.[5] For her the fall and winter of 1928 were times of worry, of managing hospitals and illness, and of living with a brother who was "living in sin."

From the beginning, Giorgio and Helen's relationship was considered scandalous. Helen was eleven years older than Giorgio, Jewish, and married, but the disturbing emotional dynamics of the affair were even more complicated than many people knew. Myron Nutting remembered how he first learned about the couple: "On our return to Paris from one of our many short trips, Richard Wallace told me the James Joyces were running quite a temperature. Giorgio was discovered in an affair with Helen Fleischman. Richard Wallace's comment was that it was interesting that, for people supposed to be so unconventional, the Joyces' reaction was one of proper middle class distress. Nora may have confided in Helen Nutting, probably did, but I don't remember being even interested. Helen Fleischman was then seen at the Joyces and was always treated with kindness and courtesy so far as I could see. I always had a feeling of vague discomfort in her presence at the James Joyces as I could see little temperamentally in common between her and any of the Joyces."[6] Nino Frank considered that Helen had set her sights on "Joyce *père*," that she was "really married to father not son." He also remembered that in 1926 and 1927 Helen was interested in neither the elder nor the younger Joyce but was being courted by Philippe Soupault.[7] Giorgio thought he had met Helen in 1922, when he was seventeen,[8] but Helen put the date several years later, and at least in her unpublished memoir, she surrounded it with a drama of betrayal and deception.

There is no doubt that Helen's initial excitement about meeting the Joyces had to do with Joyce senior. The "We Meet" section of her memoir is not about meeting her new lover, future husband, and father of her next child but about meeting her future father-in-law. He told her "in no uncertain terms" that he found her attractive, and she felt that her fate would "be inextricably woven with the destiny of the man I had met that night."[9] Helen quickly became a member of an inner circle of the Joyce family, knowledgeable about their birthday rituals, intimate parties, and the gossip festivals that invariably followed these gatherings. She was in on the Bloomsday lunch that Adrienne Monnier and Sylvia Beach gave at the Hôtel Léopold to honor Joyce in June 1929 and the Bal de la purée (Ball of the Busted), which Joyce (whom she called "Babbo") invented as a response to the crash of the American stock market that October. Everyone was to come in rags. Instead of fearing shabbiness, the guests were to flaunt it. Eventually she recognized that it was Giorgio—and not his father—who would furnish the next chapter of her life.

Although some of her own relatives were unkind and spoke of Helen as sexually voracious (to her brother's wife, Ellen, "she was a sexual vampire, a bloodsucker"[10]) Helen reversed these roles, casting Giorgio as the one on the make. In her memoir, she pictured him at the end of an evening party at square Robiac, standing beautifully erect, fixing her with an intense, knowing look, and singing an old Italian song, "Amaryllis," to the accompaniment of Arthur Laubenstein. She was charmed. "I knew, as his father knew, that he was in love with me." She returned his gaze with "equal intensity," sensing that a "new phase" of her life had begun. She was embarrassed but equally certain that all the guests could see that Giorgio was very taken with her.[11] In her memory, Joyce became "perhaps the *deus ex machine* [*sic*] that was then shaping our ends." "It was the old game that I loved," Helen admitted. "But this boy was so young, so sweet. I did not want to hurt him."[12]

In one passage after another, Helen's retrospective memoirs tried to make the "rough places smooth." She pictured Nora, whom she came to dislike before her marriage to Giorgio was over, as the model young wife, charming and witty. Lucia was "sweet, pretty, slightly cross-eyed

. . . with warm, friendly eyes . . . and an adorable little accent when speaking English."

According to Helen, she was not Giorgio's first lover, and their ability to share stories about their previous erotic experiences formed the foundation of their later intimacy.[13] She claimed that Giorgio's sexual initiation had been with Lillian Wallace, Richard Wallace's wife, who had first come on the scene as the Christmas benefactor of Lucia and Giorgio in 1920.[14] Wallace, she said, was an attractive, cultured man, but Lillian she found common. She characterized her as having a harsh voice, a "tense rather horselike face," scruffy hair, and big teeth. But she acknowledged a reason for her animosity. "Dear Lillian had been Giorgio's first romance. I think she seduced him but perhaps that is unkind." Helen easily got him away from her.[15]

This rather vindictive account is contradicted by Myron Nutting, who saw Lillian Wallace as "slender and quite chic looking." He remembered that she was English, the daughter of an Anglican parson, and that Richard Wallace had met her in Paris when she was performing with a theatrical troupe: "She was good-looking, dressed smartly and tastefully. She was good company, jolly, but shallow. Lillian always called James Joyce 'Jim.' I can't be sure but don't think even Richard Wallace used his first name. I had an idea from Nora that Joyce got several ideas from Lillian Wallace, but aside from the 'yes' of Molly's reverie, I don't recognize anything."[16]

And Helen's manuscript recollections differ from the well-groomed pages that she eventually typed and edited to form a coherent memoir. Its distinctiveness comes from the press of sentiment. It seems to be composed of unedited flows that capture the sting of raw, unprocessed emotion. It is self-aggrandizing and melodramatic. Her dislike of Lillian Wallace was real, and she later would explain her crucifixion upon the cross of gossip during 1926 and 1927—years when she was shunned by the elder Joyces in public—as due in part to Wallace's desire for revenge.

The Joyces, as Helen remembered them, were accustomed to combining teacups with intellectual scalpels. Their evening parties were always served up a second time for "cruel analysis" at tea the next day, when "we would figuratively wipe the blood of our victims off our mouths and hands . . . on dainty napkins." When she was included as a commentator in these postmortems, Helen considered herself one of the

elect and this the best part of the fun. Nora would start by disparaging
the behavior and looks of the women guests: " 'Did you see' . . . and so on
down the list with hardly a kind word for anyone."[17]

When she had to imagine herself as the dissected "corpse," Helen collapsed in misery until, in one remarkable intellectual move, she recognized that Joyce used his family's gossip fests in *Finnegans Wake*. "O tell
me all about Anna Livia! I want to hear all about Anna Livia. Well, you
know Anna Livia?" (*FW* 196.1–4). Helen concluded that she herself was
the heroine of Joyce's novel. "Babbo," she thought, had transcribed her
life in *Finnegans Wake* in the character of Anna Livia Plurabelle, just as
Nora's penchant for criticizing her guests was transformed into the gos-
siping washerwomen "eagerly ripping me apart and washing their own
dirty linen." In Helen's imagination Joyce became H.C.E., "trying to
catch my slim young form which was chasing after Giorgio," all the
while himself fearing that "love and life . . . youth and beauty" were
passing him by.[18]

Helen apparently worked on this memoir after her separation from
Giorgio in the late 1930s, and she no doubt needed to recapture a happy
world that had disappeared. But her narrative does show us a young
woman who is actively aware of intergenerational sexual currents, and it
gives us some new information: Giorgio was already accustomed to adulterous assignations.

Did the other Joyces know about Lillian Wallace's reputed relationship with Giorgio? It is difficult to imagine that Nora, who became upset with Helen Fleischman, would have continued to be Lillian's friend
if she had known. If Joyce knew, he did not tell anyone, and Lucia's un-
sullied memory of Lillian lasted a lifetime. In the late 1950s and early
1960s, she remembered her simply as a family friend—significantly identified as "a Yorkshire girl"—who had treated her "like a princess." Of
course this need not mean that she had no contemporary sense of the onset of her brother's erotic life.[19]

Lucia's assessment of his relationship with Helen was instant and unsparing. Giorgio was now a "gigolo."[20] This recognizable type was newly
popular because of the movies and lifestyle of the Hollywood film star
Rudolph Valentino, who began his career as a professional dancing partner at Maxim's. Both on and off the screen his erotic good looks seemed
to symbolize "everything wild and wonderful and illicit in nature." In

film after film—*The Sheik* (1921), *Moran of the Lady Letty* (1922), *Monsieur Beaucaire* (1924), *The Eagle* (1925), and *The Son of the Sheik* (1926)—Valentino captured hearts with his photogenic elegance, style, and grace. And in his second marriage to Natacha Rambova, heiress of the cosmetics manufacturer Richard Hudnut, he captured extraordinary wealth as well.[21] By the mid-1920s, a "gigolo" was a nightclub dance sensation in Paris as well as a career choice for otherwise aimless young men. In *L'Apprenti gigolo*, written by Jean Marèze in 1926, the protagonist is a Parisian who is picked up as a dance partner at Le Bœuf sur le toit by Lucienne, a wealthy and significantly older woman. Money is exchanged; she suggests that the young man leave his family. In the winter, she takes him with her to Nice, where she drops him with "profound indifference" because he has stayed out all night with someone else.[22]

Lucia did not mean that her brother literally solicited dancing partners, but she did understand that wealth and age were important factors in his relation to Helen Fleischman. Now living with the two of them in Helen's rue Huysmans apartment, Lucia came to know many details of their life together. Who could miss the Talbot car, the china, the silver, the good linens, the food that was both well cooked and well served? She noticed the couture clothing, the leisure, the travel, and the freedom from worry and read it all as a private morality play that made no sense to her. Like her father with Miss Weaver, Giorgio had found a wealthy woman "patron"; but unlike her father, he seemed not to use money to support the practice of art. Lucia understood Giorgio's share in the arrangement with Helen not as music, but as sex.

Stuart Gilbert, who had joined the Joyce family's inner circle of friends during 1927, also wondered about Helen Fleischman. He was recently returned from many years as a judge in Burma,[23] and perhaps by temperament, perhaps by training and habit, he was cynical of human motives. He was unsympathetic to the general "philandering" of the times, and this lack of sympathy permeates his Paris diaries. He was hard on himself and he was hard on those around him, seeing them as "a world of barbarians and callow exhibitionists." He was equally hard on the Joyces. He thought Helen an excellent secretary to Joyce and considered their hostility to her—apparently maintained for years—boorish. In December 1930, he wrote in his diary, "The family still hostile to Mrs. F. . . . Anyhow Mrs. F. is marrying George J. on Wednesday (the 11th) and can snap her fingers. I foresee a swift reconciliation. Mrs. F.'s presents are worth to the Js at least £200 a year. They cannot do without her or someone like her."[24] But this raw calculation did not include Lucia.

The immediate effect on Lucia of Giorgio's liaison with Helen Fleischman was to catapult her into a sexualized world in a position of loss, a world where most of the players were considerably older and certainly more experienced. William Bird, at one of the Joyces' parties after Nora recovered from her surgery, was surprised to hear Lucia describe herself to him as "sex-starved." "That's rot," he remembers having replied to her. "What have you been reading?"[25] It was a good question. Everyone in Paris had been hearing about the surrealists' research on sex, and she in particular had been reading *Lady Chatterley's Lover*, published in 1928. She might also have answered that it was hard to avoid the scandal that her father's books and manuscripts seemed to generate.[26]

If the sexual freedom of women like Helen Fleischman and Peggy Guggenheim had begun as a reaction to the bourgeois imperatives of their families, the surrealists' sexual explorations were culturally more far-reaching. In early 1929, they conducted a series of twelve sessions of what they called "Recherché sur la sexualité," and in March they began to publish the transcripts of these conversations in their journal *La Révolution surréaliste*. Previous issues had recounted experiments about the narration of dreams, and experiments with language and with automatic writing, as part of a generalized revolt against "family, country, religion." They wanted to think about the whole human psyche and to understand how one might gain access to hidden, subconscious parts of the self through dreams and even madness. Their extraordinarily frank conversations were considered part of a scheme to separate love from "the normalization of sexuality within marriage." They also wanted "to resist the construction of woman as mother" and ultimately to challenge the Oedipus theory that lay at the heart of Freudian psychoanalysis. One of the main questions that André Breton wanted to answer was about the reciprocal nature of desire and pleasure. "To what extent and how often can [a man and a woman making love] reach orgasm simultaneously? . . . Does the frequency vary according to how accustomed you are to making love with a particular woman?" and "Is this simultaneity desirable?"[27] For young people who considered themselves part of the surrealist "revolution," the importance of these sessions lay not in any particular question or answer but in the explicitness of the dialogue itself and in the willingness of men (in this case) to examine the nature of their intimate experiences.

D. H. Lawrence's message was similar. In 1928 a cheap popular edition of *Lady Chatterley's Lover* was published in France, offered to the public at sixty francs. Lawrence's intention, like Joyce's in publishing *Ulysses* in Paris, was to outwit the American firms that were pirating the book and, at least in Europe, to reap the income from his own work. But his concern in writing the novel had been to "speak the body" without embarrassment. "And this is the real point of this book," he wrote in explaining his aims. "I want men and women to be able to think sex, fully, completely, honestly, and cleanly." Only in this way, Lawrence thought, could "consciousness of the act and the act itself" get into harmony. "All this talk of young girls and virginity, like a blank white sheet on which nothing is written, is pure nonsense," he continued. "A young girl and a young boy is a tormented tangle, a seething confusion of sexual feelings and sexual thoughts which only the years will disentangle." In Lawrence's opinion, lifting the taboo on speaking about sex would lead not to licentiousness but to its opposite. Only when thought was avoided would a person get "all messed up with physical reactions that overpower . . . him."[28]

Lucia was one of those who talked about sex. Several years later Stuart Gilbert was appalled by her conversation. "Meanwhile she [Lucia] worried the maid by her curious questions. 'Have you had a lover? Do you think every girl should marry?' " Gilbert thought this candor in bad taste. "This sort of question strikes the amateur psychologist as rather insane," he said. "To me it seems merely Joycean: the expression of whatever comes into one's head without the least shyness, indifferent to what people may think (except for a certain joy in shocking them)."[29] In Lucia's circle, there was nothing extraordinary about discussing sex. It came as part of one's Parisian youth in the 1920s.

But the ability to chatter and the ability to express difficult feelings are not commensurate. Joyce attributed the greatest importance to Lucia's relationship with Giorgio. In later years, when he was trying to create a coherent narrative of his daughter's life for one of her doctors, he commented, "She loved her brother in an extraordinary way. When he fell in love with and finally married an attractive, rich and previously married woman, she went through many hardships."[30]

In 1924, in a first-draft version of *Finnegans Wake*, Joyce had created an imaginary scene of a brother and sister parting, which he described to Harriet Weaver in this way: "Shaun, after a long absurd and rather incestuous Lenten lecture to Izzy, his sister, takes leave of her 'with a glance of Irish frisky from under the shag of his parallel brows.' "[31] The brother, figured as Shaun, advises "Sister dearest" to let the universe perish before she parts "with that vestalite ~~jewel~~ emerald ~~of yours~~ which you have where your two nether extremes meet."[32] In turn the young girl, figured as Izzy, gives "Brother dear" a "**handkerchiefduster**," asking him to remember her by it, and then requests that he "*teach how to tumble dear, & teach me whom to ~~love~~ lure*." Shaun leaves, "[t]ill we meet to part no more," but reports that "**I'm leaving** my proxy behind for you. *Dave the Dancer . . . Be sure & love him my treasure as much as you like*."[33] In later versions of *Finnegans Wake* the coherence of this dialogue is obscured, elaborated, and intercalated with other material. Its lines become scattered over thirty or so pages of the final narrative, but in the father's imagination the figure of the son remained as an erotic tutor who must envision his own replacement. Dave the Dancer, later Dave the Dancekerl, steps in to take the place vacated in an abandoned heart. But as is always the case in Joyce's book of the dark, it is not clear whether the proxy steps into a bed or onto a dance floor or simply represents the heart turning to the dance in love of another more focused and sublimated sort.

For the flesh-and-blood child, the love of dance remained. On Christmas Eve 1928, the last Christmas that Helen and Myron Nutting spent with the Joyces before their return to America in 1929, Helen pictured the family and their friends in a moment of reprieve from pain of any sort:

A room full of soft lights, a piano and four Irishmen. Redmond . . . Tuohy . . . Power . . . All interested in Joyce, who with a pink paper cap on his head, thin-faced, subtle, and keen, was entirely at ease with his countrymen. He sang old ballads . . . then Redmond would say, "Do you mind, Mr. Joyce, if I sing you a ballad? I never heard it but from my old nurse, and she was from the south of Ireland." Then Joyce would say, "Now, Tuohy, sing your song," and Tuohy, with no graces at all, would make his contribution. . . . So the evening went, Lucia curled up in a chair, at times bursting into spasms of laughter over Tuohy. She danced a Charleston, after we had sandwiches and champagne. Tuohy was anxious to learn it, and she gave him a lesson. He never got the step, but with infinite patience, with rosy cheeks and coattails at angles, he did his best. Lucia sweetly and most politely saying, "Now you must do this," winking over his shoulder when his head was turned. George came in at midnight and we all sang carols. So ended an unforgettable evening. One felt the deep bond between Joyce and Ireland, the intimate charm of the home, the melancholy charm of music. Nora, handsome and hospitable; Lucia, half-child, half-woman, vital and audacious, gifted child of a gifted father.[34]

II. LUCIA, THE SILVER FISH

In spring 1929, with Nora recovering from her surgery and the flat at square Robiac open once again, Lucia prepared for her first solo competition. As her father had already noticed, dance had kept her emotionally alive and focused during a time of terrible anxiety and suffering for her parents. "Lucia dances through it all," he had written to Harriet Weaver.[35] Now she entered the first international festival of dance at the Bal Bullier on 24 May, a contest sponsored by *La Semaine à Paris* to promote the status of rhythmic dancing among the arts.

The Bal Bullier was an immense dance hall at the end of the boulevard Saint-Michel in the Latin Quarter, and it was customarily a place for social dancing. Joyce and Nora, the Nuttings, and the Wallaces had all been there for evening soirées, and a reviewer for the *Courrier du soir* described it as a place that almost all Paris students remembered with fondness as a part of their university days. In 1929 it was the place where couples went to practice the tango and the blues—two contemporary crazes—and the *Courrier* reviewer thought its walls had heard *fleurettes* (sweet nothings) in every possible language. "The old Bullier," he said, was "accustomed to a long tradition of lovers' discourse, simplicity, and French intimacy." It was a wonder to him that it had been turned into "a brilliant theater" for such a competition.[36]

A stellar panel of judges had been assembled for the event, headed by Charles de Saint-Cyr and Emile Vuillermoz, another noted dance critic. The other judges were dancers who had well-established reputations. Madika, "the Hungarian," was there, described as a "dark woman of a sympathetic grace," as well as Djemil Annik, Marie Kummer, Claude-Fayard Puis, Tristan Klingsor, and the Hindu dancer Uday Shan-Khar,

Lucia Joyce, Julia Tcherniz, and Kitten Neel in *Le Pont d'or*, Paris, 1928. Photographer unknown. (Courtesy of Special Collections, McFarlin Library, University of Tulsa)

Business card of Lucia Joyce and Kathleen Neel, Paris, circa 1930. (Courtesy of the Sylvia Beach Collection, Department of Rare Books and Special Collections, Princeton University Library)

KATHLEEN NEEL, LUCIA JOYCE

PHYSICAL TRAINING

PRIVATE LESSONS

PHONE FOR PARTICULARS, 2 TO 3 P.M.
SÉGUR 95-20

with his "swarthy, violently sculpted appearance." Of the luminaries assembled to judge the competition, the only remarkable absence was the
Indian dancer Nyota Inioko, who had been detained in Geneva.[37]

Six young women made it to the finals: three Parisians, one Norwegian, one Greek, and Lucia Joyce, "looking delicate as periwinkles, the
daughter of the celebrated writer. [Lucia made one] dream of Ireland
with her lilting chant, modulated with a voice in which lingered an Italian accent." For the final rounds of the competition, the girls had to perform twice. The first time each was to interpret Schubert's "Marche
militaire" in her own fashion. One journalist was amazed at the range of
responses as the girls created their "fictions of war" and expressed the
"glorious spirit" of the music through their gestures and movements.
Next each competitor had to present an original improvisation that had
been developed "in secret."[38]

It was at this point that Lucia leaped into the imaginative graces of
the audience, for she suddenly appeared before them arrayed as a blue,
green, and silvery fish. She had created a remarkable costume with a
moiréd cloth sequined as if in scales. It was sleeveless, to emphasize the
creature's slender evanescence, and from her hips protruded delicate
gills. Her head was covered with a rounded cap of the same material,
from which she had suspended long silver tresses dangling to her waist.
The wit of the costume was in its "leggings," for Lucia had swathed only
one leg in sequined cloth, leaving the other free to appear and disappear
nakedly behind the first. As everyone knows, the allure of a mermaid
arises from the frustration of sexual longing that the single tail ensures.
Dancing to the music of an English composer, Lucia was a *feu follet*—a
will-o'-the-wisp, a beautiful creature representing our desire and the im-
possibility of sustaining it in the commonplace world. A will-o'-the-wisp
disappears at the point when one reaches outside the dream to hold on to
it. It beckons, it inflames, and it leads only to disappointment, coloring
the mind with an image of loveliness that, though it can be imagined,
can never be secured.

The audience was an opinionated and vocal crowd. A reviewer noted
that the orchestra had to play a piece by Beethoven during the intermis-
sion to calm the restive nerves of the gathering. When the winner was finally announced—it was one of the French girls, Janine Solane—the
audience booed and heckled, announcing that they preferred "l'Ir-

landaise! Un peu de justice, Messieurs!" ("The Irish girl! Gentlemen, be fair!")[39] Joyce noted with pleasure the audience's spontaneous support, then whisked Lucia, along with Alan and Belinda Duncan, Tom Mac-Greevy, and Samuel Beckett, to a private celebration.[40]

Charles de Saint-Cyr's evaluation of the contest identified Lucia as the only contestant with the makings of a real professional dancer.[41] "This very remarkable artist," he wrote, "totally subtle and barbaric, gives proof of an unmistakable personality. Barbaric, she forcefully performed to the *Marche militaire*; during the choice morsel of *feu follet* . . . she was subtle." He was not the only judge who was of this opinion, for the Hungarian juror, Madika, invited Lucia to study with her in order to prepare for the second international competition in 1930. Lucia decided to accept. Madika was a "fugitive from the classical style" who had left the ballet to study with Rudolf Laban in Germany.[42] Then Lucia made an even more remarkable decision, not unlike the one Zelda Fitzgerald had made several years earlier: to retrace her steps, so to speak, and to train vigorously in ballet.

But while Lucia was making plans, she faced an invisible foe that we, in retrospect, might call the giant "Over Shadow." Everyone had seemed to like her dancing. Samuel Beckett remembered the excellence of this particular performance and kept his photograph of Lucia in costume for the rest of his life.[43] And Stuart Gilbert, who apparently had seen her at an earlier stage of the competition (on 23 May), wrote in his diary that though his own interest in the ballet was languishing, he thought Lucia's dancing "good—if a little too acrobatic." "Ballet yesterday; *fils prodigue* is a compromise between *pas d'acier* (steps of steel) and neo-Stravinsky."[44] He was also quick to console Joyce, who thought she should have won, by remarking that it was only the current passion for "Negroid dancing" that had disqualified her.[45] But no further support seemed to come from her home. Her small triumph seemed to fall into a void.

Undoubtedly it was a busy spring for the Joyce family. In April Giorgio had made his singing debut as the pupil of George Cunelli.[46] He was already singing in the choir at the American Pro-Cathedral, and his teacher thought that a stage career might also be possible. This recital was intended to launch his professional life. And Joyce himself was once again intensely busy promoting his own work. In the same month as Lucia's competition, Shakespeare and Company published the first book of critical essays about *Work in Progress*, a book with the whimsical title *Our Exagmination Round His Factification for Incamination of "Work in Progress."* Not only did Joyce "choreograph" each of the twelve essays in the book, but he also commandeered more essays for the future. In addition, he was arranging for Harry and Caresse Crosby to bring out a limited edition of *Tales Told of Shem and Shaun* at their Black Sun Press.[47] And along with all these projects, Sylvia Beach and Adrienne Monnier conspired to hold a Déjeuner *Ulysse* to celebrate the publication of the French translation of *Ulysses*. On 27 June these two inimitable ladies chartered a bus to take all their guests to the town of Les Vaux-de-Cernay where they would all dine together at the aptly named Hôtel Léopold.

Helen Fleischman remembered this as a marvelous party. She, Giorgio, Samuel Beckett, and Tom MacGreevy were together in the bus, and the young men she met at the party were "very attractive." She flirted, drank copiously, and had "a perfectly wonderful time."[48] But to Lucia it was yet another detour from her own life and from the six hours a day that she was now working with Madame Egorova, her new ballet teacher.[49] If she looked dejected or abstracted in the photograph taken to commemorate the occasion, there was reason. Her position in the photo speaks for itself. She was in the back row on the side—obviously an unimportant person to whoever arranged the photograph. And Helen, who is leaning her weight on the shoulders of Philippe Soupault, displaces her quite directly and even physically.

Lucia probably experienced the family trip to Torquay, a seaside resort in southwestern England, later in the summer as a similar disruption. Joyce was using the trip as an occasion for research as well as pleasure. He visited Kent's Cavern to see prehistoric remains that would fit into his fictional portrait of H.C.E. as a giant lying beneath the earth dreaming of the course of human history. He also collected a "series of strange newspapers and magazines: *The Baker and Confectioner, Boy's Cinema, The Furniture Record, Poppy's Paper, The Schoolgirls' Own, Woman, Woman's Friend, Justice of the Peace, The Hairdressers' Weekly,"*[50] which he planned to use in the second section of *Work in Progress*, devoted to children. But to the children at his side he paid scant attention. In England, according to Gilbert, "the Great Man interested as usual in himself only. Pleased to have two secretaries, Mrs. Fleischman and me."[51] In Lucia's own mind, she shouldn't even have been there. Madame Egorova "was a pitiless teacher [who would not understand] if you didn't want to spend the summer with her, because the profession demanded that you force yourself and subdue the body."[52]

By December 1929 Lucia's sense of artistic displacement was almost complete. Disregarding the development of his own children, Joyce had taken up the cause of John Sullivan, a "dramatic tenor" at the Paris Opéra, who became a surrogate son to him despite their closeness in age. "J.J. is now all Sullivan," Gilbert wrote in his diary, noting Joyce's ploys to get audiences and publicity for his protégé. Lucia, bent as she was on her own artistic journey, might well have been a modern-day Antigone. She watched as her blinded father skipped over her years of intimacy, gentleness, dedication, and internal fire to impart his blessing on a stranger.[53]

Lucia was persisting nonetheless in her work at Egorova's studio six hours a day. Lubov Egorova, wife of Prince Troubetzkoy, had come to Paris in 1918 with Diaghilev's Ballets russes. She had established a school in Paris that dancers considered a "feed" school for the Ballets russes, and by the time Lucia studied there, the studio on the rue de La Rochefoucauld was a multifaceted operation. Madame Egorova directed the ballet classes herself, delegating the classes for children, salon dances, and character dancing to others. She also offered her students advanced courses on "plastique et de mimique" as well as lessons in choreography "pour théâtre de toutes les époques et de tous les styles."[54]

For a young woman to recognize "that she lacked a classical formation" and to begin to train in ballet at the age of twenty-two was as remarkable as it was difficult. When Lucia chose to learn "the strict and harsh tradition of the théâtre marie [formal ballet],"[55] she began at a disadvantage, since most ballet dancers begin the arduous process of "turning out" the body, more particularly the legs, at the ages of eight or nine. As André Levinson explained, "The arms and the legs stretch out, freeing themselves from the torso, expanding the chest. . . . The dancer spreads the hips and rotates both legs, in their entire length from the waist down, away from each other, outward from the body's centre, so that they are both in profile to the audience although turned in opposite directions."[56] The purpose of this training is to free the dancer from the usual limitations upon human motion. Instead of being restricted to simple backward and forward motion, the leg turn-out permits free motion in many directions without loss of equilibrium. Levinson understood that "to discipline the body to this ideal function, to make a dancer of a graceful child, it is necessary to begin by dehumanizing him, or rather by overcoming the habits of ordinary life." He thought of the classic dancer as a machine—"a machine for manufacturing beauty, if it is in any way possible to conceive a machine that in itself is a living, breathing thing, susceptible of the most exquisite emotions."[57]

Lucia was embarking on an artistic path that was startlingly similar to the one Zelda Fitzgerald had chosen two years earlier and commemorated in the only novel she ever wrote, *Save Me the Waltz*.[58] At the even later age of twenty-seven, Zelda had also decided to begin classical ballet training in Paris with Madame Egorova. In the novel, "Madame" drives her students mercilessly, expecting nothing less than total commitment. With the protagonist, Alabama, she is especially harsh, since she is "too old":

> "You will have the piano when you have learned to control your muscles," she explained. "The only way, now that it is so late, is to think constantly of placing your feet. You must always stand with them *so*." Madame spread her split satin shoes horizontally. "And you must stretch *so* fifty times in the evening."
>
> She pulled and twisted the long legs along the bar. Alabama's face grew red with effort. The woman was literally stripping the muscles of her thighs. She could have cried out with pain. Looking at Madame's smoky eyes and the red gash of her mouth, Alabama thought she saw malice in the face. She thought Madame was a cruel woman. She thought Madame was hateful and malicious. "You must not rest," Madame said. "Continue."
>
> Alabama tore at her aching limbs. The Russian left her alone to work at the fiendish exercise. Reappearing, she sprayed herself unconcernedly before the glass with an atomizer.
>
> "*Fatiguée?*" she called over her shoulder nonchalantly. "But you must not stop." . . .
>
> Alabama rubbed her legs with Elizabeth Arden muscle oil night after night. There were blue bruises inside above the knee where the muscles were torn. Her throat was so dry that at first she thought she had fever and took her temperature and was disappointed to find that she had none. . . . She fastened her feet through the bars of the iron bed and slept with her toes glued outwards for weeks. Her lessons were agony.
>
> At the end of a month, Alabama could hold herself erect in ballet position, her weight controlled over the balls of her feet, holding the curve of her spine

drawn tight together like the reins of a racehorse and mashing down her
shoulders till they felt as if they were pressed flat against her hips.[59]

Keeping the rigors of Lucia's training in mind, we can turn back to
Joyce's "month of tears" letter to Harriet Weaver written on 19 October
1929 and ask again why "Lucia turned down the Darmstadt offer and
seems to have come to the conclusion that she has not the physique for a
strenuous dancing career."[60] If an aversion to the ideology of the Elizabeth Duncan School made Lucia decide not to return to it as an instructor, then Madame Egorova's studio was the place where a talented young
woman who had been a gymnast for seven years might question her own
stamina. Zelda Fitzgerald had gone through a similar testing, which she
represented in her fiction as a dialogue between a dedicated dancer and
her skeptical husband: " 'you wouldn't understand,' she answered egotis-
tically. 'You will just see that I am given only the things I can't do and
discourage me.' The dancers worked always beyond their strength.
'Why déboule?' Madame expostulated. 'You do that already—passably.'
'You're so thin,' said David patronizingly. 'There's no use killing yourself. I hope that you realize that the biggest difference in the world is between the amateur and the professional in the arts.' "[61]

Lucia's fatigue, her sense of a body bruised and limited by the years of
lost training that cannot be recouped, her sense that "she has thrown
away three or four years of hard work and is sacrificing a talent" was
well expressed by Zelda Fitzgerald. Her protagonist, Alabama, wishes
"she had been born in the ballet or that she could bring herself to quit altogether. When she thought of giving up her work, she grew sick and
middle-aged. The miles and miles of *pas de bourrée* must have dug a path
inevitably to somewhere."[62] Even after Fitzgerald herself collapsed and
was hospitalized, she continued to be obsessed with her failure to make
the grade in what she called "a desperate school." "If you could write to
Egorowa a friendly impersonal note," she wrote to her husband, Scott,
"to find out exactly where I stand as a dancer, it would be of the greatest
help to me."[63]

No one in Lucia's circle could give her similar help. The giant "Over
Shadow" had by this time turned into a more active pressure. According
to Helen Fleischman, Lucia never decided to stop dancing, nor did Joyce
discourage her. It was rather "all Nora's idea." The mother "nagged and

bullied until she got Lucia to give it up." She thought Nora was jealous of the attention Lucia was getting.[64] Eileen Schaurek, the aunt with whom Lucia was most intimate, agreed. She told Richard Ellmann in the 1950s that she had asked Joyce why Lucia later turned against her mother: "I said that daughters were usually jealous of [their] mother—he [Joyce] said it was more a case of mother jealous of daughter. Joyce doted on Lucia."[65] Dominique Maroger's analysis of the situation in 1929 was more complex, but it too voiced a suspicion that the pressure on Lucia to stop dancing contained an element of "vengeance of the adult on the gifted child, the creative child."[66] But she also remembered that it was not until 1931 that Lucia succumbed to external pressures to abandon the dance "on account of an accident of health."[67]

In a letter of November 1929, Joyce reported to Harriet Weaver that Lucia wanted to teach dance and hoped to work for Margaret Morris, who was planning to open a school in Paris.[68] Brenda Maddox tells us that Lucia decided to "narrow her sights"[69] to teaching. But no one in Lucia's rhythm and color group would have seen it this way. Dance was a vocation whose "secrets," unlike those of writing, were always to be shared; they implied a community.

So Lucia's decision not to go to Darmstadt was hardly a diminution in her commitment to dance. And it is extraordinary to see the extent of her success. Though Richard Ellmann and Brenda Maddox neglect her story in 1929–31, implying that emotional collapse followed closely upon the failure of her "career," Margaret Morris, who finished writing her autobiography in 1969, remembered Lucia well. "I had long wanted to open a school in Paris. . . . As a qualified physiotherapist, it would be much easier for me to approach French doctors. I had two teachers with me in Paris, and both were fully employed . . . one English girl who later married the portrait painter, James Gunn, the other Irish, the daughter of the writer James Joyce."[70]

Morris's studio was located in a top-floor flat in the rue de Sèvres near the boulevard Montparnasse, and here she continued the work that had made her famous in England.[71] "In Paris," she later wrote, "I demonstrated how all athletic movements were inevitably based on the opposition of one group of muscles to another as shown and accentuated in [Raymond] Duncan's Greek positions."[72] Lucia was in familiar territory, for every bone and muscle in her body understood these sets of opposition. She had practiced them for years, and the body has ways to store memories for which no words exist and which lie dormant until they are needed and called again into being.

In the circles around Raymond Duncan, posturing in profile and creating tensile oppositions within the body had served an aesthetic purpose. They were ends in themselves. In the hands of Margaret Morris, these same gestures were fit into an explicit system of health care and given remedial purpose. Morris gave lectures to French midwives and to women who would need to understand movement in relation to childbirth. She spoke of the benefits of movement for children with tuberculosis. It was a kind of thinking that, in her own estimation, brought "something quite new to France."[73]

It was her teaching position with Margaret Morris that Lucia eventually left in 1931. Dominique Maroger remembered that Lucia took her to see a Morris performance in 1931 and that she "applauded frequently at my side, convinced, trying to drag me along, to vanquish my stupor in the face of so much novelty. Her eyes brilliant, she could barely contain herself until finally, when the performance ended, we could applaud the artists. I discerned that while Lucia pretended to have deliberately quit her dance career to devote herself with joy to design, her heart and her body would not let her forget the art in which she had achieved her primary success. Dance was where she belonged."[74]

Maroger's memoir gives us a glimpse of two more years of Lucia's accomplished work and two more years of her struggle against a growing network of opposition. For Maroger, her friend's later struggles were born of conflict that had been internalized and buried until, like the young hysterics whom Freud treated in the early days of psychoanalysis, it issued in another kind of performance that we call "symptoms." We can imagine Lucia's body as that of a continually responsive dancer, who without an appropriate, self-chosen, and socially acceptable stage, nonetheless continued to dance, acting out the more sinister choreography of the unconscious. Maroger's memoir pictures Lucia at a pivotal moment in life when she was encouraged by doctors to walk the city in pursuit of health but not to dance upon a stage in pursuit of it.[75] It captures Lucia at the onset of a crisis, still unrecognized, when she could not permit herself to dance and also could not stop her desire to dance.[76]

In addition, we can see the actual historical conditions that may explain Lucia's eventual crisis, for according to Maroger it was the daughter's success as a dancer, rather than her failure, that created strife in the Joyce household. For Lucia, the years 1929–31 were framed not by ineptitude and desperation but by the sensitivity of her mentor Margaret Morris and by the practical exertions of the bending, stretching, and breathing bodies of women in pursuit of their own health. It was for others, not herself, that "the situation of an instructor at the Margaret Morris school was too brilliant."[77]

Sometime before 10 April 1931, Lucia made another decision: She and Kitten Neel, her friend from Les Six de rythme et couleur, would establish a practice together: "Kathleen Neel, Lucia Joyce. Physical Training. Private Lessons. Phone for particulars, 2 to 3 p.m. Ségur 95–20."[78] Their slender business card lets us see that Lucia had far more at stake in wanting to stay in Paris than a personal preference for stability or for one city or another. Square Robiac was to provide her with the means of her own support and the basis for self-respect. Her planned entrepreneurial venture would put her and Kitten on a footing with their teachers and establish them as originators of movement training.

But on 11 March 1931, Joyce wrote to Harriet Weaver that he was storing his furniture in preparation for moving his family to London.[79] He does not seem to have acknowledged that this decision might have profound consequences for his daughter; nor did it occur to his biographers that Lucia might have had reasons to resist getting on the train when he left Paris the following year.[80] A temper tantrum, a wail of despair, or a sense that life is now empty of purpose is very different from the collapse of sanity.

Lucia Joyce, Paris, 1926. Photograph by Berenice Abbott. (Courtesy of Commerce Graphics Ltd.)

8

STEPPING OUT

PARIS 1931–32

I. LUCIA, SAMUEL BECKETT, AND THE MIRROR

By the end of the 1920s, the circle around Joyce and his family had begun to shift, as old friends like the Nuttings left Paris and others, keen to play their own special roles in the creation of modernist literature, arrived and introduced themselves. On New Year's Eve 1929 Stuart Gilbert, who kept a diary, noted that the "inner circle" now included Helen Fleischman (whom he referred to as "Mrs. Butcher"), Mr. and Mrs. Huddleston, and Padraic and Mary Colum. His writing also shows us that Joyce's eyes were not the only ones fixed on Lucia in these years.

In effect, Gilbert made Lucia into his model of the young flapper, seeing her as an avatar of a postwar urban generation of women or, as he put it, "the typical girl left to herself and developing in all her selfishness."[1] In his journal, he noticed major events in Lucia's life, like Giorgio's marriage in December 1930, Lucia's hostility toward Helen (which he read as a form of anti-Semitism), and the elder Joyces' reconciliation with Helen, symbolized by their agreement to have Christmas dinner at her home that December. He knew about Lucia's increasing worry about the strabismus in her eye[2] and wrote down the conversation he had with Joyce when he learned about a "domestic battle" over Lucia's eye and a small scar on her chin.[3] A few days later he remembered seeing her with a bandage on her eye, the result of corrective surgery. She was understandably anxious about both her vision and her looks.[4]

As Gilbert watched her, he found himself regarding a young woman who was increasingly preoccupied with her own sexual attractiveness. Where once she had stood at the ballet barre, using the mirror to study her dancing body, watching herself perfect the grace and precision of her own movements, she now began to consider her body as a mirror, capable of reflecting back to others the nature of their own desire.

Gilbert was quite critical of Lucia. In 1932 he wrote, "Only her conceit and idleness prevented her from trying for either of the things she wanted, becoming another Pavlova or making a good match. . . . She cultivates her father's imperious airs and spells of silence. And few young men in these times of free and facile conjugation would put up with that. Illiterate in three languages, professing the feminist desire to 'work' and having the feminine aversion for any work that is not directly exhibitionist or concerned with embellishing her body—'work' as she sees it, meaning a well-warmed and elegant office where she, the Worker, shines like a jewel before the admiring gaze of employer."[5]

Although "the Girl" of the Parisian 1920s provided him with categories for seeing the longings and desires of his friend's young daughter,[6] Gilbert caught Lucia at a shifting and yet singularly important moment in her life. Where Gilbert generalized, seeing exhibitionism as a typically "feminine" trait, and the desire to work for admiring men as a "feminist" one, Lucia's posing for "the gaze" of men magnified and focused the behaviors of a lifetime spent as an artist's child. Her father captured these tendencies in the book he was writing, where the daughter becomes "Show 'm the Posed" (FW 92.13) and then "the dotter of [her father's] eyes" (FW 372.03). The girl who once delighted in herself as a center of energy, organizing her own forces of creativity and finding an authentic way of being in the dance, has begun to slip away. She is becoming a girl aware of herself dancing, thinking instead about how the dance looks to the observer.[7] Her father saw this, too. Issy, the fictional daughter, "smiled over herself like the beauty of the image of the pose of the daughter" (FW 157.34–35). By the late 1920s Lucia seemed to be aware of the erotic dimension of this looking back and forth. She was beginning to pay attention to eyes other than her father's "fishy eyes" (FW 75.13) and "fathomglasses" (FW 389.26–28) and "deepseapeepers" (FW 386.16–17) even though these were the eyes that had watched her grow from childhood into a woman who could re-create herself as a beguiling, dancing silver fish. When she came to relate to other men as possible suitors, they too noticed her propensity to think of herself in terms of her own impression.

In 1929, as Gilbert's diary attests, Emile Fernandez was still one of Lucia's companions, but his place in her life was increasingly eclipsed by a young Irishman newly arrived in Paris named Samuel Beckett. He had been introduced to the Joyces in November 1928 when Tom MacGreevy, who had been helping Joyce with his writing, brought him over to square Robiac.[8] At that time, both young men held teaching positions at the Ecole normale supérieure, and both lived in rooms facing the rue d'Ulm. Thirty years later, Beckett remembered the exact location of the Joyces' flat, their telephone number, and his first "overwhelming" meeting with Joyce.[9] He soon found himself embroiled in Joyce's writing life. He came nearly every day to read to him, to translate some of *Work in Progress* into French, and eventually to write one of the first critical essays about Joyce's new work. In "Dante . . . Bruno, Vico . . . Joyce" he noticed a relationship between writing and movement. "When the sense is dancing," he claimed, "the words dance."[10] He soon found himself dancing in the Joyces' personal lives as well.

The story of Lucia's crush on Beckett has been told often.[11] We can see the attraction that Beckett would later describe in fiction as "besotted."[12] He was two years older than she, twenty-three to her twenty-one, of the same nationality as her parents, fluent in French and Italian, a linguist and an aspiring artist. He frequently saw Lucia on his visits to the Joyce flat; they went out together *en famille*, making a third couple with Joyce and Nora, Giorgio and Helen. He was with her at important family occasions like Giorgio's singing debut in April 1929 and at many Opéra performances of John Sullivan; he came to her dance competition at the Bal Bullier. As Beckett's letters from Paris attest, Lucia used to stop by to have tea with him at the Ecole normale supérieure, and they went together to restaurants like the Brasserie Universel, to the theater, and to the cinema.[13] Hidden among such facts as these are the familiar threads of human interaction—the smiles, the touches, the personal admissions that either create a web of intimacy or else fail to coalesce. In the end, Lucia and Beckett could not forge a lasting bond, but the path to this realization was not uncomplicated, and it did not have the same trajectory for each person.

For Beckett Lucia was one of a number of erotic relationships that crowded his "salad days."[14] He met her at a time when he was already involved with another woman and when sex was important to him for itself and not necessarily identified with love. He admitted that he did not know if "his soul, by implication, had as many brides as his body."[15]

For Lucia it was similarly a time of conflict, but her feelings for Beckett were more tenacious and the consequences of her unrequited love for him much more serious. No account of their relationship exists from Lucia's point of view beyond the memory of her middle age: "My love was Samuel Beckett. I wasn't able to marry him."[16] Perhaps the most interesting version of their affair, giving a sense of its emotional tenor and the complicated network of circumstances surrounding it, is encoded in Beckett's posthumously published *Dream of Fair to Middling Women*. In this novel Lucia appears as the Syra-Cusa, one of the book's three "capital divas."[17]

Written in 1932, Beckett's *Dream* is structured around a young man's experiences with three women who are identified as the Smeraldina-Rima, the Syra-Cusa, and the Alba. With all of them, Belacqua weighs, measures, and builds distinctions between love and physical passion, but each woman presents him with a slightly different dilemma. Beckett's biographer, James Knowlson, claims, "The novel is not, strictly speaking, a *roman à clef*, but it comes very close at times to that genre."[18]

The Smeraldina-Rima is based on Peggy Sinclair, Beckett's German cousin (and daughter of Harry Sinclair, who had given Beckett a letter of introduction to the Joyces).[19] Beckett had met her during the summer of 1928, when she had vacationed in Dublin, and had visited her in Austria, where she was studying eurhythmics, before coming to Paris in the fall. In the novel she is an odd kind of virgin rapist. She is "blithe and buxom and young and lusty, a lascivious petulant virgin, a generous mare neighing after a great horse, caterwauling after a great stallion and amorously lay open the double-jug dugs. She could not hold it."[20] "She violated him after tea."[21] In the narrative, this relationship is described as a "gehenna of sweats and fiascoes and tears and an absence of all douceness" that eventually breaks up because the young woman was "[l]ooking babies in his eyes."[22]

Whatever the discomfiture of this relationship, Beckett was deeply engaged in it when he met Lucia in November 1928. At Christmas, scarcely a month later, he went back to Kassel to see Peggy, and he spent Easter 1929 and the summer of 1929 in her company as well. She handled the intervening months of separation by writing hundreds of passionate letters to him.[23] It was scarcely the moment for another—any other—young woman to make a lasting impression.

Not surprisingly, the Syra-Cusa first appears in Beckett's narrative as a figure that invites comparison:

> On my right, the powerfully constructed Smeraldina-Rima; on my left, the more lightly built Syra-Cusa. Beautiful both, in so far as before the one as before the other, I find myself waxing pagan and static, I am held up. If it be not beauty, the common attribute here that dynamises, or, perhaps better, inhibits me, then it is something else. . . . The important thing is that I may, may I not, suppose that these two dear measures of discrete quantity could be coaxed into yielding a lowest common one of the most impassioning interest in the sense that in it might be expected to reside the quintessential kernel and pure embodiment of the occult force that holds me up, makes me wax pagan and static, the kernel of beauty if beauty it be, at least in this category (skirts).[24]

The narrator can't decide what to do. He considers going to a brothel, continues to spend money on Parisian "concerts, cinemas, cocktails, theatres, aperitifs," and then decides that it is all "Égal. ÉGAL."[25] He is weary of the entire scene.

> That was when they were not too busy doing something to you, raping you, pumping your hand, troling you like a cat in rut, clapping you on the shoulder, smelling at you and rubbing up against you like a dog or a cat, committing every variety of nuisance on you, or making you do something, eat or go for a walk or get into bed or get out of bed or hold on or move on, too busy committing nuisance on you or chivvying you into committing nuisance on yourself.[26]

The figure of Belacqua is already leaning toward the lethargy of the characters that populate Beckett's later writing. He is paralyzed by the need to act, make decisions, and interact with people. He finds sexual demands annoying and intrusive. Given these attitudes, neither woman is likely to "win" Belacqua's allegiance, and in the end neither does. He leaves Europe to renew his infatuation with a Dublin woman, the Alba, who was based upon still another of Beckett's friends, Ethna Mac-

Carthy.[27] When she refuses to have him, he ends the evening (and the book) sitting on a sidewalk, mesmerized by his own (empty) hands.

The identity of the model for the Syra-Cusa has been debated. Terance Killeen, in an article in the *Irish Times*,[28] thought her to be Nancy Cunard, but Knowlson considered Lucia Joyce more likely.[29] To anyone steeped in the lore of Joycean identity, there is little room for question. The sections about the Syra-Cusa read like a private catalog or a covert confession of the intimacy that Beckett enjoyed within the Joyce family in the early 1930s. The most profound "clue" is simply the character's name, for Lucia Joyce had been named for Lucia, martyr of Syracuse,[30] patron saint of eyes, light, and lucidity. Joyce had also been mindful of Lucia Mondella, the heroine of Alessandro Manzoni's novel, *I Promessi Sposi* (*The Betrothed*).[31] In Beckett's hands, what the Syra-Cusa needs is a "well-stocked gallery of . . . sposi manzoneschi whose names we forget and such type."[32] That is, she needs to have actual men behave in the predictable ways of characters in romantic fiction, characters like Manzoni's Renzo Tramaglino, who defends Lucia Mondella with unwavering loyalty.

Knowlson points to physical and behavioral traits to support his identification of the Syra-Cusa. He notices, for example, that the character is as graceful as a dancer and that she pukes into her napkin at meals, as Lucia was remembered doing.[33] Beckett alludes to eyes as "wanton" as Lucia's: "They rolled and stravagued, they were laskivious and lickerish, the brokers of her zeal, basilisk eyes, the fowlers and hooks of Amourr."[34] And in a masterful piece of detective work, Knowlson discovers that the book Belacqua gives to the Syra-Cusa coincides with the copy of Dante's *Divina Commedia* that Beckett once gave Lucia as a mark of esteem.[35]

But the Syra-Cusa is not simply graceful; she is graceful in the ways of her father. From the first sentence she appears in the context of Joyce's writing. She is like a river in a dream, that is, like Anna Livia Plurabelle in *Finnegans Wake*. Beckett writes that "she flowed along," "her body more perfect than a dream creek," and he uses the words "dream dive" and "dream water" to further situate her in the imagination. In his mind's eye, she is playing her role in the *Wake* as a daughter of the night, whereas with Belacqua, who is not the father-creator, "Night had no daughters."[36] He writes, as an in-joke that would have been recognized by the twelve contributors of the first book on *Finnegans Wake* (1929), that her "fetlocks" are like a "Brancusi bird."[37] Brancusi was the artist whose abstract rendering of Joyce graced the first edition of *Our Exagmination Round His Factification for Incamination of "Work in Progress."*[38] And Beckett refers to the "abstract drawings" that keep the Syra-Cusa in her room.[39] These are the lettrines that Lucia was making to illustrate Joyce's *Pomes Penyeach* in 1929.

If the Syra-Cusa's context is her famous father's work, her conduct seems to be distinctly her own. In the words of the novel, the Syra-Cusa "had a lech on Belacqua, *she gave him to understand as much*."[40] He describes her as someone who wants to "titillate and arouse," who "flounce[s] with a bright gay swagger and clang."[41] "Her grace was supplejack, it was cuttystool and cavaletto."[42] She is "always on the job, the job of being jewelly,"[43] Beckett writes, picking the same word that Gilbert had used to describe the bright, performative quality of Lucia's character (needing "to shine as a jewel before the admiring gaze of her employer").[44] Belacqua finds this sexual forwardness both alluring and a "cursed nuisance." He pauses to wonder if she is a virgin ("would she sink or swim in Diana's well?"). And he describes himself in relation to her as "trembl[ing] as on a springboard, jutting out, doomed, high over dream-water."[45]

Were Lucia and Beckett lovers? Did Beckett ever answer the question about Diana's well? We cannot know. But we can notice that Belacqua knows the Syra-Cusa's body intimately: "The fine round firm pap she had, the little mamelons, gave her an excellent grace. And the hips, the bony basin, coming after the Smeraldina-Rima's Primavera buttocks . . . were a song and a very powerful battery." We can notice that he calls her "puttanina," a little whore, and that his termination of the relationship with her fails to stay in place: "We thought we had got rid of the Syra-Cusa. No such thing."[46]

But as Beckett well knew by 1932, the important question was not whether the two of them had slept together but whether they had created lasting emotional ties. In the terms of understanding projected in this *Dream*, neither partner is equipped for such a relationship. The narrator of Beckett's text is hard on himself. Having entangled the emotions of three women, he explains that he is "trine."[47] He cannot choose one woman over the others; he cannot experience one of his "trine" selves as more authentic than the others. The choices he sees before him are to continue "the dreary fiasco of oscillation" or, because he is "really unable to rise to such superlative carnal occasions,"[48] to withdraw in a "slough of indifference and negligence and disinterest."[49] He understands that he has been inconsistent. "The hand to Lucien and Liebert and the Syra-Cusa [has been] tendered and withdrawn and again tendered and again withdrawn."[50] And he entertains the idea of passing the Syra-Cusa off on another man: "she might even, at a stretch, be persuaded to ravish Lucien, play the Smeraldina to Lucien's Belacqua. She could be coaxed into most anything."[51] Later, he looks back on this idea as "crass," not because of its possible effect on the Syra-Cusa but because one could not suppose that "Lucien might play his part like a liu" (lieu/substitute). "We were strongly tempted, some way back to make the Syra-Cusa make Lucien a father. That was a very unsavory plan."[52]

To the extent that Beckett's narrative is a self-portrait, it is a self-censoring one. As the book's ending reveals, his goal had been to explain how three loves could nonetheless leave him with empty emotional hands. He also faces the pain that the protagonist's "dirty confusion" caused to the women whose emotions he engaged.[53] By dramatizing their distress when he culminates each affair, it implicitly acknowledges responsibility and asks forgiveness. For these reasons, its admission that the protagonist played with a young woman's possible pregnancy is chilling. And it reminds us that the underside of the 1920s' changing sexual mores—the license it condoned, the experimentation it encouraged, the "free and facile conjugation," as Stuart Gilbert called it[54]—was precisely the burden of unwanted pregnancy. Peggy Guggenheim's memoir of these years, *Out of This Century*, was considered outré not simply because it named her many lovers but also because she admitted she had undergone abortions as a consequence of her lifestyle. "I had so many abortions. . . . I think I had seven abortions. . . . I had most of them with Holms . . . I didn't want to have a child, because I wasn't married to him. It was stupid, I think now, but in those days it meant more."[55] She even described the procedure for getting one: "I had had an operation performed in a convent by a wonderful Russian doctor called Popoff . . . who was supposed to have been the *accoucheur* of the Grand Duchesses of Russia. [He] admitted one to this convent for needing a *curetage* and then was credited with saying suddenly, in the middle of the operation:

'Tiens, tiens, cette femme est enceinte.' " ("Well, well, this woman is pregnant.")[56]

Nothing in Beckett's text suggests such a secret, though it reminds us of the anxiety surrounding the issue of pregnancy from a male perspective. About pregnancy from Lucia's viewpoint, we are free to notice a constellation of images that remained in her memory about her years of courtship. Many people have remarked about her sense of being fragile.[57] But to Dominique Maroger she spoke not about being too fragile to dance as much as being too fragile to bear a child. "Then I knew Sempo in Locarno," Lucia admitted to her old friend. "Sempo had tuberculosis. I don't understand. He was going to give me a baby. It was dangerous for me to become pregnant. In order for me to grow up, he wanted me to have a baby. And I was not able to have the child (she displayed her abdomen, still very normal, but which to her seemed too small). I am very petite, very frail."[58]

Maroger did not take these comments as factual but thought of them as examples of "the regrets that continue to torture her—the reasons why she suffers."[59] In another essay she wrote that the reason Lucia was no longer dancing was "an accident of health" that occurred sometime in the early 1930s.[60] We may also note that the Joyces at this time chose a noted obstetrician, Dr. Henri Vignes, as a doctor for Lucia. Together these facts suggest a disturbing and totally unverifiable network of meaning around the issue of Lucia and unprotected sex. This is the circumstance that Beckett refers to in his *Dream* as the "absence of all douceness."

According to the explanatory system established in the narrative of Beckett's *Dream*, the Syra-Cusa's problems with Belacqua come not from anxiety about the consequences of pregnancy but because she is preoccupied: "she belongs to another story, a short one, a far better one."[61] Beckett adds that "she might even go into a postil" and that "she remains whatever way we choose to envisage her, *hors d'œuvre*."[62] That is, she belongs in a marginal note or comment upon a text of scripture but she is not herself the sacred text; she is like the prelude to a meal but not the main course. These metaphors both support the apparently callous end of Lucia and Beckett's affair as it has been previously told.[63] As the story goes, Beckett finally had to tell Lucia that he came to square Robiac because he was interested not in her but in Joyce and his writing. The chatty young girl who opened the door to the apartment, whose talk and

admiration led to the more substantial preoccupation of both men in the
project of writing *Finnegans Wake*, was only a tempting morsel that preceded real sustenance. The "postil" was a footnote or addendum, which,
as Beckett probably knew, was the structural position that the father-
creator gave Issy, the daughter figure in the *Wake*.[64] Lucia belongs to
"another story"—that of her famous father—but only as an annotation.

Beckett also noticed something else about Lucia's emotional world. It
was not simply that he saw her as a subsidiary of genius but also that
she herself continued to be preoccupied by genius. In an interesting leap,
the narrator of *Dream* understands there to be a relationship between
Lucia/the Syra-Cusa's erotic desire, what he called her "priapean whirlijiggery-pokery,"[65] and Joyce's writing practice: "The Great Devil had
her, she stood in dire need of a heavyweight afternoon man."[66] On the
literal level, she presumably needed an afternoon man because Joyce required her, like her mother, to keep the house quiet during his writing
time. On another level, Beckett could see that sex was profoundly am-
bivalent for her, motivated by a young woman's desire to leave the father's emotional sphere and at the same time implicitly admitting that
sphere's seductive power. For the Syra-Cusa, as Belacqua understands it,
a lover becomes an implicit counterpart or substitute for the father, a role
he is unwilling or unable to play. He describes this situation as the Syra-
Cusa needing "a liu man"—an instead-of man. "Something might yet be
saved from the wreck if only he would have the goodness to fix his vi-
brations and be a liu on the grand scale."[67]

The narrator jokes about needing a tuning fork to create harmony
out of these people who are so at odds with one another, but he is identifying a real problem. As much as she seems to resist platonic esteem (the
Syra-Cusa does not want Belacqua's copy of the *Divina Commedia*; she
leaves it behind in a bar), as much as she seems to want sexual relation,
she is not emotionally available to compose a new "story" of her own:
" 'She lives,' said Belacqua, altogether extenuated, one day behind her
back to Lucien, 'between a comb and a glass.' "[68] Someone's eyes, as she
already knows, are always upon her. She lives, self-consciously and nar-
cissistically, as she finds herself reflected in her father's art.

The real Samuel Beckett took the blame on himself. Years later,
when he became intimate with Peggy Guggenheim, he told her that "he
was dead and had no feelings that were human and that is why he had

not been able to fall in love with Joyce's daughter."[69] And the real Lucia blamed him. She grew distraught and called her parents, who were then in Zurich; Nora flew to her defense.[70] But though the elder Joyces took her side, banning Beckett and also Tom MacGreevy from the house, Lucia's relationship with Beckett did not end cleanly in 1929. Beckett saw her in London in 1931, where he was disturbed by how unwell she looked—"knackered" was the word he used to describe her then.[71] He continued to write to her. His invitation to Joyce's fiftieth birthday party in 1932 was seen at the time as contributing to Lucia's huge tantrum on that day. He saw her several times in London in 1935. He continued to write while she was in Ireland, although by this time he had gone on to have still another affair with their common friend Nuala Costello.[72] He described their reunion in London as "the Lucia ember flared up and fizzled out."[73] Peggy Guggenheim, who became his lover in 1937, understood that the two of them had considered themselves to be engaged.[74]

At a time that is impossible to date exactly, probably in 1932, Beckett spent an entire evening trying to convince Kay Boyle that madness was something different from accumulated unhappiness. To Richard Ellmann, in an exchange of letters that followed Lucia's death in 1983, Boyle wrote,

> One day, when we chance to meet again, I want to tell you of my first meeting with Samuel Beckett. It was in the sad time of Lucia's first crisis, the beginning of it all, and Sam and I talked together at a crowded party in Walter Lowenfel's apartment in Paris. We both remember every word of that talk of over fifty years ago, a talk which lasted from nine in the evening until two o'clock the next morning, during which he convinced me that there is such a thing as madness, and that love or understanding or any emotional response to that condition is not the cure.[75]

What rueful blend of conviction and memory and affection and regret and generosity of spirit underlay the fact that Beckett was to remain Lucia's most loyal friend? Whatever he came to believe by the time he talked to Kay Boyle, no hint of madness lurks in his story about Lucia. The Syra-Cusa of his youthful imagination is a beautiful, eager, and sexually curious young woman who desires to be loved for her own character and grace. In real life, she would need to accept that Beckett would love her but never in the way that she most wanted.

II. MORE DANCING PARTNERS

Beckett returned to Dublin to take up a position as a lecturer in French at Trinity College at the end of summer in 1931. By this time Lucia had begun to change the entire focus of her life. No longer dancing in a sustained way, she had begun halfheartedly to study design and to run with a fast crowd of visual artists. Helen Kastor Joyce remembered these years as painful ones for Lucia, whose depression and aimlessness were palpable: suddenly she was adrift "without an occupation or a career," and it seemed that nothing could take the place of dancing.[76]

Stella Steyn, a young Irish artist who knew Lucia, also noticed the change in her between 1926, when they first met, and 1929, when she encountered Lucia again. "Lucia was a young girl about a year older than me," she wrote of her first visit to Paris in 1926.[77] "Pretty, with a fresh complexion, elegant and more sophisticated than a young art student. Joyce encouraged a friendship between us, as we were of an age. Lucia was a dancer and had been studying since the age of sixteen and seemed to be [as] absorbed in dancing as I was in art." Joyce also suggested a kind of barter between the girls: Lucia's fluent French in exchange for visits to the Louvre and discussions of pictures. Stella visited square Robiac several times a week, but neither the language lessons nor the art appreciation plan worked out: "I don't think Lucia had much interest in art at all."[78]

When Steyn returned for a second period of study in 1929, she expanded her repertoire to include market and street scenes. These were such a success that *Paris Montparnasse* published an article on her work. It was perhaps for this reason that Joyce asked her to do a few illustrations for *Finnegans Wake*. She was, according to her own admission, "a bit alarmed about this as I was young and was always rather afraid of Joyce." But when he read the passages of his book aloud to her, explaining what to listen to, she understood enough to make three drawings, which appeared in *transition* in the fall of 1929: "Anna Livia with her Baudeloire Maids," "The Ondt's Funeral," and "Anna Livia Legging a Jig."[79]

Later in the year Lucia came to visit Stella in Montparnasse and told her that her father had advised her to give up dancing as a career and to take up something more akin to what Stella was doing. The young

woman was shocked and asked Lucia if she could really rely upon her
father's judgment in this matter. But Lucia asserted that her father was
infallible. He "knew everything."[80] The news did not sit well with Stella
Steyn. However nervous Joyce made her, she considered this a false
move on his part:

> I don't think Joyce knew much about women. I thought Lucia's upbringing
> seemed to be very strange and less free than that of the young girls in Ireland.
> I remember she said she had to be home by 9:00 p.m. He [Joyce] also said that
> it was enough if a woman could write a letter and carry an umbrella grace-
> fully. He thought clothes and trivialities were all that mattered to them. . . . It
> seems surprisingly shortsighted to have advised her to give up dancing, which
> had been her main interest for about five years. He was undoubtedly devoted
> to Lucia. I am sure he loved her more than any other human being and
> wanted nothing but her happiness. But he had no interest in the visual arts. . . .
> I too had seen Lucia's dancing and it might have been good to have suggested
> taking other directions in dancing . . . but to abruptly take her off one form
> of art and direct her to an equally superficial aspect of the visual arts was no
> solution.[81]

She was even more shocked when she learned that Joyce had chosen
Alexander Calder as a teacher for his daughter. It showed, she thought,
the "flippant attitude" he had toward art, for Sandy Calder, an unknown
builder of mobiles then, was hardly her idea of a serious artist. If she was
bent upon this new course, she advised Lucia to study from nature,
"drawing from the model, which must take time, and to go to the museums and galleries and look at what was best in art."[82] But she reckoned
without taking account of the press of Lucia's conflicting emotions. All
the Syra-Cusa's "priapean whirlijiggery-pokery" impulses were still in
place. Dedication to art was not the only desire served by Lucia's agreement to turn her attention to drawing and to tutoring from Sandy
Calder.

Calder was part of a younger, more bohemian crowd than the people
in the Joyces' social set. In 1934 Joyce would describe them to Cary
Baynes as "a group of people who thought she ought to get away from
home more and see something of life. The group seemed to center
around an American woman and her husband, neither of whom were
desirable characters. The man's name was Pierce."[83] Joyce told Baynes
that "he had no idea what had happened to her during the time she was

running around with these people. Some one had pointed out to him the
undesirability of it and he had replied that one could not put a wall
around a person in a city of four million."[84]

"Pierce" was "Peirce." The couple Joyce referred to was the American artist and bon vivant Waldo Peirce and his wife, Ivy Trautman, who
lived at 77, rue de Lille.[85] If they were an unsavory pair, they were unsavory to all the Joyces, since Giorgio and Helen and Joyce and Nora fre-
quented their salons as well as Lucia.[86] The more accurate way to
describe them is probably to say that they belonged to the same international moneyed set as Giorgio and Helen and Peggy Guggenheim.

Peirce was an independently wealthy American from Bangor, Maine.
Born in 1884, educated at Harvard, he was a huge man, six foot two, up-
ward of 210 pounds, described by the press as a "human hurricane" and
called by his friends "the Elephant."[87] His gusto for life was as large as
his waist, and by 1930 he had lived in and around Paris for nearly twenty
years. Buoyed by large letters of credit from his mother, he had first
come to Paris in 1910, found a garret for himself, played with his name,
frenchifying it to "Pierre Waldo," and enrolled in the Académie Julien.
"It will take a good deal of pressure or prying to oust me from this city,"
he reported in 1911. The Académie Julien was a place where "[e]very-
body roars at everybody else all the time. They also work like hell. Three
expressions you hear are beat it, hairy fellow, teach the clothes off the
new student. The last is called at the models. They undress aided by the
students, mount on a table, assume two or three poses, while the *massier*
counts the raised hands. . . . If it is hot, everybody strips to the waist." By
1912 he was wearing short Greek tunics, dancing French fashion ("very
primitif") at the Bal Bullier, and reporting to his tolerant mother that
"naked models are nothing." [88]

During the war he had joined the ambulance corps, where he became
friends with Ernest Hemingway; he may also have met Richard Wallace,
Myron Nutting, or Joseph Collins. Such a network of friendships would
explain how Waldo Peirce had come into the lives of the Joyces, but it is
only a guess. By 1930 he was a kind of fixture in Paris café life. Maurice
Grosser knew him as "a large headed man who one used to see surrounded by pretty women, his café table piled high with saucers."[89]

Ivy Trautman had apparently been one of those "pretty women," for
she was Peirce's second wife. At the end of 1930 she would be replaced

Samuel Beckett, Paris, circa
1930. Photographer unknown.

Alexander Calder, 1930.
Photographer unknown.

by Alzira Boehm, who bore the painter three children. The first two were male twins, born in the American Hospital in Paris. Peirce took a house at Garnes Vallie de la Cherreuse to lodge his growing family, but in April 1931 he decided that an American country life would be better for them all. By 18 May he was back in Bangor, where he continued to paint. A New York review in his clipping file at the Smithsonian Institution described the quality of his art in terms that are totally consonant with his life: "One looks at these paintings, foaming with joie de vivre, a healthy hedonism, a gusto akin to Renoir's, a delight in life and its simplest pleasures and one almost overlooks the fact that this fizzing is merely the head of the drink: that underneath is a solid substance compounded of technical ability as great as the more obvious joy in life."[90]

Calder had met Waldo Peirce and Ivy Trautman in 1928,[91] and he apparently met Lucia then too, or in early 1929, for Stella Steyn remembered them as teacher and student in her 1929 trip to Paris.[92] In June Calder traveled to the United States, remaining there until March 1930, but by the fall of 1930, his relationship with Lucia had changed to a social one. Albert Hubbell, who also met Lucia at Ivy Trautman's, remembered that "she came with Alexander Calder who was giving her some kind of a rush at the time."[93] Lucia's own account was plainer: "We were in love," she wrote in her autobiography. "He had a strange kind of a circus which he invented himself."[94]

Although Steyn thought Calder a dilettante, his work, we can imagine, would have been interesting for Lucia in the years when she was struggling to make a transition from dance to abstract drawing. The distinctive mark of Calder's own creativity was "dancing" or kinesis of another sort. A visual artist and sculptor working in pen and ink, wire and wood, Calder was concerned to capture the movements of bodies—particularly those of dancers, acrobats, and animals.[95] He was interested in the mechanical movement of abstract forms.[96] And he had just invented the hand-operated figures in his miniature circus for which he became famous.

Like a Waldo Peirce without the money, Calder went out to meet experience with humor and unorthodox enthusiasm. In January 1929, he was getting ready for the first solo exhibit of his work at the Galerie Billet in Paris and was busy running around the *quatorzième arrondissement* on an orange bicycle and meeting friends at the Dôme. He remembered his usual guise as gray knickerbockers and red socks and when he had a cold, he "held a piece of camphor under my nose with a wire that looped and went behind my ears."[97] His friend Clay Spohn remembered an even more remarkable first glimpse of him. "Suddenly I saw someone in a bright striped suit, straw hat and cane. The suit had orange and light brown stripes that were almost one inch wide running lengthwise. It was a heavy, woolly suit and the man in it was large and stout and he had long, sandy colored mustaches and beady blue eyes."[98]

By 1929 Calder's circus had expanded to fill five suitcases; a small phonograph was also part of the getup. Different songs announced the various acts. In wire, wood, metal, cloth, yarn, paper, cardboard, leather, string and buttons, Calder re-created the circus tent in all its complexity. He unfolded little carpets and put up poles and hanging wires for the miniature trapeze and tightrope acts. He set up an assortment of planks and rings, and once they were in place, he blew whistles and made animal sounds as he manipulated the small figures. Chance and suspense played their part in each performance, and whoever was manning the phonograph had to key the blaring music to the unfolding drama. After he had watched one circus, Joan Miró told Calder that he "liked the bits of paper best." These were, Calder explained, "little bits of white paper, with a hole and slight weight on each one, which flutter[ed] down several variously coiled thin steel wires, which [he jiggled] so that they flutter[ed] down like doves onto the shoulder of a bejeweled circus *belle-dame.*"[99]

The little circus was carried everywhere. Calder took it to Berlin with him in March 1929 and later set up another performance for Joan Miró in his house at Montroig, Spain. It went back and forth across the Atlantic Ocean. Thomas Wolfe was so impressed with it that he wrote a fictionalized account of it in *You Can't Go Home Again*, and Keystone made a short movie feature about it in Calder's studio in the rue Cels.[100] But mostly it was a popular pastime in Montparnasse, where Calder charged twenty-five francs admission so that he could pay his rent.

The circus became an oddly appropriate center of social life for Calder as well. There were no flyers or formal announcements of the shows. People came because they had heard about it by word of mouth; they sat on empty champagne crates that served as bleachers; they laughed, and usually they drank. It was a tony kind of party and assured that Calder frequently got invited out in return. By 1930 the spectators included Jean Cocteau, Man Ray, Piet Mondrian, Joan Miró, Fernand Léger, Hans Arp, Le Corbusier,[101] and Lucia Joyce.

When Joyce imagined his daughter running around Paris without his supervision, at least some of the time she was running around with Sandy Calder, who made no apologies for his bohemian lifestyle. It was easy for him to remember the "bottle parties" of those years: "Everybody brought what he liked best. . . . As the night was balmy, the window was open. People would pass their bottles through it, like a *guichet* (box office), then walk to the door and come in. The bottles were the password."[102] His friend Pascin gave equally outrageous parties: "At his home in Montmartre there was a sort of entrance hall with a little narrow staircase running up in a corner. Up the staircase there was a small window, close to the ceiling, which opened onto his studio. At Pascin's parties, the little girls would go up and show their *derrières*. One evening a drunk was a bit too bold. He showed something else and everybody was horror-struck."[103] Just before Calder left Paris in 1929, his friends (whom he called "quite a gang") included artists, photographers, and writers: "I felt very much at home with them and they usually held forth at the Coupole Bar."[104] Lucia's memories of whatever life she had with Sandy Calder included no colorful details. She just remembered its puzzling outcome: "We were in love but I think he went away. Anyway he never wrote to me and I don't know what became of him."[105]

Albert Hubbell, an American whom Lucia also met at Ivy Trautman's, understood why Calder had disappeared. In 1930 Hubbell, then twenty-three, was studying in the evenings at the Art Students' League and earning money as a contributing editor for *Time* magazine. He had helped Calder organize a circus in a "tiny little theatre on the Left Bank." He told Lucia that it had "turned out to be something of a fiasco because he hadn't prepared adequately for it (a friend of mine and I had to search the bars for him the afternoon of the show)."[106] What he knew and what Lucia apparently did not was that Calder was engaged to "a girl from Boston." By 1930 Calder had met and fallen in love with Louisa James, whom he was to marry in January 1931. He had met Louisa on board the *De Grasse* when both of them were returning to the United States in June 1929. He had spent part of the summer at her family's place at Eastham, on Cape Cod. Louisa, from Concord, Massachusetts, a grand-niece of Henry James, had followed Calder to Paris in the summer of 1930 after a bicycle tour of Ireland with her friend Helen Coolidge.[107] Although Louisa spent a good part of the fall in Paris, Lucia seemed not to know that Calder was involved with her.

It was Albert Hubbell's fate to pick up where Calder left off. At a party at Ivy Trautman's, he danced with Lucia, whom he already knew as a performer. She told him she wasn't dancing much anymore, that she was drawing these days. He spoke about his classes in life drawing; they talked of Augustus John, who was coming to Paris to make some portrait drawings of Joyce. It was the normal boy-meets-girl-at-a-party talk, but it was enough for Lucia to call Ivy Trautman to see if Hubbell would like to go to the theater with her later in the fall of 1930. By then Sandy Calder had already left for America.[108] Ivy called Hubbell at his hotel, and he arranged to pick Lucia up at square Robiac. The performance of *Boris Godunov* at the Théâtre des Champs-Elysées was humdrum—no costumes, lackadaisical staging, mediocre singing. The interest for Hubbell was Lucia herself. He found her physically attractive and was charmed by her way of talking: "She had a perceptible Irish accent . . . and her solemn, almost melancholy expression . . . could suddenly break up in a monkeyish grin. She affected a certain insouciance, but she seemed quite vulnerable; she had a way of standing quite close to you, and for a moment, confiding her whole self to your care."[109]

They became lovers. At the opera, Lucia suddenly gripped Hubbell's hand, and they sat with fingers intertwined for the rest of the performance. In the taxi on the way back to square Robiac, they kissed, and that was the beginning. Hubbell was surprised by the ardor of her response.[110]

"After that," he remembered, "we started seeing quite a bit of each other." When he explained this to Richard Ellmann in 1981, he admitted that he and Lucia never discussed a future together. The truth was, Hubbell didn't know what to do. As he told Lucia at the time, he was already married, although the marriage was on the rocks. His wife, Renee Oakman, who had been a model for photographers like Man Ray and Edward Steichen, had already returned to America, and he was at loose ends. He couldn't get a job on the *Paris Herald*; he couldn't get a certificate of travel to work outside of Paris. He was truly touched by Lucia, and this in itself was a problem. "I felt then," he said, "that I could really fall in love with Lucia." But he was terrified of consequences and found himself, like Beckett's Belacqua, thinking about the "absence of all douceness" and "looking babies in his eyes."[111] "Afterwards," he said, "I was in a fever of anxiety, not knowing for certain exactly what had happened, and in a sweat over the possible consequences for us both if anything had."

In addition, he couldn't decide—and didn't apparently ask—what Lucia felt for him. He remembered their occasions of lovemaking in his hotel in the rue de Bellechasse. She initiated the first time, after they had been to the Bal Bullier with some of his art student friends; they'd both been "tight"; they were clumsy. As they continued seeing each other, Hubbell noticed "Giorgio, whom I didn't like, giving me thoughtful looks." Nora began to ask Ivy Trautman questions about him. Only Joyce seemed not to be "nervous" about their relationship. "I got the feeling that anything that occupied Lucia and made her happy," Hubbell recalled, "was all right with him." When Hubbell asked Lucia what her parents would say about her staying out till all hours, she said, " 'oh, don't worry about *them*,' not contemptuously, but with airy self-confidence."[112]

They went to art exhibits, walked around Montparnasse, went out to Saint-Cloud, and "necked in the Lanterne de Diagène and Lucia did a kind of Mary Wigman dance on the grass." Looking back, Hubbell had the impression that he did most of the talking and that sometimes she seemed not to pay attention to his words but seemed more preoccupied with the physical and intuitive nature of their bond. She would interrupt with remarks like "I like the way you look." Her emotional responses were hard for him to read. Sometimes he thought she was in love; at other times she seemed "distant, distracted, and even indifferent." He sometimes noticed in her "a profound discontent." He sometimes called her "batty," but in 1981 he was quick to add, "it was a joking remark, and I didn't mean anything by it."[113]

Eventually Renee Oakman came back to Paris to try to reconcile with her husband, and Hubbell ended his relationship with Lucia, in his own words, "not by a clean break, but more reprehensibly by just sliding out of her life." To Ellmann, fifty years later, he confessed: "For years after I left Paris, the thought and memory of Lucia kept coming back to me, sometimes in dreams. When I heard what was happening to her, first from Herbert Gorman and, later, from Oliver Gogarty . . . I couldn't stand it. A curious thing is that whether from guilt, or remorse, or dread, I stopped inquiring about her. To this day, I don't know whether or not she is still alive."[114]

For her own part, Lucia did not speak about the nature of her experience with Hubbell. When she was in emotional trouble in 1934, she hinted to her companion, Cary Baynes, that something sinister had happened to her, and she spoke of a little white dog, though the white dog belonged to Waldo Peirce, not to Albert Hubbell. When Baynes and Lucia's doctor at the time, Carl Gustav Jung, discussed whether some trauma had set off the distress that eventually sent her to a succession of *maisons de santé*, Jung thought it would be more "hopeful" if there had been some such precipitating event. But his questions suggest that he never found out what it was. To her father she admitted that she had done "terrible" things in her life, and when he told her that he had too, she replied that women could not act in such ways.[115] In her own mind she was culpable.

We can imagine that she was feeling bleak. By 1930 she had been abandoned three times in pretty quick succession. Beckett would soon be back in Dublin trying to renew his relationship with Ethna MacCarthy. Calder was married to Louisa James. Peirce had divorced Ivy Trautman, married Alzira Boehm, and left Paris entirely. Hubbell was back with his wife. Kay Boyle had married Laurence Vail and also moved away. Zdenka Podhajsky had returned to Prague to found her own school of dance.

It was a time of rupture for Lucia's parents as well. By 1930 and early 1931, many of their closest friends in Paris had moved on. The Nuttings had returned to the United States, Richard Wallace had died of cancer, and Adrienne Monnier and Sylvia Beach had quarreled with Joyce over the copyright of *Ulysses*. But soon these friends were replaced by others. Through Helen and Giorgio, the Joyces met Lucie and Paul Léon, Russian Jewish émigrés who, along with Lucie's brother, Alexander Ponisovsky, had settled in Paris in the 1920s.[116] While Alec gave Russian lessons to Joyce, Léon assumed the role that Sylvia Beach had so often played, as amanuensis and general business manager. Stuart Gilbert watched this shifting panorama of faces and thought all the Joyces incapable of sustained friendship: "They do not attach themselves to anything except ephemeral things, and tire of these so soon they are always at a loss. Thus they never, or rarely, make friends."[117] On 28 April 1930, he paused to ask himself what Léon's interest in the Joyces was. "After Lucia?" he wondered, before reminding himself that Léon was already married.[118]

During this disruptive time, we can catch only dark glimpses of Lucia. We see her in fleeting images that accost the mind but do not cohere in a sustained narrative. Zdenka Podhajsky remembered that Lucia was on the sexual prowl. In the way that girlfriends share news of their exploits with the opposite sex, Lucia had told her about secret meetings with a sailor at the Eiffel Tower, and when Zdenka had asked her what the attraction was, she replied, "Il est tellement naïf." His naïveté made her own shyness more bearable. She told Zdenka about coming on to Liam O'Flaherty at one of her father's parties;[119] and then, to Zdenka's surprise, she greeted her return from a trip with a passionate kiss—announcing that she had now become a lesbian.[120] In an interview with Richard Ellmann in 1953, Maria Jolas mentioned that "Lucia had evidently stopped [taking] dope." Had Lucia participated in smoking some of the opium that was so much a part of the lives of people like Harry and Caresse Crosby?[121] Mary Colum remembered, "We heard of her coming into a party and having been offered a drink, saying that instead of a glass of sherry she would have half a cocktail, as that would enable her to face going home."[122]

It is a strained, dissonant mosaic of experiences, but Nora reduced it to what she called her daughter's "nonsense." Her favorite jibe was, "why can't you be more like Kitten Neel? She has lots of boy friends." And "why don't you stop dancing since it makes you too nervous?" Or "why do you hang on your father's every word—he did x and y in Trieste."[123] These, at least, were Helen Kastor Joyce's memories, admittedly influenced by her own difficulties within the family. But the general drift was confirmed by Lucia in 1935 when she said very simply to her cousin, Bozena Berta: "my mother doesn't approve of me."[124]

Clearly trouble was brewing, and in light of it the larger pattern of Joyce's general preoccupation in these years, his Wakean comedy of the sleeping giant, takes on a darker, almost prescient tone akin to Karl Marx's troping of Western capitalism as a sleeping giant. Both men used the structure and language of fairy tale to identify a dormant menace of an entirely different order. When we think of the building tensions and resentments in Joyce's family, we realize that anger can go underground as much as any giant lying under the Hill of Howth. In the imagination of Lucia's father, a monolith was waiting to spring to life when least expected. When it rose into articulation, it took a swerve—attaching itself primarily to Nora, so that Lucia could preserve an unadulterated image of her father. Lucia would continue to love him and to resent the centrality accorded to his talent, holding each position vehemently and without apparent concern for their contradictions. As if to add to a "sea of troubles," the year 1931 brought further dislocation. Instead of the marriage she had longed for, Lucia was astonished to witness that of her own parents.

III. IN THE WINGS

Only at the point of Giorgio's marriage to Helen Fleischman was Joyce forced to confront the legal consequences of choices he and Nora had made in 1904. Guided by the social commentary of Henrik Ibsen, by roughly conceived notions of natural law, by private dissatisfactions and intuitive longings for freedom from social and religious convention, they had eloped to the Continent and to a kind of legal anonymity that suited them both. True, they were accustomed to celebrating their marriage anniversary on 8 October, but there had been no marriage to celebrate. Their children, raised largely outside the institutions that had occasioned their parents' revolt, had no way of appreciating the restrictions and hypocrisies that had led them to seek relief. If Stephen Dedalus, the child of Joyce's imagination, had left Ireland in search of "unfettered freedom," the real children of Joyce and Nora had been raised knowing little else. But neither child could see things in this perspective. Giorgio and Lucia read the circumstances of their own births in the light of appearances, assuming they were the legitimate children of a legitimate union. That their parents would need to get married was unthinkable.

How did this remarkable midlife marriage come about? Joyce's biographers have assumed that Helen Fleischman brought up the subject of the Joyces' legal status because she wanted any future children to bear Joyce's name. But this cannot be the exact scenario, for her memoirs attest that she, no less than Giorgio, presumed that 8 October commemo-

rated a real occasion. So we must imagine Joyce or Nora beginning to
think about the issues of progeny and inheritance and asking about the
tangible consequences of their youthful decisions. However the subject came to mind, on 11 March 1931 Joyce wrote to tell Harriet Weaver
that he was preparing to go to London.[125] He was going to establish
British domicile in order to marry Nora under British law, and he intended to make a will that would stipulate the terms of inheritance for
his descendants.[126]

Square Robiac was packed up, the furniture put in storage—and
with it Lucia and Kitten Neel's hope of having their own physical-
culture training program in Paris. Lucia came along to live in London in
yet another rented flat, this one at 28b Campden Grove, on Campden
Hill in Kensington. She was enrolled in the Grosvenor Art School to
keep her occupied, but it didn't matter. Nothing mattered in comparison
to the humiliation of discovering her illegitimacy. In the days preceding
their departure, Lucia finally lost the veneer of quiet shyness that had
characterized her early youth. When Nora nagged or shouted at her, finally yelling, "You bastard!" Lucia shouted back, "If I am a bastard, who
made me one?"[127] Legally she neither bore her father's name nor stood in
the line of material succession. According to her cousin, she was still suffering from the "shock" of it in 1935.[128]

Her father chose 4 July as his wedding day. He applied for a license
that required only a day's notice, hoping to elude the press but instead
found the family swamped with public attention. The *Daily Mirror*
headline that morning was "Author to Wed: Mr. James Joyce Who
Wrote *Ulysses*," and that was only the beginning. Moira Lynd, whose
parents were among the few people to be told in advance of the odd little
wedding, took one look at Giorgio and Lucia at a party the following
week and pitied "the two silent grown-up children."[129] Joyce joked about
the occasion—to Padraic and Mary Colum he wrote, "while the king
was signing the Marry-Your-Aunt Bill" (a new law that allowed for previously forbidden marriages between certain relatives), "he should now
sign a Marry-Your-Wife Bill."[130] But neither Giorgio nor Lucia shared
his humor, and neither of them wanted to be there.

Giorgio rushed back to France to be with Helen, who was in the
throes of a difficult pregnancy. When it was clear that Helen was
all right, they invited Lucia to join them. "We are expecting Lucia

here every day," Giorgio wrote to his father from La Vanne Rouge in Montigny-sur-Loing on 18 August, "but I suppose with the three of you watching and discussing the channel, she will probably spend the rest of this wintry summer in Dover." He added a description of his summer lifestyle with his wife: to bed at ten, up at twelve, sleep in the afternoon, and spend the rest of the time eating, and he mentioned that their friend Alec Ponisovsky had been down to share an indolent weekend.[131] He needn't have worried. By five-thirty that afternoon, Lucia had arrived. "I tired of England" was all she said to Zdenka in a postcard sent on 22 August. "I'm visiting with my brother and will probably stay until September."[132] It was clear she didn't intend to return to England, but no one seemed to know what she had in mind as an alternative.

IV. BROODING TENSION

By the end of September 1931, Joyce and Nora had had enough of English life as well. They decided to sublet the Kensington flat until the following April and return to Paris for the winter. Joyce told Harriet Weaver that people seemed surprised when they came back, but he insisted he had intended this all along.[133] The family looked back on their sojourn in London with macabre humor. In their private parlance, Campden Grove became "Campden Grave"; it was inhabited by mummies; the estate agents Marsh and Parsons became "Messrs. Mashed Parsnips"[134] and the house itself "Chicken from Barkers."[135]

In the middle of October he and Nora moved from La Résidence on the avenue Pierre to a small furnished flat at 2 avenue Saint-Philibert. Lucia joined her parents there, but she was completely at loose ends. She still wanted to have a life of her own, to marry, and to express herself in art. She tried to pick up the pieces of her life, going around Paris with Helen and Giorgio's friend Alec Ponisovsky, on whom she had had a crush for years, and talking with him late into the night. Her social life revolved more and more around her brother's circle of friends. We used to talk "until 2 or 3 o'clock in the mornings in the rue Huysmans," she remembered in 1961.[136]

Joyce now came up with a plan of asking his daughter to design illuminated initial letters for special editions of his poetry. Limited edition

books were everywhere in Paris in the 1920s. They were attractive because of the high quality of the papers and bindings, the careful designs,
and the original art that the publishers commissioned to accompany the
texts. This generous complexity of production could turn books into
small *Gesamtkunstwerke*. Matisse, for example, later drew six etchings to
accompany a Limited Editions Club version of *Ulysses*,[137] which paradoxically elicited Joyce's bitterness, for he genuinely thought Lucia's
work beautiful and could not see why Matisse's got such a high price.
And aspiring printers surrounded him: William Bird ran the Three
Mountains Press, Harry and Caresse (and later just Caresse) Crosby had
the Black Sun Press, and Jack Kahane the Obelisk Press.

Joyce's specific idea came to him in conjunction with a new book that
Oxford University Press was about to publish called *The Joyce Book*.
Herbert Hughes, its editor, had invited thirteen different composers to
write musical settings for thirteen poems.[138] In November 1931, they
were still waiting for one, and Joyce assumed there would be time to include Lucia's work, but this proved not to be the case. In November Lucia drew the illuminated letters—or lettrines, as they were called, one for
the beginning of each of the poems in *Pomes Penyeach*—and Joyce forwarded them, but Hughes very quickly returned them because the text
had already been set in type. Stella Steyn, who learned of Joyce's plan,
wasted no time in criticizing it. She considered that graphic art of the
type Joyce proposed for Lucia was a minor decorative art form; true visual art demanded as many years of dedicated training as dance or writing did, and she thought Lucia unsuited for such a project in any case. It
had been her experience that Lucia had no discernible interest in the visual arts.[139]

It was a stopgap measure at best. Joyce readily admitted that he had
ulterior motives. He wanted Lucia to earn some money from her work.
He wanted to help re-create a purposeful sense of identity to replace the
one that, he could now see, had been sacrificed when she stopped dancing, and he hoped that she would once again derive pleasure from the
pursuit of art. Discomfort began to plague him as he realized all that had
been sacrificed in leaving Paris and ignoring the path Lucia had chosen
for herself.

He had meant well, but he had not foreseen the consequences of tear-
ing people from their accustomed lives so many times. Joyce's "fifth he-

gira," as he called the trip to London,[140] was a turning point, and it became an unmitigated disaster, the final straw that made people depart from their customary civility and speak their minds about their service to "Himself." Urging Lucia to make these lettrines had made visible the structural parallel of their relative positions in life, at least as they existed in Joyce's unexamined consciousness. Drawing illuminated letters for the work of one's genius father, copying and magnifying the words of a "great" man, could in no way replace dancing on her own. As Dominique Maroger could see, dance had been Lucia's vocation as much as Joyce's calling to be a writer. It "was her life."[141] Lucia was very clear about it. In another letter to Zdenka in Prague, written in December 1931, she wrote bleakly that she hoped to earn some money from what she was doing, but that she in no way liked it as much as dancing.[142]

In any event, nothing came of Joyce's plan. When the lettrines came back from Oxford University Press, he showed them to Caresse Crosby, who proposed to print an expensive edition with the texts of the poems in a facsimile of Joyce's handwriting: either an edition of twenty-five copies for $60 each or an edition of fifty copies for $30 each.[143] At the time, Joyce was pleased. "I have done a good job for Lucia," he wrote to Harriet Weaver. When he looked around him, all seemed calm. "Everything seems now to be well disposed," he said. He was working very hard; his children seemed engaged in life; and he and Nora were anticipating the birth of their first grandchild in February.[144]

But Caresse Crosby backed out of the deal when her publishing plan met with indifference in America. Joyce's serenity turned into tiredness and dejection.[145] Then it turned into deep melancholy and self-recrimination when on 29 December his father, John Stanislaus Joyce, died in a Dublin hospital. Joyce could think of little else than the love he bore for his father, the creative heritage he had received from him, and the grief ensuing from his having neglected to visit him for eleven years. He put aside his concern for Lucia. When Dominique Maroger looked back on this period in the lives of the Joyces, she saw more than sorrow; she saw danger. Where was Lucia in Joyce and Nora's emotional economy? "What devastating rage brooded then over his tranquility?" she asked.[146] Finnegan was about to wake.

PART TWO

THE DANCE OF DEATH

Lucia, James, and Nora Joyce in Feldkirch, Austria, 1932. (Courtesy of the Eugene and Maria Jolas Collection, Beinecke Rare Book and Manuscript Library, Yale University)

9

LASHING OUT

PARIS AND FELDKIRCH 1932

I. THE DANCING SHIFTS

For a time at the beginning of 1932, Joyce's preoccupation with his father's death disrupted the foundations of his life. He considered not finishing *Finnegans Wake*, and on another level he was so thrown off track that he feared there would be no 2 February celebration of his fiftieth birthday. Helen, a few weeks away from the birth of her child, could do nothing for the event, but as the time approached, Maria Jolas came through with a party and a splendid cake with *Ulysses* represented in blue frosting.

On 2 February, Lucia, dangling irresolutely around the edges of her previous life, suddenly leaped from her liminal position to the forefront of everyone's awareness by throwing a chair at Nora. She was not dressed in a costume, but she might just as well have been performing on a stage. The theatricality of her feat caught everyone's attention.

When they talked it over, those people closest to the family understood Lucia's hostility to stem from her parents' having invited Samuel Beckett to her father's party.[1] She had expected a longer-lasting loyalty from them. She still had feelings for Beckett; his presence would make her anxious and unhappy. But it was not so simple. Beckett had long-standing friendships in the Joyce circle, aside from Joyce himself, and he had been careful to maintain them. On 25 March 1931, he had come to

Paris for one night for a party honoring *Work in Progress*. He had also gone to see Giorgio and Helen in July on his way back from a trip to the south of France with his brother and Tom MacGreevy.[2] In January 1932, convinced that he was ill suited for the life of a university professor, Beckett had given up his job at Trinity College Dublin and had once again headed for Paris. He was hoping to write the book that was to become *Dream of Fair to Middling Women*,[3] but his own life, both personally and professionally, was pretty much in shambles.

Not to Lucia. She read his invitation to the party as a sign of preference or displacement—there was one of those Sullivan-like sons again— or as a personal betrayal. She was furious, and her gesture was as eloquent as it was futile. Here was expressive energy with no aesthetic purpose. Here was the press of emotion with no shaping direction to its flow. Here was a dance, so to speak, that was as menacing as Mary Wigman's squat, abrasive *Witches' Dance* performed on the *Tanzbühnen* of southern Germany, something ugly and unbefitting to a well-bred young woman. Amid the dismay that her behavior caused within the family, Giorgio alone responded to her action without hesitation: he took her immediately to a *maison de santé*. He thereby changed her fate.

It is extraordinarily difficult to inflect the emotions of past events, but it is unlikely that anything earth-shattering seemed to be happening at the time. Joyce was dour at his party, and Nora was unsettled. But in a few days Lucia returned home and was once again thrown into the events of her family's life. In late January, Helen's brother, Robert Kastor, had brought Joyce a contract for publishing *Ulysses* in America, and on 15 February, Helen gave birth to a boy who was named Stephen James Joyce after his grandfather. It was an auspicious moment: Joyce was experiencing a double happiness that seemed in some measure to compensate for the death of his father. In imagination he linked the two events as the poles of "joy and grief" that tore at his heart.[4]

Though she registered these events, Lucia remained aloof from them. She knit little Stephen a sweater. She was hurt, just as Lillian Wallace and Moune Gilbert were, that Helen's German nurse refused to let her hold the baby, but primarily she was preoccupied with her own life. She was thinking of getting married, though it was not going to happen in the way that she had once imagined it would. Padraic and Mary Colum could see that Lucia, despite her Irish parents and the eclecticism of her upbringing, had grown into a young French woman and had assumed the values of other *jeunes filles*. "For all her Italian look, Lucia . . . had taken on the French values of the young girls she knew in Paris and the question of a *dot* (marriage portion) became all important for her."[5] Mary Colum (Molly to her friends) in particular had responded to Lucia's loneliness and longing for independence by suggesting that Joyce settle a dowry on her and, in this way, arrange a marriage in the old world style. It was something to consider, and while Lucia was weighing this plan, Paul and Lucie Léon put pressure on Alec Ponisovsky to turn to marriage to Lucia as a path for his own life as well.

Alexander M. Ponisovsky was known to the Joyces primarily through the Russian lessons he had been giving to Joyce since 1928.[6] He had come to Paris by a circuitous route. Leaving Russia in 1918 to avoid the revolution, he had gone first to Cambridge, England, where he took a degree in economics. He was one of a set of twins, with a brother named James. In the early 1930s, he worked in the Banque franco-américaine. In the account that Joyce and Paul Léon later wrote about this period of Lucia's life for Jung, Alec was "a young man whom she had loved for many long years, but who had never brought anything to a conclusion with her."[7] But in Paris more generally Alec was usually associated with Hazel and Peggy Guggenheim and their crowd.

The Guggenheims had known about Alec for years before they even met him, for their aunt Irma Seligman (their mother's sister) had married into his family. In 1908 Gregory Wilenkin, Alec's uncle, had been sent from St. Petersburg to New York as Tsar Nicholas II's minister, whose job was to secure loans from J. & W. Seligman and other banks.[8] He had gone one better and secured for himself a Seligman wife, making all the Seligmans cousins of sorts with the Ponisovskys. Their families had become more deeply entwined when Peggy's younger sister, Hazel, had married Hugo Seligman, whom the Guggenheims referred to as "Siggy."[9] It was to be the first of many marriages for Hazel, but at the time it put the Guggenheim sisters in the Seligman-Ponisovsky circle when they came to Paris. Many years later Hazel Guggenheim wrote a memoir in which she speculated about what would have happened had her father not died on the *Titanic* in 1912. "I suppose," she mused, "if father had lived, Peggy would have married bourgeois men and I would have stayed married to them."[10] Where Peggy delighted in lovers, Hazel preferred to marry the men she loved. One exception was Alec Ponisovsky. To her he was "charming, well educated, and about the nicest person I ever knew."[11] But everyone "in the know" in Paris in the 1930s knew that Alec was desperately in love with Hazel and had been for years.

Maria Jolas, who looked down on the Guggenheim circle in general, had kind words to say about Alec. Of the group as a whole, she remarked, "It was a frivolous, less psychoanalytic group looking for one thing—titillation. There was a tremendous amount of lesbianism, the beginning you might say, the first rivulets of the wave of sexuality. Rules were to be flouted and the body abused."[12] But if Jolas knew about Alec's participation in this lifestyle, she did not admit it. To her he was a "devoted friend of Peggy's sister, Hazel," and she said that she "found his conversation astoundingly intelligent. He was personable, kindly . . . and always helpful to other people."[13] Alec was eventually to be picked up by the Nazis in Monte Carlo and presumably killed, but Maria Jolas knew that personal danger had not affected his generous outlook. In the summer of 1940, she remembered thirty years later, Alec and Giorgio Joyce were instrumental in getting Peggy's art collection out of Paris.

In 1932 Alec Ponisovsky, for all of his fine and sympathetic qualities, was still in love with Hazel Guggenheim. Yet the Léons convinced him to propose to Lucia on the grounds that she was a well-raised, bourgeois girl to whom one could not show attention without its being misconstrued. Helen Kastor Joyce looked on the scene being acted out in Paris and saw the futility of the gesture. Alec "was certainly never in love with Lucia," she wrote to Richard Ellmann in 1959. She said Ponisovsky still loved Hazel Guggenheim, and that they had had an affair "for about three years."[14]

What Joyce and Nora Joyce knew about the hearts of their children is unclear. A few years later, Léon's and Joyce's account for Lucia's doctors said that Alec, after years of enjoying Lucia's affection, "disappeared from the picture and often had affairs with other women. When he reemerged on the scene in 1932, he proposed to her, whereupon Lucia became psychotic for the first time."[15]

Stuart Gilbert noticed that sometime early in March there had been an engagement dinner at the Restaurant Drouant at which both Joyce and Paul Léon got "royally drunk."[16] To ask what happened next and why the engagement was eventually called off is to invite conflicting stories from everyone who knew the young couple. Paul and Lucie Léon thought Lucia was a talented, sweet girl, and obviously, having helped to engineer the engagement, they approved of it.[17] Helen Joyce approved, too. According to her, she, Giorgio, and the baby were in the south of France when Joyce telegraphed the news. Giorgio immediately asked, "What the hell does this mean?" And she said, "We'd better send a wire to congratulate them"—an idea that Giorgio vetoed.[18] According to Giorgio, he immediately returned to Paris to argue against the engagement with his father. "You can't talk about engagement with a girl in Lucia's condition," he later remembered telling his parents—a remark that shows he had stigmatized his sister before any doctor had offered a professional opinion about her state of mind.[19]

Stuart Gilbert had a different take on the situation. With a curious, seemingly twisted logic, he considered the collapse of Lucia's marriage plans to be another chapter in the history of the Joyces' alleged anti-Semitism. He believed that the force driving a wedge between Lucia and her beau came from Helen and that she had persuaded Lucia to drop Alec. "Though [Lucia's] fiancé is an intimate friend of George J.," he wrote in his diary, "the latter's wife dissuades his sister from the marriage—the repugnance of the rich Jew towards the poor and well-bred one. For Alex Poniatowski [*sic*] belongs to the Jewish 'aristocracy' in Russia and has got a Cambridge degree; he speaks English with hardly any accent. All of this is irritating to a German Jewess of New York."[20] Lucia remembered that her mother "liked [Alec] she said he was good enough for me. His sister was a very pretty woman married to a lawyer. They were also Jews. Alec took me to restaurants and to the cinema. He had a beautiful speaking voice very low." But then, "I had a breakdown and had to give up the idea."[21]

After the engagement party, according to Lucie Léon, Lucia returned with her to the Léons' home on the rue Casimir Périer, where she lay on the sofa for several days without responding to her surroundings. Her behavior was called "catatonia"—the refusal of gesture—which, in the case of a dancer, is an extraordinary form of eloquence. But a month later, when she was staying with Mary Colum, she was actively questioning her own motives, weighing the differences between sex and love, between love and marriage, asking herself and those around her if every girl should marry.[22] Perhaps initial torpor had been her body's way of expressing a contradiction that she was consciously unprepared to accept: that she wanted to marry, there was no one else to marry, but she did not want to marry Alec Ponisovsky. Or perhaps she did understand the difficult truth—that both of them were on the rebound, urged by their families to do the correct thing when their hearts were clearly not in it. Those who knew them understood that Lucia was still obsessed with Beckett and that Ponisovsky still loved Hazel Guggenheim.

It is important to note that the scenario for this drama was already scripted. As her young cousins Bozena Berta and Nora had noticed in their 1928 visit to Paris, Lucia was so enamored of a Donizetti opera that she carried its libretto around with her.[23] Like her namesake, Lucia di Lammermoor, Lucia changed from being a passive younger sister to being an active and "dangerous" woman at the very point when a public blessing was given to a union that had no inner integrity. She knew what to do when she recognized a betrothal that was emotionally wrong, but she could not follow the entire plot. Donizetti's Lucia killed the lover forced upon her before going mad. The real Lucia could not harm the men who had betrayed her, but she knew that faulty human connections could lead to unspeakable rage.

No decisions were immediately made. For the next several months, Lucia and Ponisovsky both understood themselves to be engaged. The two of them were still going around together in May and still gathering opinions about the appropriateness of their marriage. When she met him in late April, Mary Colum respected Alec Ponisovsky, even though she thought him "rather too much on the correct side" for someone of Lucia's temperament.[24] But before this, another crisis had occurred: Lucia had thrown a huge tantrum at the Gare du Nord on 17 April, refusing to go to London again, and the senior Joyces had had to take their luggage off the train and stay. Gilbert, who arrived at the station at that very moment, wrote in his diary, "the truth is none of them really wanted to go. We all went to lunch at the Mariniers."[25] He very quickly read Lucia's conduct as a symptom for the whole family, daring now to express what none of them had been capable of saying to this point. Not only did they find life in the dark "mummy" flat at Campden Grove alienating, but they also resented the more general circumstance that had repeatedly driven all of them from one place to another. For Lucia and her mother,

Joyce's nomadic pursuit of his own genius had to end. They had paid enough.

Not everybody who heard about this incident took it as matter-of-factly as Stuart Gilbert. Padraic Colum remembers hearing about it at Sylvia Beach's bookshop. "They didn't get off," Beach told him, and he laughed because "the Joyces' unpredictability had become a joke. There we were, believing that at that moment they were having tea in Piccadilly, and they hadn't got off."[26] Just when they were laughing, however, Joyce walked in, stood on his dignity, and described the seriousness of Lucia's hysteria. And indeed it was serious enough to set off a chain reaction that affected him greatly.

Within a fortnight, in the first week of May, Nora was also threatening to leave him, packing suitcases, making her own version of a scene, and admitting that she too had come to the end of her rope. On 6 May, on the way home from a performance of *Châtiment*, Gilbert found himself embroiled in another Joyce family drama, this one staged by Nora. "Mrs. Joyce," Gilbert observed, "who is nearly as jumpy as her daughter, got more and more *énervée*, blaming him for everything—that they have no home, that the girl was ill and so forth. Unjustly, as I think—for she is just as fretful and capricious."[27] He described the drama of returning to the Hôtel Belmont with Joyce, Joyce's worry that his wife had carried through her plan to desert him, finding no one in the room, going to tea, returning, and waiting in the reading room. "After a quarter of an hour porter asks me to go up. Mrs. Joyce is by herself. Tells me it's all over, she won't live with him any more . . . Says he gives her and Lucia an unbearable life." The show of emotion was quickly over. By the next morning, when Gilbert telephoned, Nora told him that she had "given in again."[28]

All the Joyces were tense, but Lucia's anxiety had the force of being a repetition. Nora and Joyce had heard the story before: She did not want to live with her parents any longer. The first trip to London had kept her from becoming a Margaret Morris instructor; the current trip would separate her from Alec. The previous year at least she had had Helen and Giorgio's flat in the rue Huysmans as a fallback position when things got too contentious at home. Now, with the birth of Stephen, who had a live-in nurse, she had no place to go. To break the impasse, Joyce asked Lucia where she wanted to live since she was so unhappy at home. She tried returning to Paul and Lucie Léon's flat. When that proved too crowded and nerve-wracking, she asked to go to Padraic and Mary Colum, who had taken over the Jolases's old place in the rue de Sévigné.

On 24 May, Stuart Gilbert wrote in his diary: "The interest has centered for the last twenty days round Lucia." Once she was living with the Colums, everyone in the Joyces' circle seemed intent upon interpreting her conduct. Gilbert thought that she was "selfish," that she "cultivate[d] her father's imperious airs," and that she had, for the first time in her life, "run up against realities." He also thought there was something theatrical about her responses to those realities. She was merely "profess[ing]" sleeplessness and anxiety. He disapproved of the attention the Colums were giving to her, and he noted that "she came to lunch here and was quite cheerful and normal; realized, I suppose, that we are not impressed by hysterics."[29]

Padraic and Mary Colum saw things differently and disagreed with each other about what they saw. Padraic thought Lucia was "distinctly a pretty girl" and remembered that a houseguest whom he'd taken to the Joyces had remarked, "*Mademoiselle de la maison* is the most charming of the girls there." Perhaps because he found her "a normal and attractive young woman"—even if somewhat "hesitant and solitary"—he was surprised by the vehement emotions she directed at her father: "Once when we suggested she come some place with us, she said, 'If anyone talks of my father I'll leave.' " Certain isolated incidents seemed ominous to him although he could not explain why. Lucia had impressed him when she explained her name: " 'Lucia,' she once said to me . . . 'It means Light—like Paris, the City of Light.' " And he found himself lingering over an image of her staring out the window at a particular star, as if it meant something special. He noticed how she slipped in and out of languages: "She would slip from English into French, and from French into Italian, in the course of going from one side of the room to the other." And he noticed that her English idioms were sometimes wrong. He remembered that she had religious longings and that Joyce, on learning she'd gone to Mass, had said, "Now I know she is mad."[30]

Mary Colum, in contrast, was not bothered in the least by faulty idioms or isolated odd behaviors. She tried instead to see the world from Lucia's perspective and to offer the external stability that would allow Lucia to sort out her confusion. Lucia had instinctively turned to a genuine ally. Young, recently married, an American in Paris by virtue of a

Guggenheim Foundation grant, Mary Colum was an empathic person, and like Helen Nutting she genuinely liked Lucia in and of herself. She had studied with the great French psychologist Pierre Janet, and of all the amateur psychologists in the Joyce circle (and there were many), she was one of the best equipped to understand Lucia's problems. She could see that Lucia was anxious—she even agreed to sleep next to Lucia in bed, safety-pinning their nightdresses together—but she believed that experience, not some inevitable bias toward madness, had played against her. Unlike Giorgio, she did not stigmatize Lucia with the label of mental illness. Had she herself not been seriously ill—she had a tumor that required surgery—she thought that her home could have provided Lucia with the quiet, settled atmosphere she needed to sort out her emotions and renew her sense of vocation.

When she looked back on this period of her life, Mary Colum was wracked with guilt, for she thought Lucia had been treated dishonestly. She had been falsely manipulated, and the Colums had participated by agreeing with Lucia's parents to act as her jailers. Joyce and Nora had insisted that they keep her under surveillance and forbid her the freedom to move around in the world outside their home.

In her memoirs, Mary Colum described a scene in which Lucia tried to break this restriction and go out with Alec Ponisovsky, who was there for a dinner that Lucia and Mary had cooked together. Lucia put on her hat and coat to go out. " 'Where are you going?' my husband asked. 'Alec and I are going to the theater.' Not a word from Alec, who stood as if ready to leave. 'I have promised not to let you go out,' my husband said. 'Have I left my father's to be ordered about by you?' Lucia replied." Lucia refused to accept his order and, as she departed, cried, "I will go out!" Colum chased her down the stairs, intending to bring her back into the house, when Lucia stopped, became quiet, and said, "You win."[31]

This scene functions as a *tableau vivant*, a living demonstration of the forces that were arrayed against Lucia Joyce at this time in her young life. Members of her immediate family questioned her competence. Padraic Colum was against her. (Mary wondered why her husband had been so authoritarian and unyielding, and she reproved herself for not standing up to him.) Alec Ponisovsky not only did not help her but abandoned her, indeed vanished. (Mary Colum couldn't imagine how he had left that evening without their seeing him do so and conjectured that he must have gone up to the roof and then descended to the street from another stairwell.) "You win" was neither a confession of madness nor a tacit admission of guilt, but a straightforward reckoning of her position. Lucia was alone at the foot of the cultural stairs, and she was facing another closed door. In a few days, on 29 May, her own brother tricked her into going to the sanatorium of Dr. Gaston Maillard at L'Haye-les-Roses, where she was held against her will.[32]

Mary Colum's feeling of guilt extended beyond the regret she harbored for having restricted Lucia's freedom, for in other ways she had deceived Lucia. Joyce and Nora, having listened to Giorgio, decided to have Lucia observed by a nerve specialist, but they did not want Lucia to know this. With Mary Colum's cooperation, they devised a ruse: Each day the psychiatrist whom the Joyces had selected, Dr. Henri Codet, would come to the apartment ostensibly to examine Mary. Mary would claim she needed Lucia to act as a translator, and in this way Lucia would have to interact with the doctor. Posing as the patient, Mary would sometimes answer and sometimes wait for Lucia to reply to his questions about the relation between anxiety and creativity. The psychiatrist would say that nervousness was often coupled with artistic sensibility—"Madame est très nerveuse," and "Madame est artiste"—drawing Lucia out until she interposed, "Mais, Monsieur, c'est moi qui est artiste." ("But, sir, it is I who am the artist.")[33]

Mary Colum thought that no doctor could pass judgment after such a short observation. "Frankly, I had not much faith in the proceedings. The psychiatrist did not understand Lucia, and indeed I have never been able to comprehend how such a person, after a couple of interviews and without having known the patient previously, could come to any real conclusion about anyone's malady." But in any case Dr. Codet's judgment was, interestingly enough, that "there was not much the matter with the girl, and that, whatever it was, she would soon get over it."[34]

Each day, whenever Lucia went out, Joyce would telephone or come over to talk with Mary Colum about the doctor's visits. He professed to be shocked when he learned that Codet had said that Lucia "seems to have been hearing a good deal about sex."[35] Mary was not shocked by Lucia's interest in sex so much as by the general conclusion that nothing special needed to be done for her. She thought that it would take a long time for Lucia to get her emotions in order and that "she could get well only in new surroundings, where there was an atmosphere of affection and interest in her."[36] The Colums had listened carefully to Lucia's complaint that the young men who came to visit the house treated her as an "hors d'œuvre" and were, like Beckett, primarily interested in talking to her father. They could also see that Joyce had, for many years, reserved his intensity for his work, without attending adequately to his "human commitments."[37] They faulted him as a parent; and Mary at least wanted to take care of Lucia.

But Mrs. Colum's own physical health prevented her from carrying out her good intentions. "And so," she admitted, "with her brother, I accompanied Lucia to a sanitarium. I did not tell her the truth about where we were going, though I hated more than anything to deceive someone who trusted me. But I was obeying orders, and did not know what else to do. . . . We entered the office of the director of the sanitarium and as he began to talk to me, Lucia threw me a look of bewildered appeal that I can never forget." Her misery was somewhat assuaged by the appearance of a young nurse who was just Lucia's age and who promised she would stay with her. "Her presence in the room made the good-by I had dreaded pass off more easily."[38] Looking back twenty years later, Mary Colum did not spare herself. She inscribed that scene as a final deception in a long list of betrayals. The Lucia Joyce whom she knew was confused but in no way insane. She had simply run out of resources.

Through all the vicissitudes that lay ahead for Lucia, the eloquence of her body did not diminish, and she did not ever lack an audience. In illness as in health, Lucia continued to experience the lessons of the dance world and to use its wisdom in her response to experience. Western culture is built upon a system of exclusions, and the expressive, "dancing" body is regulated, disciplined, normalized, and individualized in proportion to the fears it arouses about transgression. As Nietzsche's Zarathustra knew, the body can also be considered a locus of power or a site of resistance that threatens to subvert the laws that dictate its exile: "She is changeable and defiant; I have often seen her bite her lip and comb her hair against the grain."[39]

The figure who haunts this story is Friedrich Nietzsche. He hovers behind Lucia like the spiritual father who guided Stephen Dedalus on his
way at the end of *A Portrait of the Artist as a Young Man*: "old artificer,
stand me now and ever in good stead" (*P* 253). Years after he had finished writing *A Portrait*, Joyce disclosed his unwitting association of his
daughter with Stephen Dedalus: "The poor child is not a raving lunatic,"
he claimed in 1934, "just a poor child who tried to do too much, to understand too much."[40] Like Icarus, he seems to say, she flew too near the
sun and was burned by what she could not sustain. Indeed, if we think of
the sun as Dionysos, in the way that Nietzsche understood Dionysos, we
can use this metaphor to measure the dangers inherent in Lucia's early
life choices. To worship Dionysos, as the dancers of the early part of this
century almost invariably did,[41] was to risk dissolving the self in a mystic
circle. In fact, dissolving the rational self was often the goal of dancing
when conceived as a collective rite and the dancers' gift to modern culture. They saw themselves as the bearers of wisdom, the vehicles of
tragedy, restoring a bacchic spirit to a world diminished by too much science, too many machines, and too many alarm clocks. "The Greek mind
manifests itself in dance," Nietzsche asserted, "since in dance the maximum power is . . . potentially present, betraying itself in the suppleness
and opulence of movement."[42] "The mystical jubilation of Dionysos
breaks the spell of individuation and opens a path to the maternal womb
of being."[43] Nietzsche's descriptions of this underlying wholeness
abound. "While the transport of the Dionysiac state, with its suspension
of all the ordinary barriers of existence, lasts, it carries with it a Lethean
element in which everything that has been experienced by the individual
is drowned."[44] "The dithrambic chorus . . . is a chorus of the transformed, who have forgotten their civic past and social rank, who have
become timeless servants of their god and live outside all social
spheres."[45]

Isadora Duncan, Raymond Duncan, and other modern dancers believed that their movements constituted a kind of universal language and
a rhythmic embodiment of the spirit of music. They understood themselves to be returning for inspiration quite literally to the ancient, pre-
Socratic Greeks who could, as Nietzsche claimed, "teach [them] what

such a sudden miraculous birth of tragedy means to the heart and soul of a nation." Their tunics and loose wraps were not simply signs of emancipation from bourgeois values but tributes from "timeless servants of their god."[46]

In opposition to this collective rapture, Nietzsche had placed the world of positive science. "Our whole modern world," he wrote, "is caught in the net of Alexandrian culture and recognizes as its ideal the man of theory, equipped with the highest cognitive powers, working in the service of science, and whose archetype and progenitor is Socrates."[47] For Nietzsche Socrates' values had led the Western world into constriction and error. He could see the many consequences of that false turn wherever one found "optimism which believe[d] itself omnipotent," wherever "the belief in general happiness and in the possibility of universal book knowledge reigned."[48]

Because the contemporary world was built upon an absence of myth, it became, for Nietzsche, a kind of illness. Any kind of secular activity was "feverish and frightened"; a thirst for knowledge was "insatiable"; curiosity is similarly "insatiable"; the drive for secularization is a "greedy rush"; and these impulses are, collectively, "symptoms of a state of morbid growth." Reversing the terms of sickness and health, Nietzsche created a picture of a culture that had repudiated its "original oneness." In such unhealthy circumstances, any orientation that can undermine the status quo is valuable, and in *The Birth of Tragedy* an "unruly lust for life" or "orgiastic abandon" or "living recklessly . . . in a wilderness of thought" can lead one back to a "marvelous ancient power."[49]

Nietzsche anticipated that a struggle would ensue before the modern world could once again acknowledge its full heritage. The goal of Western culture might be the union of two ways of being in the world or, as Nietzsche put it, a marriage of Apollo and Dionysos. But the path would be difficult because the logic that supported contemporary culture would not relinquish its hegemony without strife. It would repress and stigmatize alternative values. It would denigrate whatever was unruly, orgiastic, or without proportion: "Any type of existence that deviates from this model has a hard struggle and lives, at best, on sufferance."[50]

We could say that from this point in her young adult life, Lucia Joyce lived on sufferance, and the lines of battle for her allegiance had been already drawn before Giorgio turned her over to the psychiatrists. In certain ways, they were drawn as far back as the youth of her father, who had left the ailing institutions of the British Empire and the Catholic Church in order to discover a life that was reunited with myth and that admitted the possibility of tragedy. Where Nietzsche spoke about the danger of being "caught in the net of Alexandrian culture," Joyce located his nemesis in "the nets" cast by church and state in Dublin. But their images of cultural imprisonment and the need to escape coincided, and they implied a style of politics that looked to his contemporaries like "indifference, or even hostility, towards political instinct," as Nietzsche put it.[51] "The affair doesn't interest me in the least," says the fictional Stephen Dedalus wearily, as if speaking for Joyce himself. "You know that well. Why do you make a scene about it?"[52]

Joyce, like his young invented hero, actually left Ireland, bent on discovering more exciting allegiances, but he left the task of carrying on Stephen Dedalus's project of "unfettered freedom" to his children.[53] It was they who lived out the consequences of being cultural nomads. It was as if Joyce could imagine but not embody liberation. It was as if, as Mary Colum said so well in her memoirs, Joyce's mind remained steeped in the very traditions he had abandoned, shaped more by the effort of undoing belief than by any novel alternative. Giorgio and Lucia were the ones who could live in "a wilderness of thought,"[54] for they never knew any alternatives. They had always lived without religion and outside the bureaucratic restrictions of colonialism. Little did Joyce imagine that his children might be lonely or unhappy in their freedom.

Nietzsche had seen, as Joyce had not, that the Dionysian life could be sustained only in a community. Nietzsche's image of the transformed future was a social one. The daemonic could come into being only through and among people moving together. Rudolf Laban had understood this when he established his circle in Ascona. His protégée Mary Wigman thought of dancing not only as a festival "at which all [are] participants in communal thinking, feeling and doing" but also as a way of life that had to satisfy personal needs within a self-sustaining group. You could avoid "be[ing] sucked back into the social system" only if you were not alone.[55] Lucia wasn't part of a group until she met Lois Hutton and Hélène Vanel, so it is not hard to imagine the implications of her loss when it was decided, however it was decided, that she would no longer perform with them. It was as if dancing had unleashed an energy that did not cease to flow when she no longer mounted a stage and enacted its release.

We can imagine a continuum between Lucia's dancing experiences, which were by bourgeois standards already excessive, and the physical violence that periodically characterized her later conduct. Her life had no rupture or psychotic break but rather a transposition of energy that was no longer restrained and purposeful. It was as if she retained an instinctive loyalty to Dionysos. We can imagine her falling like Icarus, drowning in the "Lethean element" that threatens anyone who risks "the dissolution of the self" in bacchic activity. "Ecstatic reality . . . takes no account of the individual and may even destroy him,"[56] Nietzsche had admitted. Joyce, as if in parody of the same idea, had followed his description of the "radiant," "purified" flight of Stephen Dedalus's soul with "o, cripes, I'm drowned!"[57]

The problem for the Joyce family was really a practical one: Lucia was too noisy. She created too much commotion, set too many nerves on edge, as she inserted her energy into her mother's west-of-Ireland common sense and her father's need for quiet in which to write. It is one thing to glorify the life force as a kind of "Blakean tiger of the night."[58] It is another to live with it day by day. "But you can think in what a state my wife's nerves are after four years of it," Joyce wrote to Harriet Weaver in 1935. "And that is the problem, the whole problem, and nothing but the problem."[59] Nora could barely tolerate her husband's bouts of drinking in the evening, and she was not equipped to deal with the personal accusations that her daughter hurled at her as rudely and forcefully as chairs across a room. She could certainly not deal with the chair itself once it was thrown. To someone like Nora, who didn't read books and didn't think about deciphering body language, it must have seemed as if her daughter's sanity had collapsed.

When Giorgio, in sympathy with Nora's position, decided to put Lucia into the hands of doctors, the battle between two hostile principles was joined. For mental health professionals in the early twentieth century were Apollonian men par excellence. They had dedicated their lives to what Nietzsche called "Apollo['s] demands": "self-control, a knowledge of self."[60] In Nietzsche's words, they worshiped "the god of engines and crucibles" and believed the world could be corrected through knowledge and life guided by science. They also believed, to Nietzsche's dismay, that "it is actually [possible] to confine man within the narrow circle of soluble tasks, where he can say cheerfully to life: 'I want you. You are worth knowing!' "[61] Once they had decided that Lucia was "worth knowing," she could not escape surveillance. No matter what she, or her friends, or Nietzsche for that matter, thought of psychiatrists, she existed from this point in her life on their sufferance. Already a cultural logic was at work that would control Lucia's fate. The body must be observed, categorized, and subdued. This child of Dionysos, dancing out, in whatever hesitant way, the fate of Icarus when he hurled himself against the forces of gravity, would not be released until discipline had been internalized and her mind and habits regulated by rules she had neither made nor accepted. Nietzsche may have regarded the cultural accomplishments of doctors of medicine as "degenerate" and "atrophied. . . . How cadaverous and ghostly their 'sanity' appears as the intense throng of Dionysiac revelers sweeps past them."[62] But it is their judgment about Lucia that the world remembered.

III. THE UGLY DOCTOR

The Joyces did not deal with Lucia's "illness" in a logical or sustained way. For one thing, it was not immediately clear to them that their daughter had any identifiable disease. That she was unhappy was obvious from what Joyce called her "King Lear scenes."[63] Lucia had lost none of her flair for staging interiority, and her emotional style remained theatrical. Even when she wouldn't speak, leading those who were trying to understand her emotional life to believe her uncommunicative or "catatonic," she retained her flair for mime and for somatic expression. But the boundaries between suffering, even suffering expressed hysterically, and what we have become accustomed to calling mental illness are difficult to draw, especially when you are in the midst of experiencing them. For another, the line between illness and health was not yet understood in any consistent way by doctors either.

As in her experience with modern dance, so in her illness (if that is what it was), Lucia was destined to be a pioneer—someone surrounded by new social forms, new institutional practices, and innovative ideologies. That Lucia's many doctors failed to agree with one another had as much to do with the lack of uniform diagnostic categories among physicians as with inconsistencies in her behavior. When Eugen Bleuler looked around him at the fates of suffering people in the 1920s, he could see that "with many patients, the number of diagnoses made equals the number of institutions they have been to."[64] Nonetheless, few doctors hesitated to label Lucia. Their judgments tended to divide along national lines, the French and German and German Swiss having the most distinctive attitudes and practices.

Jung's first experiences in dealing with schizophrenia had come from working with Eugen Bleuler, the doctor responsible for creating the modern system of classification for schizophrenia. In fact, they "were collaborating in the years that preceded [Bleuler's] famous book on dementia praecox."[65] Because Joyce disliked Jung, he placed Lucia in his hands relatively late in his search for a cure, but Jung's clinical orientation would have been similar to that of many of the other doctors who had already been treating her, for like Jung, they too had been trained by Eugen Bleuler. German and German Swiss doctors were, so to speak, all sons of the same intellectual father.

It is hard to reconstruct what actually happened to Lucia at the beginning of this period of turmoil. As Richard Ellmann tells the story, Giorgio was the first person to intervene and to set a limit on what kind of behavior the family would tolerate. No records survive of Lucia's stay in the *maison de santé* on Joyce's fiftieth birthday. But Paul Léon's papers in Dublin contain a Swiss residence permit for Lucia granted on 5 February 1932, and due to expire on 31 March 1935, for staying in Dr. Theodor Brunner's sanatorium in Küsnacht, outside Zurich.[66] This document suggests that the Joyces knew about the place long before 1934, when they sent her there.[67] How did they learn about it? Who applied for this permit? Was it used? The mystery remains unsolved.

The first surviving document that charts Lucia's residence in an institution is dated 29 May 1932, at L'Haye-les-Roses. Throughout that year she seems to have been unhappy enough to seek help from professionals, but she did not do so consistently, and only during brief respites did she stay away from her family. As we know, her first experience of institutional life was imposed on her against her will and with deceit. In this circumstance she was unfortunately not alone.

Mental patients seldom came to the main psychiatric hospital in

Paris, the Salpetrière, of their own accord. Like the Burghölzli in Zurich, the Salpetrière had a sinister reputation based on accounts of what happened to people once they were within its walls, where drug addiction, solitary confinement, treatment with leeches, electric shocks, and daylong baths were common.[68] Annie Barnacle, Lucia's grandmother, and Michael Healy, her maternal uncle, had seen the permanent damage done to Nora's sister Dilly after eighteen months in Ballinasloe, a lunatic asylum in Ireland. They wrote urgently and apparently as often as once a week about Lucia, imploring, "No doctors, no sanatorium, no blood examination."[69]

Despite such warnings, Giorgio chose to follow a pattern that was common in France at the time: A family member, an employer, or a police officer could commit a patient "voluntarily."[70] Although biographies of the Joyces have emphasized Lucia's "voluntary" status as a patient, this was not the case, or at least it was far from what we now understand as voluntary. Once installed in an institution, French patients lost their status as adults with full legal rights and became, instead, legal wards of their doctors, who could, simply by a professional judgment, prevent them from leaving. The doctors were endowed with wide and almost exclusive powers of decision-making, whether the institution was private or public.[71]

This wide-ranging power rested on the idea of "therapeutic isolation." Medical authorities argued that patients should be placed in special sites of detention for their own good, and in fact isolation came to represent the attempted cure and then later to indicate the very nature of insanity itself. Someone who was incarcerated was de facto insane; in like manner, one who was legally discharged left his or her mental illness behind.[72] The Joyces repeatedly heard this rationale for Lucia's treatment as they sought help for her over the years. This legal circumstance—that once in professional care a person's status could, at the drop of a pin, change from voluntary to compulsory placement—explains why Joyce had to smuggle his daughter out of L'Haye-les-Roses in 1932 when he decided that institutional life was harming her.

At the clinic, Dr. Gaston Maillard examined Lucia and, agreeing with Thérèse Bertrand-Fontaine, who had already prescribed solitary confinement for Lucia, decided that she should remain in bed for several weeks. He diagnosed Lucia's case as "hebephrenic psychosis with serious prognosis."[73] Joyce reported to Miss Weaver that Nora hated Maillard's associate, Dr. Henri Codet, for being so ugly,[74] but he was the doctor whom the Joyces should have trusted. He at least had specialized in the treatment of emotional problems. He had been one of the nine founding members of the Société psychoanalytique in Paris and was known for having written *Psychiatrie*, a general handbook for the diagnosis and treatment of mental illness, published in 1926. In the mid-1930s Codet began to read Freud and integrate psychoanalytic theories into his writing, but in 1932 when he worked with Lucia, he had only a nodding interest in Freudian talk therapy. Instead he pursued a brand of psychiatry that relied on careful observation and what he called "medical common sense."[75] He spoke to patients only to discover a pattern of symptoms in their lives.[76]

In his handbook, Codet gave impressionistic advice to physicians faced with psychiatric admissions to their clinics. He began by warning that the term "lunatic" ("*folie*") should be superseded by a more scientific, clinical vocabulary. This, in turn, could bring new worries, for the field of psychiatry was fraught with "complicated words" from different authors who contradicted one another. He proposed to show the practical application of a few terms and techniques that were sufficiently precise and well-defined. When doctors examined patients, they should try to elicit three types of information by asking about heredity, the past circumstances of the subject's life, and the current state of the patient's "organic" health. The idea was to proceed with patience and "perpetual control" to find out how the patient exteriorized her inner, emotional life. "In all cases," Codet said, "one should observe the general demeanor of the subject, [her] mimicry with the expressions that are conveyed, [her] gestures; one should study [her] manner of being, [her] comportment."[77]

In an almost grotesque parody of dance performance, Lucia's body would now show the signs of inner-feeling states that alerted the observer not to creativity but to pathology. She was no longer Charlie Chaplin at her father's parties but a mime nonetheless. Instead of seeing an inventive recital, men now watched her in order to probe the most intimate recesses of her psyche. Lucia later referred to this surveillance as "try[ing] to get hold of my soul."[78]

Lucia had reason to be apprehensive: Codet did not stop his research with her. He believed in involving the family of the patient in his tête-à-têtes, using them to provide information that the patient herself might withhold since "many timid or defiant psychopaths immediately rebuff an interrogation that is too categorical."[79] It was a world in which the ideal patient was completely transparent and completely docile with regard to the doctor's verdict. Resistance was itself a sign of illness; insurrection was read as malady, and one's compliance with the asylum's daily regimen was a necessary prerequisite of being "cured."

There is no doubt that Codet was condescending toward his patients, but at least he believed in being scrupulously honest with them. He recognized that a patient's family would want to know not only what his diagnosis was but also what to expect about the progression of the "disease," its dangers, complications, and general prognosis. In no case should the doctor deceive them. To the contrary, the physician had the responsibility to inform them of the measures that might be necessary to effect a cure: "relative quiet, cessation of work, observation, isolation or internment, depending on the case."[80] He should even be prepared to make weighty judgments about whether the patient should ever marry or have children, even if he or she had recovered from the "illness" that first presented itself. He considered that the tendency toward degeneration might be inherited and that people with a history of mental illness should not bear children. The Germans were not alone in their concern for genetic programming in the interests of race.

Codet considered *démence précoce* to be one of the most difficult diagnoses, and he defined it by six characteristics, which he admitted could be symptoms of other diseases as well. Above all, the condition was insidious and was often signaled to those in the sufferer's circle of friends by a "fantastic" change in character; he or she might show an atypical excess of excitement or depression; might become frequently confused, in a manner similar to the intoxication produced by alcohol; or might become antisocial, manifesting "violent and unjustifiable, astonishing or pathological" behavior.[81] He or she might grow suicidal or show signs of delirium; or might act as if obsessed or phobic. In the end, Codet relied for his diagnosis on a general sense of discordance in the patient's behavior, as if the disease suddenly threw a psychological monkeywrench into customary behavior or thinking that remained otherwise quite correct.

Like Karl Jaspers, Codet considered that incomprehensibility was the deciding factor in making a diagnosis of *démence précoce*, for if the doctor could not understand a patient's behavior or speech, it must certainly be irrational: "On observing tics, grimaces, excess of weeping or smiling without an explicable motive, very often the expression of a mimic is in complete discord with the idea expressed."[82] The patient might refuse to eat, might be irritable when approached, or might attach great importance to something that another might consider trivial and vice versa. In intervening times, the patient might appear to be entirely lucid, but lucidity would give way to confusion and finally, according to Codet, to indifference and apathy.

We can assume that Codet talked to the Joyces about these issues because in 1932 Joyce in his letters began to classify Lucia's behavior and to notice whether her thoughts seemed disjointed and whether she fell into apathy. On 6 August 1932, Joyce confided to Harriet Weaver, "What I find disquieting in [Lucia's] letter is not so much its exaltation. . . . It is the lack of even casual connections. . . . when she heard vaguely of what Vogt [Joyce's ophthalmologist] said she had a violent fit of crying and said she should come to Zurich to stay with her mother. Anything, even weeps, which takes them out of absorption in themselves is a good sign."[83]

IV. LIMBO

To the distress of some of his friends, Joyce smuggled Lucia out of L'Haye-les-Roses in July, and she went to live with a nurse companion, Mathilde Wönecke, in Feldkirch, Austria, where Maria Jolas and her family were spending the summer. (Wönecke was the young woman whose presence had reassured Mary Colum when she brought Lucia to the clinic.) Joyce had followed Dr. Codet's recommendation that a person with Lucia's symptoms should be separated from the circumstances in which they had initially arisen, and he did not bring her back to live with him.[84]

Stuart Gilbert, looking on from the sidelines, was surprised by this whole turn of events. He had thought Lucia difficult and selfish, but it had never occurred to him that there was anything abnormal about her. In July he recorded an incident that supported his view of her and of her father's manipulative natures: Lucia had spent a day and a night in a hotel in Passy before going on to Austria. There Joyce had staged a scene in which Mathilde Wönecke pretended to pay for her own trip to Austria, as if she, too, like Lucia, were simply going on holiday. The scene was necessary because a week or so earlier, when Joyce had proposed this trip, he had suggested that Lucia pay part of Wönecke's expenses, but she (accepting the ruse of nurse-equals-friend) had refused, saying each person should pay her own way.[85]

Gilbert mused about the nature of sanity, continuing and extending his earlier observations about Lucia's theatricality and her need to be the object of attention. It seemed to him that he was watching a variation of an American comedy film, albeit a subtler one than those on the silver screen: "It seems that L[ucia], by playing her part so well, has come to be dominated by it and is, in some respects, genuinely out of her wits. Probably, *au fond*, everyone is insane and sanity (as we call it) is instilled into us by the teachers of self-restraint and proper sentiments. Once we repudiate these there is no knowing how far we shall go—murder, melancholia, suicide, all are possible. After all, one's first emotion, when a desire is denied, is to mope or curse or break things." "What restrains us?" he asked himself, thinking of Lucia as one whose impulse to pose— or in Beckett's words, to live between the mirror and the comb—had finally become synonymous with her most basic experience of selfhood.[86]

Lucia was being treated ambiguously, for no one was quite sure if she had lost the self-possession that underlies one's status as a functioning, sane adult. As Codet himself said, *démence précoce* is a disease that "simulates simulation." "Reciprocally," he continued, "certain simulators may be, for the same reason, like *démence précoce*. This is a diagnostic mistake that is easy to make. And it is also the case that the various affections may simulate organic diseases—through examination one may discover the cause: alcoholism, intoxication, uremic poisoning, a cerebral tumor, meningetic tuberculosis, general paralysis."[87]

How should we think about Joyce's plan for Lucia to go to Austria with the Jolases? Sending one's daughter of twenty-five to live in a resort village with a companion to supervise her day may be perfectly reasonable, or it may be considered overly protective. Lucia felt, at this point and at many other points in the future, that her sense of integrity was being violated by the strictures her parents placed upon her. One feels an

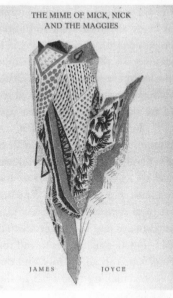

THE MIME OF MICK, NICK
AND THE MAGGIES

JAMES   JOYCE

Illustration by Lucia Joyce for *The Mime of Mick, Nick and the Maggies*, 1934. Copyright the Servire Press. Notice the dancing body in a configuration similar to Margaret Morris's costume, below. (Courtesy of Special Collections, the McFarlin Library, University of Tulsa)

Margaret Morris,
Juan-les-Pins, 1928.
Photograph by Fred
Daniels.

extraordinary sadness when imagining her task, there in those high mountains, of forging a new identity as an ex–mental patient and of re-organizing her view of the past. Compared with this task, Stephen Dedalus, forging the "uncreated conscience of [his] race," had light work. Lucia had to integrate her memories of the beauty and forceful-ness of dance with the more recent stigma of the asylum and its judg-ment. She did not know if she could fix the condition that she was identified as having. She did not know if she had a condition or if she lived according to a private set of countercultural values, as it had seemed to her during her days with Raymond and Elizabeth Duncan, Jean Borlin, Margaret Morris, and Hélène Vanel and Lois Hutton. In-deed, it is only if one suppresses the memory of a young girl's dancing body that one can view her retreat to Austria with any hope. How was that isolated sojourn with a single companion going to replace all that was lost of her creative life? How could being an amanuensis to and for a genius who was one's father replace a group, a social identity, and the soaring leaps of young women intent upon remaking the world in the image of their own vitality?

To Lucia, the time in Feldkirch seemed more like a vacation or an in-terlude than a period of work. She took up drawing letterforms again, but her heart was not in it. Photographs taken there show her lunching outdoors with the Jolas children and with her parents, who came to visit in early August, or promenading by herself or on motoring trips in the Jolases' car, which she referred to as "Our Rolls Royce." "Isn't this a scream?" she wrote on the back of another picture that had caught her unawares. "We are looking at a mountain and were snapped by surprise. Jolas on the extreme right."[88] Kay Boyle and her new husband, Laurence Vail (formerly Peggy Guggenheim's partner), came for a visit. She wrote letters to Harriet Weaver and to Zdenka Podhajsky, whom she invited to visit if she could get away from the school of modern dance she was set-ting up in Prague: "It's very jolly and not too expensive. There are mar-velous walks and the food is good."[89]

But deeper emotions were at play than these chatty letters suggest. In a private communication to Mathilde Wönecke, Lucia admitted her in-terior destitution. "This body, which you see is devoid of soul. It has left me," she explained, "and I hope that it has gone to a better place than this earth which is full of suffering and unfortunate beings." Wönecke had apparently cautioned Lucia to lower her sights, to be content with less, to compromise with life. "You speak as if one's fate were a mere nothing, as if the mountains are inaccessible, and you insist that one can be content to gather a single strawberry in the lovely forest. Happy Creature," Lucia wrote. But she was unconvinced by such a restricted vision. "I prefer abundance," she countered. "I need to disabuse you, for the clouds are not inaccessible and I have seen the mountain peaks and the ocean, its surface like a ripe fruit, with my own eyes."[90] She was not ready to relinquish her private sense of vocation, her identity as a creative artist.

When Mathilde Wönecke forwarded this note to Joyce, he in turn sent it to Harriet Weaver. This was the letter about which he said he worried less about its "exaltation" than about its lack of "causal connections." But in many ways, Lucia's prose is reminiscent of the words Joyce had used in his own memoir of youth. In *A Portrait of the Artist as a Young Man*, Stephen Dedalus uses similar metaphors about his extraordinary sense of vocation: "His soul was soaring in an air beyond the world and the body he knew was purified in a breath and delivered of incertitude and made radiant and commingled with the element of the spirit."[91] These words are not so distant from Lucia's way of describing a vision of life's potential abundance. In a moment of extraordinary candor, she personified her anxieties as "grimacing figures, exaggerated masks of strange people."[92]

Joyce's anxiety on Lucia's behalf took the form of further manipulations behind the scene. "Each phrase" in her letters "could bear a rational meaning," he claimed to Harriet Weaver, and one meaning he attended to was his child's need to reclaim what had been taken from her in dancing. He understood that her inner emptiness and her glimpses of having a singular destiny were related, and if he could not restore the dance world to her, he could at the least attempt to open the way for bookbinding and design.

V. THE CAREENING LETTERFORMS

Joyce had already found a publisher to replace Caresse Crosby in his *Pomes Penyeach* collaboration with Lucia: Jack Kahane and Desmond Harmsworth at the Obelisk Press had agreed to bring out a beautiful limited edition of a facsimile manuscript. They combined Joyce's hand-writing with Lucia's illuminated letters, printed them together on Japan *macre* paper by a stencil color process known as *pochoir*,[93] and placed the twenty-five copies in a casing of light green watered silk.[94] Joyce signed the editions, and Obelisk set the price at £12. Lucia had designed seven new illuminated letters while she was at L'Haye-les-Roses.[95] Now in Feldkirch, with her father's encouragement, she worked her way up to the letter O on the understanding that a complete alphabet could eventu-ally be integrated into a children's book of some sort.[96] In August she balked and asked for some kind of contract or compensation for her work.

Despite Lucia's ambiguous feelings for these drawings, they were to become a thread of fragile hope as the years passed. They were a solitary and portable occupation, and to the extent that her father could manage it, they connected her to a community of book manufacturers, readers, and reviewers. For the next six years, Joyce attended to one or another aspect of this enterprise, sending her payments (both artificially arranged by him and formally contracted), reviews, and lists of subscribers. Cast-ing his daughter as his own collaborator, he formalized and made visible the collusion in place between them. The child was the progenitor and vehicle of the sire's text, both inspiring and rendering the form of the let-ters' delivery. Lucia's solitary occupation in the open air of Feldkirch and later in Paris and in the confinement of various asylums served as a metaphor of their relationship and of the fantastical meeting of their in-terior lives.

As she worked, Joyce worked on her behalf. Since, aside from his love of the Irish Book of Kells, Joyce knew nothing about illuminated letters, he described himself as "a blind man walking in a fog."[97] What-ever he had done on behalf of Giorgio or for John Sullivan seemed a model of clarity compared with the intricacies of manufacture that now demanded his attention. In the summer of 1932, while he and Nora lived in Zurich, he showed Lucia's designs to Edmund Brauchbar, a silk mer-chant, in the hope that they might be used for fabric design. He sent still others to Daniel Brody, an editor at Rheinverlag, the German publisher of *Ulysses*, who in turn forwarded them to a German wallpaper com-pany. He arranged to send a copy of the completed book to Helene Vogt, the daughter of his Zurich eye surgeon, and was persistent in gathering names for subscriptions. By August he was able to write to Robert McAlmon that he had the names of seven subscribers, among them himself, McAlmon, T. S. Eliot, Harriet Weaver, and others about whom he felt confident, among them Lady Cunard, Nancy Cunard, Wyndham Lewis, George Antheil, and Mrs. Herbert Gorman.[98]

In the fall, after the little book was actually published, he was even more forward in calling attention to it. On 22 September, he wrote to Stanislaus that "Lucia's book" was "exquisite."[99] He sent a copy to T. S. Eliot, asking him to speak to his literary agent about Lucia's work. Another copy went to Frank Morley at Faber and Faber, and one to Hubert Foss at the Oxford University Press, both in hope that the quality of Lucia's craftsmanship would lead to further commissions. In February 1933, he sent a copy to his own agent, Ralph Pinker, instructing him to present it to the British Museum Library. He had already arranged for it to be given to the Bibliothèque nationale.[100]

Lucia kept to her work through the summer and into the early fall, even as she and Mathilde Wönecke moved from Feldkirch to Vence, where they went to visit Lois Hutton, who was still running the little dance theater that had first made her famous. The elder Joyces moved in her trail, settling into the Hôtel Metropole in Nice, where they stayed until late October. Helen and Giorgio joined them with the baby for part of that time. In early October, Padraic and Mary Colum came down; Mary had chosen Nice as a place to recuperate from her surgery. Lucia occasionally went walking with Helen and joined the Colums for tea. Mary renewed her invitation to have Lucia make a home with them, but this time, while no one refused, the subject was quietly let drop.

In early October Joyce sent the Colums a letter that showed that he was mulling over the events of the previous six months, trying to understand what had happened in his family. He wondered whether Dr. Bertrand-Fontaine had been thorough enough. He reported that "Dr. F." claimed Lucia "has or had nothing wrong with her. There is nothing mentally wrong with her now."[101] He had also been in touch with Dr. Codet, sharing, seeking guidance, asking questions. He understood the nature of the responsibility he had assumed by taking Lucia out of the clinic, and he was careful to point out to Giorgio that Dr. Codet did in fact agree with him that Lucia might improve in less clinical surroundings than those at L'Haye-les-Roses.[102] He asked Harriet Weaver, to whom he had apparently sent Codet's answer, to forward it to Giorgio, who was vacationing with Helen in the Maritime Alps. It confirmed that Codet was not inflexible about the treatment he prescribed for nervous disorders and in his assessment of their cure.

Giorgio was convinced that Lucia's life was unsalvageable, but Dr. Codet did not agree. First of all, the nature of her nervous disorder was not clear. Maillard's diagnosis of hebephrenia was not a worst-case diagnosis, and even if Lucia had been diagnosed with *démence précoce*, Codet considered that it could go into remission, and he was realistic about what treatments were available in the first place. Unless there was an underlying organic illness, nothing could be done for a dementia patient no matter where he or she lived. Clinics were, in his judgment, merely custodial institutions, and the reasons for placing a patient in detention had as much to do with preserving decorum within the family as with "cure."

The only advice he offered his colleagues in his clinical handbook was that one should go through certain procedures in case a physical malady had caused the irrational behavior: "With forms that are at the beginning, 'toxi-infectious,' a therapy of the causal ailment is required that may notably diminish the chances of them recurring. On the other hand, opotherapy [a form of treatment with the glands of animals] may be systematically attempted at the onset, oriented toward the physical signs of endocrine trouble if it exists, based principally on extracts of 'thyroïdien,' 'orchitique,' or 'ovarien.' "[103] If the young person was suffering only from unbalanced hormones, Codet thought the "disease" might not advance to incurable *démence précoce*, and psychotherapy, which he called "moral treatment," was useful if the trouble had an emotional origin.

In other words, Codet hedged his bets. He did not know whether *démence précoce* was a physical illness; he did not understand its origin; and aside from the hormone treatments, he did not know what to do beyond maintaining as much order as possible for all concerned. Using that "medical common sense" that he had advocated for all diagnosticians, he recognized that the condition usually required that the patient be committed to an institution. "Nevertheless," he admitted, "when the condition is not too violent, when the patient does not appear very affected to his relatives, one may advise placing [him or her] under observation in an outpatient clinic or in a *maison de santé*. And even with certain kinds of surveillance, there may be those patients who may be kept at home." Codet only warned that the patient might, at any moment, turn erratically into the unreasonable creature that the doctors had first seen, being subject to "dangerous impulses, fugue states, tantrums, excessive, violent agitation, refusal to eat, senile decay, suicide attempts."[104]

While Codet did not think that Lucia was incurable, he did make the Joyce family into his cohorts, forever on the alert, waiting as if in ambush for further signs of senile decay. They joined the ranks of professional observers who waited for the behavioral signs that would signal the presence of some underlying pathology. From Feldkirch Joyce wrote to John Sullivan on 25 August, telling him that Lucia was better "but will need many months of surveillance."[105]

When the Joyces returned to Paris at the end of October 1932, they rented a furnished apartment on the rue Galilée, off the Champs-Elysées, and Lucia set to work trying to pick up the pieces of her life. She was pretty shaken. In Feldkirch she had come to terms with the end of her engagement to Alec Ponisovsky. Little of her former life remained. By this time, the family had asked Mathilde Wönecke to leave and had asked Myrsine Moschos to serve as Lucia's companion for three hours, from ten to one o'clock, each day. Another young French woman came in the afternoon, and Moschos apparently returned to spend the nights with Lucia, for Joyce speaks about her sleeping in the same room with Lucia and being the only early riser among the Joyce women.[106]

Companions aside, drawing was one of the few occupations left to Lucia. By 23 October, she had finished the new alphabet, and Joyce, after casting about for months, finally decided that they should accompany a Chaucer hymn to the Virgin Mary. The art critic Louis Gillet, having seen Lucia's illuminations for *Pomes Penyeach* and heard from her father about their possible future collaborations, had come up with the suggestion, for he knew of the French version of the prayer by Guillaume de Deguilleville, who had been a monk at the Abbaye de Chaalis.[107]

Being the father of Lucia's friend Dominique, Gillet shared Joyce's concern for the welfare of daughters, and he expressed his appreciation of Lucia's first venture into the art world, both in a letter he wrote to Joyce in June and later in a review for the *Revue des deux mondes*. "I admire these lettrines as a marvel of atavism," he wrote. On seeing them, "one believes in [the reappearance of] the caprices of an ancient Irish illuminator. The 'T' is particularly stunning." "You should tell me what to do," he added in the letter, wondering if other contemporary artists would have the insight "to learn from a young girl who is guided by the hand of a St. Patrick or a St. Columbo."[108] Joyce pressed the advantage by asking Gillet to write a short introduction to the book. He agreed, and Joyce began to look for a publisher.

Given all the high drama of the spring and summer, it was not such a hopeless time. In early November, Joyce invited John Holroyd-Reece, who headed the holding company that controlled the Albatross Press, to come to dinner to meet Lucia. Holroyd-Reece was, as it turned out, an expert on Italian illumination, and he liked Lucia's alphabet enough to use his influence on her behalf with the manager of Burns and Oates, a London publisher. First he suggested that Burns and Oates issue a reprint of the *Chaucer A.B.C.* with Lucia's letterforms, and then he sent Lucia a stack of books about illumination. She herself bought books on Chinese and Japanese art; her father bought her a copy of Aubrey Beardsley's *Under the Hill* as a way of encouraging her to see black and white as active design elements; and Lillian Wallace lent Lucia one of her late husband's books on letterforms.[109]

Jack Kahane was also instrumental in getting *Pomes Penyeach* reviewed. By the end of 1932, Fritz Vanderpyl, another of Paris's leading art critics who took a special interest in contemporary gravure,[110] had written a one-page notice of Lucia's lettrines. Like Gillet, he was struck by her revival and transformation of an ancient art form. In the wake of Vanderpyl's essay "Pulchritudo Antiqua Etam Nova: Les Lettrines de Lucia Joyce," Carolus Verhulst, the owner of the Servire Press in the Hague, wrote to Joyce to propose publishing still another deluxe edition of his work in combination with Lucia's illuminations.[111] This would be a commercial venture: Verhulst would finance the edition himself, and he proposed royalties of ten percent to be paid to Lucia and thirty percent to Joyce.[112] Encouraged by this unexpected turn of events, Joyce asked Paul Léon to prod Burns and Oates about the *Chaucer A.B.C.*[113]

Once more looking over the shoulders of the Joyces, Stuart Gilbert watched these developments. On 5 November 1932, he wrote in his diary, "The neurotic L seems to have quite recovered and is interested, above all, in her publicity. She has, I think, some talent, and if she worked for the glory of God, not her own, would make a little name in the world of missals, evangelaries and the like. And that is, perhaps, what she will do."[114]

Pomes Penyeach did not receive much publicity, but what it did was good. By Christmas 1932, aside from the notices of Gillet and Vanderpyl in *Revue des deux mondes* and *Mercure de France*, the *Paris midi*, the *Herald Paris Sunday*, the *Daily Telegraph*, and the *New York Herald*[115] had all carried interviews occasioned by the publication of Lucia's work. The interviewer with the *Daily Telegraph* perceptively recognized that Lucia saw the world through the lens of dance. Not only did she still identify herself as a dancer, but she explained that dance had informed the rhythms of her visual work: "Reading made a dancer of the daughter of the poet James Joyce and dance incited her to painting." She said that seeing the Book of Kells had been an event of great importance in her life and that its flowing, rhythmic calligraphy had led her to admire dance, then to learn dance, and finally to let dance guide her pen and brushes: "reading it made her love dance . . . and the rhythm of her dancing gave her another inspiration. She began to do design." She could only have been fifteen when she first saw the Book of Kells, when her mother took her to Ireland. But in the intervening years, Lois Hutton and Hélène Vanel had done their work well: Lucia recognized the rhythmic quality of all human effort and translated the impulses of one art form into the gestures of another.

The *Daily Telegraph* interviewer also noticed the extraordinary nature of the collaboration between Joyce and his daughter, casting them in the roles of Oedipus and Antigone: "It is easy to picture them: the serene old man guided by the beautiful devout young woman. But times have changed since Homer and Oedipus, and though our century is a barbaric and ignorant one, the poet is no longer unrecognized. Antigone is no longer suppliant, anxious and fearful." And it was true that there was nothing apprehensive about the execution of Lucia's drawings. In them —and especially in the cover for *The Mime of Mick, Nick and the Maggies*—we can see the lift and the glide of a dancing body. We can see that Lucia had understood the "secrets" of her teachers. She knew how to use gravity to positive effect, so that one need not fall without recovery.

But the heart often has more complexity than the hand has means. Already the seeds of discouragement were being strewn, and none of them by Lucia herself. Joyce could see some of the trouble coming, but a world that would confound Lucia's desire to express herself in art never failed to stun him. Opposition came from legal contracts about copyright, from private controversy generated by amateur psychologists, and from simple but infuriating human error. In November Joyce wrote to Harriet Weaver that "wherever I walk, I tread on thistles of envy, suspicion, jealousy, hatred, etc."[116]

One small book was out and two more were seemingly in the works. Lucia's Chaucer alphabet was finished, and when Burns and Oates received it, they agreed to publish it. They were not the firm Joyce had hoped for—he had been privately holding out for the Oxford University Press. Neither did they offer him the terms he had wanted. He would have to pay production costs of £225. It was essentially a vanity press arrangement, but at least the project was under way. The Servire book seemed close at hand; and for that book, which Joyce decided would be called *The Mime of Mick, Nick and the Maggies*, Lucia would have to design a cover and several new illuminations.

At this point Lucia enrolled in classes with Marie Laurencin. Laurencin was hardly a new face in the Joyces' world. Arthur Power remembered the evening in the late 1920s when Laurencin had asked to paint the young Lucia's portrait—they were all dining at Fouquet's—and he remained disappointed that he had never seen the finished painting.[117] As a fledgling dancer, Lucia had been Laurencin's ideal subject, for Laurencin's reputation had been made by her paintings of adolescent females—many of them dancers—with slender, fluid, undeveloped bodies, rendered in intense, undiluted color. Her images played with the seeming paradox of young womanhood as a state that combined malleability and power, suppleness and outrage. Laurencin had begun her career as an intimate in the circle surrounding Pablo Picasso and Juan Gris. For many years she had been the lover of Guillaume Apollinaire, and her life overlapped with Lucia's through her father's friends Valery Larbaud and John Quinn. (The former had been Laurencin's lover, the latter her patron.) She also knew of the Joyces through her affiliation with Nancy Cunard and the Black Sun Press and more immediately through her friendships with André Salmon, Emile Fernandez's friend, and Jules Pascin, Sandy Calder's friend.

In 1932–35 Laurencin offered classes in painting and design through the Académie du XVIe, her only venture into teaching. It was a considerable boon to Lucia, for she had overlapping interests in performance art, stage design, and book illustration. In the early 1930s in Paris Laurencin was still remembered for the costume designs she had made for Diaghilev's ballet *Les Biches* and for her ability to transform the vitality of performance into the stillness of a single image. Like Toulouse-Lautrec and Renoir, she seemed drawn to the arts as the subject of her paintings. And perhaps because of her long affiliation with Apollinaire, she understood the intimate relationship between painting and poetry. Rousseau's 1909 portrait of her with Apollinaire had been entitled *La Muse inspirant le poète*. She was well aware of the importance of women in inspiring the arts.

In 1932 Laurencin had just finished a series of illustrations for limited edition books—all of them for texts that shared her fascination with the quiet, imaginative power of young girls. For Nancy Cunard's edition of *Alice in Wonderland*, she had created six lithographs; for René Crevel's *Les Sœurs Brontë, Filles du vent*, five lithographs; and for Jacques de Lacretelle's *Luce ou l'enfance d'une courtisane*, six drawings. There had been few years since her debut as a book illustrator in 1919, with lithographs done for *Les Choses qui erroné vielles* by Louise Faure-Favier, when she had not contributed to a book project. In 1924 Albert Flament, noticing the distinctive quality of these books, had written an article about her arabesques for *La Renaissance*. Fate could not have handed Lucia a more perfectly suited teacher if she was ready for any design teacher at all.

Lucia set to work on the art for *The Mime of Mick, Nick and the Maggies*, but then one complication after another fouled things up. In January 1933, barely two weeks after two new book contracts seemed assured, Ralph Pinker wrote to say that B. W. Huebsch, who had contracted to publish *Work in Progress* in the United States when it was completed, objected to having any parts of the text published in book form before then. Paul Léon immediately wrote back to defend the publication of these fragments on the ground that they would help familiarize the public with the language of the forthcoming book.[118] But it took two months of active negotiation to work out the terms for Servire's publication of the *Mime* fragment, and only after Faber and Faber in London decided not to bring out a limited edition itself.[119]

In the interim, Joyce worried about Burns and Oates because they were slow in sending a written contract. In February he asked them to return Lucia's alphabet. Holroyd-Reece assured him that Burns and Oates would in fact publish the *A.B.C.* and that he personally would oversee its production by the same process that had been used in *Pomes Penyeach*. Somewhat placated, Joyce arranged for Chaucer's poems and Gillet's preface to the book to be sent to him, then presumed that production was under way.

Neither Lucia nor Joyce had any way of knowing the error of their faith, but as time passed, it became clear that Carolus Verhulst at the Servire Press was the only professional person they were dealing with. Jack Kahane, at the Obelisk Press, did little to encourage the subscribers of *Pomes Penyeach* to pay for their copies. Since Joyce had subsidized the edition and had sent him a thousand francs to forward to Lucia for her work, Kahane was not out of pocket—the money owed was owed to Joyce. But in November 1933, Paul Léon was still writing to Kahane to find out how much money had been collected for actual copies sold. Burns and Oates would prove no more reliable. After many delays, Joyce apparently spoke to Carolus Verhulst about the *Chaucer A.B.C.*, for in December 1933 Paul Léon wrote a second time to Holroyd-Reece, thanking him for his efforts on behalf of the Joyces but asking him once again to return Lucia's alphabet and Gillet's preface.

While this correspondence was in progress, the Servire Press had produced *The Mime of Mick, Nick and the Maggies*. Verhulst had worked out agreements with both Faber and Faber and the Gotham Book Mart in New York whereby his deluxe edition would be followed by trade editions for English and American readers. He apparently had few doubts about the saleability of the project. The first edition, copublished with Gotham, appeared late in 1933,[120] a thousand copies printed on antique Dutch paper. Lucia specially designed the initial letter, the tailpiece, and the cover. This deluxe edition was followed in 1934 by the trade editions in unspecified quantities printed from the plates made at the Servire Press. Verhulst offered to bring out the Chaucer book under a similar arrangement at no cost to the Joyces. With such technical experience and marketing intelligence behind them, father and daughter felt, understandably, on the verge of a good thing. Nino Frank, running into Lucia on the Champs-Elysées in early 1933, remarked that he "had never seen her so pretty, so gay, so strangely tranquil. We exchanged a few joking words, then I watched her move off with a lithe, startlingly light step."[121] Carelessness, plain and simple, was now to stand in the Joyces' way: Burns and Oates had lost Lucia's lettrines.

Between February 1933 and September 1934—that is, for almost one and a half years—Joyce tried doggedly to locate his daughter's work. It took more than a year for Holroyd-Reece to return Louis Gillet's preface and two photographs of Lucia.[122] Then he began an elaborate set of apologies for not sending on the lettrines. They were in his safe in Grasse; they were not in his safe in Grasse; they must be in England; no, they were apparently sent to Paris; they weren't there either; the matter was now in the hands of the Paris postmaster general. During this time Léon tried every strategy he could think of to compel a response, including the threat that if the lettrines were not sent to Holland, the Dutch editor would press Holroyd-Reece for damages. Nothing worked. Holroyd-Reece claimed that his feelings were hurt and that he would no longer write to Léon because of his "commercial, threatening attitude."[123] In August Joyce hand-wrote a letter to Holroyd-Reece himself, reviewing the dark trail of human error that had endangered the lettrines he so admired, which were "also a family document of great value to me and I regard their eventual loss in the same light as I should regard the loss of one of my own mss."[124] He noted that they had already missed the Christmas market. He could soon add that the fiasco had scotched Servire's interest in the *Chaucer A.B.C.*[125] He and Lucia did not find another publisher until Jack Kahane made another "no cost to himself" agreement for the Obelisk Press to bring the book out in 1936 in a limited edition of three hundred.[126] But by then the rationale of the project—its role in reconfiguring a *vita nuova* for Lucia—was destroyed beyond repair.

VI. UNMAKING PAIN

Years later, when Richard Ellmann came to write about Joyce's concern over Lucia's lettrines, he described him as manipulative and self-deceiving, devoting "his thoughts frantically and impotently to his daughter."[127] But this description misrepresents both the purpose and the tenor of his project. By 1933 Joyce was beginning to rethink his relationship to his children and was trying to understand his role in forging their identities. Encouraging Lucia to design books was based on a profound understanding of Lucia's nature and of what might "unmake" her pain. It demonstrated compassion and shows us a man grappling with the essential work of culture in alleviating suffering.

We might think of Joyce's labor on behalf of Lucia in terms set forth by Elaine Scarry in *The Body in Pain*. Made objects are a projection of the live body; they reciprocate the live body by containing within themselves a "material record of the nature of human sentience out of which [they] in turn [derive their] power to act on sentience and recreate it."[128] Another way to say this is that made objects are implicitly manifestations of "perceived-pain-wished-gone."[129] In the case of Joyce's collaboration with Lucia, the small books of his fantastical writing combined with, and interpreted by, the wonderful arabesques of her imagination can be seen as a form of cultural self-dramatization. They combined two gestures: Joyce's "this is for you" with his "this is by you." They coupled parental generosity with a realization that Lucia too identified herself as a maker. If the years since 1929 had been a mistaken deconstruction of Lucia's life as a creative dancer, then some form of "making" was the only activity that could recuperate that loss. As Scarry reminds us, "in work, a perception is danced; in the chair, a danced-perception is sculpted."[130] In Joyce's collaboration with Lucia's lettrines, a private wish was made sharable; in the artifact the shared wish came true.

As Joyce's letters indicate, his view of Lucia's artwork and what it could achieve changed over time. In 1932 he hoped that Lucia could work in a publishing house, transferring the skills that she had developed with him to the interpretation of the writings of other authors. He was particularly hoping that Frank Morley at Faber and Faber or Hubert Foss at the Oxford University Press might find her a "position," not just a contract or a commission.[131] Neither press made an offer. In time the possibility of her getting such a job diminished, but Joyce did not cease his labor on her behalf. In 1936 he explained his motives not in pragmatic but in existential terms. Still struggling to bring the *Chaucer A.B.C.* to fruition, he wrote to Harriet Weaver, "My idea is not to persuade her that she is a Cezanne but that on her 29th birthday . . . she may see something to persuade her that her whole past has not been a failure.

The reason I keep on trying by every means to find a solution for her case . . . is that she may not think that she is left with a blank future as well."[132] A similar motive would guide his preparation of *Storiella as She Is Syung*, published by the Corvinus Press in 1937.[133]

The pain that Joyce was able to imagine on Lucia's behalf tells us something important about his own early life as well. The extent of his empathy for the pain of being separated from the benefits of one's own work suggests anew the suffering of his own younger years when he had struggled unsuccessfully to get his writing published. The earlier "unfamous" self arose, so to speak, and tried to prevent a recurrence of that situation for his child. That his own self-realization in the pursuit of writing was in some way implicated in her unhappiness he did not yet see. Years later he was to tell his friend Jacques Mercanton that he saw a profound connection between the writing of *Finnegans Wake* and Lucia's suffering. "In that night wherein his spirit struggled," Mercanton later recalled, "in that 'wildering of the nicht' lay hidden the poignant reality of a face dearly loved. He gave me details about the mental disorder from which his daughter suffered, recounted a painful episode without pathos, in that sober and reserved manner he maintained even in moments of the most intimate sorrow. After a long silence, in a deep, low voice, beyond hope, his hand on a page of his manuscript: 'Sometimes I tell myself that when I leave this dark night, she too will be cured.' "[134]

VII. CONSPIRACY

While Joyce worked with Lucia to lay the fragile foundations of a recovered life, Stuart Gilbert noticed not only her talent and her supposed vanity but also the machinations of those who had no faith in her. Joyce knew that Lucia's way would not be smooth, for she had become outspoken and abrasive with friends and family, he told Harriet Weaver, "and as usual I am the fellow in the middle of the rain holding out both hands though whether she is right in her blunt outspokenness or not is a question my head is too addled to answer."[135] He expressed his anxiety through sleeplessness and stomach pains that Dr. Bertrand-Fontaine mistakenly ascribed to nerves,[136] but gradually he recognized the weight of opinion amassing against Lucia. He continued to see the emotional ca-

pabilities that had allowed her to triumph at the Bal Bullier. Writing to
Harriet Weaver, he referred to her as that "subtile et barbare person"—
using the same descriptive phrase which Charles de Saint-Cyr had used
to describe the force of her performance in 1929.[137]

In November 1932, Stuart Gilbert noticed a counterpart to Lucia's
new achievements: "Meanwhile, there seems to be a conspiracy on foot to
send her back to observation, i.e. a half madhouse. Her charming sister-
in-law is in the movement, also the woman doctor Bertrand-Fontaine.
The Jolases, always on the scent of neuroses, hallucination and the like,
adorers—like all good Americans—of the medicine-man, concur." In
Gilbert's dour judgment, the situation grew out of straight projection.
Those who refused to acknowledge their own excesses, hostilities, and irrational desires were the first to cast them onto others, or as he put it,
they tended to "set a thief to catch a thief." "Set a thief to trap an honest
man is no less true," he continued, "and people who themselves are
touched are quickest to see insanity in others."[138] He listened to the gossip of amateur psychologists in the circle around the magazine *transition*,
and decided that he was witnessing another witch-hunt of the type
brought to prominence in colonial Salem.

The single most influential person outside the Joyce family who was
convinced that Lucia was "insane" was Maria Jolas, and she had been of
this opinion since early in 1932. She had met the Joyces in 1927 through
her husband, Eugene, and her life was to be closely intertwined with
theirs until war drove them all from Paris and to separate destinies.

An American from Louisville, Kentucky, Maria Macdonald Jolas had
come to Paris when her New York singing teacher moved there in the
early 1920s. "I was reared when there was a good deal of sniffing and
snorting about women writers," she recalled in 1970. "All one asked of a
daughter was to look pretty and smell sweet." Singing was one of the
few pursuits that the Macdonald family had considered appropriate for
women. "When I got a scholarship to the University of Chicago, my
family laughed their heads off and it never occurred to any of us that I
should take advantage of it." She had met Eugene Jolas in 1925, and
though he was committed to experimental literature from the first, she
had understood that her own role would be that of wife and mother. "I
said to my husband when we were married, 'I promise you I'll never
write.' " Later in life, she found herself correcting proofs, writing letters,

and doing translations. "But as a rule in our circle the men did the creative work and the women kept house."[139]

She was nonetheless a woman of formidable talents and strong opinions. Reluctant to put her first daughter into the French school system, she had sought out a play school in Neuilly for her and then, when its director left, had taken it over herself and made it bilingual; by 1939 she was supervising twenty faculty members and one hundred students. While her husband delighted in Joyce's *Work in Progress*, which he thought was the most important modernist text of his time and featured repeatedly in *transition* magazine, Maria's interaction with the Joyces was more personal and based, at least with Joyce himself, on a love of vocal music. Ellmann's biography of Joyce is filled with examples of Maria Jolas's ample hospitality and quiet authority. She is described as "tall, laughing-eyed, radiating mingled good humor and efficiency,"[140] though not everyone who met her found her equally charming.

Stuart Gilbert, who considered her an egregious type of modern woman, did not like her any better than he liked Lucia. Thinking of Maria Jolas and her mother, he wrote on 19 August 1932, "Yet in the plain common sense and energy of these ladies one sees the germ of the new Americans—dogmatic, callous, egotistic. . . . Men are sweating in America and their machines are ruining the economies of the civilized countries just in order that these noisy and ignorant women may dash from Edinburgh to Salzburg, to Cannes, Paris and Copenhagen, and play the little autocrat wherever they go. . . . Even Frenchwomen," he added, perhaps thinking of his own French wife, Moune, "are infected by their restlessness—their empty heads and hearts."[141] Despite Gilbert's sense of Jolas's autocratic nature or perhaps because of it, it is easy to see how her opinions would carry weight with the Joyces; and for Joyce himself, this was precisely the problem, for on the subject of Lucia, he did not agree with her.

In an interview with Ellmann in 1953 Maria Jolas said she considered Lucia's first sign of illness to be the chair that she threw at Nora on Joyce's fiftieth birthday. "Maria tried to reason with them, convince them how sick she was," Ellmann noted, and it "took four or five years"[142] to succeed, as if it were self-evident that locking Lucia up was a form of success. She, like Paul Léon and later Harriet Weaver, was bent on restoring Joyce to the quietness and peace that would benefit his writing.

Joyce listened to the maelstrom of opinions whirling around him. In November 1932 he told Padraic and Mary Colum that "the nurse, Helen, Mrs. Jolas, Dr. Codet and Dr. Bertrand-Fontaine think that Lucia's mind is deranged."[143] But with the vocabulary of abnormality careening from voice to voice—neurosis, derangement, insanity, relapse—his most honest response to his daughter was that her situation was ambiguous and delicate; and the more he listened, the more he felt thrown back on his own judgment. When he and Giorgio went together to visit Dr. Codet, he thought their talk with him had led "to nothing."[144] He decided to act conservatively and to combine some kind of treatment of her condition—though he did not know what her "condition" was—with continued encouragement in her new interest in bookmaking. He would attend to "pathology" and to Lucia's need to find a creative place in the world at the same time. As he understood it, his project in life was now, as it had been for the last number of years in writing about the sleeping giant of *Finnegans Wake*, the resurrection of the spirit, not its burial.

By 1933 Lucia had his attention—not that she had ever been far from it—but this time in terms of her own need for autonomy, creativity, sufficient love, and support. For Joyce, to deal with the intensity of his daughter's desires and the poverty of her resources was to relive a nightmare of his own devising. It was as if the lithe "bird" girl on Sandymount Strand in the Dublin of his youth, whose "eyes had called him," had changed before his very eyes into the pitiable figure of Dilly Dedalus buying a French grammar for a trip she would never make. It was as if the "wild angel of mortal youth and beauty" who had inspired Stephen Dedalus to enter "the fair courts of life" had turned around and told him she would no longer "suffer his gaze"[145] but instead wanted to borrow his wings.

Lucia confronted Joyce with the fallacy of his own imaginative construct of "the Girl" as muse. He had assumed that being the subject and inspiration of an artist's creativity was her appropriate role, but she turned the tables and showed him what had been sacrificed in order to build his world. Where once he had wanted to "cast his shadow over the imagination of [Irish] daughters, before their squires begat upon them,"[146] Lucia made the outrageous and stunning claim that she wanted to stand in her own light. As this interior drama between father and daughter played itself out, Maria Jolas, with her "plain common sense and energy," her lifelong conviction that daughters should "look pretty and smell sweet," and her assurance that a university education was inappropriate training for her own mind, looked over the Joyces' emotional shoulders and decided that a book was more important than a girl's life.

In March 1933 Paul Léon reported to Harriet Weaver that a new doctor, Henri Vignes, was "pleased and hopeful" about Lucia's prospects. But in the same letter he made visible the web of skepticism surrounding father and daughter. When he describes Joyce as "acting single handedly against the opinion of the rest of the family,"[147] he is showing us something else important. The Joyces were living along an emotional divide that had been drawn more than twenty years earlier and that Lucia's illness was making apparent. Nora and Giorgio tended to remain as united as they had been in the years when Nora had nursed him, while Joyce would look to other women, and increasingly to himself alone, to help provide for Lucia—as he had done in Trieste, when she was newborn and he brought his sisters from Dublin to care for her.

Léon's letter also disclosed his own bias. He had already fallen into an explanatory scheme that would continue to characterize his letters to Harriet Weaver: Lucia was the scapegoat, the cause of everyone else's tension; thought was not given to the idea that she might be responding to the emotional tensions writhing around her. That distrust, duplicity, and talking behind her back—characteristics, indeed, of Léon's letters—might form an emotional register that she experienced, recorded, and in some way mirrored back to those surrounding her was not considered. Already, in Léon's eyes, her father's solicitude was a fault; already her life was a liability. "For I do think," Léon continued, "Mr. Joyce belongs to his work and unless he is able to do it he will not get well."[148] This had been Joyce's own judgment about Lucia: unless she was able to do her work, she would not get well. In Paul Léon's mind, there was only one nervous person who needed to be restored to the conditions that permit creativity. In Joyce's awakening sensibility, as he struggled to learn from this much-loved child, there were two.

So it was arranged that, along with her design classes with Marie Laurencin, and along with a fur coat that Joyce thought would please her ("my wish for you is warmth and beauty"), Lucia would take injections of sea water as prescribed by Dr. Vignes. His opinion, according to

Léon, was that Lucia had "ruined her nervous system by five years dancing strain something which [Joyce] always combated and tried to discourage as far as he could while recognizing her great talent."[149] The injections had no discernible effect one way or another, but in April 1933 Joyce became dejected. Half of his plan seemed not to be working. The ever diligent Léon reported to Harriet Weaver that while Lucia was well enough, she had stopped going to her Laurencin classes.[150] The substitution of the visual arts for dancing was not giving her a renewed sense of vocation. It must have been evident to all of them that new roots could not be put down so quickly. Lucia remained unfocused—but then in 1933 none of them had any fixed plans or any fixed place to live.

Nora and Joyce did not invest in an unfurnished flat and unpack their furniture until February 1935.[151] In the spring of 1933, Joyce wrote first to Valery Larbaud and then to Carola Giedion-Welcker asking if their residences would be free for his family to borrow during the summer, and then in May he and Nora took Lucia with them to Zurich, where Joyce was to have another eye examination with Dr. Vogt. For the time being, Dr. Vignes was left behind and, along with him, one of the most puzzling moves in the Joyces' many attempts to help Lucia. Dr. Vignes was not a nerve specialist but an obstetrician/gynecologist.

There is no question that Vignes was a distinguished man. He had begun his career in 1903 as an *externe des hôpitaux de Paris* and had been granted his medical doctorate in July 1914. By 1919 he had risen to be head of the faculty clinic in Paris and the following year he was named head of obstetrics for all Paris hospitals. In 1933, when he was consulted about Lucia, he was head of obstetrics at La Charité. He was a member of many learned societies who held military titles and medals of distinction, being honored for a distinguished career in public service and recognized for his pioneering work in obstetrics, especially in problems during pregnancy and anomalies of birth, about which he wrote many books. Some of their titles are *Obstetrical Physiology, Normal and Pathological* (1923); *The Hygiene of Pregnancy* (1942); *Maladies of Pregnant Women* (1948); and *The Sufferings of Childbirth* (1951). In 1933, the year he treated Lucia, his two books *The Duration of Pregnancy and Its Anomalies* and *Premature Babies* were published. Nowhere in this long career and in the records of his extraordinary life as a doctor and writer does there appear a trace of interest in the mental health of young unmarried women.

According to financial records in the Paul Léon papers in Dublin, Lucia was again in Dr. Vignes's care in December 1933, but we don't know why. We find isolated glimpses of her in various letters written in December. She had designed the Christmas cards the Joyces sent to their friends; Joyce reported to Stanislaus that "Lucia is much better (touching wood) in excellent health but as *stramba* [extravagant] as a March Hare and as proud as ever she can be. But devil a hapworth else that I can see after ten doctors."[152] Amid other family chat—Nora has made four plum puddings—he cautioned his brother, "Don't talk to her either about dancing or diseases. She is beginning to forget about both, thank the Lord."[153] Then Ellmann's biography states that "Lucia . . . ran away from home in January 1934" and was "persuaded to return only by threats of police intervention."[154] But Ellmann provides no notes or corroborative evidence for this story, and in fact the scant evidence suggests another story altogether.

From 2 January through 8 January 1934, various financial records tell us that Lucia was at the Château de Suresnes, at 10 quai Gallieni.[155] From these two circumstances—the choice of Dr. Vignes and a week-long sojourn in Suresnes—it is possible to construct a totally speculative scenario that at least accords with the facts. In the spring of 1933 and then again at the turn of the years 1933–34, Lucia was a young woman under the care of an obstetrician/gynecologist, and in January 1934 she was sent away for seven days. If we connect these circumstances with Dominique Maroger's memory that Lucia stopped dancing "on account of an accident of health"[156] and with Lucia's own memory that "it was dangerous for me to become pregnant. . . . And I was not able to have the child,"[157] we might have a ghost story that underlies and explains both the silences in the available record and the inconsistencies in the account that Ellmann constructed. How can one explain the seemingly unmotivated suffering of a talented young woman who, though healthy, strong, and unafraid of sex, could neither dance nor marry? The consequences of a cover-up, so to speak, would have to have been immense. One can see that a young woman undergoing the physiological and emotional changes brought on by pregnancy and its early and secret termination would have ample reason to be distraught. But we shall probably never know what really happened. And it is a subject on which the Joyces and their friends—all of them loquacious, argumentative people in other circumstances—agreed in silence.

Lucia's story was complex and tangled even without gynecological complications, for in the summer of 1933 she had thrown another tantrum. She and Nora had stayed in Zurich with Joyce from late May until early July while Joyce weighed the pros and cons of further eye surgery and worked on the children's homework lesson in *Work in Progress*. Then they all went off to the Hôtel Savoie in Evian-les-Bains, a break that was intended to soothe their nerves. On their return, Lucia staged another one of her grand scenes of protest in the train station at Zurich. This time, because they were in Switzerland, her parents took her to the place where modern Europe focused the most attention on schizophrenia as a disease. They took her to the Burghölzli.[158]

10

PLAYING WITH FIRE
ZURICH AND GENEVA 1933-35

I. CLASSIFYING AND CONSTRAINING

When Lucia went to the Burghölzli Poliklinik on 19 July 1933, it was an institution in transition. Directed by Dr. Hans Wolfgang Maier, who had been a medical student under Eugen Bleuler, it was at the cutting edge of research on schizophrenia and what was then known as the "moral treatment" of mental patients. But in the minds of ordinary people, it was still what it had been for many long years: an insane asylum, a house of lunacy, a place of madness, of screaming and despair.[1]

Lucia went there only for a consultation, a diagnosis, and a referral. Since in Maier's judgment Lucia was "not lunatic but markedly neurotic,"[2] he suggested that the Joyces take her to Les Rives de Prangins, outside Geneva in the town of Nyon. Prangins was another of the twenty-eight hospitals that the Swiss maintained for the care of people with mental and spiritual problems. Though his care of Lucia was fleeting—a judgment, a suggestion—Maier was a pivotal figure in Lucia's life, for it was through him that she was handed into the care of other doctors who had been trained by Bleuler.[3] He was, consequently, responsible for whatever consistency of diagnosis Lucia received.

How would Maier have looked at Lucia? What could he do for her? Although his colleagues often considered Maier a "weak" scientist, he was a superb administrator, famous for redesigning the therapeutic

Lucia Joyce's passport photo, circa 1932. (Courtesy of the Beinecke Rare Books and Manuscript
Library, Yale University)

structures that surrounded and "contained" mental patients in central Europe during the early years of the twentieth century. Directing the Burghölzli at a time of stunning transitions, he made available a wide variety of treatments to his patients—from sleeping cures to insulin injections and electric shock therapy. He rejected none of the approaches then considered credible, and he supported young doctors who wanted to explore the new possibilities offered by Freudian psychoanalysis.

He was following the example of his predecessors Eugen Bleuler and August Forel, and his senior colleague, Carl Gustav Jung. Maier had begun his work at the Poliklinik at Burghölzli in 1905 as an assistant doctor. In 1909, when Jung left the clinic, Maier was promoted and given unusually heavy responsibilities, since his boss, Bleuler, wanted to work on his textbook on psychiatry and left his protégé in charge of day-to-day operations. One of Maier's most important duties during this time was examining young women who had unwanted pregnancies in order to make recommendations about abortions. His criteria for deciding what to do were used for the next sixty years in Switzerland.[4]

Maier remained chief physician of the Poliklinik until 1927, when he was selected to succeed Bleuler as director, but he had to fight for his position. Many other candidates were more highly esteemed as researchers; indeed, Maier's only significant publication at the time was a book on cocaine addiction (1928). But in the end the selection committee opted for continuity. Since Maier had been trained so thoroughly by Bleuler, they thought he would carry forward his mentor's methods of working. They were correct. Maier never did become a prolific writer or an original thinker. The few essays that he did write on psychiatry in his early years were never published, and those that he delivered at Freudian psychiatric congresses were apparently considered so controversial that he was asked to leave the society.[5] Nonetheless, Maier knew Burghölzli with a thoroughness that none of the other contenders could rival, and he had the endorsement of Bleuler, who, having defended Maier against the psychoanalytic society in 1911, continued to support him as an administrator. In favoring his own disciple, Bleuler was, in effect, ensuring the future of his own diagnostic categories.

Given these circumstances, we can assume that when Lucia came to the Burghölzli in 1933, she was seen in the light of Bleuler's research on dementia praecox. His book, first published in 1911 as *Dementia Praecox or the Group of Schizophrenias*, had attempted to clarify Emil Kraepelin's taxonomy of mental illnesses so that physicians would be able to distinguish between diseases with good and bad prognoses. That Maier found Lucia to be "neurotic" but definitely "not lunatic" is an interesting sign, for if anyone in Europe had been trained to recognize schizophrenia at that time, it would have been Bleuler and his associates.

What did people mean by the term *schizophrenia* in the 1930s? Bleuler's textbook is notable for its carefulness, its tentativeness, and its intellectual modesty. "It must be emphasized," he wrote, "that the experiences of one or two decades and of relatively few observers [do] not suffice to enable us to voice definite opinions on every aspect of this disease."[6] Like his predecessors Emil Kraepelin and Karl Kahlbaum, Bleuler adopted the view that schizophrenia was an organic disease whose somatic origin had not yet been discovered. Hence even as he carefully aligned symptoms and grouped them into primary and secondary characteristics, he regarded himself as making, in the words of Karl Jaspers, "stopgaps until the time when experiment, microscope and the test tube will have rendered everything accessible to objective investigations."[7] In theory, the primary symptoms of the disease were caused by bodily processes, while the secondary symptoms were "partly psychological functions under changing conditions and partly the results of more or less successful attempts to adapt to the primary disorders."[8] Convinced that he was really looking for an infection or a kind of poisoning, Bleuler maintained that life events, experiences, or conflicts might spark off the symptoms but were not the disease itself. "Where no substitutes could be found for them, they [symptoms] are being employed in full awareness of the fact that they are merely temporary formulations, not diagnoses." Given that psychic events were only signs pointing to some unknown organic origin, Bleuler was not surprised that physicians were often vague and arbitrary in their diagnoses. "What one observer considers as important, another may hardly notice. . . . Indeed, it happens frequently that one physician does not note a symptom which another finds immediately striking."[9]

When, after years of consultations and conflicting diagnoses of Lucia's condition, Joyce spoke of her as having "one of the most elusive diseases known to men and unknown to medicine,"[10] he was exactly right. One wonders if knowing Bleuler's candid assessment of the clinical picture might have mitigated his despair. For Bleuler thought that "with many patients, the number of diagnoses made equals the number of institutions they have been to." In his judgment, the diagnostic situation was dire and was likely to remain so until some uniformity in classification was accepted:

> It is obvious that every author of a textbook was obliged, above all, to construct his own system of classification since the systems established by his predecessors were useless to his way of thinking and to his method of observation.
>
> Even within the very same school, one physician defined as paranoia what another terms a melancholia. The in-between forms, the atypical cases, had to be fitted in somewhere, if need be forcibly. Situations as the following are rather common: In a certain hospital there would be a big pot, labeled "dementia." Now along comes a new physician who enlarges the pot standing alongside the other one, and labels the second pot, "paranoia." He then carefully proceeds to seize the old inmates of the institution by some vestige of a delusion and puts them, one by one, in his new pot—and in doing this believes that he is correcting the errors of his predecessors.[11]

With such a chaos of theory around them, the Joyces had received a great blessing. Lucia could not have chosen a better location for her temper tantrum than the Zurich railway station. Whatever help there could be in naming her problem in 1933 was to be had in the quiet discipleship of Hans Wolfgang Maier, who still adhered to his teacher's diagnostic categories.

What he could do to help Lucia feel better or understand her situation more clearly is another question. Even Bleuler had not intended his systematic description of symptoms to serve the interest of the patient in any direct way. He was trying to codify behaviors as a way of laying the foundation for further physiological research. The people who would benefit from his work were not the ones whose lives stood so fragilely exposed to his classifying eye, but people living in some future time whose problems would be expertly recognized.

For Bleuler the essential issue posed by the patients he called schizophrenic was the disturbance of reason.[12] He considered the absence of the ability to make reasonable associations to be the central psychological manifestation of disease. The second most important index of disease was emotional deterioration. Such patients might lack affect; they might seem indifferent to their circumstances or respond to situations with inappropriate emotions. They might suffer uncontrollable mood swings, irritability, or fury. Bleuler's catalog of emotional deviance reads rather like a list of unacceptable social behaviors, and one can immediately see the possible diagnostic confusions, for both lack and excess of affect supposedly indicated the same underlying pathology. Extrapolating from these two basic anomalies, Bleuler observed that any function that resulted from the coordination of thinking and feeling—attention, intelligence, will power, and action—would also be altered by schizophrenia. Of these, he considered autism the most common. He had observed patients who detached themselves from reality, giving such predominance to the inner life that their outer aspect could be described only as a stupor.[13] They might do this because their feelings were so powerful that they had to avoid everything that might arouse their emotions, or because their fantasy worlds were more compelling than their surroundings. If they were so engaged with a delusional interior life, they might seem to others to lack attention, will power, goals, or initiative. In none of his patients, however, did Bleuler find disturbances of perception, orientation, or memory.[14]

Bleuler's descriptive abilities were exceptionally good. He was able to conjure for contemplation the most varied behaviors, and for this very reason his chapter on diagnosis is unsettling. For having set out the full array of possible symptoms, he remarks, "Schizophrenic symptoms are not necessarily present all the time. In no other mental disease is it so uncertain whether or not a specific symptom will be present at any given moment."[15] And of the many symptoms that might be observed, few belonged solely to schizophrenia. "The systematic splitting, with reference to personality, for example, may be found in many other psychotic conditions; in hysteria they are even more marked than in schizophrenia. . . . Stupor . . . also occurs in organic brain diseases, in manic-depressive psychosis, epilepsy, and hysteria."[16] Bleuler added that any of these symptoms could be produced intentionally. A patient could give false answers on purpose or feign illness, so that even the distinction between conscious and unconscious symptoms could not be assumed: "Schizophrenia cannot easily be distinguished from malingering since a definite boundary between conscious and unconscious symptoms does not exist in this disease anymore than in hysteria."[17] A conscious withdrawal from surroundings might easily be mistaken for lack of interest, or hostile attitudes toward the environment might give the impression of a false conception of the environment.[18]

If one could not be sure that a given symptom identified schizophrenia beyond doubt, then one certainly could not make an unerring prediction about the course of the disease. "We have to be content," he cautioned, "with a diagnosis of the extent of the deterioration that has already taken place; that is, we have to determine how far the 'incurable' deterioration has already gone and how many of the acute symptoms may be expected to disappear."[19]

This was the best that psychiatry could do for Lucia in 1933. It could classify and it could constrain without knowing what could ameliorate her suffering or what its outcome would be. Hans Wolfgang Maier, with his patient observation according to the most thoughtful classification system then in existence, could only suggest to the Joyces that Lucia might benefit from spending some time away from them. He thought she was *not* schizophrenic; he saw no signs of psychosis.

Consequently he knew that his plan of action was only a stopgap measure for a small group of adults who were desperately unhappy in one another's company. Les Rives de Prangins, outside Geneva, he suggested to the Joyces, was a very well run establishment under the direction of Oscar Forel. The Joyces could rest secure with Lucia in his hands. On Maier's recommendation, they all went to Geneva, where Lucia was admitted to Prangins while her anxious and weary parents waited to see what would happen.

II. PRANGINS: A HOUSE OF SCREAMING AND DESPAIR

And so Lucia went to see yet another well-meaning doctor, one whom she would remember, even in middle age, as a man she had a huge crush on.[20] Oscar Forel, whom Maier had recommended so highly, was the son of another physician of renown, August Forel, who had written influentially about issues raised by contemporary sexuality.[21] The son was also a writer of distinction, his most original contribution to psychiatry being two books about the care of mental and "nervous" patients. He had pioneered in the reform of asylums and in the training of service personnel.

With the newly emerging understanding of mental illness, one could anticipate treatments that might prove therapeutic in themselves. Given the options for people in Lucia's position whose families were determined to help them, there could have been no better place for her to stay.

She arrived at Prangins on 30 July 1933 and stayed until 4 August, left, returned on 7 and 8 August, and then remained away until 10 February 1934, when her parents decided she should be institutionalized again.[22] Contrary to Dr. Maier's judgment just eleven days before, the admissions officer at Prangins thought Lucia might be schizophrenic with "pithiatic elements," but capable of being cured by persuasion and suggestion.[23] And with this, he directed her into an institution that, like the Burghölzli, prided itself on being at the forefront of caring for people suffering from emotional and spiritual problems. But the Joyces reckoned without Lucia's response to incarceration. Whatever she saw or experienced in her first four days sent her back into the arms of her family.

Like the previous autumn in Paris, the autumn of 1933 was filled with unforeseen difficulties for Lucia. The year before she had had to deal with her father's illnesses, her mother's frayed resentment, and the hostility she aroused by her bluntness. Now the family would prove that none of them knew how to change the dynamic of their life together. They stumbled on until news of Judge John M. Woolsey's favorable ruling in the *Ulysses* obscenity trial in the United States reached them in December. *Ulysses* was finally going to be published in America. As her father's friends called to congratulate him, Lucia cut the telephone wires and then cut them again.[24] The commotion seemed to cast her back into the same despondency that had afflicted her on Joyce's fiftieth-birthday celebration.

Cutting the telephone line was a poor, rash action, but it also had a kind of perverse expressive meaning. Few actions could have spoken so eloquently about the faulty lines of communication in the Joyce world. And few gestures could remind us better of the symbolic violence of Joyce's decision in 1931 to move his family from the square Robiac apartment, cutting off service to the telephone line that was the foundation of Lucia's first business venture: "Kathleen Neel, Lucia Joyce. Physical Training . . . Ségur 95-20." One kind of violation led to another, but only the daughter's pantomime was noticed and rebuked.

When Lucia slapped her mother on 2 February 1934, repeating the hostile gesture that had led her to be institutionalized two years before, the other Joyces reiterated their accustomed roles as well. They sent her away. This time Giorgio apparently made his father promise not to remove Lucia from the asylum without first consulting him. Joyce let himself be persuaded that for Lucia to spend time away from the tensions of their Paris household would do her good. He engaged a nurse, Pauline Browne, to take Lucia back to Prangins.[25] This time she had seven months of asylum life, and by the end of it she had internalized the meaning of her mother and brother's conduct. "I will never be able to live in a big city," she conceded, "but we could try and if I do not behave you can give me up."[26] She knew she was now a disposable person.

Despite Lucia's hatred of Prangins, it was a well-run place and Oscar Forel a distinguished psychiatrist. He was then a *privat dosent de psychiatrie* and also on the faculty at the University of Geneva. In collaboration with Walter Morganthaler, he had written two books that revolutionized the nature of mental health care in Switzerland in the 1920s and 1930s. We can get the flavor of Lucia's experience at Prangins by seeing how her caretakers understood what they were doing with her.

The first thing they were doing was classifying. Forel and Morganthaler's first book, *The Treatment of Nervous and Mental Patients*, first published in 1926, was designed for people in the health care professions, for parents, and for anyone in the general public who wanted to learn more about mental illness. They used Bleuler's classification scheme, and their recommendations included treatments for congenital defects, organic diseases, senility, brain injury, substance abuse ("poisoning"), endogenous psychoses, and borderline areas where behavior might be understood as an adaptation to other illnesses.

Forel and Morganthaler's second book, a statistical study of asylum patients from 1927 to 1932, summarized the results of their own complete redesign of the curriculum for training mental health workers, their installation of a program that offered a degree only to those who passed a standardized examination. In six years, they had modified the whole orientation of nurses, changing them from custodians to active participants in a health care team. Their daily presence among patients gave them opportunities to observe and to interact that doctors did not have. Rather than act simply as guardians, whose function was to maintain order, they were to become extensions of the doctors' eyes, watching everywhere for signs of illness that might otherwise go unnoticed.[27]

This training meant that a patient could be subjected to almost around-the-clock supervision. Doctors could count on uniform, rational procedures to monitor patients' entry into the asylum, their daily routines, and the responses they had to their experiences. How did Lucia look after her clothes? How did she care for her body? What did she eat? How often did she bathe? Did she have a positive outlook? Did she maintain a consistent weight? What did she think of her doctor? Almost no aspect of her existence was ignored.

But primarily the nurses were taught to regard the body as a text whose meaning could be deduced from outward signs. Forel and Morganthaler carefully explained the terms of their semiology. Distinctions were made among sensations, feelings, perceptions, comprehension, and imagination, between memory and thought, between intelligence and fantasy, between attention span and expression, between drives and instincts. Every symptom was used to decipher the book of sicknesses, to distinguish among all possible causes of malaise. Some patients had congenital disturbances; some had organic disturbances. Some were senile; some had suffered brain injuries. Still others were living with the deleterious effects of alcohol, morphine, or cocaine addiction. The asylum was a place to house epileptics and those who, like Lucia, were thought to have endogenous psychoses like schizophrenia and manic-depressive disease. But above all the nurses were to observe—accurately, faithfully, indeed vocationally. In the opening section of their textbook, Forel and Morgenthaler asked them to consider the nature of their calling, for not everyone possessed the keen wit and unobtrusive demeanor that marked the talented watcher of the night.

One passage in their first book, entitled "Observation and Notification," emphasizes, "To be able to observe correctly and to notify correctly is one of the chief assignments of the attendants and nurses."[28] Attendants were decisive in providing physicians with accurate materials. If you were withdrawn or daydreaming, you couldn't become a good observer, for you had to be sensitive to many impressions that might at the time seem unimportant. You had to be selective and able to learn from experiences with hundreds of patients. Which details were of primary

importance and which were subsidiary? You also had to be mindful of
the distinction between clear observation and idle gossip. Your job was to
provide information and not to engage in premature, unprofessional
judgments.

Forel's instructions remind anyone with the least penchant for solitude or privacy of the spirit of Mephistopheles standing behind the
shoulder of Faust. You must be mindful of the importance of first impressions, he told his staff. From the very first moment you must attempt
to discern if the sick person has any proclivities to which you must pay
special attention. Is she in danger of escaping, hurting others, or harming
herself? How does she react when approached? Does she care for her
personal needs in a well-regulated way? Does she have any physical ail-
ments? Does she have any infections? How does the patient orient herself in the new environment? What makes an impression on her and
what not? What does she inquire about first, what later on?[29]

> One must get to know the patient better . . . The first impression must be
> deepened, enlarged, corrected; one must try to bore into the patient's inner
> life. One who is capable of empathy and who has long experience will succeed
> in approaching the actual being of the patient. Is he or she apathetic by na-
> ture? Is he or she sunk in deep self-absorption? Is he or she unruly, angry, sen-
> sitive, in need of love, distrustful?[30]

The attendant was to persevere so as to be able to predict what would
upset the patient or bring relief. All of this was to be accomplished, if
possible, without the patient's knowing that any such inquiry was under
way.

But Lucia was not deceived. By the following year, when her parents
urged her to consult Carl Gustav Jung, she could recognize these ploys
for what they were: the attempts of men of science to "get hold of my
soul."[31] She knew what had been happening to her.

Oscar Forel also attempted to restore order to people whose lives
were obviously disturbed. He wanted the institution to be a place where
patients could relate to other people without fear of being hurt or
ridiculed. No matter what the provocation, psychiatric nurses were to respond calmly, never taking belligerence to heart but regarding it always
as a sign of illness. They were to try to replace faulty emotional habits
with firmness and discipline. In effect, the asylum reduced each inmate

to the status of a child and tried to give him or her a new start in life. This goal explains why Lucia had to work every day. Forel believed that an orderly schedule and assigned tasks would contribute to a more organized interior life. She would school herself in moderation and responsibility with rakes and hoes, with needle and thread, and with carefully kept hours.[32]

It is no wonder that Joyce and Nora so often felt stigmatized in the eyes of the psychiatric profession. In a letter to Harriet Weaver in September 1933, Paul Léon reiterated Joyce's dismay: "Every time I meet him some new origin of her condition has been discovered the only thing which does not vary is the fact that he is the culprit."[33] Whatever Léon may have thought when he reported this, Joyce was not begging for sympathy. He, like his daughter, had assessed his assessors correctly. In the eyes of the medical profession, he and Nora were responsible for the unruly psyche of their child, and Lucia's prospects hinged on her ability to forsake previous habits and submit to a complete overhaul of her emotions and conduct.

We do not know what Lucia herself wanted. While Joyce wrote patiently to his daughter as if she were spending a holiday at a pleasant resort—telling her of dance performances he had seen, talking of music, typewriters, new clothing—Lucia was being held in solitary seclusion, often under physical restraint. No surface gentility could disguise the penitential nature of her exile. And no landscaping or civilized custom could hide the fact that the caretakers at Prangins had been trained to handle violence as well as hygiene. Forel's handbook contained detailed and explicit instructions for dealing with unruly inmates. (In the 1950s, when he updated it, psychotropic drugs would tranquilize them, but Lucia entered Prangins just before these drugs became available.) Restraint took the form of physical intervention. Two or three men would hold and carry them, force them to wear leather mittens, put them in straitjackets, make them bathe for five to six hours at a time, and keep them in solitary confinement.

The surviving reports that Joyce and Nora received from Prangins, like Lucia's letters, offer isolated glimpses of fury and desperation laced with purposeful activity. But we know that she made a close friend at Prangins, someone whom her parents described as "some undesirable gent . . . who either lives in Dublin or London."[34] Asylum authorities disapproved of romances between "ill" people and separated them. Lucia became upset; they argued that she would soon get over him, but she began to experience states that her doctors described as "pseudo-hallucinative dissociations" of mind.[35] They tried a *Pyrifekur*—cure through an induced fever—that she detested and struggled against. She tried to escape several times and once succeeded in getting outside the institution's grounds and as far as the French border, where "she tried to seek refuge in a peasant hut, intending to cross the border next day, but was found and brought back."[36] She eventually found a measure of peace when her therapy began to include sports.[37] But whether Lucia languished because of disease, because she was violently removed from everything that was meaningful to her, or because she loathed solitary confinement or the violence that constrained her body is a question that cannot be answered easily. It was Paul Léon's view, and apparently Joyce's, that asylums were places that dismantled the self rather than rebuilt it; and when Joyce and Nora went to pick up Lucia seven months later, in September 1934, his worst fears were confirmed.

In the meanwhile back in Paris, Léon reported on 11 March to Harriet Weaver that Lucia's internment had not had a simple and beneficial effect on Joyce:

> But as far as he is concerned primarily the important event in his private life is the departure of Miss Joyce to the Sanatorium in Nyon. This affects him, so it seems to me, in two divergent directions. This departure has first of all created the feeling of emptiness in the house and this is quite understandable after having been for the last three years in the center of all his worries and of daily if not hourly thought and reflection. Miss Joyce even while absent causes enervation which is perhaps the more tantalizing as she is not there and communication with her or even with the doctors are both scarce and merely medical in character.[38]

Léon hastened to add that the medical news that they had received was guardedly optimistic, in spite of Lucia's attempt to run away, and that her doctors seemed "to be satisfied with the first month of her stay." For him as for Harriet Weaver, Lucia seemed to be a management problem, and his attention to what should be done about her had to do primarily with the problem of how *Work in Progress* could most reasonably progress.

The second influence of this departure and the consequent feeling of emptiness in the house is to my mind even of greater importance. Mr. Joyce's
thought actuated by this feeling has turned to his work and the last three years
of unceasing worry about Miss Joyce, which have caused him almost to abandon his work. It is remarkable that he was even able to accomplish what he
did. . . . But what is obvious is that owing to whatever influences it may have
been he has neglected that part of his work. . . . [H]is daughter's health . . .
should be kept in as satisfactory circumstances as possible though even mate-
rially it involves a great sacrifice. Mr. Joyce will never be calm unless he
knows his daughter is taken good care of even be it at the sacrifice (as he is doing now) of 7,000 francs monthly.[39]

When Joyce first began to write to Lucia at Prangins, he had thought
her worst problems there were melancholy and passivity. In June he had
written, "Why do you always sit at the window? No doubt it makes a
pretty picture but a girl walking in the fields also makes a pretty picture."[40] His letter is as interesting for its tacit presumption that, whether
sitting or walking, Lucia would experience herself as being observed, as
for its explicit advice.

When he and Nora finally returned to Geneva to see her at the end of
August 1934, Lucia was distraught with grief and beside herself with the
joy of being reunited with her parents. Although the Joyces had planned
to sneak into the clinic for a private talk with Dr. Forel before seeing her,
Lucia had learned of their arrival and fell upon them in tears. "Babbo!"
"Mama!" For seven months she had been held, as Joyce was to describe it
to Carola Giedion-Welcker on 2 September, "under restraint, that is, her
windows are barred, and she is always *surveillée*."[41] Joyce was appalled at
the meager young woman who stood before him, a mere ghost of her
former self.

Joyce's discussions with Dr. Forel did little to alleviate his distress at
the condition of his child. The doctor had no diagnosis to offer him.
Carola Giedion-Welcker, Frank Budgen, and Giorgio all received versions of the same report: Forel said he could not make a diagnosis; "he
could not sign his name to a conclusive statement about her. . . . The only
hold she seems to have on life is her affection for us. . . . I feel if she stays
there she will simply fade out."[42] Separated purposefully from the one
friend she had made at Prangins, Lucia was found lacking in "affect."[43]
Divided from whatever world she had possessed before she was institu-

tionalized, she was noticed to be unconnected to life. In Joyce's eyes, seven months at Prangins had eroded her already fragile sense of self.

III. FIREBIRD

Dr. Forel tried to mitigate the Joyces' devastation by telling them about a physical abnormality in Lucia that puzzled him. She had too many leuko-cytes or white blood cells, a circumstance that seemed to indicate some kind of lingering infection that they could not find. Though this worried Joyce, his first order of business was to get her out of Prangins altogether. Forel suggested a colleague in Geneva, a Dr. Loy, who would care for Lu-cia under a *cure libre*, that is, without physical restraint. But before this transfer could be effected, Lucia staged her most incendiary performance. She set fire to the tablecloth in her solitary confinement room.[44]

The immediate and practical consequence of this startling behavior was to close the doors of Dr. Loy's clinic. Few doctors want to offer free-dom to a woman whose irrationality takes a dangerous form. But we should notice that Lucia waited to stage her protest until her father was among its witnesses and that she chose to make a Ring of Fire, as if she were enacting a scene from the Wagner operas of which she was so fond. When Joyce asked her about her "prank," she said that she had used the fire to show her need to get out of the confinement room, reasoning that she had created a circumstance in which the door would be opened. It was as if she had decided to personify the "Prankquean," one of the char-acters in her father's *Work in Progress*, who "lit up and fireland was ablaze. And spoke she to the dour" (*FW* 21.15–17). She later remarked that fire was red and so was her father's face. The blaze of genius, the fires of consciousness, the heat kindled by a Lucifer ("Lausafire" [*FW* 621.03]), the father a devil, the room a space that she occupied in a pas-sionate but dark and unviable emotional economy, a misdirected love, a preoccupation that she could neither accept nor escape—her act res-onates with manifold symbolic qualities. She seemed to speak with the "dancetongues of the woodfires" (*FW* 404.06). But in the report from the clinic, the fire was a cryptic gesture about which the patient refused to speak,[45] and which for that very reason became the focus of further in-tense inquiry.

Lucia's dilemma was her dependence upon the father whose love confined her in the unhappy and solitary rooms of consciousness. Whatever dark recrimination he read in his daughter's behavior, Joyce now chose to deal with the problem he could address immediately: Lucia's physical condition. Remembering that Frank Budgen had once spoken to him about a friend who had been treated for a reduction of white blood cells, he wrote asking about the condition and the doctor who had treated it. The friend, Fritz Fleiner, put him in touch with Dr. Otto Naegeli, a blood specialist in Zurich. And once he was in Zurich, Joyce decided, after years of resistance, to take Maria Jolas's suggestion and to consult Dr. Carl Gustav Jung.

IV. THE BIG MATERIALISTIC DOCTOR JUNG

The Zurich to which Lucia Joyce returned in the fall of 1934 was very different from the city that had sheltered her as a child during the Great War. Once the site of youthful friendship and awakening aspiration, it was now the site of further dreary probing. What was wrong with her? Why did she play with fire? What made her so angry? She came stigmatized, and she left, according to her new doctors, with no deeper insight into her own spirit. Neither Maier, who examined her again, nor Jung was able to establish a therapeutic relationship with her. In the absence of such rapport, Maier now called her "catatonic," and Jung conceded that he could think of nothing to lessen her suffering. To one doctor, she was withdrawn and unreachable because of her apparent self-absorption; to the other, the lack of "transference" signaled the limit of his art. The one doctor categorized her according to his belief about the body's relation to behavior; the other was the first to practice analytic psychology on her. Jung's task was to ask serious and systematic questions about the psychogenesis of Lucia's problems. To each of them, Lucia responded with an antagonism that her father recognized as characteristic. He and Léon admitted in the *Anamnese* that they submitted to the Burghölzli that she had "a great aversion to all doctors and wants only to be with her father, to leave with him, to show the doctors that the two of them are stronger than medical authority."

The first order of business was, however, Lucia's blood count. To this end, the Joyces hoped that Dr. Otto Naegeli, then director of medicine at the Clinic of the University of Zurich, could help them distinguish symptoms that had an organic origin from psychogenic ones. Their hope was well founded, for Dr. Naegeli had made his reputation by helping physicians make just such distinctions. He had written a manual that described the differences among patients suffering from the aftereffects of traumas, from lingering fright, from hysteria, or from inborn nervousness.[46] His diagnosis of Lucia has been lost or destroyed, so all we can know is that he first saw her on 22 September 1934 and continued to treat her until March 1935, months after she had stopped having psychoanalytic sessions with Jung.[47]

Only within the immediate family did the Joyces admit to what they feared this consultation would produce: They thought that Lucia had syphilis. To Giorgio, Joyce wrote,

> Try to understand what I am going to say and don't get it all wrong. Lucia has constant leukocytes . . . a superabundance of white blood corpostles [sic] . . . Hers is not a disease at all but a symptom. He says that white corpscles [sic] among other things are the police of the body . . . Lucia's blood is always over policed. They say, therefore, there must be a form of infection. Nothing is absolutely sure . . . [but] the chances are 9 to 1 against syphilis. . . . Physically her case is as baffling as it is psychologically.[48]

Lucia herself was preoccupied with the physical aspects of her case, and she considered her appointments with Jung to be fruitless. Cary Baynes, whom Jung engaged to serve as a companion to Lucia during her months of treatment with him, remembered that Lucia bridled at Jung's insistence on remembering dreams. Such a doctor could do nothing for her, she said, "because my trouble is somewhere in the body."[49] Baynes, trained at the Johns Hopkins Medical School, was impressed that Lucia asked about leukocytes by their proper name, and Baynes talked to her about their function, which was to stave off local infections like appendicitis. "But," she assured Lucia, "you have no such place like that so they do not know why you should have so many of these cells."[50]

Baynes's diary of the several months she spent in Lucia's company is one of the few documents in which Lucia's own speech and self-understanding survive, and aside from this immense importance, it provides the clearest circumstantial evidence that Lucia did not in fact have syphilis. The absence of Naegeli's medical report has left some Joyceans free to speculate that Lucia's erratic behavior might be explained as paresis, a form of neurosyphilis that leads to insanity.[51] But Baynes, who knew explicitly that Lucia had been undergoing blood tests for syphilis,[52] assured her that this was not so.[53] And had Naegeli discovered syphilis, there would have been no reason to lie to Lucia about it.[54]

We are left with another dimension of the issue, the fear of syphilis evidenced in the exchange between Joyce and Giorgio, equaled only by Lucia's own worry that she had contracted the disease. By mid-December, Baynes noted that she thought "the hammering" she had given Lucia about the probity of discussing bodily functions was beginning to take effect, and that Lucia had broached the subject with her father: "And then she told him [Joyce] that she had syphilis . . . explain[ing] to him that he was not to think she thought she had inherited it from him—it was her own fault that she had it."[55] Joyce was equally quick to reassure Lucia that she had been very carefully examined for it, but she was not convinced.

Baynes tried everything she could think of to gain Lucia's confidence. There was nothing shameful about discussing the body, she said. But Lucia would have none of it. She could allude to the kind of sexual experience that might lead to syphilis without being able to discuss her own sex life directly. Baynes recorded her frustration as time and again Lucia began to talk, only to censor herself and then withdraw.

Whatever Naegeli's tests revealed, Lucia could not abide staying in the Burghölzli Psychiatric Clinic. Despite Maier's extensive program to upgrade its facilities and to affiliate it with the University of Zurich, the Burghölzli remained a large cantonal facility, similar to a state hospital in the United States. Its "hysterical" patients were, as one writer has described them, "uneducated and came largely from the lowest classes. Their numbers were relatively small compared with the other patient groups, such as the dements, tertiary syphilitics, and schizophrenics, that made up a state hospital's usual run of cases at that time."[56] To the Joyce family—mindful more of the Burghölzli's dire popular reputation than of the ground-breaking psychiatric work that had been accomplished within its walls—it was the kind of place to be resorted to as a stopgap measure, and unsuitable for a longer stay. On September 28, Lucia moved out to the private sanatorium run by Dr. Theodor Brunner in Küsnacht, a suburb on the shores of the Lake of Zurich.

We can only guess what Joyce and Nora thought about this move. Brunner's clinic was an extension of his home, it was quiet and genteel, and it offered Lucia privacy. Theodor Brunner (born in 1877) was an important figure in the political life of Zurich, the fifth generation of a family of well-known physicians. His grandfather had founded the sanatorium in the 1840s, and he himself had wide experience in medicine, surgery, and obstetrics. In his hands the clinic focused on nervous disorders, and he specialized in intrathecal treatments of parasyphilitic affections of the nervous system, among other things.[57] Yet there is no evidence to indicate that the Joyces chose the sanatorium on account of Brunner's specialty. Cary Baynes never saw any treatments take place there, but she did say that it was a place where family friends like Carola Giedion-Welcker could visit Lucia in a civilized environment. She also mentions that Jung's home was only a few doors away. This was important, for Lucia was now going to try a talking cure. She was going to submit to psychoanalysis.

Her father had serious reservations, for Jung had followed on the heels of Joyce's artistic career in many unwelcome ways. But he told Carola Giedion-Welcker, "my daughter is not myself. I wouldn't go to him, but maybe he can help her."[58] Perhaps he was remembering Jung's earlier interference in his life. When the Joyces had lived in Zurich in 1914–18, Edith Rockefeller McCormick, one of Joyce's patrons, had suggested that Jung psychoanalyze him, and when Joyce refused, Mrs. McCormick had immediately stopped sending her monthly checks. For many years, Joyce had harbored the suspicion that Jung convinced her to withdraw her financial support.[59] No one knows if this is true or not, but Joyce had many other reasons to mistrust Jung. Chief among these was the doctor's negative opinion of his writing.

Carola Giedion-Welcker shared Joyce's indignation. She had written an essay about *Ulysses* in 1928,[60] and in 1930 she decided to attend a public lecture that Jung gave about the book. Jung claimed that the language of *Ulysses* could have been produced only by a proglottid, a creature "with severe restriction of cerebral activity." Joyce's work had, he said, "the character of a worm cut in half that can grow a new head or a new tail as required." Joyce was capable only of "visceral thinking," could write only "with the sympathetic nervous system for lack of a brain." Like some "transcendental tapeworm," the chapters of *Ulysses* proliferated senselessly in a "rippling, peristaltic, monotonous" fashion.[61]

Joyce's inclusion of so many encyclopedic details in *Ulysses* Jung treated as a symptom of what the French psychologist Pierre Janet called *abaissement du niveau mental*—the lowering of the threshold of consciousness, a mental state supposedly characterized by a proliferation of "rich . . . and grotesque profundity." He saw the reality function as having abandoned control of the mind and admitted such a plethora of sensation that one felt in the presence of someone who had abandoned "any communicable meaning." Such ranting was his "daily bread," Jung reminded his audience, and though he claimed that "the clinical picture of schizophrenia is a mere analogy," his lecture makes clear that he thought Joyce's work fit the mold.[62]

Giedion-Welcker was so angry that she wrote Jung a letter. In her opinion, Jung hadn't a clue about modern art. It wasn't simply that he had compared Joyce to a schizophrenic but that he had disguised prejudice as professional judgment. "It seemed to me that your negative judgment dominated your lecture from the beginning," she told him. "You said that you fell asleep while reading the book, but nothing, absolutely nothing, about the substance of *Ulysses*."[63] In her judgment, it was Jung, and not Joyce, who had been carried away by uncontrolled unconscious impulses in his writing. He was responding to *Ulysses* as if it were a patient begging for psychoanalysis and refusing it at the same time. He had admitted, "Joyce has aroused my ill will." The examples of this ire were so numerous that even Jung had asked himself in the lecture what lay behind it:

> Irritation means: You haven't yet seen what's behind it. Consequently we should follow up our irritation and examine whatever it is we discover in our ill temper. I observe then: this solipsism, this contempt for the cultivated and intelligent member of the reading public who wants to understand, who is well-meaning, and who tries to be kindly and just, gets on my nerves. There we have it, the cold-blooded unrelatedness of his mind, which seems to come from the saurian in him or from still lower regions—conversation in and with one's own intestines.[64]

To Giedion-Welcker this passage was unnerving because it revealed that Jung could not distinguish between irrationality as a sign of illness and irrationality as a purposeful strategy of representation.

If Jung couldn't understand Joyce's writing, what was he going to make of Joyce's other creation—the blunt, ardent, modern daughter who had spent her teenage years in the fast-running company of young Parisian surrealists? How could a man with so little insight into the expressive forms of modern art claim to fathom a young woman who had grown to maturity with Joyce's verve and virtuosity of wit as her daily bread? How would he read sensibilities and ambitions that had been nourished by dancing with rhythm and color? How would he communicate with a young person who babbled comfortably in Italian, her native tongue, and in English, the language of her parents, but whose German and French had been acquired in exile?

Something else was also on Giedion-Welcker's mind. Jung himself was a man with a distinctive psychological style. He needed to feel in control, and he responded poorly to frustration. When he was bored or unable to decipher the meaning of the text, he blamed the words rather than himself. "One should never rub the reader's nose in his own stupidity," he lectured, "but that is just what *Ulysses* does."[65]

The text was not, in short, something over which *he* could maintain control. As everyone in the Joyces' circle by that time knew, control was the one psychological style that aroused Lucia's fury. She hated being locked up; she hated being under continual surveillance; and she might be predicted to respond poorly to a symbolic domination as well. A young woman with an unruly heart was on the threshold of psychoanalysis not only in its early stages of development but with a therapist who insisted upon interpretive control and who responded, to judge by his encounter with *Ulysses*, with irritation to texts that eluded him.

Things didn't look good. We can think of the elements aligned for further confrontation in September 1934: the Apollonian Jung, the Dionysian Lucia; a doctor fascinated by the daemonic but committed to control as a psychological style; a young woman schooled with and by dadaists who was accustomed to performing with her body as a text; and a father who already knew how much his child hated psychiatrists. Joyce could discern the subtlety and barbarity of which his daughter was capable, the control of interpretation that Jung found essential to his own equilibrium, and the fragility of the hope they placed on the famous doctor's shoulders. Like the *Ulysses* of Jung's previous experience, Lucia Joyce would soon "turn [her] back on him," "prove uncooperative," and provide him with another equally infuriating kind of illegibility. Like

Marie Laurencin, Paris, 1927.
Photograph by Man Ray. (Courtesy of
the Man Ray Trust / ARS / Telimage, Paris)

Symphonie ou Les Danseuses
by Marie Laurencin, 1921.
(Courtesy of the Artists Rights
Society)

her father's other intricately wrought handiwork, she would act as another tantalizing cipher, provoking Jung to recognize in his situation the intelligent reader's "maddening defeat."[66]

V. A MOTHER, A FATHER, AND A DOCTOR BATTLE IT OUT

Lucia's program of therapy with Jung lasted more or less four months—an interesting length of time, since it indicates that Jung neither dismissed her case nor made a full commitment to it. In the end, Lucia and Jung didn't establish a satisfactory therapeutic relationship. Aside from a brief period at the beginning, when Lucia apparently spoke openly and happily with him,[67] Jung neither impressed her as wise nor gained her confidence. To her, the doctor and her father seemed equally "old fashioned."[68] And the solid bourgeois comfort in which he worked, so different from the series of apartments in which she had been raised, apparently aroused her resentment.

Very few people shared her low opinion of Jung. In the 1930s Jung's practice had the aspect not only of a thriving clinic but of a religious cult as well. From all accounts he was a man of tremendous vitality, wit, and erudition, and his catholic array of interests in occult subjects attracted an international train of disciples. Most of them were women from prosperous homes who had the resources to live abroad and to "pursue their souls."[69] Emma Jung, Toni Wolff, Linda Fierz-David, Dr. Marie-Louise von Franz, and Dr. Liliane Frey were among them, collectively forming what Jung called his "Anima." Charles Baudouin remembered finding them a strange entourage. In his 1934 journal he noted, "But when someone raised the objection that a majority of his disciples were women, Jung is said to have replied: 'what's to be done? Psychology is after all the science of the soul, and it is not my fault if the soul is a woman.' A jest; but for anyone who has followed his teaching, a jest which is itself charged with experience, and behind which one sees arising in all its ambiguous splendor the archetype of the Anima."[70] One thinks back on these women who formed the inner circle around Jung—variously referred to as the Vestal Virgins, the Maenads, the Jungfrauen, and the Valkyries[71]—and wonders what separated their deep investment in analysis with Jung from Lucia's eventual forlorn hostility.

A profoundly simple answer would be her father. Lucia worshiped at another shrine and consequently lived beyond Jung's sway. In later years, Jung explained the failure of Lucia's analysis in terms of his theory of the Anima. Lucia, he said, was Joyce's inspiration: "If you know anything of my Anima theory, Joyce and his daughter are a classical example of it. She was definitely his *femme inspiratrice*, which explains his obstinate reluctance to have her certified. His own Anima, i.e. unconscious psyche, was so solidly identified with her, that to have her certified would have been as much as an admission that he himself had a latent psychosis. It is therefore understandable that he could not give in."[72] He recognized that a good part of Lucia's dilemma duplicated the experiences of his own young women analysands in relation to him, with the crucial difference that Lucia was not available to him. Here we are, back at Samuel Beckett's perception of Lucia: "She's already part of a better story." Anyone who wanted to get close to Lucia could only be an "in liu man." The question for Jung was whether he could pull her out of her father's orbit.

From the notes that Cary Baynes made for herself as she carried out her part of Lucia's overall treatment, we can deduce the general shape of Jung's therapeutic program,[73] which had many aspects—dream analysis, writing, self-objectification, and various kinds of transferences, both male and female—and many people involved. Aside from seeing her himself, Jung involved two other analytic psychologists in her care: Kristine Mann and Archibald McIntyre Strong, both of whom were independently qualified to see patients and who were also participants in the seminar Jung was then conducting on Nietzsche's *Thus Spoke Zarathustra*.[74] Cary Baynes, a third seminar member, was not an analyst, though her life revolved around Jung and the Zurich Psychology Club.

On the surface of it, Baynes's role in Lucia's life was rather analogous to the earlier one of Mathilde Wönecke, who had accompanied Lucia to Feldkirch in July 1932. She drove Lucia around Zurich in her motorcar, went to the theater with her, had tea, took walks, and generally acted as a bridge to the ordinary social world that had been denied her at Prangins. The very fact of her participation in Lucia's therapy is a mark of the optimism that Jung must have had about Lucia's ability to reintegrate herself into ordinary social life, for he understood that a patient's renewed health partially depended on having a sense of a world to return to. Jung had also apparently asked Baynes to act as an older woman friend who could, he hoped, effect a transference. She was supposed to act as a kind of "good mother" or surrogate for Nora, with whom Lucia was known to have a hostile relationship.[75] She was evidently supposed to engage Lucia's emotions, guide her thinking, try to broach subjects that were difficult to talk about, and attempt to create a sense of safety in female companionship that had been lacking in Lucia's life. She helped Lucia get bookbinding equipment so that she would have something purposeful to do. Above all, she acted as a second set of eyes for Jung.

In 1934 Baynes (born in 1883) had been living in Zurich, with several long breaks, for close to thirteen years. She herself had a sixteen-year-old daughter, Ximena, the child of her first marriage, to Jaime de Angulo. Being twice divorced, she knew what it was like to have difficult relations with men and to have to establish an independent female identity in a world that remained oriented toward married women.

Like the Joyces' family friend Maria Jolas, whose childhood friend she was, Baynes had been raised in Kentucky, though she had no leanings toward an expatriate life as a young woman. She had graduated from Vassar College in 1906 and had gone on to earn an M.D. from the Johns Hopkins University in 1911. At Johns Hopkins she had married a fellow medical student, and the two of them had gone to live in California, where Jaime de Angulo had studied anthropology, focusing on American Indian languages. Neither chose to practice medicine. In 1921 Cary left de Angulo and took Ximena with her to Zurich, where her old teacher from Vassar, Kristine Mann—by this time a physician herself and an adherent of Jung's ideas—had persuaded her to study with Jung.[76] Initially her intention had been to try to understand the failure of her marriage,[77] but her participation in Jung's various seminars led to her second marriage, to Helton Godwin Baynes, a British analyst who was Jung's assistant in the 1920s. Together she and Baynes translated Jung's *Contributions to Analytical Psychology* (1928) and *Two Essays on Analytical Psychology* (1928). When she met Lucia, she had recently finished the English translation of Richard Wilhelm's *The Secret of the Golden Flower* (1931) and (with W. S. Dell) Jung's *Modern Man in Search of a Soul* (1933). Throughout the 1930s, she continued to work on the translation of Wilhelm's version of the *I Ching* (which was eventually published as part of the Bollingen series in 1950). She also helped Olga Fröbe-Kapteyn manage the Eranos conferences in Ascona, and she participated actively in the Psychology Club in Zurich.[78]

When asked why she did not become an analyst, Baynes gave two

standard answers: She had never had any experience of the collective unconscious, and Jung had advised her against it, claiming that "no one
should engage in analysis who was not backed by a very strong relationship to a partner, to keep him from being sucked into his patients' problems . . . and from losing his grip on reality."[79] If she did not have a
partner in a conventional sense, she had nonetheless set up a household
with her sister, Henri Zinno, and their home became a meeting place for
foreign visitors who were undergoing their own analyses with Jung.
Joseph Henderson, who was one of their guests, remembered Henri, the
artist, as humorous, hospitable, and of great charm; Cary was the intellectual who delighted in spirited discussion. Jane Wheelwright, another
houseguest, could never understand why Cary "couldn't have been an
analyst. She was the Rock of Gibraltar."[80]

It was this "Rock of Gibraltar" whom Jung chose to be Lucia's companion. A mother, a doctor, an artist's companion, and a woman with an
independent and productive life, she was beautifully suited for the task
at hand, and her memories of Lucia give an astute and candid picture of
her young charge and of Lucia's interactions with her parents. Baynes
noticed Lucia's moods, listened carefully for the subjects of her conversation, the level of her self-awareness, her ability to sustain continuous and
coherent dialogue, and the signs of unarticulated preoccupations.[81] On
29 October, for example, she noted after a two-hour car drive:

> All of that time she was very talkative, even gay. There were a good many
> breaks in the thread of her conversation however, and usually when I asked a
> direct question which had anything to do with her she did not reply. But my
> whole impression of her was of an immense improvement both physically and
> mentally since I had seen her a month or five weeks ago. I asked her on this
> drive if she did not like the flowers in the gardens here and she said, "No, I
> don't like either flowers or vegetables, they are so messy. I like churches and
> cemeteries." "Ah, wie herrlich melancholisch!" ["Oh, what splendid melan-
> choly"] I said and then she laughed delightedly, as if she had fully caught the
> nuance of the situation.[82]

When the two women returned to the sanatorium, Lucia became
morose, and this mood persisted into the following week, when Cary
Baynes returned. Instead of a gay, engaged young woman who participated in the delights and ironies of language, Lucia was lonely, with-

drawn, and without a sense of purpose. She walked up and down the halls alone, and "everything went *schief* [false, distorted] . . . I could get no contact with her . . . She remained inaccessible."[83]

Baynes returned again and again to certain themes. Silence and talkativeness frequently formed the poles of her analysis, and we can see that she did not consider quietness to be a natural way for Lucia to respond to experience. It was suspicious. What was she thinking? What were her fantasies?[84] Baynes also watched for Lucia's orientation to the environment and seemed surprised when Lucia was lucid. On 20 November, for example, she spoke about meeting Lucia and her nurse on their way into Küsnacht to buy something for Lucia to sew. She noticed that "she was entirely withdrawn and did not speak on the way there nor on the way back unless I spoke to her, and then reluctantly." Then Baynes added, "But in the shop she asked for the thing she wanted and appeared to be perfectly orientated." On another occasion Baynes realized she had misread a situation. "The only 'off' thing she had said was that she had my address when I had said I would like to give it to her. She opened her desk drawer and pulled out a notebook and said she had the address there." But Lucia's father explained to Baynes that this was in fact true: he had given it to her only days before. Baynes had the honesty to admit, "Evidently one is inclined to think that she is more confused than she actually is."[85]

With Joyce and Nora and with Lucia herself, Baynes approached and reapproached the possibility that a sexual trauma in the past had initiated Lucia's problems. She would lead toward this subject, only to discover time and again that none of the Joyces spoke comfortably about intimate experiences. Nora and Joyce, with whom she often had tea, reported that Lucia had run with a fast crowd when she lived in Paris. Baynes did not pick up their names, only that they drank cocktails and that "the group seemed to center around an American woman and her husband, neither of whom were desirable characters." Baynes thought the man's name was "Pierce" and then remembered that Lucia had mentioned him "in connection with a little white dog." "I noticed at the time that she laughed in a significant way when she was telling about this man and the dog, as if a good deal was going on in her mind which she was not saying." But though she surmised that Lucia was harboring an unarticulated preoccupation, she could not confirm it. Baynes knew from Joyce that Lucia had told him "she had done dreadful things in her life, and he said, well for that matter he had too. 'Yes,' she said, 'but a girl can't do things like that.'" When Baynes reported these suggestive fragments to Jung, thinking that the "Pierce" person had perhaps lured her into a sexual relationship, he listened closely. A precipitating event would lend the case more hope.[86]

Baynes insistently returned to the subject of candor about the body. Twice Lucia emerged from her reticence to mention that "she had had an unfortunate experience when she was a child." Baynes listened attentively, imagining that Lucia saw some connection between what had happened to her then and her current condition. But Lucia then grew "silent and said after a little while that it was not very pleasant to speak about." No amount of encouragement could puncture this reserve. Lucia asked, instead, if Baynes knew what a *sondage* was. Baynes did not know. One feels led to the edge of the mystery, for *sondage* refers to the probing of an open wound.

Baynes missed a lot of cues because she thought she was dealing with classic repression, with painful memories of the body subdued and pressing, sickly, to be released: "I said to her that it looked to me as if she had tried to live her life in her head and maybe she had got sick because her body had got tired of this state of affairs. She laughed a great deal about this." To Baynes, ignorant of Lucia's life as a dancer, laughter was an inappropriate emotional response. To her, steeped as she was in Jungian ideas, the unconscious was the great enemy, the ocean that threatened to engulf Lucia, as it was judged to have engulfed every other individual diagnosed as schizophrenic.[87] When Lucia lapsed into silence, when there were broken threads in her conversation, it signaled the existence of "autonomous complexes," that is, constellations of unconscious thought that evaded the control of the ego and threatened to fracture the unity of the personality. Psychology was the great savior for Baynes, and psychology was above all a matter of articulation, of speech that could bring in its wake a conscious image of the self and its previous vicissitudes.

To Lucia, former dancer, scamp, and sexual adventurer, the mere suggestion that she had not lived fully in her body was laughable. She could remember years filled with movement, desire, and a vision of an extraordinary fate. But she did not always put things into words as she sat quietly or with agitation, morosely or with pleasure, in the car that took her and Baynes to their various adventures in Zurich.

Sensitive, intelligent, scrupulous in her attention, Baynes pushed forward, searching for ways to reach Lucia and to make her feel comfortable talking. On 12 November she recorded, "I told her I thought the trouble with her was that many things had happened to her, which she did not understand." Lucia responded enthusiastically, as if she had finally been given something to grab hold of. "Oh, yes," she replied, "it is just as if you had been very rich, and collected many valuable things, and then they were taken away from you." She had lost not only her life in dance but her prospects for love as well. She retained a fierce sense of the injustice of it all.

Joyce and Paul Léon had tried to convey this sense in the *Anamnese* they wrote for the Burghölzli, when they observed that Lucia had not only loved her brother and lost him in marriage but had repeatedly compared herself to him, finding it incomprehensible that his good fortune should be so much greater than her own: "The patient insists that despite her diligence, her talent and all her exertions, the results of her work have come to nothing. The brother, her contemporary, whom she previously idolized, has never worked at anything, is well known, has married wealth, has a beautiful apartment, a car with a chauffeur and, on top of it all, a beautiful wife."[88] She then turned her situation into metaphor, seeing the previous prosperity of her life as the Eiffel Tower and the intervening experiences as the tower's collapse.

Baynes used the circumstances of driving to suggest that the danger of the car might be thought of as an analogy to other kinds of danger in one's life. Liking dangerous things could indicate that "you don't value your life," Lucia replied. And then Baynes returned to the subject that everyone in Zurich was concerned to understand: Why had Lucia set fire to her room in Prangins? Lucia asked her what she thought fire symbolized. In retrospect, Baynes faulted herself for giving "very stupid answers," saying to Lucia that for many people fire was the symbol for God. But she lets us see the configuration of her real thought on the subject: Fire was the universal "symbol of passion," and Lucia had acted out a symbolic desire. The flaming room had been the expression of an engorged heart, out of control and dangerous.

That this danger was connected in Baynes's mind with Lucia's father is revealed in her observations of Lucia on Thursday, 13 December, the commemorative day for her namesake, Saint Lucia. That morning Baynes took Nora out to see her daughter and watched as Lucia, who had not seen her parents for three weeks, greeted her mother affectionately. Lucia "was dressed as I thought," Baynes noted, "but her mother told me afterwards that she had on an evening dress under her coat, and this she kept on all day." When Nora asked Lucia if Joyce should come for a visit in the afternoon, Lucia laughed and said, "Tell him I am a crossword puzzle, and if he does not mind seeing a crossword puzzle, he is to come out."[89]

Joyce did come to visit, and Baynes recorded what he told her of his conversation with Lucia that afternoon: This was when Lucia told him she thought she had syphilis. Baynes characterized Joyce as blind to the pathology of his own intimate relations: "She was careful to throw back her coat and show herself to him in evening dress. I thought he would get the significance of this but he did not." In Baynes's estimation, Lucia's evening dress was cut from the same cloth as the fire in her room in Prangins. Both were displaced enactments of the sexualized nature of Lucia's attachment to her father, and both explained the animosity between mother and daughter. Incest had reared its tangled head in Baynes's imagination, although she used the Jungian language of "Anima" and "Animus" to explain the psychic system that bound father and daughter together.

Cary Baynes interpreted what she saw as a scene of seduction played out by a young woman whose illness was caused by her illicit desire for a man who refused to understand its importance. Her sister Henri agreed: "At tea I tried and Henri tried to get Joyce to turn his attention for a moment to the meaning of her condition, but it was not possible to make even the smallest dent in the wall he has erected against the understanding of it. He gave some further details of her behavior which show I think how much of an anima situation it is." Then Baynes went on to describe what others attuned to the substance of Joyce's writing have long suspected without having proof: that there was a recognized collusion between Joyce and Lucia in the creation of *Finnegans Wake*. Lucia "asked him if he were stuck in his work and he said he was. 'You mean,' she said, 'that you have not had any new ideas?' 'So,' she said, 'you cannot find anything new, well maybe you can through me.' 'And who knows if I won't?' was his comment to us."[90]

What is revealed in this scene? Where did Lucia's behavior come from? Baynes, immersed in the world of analytic psychology and its newly developed theory, saw what that theory led her to expect. Here was Oedipus/Elektra; here was the child's overinvestment in one parent and murderous rage at the other, with the bizarre twist that Lucia's supposed psychosis had banished all repression. "Henri took up this theme," Baynes noted, "and told [Joyce] if he would but understand what was transpiring in her mind he would indeed have the clue to a new idea, but he could not get it." Here were the Joyces, "erecting walls," refusing enlightenment, persisting in pathology even as the means of salvation sat earnestly across the table, offering clues, as if on a platter, that they would not accept. To the sisters it was all there. The hatred of the mother: "After Lucia had deviled her mother so that she had to leave the room, she said to her father, 'She is jealous of me.' " The parents' blindness; the child's immersion in the unconscious: "This of course is true—both of them tend to think of her as a perfectly responsible agent."[91]

But there is another way to understand what had been going on. It is a liaison whose origins lay in the ancient history of the Joyce family. Think back: a young girl, "[a] wild piece of goods. Her slim legs running up the staircase. Destiny. Ripening now. Vain: very" (U 66). The unselfconsciousness of youth. Lucia. Milly. The eyes of an attentive father, loving, watching, transcribing, seeing always with the needed transpositions of art pressing against the spontaneity of the moment of lived experience. The child growing into consciousness with those eyes trained upon her. The child growing into consciousness *of* those eyes trained upon her. "The circumstance that she bears the name of a famous father is relevant to the consideration of her highest aims."[92] The knowing, half-intuitive dynamic between creative father and responsive daughter. The girl waking slowly but inexorably to a knowledge of her place within an imaginative economy of the most extraordinary kind, neither Elektra nor Antigone but Milly, Issy, the Rainbow Girl, the child before the cracked looking glass not of schizophrenia but of her father's art.

"Tell him I am a crossword puzzle, and if he does not mind seeing a crossword puzzle, he is to come out." "Well maybe you can [find something new] through me." Can you use my evening gown when I wear it in the morning? Yes, I am writing a book of the dark in the day. Can you use my face painted with black ink?[93] Yes. Will the telegrams I invented out of my boredom amuse you as well? Yes.

Joyce went over the telegrams that she had written explaining them to me
[Baynes]. They were all more or less satirical and he could understand all of
them, except part of one. They referred to things he knew about, and were directed to various people including her brother. He says she told him she knew
they could not be sent, though she handed them into the office, but that she
had to do something to amuse people out there . . . she was pretty excited
however after her father left and danced and sang quite a bit.[94]

The daughter had transposed and was willingly transposing herself into
a mother of sorts, participating in the creation of a child that the world
would later call *Finnegans Wake* but that Jungian psychology reduced to
the banal desire for illicit sex.

Baynes, to her credit, did try to integrate what she knew of Lucia
with her knowledge that she was the child of a famous writer, but here
again Jung's views intervened. She saw Lucia's writing only as an imitation of her father's. How could she have done otherwise? Jung was using
the Joyces' joint presence in Zurich as a pretext for discussing Joyce's
work once again, this time in the context of his seminar on Nietzsche.
Baynes went from a discussion of Joyce's writing on one day (7 November) to seeing his daughter on the next (8 November), an alternation that
continued through the fall and into the winter. "Of course," Baynes observed, "all that [Lucia] wrote referred to outside things, this and that
dish she had eaten in Trieste or in Brittany, *kinos* [movie theaters] she
had been to, people she had seen—it was very much the sort of record of
sensations her father likes to write, and reminded both Henri and me of
his writing. It was as though she were trying to be him."[95]

We must remember that Jung considered *Ulysses* to be written out of
an "atrophy of feeling," the creation of a writer "as unconscious as a
sleep-walker." We must remember that he thought Joyce's writing was
filled with "unavowed resentments of a highly personal nature," "the
wreckage of a violently amputated boyhood," and "a delirious confusion
of the subjective and psychic with objective reality." "In all the book,"
Jung had claimed, "there is nothing pleasing, nothing refreshing, nothing hopeful, but only things that are grey, grisly, gruesome, or pathetic,
tragic, ironic, all from the seamy side of life and so chaotic that you have
to look for the thematic connections with a magnifying glass."[96] Lucia
never had a chance.

Baynes, like Jung, considered Joyce himself as the progenitor of his child's malady. On 20 November, she wrote: "Lucia had the negative thought brought into the very midst of her life, not once-removed in books, but in her own father, that fact coupled with the whole incest situation and her lack of any orientation about life anyway . . . was more than she could deal with."[97]

In the midst of this imagined darkness, Baynes paused to notice that Lucia had given her a small hand-painted box—a gesture of generosity and human connection. In Baynes's language, it was the beginning of a transference. She went to see Dr. Brunner in order to find out his impression of Lucia. "He thinks she has made a steady improvement since she has been there, and says he does not think it out of the question that she might get back into life." Lucia's nurse, consulted on Saturday, 15 December, was of the opinion that "she had not regressed." The Polish assistant at the sanatorium "said he had spent an hour and a half with her that [same] morning—could hardly get away so attractive had she been and that she was quite unrecognizable as the person she had been before."[98] Jung, as we can imagine, was not sanguine, but still Joyce thought he wanted him to carry on.[99]

VI. ALONE WITH JUNG

Elizabeth Shepley Sergeant, who wrote a portrait of Jung for *Harper's* magazine in 1931, remembered the place to which Lucia came for her sessions in Küsnacht—his "sober, book-lined study, with its Oriental paintings and Christian stained glass."[100] She wrote about coming to visit on a steamboat that landed amid gulls and wild ducks, a ten-minute walk from "a yellow country house standing well within walls and gardens on the edge of the lake of Zurich." One "must pull a shining brass bell, of old fashioned mold, and [wait] while its fateful ring resounds through the house—as obviously a hospitable, family mansion as the other [the tower at Bollingen] is the isolated domain of the creator-scholar."[101]

For Jung himself, the immediate task was to try to break the tightness of Lucia's bond with her father. Without this separation, she could not become therapeutically "available" and able to relive the traumatic or submerged aspects of previous relationships that had presumably contributed to her breakdown.[102] Later in his life, looking back on specific problems in psychotherapy, Jung proudly remembered that when he met Freud in 1907, Freud asked "out of the blue," " 'and what do you think about the transference?' I replied with the deepest conviction that it was the alpha and omega of the analytical method, whereupon he said, 'Then you have grasped the main thing.' "[103]

What Freud had in mind, and what Jung never questioned despite his later quarrels with Freud, was "the intensity and tenacity to the bond with their fathers" that characterized the emotional landscape of many young women. He was also thinking of the equally stunning discovery that such young women could be induced to transfer these intense feelings to their doctors in the course of their "talking cure."[104] Jung gave this phenomenon his own mythopoetic twist, using the language of alchemy to describe the "mystic marriage" thus achieved between patient and doctor, but the practical effects were the same as those Freud described. Without them little could be accomplished.

In some general way the Joyces knew this was part of Jung's treatment plan. To facilitate Lucia's psychic investment in the new people in her life—Baynes and Jung—Nora and Joyce were repeatedly urged to leave Zurich. Though they never did leave, they did *pretend* to leave between the last week of November and 13 December.[105] On 17 December Joyce wrote to Harriet Weaver that he had once again been urged to go away—"The idea is to efface myself"—but he remained skeptical. Leaving his daughter in Prangins for seven months had resulted, as he saw it, in "almost irreparable" damage, and now "Lucia has no trust in anyone except me and she thinks nobody else understands a word of what she says."[106]

On this matter, the Joyces and Jung were at loggerheads. Without a clear sense of the clinical importance of Jung's maneuver, Joyce experienced the attempted separation from Lucia as an effort "made by more than one person to poison her mind against me."[107] That Lucia herself was worried about the same issue and that someone had reassured her that affection for one man need not constitute betrayal of another can be surmised by a letter she wrote in October: "Father, if you want to go back to Paris you would do well to do so. . . . If ever I take a fancy to anybody I swear to you on the head of Jesus that it will not be because I am not fond of you. Do not forget that."[108] And so, with the anxieties of parents and child at least partly assuaged, and with the father having been told of the difficulty of the case, Jung set to work.

We will never know exactly what Jung thought Lucia's problem was, in part because he scrupulously destroyed all of his former patients' files[109] and in part because she probably defied the clarity of his classification schemes. We can, however, infer some of his suppositions through his guidance of Cary Baynes. Her notes make clear that she was to evaluate Lucia according to Bleuler's seven signs of "schizophrenic negativism"—not that this was Jung's diagnosis, but that it was the hypothesis to test. Even Cary Baynes was confused by her experiences. "Evidently one is inclined to think that [Lucia] is more confused than she actually is," she had reminded herself on 8 November. We also know that Baynes acted as the "dream collector," for she records asking Lucia about them. And we know that self-objectification—the ability to stand away from one's experience and to see it analytically—was something that was prized when Lucia was able to do it, as when she spoke of her life as the Eiffel Tower.

Jung had cautioned Joyce that Lucia's case would be difficult to handle. In order to free a neurotic person of his or her neurosis, he considered it essential to delve into the unconscious origins of the problem, and he concurred with both Bleuler and Freud that those origins were sexual. Since he considered dreams a direct expression of unconscious psychic activity, their interpretation could be an important part of therapy. But Jung was always on the alert to recognize patients with more intractable problems for whom confrontation with the unconscious might be overwhelming. In such cases, he said, "the patient ha[s] to be rescued from the already menacing invasion of the unconscious by effecting a drastic change in her present situation."[110] In the one case, patient and doctor moved forward together to explore the contents of the unconscious. In the other, the doctor alone, having judged that such a course of action might lead to an emotional relapse, worked instead with methods that could distance the patient from his or her interior life. One might paint pictures, for example, or think of oneself as an object like a tower to create a space of safety. "In this way," Jung wrote, "the apparently incomprehensible and unmanageable chaos of [the patient's] total situation is visualized and objectified; it can be observed at a distance by his conscious mind, analyzed, and interpreted."[111]

In which direction was Lucia Joyce to go? The fact that dreams were a part of her therapy suggests that Jung himself had not decided, at least at the outset. Was she capable of the interior journey? Could the secrets of her unconscious be faced, accepted, and integrated into a holistic sense of selfhood? Or would she fall apart if pushed in this direction? Jung undertook to answer these questions when he decided to try to effect a transference. Whatever lay at the origin of Lucia's disturbance, experience had shown Jung that it would be projected onto him.

By 1934 Jung had developed arcane interests that separated him forever from Freud and the world of Viennese psychoanalysis. He had veered off into realms of mysticism and the study of alchemy. He had no compunction about describing his methods of relating to patients in terms of ancient formulas for refining matter. The unconscious was the *prima materia*, or the chaotic, undifferentiated earth, and the process of therapy reiterated the stages of transformation by which ancient sorcerers moved from *separatio* or *divisio* or *disiunctio* of the body to a *res simplex*—a simple and unified nature.

Jung's theory of the archetypes of the collective unconscious and his belief in the transpersonal psychical heritage of humanity cast his explanations of the transference in an ambiguous light. It was not simply that he borrowed a system of metaphors that would let him render an invisible process more concretely. It was also that he seemed to think of what happened to his patients and himself as a search for integration that was endlessly repeated by each generation in transfigured form: "Alchemy describes not merely in general outline but often in the most astonishing detail, the same psychological phenomenology which can be observed in the analysis of unconscious processes."[112] Although no psychic illness was like any other, the remission of each illness involved the same kind of struggle and the same vision of health. One did not defeat the monsters of the unconscious so much as integrate them into a holistic picture. The healthy self was imagined as a peaceable kingdom where the lion and lamb of conscious and unconscious material coexisted without denial and without strife.

The first strategic move of the therapeutic process was an act of reclamation that was at the same time an act of disintegration of previous psychological habits. Psychically ill people, Jung believed, had a specious unity to their personalities that had been achieved by projecting their own negativity onto other persons, typically their father or mother. Someone else was to blame, and one's battle in life was falsely perceived to be with the other person. We can think here of Lucia's tirades against Nora and of her insistence that Joyce was responsible for her condition because "he had given her no morale."[113]

According to Jung, the patient had to come to the recognition that "he himself has a shadow, that his enemy is in his own heart."[114] That is, Lucia had to reclaim agency for the darkness of her own life and to understand that her pain was the result of an internal battle, a conflict not yet articulated, a fight between a consciously acceptable image of herself and her repressed desires and fears. Jung used the metaphor of "passing through the valley of the shadow [of death]" to describe this reclamation of the unconscious. One could not proceed directly to this new recognition. First one projected the old conflicts and negativities onto the therapist. Then the therapist, by his superior awareness of them and refusal to bear them, could help the patient examine them and bring them back into his or her own psychic economy.

It is not necessary to continue with this description, for nothing of the kind seems to have happened to Lucia. Jung apparently knew after several months that it was not going to work. One could not force a transference to occur. "Any analyst who inculcates such things . . . is entirely forgetting that 'transference' is only another word for 'projection.' No one can voluntarily *make* projections, they just *happen*."[115] The affection Lucia bore for her father was not something she would or could reassign to Jung.

Instead of accepting Joyce's absence quietly, she threw another fit that Harriet Weaver later described to Paul Léon as "a repetition of the fire scene at Prangins in a more unpleasant form."[116] Almost twenty years later, looking back on this experience in an interview with Patricia Hutchins, Jung explained Lucia by claiming that she remained caught in Joyce's psychic system and could not emerge from it into an independent and whole sense of being. She was his *femme inspiratrice*, his Anima. If any mystic marriage was occurring in her life, if any alchemical merging of antithetical elements was transpiring, it was not in the therapy room but with the singular man who was her father. And having so identified her, Jung closed his books.

In January 1935, he agreed that Joyce could take her out of the sanatorium, even though Dr. Brunner, who thought she was making good progress, wanted her to remain. Joyce explained to Giorgio and Helen that Jung "told me nobody could make any head of her but myself as she was a very exceptional case and certainly not one for psychoanalytic treatment which he said might provoke a catastrophe from which she would never recover."[117]

VII. A MYSTICAL MARRIAGE

In later years Jung did not recall the failed transference or even much about Lucia herself but spoke instead about the role Lucia played in her father's life. The doctor, who had made his reputation in the diagnosis of schizophrenia, did not use the language of psychosis to identify his patient but reverted to the language of the soul. Jung was more accustomed to thinking about the relationship of son to mother when he spoke about the Anima, but he never doubted that the Joyces, father and daughter, stood in this relation to one another. Instead of thinking about Joyce and his mother or Joyce and his wife, Nora, Jung thought about the intensity of the father-daughter bond in the Joyce family, and he saw pathology instead of health. He thought, in other words, that Lucia was the symptom of Joyce's problem.

When Jung developed his theory of the archetypes, he decided that the unconscious mind contained virtual forms or receptacles that derived from the collective experiences of the human race and that could function autonomously without the knowledge or will of the individual. He identified a series of figures that supposedly structured each person's individual experiences. The Anima was the image of woman in the male psyche, a sort of a priori category, almost a racial memory, into which each man poured his actual experiences of real women. Jung's published examples presumed that men began life with the image of their mothers shaping the Anima and that their wives or partners in love later determined its form.

But regardless of the origin of a man's unconscious image of woman and regardless of the actual woman who eventually bore the weight of it, the Anima was always "inseparably" related to him through opposition. "The persona," Jung claimed, "is inwardly compensated by feminine weakness, and as the individual outwardly plays the strong man, so he becomes inwardly a woman. . . . The more he is identified with the persona, the persona's counterpart, the Anima, remains completely in the dark and is at once projected, so that our hero comes under the heel of his wife's slipper. If this results in a considerable increase of her power, she will acquit herself none too well. She becomes inferior, thus providing her husband with the welcome proof that it is not he, the hero, who is inferior in private, but his wife."[118]

In Jung's eyes, Lucia was "inseparably" related to her father through opposition, acquitting herself "none too well . . . inferior." She existed as a necessary counterpart to Joyce's genius, almost, one might claim, as the grounds that permitted that genius to flourish. Unaware of his own madness, unwilling to face it, reluctant to ferret out darkness or perhaps needing that darkness to spur his own creativity, Joyce held Lucia in thrall and in turn was captivated by her. "You behold," Jung said about the mystical marriage between a man and his Anima, "the secret conspiracy . . . and how each helps the other to betray life." "Where does the guilt lie? . . . Probably with both."[119]

According to Jung's construction, if Joyce was a genius, Lucia was a girl with no artistic talent. If Joyce's writing was conscious, Lucia's writing was unconscious. If Joyce was diving into a river, Lucia was falling. All his descriptions of father and daughter are expressed in terms of such antitheses. No matter that Joyce quietly insisted on what he recognized—the new or avant-garde quality of Lucia's prose. No matter that other readers of Joyce's work recognized his unprecedented ability to acknowledge and represent the interior lives of ordinary men and women. In Jung's imagination, Joyce flourished on sensations, lacked introspective abilities, and projected the unexamined contents of his own unconscious in proportion to that lack of self-reflection. Man and Anima. The two were inseparably related through opposition.

What we see here is, of course, Jung's compilation of theory upon theory. Each theory was based on presumptions about the superiority and agency of men, the proper role of women as helpers of husbands, and the subsequent illegibility of truly original and creative women. Even the "Valkyries," the circle of women who surrounded Jung with adulation, talked about Jung's sexist tendencies.[120]

But it is also important to see that the particular cast of Jungian theory left Jung repeatedly at odds with the nature of Lucia's lived experience. Jung found in her what he was intent on finding. Yet she just as actively resisted his classifications. She did not want to be under surveillance; she did not want her energy forcibly bound; she did not want to be restrained in institutions or by intellectual categories. Indeed, we might say that classification and resistance to it characterized their respective psychological styles and predetermined the collapse of their working relationship. As Joyce himself realized even before he brought her to Zurich, she was intent to prove that she and her father were stronger than medicine. Where Jung saw a young woman who was the victim of unconscious impulses, participating in a psychic marriage with her father that constituted a betrayal of life, she considered herself to be engaged in purposeful theatrics. In her own mind she remained the willful dancer and the child of genius, consciously participating in unprecedented creative activity. She was acting for the benefit of a man whose work would be enriched by her contributions to it. "I am a crossword puzzle." "Come to see me."

Amid all of Jung's theory, Lucia was lost in the picture. And since Jung read her life only in terms of his negative assessment of her father, her experience with him simply reiterated the dynamics and frustrations of her previous life experiences. Whether their judgments were positive or negative, everyone was preoccupied with her father and not with her.

Cary Baynes, her only consistent companion, noticed that Lucia herself was becoming more and more disconsolate. By 20 November, she complained about the sanatorium, using her father's penchant for black humor by saying that she wanted to murder someone so that she would be put into prison.[121] At this point, an incarceration that she deserved seemed more comprehensible than one that ensued from no fault of her own.

What would it take for someone, aside from Joyce, to treat her desire to distinguish herself seriously? In October she wrote to her father that doing something simple like selling shoes would be preferable as long as she could do it with integrity. She wanted a quiet life—a house with a garden, a dog.[122] But whose voice speaks here? Had Jung or Baynes been trying to reorient her and help her to value a life lived without art? As soon as she wrote this, Lucia seems to have edited her own thoughts, thinking back to women artists whom she had seen during her seven earlier months in Geneva. "At Prangins I saw a number of artists, especially women who seemed to me all very hysterical. Am I to turn out like them?" she asked.[123] What was it in her discussions with Jung that made her remember other women whose creativity she associated with illness and enforced restraint?

By her own assessment, Jung was not the right physician for her. Lucia had been surprised when Cary Baynes admitted that she too had gone to Jung for help, a confession to which Lucia responded by saying, "she did not think her trouble was to be helped by working with her hands but by sport." Baynes, like Jung, did not recognize Lucia's investment in the cultivation of the body, nor did she respond to Lucia's concern that Jung did "not look after physical things." But she did record her charge's sense of her life's diminishment in Zurich.[124]

Baynes leaves us with a haunting image of Lucia's acute interest in visiting the Zurich Zoo. As Lucia watched the bears, she asked, "What sort of God does that fellow have, do you think?" Her attention did not wander, and her remarks were "apt." But there was more. The dancer who could "leap no more," the woman whose love and desire for physical culture fell repeatedly on deaf ears, saw her fate in that of the animals. She had once pursued a Dionysian ecstasy that Nietzsche described in terms of lions and panthers, and now she was asking about the cosmic justice of domesticating joy. The Apollonian Cary Baynes saw a young woman behaving properly. But Lucia saw the cage.

Vaslav Nijinsky, age fifty-one, jumping in his asylum. (Courtesy of the Roger Pryor Dodge Nijinsky Photograph Collection, the New York Library of the Performing Arts)

11

LOCKING UP DANCERS
LONDON 1935

I. NIJINSKY'S FATE

Lucia spent Christmas Day 1934 with her parents at the Hotel Carlton Elite in Zurich. They had a dinner of ham, turkey, plum pudding, and champagne and then went for a drive. Joyce wrote to Giorgio and Helen that people were charmed by her grace. "She was all dressed up and powdered and perfumed." On Boxing Day, she came back again from the clinic, this time to sing in the music room of the hotel, entertaining the other guests with what her father referred to as "all my Irish songs to my Liszt-like accompaniments."[1] Despite the loveliness of her concert, it was Lucia the dancer whom the circle of her parents' friends had in mind that winter. They were reading the biography of Vaslav Nijinsky written by his wife, Romola, that had just been published that season, and wondering if Lucia's fate was to be like his.

Since its publication in 1934, Romola's account of her husband's fight against schizophrenia has been severely criticized. Peter Ostwald, a contemporary psychoanalyst who reviewed the documents chronicling Nijinsky's supposed madness, decided that Nijinsky had had strange attitudes but was basically sane. He believed, as many of his doctors at the time had also done, that nothing prevented Nijinsky's return to domestic life except his wife's refusal to live with him.[2] But Joyce's friends saw a sad analogy between two dancers whose aberrant energies had brought them from the stage to the asylum. On 11 November, Harriet Weaver told Joyce she had just finished the book and had found its epilogue "depressing reading."[3]

At the end of the biography Romola Nijinsky presented the scene of diagnosis at the Burghölzli as a bitter melodrama, describing Dr. Bleuler's brittle smile, false heartiness, and a judgment that followed after ten minutes of conversation: "Now, my dear, be very brave. You have to take your child away; you have to get a divorce. Unfortunately, I am helpless. Your husband is incurably insane." Nijinsky himself responded, as she dashed from the consultation room, "*Femmka*, you are bringing me my death-warrant." The epilogue that followed began with the words, "Fourteen years have elapsed since the day that Nijinksy's mind became shrouded in darkness, when he withdrew from this world."[4] It continued with a scenario that would have seemed darkly familiar to Harriet Weaver and to anyone else who tried to follow the Joyces' long-suffering concern for Lucia—the saga of Romola's attempt to find a cure and to return Nijinsky to the semblance of a normal life. "The greatest specialists in Europe and America were called in," she reported. "They all agreed it was a case of Schizophrenia. . . . Then I turned to desperate means—fakirs, healers, Christian Science—but everything failed. We took him to the theatre, to see the Ballet, to Balieff's Chauve-Souris, to clubs where Cossacks danced, and, when he saw these, his expression changed, and for a few minutes he became his old self again. But there were weeks of great violence, and then he had to be taken to a sanatorium, to which I followed him, and unfortunately found out that in all other places except Kreuzlingen he was either neglected, badly nourished, or even occasionally ill-treated."[5]

Harriet Weaver may have considered these experiences prophetic, but she encouraged the Joyces in their hopes and supported their belief in Lucia's exceptional nature. "The example you gave of her clairvoyance was indeed extraordinary," she wrote in the same letter. "And as for her letter, so affectionate and docile in tone, reading it, it is difficult to picture the violent scenes that occur at times and that are so devastating to her and to her parents when witnesses of them."[6]

But she reckoned without Joyce's determination to remain in contact with his child and to believe in her regardless of professional judgments about her normality. Romola Nijinsky accepted the pronouncement of the medical profession as a godlike dictum, terrible but infallible. Joyce believed he understood Lucia better than anyone who had the temerity to classify her on the basis of a single interview, and he did not condemn his child for falling prey to a malady that he shrewdly called "one of the most elusive diseases known to men and unknown to medicine."[7] Joyce was very accurate in this judgment.

In the 1950s, Jung would look back on a lifetime spent in the diagnosis and treatment of schizophrenia and remark, "It would be a mistake to suppose that more or less suitable methods of treatment exist. Theoretical assumptions in this respect count for next to nothing. Also, one would do well not to speak of 'methods' at all. The thing that really matters is the personal commitment, the serious purpose, the devotion, indeed the self-sacrifice, of those who give the treatment. I have seen results," he added, "that were truly miraculous as when sympathetic nurses and laymen were able, by their courage and steady devotion, to re-establish psychic rapport with their patients and so achieve quite astounding cures."[8]

As 1935 began, the Joyces were thrown back upon their own resources and upon the "courage and steady devotion" of a father who had come to the realization that he must walk a fine line in relation to his child. Neither too intimate nor too distant, he must rekindle her interest in life and build her confidence in its success without usurping the emotional energy that should ultimately be directed outward toward other loves. Aside from this solitary burden he placed on his own shoulders, Joyce faced financial devastation. He estimated that Lucia's care in the previous three years had cost £4,000. During that time she had had twenty-four doctors, twelve nurses, and eight companions and had been in three institutions.[9] And his London solicitor wanted him to put Lucia "out of harm's way." Though Joyce did not elaborate on his meaning, Baynes had discovered through Maria Jolas that Monro Saw was of the opinion that Lucia should be sent to live in a Belgian village that for several generations had done penance for some crime against God by taking insane or half-sane people into their families.[10] What Joyce had no way of knowing was that the absence of uniform diagnostic categories in the 1930s made the variety of opinions that he repeatedly encountered inevitable. In 1958 Jung could still see the predicament of families like the Joyces. "There are some—in my view—premature attempts at theory-building," he observed, "but they are frustrated by professional prejudice and by insufficient knowledge of the facts."[11]

Joyce quite rightly saw himself as a "minority of one." Not even the girl's mother seemed to want to save her. Nora, who had borne the brunt of Lucia's antagonism through the years, wanted to send Lucia back to Dr. Brunner in Küsnacht. It was not simply that Lucia's care would otherwise fall on her shoulders[12] but that her daughter was, increasingly, replacing herself in Joyce's emotional and artistic landscape. Lucia seemed more and more to be the daughter-wife of *Finnegans Wake* embodied in a flesh-and-blood child. If she was not an Anima in the Jungian sense of the term, she was nonetheless an inspiration, a preoccupation, a "princeable girl" (*FW* 626.27), a collaborator in a work that Nora herself found illegible. Lucia had not been wrong: her mother was jealous.

Joyce seems to have relied on Annie Barnacle's weekly letters from Galway to thwart his wife's active opposition to his plans for their daughter. Meanwhile he had to weigh evidence, weigh options, think of his wife's peace of mind, take into account his daughter's own longings and desires, gather strength for the next journey into uncharted waters. Even twenty years later Jung himself would speak candidly about the "pioneer" status of all psychological investigations in the 1930s and admit that "how one could penetrate further . . . into the structure of . . . schizophrenic disturbances . . . remained unanswerable."[13]

What had it meant to label Lucia schizophrenic? In none of the medical records that have survived is there mention of her having hallucinations, hearing voices, or exhibiting the language disturbances that were then believed to characterize schizophrenia, nor is there evidence of a "psychotic break." The one "terrifying dream" of Lucia's that Joyce mentions did not conjure disembodied phantasms but reflected the very real fear that one of her lovers had given her syphilis. James Joyce was a writer, but in this most private dimension of his life, his task was to become an attentive and effective reader of the text of his daughter's life. It was up to him to find coherence in behaviors and demonstrations of desire that everyone else considered illegible. Of course he had been doing this her whole life, but it now became his solitary preoccupation.

Joyce took Lucia out of Dr. Brunner's sanatorium on 14 January 1935 and arranged for her to live temporarily in the annex of the Carlton Elite with a nurse companion while he considered what to do next.[14] It was a short-lived solution, for in her newly won freedom, Lucia proved to be as obstreperous as she had been with her family in Paris. Far from lapsing into the apathy that her parents had been taught to recognize as schizophrenia's primary symptom, she was willful and without social grace. She still hated her mother; she walked out of a restaurant; the nurse immediately resigned.[15]

Trying herself to think of a suitable companion, Lucia came up with the idea of her aunt Eileen. It is a mark of Eileen Schaurek's continued love for her niece that she came to Paris to look after her, for she was then a widow with three teenaged children of her own to support. It was an improvised, short-term arrangement; Lucia thought of her aunt as "a bit loony but so am I, they say"[16] ("loonely in me loneness" [FW 627.34]). Lucia's remark lets us see that she was now beginning to identify herself as much by her experiences of being locked up as by her desire to create.

By this time, Lucia must finally have talked to her father about her relationship to Alec Ponisovsky, admitting more than the fear that she had gotten syphilis.[17] (The first time she had brought up the matter, on 20 November 1934, Cary Baynes had despaired at the Joyces' inability to communicate about intimate matters of the highest significance. Joyce had swerved away from his daughter's confidences "as though he had a deadly terror of knowing what actually had happened to her." "Then she said her ex-fiancé deserved six years in prison for what he had done to her, and told her father he must sue him for all the money he had had to expend on her. Her father told her he knew nothing of what had passed between the fiancé and herself, and she said, 'I will tell you.' Then he like a fool instead of encouraging her to tell him changed the subject."[18]) But now, on 16 January, Joyce arranged for Lucia to talk to W. Rosenbaum, Switzerland's leading criminal lawyer. The result of this conversation, as Joyce reported to Paul Léon that evening, was that she decided to drop the idea of a lawsuit against Ponisovsky but was feeling suicidal.[19]

Long before this moment Paul Léon and Joyce had recognized the complicated nature of Lucia's relationships with men, writing in the *Anamnese* that men had "generally badly treated" her.[20] According to them, Alec Ponisovsky had been the love of Lucia's life for many years, even when he had disappeared from the scene, ignored Lucia, and was having many affairs with other women.[21] And it was when he proposed to her in 1932 that she first became psychotic.[22] The life summary went on to say that this event precipitated her first stay in a sanatorium and re-sulted soon afterward in a lesbian relationship with one of her nurses.[23]

While Joyce dealt with his daughter's self-doubt and anger, arranged to return to Paris, and waited for his sister to arrive,[24] Paul Léon and Harriet Weaver continued writing to each other about the effect of Joyce's concern for Lucia upon his writing. It is their construction of the meaning of the father-daughter relationship that colored subsequent bi-ographies of Joyce and that colored the generally held view that the story of Lucia's illness and the story of *Finnegans Wake* were antithetical narra-tives. Throughout the fall of 1934, they had discussed how to lure Joyce back to his flat in Paris. On 5 October, Weaver had agreed to write to Joyce to urge that they return to Paris "at the earliest possible moment." She wanted him to settle down to work after the summer. But she cau-tioned Léon that Joyce would be "too much overwrought" to make the decision to leave Lucia, and when Léon said that Joyce was determined "to stand by his daughter to the end," she worried.[25]

They were not sure what arguments to use that Joyce would listen to. Both agreed in the vulgarity and futility of using a financial argument to leave Zurich. Both wondered if they could suggest that affection for Lu-cia required him and Nora to leave. Both waited anxiously for Jung to come to a decision about Lucia's condition, agreeing that indecision was worse than a bad verdict. Intent in their view that Joyce needed to sepa-rate from his daughter in order to write, neither Weaver nor Léon con-sidered the significance of what was before their very eyes. "On Tuesday evening," Weaver reported on 20 December, "I received, very unexpect-edly, a long letter from Mr. Joyce enclosing a batch of ms. of the piece he is working on."[26] Even as they declared Lucia to be the cause of Joyce's enervation, they had evidence that this was not true. Even in Zurich, Lu-cia and creativity went hand in hand.

Six weeks later, Miss Weaver and Léon were still at it. They saw Lu-cia as the primary obstacle to her father's ability to work. On 6 February, with the Joyce family back in their rue Edmond Valentin flat, Léon wrote to tell Miss Weaver that "Miss Joyce" was "decidedly and obvi-ously better." "I think there is no doubt that Mr. Joyce has up to now suc-ceeded where all the doctors have failed and even against their opinion I mean he has averted the dangers of schizophrenia. Miss Joyce can now talk intelligently, be out with people, enjoy the cinema, the theater etc." His opinion was that "Mr. and Mrs. Joyce [were] decidedly worse" and that to leave them in the present condition would seem to be "fatal." The problem was between Lucia and her mother. "Though Miss Joyce is not doing anything extravagant the strain between her mother and herself is very great indeed. . . . Mrs. Joyce reprimands Miss Joyce for any gesture or word she uses or makes and this renders the strain almost unbearable."[27]

Léon then suggested that Miss Weaver invite Lucia to visit her in London, seeing a separation from her parents as the only possible means of restoring to Joyce some semblance of domestic peace: "Excuse me if I am suggesting something disagreeable to you but it occurred to me to be the best solution when she spoke yesterday of going to London as her very sincerest wish."[28] All the Joyces could see that Paris contained many painful memories for Lucia, and so they were receptive when Miss Weaver proposed that Lucia visit her. Evidently they did not suspect the connivance between Léon and Weaver that, however well intentioned, now steered their fates into another kind of calamity.

II. MISS WEAVER: "A GOVERNESSY GRANNYMAMA"

In Paul Léon's opinion, sending Lucia to London was a "safe" kind of option because Lucia would associate Miss Weaver with her father and with his work. As his benefactress and publisher, she had shown the kindest regard for the Joyce family for many years. But this was amateur psychology at its worst, for it would be hard to imagine two women more unlike each other than Lucia Joyce and Harriet Weaver.

Born in 1876 in Cheshire, England, six years older than James Joyce, Harriet Weaver was his antithesis in almost every way. A child of privilege, of a well-ordered and abstemious background, and highly reserved in her social bearing, she had devoted her life to the well-being of others. Jane Lidderdale, her friend and goddaughter, spoke frequently of Miss Weaver's conviction that unearned income was a form of usury, and in the biography she wrote of Miss Weaver she tried to demonstrate an underlying unity to Weaver's life as she moved from being a social worker, to editor of the Egoist Press, to patron of the arts, and finally into the so-cialist movement.

By 1935 Harriet Weaver was well acquainted with Lucia's problems, mostly through Paul Léon's letters. Some combination of duty and gen-uine kindness must have called her to respond to Léon's request, but it could not have been an easy decision. She liked quiet and order and was even uneasy in the presence of people who used alcohol or cigarettes. Her Quaker upbringing made her uncomfortable among bohemians, and Ezra Pound liked to laugh at her inability to distinguish between high spirits and malice.[29] Like Jung she was a reluctant reader of some of Joyce's prose, although the book that made her anxious was not *Ulysses* but *Finnegans Wake*.

If Weaver was awkward in company, she was good at nursing. Peo-ple admired her for her quiet and reassuring demeanor in the sick-room.[30] Yet whatever made her calm, soothing, and practical in outlook left her ill equipped to chaperone a now-twenty-eight-year-old woman who was restless, angry, despairing, and in no mood to be watched over as an invalid. Miss Weaver's quiet courtesies were no match for Lucia's unbridled tongue. A disenfranchised Parisian flapper, a friend of the avant-garde, a frequenter of communes, a reader of bohemian newspa-pers, an ex-dancer, an ex-asylum inmate, she was a young woman thwarted in love who continued to think of herself as the undirected but ambitious child of a genius. Her father had made a career out of his dis-regard for bourgeois thrift and convention, and so would she.

Lucia and Eileen Schaurek arrived in London on 14 February 1935. Jane Lidderdale wrote that Lucia lived in the back room of Miss Weaver's apartment at 74 Gloucester Place while Eileen stayed at a small hotel, the Mascot, around the corner in York Street.[31] But Joyce's own letters refer repeatedly to paying for room and board for both women to-gether.[32] An educated guess might be that Lucia stayed with her aunt at the hotel until Schaurek returned to Dublin to check on her own family on 24 February and only then went to Miss Weaver's.

From the beginning, the visit was fraught with good intentions gone awry. Lucia had a private agenda of friends and family to see. She wanted to see Samuel Beckett again,[33] and she experienced Harriet Weaver's careful companionship as a choking restriction on her freedom. She behaved erratically. Miss Weaver had an anxious and inhibited disposition even in less trying circumstances and did not know how to measure Lucia's unruliness. What is clear is that the two women lived within a circle of mutual mistrust that brought each of them distress, that Miss Weaver had none of the humor or quickness of wit that made Eileen Schaurek a less irritating companion, and that the story of what happened got distorted in the telling.[34]

The problems started when Eileen Schaurek left London for a week. At first Miss Weaver reported only that Lucia was quite understandably depressed and had difficulty concentrating: "But that anyone could call her insane seems to me (so far) absurd."[35]

On 26 February, Lucia and Miss Weaver set out to visit a urologist, Dr. John Joly, in Harley Street.[36] Miss Weaver wrote to Joyce, "At Dr. Joly's Lucia told the story of her illness and made the assertion she had been a lunatic. I demurred. Whereupon she turned round and gazed at me with a dark and ambiguous expression on her face. I did not at the time know that she liked to pose as having been insane, as your sister told me later she did."[37] At the end of this "posing, mad-cap" interview, realizing that they were close to another doctor's office at number 145, Lucia stopped in to see if an appointment scheduled there for 7 March could be set for an earlier date. Then the two women went to lunch at a Swedish restaurant that Lucia loved. She ate quietly and then told Miss Weaver that she wanted to go to Piccadilly by herself. Miss Weaver said that she would go with her, but Lucia insisted that she preferred to go alone. In writing to Paul Léon, Weaver was concerned to justify herself for letting Lucia do this, but her letter tells us that Lucia was accustomed to going out alone in Zurich and Paris and previously in London.

When Lucia did not return for dinner, Weaver panicked. She feared that Lucia "might have been run over or else kidnapped and drugged by some rascally person." All her worries surfaced. Lucia had said she hated the traffic in central London. Lucia might not know her current address. She might have taken the night train to Dublin—although how someone who supposedly did not know her own address might find and book passage on an international train seems not to have struck her as illogical. She called her friends Mr. and Mrs. Yeates to ask for advice; they considered that Scotland Yard should be notified. Informing Miss Weaver that no accident involving a young woman had been reported to them, Scotland Yard in turn suggested calling the local police. Leaving her telephone in the care of a French neighbor, Miss Weaver went to the police that evening and then thought to telegram Eileen lest Lucia should somehow arrive in Dublin.[38]

At 12:50 the next day, she knew that Lucia was safe, for Lucia telegraphed to say she had gotten lost and would be home later in the day or on the day following. The postmark showed that the message had been sent from the Baker Street telegram office, so Miss Weaver made the rounds of local hotels. Not until the crisis had been resolved did she notify Joyce.

It is interesting, given that this story has been used as evidence of Lucia's madness, that she had simply gone to a small private hotel right on Gloucester Street, not two hundred yards from Miss Weaver's flat. She had paid the bill properly and left the next morning. She had not telegraphed earlier because the telegraph office had not been open the previous evening. After sending the telegram on the morning of 27 February, she went to visit her uncle Charles, then returned to 74 Gloucester Place by early evening.[39] In Ellmann's account, this series of events became one of many "mad maneuvers," and he wrote that Lucia had "slept in the street."[40] Jane Lidderdale claimed she slept "apparently in the open."[41] Brenda Maddox did not say that Lucia and Miss Weaver had had a quiet lunch where they agreed that Lucia would spend the rest of the day alone. Instead she portrayed her as stomping out of Dr. Joly's office, as if angry that Miss Weaver was in a conspiracy with the doctor.[42]

None of these narratives agree with Miss Weaver's own account of these several days, though they pick up on and amplify her anxiety. And none of them concur with what Lucia said to Eileen when she came back to London several days later: that she both wanted solitude and was wary of infringing on Miss Weaver's hospitality. "She told your sister," Miss Weaver wrote to Joyce on 4 March, "that she felt she was in the way here, gave too much trouble. Hence her absenting of herself. This in turn gave me the idea that she did not like being here."[43] She herself had thought this a week earlier when, with characteristic self-scrutiny, she had told Joyce, "I think my attitude has probably irritated her to some extent—a kind of governessy grannymama."[44]

We can see the tensions, plans, and energies working at cross-purposes here, the suspicions and countersuspicions, the movements of fear. We can also understand the nuances of sympathy and credence that eventually form a historical record out of events that were ambiguous and unhappy to those living through them. Miss Weaver's character was unimpeachable; Lucia's was stigmatized by her having been in an institution. What she said about herself from this point on was all too often deemed evidence of deviance or self-deception. Her testimony was untrustworthy. Richard Ellmann, and then Jane Lidderdale and Brenda Maddox following him, reported that Lucia Joyce slept on the street. This statement is not correct, but it offers us a metaphor for her exile from the community that claimed to determine the meaning of her life.

Eileen Schaurek returned to London on the evening of 1 March. She was tired but spent most of the next day with Lucia, who told her about her difficulty with Harriet Weaver's hospitality. Miss Weaver described this time as "three days of racketing about"[45]—a phrase Ellmann transposed into Lucia's having "disappeared again,"[46] although Weaver also made clear that Lucia had spent the previous day with her aunt.[47] Soon she told Joyce that she and his sister agreed that London was too exciting for Lucia and that Lucia herself wanted to get away.[48]

Their plan was to go to Tully Wells Farm at Offham, near Lewes, Sussex, but they never got there because Lucia took matters into her own hands. She got on a bus going to Windsor. Eileen came with her, telephoning after their arrival to ask Miss Weaver to send them some clothes. The impetuousness of the trip upset both older women, but we can see from Weaver's letters to Léon that she was watching Lucia closely and working out terms for hiring more professional help: Edith Walker, a nurse whom Weaver had met in her days as a social worker in south London, was going to come with them to Sussex. From the Star and Garter Hotel, Lucia wrote to explain, "I'm afraid I cannot keep by you in London. . . . I certainly must appear to you like the most disgusting creature that ever walked on this earth." But she asked Miss Weaver to remember, "One of the doctors I was in contact with said I really had a great wish to live and an immense love of life. He was right, and perhaps you know somebody who will explain this to you quite carefully." She signed the letter, "With kindest regards, yours sincerely."[49]

When Lucia did come back to London and to Miss Weaver's flat, she was increasingly moody until she erupted in a "hysterical crisis" to which Miss Weaver responded by asking a doctor to sedate her. "Today," she wrote to Paul Léon on 9 March, "the doctor gave a strong injection, which this afternoon seems to be taking effect. She is much calmer and is actually drawing some large initials at the moment and asked for the Book of Kells."[50]

What was going on? Harriet Weaver's way of being hospitable increasingly included supervision, secrecy, and sedation. By now Lucia could recognize these maneuvers with uncanny swiftness. Within a month, in conversation with her cousin Bozena Berta, Lucia described her visit to Miss Weaver as being held "prisoner."[51]

When Eileen Schaurek announced that she had to return to her job in the *Irish Sweepstakes* office in Dublin, Lucia was ready to go with her. Eileen was of two minds, first asking Joyce to endorse the plan, then almost immediately wiring her brother to forbid it. On 14 March, Joyce sent his approval and arranged to finance the trip through Miss Weaver. Lucia wrote a thank-you note to her: She felt chagrin about her behavior, she said, and described herself to Miss Weaver as a "lout."[52] Finally she was off to Ireland.

III. SILENT INTERLUDE

To follow Lucia Joyce at this time is to walk directly into silence. Harriet Weaver had recorded the image of Lucia writing: "This morning . . . she was in and out of the rooms . . . washing gloves then writing at my desk while I went out on some errands."[53] But she later destroyed those pieces of Lucia's writing. Almost all Lucia's letters have been deleted from the copious archive that Miss Weaver left to the British Museum, although Joyce had said these were the ones he most valued.[54] On 7 April 1935 he wrote to Weaver, "I am grateful for your letters but the only ones which enlighten me, even if they are wild, are Lucia's own."[55]

Interpreting Lucia requires one to follow not just words but also the course of intensities. Lucia spoke in a kind of body language that expressed pain and suffering and unspoken desires. She expressed life as a dance of false starts and small triumphs, of emotions lifted, of hopes deflated, of steps taken, however tentatively, toward health. As his daughter's primary spectator, interlocutor, and dancing partner, Joyce was learning the measure of his own love for his child. He let her teach him;

he listened to her; he changed; and above all he persevered. He also learned to distinguish between suffering and being sick, between personal (mis)behavior and physiological dysfunction. He learned the difference between controlling deviance and curing disease. He, like Jung, reverted to the language of the spirit as he tried to explain to others what he understood about Lucia and what he hoped that he could help her achieve.

Among all the letters that were destroyed, there was one, I like to imagine, that expressed Lucia's gratitude to her father for persisting in his belief in her. Our contemporary Kay Redfield Jamison has written about her mother, who did the same, in this way: "She could not have known how difficult it would be to deal with madness; had no preparation for what to do with madness—none of us did—but consistent with her ability to love, and her native will, she handled it with empathy and intelligence. It never occurred to her to give up."[56] Jamison is telling us, as anyone who has ever suffered through the kind of turbulent emotions that plagued Lucia can attest, that the steadiness of uncompromising love is itself a medicine.

At home in Paris, waiting daily for news of Lucia's new life,[57] Joyce was more abstracted and unable to focus on his work than he had been when her daily vicissitudes unfolded before his eyes. Léon and Miss Weaver's benevolent scheme on his behalf had backfired. He worked sporadically and described himself as penning five words a day while Nora ran around Paris with her friends. To Miss Weaver, after all her kindness, he wrote a nasty letter, asking her if she had actually liked Lucia, for he could sense that her intention had been to facilitate his writing rather than to enjoy Lucia's company. He knew already that his daughter had a savage tongue and that, "not having been brought up as a slave and having neither Bolshevik nor Hitlerite tendencies,"[58] she would not behave in ways intended to placate convention. "She certainly does not flatter like the ladies of the rue de l'Odéon," he wrote to Miss Weaver, who to her credit readily conceded her lack of "imaginative and consistently sympathetic understanding of Lucia's mental state."[59]

By this point, Joyce knew there was no one else to rely upon. After twenty-odd attempts at diagnosis, he no longer had faith in any doctor. Nora was no help. Although Joyce had set up the apartment at 7 rue Edmond Valentin so that Lucia would have a home, Nora now refused to let her daughter live there. "She should be in this house, which was set up for her," he wrote to Harriet Weaver. "But you can think in what a state my wife's nerves are after four years of it. And that is the problem, the whole problem and nothing but the problem."[60] He and Nora were at odds about their child—Joyce wanting and needing Lucia near him; Nora hostile to the mere thought of renewed proximity. Paul Léon captured the bleakness of their lives and the altered focus of Joyce's emotional preoccupations. Far from relishing his private life with Nora, Léon claimed, Joyce was languishing. He was "suffering from solitude" without Lucia; he was living with a "sense of desertion"—as if he had been abandoned by a lover. There has "developed a peculiar atmosphere here," Léon confided to Miss Weaver. "Mr. Joyce trusts one person alone, and this person is Lucia."[61]

Who can measure the resonance of a father's love for a daughter? Who can decide whether an emotion is "proper" or "improper," "enough" or "too much"? In these years, Joyce seems to have come to understand that if Lucia was to survive and flourish once again, he could help her to puzzle out the way, and to see that freedom had to be the ground of her recovery. Several months later, he described the various strategies used with her to Nora's uncle, Michael Healy, explaining, "Rigid surveillance was a complete failure and slack surveillance only a partial success. The plan of allowing her her own way as much as possible using only the force of persuasion has apparently been more successful."[62] He did not cease to watch over her, but he did so from afar, maintaining his connection to her through constant letters, books, and suggestions about activities, people to meet, and places of beauty to visit. He harbored no illusions, knowing that others called her malady schizophrenia, but he continually refused to sentence his child to exile.

To Giorgio, who still thought that Lucia should be put away, he wrote that her experiences at Prangins and the Brunner sanatorium had made her worse, not better. And summarizing the situation to Michael Healy, he said that her problems were not in the violence or hysterics or setting of fires, difficult as these were to deal with. "The real danger is torpor," he wrote, the danger of Lucia's coming to live entirely in "her inner world, losing more and more contact with the outer world."[63]

By this time, Joyce was conceding that Lucia had no future as measured in conventional ways. She was presumably destined for the life of a single woman. However sad and lonely her prospects, he himself would not abandon her.

As Carola Giedion-Welcker was to remark many years later, Joyce's models for understanding Lucia were taken from Ibsen, Hauptmann, and Wedekind. Artists, not psychologists, would win the day, and he turned to the theater to gain insight into the troubled histrionics of his own family. Lucia had neither practical instincts nor decorum, but like the European drama he had so valued in his own youth, Joyce considered that "her mind [was] as clear and as unsparing as the lightning." "She is a fantastic being," he continued, as if describing actress and playwright alike, who speaks "a curious abbreviated language of her own." He knew the singular importance of his own role as spectator. "I understand it or most of it," he claimed, which placed him ahead of any of the psychiatrists who stood darkly before the curtained minds of other patients like Lucia, unable to penetrate the symbolic nature of their self-representations.[64] In adolescence Lucia had been his Wild Duck, his Hannele, the troubled youth of *Spring Awakening*.[65] Now Lucia came to him, as Paul Léon reported to Harriet Weaver, as the figure of Irene from *When We Dead Awaken*.[66] He stood before her turbulence as if before the dramas beloved in his youth for their unsparing honesty and disdain of convention. He saw in her life "the interplay of passions to portray truth,"[67] yet the idealism he had embraced as a young man would not serve him now.

Years earlier, long before he had had children, Joyce had read Ibsen's *The Wild Duck* and remarked that it was not possible to criticize such a play but only to "brood upon it as upon a personal woe."[68] Ibsen was an artist who stood as "a mediator in awful truth before the veiled face of God."[69] When his own daughter called him to stand in the same unsparing place, Joyce could understand that she would teach him nothing about romance, beauty, or ethics but only, like Ibsen, about desire as the expression of necessity.

Whenever agitation had characterized her earlier life, Joyce had placed Lucia in the company of a group of fictional characters whose various awakenings revealed to him the traumatic nature of female coming of age in contemporary Europe. Ibsen's Hedvig Ekdal, Hauptmann's Hannele Mattern, and Wedekind's Wendla Bergmann (all fourteen-year-olds) suggested that Lucia would find no Victorian gentility to buffer her entry into adult life and indeed that such gentility often masked the barbarity of acts that were supposed to protect children.

Wendla, Wedekind's young protagonist in *Spring Awakening*, asks her mother how children come into the world and must hide her head under an apron while her mother prevaricates. "To have a child," she tells her curious daughter, "the man—to whom you're married—you must—*love*—love, you see—as you can only love your husband. You must love him *very much with your whole heart*—in a way that can't be put into words. You must *love* him; Wendla, in a way that you certainly can't love at your age . . . Now you know."[70] Not knowing kills this child, for she has had sex with a schoolmate without understanding the ramifications of what she was doing, and then dies from a botched abortion. The same mother who tells her that she is merely anemic is the one who administers the purgatives that bring about her death.

Hedvig, Ibsen's adolescent in *The Wild Duck*, fares no better, though in her case the unnamed specter that haunts her life is syphilitic blindness. When her father learns that his wife had premarital sex with a previous employer and cannot vouch for the paternity of their child, he rejects them both. Hoping to recoup some of the damage brought about by this awful truth, a friend of the family tells the daughter, Hedvig, that the sacrifice of her beloved wild duck will restore her father's affection. But she chooses instead to act like the duck rather than kill it. When wounded, as Ekdal tells his childhood friend, wild ducks "shoot to the bottom as deep as they can get . . . and bite themselves fast in the tangle and seaweed—and all the devil's own mess that grows down there. And they never come up again."[71] Even before she has had to face the inherited affliction of her life, the child kills herself, opting out of a world that is devoid of sky and sea. She can see no path through the mess of dark and tangled human relationships that marked her even at birth.

In Hauptmann's drama *Hannele's Ascension* we find a similar situation. Hannele takes her own life rather than return to a father who abuses her. "Have you nothing to reproach yourself for?" a divine stranger asks the drunken man. "Have you never torn her from her sleep at night? Have you never beaten her with your fists until she fainted?"[72] We may never know what specific knowledge of Lucia's young life prompted Joyce to associate his child with syphilis, abortion, and suicide, but we can notice the darkness of his imagination and the extremities of experience that he accepted as natural aspects of the youth of women.

But the most singular aspect of his daughter's fate and his own role in it could easily have dawned on him years later as he reread the play most beloved by him in his own adolescence, *When We Dead Awaken*. In 1900, at the age of eighteen, he had written to thank Ibsen for noticing his essay about it in the *Fortnightly Review*. "The words of Ibsen I shall keep in my heart all my life."[73] The play that had once inspired a young man to "inward heroism"[74] in the face of public indifference now returned to haunt him, as if it were both prophecy and personal indictment, occasioning feelings of responsibility and remorse. "Lately there has been a good deal of talking on Ibsen," Léon wrote to Harriet Weaver in July 1935. Lucia had written to ask her father to write a play. The result was "a remark let fall today inspired by Ibsen's *When We Dead Awaken* to the effect that whatever sparkle of gift Mr. Joyce had he transmitted it not to his son but to his daughter and that this sparkle has kindled a fire and storm within her brain—hence . . . the desire to still that spiritual thirst which he considers he set afire within her."[75]

Where once Joyce had read the play from the perspective of a young man anticipating the heights to which his creativity might take him, he could now have a retrospective insight into the damages that such a life in art might impose on those who followed him in its exacting path. If ever he had neglected his daughter, if ever he had thought her pursuit of the dance a mere pastime or that artists were properly sons like Giorgio or surrogate sons like Samuel Beckett or John Sullivan, he could now see the error of his ways. This child returned him to the drama of his own unexamined assumptions and to the cost of his life's priorities. Léon saw him struggling with these issues. "You know," he confided to Harriet Weaver, "that if there is a feature in his life it is that he never belonged to himself, his family, his friends, but has always belonged to his work."[76] Léon persisted in thinking that no conflict existed between Joyce's work and "his most real and deep affections." "The more successfully his work will shape itself," he reasoned, "the more successful will his influence be on his surroundings and eventually if possible on his daughter."[77]

But Joyce's renewed attention to *When We Dead Awaken* tells a different story of an artist who, late in life, begins to reckon with mortal error. Lucia could have spoken Irene's lines: "(*rises slowly from her chair and says quiveringly*). I was dead for many years. They came and bound me—lacing my arms together at my back. Then they lowered me into a grave-vault, with iron bars before the loophole. And with padded walls, so that no one on the earth above could hear the grave-shrieks."[78] Lucia did not openly accuse Joyce of anything, but what better way would there be to describe her seven-month stay in Prangins, with its straitjackets and solitary confinement rooms? Nor could Joyce have missed the fictional Irene's unflinching assignment of blame: "[I hold you] guilty of making my death inevitable."[79]

Thirty-five years earlier, he had thought the play almost perfect: he had seen it as a drama about a sculptor's violation of the possibilities of his own life. Professor Rubek was, to the young Joyce, an artist who achieved "mastery of hand linked with limitation of thought."[80] The dramatic action of the play's three acts was, he thought, to wake up the sculptor to his own capacity for greater fulfillment. At the play's opening Joyce identified Rubek as a man whose life has all the trappings of worldly success: seated in luxury at a spa in Norway, he is resting from the furor created by his latest sculpture, "The Day of Resurrection." Basking in critical acclaim, enjoying his new affluence, he is nonetheless bored with his marriage to a younger woman and can find nothing among all his new experiences to hold his attention. He has stopped doing serious work and brings in money by making portrait sculptures of the fawning public.

To the eighteen-year-old Irishman, Rubek was a Faustian figure who had squandered his own spiritual legacy, the image of the future that he, James Joyce, would avoid by his truer sense of vocation. The spiritual crisis of the play is initiated when Maja, the young wife, goes off into the high mountains with a bear hunter, while Rubek renews his acquaintance with Irene, the model who inspired his work before his marriage. In conversation he learns that she harbors a murderous rage against him for not esteeming her in the past. He can see that she is ill and that she travels always in the company of a Sister of Mercy, habited in black, who trails her like an ominous shadow. Rubek regards her appearance as a new lease on life. Together they will evade the Sister and ascend into the mountains, seeking the heights of spiritual glory that his ignorant and compromising choices have prevented before this.

The young Joyce read the play as a waking into the full possibilities of life. While he appreciated Ibsen's rendering of the female characters, his own imagination remained riveted on the sculptor, whom he regarded as "dead, almost hopelessly dead, until the end, when he comes to life."[81] His appreciation of Rubek's new sentience seems, in fact, to herald Stephen Dedalus's own awakening to the "call of life to his soul."[82]

But what Joyce missed in the play is as interesting as the aspects that clearly influenced him. In his adolescent enthusiasm he had not seen, or at least had chosen not to emphasize, the death-in-life of Rubek's former model. And indeed, the only significance that he had attributed to Irene was the violation of bourgeois convention implied by her decision to pose as a model in the first place. "It will be considered by some as a blemish that she—a woman of fine spirituality—is made an artist's model," he conceded, "and some may even regret that such an episode mars the harmony of the drama." But, he continued, defending Ibsen's artistic restraint and sympathy, "He sees it steadily and whole, as from a great height, with perfect vision and an angelic dispassionateness with the sight of one who may look on the sun with open eyes."[83]

However, Irene stole Joyce's attention in his middle age, when weary experience had given him a vantage point closer to Ibsen's. *When We Dead Awaken* had been the work of an aging playwright whose final effort had been to look unsparingly on the cost of his life's dispassion. The violation explored in the drama is endured primarily by the young woman who had once been Rubek's *femme inspiratrice*. It is she who reveals the harm of the very commitments and priorities that made Rubek famous; and it could not have escaped Joyce's notice that she, and not the artist bent on his own salvation, articulates the irrevocable nature of their loss:

> IRENE: . . . it flashed on me with a sudden horror that you were dead already—long ago.
> RUBEK: Our love is not dead in us, it is active, fervent and strong.
> IRENE: The love that belongs to the life of earth—the beautiful, miraculous life of earth—the inscrutable life of earth—that is dead in both of us.

While Ibsen's drama unmistakably explores the shortsightedness of a man who chose to wed himself to his art instead of to a flesh-and-blood girl, the play brings into focus the more general dynamic created between an artist and his subject. In his boyhood essay Joyce had noticed the relation between the sculptor and his model. He had quoted Irene's line, "I exposed myself wholly and unreservedly to your gaze (*more softly*) and never once did you touch me,"[84] but he had placed it in the context of forfeited love. He had not followed the dark subtext of the play, in which surveillance becomes a kind of secret sharer, as if it were an independent character, blocking relationships, meliorating the expression of emotion, and destroying reciprocity. It is not simply that Rubek does not understand the nature of Irene's love (who among us has not suffered from a similar failing?) but that his pursuit of art has become a form of predation. He takes unceasingly from Irene, subjecting her nakedness to a transforming gaze, but does not consider the effect of making someone else into an object of such inspection. As she explains to him, she "died" not from lack of his love but from a spiritual avarice that left her with no interior life of her own. "I gave you my young living soul. And that gift left me empty within—soulless (*looks at him with a fixed stare*). It was that I died of, Arnold."[85]

In 1935, at exactly the time when his own daughter, the subject of his art from her earliest years, seemed incapable of integrating herself into a satisfying adult life, the figure of Irene "rearrived" to speak about a dilemma that Lucia herself could not articulate. Modeling, in Irene's sense, had little to do with the poses of the body but instead with a spiritual dynamic: the lilt of the voice, a characteristic lift of the chin, the inflection of one's walk, the vagaries of the heart, the exposure of one's most intimate experiences offered as the precondition of another person's creativity. In *When We Dead Awaken* Irene made this offering as a young adult. Lucia had grown to the awareness of herself with such a gaze fixed always upon her. And in Irene, as Joyce could see from his renewed acquaintance with the play, four years of bearing such "dispassionate" scrutiny had provoked enough rage to generate a lifelong illness.

In the play, Irene asks Rubek about "their child," which Joyce realized, even at eighteen, meant the statue: "To her it seems that this statue is, in a very true and very real sense, born of her. Each day as she saw it grow to its full growth under the hand of the skilful molder, her inner sense of motherhood for it, of right over it, of love towards it, had become stronger and more confirmed."[86] To her astonishment, she learns that Rubek has altered and obscured her image in the pursuit of what he calls his "changed conception."[87] When she reminds him that her "entire soul" was in that lonely figure, Rubek tries to dispel her agitation by pointing out that he had represented himself in the work as "a man weighed down with guilt." "I call him remorse for a forfeit life," he confesses.

One thinks of the unsparing commitment to the truth that Joyce shared with Ibsen, a commitment that had drawn him to value Ibsen in the first place. We can imagine the resonance with lifelong experience that an anguished father found re-presented in this drama. "The Day of Resurrection"; *Finnegans Wake*. Young women waking from sleep and death. The beloved as model; the daughter as model. The model turned partner; the daughter turned wife. The damage of creation measured in forfeited love, issueless effort. Imaginative transformations that in no way make up for the renewal of life that should have unfolded in their place.

> IRENE: But I was a human being—then! I, too, had a life to live. . . . All that I put aside . . . threw it all away in order to serve you. It was suicide. A mortal sin against myself. . . . I should have borne children into the world . . . not such children as are hidden away in grave-vaults. . . . I ought never to have served you—poet.[88]

These correspondences and recriminations are all present in Joyce's stark admission to Harriet Weaver during that terrible spring that he was "only too painfully aware that Lucia has no future."[89] Others might accuse him of neglecting his children—the interrupted schooling, the poverty and anxiety, the absence of domestic routine, the preoccupation with his work—but who among them could see the inner logic of the pattern that Joyce was beginning to understand? Scrutiny had been his daughter's constant companion, the invisible partner claiming more and more of her psychic energy until surveillance of any kind elicited inordinate and colossal rage. Like Irene, Lucia seemed poised *"to strike him with the knife,"*[90] though she needed no instrument sharper than her "wild and unrestrained feelings" to effect a wound to the soul of her father/creator.[91] "People talk of my influence on my daughter," Maria Jolas remembered Joyce saying during these months, "but what about her influence on me?"[92] Even Paul Léon, who was a relatively new friend to the Joyce family, considered that "some of the former attitude of his daughter to him, when she hated his glory, hated his success, may have led to the present state."[93]

One is tempted to ascribe predictive value to Ibsen's drama. *When We Dead Awaken* shows us in the untimely demise of Irene and Rubek that insight cannot always redirect the lives of those who struggle to face truth, however savage. Irene speaks of the irretrievable nature of her problems, even as she takes the hand of the sculptor and agrees to ascend with him into the high mountains. Ibsen transposes the avalanche of feeling unleashed between these two into the literal snowfall that destroys the couple: "*Suddenly there is a roar as of thunder from high up on the snowfield, which begins to slide and tumble down at terrifying speed. Rubek and Irene can be glimpsed indistinctly as they are caught up and buried by the mass of snow.*"[94]

Ibsen gives the last word in the play to the Sister of Mercy who, despite Irene's attempt to evade her, follows inexorably. No matter how singular our efforts to elude the eyes of the moral order, no matter how exalted the vision that compels us to pursue a private destiny, Ibsen would have us understand, we cannot escape the judgment of collective humanity. Functioning like the chorus of ancient Greek tragedy, the Sister of Mercy quite literally shadows Irene, secure in her judgment about the boundaries of rational and permissible behavior. It is Irene's fate in Ibsen's final drama to exchange the gaze of the artist for the gaze of social opinion and to find rescue only in death.

In the spring of 1935 Joyce seemed to anticipate that the time left for his daughter would be circumscribed, not by their own endurance, but by some future offense that Lucia might give to the outside world's sense of propriety. By April he had succeeded in convincing Paul Léon that "if anything can be achieved at all it is in keeping her free." "This naturally involves certain risks," Léon continued to explain to the ever receptive Harriet Weaver, "but I do not think these are of a suicide but much more of a public row which will lead to a definite landing into a sanitarium."[95]

Most of Joyce's friends worried about Lucia's trip to Ireland, anticipating that her behavior would jeopardize her father's name. Joyce alone paused to ask how the attitudes of the Irish might distort *their view of her*. "How well I know the eyes with which she will be regarded," he admitted to Harriet Weaver. "Léon is concerned with what she may do to prejudice my name there and my wife . . . thinks that this is the chief reason for my constant state of alarm. So far as I know my-self it is not so."[96]

In the meanwhile the child of Joyce's body continued to inquire about the child of their souls. Amid her supposed lunacy, Lucia paused, as she had in London, to ask how *Finnegans Wake* was coming along. Would he please send her the latest portion of it? No matter where she was, Lucia was acting on her father's behalf.

Lucia Joyce, mid-1930s. Photograph by Zdenka Podhajsky. (Courtesy of Special Collections, McFarlin Library, University of Tulsa)

12

ACTING ON
HER FATHER'S BEHALF
DUBLIN AND BRAY 1935

I. "SHE HAD GREAT SCOPE TO HER"

Brief memories from her own childhood, endless stories from her parents, and a lifetime of imaginative investments pressed against personal despair as Lucia Joyce headed for Dublin. She had not been in Ireland since 1922, and this was the first time she was old enough fully to appreciate the complicated relation between her father and his homeland. Her mother's anxiety about her visit she knew only too well: Nora worried that her people in Galway would look askance at her daughter's lack of religious training. But Joyce's dense network of associations, his long-harbored resentments, his secret loves, his obsessions, and his avoidances were not easily to be reckoned with. What Lucia knew of Ireland, she knew primarily through him, through family conversations, and through his fictional representations of the past. But the world that met her and the resources available to her for meeting it were far different from those that Joyce had left behind more than thirty years before.

At a time when most of her peers had settled into marriages and into commitments to actual places, Lucia could cling to wavering hopes as these arrived primarily through the spidery lines of her father's letters, emblems of her predicament. Composed in Paris, written in Italian, and sent to Ireland, often bearing news of America, each one bore witness to the displacement that destabilized even her simplest plans. Unmarried, almost thirty, disenfranchised, without independent means, accustomed to the lifestyle of artists, comfortable with the sexual license that characterized her generation on the continent, lonely, unhappy, Lucia faced the empty hours that stretched before her in Dublin.

At first she thought she would study art, so Eileen Schaurek changed her hotel from the Gresham to Buswell's on Molesworth Street so that she could be near the College of Art.[1] But once again, as in London, Lucia was unable to concentrate. It took her very few days to discover the changes that had taken place in her family on her father's side. Of all the relatives who had coddled her on previous visits, few were left. John Joyce, the grandfather who had cried over her as a small child, had died in 1931. Her uncle Charles now lived in London; Stanislaus was still in Trieste. Poppie had taken holy orders and was now a Sister of Mercy in New Zealand. Baby had died of typhoid in 1911. Aunt Josephine Murray had passed away in 1925. Of the loquacious, musical family that Joyce had commemorated in the portrait of his own youth in Dublin, only four sisters remained: Eva and Florence, May (now Mrs. Monaghan), and of course Eileen.

If she had gone to Galway, as she had at first thought she would do, Lucia would have found a similarly depleted family on her mother's side. Her grandmother, Annie Barnacle, was now old and almost totally dependent on her daughter Kathleen who had married John Griffin and stayed in Galway. Her aunt Mary had married William Blackmore and moved away, as had her uncle Thomas. Though Bridget (called Delia or Dilly in the family) had married, she continued to experience the emotional problems that had first emerged after the trauma of her twin sister Annie's death in 1925. Peg remained unmarried. Sensing that Galway would offer no more cheerfulness than Dublin, Eileen urged Lucia to take up the one option that seemed to offer gaiety and youth. She could stay with her own two daughters, Nora and Bozena Berta, who were then living to the south of Dublin in Bray.

In 1935 Bray was still an elegant seaside resort whose clientele came from England, France, Germany, and Italy to enjoy its bracing air and natural beauty. At one point in the 1700s Bray had served as a garrison town for the British, but quite early in its history people of means had recognized the extraordinary resources of the area: the sea, the protected shore, and the majesty of the Cambrian rocks on Bray Head that jutted out into the harbor. Joyce commemorated Bray Head in *Ulysses* when Stephen Dedalus notices that it "lay on the water like the snout of a sleeping whale."[2] The fictional Molly Bloom recalls it as an awkward scene of courtship with Bloom, who could not row a boat. She was typical of many in her generation who came down to Bray from Dublin for the day.

Eventually, as it was joined to Dublin by the railways, Bray became the full-time home of prosperous professional families as well. In the late 1880s, Lucia's paternal grandparents lived there, and though financial difficulties forced them to give up their house on Martello Terrace by 1891, for a few years they enjoyed the lively town with its long esplanade for walking along the seafront, international hotels with bandstands, flower beds, and palm trees. The town's development had been purposeful. City fathers, who had consulted British bylaws in constructing its civic code, referred to their home as "the Brighton of Ireland." J. Gaskin would describe Bray in *Irish Varieties* as a "magnificent mile long promenade . . . framed on one side by a shelving beach with a variety of rare and curious pebbles and shells. Opposite are beautiful and stately marine villas, well arranged terraces and mansions of noble proportions and architectural beauty, palatial hotels and oriental concert halls. These elegant and curiously embellished structures were originally designed for Turkish Baths where invalids and convalescents might not only face the breeze and catch its sweetness, but revel in the luxury of an Eastern bath with all its anodyne accompaniments and restorative qualities."[3]

Bozena Berta reminisced about "galas on the seafront, fireworks, boats illuminated at night, fancy dress swimming parades and always the music from Bray Head with loudspeakers everywhere."[4] Across the Dargle River in Little Bray, working-class people lived in thatched and poorly ventilated cottages and suffered high rates of tuberculosis. But on the Meath Road, where Eileen Schaurek had established her daughters, even middle-class people could enjoy a cosmopolitan seaside life. The girls took life on easy terms, but they knew that no amount of time or familiarity would ever alter their status: "No matter how many years we've lived in Ireland we [were] still 'foreigners,'" Bozena Berta remembered.[5]

Lucia's first impressions of Bray were of its natural beauty. In April 1935, she wrote to her father that it was "un luogo magnifico pieno di fiori" ("a magnificent place filled with flowers").[6] The hills were covered with heather, and as Sir James Ware noted in *Antiquities of Ireland*, "rare plants, species and wild life" were abundant.[7] She must have taken the Cliff Walk around Bray Head, for in May Joyce wrote to her about the Naylor baths—later called the Bray Cove Baths—which are to be found directly beneath the start of the walk. His own memories of Bray were vivid; he recalled to her "the damp clothes, the keen air and the smell of the salt water," though he also expressed amazement that his children enjoyed swimming, for he himself abhorred it.[8] She took a room in the Bray Head Hotel, one of the classic Victorian structures that had been erected at the northern end of the strand in 1860, during the first flurry of tourism. But as so often happened, she could not sleep there and left it to stay in the semidetached bungalow where her cousins were living. They had been expecting her, for their mother had written from London asking them to rent the apartment that adjoined their own.

But Lucia was not used to taking care of herself. Her cousins, her juniors by more than a decade, were much more accustomed to the tasks of everyday life. And as the adolescent daughters of a widow, they were woefully aware of the cost of it. Joyce had written to Eileen that Lucia should become accustomed to managing money, expecting that she would initially mismanage it, and he was right. She was horrible at it and as extravagant as her parents. Some of the incongruities in her behavior in Ireland can be understood by remembering that she thought of herself as a sophisticated tourist while her younger cousins were living their normally frugal everyday life.

The dissonance between their expectations of her and her own expectations of herself was the dissonance of Bray itself. On the one hand, it catered to an international elite, and on the other, it harbored the working poor. Even Lucia noticed that not everyone was like herself with her four pounds of discretionary money each week. But it cannot have been easy for her to read the codes of class and decorum that applied to the Schaureks. They could afford two homes, had the means for tennis and club fees and enough leisure to pursue these pleasures, but they seemed nonetheless to have no money beyond what was immediately required for survival. She may have heard the stories that Bozena Berta told about having to hock the family silver in order to get enough to eat when her mother was in Paris and London. But then Lucia's own immediate family constantly displayed similar ambiguities of class and status. Nora Joyce had never had a job, ate at the finest restaurants, went to the opera, and interested herself in Parisian haute couture, but she could not tell from one year to the next whether she and her husband could afford to rent an apartment.

If Lucia couldn't see the rules that governed the values of her own convent-educated cousins, then neither could she read the codes by which the more general population signaled their status as Protestant or Catholic, middle-class or worker, for or against the union with Britain, and respectable or not within any of these categories. Niall Rudd, in his memoir of a bourgeois, Methodist upbringing in Clontarf during the 1930s, remembered that the confusions of his youth remained mysterious long after they needed to be because of his family's reticence about asking personal questions. "Yet I knew," he recalled of his family's housemaid, "that in some respects Maggie was different. She had that red heart and the holy water, and we didn't. Moreover, she went to mass and confession. What *was* mass? And what did you have to confess? From time to time I wondered about such questions, but something told me it would be rude to ask her."[9] From earliest childhood Rudd noticed the various ways that religion, class, and politics permeated the simplest aspects of everyday life, governing neighborhood demographics, education, private reading habits, shopping patterns, choices of restaurants, and even preferences in sport. For a Methodist child, it was unusual to memorize "The Burial of King Cormac" or learn about Finn Mac-Cumaill, but West-Briton boys were expected to read about King Arthur, Robin Hood, and *The Jungle Book*. Their families read the Protestant and pro-British *Irish Times* but not the Catholic and republican *Irish Press*. They shopped at Arnotts and Todd Byrnes's but never walked through the colorful market on Moore Street. As he was "massively incurious" about shopping, Rudd did not ask why. "But retrospect suggests an unstated system of 'yes's' and 'no's.' There were Switzers and Brown Thomas's (yes) and Clery's and Guiney's (no). . . . The Metropole, Capital and Savoy cinemas (yes) and the Corinthian (no). The Gaiety Theatre (yes), and the Olympia (no). The system," he said, "was unstated; it may not even have been consciously formulated"; but no aspect of life escaped it.[10] As he grew, he came to see that the choice of games could tie one to the United Kingdom "and to what was still known as 'the Empire' " or cause one to be shunned because he was Gaelic.[11] Dress and manners were similarly tied to codes of gentility and gender.

So Lucia didn't fit in. Nora and Bozena Berta thought of Lucia as someone with many moods that seemed to play on the surface of an underlying loneliness and sadness. She seemed even more an outsider than they were, and she would have been no matter what her social skills and emotional frame of mind, for no one can learn to read the ingrained codes of cultural identity in a new place without practice. Moreover, she was the daughter of a heretic who disdained convention. And on top of that she was rude. People might come to see her in order to meet the daughter of James Joyce, but she was sick of accommodating Joyce groupies. Nora and Bozena Berta wanted to show her off to their friends, but Lucia had no interest in being valued for the achievement of a parent. She'd been having fits about this kind of thing long before she came for this visit. Living in Bray was a time for herself, outside the limelight of her parents and, oddly and sadly for a woman almost twenty-eight years old, the first time in her entire life when she was not living under adult supervision. She told her cousins that her supposed "visit" to Harriet Weaver had been a "prison,"[12] and they, with their mother's consent, were willing to let her be. She did as she pleased even if her pleasures were outrageous.

Throughout her stay in Ireland, Lucia was plagued by insomnia. When she couldn't sleep, she often sang to herself, but night skies and the sound of the sea seemed to comfort her, and she arose at five each morning to swim. Like the characters of Ibsen's later plays, she "had a tendency to get out of closed rooms."[13] When the weather was fine, she would sleep in the open air, and she took pleasure from bathing in the sea. Like the well-trained convent girls they were, Bozena Berta and Nora were scandalized that she would not sleep each night in a bed, but then, they didn't have memories of locked rooms and straitjackets.

What was normal behavior for men was disreputable in Lucia. She liked to skinny-dip. The girls were placated only when she assured them that at dawn the beach was deserted except for an old man who also liked solitude. During the days, she often lolled about in a dressing gown in front of the gas heater. She read, she wrote occasional letters to her family, she bought fruit and champagne. She was on vacation. Bray gave her a chance to recover some balance in her life. Would Niall Rudd have been incensed by her ways? Looking back on his own family's summers on the shores south of Dublin in the same era, he observed, "People somehow looked and behaved differently in Ballymoney; there were Ballymoney clothes and games, and even a special kind of Ballymoney boredom."[14] He remembered girls who did stripteases; normally modest hostesses who wore extravagant evening gowns and served exotic cocktails; otherwise frugal people who kept ponies; the advent of radio with programs like " 'Band Wagon' with Big-hearted Arthur Askey and stinker Murdoch." He remembered pop music like "Old Faithful," "Wagon Wheels," "South to the Border," and "The Isle of Capri." He remembered kids who tried out yo-yos, climbed rocks, fished for crabs with limpets on a bent pin, and slid down cliffs with surfboards.[15]

While in Bray, Lucia wanted a pony for herself; she wanted to learn to play the Irish harp; she fished in a neighbor's pond with a safety pin. She never paid attention to propriety, but people like the Rudds would have recognized some of her conduct as the accepted repertoire of summer vacationers by the sea. Other aspects of her behavior were pretty batty. If she felt like pouring oatmeal in the stew, she did; if she didn't want to wear underwear, she didn't; if she didn't like someone, she minced no words. Of all the many things that had comprised her scatter-shot education, the countercultural ways of Raymond Duncan seemed closest to her natural temperament. If given a choice between her mother's penchant for haute couture and Duncan's insistence that modern dress was a form of unsanitary madness, she was with Duncan and his campaign against contemporary underwear. None of this was guaranteed to win her friends among respectable people, and it didn't.

Amid all her tentative movements toward health, Lucia remained a sadly isolated figure. Bozena Berta and Nora were clearly unnerved by her sexuality, and she, it appears, by theirs. They hated taking her on jaunting carts because she didn't wear underwear. They became wary of bringing their boyfriends to the bungalow because Lucia sat on their laps or tried to unbutton their trousers. Bozena Berta remembered that her cousin would stay in the living room, singing far into the night when her own boyfriend was with her; she explained to herself that Lucia didn't want them to be alone together. The lyrics were in French, Italian, German, and English. "You're the Cream in My Coffee" over and over again. Once Lucia tore up Nora's boyfriend's monthly train ticket. The

girls "tested" her "with Paddy Collins who reported she was sexy."[16]
This was Patrick Collins, an Irish painter, who has left us with one of the
few independent views of Lucia in these months. He "marveled at the
way she walked, wearing a camel's hair coat and carrying a stick, 'as if
she owned the whole bloody world.' He found her strange but great fun.
He met her once when she was carrying a bottle of champagne, and she
offered him a drink. Her voice was lovely. 'It bubbled up as if from a
deep country well. She had great scope to her.' "[17]

A volatile, unruly body. A constellation of odd behaviors about sex.
What memories were behind her actions? What was being unhappily or
anxiously repeated? There are no answers beyond recognizing that she
had been in similar situations in the past. Lucia had spent years sleeping
in the same room with her parents. She could have remembered being
the third party after her brother married Helen Fleischman. She had
been afraid to sleep alone in Paris and had asked her mother, night after
night, to sleep with her, explaining, "la fenestra, la fenestra" (the window, the window).[18] Later she had repeated the same anxiety at Mary
Colum's. Who or what had disturbed her sleep? Joyce read the tension in
her handwriting, which always deteriorated when she was agitated.
How could someone who had produced illuminated letters of such integrity and clarity be capable of such scribbling? Did she write, he asked
her, with a "Japanese umbrella dipped in . . . the gulf of Neo-Naples?"[19]

Amid these eruptions of erratic behavior, Lucia continued to look for
more abiding interests. She wanted an animal, perhaps a pony, like the
ponies that drew the cabs in Bray. Joyce treated this as a joke, though he
encouraged her idea of learning the Irish harp. If an ad in the paper did
not produce a teacher, he suggested, she should try the Royal Irish Academy of Music. Lucia read the papers and took an interest in current affairs, writing to her father about a fire that had broken out in a square in
Dublin, threatening one of the hospitals, about the Irish Sweepstakes,
and about a tram strike. Joyce replied to her in a Wakean code that he
presumed she shared by saying, "the lady Anna Livia did not do her duty
even if the fireman did theirs."[20] Though he was referring to *Finnegans
Wake*, he can also have been reminded of the earlier tram strike that he
had used in writing *Ulysses* to signal the psychological paralysis that
characterized Dublin as he imagined it in 1904.

From Paris he sent other recommendations for her amusement. She should join the library, take out a membership in the golf club, visit coves that were remembered to be beautiful or marked by some historical adventure. As he did with Giorgio and Helen, who were now in America, Joyce sent her magazine articles, newspaper clippings, and the latest editions of *transition* with its installments of *Work in Progress*. He sent her books to read and packets of medicine.

But if leisure, extravagance, and gusto characterized her outer life, Lucia's inner life was quite different. Troubles, whether of nations, families, or the self, are about inner divisions. To her father she wrote about her old friend Emile Fernandez, recently married to a young Italian woman, who continued to haunt her. Joyce made light of her reference to him, saying he never thought about that "defunct cavalier,"[21] but here his plan for dwelling only on positive aspects in Lucia's life didn't work. Almost thirty years later, when Lucia wrote a short essay about her life for Richard Ellmann, she still remembered Emile and said she was sorry not to have married him. She remembered dancing with him in Paris when he had composed the music for *Le Pont d'or*, his home near the Champs de Mars, his physique, his manner of dressing, his talent, and his large family of aunts and uncles who had frequently invited her to tea. Hoping to keep her mind focused on the present, Joyce wrote on 7 April, to tell her that her brother and his family were well,[22] and he sent with his letter a copy of a small article about them that had appeared in *The New Yorker* in January.

All hell broke loose. The article upset the fragile balance that Lucia had been making for herself and plunged her into despair. By 10 April, she had brutally ripped the picture of Giorgio out of the magazine and sent it back to Paris along with a suicide note. She was going to kill herself; would Joyce greet all her friends for her? At the same time she sent another note to Constantine Curran, an Irish barrister and her father's friend from University College Dublin, and enclosed her house keys. She would no longer need them.[23]

The Joyce circle went into crisis mode. But before they could form a plan, Lucia wired them. She was all right but needed extra money for the week. In the interim, Curran had also learned that the crisis had passed. He had not gone down to Bray personally but had gotten word, presumably through Eileen Schaurek, that Lucia had conquered her despair. He took the liberty of inquiring about a "mental specialist" in

Dublin and finding out about a sanatorium for Lucia should she want one. Joyce was grateful, but he was through with "mental specialists." Instead he wrote a letter of thanks and sent as a token of his esteem a copy of *Pomes Penyeach* with lettrines designed by Lucia.

In May Curran wrote a beautiful acknowledgment of the gift to Paul Léon:

> the illumination is highly interesting. In reading our friend's work I have always amused myself with the idea—which some other people have also noted—that his work, revolutionary in so many respects, is at the same time profoundly influenced by traditional elements from the illuminated work of our old Irish scribes. Its variety, its grotesquerie, its apparent paradox of profuse license and invention with a rigorous sense of form, the perpetual metamorphosis of forms deriving from different worlds—all these things seem to us Irish in a degree which, I imagine, you, for example, could with difficulty appreciate. It is this which makes Lucia's decoration so interesting. Because here also I find—without slavishness to the designs of the Book of Kells—in a similar though less resolute metamorphosis and an independent and modern note in harmony with her ancestry and with it all a grace and delicacy in colour and form so entirely appropriate to this daughter of a poet—I hesitate to write, of a submerged poet.[24]

But what had caused the crisis? Curran added that he had once again seen Eileen Schaurek in town and that she had reassured him that Lucia was healthy and making progress. But a crisis there had undoubtedly been, and Lucia's self-loathing had been aroused by news of Giorgio.

The *New Yorker* article was not in itself controversial. In a chatty, conversational style, it reported on Giorgio, speaking briefly about his lifestyle and his ambitions as a singer, and then it passed on to what New Yorkers presumably wanted to hear: gossip about his famous father. "The Giorgio Joyces have been living quietly in and around town since they arrived with their small son on the Bremen last May," the article began, and then it mentioned the songs Giorgio had sung on his radio debut. Nothing more about his own life or that of his American in-laws, the well-to-do Kastors, was mentioned, but small glimpses were given of James Joyce at work in Paris, showing them an artist coping with the effects of near blindness. His father had to write with crayon on large sheets of white paper or listen to friends read to him out of dictionaries, encyclopedias, and other reference books. His parents rarely entertained,

Giorgio reported. They had a small circle of intimates; they dined at Fouquet's; they liked the opera; his father's favorite drink was white wine; and so on. His sister was mentioned as a member of the Joyce household in Paris: Joyce's "other child, Lucia."[25]

This was enough to inflame Lucia's rage. By this time Joyce recognized Lucia's suicide threats as a form of theatrics. She was demonstrating, to borrow the words of Susanna Kaysen, "externally and irrefutably, an inward condition."[26] While Giorgio made her feel worthless, it was not Giorgio for whom the demonstration was intended, but her father. Here is the cause of my pain, she seemed to indicate with the mutilated image, and here is the life-damaging extent of it. To Curran, who saw her as a true child of Ireland in a way that she probably could not see herself, she sent another message that would have been legible to those who understood Joyce's fiction: "Here are the keys." This was the Joycean gesture of usurpation: Ireland by the British and other hordes of invaders; Molly Bloom by an adulterous lover. This was a sign of the motherland or the female body violated by the unwanted attention of suitors.

Who were the suitors? Lucia's gesture reveals an emotion and its origin but no more. At the least, Giorgio was the person who had introduced her to the young men who became her lovers. Emile Fernandez, Samuel Beckett, Sandy Calder, and Alec Ponisovsky had all been his friends before they took notice of her. A few years later, when his marriage was on the rocks, Giorgio went to live in Alec Ponisovsky's apartment. His circle of friends had remained intact, having simply closed ranks without Lucia. Helen was the best friend of Peggy Guggenheim, who was eventually to dally with the love of Lucia's young life, Samuel Beckett. Out of these encounters with the children of international privilege, Giorgio had forged his life. He had found a rich wife, fathered a son, and lived in opulent leisure on his wife's money. Out of Lucia's experience with the same group had come sexual knowledge, rejection, and possibly what she experienced as abuse. Although she had been eager to learn about sex, she seemed to meet young men who slept with her and seemed to promise a future that they never delivered. Or as in the case of Albert Hubbell, she met married men who slept with her, seemed to care for her, and then went back to their estranged wives. Collectively they seem to have left her ashamed.

When Lucia looked back on her subsequent life, she might well have seen another pattern as well. It was her brother, and not her father, who had always wanted to send her away and lock her up. It was he who had tricked her into going to L'Haye-les-Roses in 1932. It was he who had insisted that she break her engagement to Alec.[27] He had also wanted to incarcerate her at Les Rives de Prangins. It is hard to know how much she knew of his attitude in 1935, for Joyce seems to have decided to give his children only the most superficial news of each other. But even from America, Giorgio continued to lobby for the end of his sister's freedom and thus for the end of her young life.[28] If Lucia had once loved him, as undoubtedly she had, the brother was now the fickle lover, the turncoat, the betrayer. Only Lucia could have known the motive that drove him to try to silence her. Even Nora with her frayed nerves did not reach across the ocean to snatch her daughter away from life. It was Giorgio's image that Lucia shredded, sending it as evidence to the father, who stood as the silent but scrupulous witness of her existence.

II. MASTERS AND SERVANTS

No matter what Joyce understood Lucia's gesture to mean, he responded to it as the effect of jealousy. To Giorgio, Joyce wrote saying he would not answer his questions about her "because I did not want to spoil the prospects of your career."[29] To Lucia, as he had done so often in the past, he sent his reply in a carefully chosen book. Where a few weeks earlier he had sent Dante's *Vita Nuova*, calling his daughter's attention away from sexual experience to the satisfactions of spiritual love, now he made her a gift of the short stories of Leo Tolstoy. He recommended "How Much Land Does a Man Need?" as the best short story ever written. He also asked her to read "Masters and Servants."[30] Each tale takes a prosperous man to consciousness at the brink of death, and in each a father wishes for a child's well-being. Joyce imagined Lucia as the reader who gains insight before it is too late. His choice of book also shows a father's anguished glimpse of himself as the overreaching protagonist who has brought extremity upon himself and thus the need for insight.

In the first story Tolstoy created a simple but profound allegory about the overarching pursuit of material well-being and the self-defeating rewards of greed. The action is initiated by the rivalry of siblings. An elder, well-married sister visits her younger sister, the wife of a peasant. The elder begins to boast about the advantages of town life, saying "how well they dressed, what fine clothes her children wore, what good things they ate and drank, and how she went to the theatre, promenades, and entertainments."[31] The younger woman defends the safety of a peasant's lot, but her sister goads her, pointing to her lack of elegance and manners and to the end of such an existence: "You will die as you are living—on a dungheap—and your children the same."[32] The actor in the story is not the younger sister but her husband Pahom who, overhearing the conversation, thinks of gaining more land. If he had enough land, he wagers, he would not fear the devil himself. Tolstoy's plot is about plotting in the senses both of conniving and of measuring out land. Pahom schemes, first about acquiring acres close to home and then about gaining remote grasslands that seem more productive, more economical, more immense. Finally, while measuring out a huge field of virgin soil by running around its perimeter, he dies from exhaustion. "His servant picked up the spade and dug a grave long enough for Pahom to lie in, and buried him. Six feet from his head to his heels was all he needed."[33] With this gift Joyce was inviting Lucia to remain with him in the kingdom of the spirit and among the elected few who understood the vanity of living for money.

The other story, which he described to her as having "a little propaganda in it," was even more telling. "Masters and Servants" focuses on another journey undertaken because of avarice. Vasili Andreevich Brekhunov sets out in a sled on a snowy afternoon with the intention of bidding for a grove of trees before his neighbors in town can make their offers. At his wife's insistence he takes with him Nikita, an old peasant, a man who is not known for the good management of his own household but who is adept with horses. As the two travel, they lose their way, and toward dusk they accept the hospitality of a family from a neighboring village, pausing long enough for Vasili Andreevich to learn that his host is in despair about the future of his family. The many sons want to divide the household, and both agree that "they used to have a proper house, but now they've split up none of them has anything."[34] No amount of sympathy and no degree of concern about the viciousness of the winter storm deter Vasili Andreevich from his purpose. Business must be done in a timely manner. But he once again loses his way, and this time even the horse cannot instinctively find its way back to the road. Confusion gives way to the desperate decision to rest until the morning light can assist them. The remainder of the story concerns the thoughts and actions of the two unsheltered men, master and servant, as they settle into the onslaught of the blizzard and wait for dawn. Nikita has no strength left and is freezing in his inadequate clothing, and he anticipates his own death. Being not only a servant on earth but a servant of God, "the Chief Master," he recognizes that whatever happens, he will still be in that Master's power. He sits with equanimity.

But Vasili Andreevich wrestles with devils. He resents his decision to bring the peasant with him, fears being held responsible for his death, measures the value of his life against that of his servant, and decides to steal away with the horse. Once again he is overwhelmed by the storm and, instead of finding shelter, discovers that the horse has led him back to Nikita. This time another kind of impulse takes hold of him. Spreading wide his warm coat, he lies down on the peasant, shielding him from the cold with his own body. At dawn he hears a "call," which signals his impending death, and his servant's breathing. " 'Nikita is alive, so I too am alive!' he said to himself triumphantly. And he remembered his money, his shop, his house, the buying and selling and Mironov's millions, and it was hard for him to understand why that man, called Vasili Brekhunov, had troubled himself with all those things with which he had been troubled."[35]

This story is another of Tolstoy's warnings about a final reckoning. Through it Joyce reminded Lucia of values other than the ones that measured Giorgio's success in the world. But as a parable, it has an uncanny resemblance to Joyce's own journey toward this moment in 1935. Like the merchant, whose preoccupation with his estate drives him out into the storm, he had followed his own calling without attending to its effects on those who traveled with him. Lucia stood in the position of the undervalued Nikita. She had been removed from one place to another, driven out into elements not of her own choosing, cheated in the various ways that Vasili had cheated his servant, and now faced some ultimate challenge for which she was inadequately clothed.

In the sleepless nights that plagued him as much as Lucia, Joyce may not have heard a voice calling him, but he seems to have been reorganizing his internal landscape, calling into question priorities that had once seemed self-evident. While Paul Léon and Harriet Weaver continued to plot out the conditions that would allow Joyce to write in peace, Joyce, in giving this story to Lucia, was measuring life's values much closer to the bone. What price was too high to pay for the practice of art? Would he, indeed, have protected her with the last heat of his own body if it would save her life? "There is not a moment, a gesture, a thought during the day or night which is not devoted some way or other to the solution of this problem,"[36] Paul Léon reported to Harriet Weaver that summer.

Joyce's letters and gift helped to avert a full-scale crisis in April, although as he admitted freely to Léon, he lived in dread of the next post from Ireland. Lucia wrote fewer and fewer letters, so Joyce found his plan to "run her" from a distance more and more tenuous. He later learned from Maria Jolas that Lucia "lived like a gypsy" with no regard whatsoever for bourgeois convention. At this juncture she formed an oddball kind of friendship with the woman who owned the Schaureks' rented cottage. Mrs. Nichols was closer in age to Lucia than her cousins, and she was probably a welcome companion. What we know of their relationship comes from the then nineteen-year-old Bozena Berta, and it is hard to know how to evaluate.

One story was about how the two women liked to have contests with phonograph records, tossing them (like later Frisbees) to see how far they would go. Lucia sent the bills for the broken records to her father. Was this good fun? Two inconsiderate women? The manipulation of a mentally defenseless woman by a feckless, opportunistic landlady? There is another, even stranger story about Lucia building a turf fire in the middle of her living room, "encouraged by the landlady, who, of course, got a new carpet from my Uncle."[37] Did Lucia and Mrs. Nichols think it was funny? Was the carpet worn out anyway, so that the landlady could calculate the money she might claim for it? Or was this the bizarre pyrotechnics of a woman for whom fire was an ever more compelling expression of fury? Bozena Berta remembered that Lucia sat in front of the turf fire as if in ecstasy. As with the incident when she cut the telephone lines after Joyce became famous, this story reads as a sign of illness, inasmuch as it forms part of an accumulating pattern of deviance. But Joyce had laughed when his daughter cut the telephone wires, and he continued to laugh about it when he reported her conduct to Swiss doctors many years later. Among the Joyces it was a family joke. The Schaureks, having decided not to tell Joyce about Lucia's everyday life, gave him no occasion for concern about this third fire.

They also chose not to report that Lucia had taken out an ad in one of

the Dublin papers advertising for Chinese lessons. Bozena Berta told Ellmann that the ad was really a coded plea for drugs of some kind, and she
remembered that Lucia eventually made contact with an Asian man in
Kilmacanogue.[38] At the time they did not understand what was going
on, but three days later Lucia was discovered in Kilmacanogue, and she
seemed to be drugged. This is probably true; for at the same time that
Bozena Berta reported on Lucia's "unpredictable" conduct, she also left
us the key to understanding it, even though she herself could not read
the signs: Lucia was hooked on barbiturates.

III. DOPE

"I send and I send and I send," Joyce wrote to Giorgio and Helen.[39] To
Lucia, along with books, magazine and newspaper articles, and her
weekly allowance, he regularly sent two medicines—Veronal and
Haemostial. At first he sent bottles with the preparation already made up
and joked about the possibility that customs officials would regard them
as torpedoes.[40] Later he switched to packets of powder, less expensive
and less likely to break in transit, but he cautioned her to be careful with
the instructions "and not to overdo the doses."[41] With this economical
gesture, Joyce put Lucia at risk: first by giving her a barbiturate without
supervision and secondly by putting her in the position of preparing the
proper strength of medication by herself.

Bozena Berta noticed the Veronal's odd smell, was curious about it,
and took it to a local pharmacist to ask him what it was. Recognizing it
immediately, he told her it was "dangerous to life as well as mind" and
threw it down the sink.[42] With this gesture, he probably threw Lucia
into a withdrawal that might have killed her. None of the well-meaning
people involved in this drama knew what they were doing, but this bitter
white powder, alternately given and withheld, insidiously affected Lucia's behavior. Clouded judgment, excitability, and emotional reckless-
ness, which were interpreted as schizophrenia, could also have been the
unrecognized effects of a chemical dependency. The effects of the attempted cure were posited as illness and then were used as the basis of
further misdiagnosis.[43]

Veronal is one of the fifty or so barbiturate derivatives that were synthesized and marketed as sedatives in the early twentieth century. First prepared in 1864, first marketed commercially in 1903, it was the only available general depressant until the early 1950s.[44] As a compound, it was categorized as a "sedative-hypnotic," that is, at different strengths it could be used to tranquilize, to induce sleep, or to act as an anesthetic. A Merck Index from the 1930s explains that the drug was used commonly and in various ways that to us now seem reckless. Doctors would prescribe it for insomnia, extreme nervousness, melancholia, coughing, vomiting in pregnancy, seasickness, cocaine addiction, alcoholism, delirium tremens, lessening the tremors in multiple sclerosis, cerebral tumors, gastrointestinal derangements, and tetanus in children. Its apparent effect was to slow people down and stop them from trembling.

Clearly doctors in the 1930s did not understand some of the simplest properties of the drug's action. Now we know that the effect of barbiturates is additive: Taking them with another depressant, like alcohol, deepens and exaggerates the induced depression. Low doses induce behavioral excitement, "a state that is often sought when a person wants to 'get loaded' or 'get drunk.' The excitement is thought to be due to a depression of inhibitory neurons within the brain, which leaves one in a state of *disinhibition*."[45] "Disinhibition" might manifest itself in overtly sexual conduct or in the violation of any normally heeded rule of social interaction. The amount and frequency of the dose could increase the likelihood that depression would be followed by a period of hyperexcitability, which "upon withdrawal of the drug, may be quite severe and might even lead to convulsions and death."[46] The body grows dependent upon the drug, and then tolerant of it, which means that more and more of it must be administered to achieve any desired effect.

A person who is intoxicated with barbiturates will behave very much as if he or she were inebriated with alcohol. The judgment may be clouded; the person may be disoriented or suffer memory loss or may seem to be in a state of euphoria; motor skills may be impaired. "Occasionally, however, as with alcohol, an individual may react by withdrawing, becoming emotionally depressed, or becoming aggressive and violent."[47] Add alcohol to barbiturates, and you have a formula for mayhem, for the two together reinforce any given effect.

With this knowledge of the drug in mind, we must realize that there is no easy way to tell Lucia's story in these months. Remember the holiday spirit that seemed at first to characterize her visit to Bray, her twice-weekly trips to the post office with its packages, and Paddy Collins's magnificent image of her striding through its streets with champagne. The past resonates with two voices. The first belongs to a displaced, unhappy young woman struggling to find a purpose for her life, and the second is the voice of a bitter white powder whose properties were not yet understood. When Joyce wrote to his friend Curran later in the summer that "it is terrible to think of a vessel of election as the prey of impulses beyond its control,"[48] he could have had various devils in mind, corresponding in some way to the idea of the Freudian unconscious. But science had no way to tell him that such impulses were probably drug-induced.

The police "thought she was drunk." Bozena Berta "couldn't get through to Lucia." She "had to struggle to keep her dressed." Lucia "couldn't sleep." "I found her sitting cross-legged in front of the fire, ecstatic." The pieces are all there: the unpredictability, the lack of good judgment, the ataxia (staggering) and loss of motor skills, the withdrawal, the euphoria, and the depressions that followed after the drug wore off. To the feelings of being unloved and undervalued, add the depression induced by an addictive drug, and one has the formula for suicide.

Lucia did feel suicidal. To her cousins, she confided that she had always felt her mother didn't love her or even like her. She spoke about the effect of discovering her parents weren't formally married and she herself illegitimate. She was "shocked" by her parents' marriage in 1931, when she was twenty-three and her brother twenty-five.[49] And although she resented her father "because of the Beckett business," her mother bore the brunt of her wrath. When Nora added postscripts to Joyce's letters that summer, Lucia "would turn up her nose at that."[50] Over the months, as Lucia's confidences to her cousins continued, resentment and anxiety fed each other, forming a web whose strands were as intricately woven as the illuminated letters that she designed for her father's writing. Lucia associated her failures with her appearance and was depressed by the failure of the surgery that was supposed to have corrected the cast in her eye. She worried about a scar on her neck. The whole summer was a continual struggle to believe in the possibilities of her future.

Bozena Berta came to understand that these anxieties were a steady undercurrent in her cousin's life. The suicidal gestures recurred night after night, as Lucia's turning on the gas tap became a ritual that was met by her cousin's repeated resourcefulness in turning it off. Bozena Berta noticed that Lucia just as scrupulously opened her window so that fresh air could counteract the toxic effects of the gas. This ambivalence suggests the theatrical nature of Lucia's gestures, even when her father, that voracious collector of dramatic conduct, was not there to benefit from it. Had performance become an unthinking habit? Bozena Berta thought Lucia's infatuation with Joyce went "beyond a daughter's love" and reported that she transformed even the landscape into the image of the parent. Lucia looked at Bray Head and saw the profile of her father.[51] Just as the Irish believed that Finn MacCool lay sleeping under the Hill of Howth, in Lucia's imagination Joyce became the giant who slumbered beneath the earth of her experience, explaining the very contours of her emotional topography.

Whatever the real and present causes of Lucia's unhappiness, they were exaggerated by the effect of drugs, and they were twisted by their withdrawal. Lucia probably had no more idea what was happening to her than those who thought that they could help her. But it was more than likely that she was addicted to Veronal—the willing subject of its sedative quality and the unwitting recipient of its mood depressions. She drank champagne, which multiplied her despondency. She grew reckless when she didn't have the drug.

How long had she been taking Veronal, and why was it prescribed? There is no exact record, but it was probably first given as a soporific. Cary Baynes had been concerned about Lucia's sleeping patterns in Zurich, and she had been relieved when Lucia was finally able to sleep without any drugs. Perhaps Dr. Brunner had tried to wean her from dependency. But whatever he had done for her in Switzerland, the prescription that was filled in 1935 was French. Perhaps she had first been given it in Paris in 1932, the year she withdrew into catatonia as a response to her broken engagement with Alec Ponisovsky. Barbital was thought to release patients from their inhibitions and was often used to break the silence of catatonia by making it easier for patients to articulate their problems. A third possibility is that the drug was given as a sedative after some kind of objectionable behavior; but being prone to violence could have been an effect of the drug and not the condition that called for its use. A muddled version of all these possibilities could have happened, since Lucia lived at a time when Veronal was, like aspirin, a kind of cure-all. It was given whenever doctors thought that patients—or their families—could benefit from their being more calm and pliable. Lucia the Rude qualified in many ways for such a prescription.

IV. THE BLACK COTTAGE: CIRCE'S LAIR

Throughout this time in Bray, and coming faintly through the fog of medication, one can also hear the voice of an original young woman of the world with an imperious flair that rivaled that of her celebrated mother. Lucia liked continental foods, and evening meals in Bray became feasts of ragout, or goulash, or gnocchi, or kipfels with sauerkraut. She inspired Eileen to take a renewed interest in life, which had seemed drab to her after her husband's death. Now, instead of coming home only by way of the church, Eileen would stop off at Kidd's in Abbey Street or go to Mr. Magill's in Johnson's Court off of Grafton Street, looking for foods they had all enjoyed in Trieste.[52]

Ever conscious of design, Lucia tried to make the cottage more to her own extraordinary liking. She worked in her own mode, choosing, like Isadora Duncan, to paint her room in the cottage black. Duncan had found the little apartment in Paris that gave her respite from her teaching particularly alluring, calling it the "veritable domain of Circe":

> Sable black velvet curtains were reflected on the walls in golden mirrors. A black carpet and divan with cushions of oriental textures completed this apartment . . . The little room was beautiful, fascinating, and, at the same time, dangerous. Might there not be some character in furniture which makes all the difference between virtuous beds and criminal couches, respectable chairs and sinful divans?[53]

Duncan owed the transformation of her home outside Paris to the avant-garde designer Paul Poiret, but Lucia worked alone. She painted a wooden table black, capitalizing on the effect of the black slipcovers, edged with gold, that were already there. As a final touch she put black phonograph records on the shelves that ran around the walls, creating an effect like that of the stage decor for Jean Borlin's *Relâche*. Her cousins found it "eerie."[54]

Eventually new people came into her life as well. At first, Bozena Berta said, "it was pathetic to see Lucia so lonely—not one boyfriend of her own, nobody she could really love. She was very unhappy at times because she felt different and out of things and we, Nora and I, tried to make her feel at home as much as possible, allowing her her freedom to come and go as she pleased because she said she had been a prisoner."[55] But she did find a male companion, and the initial loneliness gave way to a greater degree of comfort. She went out with him; she had a life with an independent shape. Nuala Costello, who had been a friend in Paris, came to visit, as did René Bailly, who had been part of Joyce's circle there. And Lucia was still writing to Samuel Beckett and he to her: "You are you because you are you and only you" was the opening of one letter her cousin remembered.[56] She also kept in touch with Kay Boyle in Nice, with Lis Brenner in Zurich, with Roger Bickart in Carnot, and with William Bird in Paris.[57] As her father remarked to her in a letter, absence can be the highest form of presence. Joyce himself continued to haunt her, and she carried with her the parts of *Finnegans Wake* that she knew were about her. When she read passages about eyes or about insanity or about being fond of various men, she cried.[58]

Finally, her own private destiny in Ireland usurped whatever relationships were tentatively calling her to a new independence. She had some kind of mission there, bound inextricably with being her father's daughter. She decided to find the addresses of various people who she thought might help her to end Joyce's alienation from the land of his youth. Maud Gonne McBride received flowers from her; then Lucia wrote to Joyce asking for the address of Patrick Tuohy, the twenty-eight-year-old painter whom Joyce had commissioned to paint the portrait of his father. (Joyce mistook her request and thought she wanted to find Dr. John Joseph Tuohy, a member of the Irish Medical Association, then in his nineties, whom Joyce referred to as a Celtic antiquity.) Later in the summer she gave some of her father's work to Trinity College Dublin.[59]

How much these small pitiful gestures were the result of medicine clouding her judgment or depended upon extraordinary naïveté is impossible to determine. At the least they echoed Raymond Duncan's odd behavior in Paris, when he had used his private newspaper to urge his readers to fight against the injustices of the modern world and to stand up against any kind of killing by the "syndicates, millionaires, political and financial interests." "Human culture," Duncan had reminded his audience, "is the result of close contacts between men. The more this contact takes place between many men and the more intimate it becomes . . . so much the better." If Lucia saw herself as a personal emissary who could breach the divisions of her father's "disunited kingdom," she was at least not alone. Duncan had for years been urging his dancers to work against the "isolation and the distance that separate men," reasoning that even his own primitive evangelism was better than the rampant nationalism raging around him.[60]

Dublin was a place so firmly rooted in Lucia's imagination that she could not remember a time when it had not seemed important. To get to know it would be to learn the source of her own existence and to see the contours of her father's mind. She decided it was time to leave Bray. She did not know that it was time for her to fall.

V. TRAMPING IN DUBLIN

She wandered. Sometimes she returned to Bray in the evenings; sometimes she didn't. Bozena Berta was worried enough that she finally wrote to her uncle in Paris. It was a progress report of sorts. Lucia was restless; she had gained a lot of weight; she herself wasn't well and was, in fact, succumbing to tuberculosis in Bray's damp climate.[61] Aside from a telegram sent on Bloomsday, Lucia herself stopped writing; so Joyce asked Nora's uncle Michael Healy to look in on Lucia at Bray and to send him his opinion of her. Healy reported that Lucia seemed to spend her days walking around Dublin, and the august old man suggested that she should stop. Joyce was baffled. What was wrong with daily walks around Dublin?[62]

Joyce himself had been a wanderer since youth. As a young man, he had personified the lure of travel as a woman calling to him with "the white arms of roads, their promise of close embraces and the black arms of tall ships that stand against the moon their tale of distant nations . . . to say . . . Come."[63] He had been recommending walks for Lucia to take along the shore and in the Wicklow Mountains for months. When she had reported about the beauties of one such outing, he had playfully written back, "*la donna è mobile*"—the lady is a tramp.[64]

Drawn by the Dublin streets, whose every door she had heard named since earliest youth, Lucia walked. When she finally left Ireland in August after six months, Joyce was moved by the power of her imagined figure: "I see you standing on the bridge of the boat and sending your farewell to the land that vanishes and your movement gives me a profound sensation. It certainly means something but I am not sure what, perhaps that which it seems. Perhaps also not. I will think, I will think again," he promised. And he added what she already knew. For him writing and insight were identical: "I am slow O yes 8 years to write one book and 18 for its successor. But I will understand in the end."[65]

There was symmetry in Lucia's journeys in the streets of Dublin, a repetition of a pattern that Joyce assumed was the key to its meaning. Lucia had tramped before. In her youth she had loved the Tramp, whose movies she had seen constantly at the Paris cinema.

Years later, when Ellmann urged Lucia to write about her life, the Chaplin film she remembered was *The Kid*. In the slums of an unidentified city like London, a "fallen woman," played by Edna Purviance, emerges from a charity hospital with a newborn infant in her arms. Unable to care for it, she scribbles a note, "Please love and care for this child," and abandons it next to a garbage can. The Tramp is the first person to come upon the baby, and the film shows his makeshift and ingenious efforts to raise the child and to make him into a street-smart partner. The boy, played by Jackie Coogan, learns to feint and jab in street fights, to break windows so that his adopted father can fix them for money, to evade the police, and to survive in style. Their idyll is disrupted only when a doctor discovers that Charlie is not the boy's natural parent and sends an orphan wagon to pick him up and eventually to send him on to his now happy and prosperous mother.

As Joyce and Lucia would have seen, *The Kid* depicts a world where the comfort of a bourgeois home supersedes the down-and-out improvisations of wayfaring, but it does not get to this point straightforwardly. In it mothers abandon children while fathers nurture, protect, and, however makeshift their efforts, bring initially helpless children into partnership. Together they collude against the world, meet the challenges of the street as a team, and learn that authority is ever present in the form of police. They thrive by shattering rules and outwitting authority with their impertinence. The drama turns on the point at which public au-

thority asserts its power to force the separation of the unconventionally
but truly bonded father and child. The return to the mother is the return
of bourgeois respectability. Though *The Kid* ends with a prosperous
and presumably happy threesome, it also makes clear that the final configuration of "the family" has been bought at the expense of the father-
child bond that not only saved the kid but also made for a kind of offbeat
happiness.

Lucia, at seventeen, had taken no notice of the film's ending. Instead
she had stressed the father figure's ability to "transport . . . Jackie to paradise" and through his "originality" to bring "a consolation for misery."[66]
Years after her Chaplin impersonation had been left behind, she was still
living as a father-identified child, turning instinctively to the male parent
for sustenance and seeing in their relationship a bond that she hoped
would prove stronger than any intervention by the state. Increasingly, as
her bohemian disposition came under medical scrutiny and as her anger
was met by forcible restraint, the state's ability to "police" the private survival strategies of free spirits and to compel bourgeois conformity must
have forced itself upon her imagination. In July, Joyce referred to her (in
a letter to Giorgio) as "that poor and proud soul, whom the storm has
so harshly assailed but not conquered."[67] Chaplin's little man could
be counted on to meet every setback with boundless optimism and to
offer, time and again, a glimpse of the road as a place where bodies
might be kicked and spirits bashed but never dominated. The tramp
might be lonely, self-pitying, or agonizingly disappointed in love, but he
could be counted on to move on with an unmistakable eagerness—a free
man with an open road unwinding before him.

If we add to these associations a particularly Irish and familial attitude toward wandering the city, we might begin to feel the allure that
Dublin streets held for Lucia in the summer of 1935. Walking down
Grafton Street, around St. Stephen's Green, past Newman House, back
around to Kildare Street and on to the National Library, seeing public
monuments, stopping to look at books in the stalls along the Liffey
would have been experienced almost as a guided tour of her father's
mind. Every place where she set foot bore the imprint of her father's
prior step. But where the young Joyce had been admitted to colleges and
universities, performance halls and private homes, office buildings and
cathedrals, his daughter had entry to none of these places. Where he had

come to understand the intricacies of Irish political allegiances, such calculation was impossible for her. Of the family whose vicissitudes had moved him to the art of poetry, only a few elderly sisters remained; of the circle of university students with whom he had honed his ideas of aesthetics, nationality, and personal identity, only Constantine Curran had remained faithful. The young Joyce had been able to write unequivocally in *A Portrait of the Artist as a Young Man*, "This race and this country and this life produced me . . . I shall express myself as I am."[68] His child knew obscurely that the same forces had molded her, but she could not articulate what they were. And if she tramped, it was because she had few alternatives. Michael Healy and shortly thereafter Maria Jolas were adamant that Lucia had to stop roaming about. For them, to be without a roof over one's head was to be without law and order in one's life. For them, tramping was unthinkable for a woman.

Of Lucia's life during her six days of tramping in Dublin, we have only one independent account, by Patrick Collins, who had met her in Bray earlier in the summer. The woman of "great scope" who had walked "as if she owned the whole bloody world" was no more. When he bumped into her in Dublin in early July, "Lucia was filthy and hungry so he took her into a cafe 'to give her a feed' and saw a sinister moon-faced man looking at her. The man, reeking of Jameson's, breathed, 'I've been following that girl for hours.' "[69]

Why was she on the road in the first place? She was probably desperate, but she also had wanted to leave Bray and go to Galway. This had always been a potential part of her plan. Even though she had been bored during her 1922 visit to Annie Barnacle, it pleased her to know that she had family in Galway, and she looked forward to seeing her aunt Kathleen again. She took the train at Bray and went to Dublin's Central Post Office to send a telegram announcing her arrival. To her amazement, when she turned around, Kathleen was standing right there. By coincidence she was in Dublin that day for some surgery. So Lucia's plan was put on hold until Kathleen was out of the hospital.[70]

But at least in part, Lucia's tramping was another attempt to escape. Joyce had decided to send Maria Jolas to Dublin as a kind of emissary, hoping she would be a more reliable witness of Lucia's situation than Michael Healy. On 6 July, Jolas left for Ireland, originally planning to return to Paris on 11 July. But Joyce had reckoned without Lucia's view of the matter. Aside from her brother, Maria Jolas was the person Lucia most distrusted in these years. Instead of receiving her civilly, Lucia absolutely refused to go to the Gresham Hotel to see her.[71] We can interpret her racketing about in the heart of Dublin, at least in part, as a tactic to evade the judgment that she knew was implied by the visit.

VI. SISTER OF MERCY

Maria Jolas was indeed in Dublin to inspect and to judge, and she did not like what she saw. Like some spectral blocking figure from Greek tragedy, like the Sister of Mercy in Ibsen's final drama, like the doctor from the orphan asylum in *The Kid*, she moved to end what she considered the disorder of the Joyces' lives. She questioned the Schaurek girls; she looked at the black room and the untended clothes; and she returned to Paris to pronounce her verdict. On 16 July, Joyce wrote to Giorgio of his new knowledge "of all the sordid squalor of the case and of the warning of the authorities that their next step would be to commit [Lucia] or intern her."[72]

How anyone could feel comfortable judging the housekeeping of a girl raised by someone of Nora's erratic domesticity is a question well worth asking. All her life, Eileen Schaurek remembered the days in Trieste when her sister-in-law had thought cleaning the food cupboard with water from a chamberpot was hilarious; and rumors of the family's erratic habits in Paris had circulated for years. Dr. Pierre Mérigot de Treigny, called on to relieve Joyce's glaucoma in 1922, remembered arriving at the furnished room at 9 rue de l'Université to find the Joyces wrapped in blankets and squatting over a pot of chicken bones on the floor with clothes strewn about everywhere.[73] But Maria Jolas had come to know the Joyces only after Harriet Weaver's bequest had made bourgeois respectability possible. She had seen polished brass and matching fabrics in Nora's household, but this was only one of the Joyces' many domestic styles.

Joyce did not care what Maria Jolas had to say about his daughter's personal living habits. He wanted to know about her spiritual health. He had asked Michael Healy to have someone send him a photograph of Lucia, not because he cared about his daughter's grooming but because, lacking the language of signs that had served as their secret bond, he could no longer "read" his child's communication.

But episodes that had drawn the attention of the Dublin police were impossible to ignore. Constantine Curran, ever the discreet and thoughtful friend, had anticipated this kind of problem and had used his personal influence to exact a promise of silence from the police with regard to Lucia. But there they all were, the great gods that Virginia Woolf disparagingly called Proportion and Conversion,[74] mocking Joyce's originality in solving the problems that had arisen during the years of Lucia's unhappy instability. Joyce saw the larger picture and quickly cut to the bone. Amid the talk of scandal and dishevelment, amid the opinions about what should be done, he selected the essentials: "She is much stronger, sturdier . . . less unhappy."[75]

Lucia was the one who finally determined the immediate shape of events. She wanted to rest. After scrupulously avoiding Maria Jolas at the Gresham, she asked René Bailly, who was also staying there, if she might go to a nursing home. On 13 July Curran took her to Farnhame House in Finglas, where she stayed until 27 July. But even in seclusion, others intervened in her fate. From America Giorgio once again pressed for her permanent institutionalization, and on 16 July Joyce once again enjoined him not to jump to conclusions or suggest some "simple" solution like severe seclusion. A month later, on 13 August, he was still resisting Giorgio's efforts: "If you had seen Lucia's condition after seven months of confinement at Nyon you would not advise me to put her back in such an institution. I shall do it when and if there is no other recourse. Nothing serious happened in Ireland. Everyone who saw Lucia there agreed that she was stronger and less unhappy. But she lived like a gypsy in squalor."[76]

In the end, Maria Jolas's view of things prevailed. She decided to tell the doctors what to think, just as she had told the Joyces. On 17 July Paul Léon sent Constantine Curran a memorandum "drawn up by Mrs. Jolas relating the clinical aspect of the illness for the last three years."[77] In this way, H.R.C. Rutherford, a general practitioner in Ireland with no psychiatric training, whose specialty was overseeing a rest home, came to a revised opinion of Lucia's case. His original view had been that Lucia was "in a restless condition and alternately exhibited symptoms of depression and excitement [and] was unable to concentrate." After Jolas's letter arrived, he came to think not of barbiturates, not of mood disorder, not of disappointment in love or anything else, but of a "general state" that "suggested that she might be schizophrenic."[78] The good doctor insisted that his summary letter should go directly to another physician and not to any layperson. He had the intelligence to add, in another letter to Curran, "I do not think however that it would be the slightest value . . . in answering . . . as the period was such a short one."[79]

VII. I HAVE FATHOMED YOUR MESSAGE

As Lucia gathered herself together, Joyce in Paris lived with a nightmare of clashing "wills gen wonts" (*FW* 04.01). Nora wanted Lucia to stay in Ireland. Paul Léon telephoned Harriet Weaver to broach the possibility of Lucia's returning to England. Miss Weaver went in search of a summer cottage, though finding a suitable place for the month of August was unlikely on such short notice, and she wrote to Lucia, inviting her to come to Sussex. The public trustee reared its head, presumably with the renewed idea of placing Lucia in the Belgian village that tended lunatics. Insomnia set in once again; after six or seven nights of sleeplessness, Joyce began to have auditory hallucinations and then real nightmares. He claimed that he felt as if he were being wound up and "then suddenly jumping like a fish out of water."[80]

Water, being out of one's depth, drowning—a network of codes for mortal struggle—seems to have been on all their minds. Lucia had sent her father the lyrics of a song called "Dublin Bay," copied out in an agitated hand, on the day before she went into the nursing home. The song recounts the story of a young Dublin couple who elope together and are shipwrecked and lost at sea. The lament of the young bride punctuates the verses: "O, why did we leave sweet Dublin Bay?" The next day Lucia wrote to her mother, for the first time in months, suggesting that Joyce write a dramatic piece based on the song's theme. It provided, as she quickly saw, an analog for the life of her own family and expressed the sorrow of exile. Whatever misery had prompted her parents to leave Ireland was nothing compared with the disasters that followed from it.

"Ho capito il latino," Joyce responded. I have understood the Latin; I have fathomed your message.[81] He could hear the pain and perceive that his daughter imagined that a reunion with Ireland promised wholeness for her. But he could not bring himself to act on the request implied in the song—come over here and be with me in Ireland—though he would do so "E se fossi convinto che quello sarebbe per il tuo bene ma proprio bene, ed a rischio di tutto." ("And if I thought it would do you good, really good, despite everything.") "Ma ho sempre paura delle aringhe," he added. ("But I've always been afraid of herrings. I fear the reproaches that would follow.")[82]

He was a father pressed between irreconcilable alternatives, seeing not only that his Irish contemporaries might harangue him for his life choices but also that "herrings" would come from his wife, his son, and people like Maria Jolas. Paul Léon tried to explain this to Miss Weaver, saying, "you know what part in Mr. Joyce's work is taken by Ireland. There is also no doubt that Ireland has crystallized at least for a certain extent one of the processes of Miss Joyce's evolution." But Léon doubted that Joyce could solve this aspect of Lucia's longing, and he wondered if "this problem [were] an elementary one for her or more likely a symptom of the evolution of her illness."[83]

In the end, Joyce did not return to Dublin or to Lucia. He could not rely on anyone else, and because of his blindness he could not act alone. He could do only what he had always done—woo his daughter with words, no more, no less. In July 1935, Joyce was a man like Stephen Dedalus in *Ulysses* who watches his sister, Dilly Dedalus, buying Chardenal's French primer for a penny. He recognizes ruefully that the only trip to France that she might have is an imaginary one. The text expresses desire and the pity of desire that will go unmet. "She is drowning. Agenbite. Save her. Agenbite. All against us. She will drown me with her, eyes and hair. Lank coils of seaweed hair around me, my heart, my soul. Salt green death."[84] *Dublin Bay*. Salt green death. She will drown me.

Icarus was down.

Lucia Joyce, Loveland's Cottage, Surrey, 1935. Photographer unknown. (Courtesy of Special Collections, University College London)

13

FALLING APART

ENGLAND AND PARIS 1935-38

After three weeks at Farnhame House, Lucia accepted Harriet Weaver's invitation to return to England, though she had misgivings.[1] When she later realized what she had walked into and asked her father why she had to be in London, he told her that she herself, "it seems," had asked to visit Harriet Weaver in Sussex.[2] But Lucia had not initiated the contact with Miss Weaver. Paul Léon and Miss Weaver had once again contrived the invitation so that Joyce could return to work on *Finnegans Wake*.

At the end of July, Léon had catalogued for Miss Weaver the sections that remained to be completed:

> There is not so much to be done. The third part is practically finished. All the additions have been done on loose sheets during the four weeks of respite Mrs. Joyce was able to influence him to have after the bad state he had been in had passed and the news from Mrs. Jolas came. The first part is, as you know with the publishers. Of the second part the section of plays is finished. The greater part of the lessons has just come out in *transition*. It leaves two sections to be done—the stories (one or two of which are ready) and the going to sleep. The Epilogue could be written while the thing went through the press. In fact I should say that six months or a year at most of labour would bring the work to an end.

But then he had asked, "but when and where would we get this lapse of time? the gaiety, the security, the moral support necessary?"[3]

Léon and Miss Weaver were repeating history, effecting once again a swerve or maneuver that placed Lucia in a false position. But repetition marked her father's style of coping as well. He asked Lucia to revisit the scenario of "Dublin Bay" and to imagine its sequel. In the original version, the song ended with the young couple drowning:

> On the crowded deck of that doomed ship
> Some fell in their meek despair.
> But some ore calm with a holier lip
> Sought the God of the storm in pray'r.
> "She has struck on a rock!" the seamen cried
> In the breath of their wild dismay.
> And that ship went down with that fair young bride
> That sail'd from Dublin Bay.

In Joyce's version, Roy Neel is a good "diver"; he does not die beneath the bay but bides his time and "remounts the salty water full of weeds and smiling happily." His joy rests on his secret company in the deep, for there he has made the acquaintance of a very smiley fish with lots of teeth. He leaves his calling card with the fish along with three thousand silver buttons from his jacket. When the fish rises to the surface to find better reading light, he sees that it is the calling card of a dentist: "Doctor George Arago, 12 bis avenue MacMahon, Paris, telephone number Étoile 14.01." The fish weeps three thousand tears, one for each button, but he cannot read further to see if his mysterious friend (who seems to have a multiple identity) in the deep were "Jacky Jakes or Jicky Jones or Jaky Jeames, so help you me!"[4]

The tale was Joyce's veiled message to Lucia at a time when he could imagine her ready to give up. He was playing parodically with Jung's distinction between "diving" and "falling" into the depths of the unconscious, and with Lucia's self-identification as a dancing fish. If you are a fish, the tale suggests, you don't need to be able to dive; you already have the requisite powers of survival. What seems like death is not death; it is only a temporary setback; get ready to rise again. You are supported by secret companionship, though "so help you me," it's hard to tell what his real name is beyond the J.J. initials.

Having buoyed his battered child's spirits, Joyce set to work once again on some kind of plan for her. To Constantine Curran and his wife he explained that the moment he embraced her after seven months at Prangins he knew that Lucia had changed.[5] And he added a note about his worry that even in physical health Lucia would have a hard time of it, "when and if she finally withdraws her regard from the lightning reverie of her clairvoyance and turns it upon that battered cabman's face, the world."[6]

In one of his crossings from Bournemouth, where the British Medical Association held its annual meetings, Curran had apparently heard of some kind of glandular treatment that he thought might help Lucia. His inquiries reinforced Joyce's own growing conviction that neither talk nor theory could counter a process within the body that affected one's moods. He once again determined that his daughter should travel a modern road. Just as he had pioneered in changing the face of literature, he understood that researchers had been transforming modern medicine, and he was willing to put Lucia in the hands of those at the forefront of the emerging field of endocrinology.

How Joyce first came to know Naum Efimowitsch Ischlondsky is impossible to determine: perhaps Ischlondsky was the physiologist whose work Curran had heard about in Bournemouth, or perhaps he was recommended by other friends. But however he discovered him, Joyce arranged to meet him in Paris sometime before the end of July and to put his daughter's case before him. In ways that would have been impossible for Joyce to foresee, Lucia's general problems turned out to fit into the pattern of clinical applications that Ischlondsky was eager to develop. Although he was a researcher with catholic interests—he had previously written about the neurological structure of the brain, about involuntary reflex action, and about the role of internal secretions in animal rejuvenation—the work that presumably interested Joyce was his inquiry into the physiological foundations of depth psychology.[7]

In 1935 Ischlondsky was preparing lectures, to be given to the Egyptian Medical Association in Cairo, that would establish his reputation as an innovator in treating various diseases thought to result from glandular deficiencies. He called his work "protoformotherapy," and he saw it as a superior alternative to the glandular supplements that were a common although controversial response to illness at the time. Instead of

suspending glandular tissues from animals in various emulsions, Ischlondsky specialized in making serums from the embryonic tissue of
mammals, and he was extraordinarily articulate about the benefits to be
had from their use.[8] He was careful to distinguish his work from that
done by others, and in light of the more general history of endocrinology
we can see the distinctive nature of what he proposed as a therapy for
Lucia.

Less than a century before, the French neurologist and physiologist
Charles Edouard Brown-Sequard had first claimed that the adrenal
glands were essential to human life. In defending his findings in the con-
troversies that followed, he gained the respect of medical colleagues in
France, England, and the United States.[9] In 1889, at the age of seventy-
two but still actively engaged in research, he announced to the Society of
Biology in Paris that he had obtained "remarkable effects" by subcuta-
neously injecting himself with a "liquid obtained by the maceration in a
mortar of the testicle of a dog or of a guinea pig to which one has added
a little water."[10] The testes, he believed, contained an active invigorating
substance that could rejuvenate old men. Within weeks "testicular extract was being given to patients with every kind of illness. Within two
years, many physicians thought that not only the testes but also every
organ of the body possessed some active principle that might be of immediate therapeutic value. Organotherapy, or the method of Brown-
Sequard, as it was often called, came to be the therapeutic hope of
physicians from Cleveland to Bucharest."[11]

Physiologists continued to work with the idea of so-called internal-
secretions[12] and to make extracts from the adrenal and thyroid glands of
various animals. Soon injections of organ extracts came to be recognized
as a general form of therapy. Serums and extractions were even available
through mail-order catalogs. Many deplored this unregulated development, for its popularity obscured the work that continued to be done by
painstaking and thorough scientists who tried to understand the "active
principles" of the thyroid and adrenal glands.[13] The Pasteur Institute in
New York, founded by the French physician Dr. Paul Gibier, seems to
have been one place that bridged the distinction between serious labora-
tory and biological supply center. It was Dr. Gibier's nephew, George
Gibier-Rambaud, whose work Joyce turned to in his efforts to understand the physiology of Lucia's ailment. In 1936 he was to buy and read

Gibier-Rambaud's recently published *Rôle de l'infection focale dans les psychoses*, and he also read Joseph F. McKaig's *Nil Desperandum: The Chemical Man as Deduced from the Biochemistry of the Human Blood* (Washington, *n.d.*).[14] Clearly Joyce was working not only with an intuitive perception of a change in his daughter's physiology but also with the nagging problem of the increased leukocyte count in her blood, which Dr. Naegali had discovered but not explained in Zurich.

In 1923 Swale Vincent, a professor of physiology at Middlesex Hospital in London, had identified three classes of people who were interested in endocrinology. The only class to survive his critical judgment was that of "scientific investigators . . . with dispassionate interest." People trying to cure disease he regarded as motivated by "a love of romance . . . which makes them delight in spinning a misty intellectual mesh which completely obscures any possible facts." Those who realized the commercial possibilities of organ extracts were simply exploiting the weaknesses of the clinicians.[15] The result, he claimed, was "that endocrine therapy is coming to bear a suspicious resemblance to mediaeval magic; the savage believes that eating the heart of his enemy will confer on him the virtues of this enemy" and so on.[16] Trying to clean intellectual house, he insisted that effective extracts could not be obtained unless the internal secretion of a gland was identified, its hormone isolated, and its metabolic action proved. For his efforts to lay down a reliable foundation for endocrinology, his contemporaries had both immense sympathy and intelligent reservations, the latter because Vincent's principles led him to reject some of the most exciting advances of their lifetime. He refused to recognize "adrenin" as a hormone because it had a "drug-like" nonspecific action, and even more surprising, he would not accept the reality of insulin, for whose 1921 discovery Sir Frederick Banting and C. H. Best in the very same year received the Nobel Prize in physiology.

Into this field of actively contested views stepped still another kind of practitioner: the man of science whose interest was the marriage of biology and psychology, and who looked to advances in physiology for the effective treatment of mental illnesses. This work was predicated on a new kind of holistic inquiry that Gustave Roussy and Michel Mosinger later described in a monumental study published in 1946, *Le Système neuro-endocrinien*. "The medical sciences," they claimed, "like the other biological sciences, have taken a new direction in the course of the last ten years. After a long phase of more than two centuries, during which the morphological, physiological and clinical disciplines had established their standards, mainly on an analytical basis, medicine today is running along new tracks. It attempts to bring together what was perhaps separated for too long. It seeks to tackle more and more ... the exercise of the large problems concerning the regulatory mechanism of the normal life of tissues and organs, and their disorders in the course of pathological processes. This is also the case in neurology and endocrinology. These disciplines tend today to run closer together to the point where the actions of the nervous regulations and of the hormonal ones become more and more intermingled in a science of synthesis."[17]

In 1935, eleven years before Roussy and Mosinger published their encyclopedic study, the desire to understand the relation between neurology and endocrinology far exceeded any researcher's ability to demonstrate or explain. If Swale Vincent had wanted to discredit endocrinologists who did not practice pure science, he would have been doubly pressed to find value in the work of those who tried to apply it to psychiatry. Those who wrote about the subject well into the 1940s admitted readily that the theoretical bases for their procedures were woefully inadequate, but they justified their work on the basis of empirical success.

At a time when most mental hospitals could give only symptomatic relief or custodial care, physical treatments offered the only hopeful prospects that many physicians could see; and beginning in the 1930s, handbooks explaining the procedures of treatment by malaria, electric convulsion, insulin coma, and leukotomy began to appear. Citing optimistic statistics (seventy percent of involutional depressives remitted with electrical treatment; fifty percent of schizophrenics responded to insulin in the first year of their illness), they pleaded for research that could explain the physiological mechanisms underlying their work. At the same time they reminded their critics that the treatments themselves were "no worse for" the absence of theoretical underpinnings.[18] They believed that mental distress was the manifestation of a more general pathology of the entire organism. While they waited for specialists to untangle the complicated relations among moods, hormones in the blood, and the chemistry of nerve synapses, they offered what relief they could. It was makeshift at best. "If one treatment fails," William Sargant and

Eliot Slater, who were considered expert clinicians, remarked without embarrassment, "the patient is passed automatically to the next stage."[19]

Naum Ischlondsky fit loosely into the category of a researcher who justified his theories by empirical success. He was not a charlatan; he did not simply administer glandular extracts bought from a supply house; but neither did he practice the kind of pure science that would have satisfied Swale Vincent. He was not primarily a psychiatrist, but since he was interested in the health of the entire body, seeing connections between the endocrine glands and the nervous system, he believed that psychiatric benefits were to be derived from his practices. His work straddled the categories that occurred to Joyce when he thought about Lucia's problems (anomalies in the blood, anomalies of mood), and we can understand the optimism in Joyce's first letters to his daughter in London, when he told her how pleased he was that she had started treatment. "I have almost the conviction that he will be for you what Vogt has been for me. That is to say the man who does his business and comes at the end of a series of 'botchers.' "[20]

Ischlondsky distinctively claimed to offer Lucia not desiccated glands as a hopeful replacement for defective hormones but a "cure." He thought he could make her better. In his work on "protoformotherapy," begun in 1924, he, like other researchers of the time, wanted to know why there had been such "meager" results in isolating the "active principle" of these glands. His answers led him to criticize the entire system of organotherapy and to conclude that therapeutic substitution could never satisfactorily replace the activity of any functioning endocrine gland. As he understood it, organotherapies of all types failed because they isolated a small part of what was originally a complex hormonal structure. The amount that could be administered by injection was too small compared with the continuous working of a living gland, but it was also, at the moment of injection, too large, if judged by the trace of the hormone that might ordinarily be found in the blood. Intermittent injections also violated the rhythmical nature of glandular secretions that could normally be expected to rise and fall with a characteristic amplitude and frequency. Organotherapy was, in short, not curative. It might alleviate a symptom, but it would leave the underlying morbidity untouched.

Few scientists would have disagreed with Ischlondsky's analysis of the shortcomings of glandular injections, but probably few would have been persuaded by the strategy he developed as an alternative. Instead of making serums from glands, he made serums from the tissues of embryonic animals, arguing in a very broad way that these cells would stimulate the entire organism to perform better. The tissues had to come from a mammal, and the optimum time for harvesting them was three to four months after gestation began, when, he calculated, the embryo began to differentiate into organs. His therapy was intended not to restitute a particular bodily function but to stimulate the entire endocrine system to do its own work more effectively.

We can see from these ideas that Ischlondsky's plan was not to treat Lucia for a particular affliction but to boost her general health, hoping that the serum would restore balance to her blood count and to her mind at the same time. He did not need to know the details of her case history; he needed to know that she was willing to become a subject for investigation.

In 1935 Ischlondsky was working with W. G. Macdonald, an English doctor whose particular interest was in the serum's application to psychiatry. Dr. Macdonald would, in his research partner's opinion, "undoubtedly create the foundation for a new chapter in contemporary psychiatry."[21] The serum was particularly effective in helping those with a congenital mental deficiency and with dementia praecox. For example, on 28 February 1935, several months before he saw Lucia, Ischlondsky reported on another patient:

> Dr. Macdonald saw the patient at Windsor for the first time. She was resistive, mentally confused and inclined to violence. She was unkempt, complexion dull and spotty (bromide); hair greasy and dull; tongue foul, hands sweating, pupils dilated. Physical examination was not possible. Dr. Miller stated that the patient was sleepless in spite of sedobrol, and that a day and night nurse had to be in constant attendance because she tried to throw herself in the fire or to set her hair on fire. She also had to be fed since she refused food. The first injection of the protoformative incret was given, and all sedatives discontinued. On March 16, 1935, Dr. Miller reported: "Miss J. continues to be much quieter and a little rational." In May 1935, the girl went to stay in a private hotel in Richmond with a nurse companion. There she became physically and mentally stronger, mixed with the guests and even played bridge. On May 12, 1935, her mother writes: "in answer to her urgent request, we brought her home here. She has played tennis for a little each day; she is taking a daily ride on her pony, and although she gets tired fairly easily and needs extra rest, she looks well and happy and has lost that worried, hunted look in her eyes."[22]

Ischlondsky made explicit that the "great scientific importance" of such cases was, in his view, the demonstration of the relationship, already suspected in the past, between mental disturbance and endocrine activity.

Joyce needed to look no further, since Ischlondsky confirmed the constellation of thoughts that had already coalesced in his mind about Lucia. The further convenience of the meeting was that Lucia need not return to Paris for the injections since Dr. Macdonald was already well established in London, and, indeed, he had already seen her before. The first mention of Dr. Macdonald with regard to Lucia had been in a letter from Harriet Weaver to Paul Léon on 9 March 1935, during her earlier visit to London. He had said then that he thought Lucia's "violent crises" would recur for six months or so and from time to time, but in an increasingly milder form.[23]

II. CONTINUOUS IMPRISONMENT

What about Lucia? She went from Dublin to London in July 1935 expecting to resume the relationship that Harriet Weaver assured her she wanted to have—one predicated upon the mutual regard of friendship. Instead she found herself prisoner of a regime of discipline and intramuscular injections that she did not want, forced into locked rooms with windows that were nailed partially shut so that she would not throw herself out of them. The very circumstances that had led her to run away to Windsor in February had been perfected: the personnel was hired, the strategies for handling one contingency or another were in place.

Another drama of "wills gen wonts" was about to unfold. Harriet Weaver and her young nurse friend Edith Walker did everything they thought appropriate and kind. Lucia continued to enact a profound ambivalence, not knowing whether to regard them as friends or jailers. She was fighting her final battle for independence and some measure of personal integrity. By the time she left England six months later, there was almost nothing of adult experience left for her to salvage. If one could imagine a kind of afterlife for Icarus after he fell from the sky—limping on the fringes of islands, not defeated but wounded by his efforts—one would see Lucia the way I imagine her in the summer of 1935. She resisted what happened to her, and resistance is a kind of life, though reactive and dependent upon circumstance. During this fragile time, Joyce seems to have experienced with Lucia the pity of a performance that would not be carried off. In his address to her, he reverted to the language of childhood: "My dear little daughter," he wrote in September, neither feigning optimism nor circumventing the subject of surveillance. He spoke openly to her about the issue of bodily restraint, using the words "continuous imprisonment" to describe the ordeal that she endured at Gloucester Place.[24]

For her part, Harriet Weaver prepared carefully for Lucia's visit. Edith Walker, her friend for many years, was a registered nurse with a social conscience. She had once worked in a hospital but had left it in protest against the conditions imposed by the current poor laws and had subsequently joined a Nurses Cooperative at Croydon.[25] The two women prepared the flat, making it safe for a person who had shown suicidal tendencies for many months. They took into account Lucia's hatred of professional caregivers, decided that Edith should wear normal clothing instead of a uniform, and considered what they should do in the case of violence—they devised back-up plans to call in help when and if it was needed. Miss Weaver thought she knew what her earlier mistakes had been; this time she would try to form a bond with her young guest. This time too she would write constantly to Joyce to avoid Eileen Schaurek's "failure" of allowing Lucia to live without making her every mood and decision the subject of scrutiny and report. It was as if Joyce were the hidden choreographer, needing to know from others what he could not observe for himself. She would provide him with ample documentation.

Dr. Macdonald, armed with his serums and injection needles, came to call at Miss Weaver's flat the day after Lucia's arrival. He quickly discovered that he had an unwilling patient at hand. His efforts to give the first injection elicited a "violent struggle."[26] He then prescribed what must have seemed to all the ladies assembled like a prescription for hell: Despite the extraordinary summer heat, Lucia was to remain not only in the house but also in bed for the seven weeks of her therapy. She was not to have visitors, and she was not to receive any communications that might upset her. She was to be taken off all other medications, including sedatives. This was standard procedure for all his patients, but in prescribing this regime, Dr. Macdonald cut the lifeline between Joyce and

Lucia, requiring her to disappear from view and ending the posturing for inspection that was her modus vivendi. In September, in answer to her complaint about the meager communications from Paris, Joyce reminded her that he had stopped writing on doctor's orders "and in your own interest."[27] But the consequences for both father and daughter were serious in ways that no doctor, looking solely for signs of physical well-being, could have foreseen.

The consequences for Harriet Weaver were also devastating, for she did not like Dr. Macdonald and, not understanding the overarching, nonspecific nature of his proposed cure, judged him harshly. Measuring him against the medical practices of her own father, a general practitioner in Cheshire, she considered that he had not shown enough interest in the particular nature of Lucia's case. As time passed, her initial discomfort turned into active hostility that no amount of self-discipline was sufficient to dispel. By the end of Lucia's treatment in 1936, each person engaged in her care felt betrayed and isolated. Harriet Weaver and Edith Walker believed they had been ill served by Macdonald. Macdonald shuddered in disbelief at Harriet Weaver's conduct. Lucia hated all of them, and Joyce realized that no person of his acquaintance had the means of dealing with his daughter's rude energies.

The protoformotherapy did not work. Whatever benefit might have been had from Ischlondsky's bovine serums was offset by the turbulence created in trying to keep an unwilling woman forcibly in bed for seven weeks. After a certain point, it becomes difficult to distinguish the effects of the treatment from the symptoms of the supposed illness. Lucia repeated her repertoire of coping behaviors. She sang incessantly in four languages, just as she had in Bray; she threw books out of windows; she struggled to break free as she had in Prangins. A second day nurse was engaged as well as a strong night nurse. Lucia was moved to a room in the back of the house. The more she was restrained, the more she struggled. As motion was exchanged for commotion, she performed the futility of the situation: she performed senseless repetition. It was Lucia's voice, not Giorgio's, that everyone in the Joyce circle noticed and remembered.

If a trauma had previously initiated Lucia's repetitive behaviors, by this time in her life it was lost in the repetitive nature of her resistance to being guarded. She wrote constantly to her father, asking for his help.

(*above*) Lucia Joyce in a
hammock at Loveland's
Cottage, Surrey, 1935.
Photographer unknown.
(Courtesy of Special Collections,
University College London)

Lucia Joyce with Harriet
Shaw Weaver at Loveland's
Cottage, Surrey, 1935.
Photographer unknown.
(Courtesy of Special Collections,
University College London)

He, through Paul Léon, asked Harriet Weaver what was going on, and she, poor woman, was reduced to asking Joyce if she might open the letters Lucia wrote in order to "interpret" them before forwarding them to Paris. Harriet Weaver's well-meaning gesture reveals her assumptions about the status of those who were mentally ill and the prerogatives of being a custodian. She thought it was appropriate to overwrite Lucia's evaluations of her own situation. Without reading Lucia's letters she already knew that she was resentful and unhappy and that she wanted to leave, but Lucia's moods changed constantly, she explained, adding that she only wrote when she was feeling bad.[28] The desperation felt by all concerned can be measured by a December letter in which Miss Weaver asked Léon what was Joyce's attitude toward "corporal chastisement."[29] In her mind and in the mind of the various women who nursed Lucia, the question of relationship had been reduced to a question of whether to hit her.

Fortunately for all of them, Dr. Macdonald agreed that they could spend the rest of Lucia's recuperative time in the country, provided that the women found another nurse capable of "policing" Lucia. In mid-September he checked her weight (seven and a half stone, or 105 pounds), blood pressure, and muscle strength, found them satisfactory, and sent them all on their way to Reigate, in Surrey. Armed with a Scottish nurse, Mrs. Middlemost, whom Edith Walker had chosen for "her splendid physique,"[30] Harriet Weaver took her unwieldy entourage to a furnished bungalow called Loveland's Cottage. There the struggle to contain the uncontainable Lucia continued for several more months until Dr. Macdonald intervened and put an end to a situation that was impossible for everyone.

III. PAPLI'S LITTLE PHOTO GIRL

At first things went quietly and well. Lucia loved the countryside, and on 7 October Miss Weaver reported that they had decided to dispense with the second nurse, who left on 16 October and was replaced with a "regular domestic general servant." The new arrangement would allow Edith Walker to devote all her time to Lucia.[31] Lucia read, took drives with Harriet Weaver, and wrote letters. She began to draw again and, because her father had sent her a camera, to take photographs.

Part of Joyce's sly motivation in this gift was undoubtedly to facilitate receiving images that could serve him in place of direct observation. He had wanted Michael Healy to send him photographs of Lucia from Dublin and had been disappointed when none had been forthcoming. But he was also once again putting tools of creation into his daughter's hands. Having sat for numerous photographers such as Man Ray and Berenice Abbott, he could appreciate the camera's denotative capacity as well as the composition implied by the frame. He hoped at least to give his child a new interest. Lucia did respond, sending him pictures of her surroundings in Surrey, her companions, and herself. Milly. Papli's little photo girl. Could the irony of life reiterating his own art have escaped Joyce's notice? Photography had been the vocation of the daughter of his imagination long before it became the avocation of his own child. But this time there was no vanity involved in sitting for a portrait and no beauty elicited by the camera's attentive eye. When Lucia forwarded snapshots to him in mid-October, Joyce saw a sullen, immobile young woman lying in a hammock with a book. Thank you, he had replied, "you look as if you did not care in the least about the terrestrial globe, absorbed as you are in your reading and swinging."[32] Emphasizing the interior life that he shared with his daughter, he wrote to Lucia about the movement of the intellect, but he cannot have missed the sadness of this image. Where once the camera had stolen moments of stasis from the purposeful evanescence of his daughter's dancing body, it now recorded immobility of a far different sort.

For me, this image—the young woman in the hammock—contains many of the nuances of Lucia's life. It is a synecdoche, a moment wrested from time, that nonetheless expresses the timbre of the whole. It lets us see the problems faced by Harriet Weaver, Edith Walker, and Lucia Joyce as they struggled to live together in the summer and fall of 1935. It also lets us see a poignant moment in modern history, a moment when modernism could not live with the consequences of its own creation. For none of these women were good dancing partners. Their well-meaning experiment was a disaster.

In the photograph, Lucia is arrested, both in the sense of "reduced to stillness" and in the sense of "held captive." Everyone who ever knew

Lucia Joyce knew that she could not bear being immobile, and yet the medical profession decreed that rest is cure. Her hammock shows the intelligence and resourcefulness of Harriet Weaver and Edith Walker, who had to ensure that Lucia obeyed the doctor's orders. Where a bed is stationary and properly positioned within walls, a hammock offers rest in fresh air where a vista can mitigate claustrophobia and swinging can lessen the opprobrium of enforced stasis. The body has been brought into the open, and yet its motion has been reduced to obedience.

A body in repose can suggest a thousand hidden directions, and yet this particular body is in pain; the intelligence of the girl is furiously directed at her book, as if the only possible direction is inward. In forcing or coaxing Lucia into this hammock, Weaver and Walker stripped her of the emotive power of gesture, denied its secret inner force, and deprived feeling of an outlet. Thus the photograph's lack of animation expresses the subject's similar lack. Where dance expresses emotion, where movement finds an evanescent voice for inward experiences, the photograph's distinctive attribute is to seize an instant and to freeze it.

The events that led to this moment and the evidence of the moment itself tell us that these women were following someone else's prescription for health. Harriet Weaver and Edith Walker, whatever their reservations about Dr. Macdonald personally and about protoformotherapy in particular, colluded in enforcing his regime. They colluded as well in reading certain kinds of social behaviors as signs of health.

Here we can extrapolate for a moment, going beyond specific evidence to imagine how the gentle and well-bred Harriet Weaver lived each day, for in decorum if not in intellect, she followed the rules of Victorian gentility, which had been instilled in her since childhood. No matter how free-thinking Miss Weaver and her protégée might have been in regard to the position of women or the lower classes in society, no matter what their courage or how radical their politics, they believed in sitting at tables, using napkins, dressing modestly, knowing how to engage in polite conversation, using discretion, being considerate, and practicing selflessness with regard to others. Why else would they have undertaken the fierce assignment of caring for James Joyce's daughter? In short, they were nice women, versions of the angel in the house, that perilously good creature that Virginia Woolf commemorated as Mrs. Ramsay in *To the Lighthouse*. It is relevant to Lucia's story to remember that Woolf knew she had to "kill" the internalized angel within herself if she were to thrive as an artist. It is also relevant to recognize that goodness can be one pole of a terrible cacophony, instrumental in creating brutal emotions, especially when it coerces or censors in the name of conformity.

IV. THE WITCHES' DANCE

Lucia was often ill mannered. Edith Walker remembered her as capable of being rude, outrageous, and ungrateful. She once overturned a tub of water on Harriet Weaver; she told both the nurses that she needed days alone, away from their company. She thought Miss Weaver, who had altered her entire life routine for her benefit, needed no time off since "she does not do anything."[33] Often her emotions were out of hand; the others lived in fear of new outbreaks of "hysteria." They worried that she would hurt herself.

We can speculate about the causes of such friction. Was Lucia rude or mad? Was she grieving because her mother and brother seemed relieved to keep her exiled?[34] Was she still mourning for the life of common affection that she would probably never lead? Was she depressed by the rejection of her various lovers? Was she trying to let go of her artistic aspirations? Probably all these problems competed for her emotional attention. But a crucial way to read this scenario is to see in it the clash between two narratives about female experience in the early twentieth century. Should that experience be veiled, its emotions hidden behind the modest "dresses" of Victorian decorum, or should it be lived starkly and without artifice? This clash was to be repeated later, when the players in the Joyce family drama decided how this part of Lucia's story was to be remembered: should it be told with the veils of consideration in place (which would recommend that certain letters should be destroyed) or in the light of uncomfortable truth?

Undoubtedly it was a turbulent time. But through the competing allegiances that were vying for ascendancy in Harriet Weaver's living room in the summer of 1935, through the boundaries of decorum that were alternately challenged and defended, we can see enacted the struggle that had led Lucia's dance teachers onto the stage and into classrooms throughout Europe and America to promote the liberation of women's bodies. The very pattern of behavior that gave structure to Harriet Weaver's life was that which Lucia's training had taught her to suspect. Mary Wigman, to give one salient example, turned not only from the classical ballet but also from the veiled fluttering of Isadora Duncan, arguing forcibly that Duncan had freed the female body from the deformations of ballet only to reinscribe it in another form of limpid eroticism. Her own repertoire of movements would eschew "the beautiful." In *The Witches' Dance*, *The Storm Dance*, *Dance of the Queen of Night*, and *Seven Dances of Life*, she would squat, claw, pulsate, and distend her body, using space as a hidden adversary, a partner that could help to express longing, lust, pain, and chaos. Through dance she would claim for women a full range of human experience. Through dance she would open up the possibility, at least in imagination, that expressions of pain or lust or disappointment or confusion or anger would one day take their place in the rounds of everyday life and no longer be considered a kind of deviance that called for restraint. The kinds of criticism that Lucia faced constantly—that she was a dilettante, that she had no skills, no knowledge, no beauty, no femininity—were also made about the creators of modern expressionistic dance. In their comparable reception we can see a strange beast struggling to be born and know that to imagine the fullness of modern female life is not necessarily to achieve it.

V. ONE REMAINS

Joyce, who still knew very little about the day-to-day dynamics of his daughter's life, felt guardedly optimistic about Lucia and returned to his writing. Knowing her self-consciousness about her appearance, he wrote to her about her healthy looks—she was at least not living like an unkempt gypsy—and he offered to have Mrs. Budgen look for a good value in a fur coat. Nora and Harriet Weaver quickly vetoed this plan, arranging for a practical tweed coat instead, but his gesture was intended to convey to her the value that at least one person continued to place in her existence.[35]

As it turned out, even a tweed coat was beside the point. By December everyone in Surrey was at their wits' end. Lucia was turning on the gas again, as she had done in Bray, and was refusing to eat. The women would go to ridiculous lengths to thwart this hunger strike: Mrs. Middlemost would sing Scottish songs and do a Highland fling so that Edith Walker could pop food in Lucia's mouth. Lucia's responses to stress and depression were not unlike the tantrums and "fidgets" that Virginia Woolf experienced in her young adult life, when she too had refused to eat, was violent with her nurses, and had tried to kill herself. She too had been unable to concentrate and she had emerged from these attacks with an enduring hatred of psychiatric doctors.[36]

But Woolf had the resources to write novels that compel us to see the relation between those illnesses and the modernist project itself. She could show both the horror of being incomprehensible and at the same time invent a language for rendering illness intelligible. Lucia's primary creative language, however, was gestural: she enacted her resistance and continued to "dance" her protest. Where Woolf had siblings—Vanessa, Adrian, and Toby—and many friends who refused to abandon her as a person, Lucia had no similar network. Her brother insisted she was incurable, and her mother refused to have her under the same roof. Where Woolf could go home after her bouts of illness, Lucia had no place to live aside from charitable arrangements made by the friends of her parents.

Only her father continued to cherish her, and he was beginning to see that his love was insufficient to meet her needs. In April 1934, he had confided to Harriet Weaver that he could not in all honesty suggest that either of his children return to Paris. By 1935 much of the expatriate community that had brought him there in the first place had disbanded.[37] Some had left as a consequence of the Depression—the money that had sustained them in Europe was gone—while others were leaving in anticipation of another European war. As real estate prices plummeted, people like the Jolases, who bought a twenty-five-room house in Neuilly, reaped benefits that would have been impossible in more certain political circumstances. The high eccentricity that had flourished in the 1920s seemed more ominous than amusing when Europe faced the possibility of a second conflagration. Lucia would have to make do.

This she did, until Dr. Macdonald came down from London to Surrey in early December. A veil is drawn over the exact nature of this visit. All who have told the story—Richard Ellmann, Brenda Maddox, and Jane Lidderdale—have reported that Dr. Macdonald wanted to send Lucia to St. Andrew's Hospital in Northampton, one hundred miles north of London, for blood tests. They concur in saying that Harriet Weaver and Edith Walker went to visit Lucia there and, while waiting for a doctor with whom to discuss her progress, discovered a report with the word *carcinoma* in it. Since this confirmed a fear that Walker had had about Lucia, so the story goes, Miss Weaver telephoned Paris, choosing to speak to Maria Jolas instead of to Joyce or Nora. Jolas, with none of Miss Weaver's compunctions, went immediately to the Joyces, thus spreading as fact a diagnosis that was unconfirmed and that later proved to be false. Alarm mounted; the Joyces summoned the doctor to Paris. Furious at the needless commotion, he broke off relations with Miss Weaver, and Joyce too decided he could no longer trust her.

These events did happen, but Paul Léon's letters show that this account serves as an alibi, calling our attention to a minor indiscretion and covering up the major drama about Lucia and those who were caring for her. When Joyce broke with Harriet Weaver in early 1936, it was not because of this mistake in judgment, which any of us could have made, but because of a more basic difficulty that frequently arises when considering how to treat people suffering from mental illness.

After the initial series of injections he administered in September, Dr. Macdonald came to visit Lucia three times in Surrey.[38] During his December visit he became concerned enough about her lack of progress to recommend that she be taken to a psychiatric hospital and undergo a second series of injections. He did not discuss this with Miss Weaver and went instead to Paris to speak directly with the Joyces. He arrived there on 9 December, and on that evening Joyce wrote to Lucia in Italian: "I have had today a long interview here . . . with Dr. Macdonald. He has come from London expressly to see me and he makes an excellent impression on me. Where you are now, as I have suspected for a time, is not doing you any good. So he will go to see you and will propose a change and I fully approve of his idea."[39] However selfless and generous Miss Weaver had undoubtedly been, both Dr. Macdonald and Joyce thought Lucia's lingering malaise resulted as much from her circumstances in Surrey as from her physical problems.

On 14 December, Dr. Macdonald returned to Loveland's Cottage to escort Lucia to St. Andrew's Hospital, where she stayed for ten weeks. Harriet Weaver and Edith Walker did not come to visit Lucia until the end of January, and the intervening six weeks were filled with tension for the Joyces, Miss Weaver, and by this time Léon. "Please excuse me if I hurt you, but I could not help feeling between the lines of your letter a certain distrust or even resentment of Dr. Macdonald," Léon wrote to Miss Weaver in early February,[40] in response to her complaints about the exorbitance of Dr. Macdonald's fees. She had initially assumed that his fee included not only the seven weeks of injections but also any follow-up visits during the six months of "policing" that were to follow. Now she discovered that he was charging for the visits to Lucia in Northampton and required payment for injections that had not been "foreshadowed" in the autumn.[41] She was disgruntled and felt that she and Lucia's doctors were at odds.

Léon was conciliatory. He thanked her for coping with the symptoms of Lucia's malady and noted Lucia's progress as measured by the clarity and purpose of her letters to her parents. His own pessimism about her was lifting, he wrote, and St. Andrew's was reaping the benefits of Miss Weaver's earlier efforts on Lucia's behalf. But something was clearly amiss long before Edith Walker and Harriet Weaver stole their peek at Lucia's diagnosis, and like Léon, we can wonder if it was not bruised feelings that led the two women to question the doctor's judgment in the first place. Macdonald had not found them professional enough in their nursing and had taken Lucia out of their hands.

Such a source of friction would explain the rifts that followed more readily than other stories that have tried to explain them. For when Dr. Macdonald learned that Miss Weaver had suggested to Maria Jolas that Lucia had cancer, he interpreted her gesture not just as an amateur's mistake but also as an attack on his professional judgment and an act of purposeful betrayal. On 7 February he wrote her a scathing letter:

It has been brought to my notice that in the past two weeks you have acted in a manner that is quite unwarrantable and, indeed, can only be described as fiendish. You have subjected a father, who has suffered so much, to a torture as exquisite and unjustified as the most malign mind could conjure up. This I cannot reconcile with the personality of the Miss Weaver that I have met, and I am forced to the conclusion that she has been unwittingly led into this appalling mess by someone who has neither knowledge nor sense—in other words, by some ill-intentioned meddler. I feel very strongly that for the peace of the Joyce family and for Lucia's smooth progress I must ask you to cease to visit Lucia, unless I am given a definite promise that such unpardonable cruelty will not be attempted in future. The insult offered to my own professional conduct of the case, in your unfortunate correspondence, is waived, but the harm that you have done without any shadow of justification I can never pardon. Yours truly, W.G. Macdonald.[42]

When he got the Joyces' distraught phone call, Macdonald went to Paris a second time to reassure them that Lucia did not have cancer. But he had to witness the emotional havoc wrought by the false alarm and to read the letters Harriet Weaver had sent to Paul Léon in January. They were puzzling. If one saw alarming information on a doctor's desk, an ordinary response would be to ask the doctor to explain it. Why had Harriet Weaver not addressed herself to Dr. Macdonald or insisted on a second opinion? We can only imagine an accumulation of mistrust or resentment, and an unacknowledged desire to discredit Macdonald, as a prelude to this breach. There would otherwise have been no motive to go behind his back.

Macdonald's harsh letter crossed with Harriet Weaver's reply to Paul Léon. Not knowing the rancor that was heading her way, she scrupulously examined her conscience and acknowledged that Dr. Macdonald had seemed to her "to take matters all along rather too casually." But within the next two weeks, she wrote again and again to Léon in an effort to repair the emotional damage she had done to her relationship with Joyce. She wanted to come to Paris. She was certain she could clear up any misunderstandings. She thought it was appropriate to do it in person rather than through the post. To no avail. Joyce seems to have withdrawn into himself, eschewing even the company of Léon. Even if Ischlondsky and Macdonald's serum improved Lucia's overall well-being, there was still the problem of how to reintegrate her into ordinary life. He decided to bring his daughter back to Paris. On 22 February Maria Jolas reassumed her role as Sister of Mercy and crossed to London, where she stayed overnight at the Great Russell Hotel, then continued on to Northampton. Lucia left Wantage House at St. Andrew's Hospital on 23 February, and she accepted Jolas's offer to live with her in Neuilly for the foreseeable future.

VI. FURTHER MERCIES

Given Maria Jolas's long-standing opinions about Lucia, and given that she was taking care of her only to give Joyce the quiet in which to write, this experiment was predestined to fail. There are two accounts of what happened to Lucia in Neuilly. In 1953 Jolas told Richard Ellmann that when she had gone to pick Lucia up in Northampton, she had been "agreeably surprised" at her improvement.[43] It had been her opinion that Lucia should remain in custody. But since Lucia wanted to leave and the St. Andrew's staff considered her well, she could not be made to stay without being formally committed. This Joyce predictably refused to do, and so the two women had made the journey back to Paris, where Lucia took up residence in the huge Neuilly home that now housed Jolas's bilingual school.

Lucia had never seen the Neuilly house before, though she had been told about it in a letter from her father the previous autumn. "She lives now," Joyce had written on 23 October 1935, "at no. 60 of the same street in a house with at least 20 or 25 rooms, all hers. You could play blind man's bluff there. Her school has now 45 boys and girls."[44] No one knows what went on between Maria Jolas and Lucia, but it was a fiasco for all concerned. Jolas's 1953 summary explained that "Lucia stayed three weeks, went completely mad, and had to be taken out in a strait-jacket." These were very sad years, she observed, for Joyce "finally had to admit defeat."[45]

The second account of Lucia's stay in Neuilly emerges from letters exchanged in 1936, and they bear out neither of Jolas's later assertions. On 22 March Harriet Weaver wrote to Léon—she was still trying to clear the way for a reconciliation with Joyce—saying that she had received a letter from Jolas: "A week ago Mrs. Jolas wrote that both Lucia and herself had been attacked by the prevalent grippe and that the former at her own request had been moved to a nursing home in the rue de la Chaise." Jolas's letter had said that "as Lucia had expressed a strong desire to go for a time to a community of nuns, Mr. and Mrs. Joyce were making inquiries as to some suitable place. I hope some satisfactory plan will be found where she can have the calmness she desires."[46] And Joyce's letters in both 1936 and 1937 tell us not that he was defeated but that he continued to believe in the integrity of his child. He looked at her in the same way that Vanessa, Adrian, and Toby looked at Virginia Woolf: as a human being who suffered under some kind of real if unnamable malady but who was not expendable. If he could have saved her by sacrificing *Finnegans Wake*, I believe he would have done so. "Of what use will any sum or provision be to her," he asked Harriet Weaver, "if she is allowed by the neglect of others, calling itself prudence, to fall into the abyss of insanity?"[47]

We have no independent account of Lucia's exit from Maria Jolas's house, so we cannot know whether she went quietly at her own request or was forced to leave. But why would someone send a violent, raving lunatic to a regular nursing home rather than to an asylum? This is what Jolas did. A statement by Dr. Pierre Leulilier, director of the Clinic Villa les Payes in Vésinet, confirmed that Lucia Joyce was there between 23 March and 25 April and that he wanted to move her because she was "dangerous."[48] Dr. Leulilier neglected to say that Lucia had been locked in solitary confinement the whole time. "They were from the beginning very apprehensive lest some scenes of violence would upset their institution. As a result they kept her closed in, in her room not letting her out [for] five weeks,"[49] Paul Léon reported.

VII. NOTHING WAS EVER THE SAME

Joyce's first thought in trying to place Lucia was to call Naum Ischlondsky, but since he was away from Paris, Léon intervened and introduced Joyce to a friend who had been a professor at Warsaw University before the Great War. Dr. Agadjanian went to see Lucia, talked to her, discussed the case with Dr. Leulilier, discussed it further with Dr. François Achille-Delmas, the director of a clinic in Ivry and arranged for Lucia to be transferred to it. He did not think that "dementia praecox" was the correct label for her, and he did not think she was incurable. He thought she had a hormone imbalance that periodically affected her moods. In early May, Paul Léon reported to Harriet Weaver, "here is the entirely considered opinion on this subject in writing and what is more his opinion is shared by the doctors in Vésinet as well as by Dr. Delmas. . . . Agadjanian defines the illness as mental disequilibrium with episodic schisoidic signs and recurrent cyclic impulsiveness and with a pronounced . . . vengeance against nurses. . . . Agadjanian emphatically maintains that there is something to be saved."[50] Eventually Agadjanian simplified this description to "cyclothymia"—circular emotions—something akin to what we call manic-depressive disorder.[51]

So Lucia's long sojourn at Dr. Delmas's clinic began. His fees—although they brought Joyce to the brink of financial ruin—were more reasonable than those at Prangins. The clinic had a large garden; Delmas knew that her previous experiences of incarceration had left her with an abiding hatred of nurses; he let her go outdoors by herself, and he encouraged her to play the piano and to sing. And once again he recommended that she take glandular treatments ten days out of every month. Somehow this combination of circumstances promoted a degree of peace for her.

Joyce raged at Lucia's incarceration. Losing the equilibrium that usually characterized his letters in even the most aggravated circumstances, he wrote to Harriet Weaver in June because "Léon says I am to write this": "my daughter is in a madhouse where I hear she fell off a tree." He then listed the bills that had to be paid "immediately if not sooner"—not only for Lucia's health care but also for that of Giorgio, who had undergone thyroid surgery for his own emotional imbalance.[52] He broke off relations with Maria Jolas. As Léon could see, the subject of Lucia had become a landmine, or, as he put it, it was like running "against some hidden cliff."[53] Years later Richard Ellmann learned that Eileen Schaurek also "blamed Mme Jolas for persuading Joyce to put [Lucia] in an asylum."[54] In November Maria Jolas left for the United States, the breach with the Joyces still unmended.

In virtual isolation and increasingly unwilling to discuss his daughter's case with anyone, Joyce now turned to reading. His patience with "mental" and "moral" physicians was as short as his faith in the attitudes of his friends and family was weak. He warned Carola Giedion-Welcker, whose own daughter was now ill, to keep away from such doctors. If he could study the history of humanity for his *Work in Progress*, he could study personality disorders that had a somatic origin. He could form a judgment of his own without the mediation of either amateur or professional psychologists, whose opinions rocketed around him, all of them founded, as it seemed to him, upon a void. While Nora and Giorgio commiserated, united in their decision that Lucia should be "shut in and left there to sink or swim,"[55] Joyce ordered books and essays. First he read McKaig's *Nil Desperandum: The Chemical Man as Deduced from the Biochemistry of the Human Blood* and a small piece by Lucia's doctor in Northampton, George Gibier-Rambaud, *Rôle de l'infection focale dans les psychoses*.[56] But the book he placed most faith in was by his contemporary Louis Berman, whose *The Glands Regulating Personality* had appeared in 1922. His final opinion after years of other people labeling his daughter was "keep clear of all the so-called mental and moral physicians."[57]

His days evolved into a familiar pattern that Helen Kastor Joyce captured in haunting terms in one of her memoirs: Everything changed after Lucia's illness, she remembered. Joyce was "punctilious" about visiting Lucia on Sunday afternoons, and though Helen never went with him, she thought she could picture the scene. "Babbo would tell us that they would dance with wild abandon together," and she imagined them singing and playing the piano together, too—"a terrible and fantastic picture." Joyce would return home from these visits completely exhausted, "near collapse." The rest of the family would hear the details over dinner at Fouquets, where Joyce would overindulge in his customary Swiss wine.[58]

The world of father and daughter was now pared to the bone, and at its center the two met in dance. A wild pas de deux symbolized the mutual responsiveness that had driven their interior lives throughout Lucia's adolescence and first maturity. In a world before the clarity of daylight, in a place beyond the intensities of "normal" intercourse, they communicated the extraordinary, sometimes corrosive, but always engrossing nature of their mutual regard. Joyce had solved the problem of the hostility between Nora and Lucia by using some of the oldest categories of his intellect. Like the young Stephen Dedalus, walking along Sandymount Strand, thinking about the primary order of the world,[59] he replaced the *Nebeneinander* with the *Nacheinander*. He substituted terms that follow one another in succession for terms that could not live in proximity. Six days of the week would be for Nora; the seventh would be for his child.

As Lucia grew more stable at Ivry, secure at least in the esteem of one parent, Joyce renewed his other efforts on her behalf. The logic of his writing had also led him to see the necessity of recirculation. He understood the human imperative to begin again, with patience, and in the spirit of hope. By now all the care for Lucia was on his shoulders; the internal division of the Joyce family was complete. Nora never went to

Ivry; and when Giorgio came once with his father, Lucia lunged at them and cried, "Che bello! Che bello!" Her anger at Giorgio was unabated.[60] Her other weekly visitors were Myrsine Moschos and Samuel Beckett, who was now involved with the woman who eventually became his wife, Suzanne Deschevaux-Dumesnil.[61]

VIII. KEEPING FAITH

After years of struggle, Joyce finally obtained Lucia's fantastical lettrines from Holroyd-Reece. He planned, doggedly, to arrange for the publication of the long-overdue *Chaucer A.B.C.* Since the loss of the lettrines had forfeited Servire's offer to publish the book, he was thrown back on a vanity-press arrangement with Jack Kahane at the Obelisk Press. He saved petty cash every which way to pay for it, and on 26 July, he arranged for Lucia to have one copy of the book for her twenty-ninth birthday.

A year later, Joyce wrote to Helen's father, Adolph Kastor, about the

Prospectus for the *Chaucer A.B.C.* with lettrines by Lucia Joyce, 1936. (Sylvia Beach Papers. Courtesy of Manuscripts Division, Department of Rare Books and Special Collections, Princeton University Library)

importance of not giving up on one's children. Kastor's oldest son, Alfred, had tried to commit suicide, and Joyce wrote plainly from the depth of his own trials as a father. On 30 August 1937, he summarized the six years of "dreadful strain on account of our daughter Lucia whose happy and promising youth has been blighted by another but perhaps even more incurable form of mental or moral derangement. I have used the word 'incurable' because it was used so often by doctors to me but it is entirely false. After that long ordeal to herself and to us she is, in the opinion of everyone, slowly coming round again." If Kastor could retain a similar faith, Joyce wrote, he would eventually "find some solace in the certitude that an irreparable loss has been averted."[62]

In August Joyce was in Zurich to consult Dr. Vogt about his eyes. There he was surprised to read in the tabloid newspapers about the supposedly miraculous cure of Vaslav Nijinsky, the former star of Diaghilev's Ballets russes, who had been diagnosed with dementia praecox. For eighteen years, the great dancer had languished in Kreuzlingen, another Swiss institution like Prangins. Now he supposedly had been returned to normal life as a result of a new kind of insulin shock treatment. Joyce's interest was caught because someone in Paris had already recommended to him that Lucia undergo a similar treatment. Joyce wrote to Helen Joyce's Swiss cousin Wilhelm Herz, asking if he knew Ludwig Binswanger or any other of Nijinksy's doctors. Convinced by now that the origin of Lucia's problem was somatic, he listened with interest to accounts of any treatment that was chemical in nature.[63]

The news about Nijinksy was premature—he was not to begin shock treatments until July 1938—but the therapy was indeed being tried throughout Switzerland, with astonishing results.[64] Binswanger was skeptical, for he believed that mental illness was "a life-historical phenomenon" and was generally opposed to the procedure because it was costly, time-consuming, and dangerous; but in the face of evidence he was eventually persuaded to give in. His colleague Dr. Max Mueller had been using insulin shock in eleven other Swiss hospitals, claiming a "full or good" remission of schizophrenia for ninety percent of the patients who had received it within the first six months of illness.[65] Nijinsky eventually received 180 shocks, given over five and a half months, before it was decided to terminate the treatment. On 2 June 1939, Dr. Mueller admitted that "during this time almost nothing has changed in his psychological state."[66] In any event, Joyce worried that the procedure was too dangerous and too experimental for Lucia. It was not one of the interventions tried in attempting a cure for her.

IX. HELEN JOYCE

In 1938 Lucia was not the only member of the Joyce family in need of medical or psychiatric care. Helen Joyce was having problems with depression. As she looked back on her life, it seemed to her that she had not lived it in a valuable way.[67] She wrote numerous soul-searching letters to her father, Adolph Kastor, casting aspersions on her life choices, finding fault with herself, and voicing various regrets. He always answered her letters but without the depth of personal analysis that she seemed implicitly to seek. In a letter that was typical of many, he countered her anguish with plain common sense. "I think you are entirely wrong in reviewing your own life," he wrote on 7 April 1939. "There is nothing to find fault with or to regret. Look to the future and be cheerful and all little troubles will be properly solved."[68]

But facile cheer was not something Helen could drum up. In July 1938 she checked herself into a *maison de santé* in Montreux, Switzerland, where she remained for two months. She returned to her life in Paris in the fall, but the problems that had set her original depression in motion had not been solved. In April 1939, she returned to Montreux, repeating the pattern of the previous year. By fall, still with a shaky sense of well-being, she was back in Paris again.

Helen's hospitalization in Montreux, like Lucia's in Prangins, had been preceded by a psychiatric evaluation by the ever-diligent Dr. Hans W. Maier of the Burghölzli in Zurich. He was, frankly, more concerned about her physical weakness than her emotional problems and worried that if she didn't receive the proper care—rest and ample nourishment—she might succumb to some kind of infectious disease.

He was not sanguine about Helen's psychic health, but neither was he unduly alarmed. "The patient is certainly not lunatic," he wrote, "nor are there any signs of latent insanity. But she is markedly neurotic." This was, almost word for word, the diagnosis he had given to Lucia six years earlier ("she is not lunatic but markedly neurotic"). Maier went on to say that the origin of Helen's anguish was sex. She had lived a sexually irregular life, and it had finally caught up with her. She was in the midst of reexamining the course of her life since infancy and felt unable either to elicit or return affection. Since she had no physical abnormality and had experienced no irrevocable trauma, Maier was confident that the patient would return to normal.[69] Just as he had in Lucia's case, Maier advised a two-month stay at Prangins; but Helen, perhaps with Lucia's dreadful experience there in mind, chose to go to Montreux instead.[70]

In Paris, according to Maria Jolas, everyone knew the origin of Helen's depression: Giorgio had stopped having sex with her. Their intimate circle was divided over the issue, and Giorgio became "very deeply annoyed" because the Léons had "sided with Helen's partisans that all she needed was for Giorgio to make love to her."[71] In 1954, debating with Maria Jolas about the disposition of the Joyces' letters still in her possession, the young Richard Ellmann wrote, "I wonder whether he [Stephen James Joyce] should have those pathetic, over-sexed letters from his mother to his father."[72]

Consider the possible causes of Helen's insecurity in the late 1930s. Her brother attempted suicide. Her father became extremely ill (she and Giorgio returned to America to see him in January 1938). Her marriage, and the literary world that it had brought to her doorstep, was in jeopardy. European civilization seemed on the verge of collapse. Yet her friends continued to engage in sexual dalliance. We have no way of knowing if this free-for-all sex seemed crazy or attractively diverting to Helen. But it continued to take its toll on the young women who engaged in it.

Helen's old friend Peggy Guggenheim remembered that she began her affair with Samuel Beckett on the day after Christmas 1937. They dined at Fouquet's with Joyce and Nora and then returned to Helen and Giorgio's for nightcaps. Beckett walked her home, and *voilà*. For the next thirteen months Peggy was smitten, even though Beckett was unfaithful to her and told her that making love without being in love was like taking coffee without brandy.[73] As soon as Beckett was out of the picture, Giorgio was apparently there to take his place. He wanted Peggy "to take a room in the hotel where he was living with his family."[74] "I certainly did not want to get so much involved with him," she wrote in her autobiography, and moved to a different hotel; but Jacqueline Weld, Guggenheim's biographer, understood that she and Giorgio had been lovers nonetheless.[75]

In April 1938, Joyce wrote to Helen that he found it odd that the two young men whom "poor Lucia" had been interested in "should now be going around with two sisters. After having got up, each of them, from a hospital bed. And that I should have gone from one bed to the other."[76] Probably neither Joyce nor Nora knew of Giorgio's liaison with Guggenheim, but in the spring of 1938 he was well aware of Samuel Beckett and Alec Ponisovsky's penchants for Peggy and Hazel, whose wealth, extravagance, and promiscuity had never escaped him. Beckett had been stabbed in the street; Ponisovsky had broken his leg; and Joyce saw with bitter clarity that he had ministered to the two young men who had broken Lucia's heart only to watch them take up with other women.

What Joyce thought of his daughter-in-law's troubles is difficult to construe, but he evidently withheld from Helen the empathy he extended to Lucia in such abundance. Nino Frank remembered Joyce telling him that Helen had a persecution mania.[77] Dr. Bertrand-Fontaine had a darker, more complicated take on it all, for Helen had confided in her and shown her letters Joyce had written, which were, in her judgment, "almost diabolically intended to upset" Helen. She believed that Joyce could not "bear the thought of his son being saddled with a sick woman," and she admitted that the Joyces had tried to get her "to sign certificates of insanity"[78] about Helen, which she refused to do. If what she remembered is true, Helen would have had ample reason to feel persecuted.

These emotional dynamics cast a mottled light over Helen's final attempt to assert a well-meaning place for herself in the Joyce family. On 2 February 1939, when Joyce expected to receive one bound copy of his finally completed *Finnegans Wake*, Helen threw him a marvelous party. She did it, she admitted, partly out of guilt. The previous Christmas, she, Giorgio, and Stephen had departed from tradition and taken a holiday in the French Alps, visiting Kay Boyle and Laurence Vail and then continuing on to Mégève, where they skated, skied, and enjoyed a robust outdoor life. She was clearly trying to save her marriage, but to do this, she and Giorgio had left Joyce and Nora alone in Paris for a gloomy holiday.[79]

The *Finnegans Wake* birthday party was intended in some way to compensate her in-laws and thank them for what she thought of as their support in visiting her in Montreux during the previous summer. The centerpiece of the party was an extraordinary cake that was decorated to represent all of Joyce's books, each with its properly colored binding, and a table decoration that celebrated the salient points of the Joyce family iconography: Dublin and Paris; the rivers Liffey and Seine; Nelson's Column and Napoleon's Column; and so on. The party served as a reminder of her intimacy with her father-in-law and shows us that her delight in Joyce remained unabated. She was also attempting to maintain the possibility of happy family life despite the family's unhappiness about Lucia. The party was a great success, a bright moment amid gathering turmoil.

Within several months, Helen was once more searching for equilibrium at Montreux. She emerged from the clinic to find that nothing could restore the affection of her husband; and in the face of his coldness, her behavior grew more and more erratic. Peggy Guggenheim wrote the most graphic description of Helen's conduct, although she was looking back on events after her own liaison with Giorgio. (She was implicated in the story; she was part of the betrayal.) By this time, Giorgio had moved out of the Villa Scheffler and was living in Alec Ponisovsky's apartment.[80]

Sometime during this period, Helen apparently bought a farm in Beynes, on the outskirts of Paris, and it was to this house (named, according to Joyce, Shillelagh) that she retreated after her return from Montreux.[81] Peggy Guggenheim claimed that Helen had an affair with one of the house painters and that she tried to seduce other men. She lived there with young Stephen and a nurse, who accompanied her into the city one night, only to find Giorgio and Peggy Guggenheim dining together at the same restaurant they had chosen. Helen created a scene; Peggy fled, then admitted that she and Alec "were terrified that Anthony [her pseudonym for Giorgio][82] was going to have her locked up. We did not realize how ill she was," she said, remembering that "we tried to prevail upon Anthony to leave her in freedom."[83] Helen's sins had been to run up dressmaking bills and insist that Joyce and Elsa Schiaparelli were spying on her. "She really was getting dangerous but I hated the thought of her being locked up. This she finally brought on herself by becoming violent," Guggenheim continued. "Anthony had removed the child, and this was too much for her."[84]

The passage of time makes it impossible to attribute the appropriate emotional nuances to this story, but it is possible to notice a kind of symmetry in it: one infidelity led to another, though who was retaliating against whom is difficult to say. When Giorgio kidnapped Stephen, driving up to Helen's house in a taxi and physically pulling the boy from her grasp, she, or any mother in a similar position, had ample reason to be upset. If she became violent, she had been treated with violence herself. In four months' time this symmetry of action and reaction was lost in the telling, and the blame for the broken marriage was laid firmly on only one partner's shoulders.

"My unfortunate daughter-in-law," Joyce wrote to Jacques Mercanton, "after having spread about her an indescribable ruin both material and moral was interned by the French authorities as dangerous to herself and others."[85] Helen Joyce left no record of her side of things, but in the list of her considerable liabilities in 1939 we find bills not only from dressmakers but from "T. P. Brennan, Court Civil & Military Tailor to George Joyce." We find bills for carpentry, painting, and wallpaper for the Beynes farmhouse, but we also find bills for liquor: "To George Joyce: stagehouse scotch whisky, browning gin London dry, sherry amontillado rico, cognac crouyer guillet, cognac crouyer guillet, and timbre, conge."[86] Clearly two people were spending her money.

Whatever the hidden emotional dynamics of Helen and Giorgio's relationship, Giorgio wanted out of the marriage by the fall of 1939. For the second time in his life, he jettisoned a young woman by labeling her mad. Paul Léon found Giorgio's attitude "incomprehensible."[87] Giorgio had Helen transferred from the "horrible maison d'aliénés," to which the police had initially taken her, to a sanatorium at Suresnes, "where she was supposed to be looked after, but of course wasn't."[88] He and Peggy then cabled Helen's brother to come and take her back to the United States. Robert Kastor flew in immediately, but Helen was too upset to travel. According to Peggy Guggenheim, Robert asked Giorgio to bring her to New York later, but he refused. "He said he could not leave as he was subject to induction into the French Army," an induction he spent the rest of the war successfully evading. So Helen "stayed all winter in that dreadful nursing home," Guggenheim continued, "and they would never have relinquished her, and all the money she brought them, if I had not again insisted that her brother send for her."[89]

Between Helen's incarceration and Robert Kastor's final success in smuggling her out of France to Genoa, where she caught a boat to New York on 2 May 1940, Germany had annexed Austria and most of Czechoslovakia. It had invaded Poland; it had invaded Norway and Denmark. France had declared war on Germany. Russia had invaded Finland and Poland, and the horror of Hitler's animosity toward the Jews had become clear. Robert Kastor pulled his sister from the edge of death. Joyce was immediately thrown into a similar rescue operation for his own family.

James and Giorgio Joyce, Paris, 1938. Photograph by Gisele Freund.

14

FACING DANGER
OCCUPIED FRANCE 1939-45

I. "SHE MUST NOT BE LEFT ALONE IN TERROR"

That Lucia might eventually be endangered by European hostilities seems to have occurred to Joyce as early as February 1938. On 19 February, a few weeks before the Germans marched into Austria, he wrote to Paul Léon that it might be possible to move Lucia from Ivry to the care of Professor Löffler, then head of the clinic at the University of Zurich.[1] His worry became more urgent in the summer, as he watched the deepening crisis over Czechoslovakia. In late September, he and Nora rushed to La Baule, on the coast of Brittany. Dr. Delmas had told them that, should there be a war, his patients would be moved en masse (105 patients, 60 staff) by the military government to the Edelweiss, an empty seaside hotel there.[2] They could find no trace of the doctor's preparations, however, and lived anxiously until the Munich Pact, signed on 29 September 1938, seemed to resolve the crisis by allowing Germany to take Bohemia, with other Czechoslovak territory ceded to Poland and Hungary. (By early March 1939, when Germany absorbed the remainder of Czechoslovakia, it would be clear that no real solution had been reached.) For the time being, Joyce's anxiety was assuaged. He and Nora returned to their flat in Paris at 7 rue Edmond Valentin, where on 13 November 1938, Joyce penned the closing sentences of *Finnegans Wake*.

Did he reconsider his wistful prophecy to Jacques Mercanton—that writing the *Wake* was somehow implicated in Lucia's illness, that her illness would end when he ceased to write? The final words of Joyce's seventeen years of work seem to modulate into the voice of a "daughter-wife" who wearily imagines a freedom that was being denied to Joyce's flesh-and-blood child. Anna Livia remembers life in terms that could equally describe Lucia's circumstances: "the clash of our cries till we spring to be free" (*FW* 627.29–30). And she speaks of uninhibited dances, which had become Lucia's way of coping with incarceration: "all our wild dances in all their wild din" (*FW* 627.24–25). Of the many stories that are brought together by Joyce's words on the last pages of his final book, one of them is surely that of the private family that had, year after year, provided Joyce with the prototypes of Tim Finnegan and his "vocably changing" relatives. Lucia haunts the final pages of the *Wake*, both as a speaker and as someone who listens to the voice of the father/creator.

Joyce ended his *Work in Progress* by imagining Anna Livia as the voice of the river Liffey as it flows into the Irish Sea. Like someone meandering on the edge of psychic dissolution, she communicates her disillusion with the ordinary rounds of human interaction: "All me life I have been lived among them," she admits, "but now they are becoming lothed to me. And I am lothing their little warm tricks. And lothing their mean cosy turns. And all the greedy gushes out through their small souls" (*FW* 627.16–19). One is reminded of Lucia's words about Jung: "To think that such a big, fat materialistic Swiss man should try to get hold of my soul."[3] And was she not the excluded one who grew to loathe not only her captivity but those who held her captive? Who would have been most "loonely in me loneness" or most aptly called "weird, haughty Niluna" (*FW* 627.28, 32)? Who would need secretly to "slip away before they're up" (*FW* 627.35) if not the young girl who disappeared from the homes of the well-meaning people in France, England, and Ireland who supervised her even when she hated it? Who needed to be saved from "those therrble prongs" (*FW* 628.05) if not the girl who had been incarcerated in Les Rives de Prangins? Who would have most worried in 1938 that "my leaves have drifted from me" (*FW* 628.06)? Who needed to be reassured that "but one clings still. . . . Yes. Carry me along, taddy" (*FW* 628.07–08) unless it was the girl left in the wake, the one whose entire adult experience could be described as a threat of extinction in the sea, in the great father, the "cold mad feary father" (*FW* 628.02)?

At the end of the *Wake*, Joyce wrote, "mememormee! Till thousendsthee. Lps" (*FW* 628.14–15). We might read this not only as an old woman's solitary resignation at death but also as a family's dialogue about anxiety and reassurance. And if we understand that Lucia is one of the people listening to this book as well as one of its subjects, we can think of Joyce ending his writing career with a promise that did nothing to hide his knowledge of the expropriations he had made in that writing. *Finnegans Wake* may then be seen as a double motion—both an expropriation of a child's experience and an act of atonement for it, a work whose progress contributed to the illness of a child and then was left as a testament to its creator's desire to assure his daughter that she was not "a way a lone a last" but also "a loved" (*FW* 628.15). "Lps" are lips without the "i" or without the ego, a way to represent the voice of the unconscious. And the key to understanding these "lps" is repetition. When unresolved conflicts return to haunt the person who has repressed them, the way to break that haunting, to lose the effect of their wake, is repetition. The interpreter "undoes" the dreamwork by interrogating the dream until it yields up its latent content. It will remain hidden until, by going over and over the same ground, the dreamer recognizes its origin. Another way to say this is that until a progenitor is recognized, recirculation is one's only course.

When Joyce began writing *Finnegans Wake* in 1922, he understood himself to be undertaking a "penisolate war" (*FW* 3.06). By the time he ended it, the meaning of his isolated writing had shifted considerably. To approach the boundary between conscious and unconscious life is one kind of project when it is undertaken from the position of consciousness. It is another kind of project when one understands that the enticements of the unconscious life are not always undertaken voluntarily. "The keys to. Given!" (*FW* 628.15) can mean to open a door, to make free, to end imprisonment. "The keys to. Given!" can mean to comprehend. If one's daughter is the imprisoned one, the keys are needed urgently. Locked as she was in a realm of ex-communication, trapped in a gestural language that no one else could decipher, Lucia needed to be reassured of her father's persistence in speaking and listening to her words, over and over again, until they were understood. With uncertainties crashing around him, Joyce left his final tribute and consolation to the child who had been his secret turbulent sharer for most of her young life.[4] If she had nothing else, Lucia would have this legacy.

There was no time to remain in reverie. In the final months of 1938 and into the beginning of 1939, while Germany built armaments and conscripted young men into the Wehrmacht, Joyce enlisted the help of anybody he could think of for the monumental task of reading the galleys and page proofs of *Finnegans Wake*. He worked with fury and with a double consciousness, seeing both the text and the context of his work, understanding how easily war could eclipse a book. He also worried constantly about Lucia. On 23 August 1939, the day the Nazi-Soviet Pact was signed, he asked Paul Léon to "ring up Loy and find out about Lucia."[5] Dr. Loy was the director of the Swiss clinic to which Joyce had wanted to transfer Lucia in 1934.

On 30 August, he and Nora rushed once again to La Baule, where, for the second time in a year, they waited for Delmas to transport his patients out of Paris. Two days later, Germany invaded Poland, and on 3 September Britain and France declared war on Germany. But there was still no sign that Delmas was providing for his patients. Joyce sent an anxious telegram to Giorgio on 5 September about Lucia, written in language remarkably similar to that which ends *Finnegans Wake*: "My leaves have drifted from me. All. But one clings still" (*FW* 628.06–07). He did not want his daughter to "be left alone in terror, believing she is abandoned by everybody," so he wanted someone to talk to her on the phone or go see her, "and if she is in danger she should be removed."[6] He was keeping his implicit promise to "mememormee!" (*FW* 628.14). On the next day, through Patrick O'Brien of the Rockefeller Foundation, he learned that there had been several night alarms in Ivry and that the government had evacuated the female patients. "At the time of writing," he wrote to Stuart Gilbert, "I have no idea where my daughter is."[7]

Mercifully on 11 September Lucia was settled at the Clinique des Charmettes in Pornichet, about three kilometers south of La Baule. Although Joyce and Nora's sole reason for being in La Baule was to reassure Lucia, she was so upset from the bombing raids that they were not allowed to see her. She herself remembered those raids: "I nearly died of fear as the noise of the thunder was so terrific,"[8] she wrote in 1959. Though she did not know it, Lucia would never see her parents again. Despite Joyce's every effort to reunite his scattered family, their lives were cut apart just as wretchedly as France was shortly to be in 1940. Within weeks ruptures of a more personal nature demanded his attention.

On 11 September, Joyce wrote to Paul Léon that he wanted his family to be together during the war, including Lucia, if a sanatorium could be found near Neauphe. On 24 September, he wrote again, saying that he would accept Helen Joyce's offer for everyone to live with her in the farmhouse in Beynes if he could find someplace for Lucia. On 25 September, he asked Léon to get in touch with Patrick O'Brien's secretary at the Rockefeller Foundation and ask her to help Helen find a sanatorium for Lucia.[9]

Then abruptly Joyce changed his tune, writing to Léon that although he understood nothing about it, he accepted the fact that Giorgio had decided to end his marriage.[10] Overnight the Joyces turned Helen from a family ally capable of housing her in-laws and aiding them in finding an institution for Lucia into someone who properly belonged in an institution herself. By 5 October, Joyce knew that Giorgio had taken young Stephen from Helen, and he wrote to Léon, asking him to try to convince Giorgio to bring the child down to La Baule. If that was impossible, then, he asked, would his and Nora's presence in Paris be helpful?[11]

At this point Paul Léon put his foot down. He sided with Helen against Giorgio. We have no record of his full judgment of this domestic crisis, but we can imagine what it looked like to a Jew already displaced by Soviet anti-Semitic politics and now menaced by Germany's anti-Semitism and aggression. Helen was not "sick," Léon told Miss Weaver, but "hysterical" about her circumstances.[12] It was the worst possible time to leave a Jewish woman alone without support. And he told Joyce that he thought it would be a poor idea for Joyce and Nora to stay with the little boy.[13] Joyce was flummoxed. What would be a better solution? he asked. He and Nora applied for a safe conduct to Paris and, when it arrived in late October, headed to the Hôtel Lutétia. Here at least they would have heat for the boy and for themselves. The rift with Léon seemed irrevocable. Joyce asked him to return whatever papers were at his home, and on 19 November, Léon wrote tersely that he had given the dossier on Miss Lucia Joyce and all of Joyce's contracts to Alec Ponisovsky for Joyce to retrieve.[14]

Once in Paris, the Joyces decided that the best thing for all of them was to send young Stephen down to Saint-Gérand-le-Puy, a village to the southeast of Varennes-sur-Allier in the mountainous Auvergne region, where Maria Jolas had relocated her bilingual school. Jolas invited

Joyce and Nora to return there at Christmas to share the holiday with their grandson. Thus it was that in late 1939 the Joyces moved to Saint-Gérand-le-Puy instead of returning to La Baule or staying in Paris. Joyce's primary goal, even while violent stomach pains increasingly sapped his energy, remained the reunion of his scattered family.

Giorgio was still in Paris, having retreated to a life beyond the horizon of anyone the Joyces regarded as a friend. Early in 1940, Maria Jolas wrote to her husband in America that "Giorgio's life is now shrouded in mystery, he gives no news of himself, lèts weeks go by without writing, and, even when he was here, gave literally no inkling as to the life he is living in Paris."[15] When Nino Frank asked Joyce for the addresses of various people he hoped to visit in Paris, Joyce could tell him Samuel Beckett's exact location but had to admit that he did not know how to find his son.[16]

Amid these uncertainties, Joyce turned his attention once again to Lucia, thinking now that he should move her closer to Saint-Gérand-le-Puy. By March 1940, he was arranging for her transfer to a clinic in Moulins, nearby. It was a state-run asylum, and he knew its impersonal standard of care would shock his daughter, but by 22 March, Lucia had given written consent to the change.[17] On 20 April, he had still not succeeded in effecting the transfer.[18] Then at some time on or before 18 June, for reasons that are not clear, Joyce abruptly postponed it.[19]

It was a fateful decision. Between the inception of his plan and the decision to revoke it, Joyce had joined a dazed nation in charting the Nazis' invasion of Norway and Denmark, the Netherlands, Belgium, and Luxembourg. On 14 May, just four days after the invasion of France and the Low Countries, the Dutch army laid down its arms; on 26 May, Belgian forces similarly capitulated. In France the Wehrmacht's advance was stunningly rapid. While a front line of French soldiers kept up some semblance of resistance, other French and English soldiers were evacuated en masse from Dunkirk in early June. Still other Allied forces retreated from Norway. Then on 10 June, Italy declared war on France and England. Soon it seemed to be all over. On 22 June, the French government called for an armistice with Germany, on 24 June, for one with Italy. The rout of France had been stunning. Within only a few weeks, between six and ten million of the country's forty million inhabitants had left their homes.[20] In central Paris, which normally had a population somewhere around three million, only about 800,000 people were left to see the German army arrive on 14 June. The circumstances that had plagued the Joyces with worry the previous September, when Lucia arrived in La Baule five days late, were nothing compared to the June exodus toward Brittany, when more than 400,000 refugees took to the road leading from Paris to Quimper.[21]

The immediate effect of Germany's lightning aggression was to separate Lucia from her parents by a boundary almost as absolute as that between foreign countries. Germany's strategy with France was to conquer and then divide it into smaller bureaucratic segments. The major division was between the occupied and unoccupied zones, but the Germans did not stop with a single line of demarcation. In the north and east, a line following the Somme and the Saint-Quentin Canal separated a *zone réservée* from the main occupied zone. A region stretching east to Charleville-Mézières was the *zone interdite*, sealed off even from ministers of the French government. The coal-rich departments of the Pas-de-Calais and Nord were declared a *zone rattachée*, directly controlled by the German High Command in Brussels. The coastal strip where Lucia's clinic was located formed a high-security *zone rouge*, which was later extended along the English Channel and down the Atlantic coast to the Spanish frontier.[22]

This complex network of administrative and military arrangements turned Joyce's simple desire to see his daughter again from a difficult undertaking to one of almost superhuman proportions. He was not alone. Thousands of French families were similarly displaced and separated. But he would need all of the patience that his years with Lucia had already taught him, and he would need to turn the intellect that had created the astonishing simultaneities of meaning in *Finnegans Wake* to meeting the simultaneous demands of two, then three, then four governments. The German occupation forces in France, the Vichy government of France, Switzerland, and England all had bureaucratic regulations run rampant. Straightforward tasks grew into seemingly unworkable requirements. History turned into a nightmare that even a man of Joyce's formidable imagination could not have foreseen.

II. HISTORY AS ANOTHER SOLUTION

Joyce's immediate concern for Lucia was her physical safety. He could see not only that the coast of Brittany had a special strategic importance to the Germans, but also that Pornichet was only some twelve kilometers from the French submarine base at Saint-Nazaire. He understandably judged her to be in danger from hostile military advances and bombardments. Unknown to him, another lethal drama was being played out behind enemy lines that put Lucia, domiciled in her mental institution, now in German territory, at almost as much risk as in the spring of 1940 the Jewish Helen was in hers.

While he was in Saint-Gérand-le-Puy, Joyce read and wrote letters. Aside from battling through a Kafkaesque labyrinth to get his family's papers in order, he tried to keep in touch with friends and family, to keep track of his career, and to keep his mind occupied. His entire personal library had been left behind in Paris, but he asked various friends to send him books that interested him. He asked Nino Frank if he could get hold of *The Life and Writings of Giambattista Vico* by Henry P. Adams and reminded him that his copy of Flann O'Brien's *At Swim-Two-Birds* was still out on loan.[23] He read Goethe's *Conversations with Eckermann*,[24] and he pestered Maria Jolas to send for Conrad Aiken's *The Coming Forth of Osiris Jones*, which he heard could be obtained from the Gotham Book Mart in New York. Among these and all the many other books that had sustained the thirty-some years of his writing life, there were no books about "racial hygiene," however. So it is unlikely that Joyce could have anticipated that the gravest danger to Lucia's life was now posed by neither bombs nor soldiers but by her very classification as a mental patient caught behind enemy lines.

Among the desires that had animated Hitler's drive to power was a radical vision of the biological and social utopia that Europe could become under his leadership. That fulfilling this dream required the persecution and eventual extermination of European Jews was becoming clear to the Allied nations by 1940. What even most German people could not foresee at the time, however, was the years of planning, trial, and error that would ensure the administrative success of the Nazis' "final solution." As Henry Friedlander has demonstrated in *The Origins of Nazi Genocide: From Euthanasia to the Final Solution*, by the late 1930s National Socialism had not only a ruling ideology but also a plan. It had a method, chosen from among many others as most effective, for the elimination of undesirable adults. In short, the Nazis had already practiced extermination on institutionalized people with handicaps.[25]

The ideological underpinnings of this program to eliminate handicapped adults had come, very largely, from a book about racial hygiene by Karl Binding and Alfred Hoche, *Die Freigabe der Vernichtung Lebensunwertigen Lebens* (*The Authorization for the Destruction of Life Unworthy of Life*), published in 1920. Binding, a legal scholar, argued that the law should permit the killing of "incurable feebleminded individuals." Whether a life was worth living, he contended, was determined by its value not only to the individual but also to society. Handicapped persons contributed nothing to their communities, and their care preoccupied an entire profession of healthy individuals, a misappropriation of valuable human resources.[26] Binding couched his argument in terms of the terminally ill who deserved, he said, the right to a relatively painless death. But this seeming benevolence, Friedlander suggests, purposefully obscured a more general belief that euthanasia was an appropriate solution for healthy but "degenerate" individuals.[27] Binding recommended that euthanasia be made available to patients, their doctors, and their relatives, but he reserved the final authority for the decision to the state, which would appoint an "authorization committee" of one lawyer and two doctors who would render an "objective expert evaluation."[28]

In the 1930s this type of thinking was still prevalent in many circles and not only in Germany, where Binding's contrast between the deaths in war of worthy young men in the service of their country and the survival of pampered, useless inferiors in institutions became a staple of eugenic arguments. A Social Democratic physician named Julius Moses predicted in 1932 that the medical profession under the Nazis would "destroy and exterminate" incurable patients because they were "unproductive" and "unworthy."[29] And indeed, this line of reasoning followed from exclusionary legislation that was put in place in 1933, when the general value of "*Aufartung durch Ausmerzung*" (physical regeneration through eradication) was given the sanction of law. In July a law requiring compulsory sterilization of "unworthy" people was passed, and shortly thereafter a Marriage Health Law and a Law for the Prevention of Offspring with Hereditary Diseases.[30] This last defined a person suf-

fering from a hereditary disease as anyone afflicted with congenital fee-
blemindedness, schizophrenia, *folie circulaire* (cyclothymia), hereditary
epilepsy, Saint Vitus' dance, blindness, deafness, deformity, or severe
alcoholism.[31]

On 1 September 1939, Hitler signed the authorization that moved co-
ercive eugenics from a policy of sterilization to a policy of killing unde-
sirables: "Reich Leader Bouhler and Dr. Med. Brandt are charged with
the responsibility of enlarging the competence of certain physicians, designated by name, so that patients who, on the basis of human judgment,
are considered incurable, can be granted mercy death after a discerning
diagnosis."[32] Four front organizations were created to hide the fact that
these killings were carried out on orders from the chancellor's office: the
Reich Cooperative for State Hospitals and Nursing Homes; the Charitable Foundation for Institutional Care; the Charitable Foundation for the
Transport of Patients, and the Central Accounting Office for State Hospitals. By 15 October, local governments in Germany were required to
list all public, charitable, religious, and private institutions holding mental patients. These institutions were in turn required to fill out question-
naires, and with the appropriate patients thus identified, they could be
transported to killing centers.[33] Often this process was disguised as a re-
location necessitated by war emergencies, so that even the surrendering
institution did not necessarily know the purpose of the transfers.[34]

These operations continued until their secrecy failed and the German
public came to know what was happening. Even "incurable" people,
however expendable they might seem to the state, had families whose
members were not easily persuaded that their relatives should die. Thus
in August 1941 Hitler issued a "stop order" to Brandt. Friedlander notes,
however, that euthanasia did not cease; it only moved. Heinrich Himm-
ler's men shifted their operations to state hospitals in the newly occupied
Polish territories, to Pomerania, to Tiegenhof, Wartheland, and to occupied areas in the east: Riga, Jelgava, Dvinsk, Aglona, Poltava, Minsk,
Mogilev, Dnepropetrovsk, Markayevo, and Kiev.[35] In Kiev alone 100,000
people identified as having hereditary illnesses were killed. Tallying figures in 1985, Ernst Klee estimated that as many as 33 percent of all the
beds that had been occupied by the mentally ill in the prewar period had
been emptied by the Nazi euthanasia programs.[36]

III. SAVING LUCIA

Lucia Joyce was, by such eugenic definitions, "life-unworthy-of-life," and by virtue of the French armistice of 22 June 1940, she was subject to a German administration that could decide upon and enforce the consequences of its own terminology. No matter that her alleged schizophrenia had not been demonstrated to have a somatic base; no matter that she had spent her adult life being a kind of psychic *aporia*, refusing to stay neatly in place in any psychological scheme. In retrospect the terrible irony of her position is evident. Only eleven years before, as a young woman pioneering in the physical culture movement, she had been asked to teach in Germany in an institution founded on the very eugenic principles that now condemned her.

Joyce moved quickly to Lucia's defense. By July he had made his decision: he would once again try to take his family to Switzerland. But by July, difficult circumstances had become even more convoluted. On 1 July, a provisional French government was installed at Vichy, to the south of Saint-Gérand-le-Puy, and on 5 July that government broke off diplomatic relations with Great Britain. Almost simultaneously German authorities cut off the post between the occupied and unoccupied zones of France. Mail was let through in only small quantities, and no personal correspondence was permitted at all until September and then only postcards of thirteen lines maximum.[37] The first immediate consequence for the Joyces was that they were cut off from income sent from London and Paris. In retaliation for the British decision to freeze all German assets in England, Germany blocked the monies of British citizens living in France. The second consequence was that they could not communicate with Lucia. On 14 September, Joyce told Jacques Mercanton that he had had no news of her for ten weeks.[38] Though Joyce never ceased to work for her release from the occupied zone, we have no evidence that Lucia ever knew of his plan to take her to Switzerland or of the resolve, which he carried to his death, never to leave her abandoned and alone.

Joyce's plan was complicated, and it changed as new pieces of information arrived in response to his many letters of inquiry. The first necessity was to find the money to live from day to day and to pay Dr. Delmas for Lucia's care. He was three months in arrears and had no way even to tell Dr. Delmas of his financial predicament. Theoretically British subjects had been transferred to the protection of the American Embassy. Accordingly Joyce wrote to Bennett Cerf at Random House, publisher of *Ulysses*, asking that his American royalties be forwarded to him through the State Department at Washington and deposited for him at the U.S. Embassy in Vichy.[39] He waited in vain, as did Giorgio, who lived in constant anticipation of money from the Kastors. Joyce then wrote to the U.S. Embassy in Paris, making use of the Vichy Embassy courier service, asking that the "dole" to which he was entitled as a British citizen trapped in alien territory be forwarded to Dr. Delmas. The maximum amount of this support was 1,500 francs per month—less than the 2,700 francs he owed Delmas—but he hoped it would suffice. The American consul, Leigh W. Hunt, replied in September that this could be done but that Joyce would have to resubmit his request each month through the American Embassy at Vichy: "Kindly note that the forms should be made out in triplicate and signed in the two places indicated on each sheet."[40]

Joyce next turned to preparing a destination for his family. Initially he hoped to return to Zurich. On 28 July, he wrote to Carola Giedion-Welcker asking her to see if the *maison de santé* at Kilchberg would accept Lucia. He added, with mistaken optimism, that he imagined that the occupying authorities would readily grant permission "to transfer a sick person, if I can arrange it."[41] He himself wrote to the previously dreaded Burghölzli asking if there was a place for Lucia there and what the cost of her board would be. And he asked Paul Ruggiero about flats for Nora, Giorgio, and himself and about French-speaking schools for Stephen.[42]

This done, he applied for exit permits for Lucia from the occupied zone and for the rest of the family from Vichy. By 11 September he was able to tell Carola Giedion-Welcker that the German authorities had told him "verbally that they would grant my daughter permission to leave the occupied zone."[43] It was only a verbal agreement, but Joyce placed faith in it. This miracle of bureaucratic efficiency left him with the impression that Germans were more responsive to ordinary citizens than other wartime bureaucrats. In the interim, replies from the Kilchberg sanatorium and from the Burghölzli arrived, and their fees were beyond even Joyce's extravagant tendencies. Kilchberg's was fifteen Swiss francs a day plus a double fee to both the institute and to the state;

the Burghölzli wanted twenty-five francs per day. Joyce couldn't afford either. The plan would have to be revised.

Joyce turned to young Jacques Mercanton in Lausanne. On 13 August, he wrote that the family had talked it over and had decided it might be better to settle somewhere near Lausanne. He could remember that there was a *maison de santé* near Vallorbe. Though he could not remember its name, he could tell Mercanton the name of the nearest railway stop. If Mercanton could make inquiries, he should say he had been given its name by Madame Fernandez, whose daughter Yva was a patient there, and by a Dr. Baruk, formerly of Paris. Joyce described Lucia to Mercanton as someone who was "about thirty-three, speaks French fluently. Her character is gay, sweet and ironic, but she has sudden bursts of anger over nothing when she has to be confined in a straitjacket. These crises are not frequent now but they are unpredictable."[44] We cannot know if Joyce paused to wonder at the internment of yet another lovely, intelligent, and original young woman, in addition to Lucia and Helen, but Lucia later remembered that Yva's fate had preceded and duplicated her own. In 1961, she wrote, "Yva the older sister went mad and had to be sent to a lunatic asylum."[45]

Jacques Mercanton came through for Joyce. A prospectus from the Pré Carré clinic, at Corcelles, arrived. There was a place for Lucia; he could afford it; the staff agreed that they could meet Lucia at the Vallorbe train station, and it seemed as if another piece of the puzzle had fallen into place. He was so anxious that this be so that he fired back another letter to Mercanton, asking if he could telephone its director, Dr. Tschantz-Chevalier, or better still, drive out to Vallorbe in person to say that he, Joyce, accepted the price.

The next problem was to arrange Lucia's transport, which evidently required that she travel with two attendants, one male and one female.[46] Joyce applied for help to the American Red Cross. They did not reply, but it is difficult to imagine what they could have done. First Lucia had to be escorted from Pornichet to Paris, which, Joyce thought, Dr. Delmas would agree to do, once he was paid for the balance of Lucia's board. Then the nightmare created by the Nazi division of France into administrative segments began. Another medical escort would have to take her from Paris to the line between the zones (then at Chalon-sur-Saône); then still another relay of nurses would have to take over from there to

Lyons and from Lyons to—and here Joyce did not know how to fill in the blank. The staff at Pré Carré presumed that Lucia would enter Switzerland at Vallorbe, where they would arrange to meet her, but Joyce learned from the Swiss Consulate at Lyons that the Paris-Switzerland train no longer passed by Vallorbe because the bridges had been blown up. He thought that the train detoured by way of Aix-Annemasse, but he wasn't sure.[47]

At this point, two of Joyce's old friends, Edmund Brauchbar and Gustav Zumsteg, came on board as part of the team that would try to bring the Joyces safely to Switzerland. Brauchbar, now an exporter living in New York, had taken English lessons from Joyce during the Great War and had become a family friend. Joyce had subsequently helped to get Brauchbar's nephew, Alfred Perles, out of Germany. Gustav Zumsteg, son of the proprietor of Joyce's favorite Zurich restaurant, the Kronen-halle, was evidently a man with a head for details who also saw the larger picture. He recognized immediately that Joyce needed money for the trip and someone to expedite the required paperwork. For the first, he offered to make Joyce a loan himself; for the second, he recommended a Geneva lawyer, Georges Haldenwang, and wrote a letter of introduction to him for Joyce. Joyce gratefully accepted the loan and promised to repay the sum to Zumsteg's father at the Kronenhalle. He told Zumsteg the current state of the Joyces' papers: his request for entrance into Switzerland should have arrived at the Swiss Consulate in Lyons "on Sunday morning," and the family's application for an exit visa from unoccupied France had been approved by the sous-préfecture that very morning, on 16 September, and forwarded to the minister of the interior in Vichy. Then Joyce returned to the problem of Lucia's transport. He asked, because he had no resources in Saint-Gérand-le-Puy, "where the railway line from Paris to Switzerland passes the line of demarcation, and how long is the railway journey across the unoccupied zone, and at what Swiss frontier station it enters Switzerland by present arrangements?"[48]

From this point, the remaining problem for the Joyces seemed to be gaining permission to live in Switzerland, for that permission had to be specific to an area or city. Of all the red tape that Joyce encountered, this was the most infuriating. Joyce initially told Haldenwang that he wanted first to live in the Vaud, near Lucia's sanatorium and near a school for Stephen, and then, having established these two, to move on with Nora and Giorgio to Zurich. He had already made this application, giving as references the names of Giedion, Vogt, Moser, and Schoeck. He had also, so he thought, arranged for Brauchbar's firm to put up the financial guarantee required, since he still had no access to funds in either London or Paris.[49] But Haldenwang considered that having a double destination would complicate the acceptance process and advised Joyce to choose one place or the other.

By 14 October, Joyce learned from Carola Giedion-Welcker that Zurich was going to prove difficult to secure as a destination. Fine. So he would begin again, choosing only the Vaud. Jacques Mercanton once again came forward as a reference not only of Joyce's good character but also of his race. Switzerland did not officially close its border to Jews until 1942, but already Jews were unwelcome, and the Zurich officials had, according to Carola Giedion-Welcker, mistakenly thought Joyce was Jewish. For his other new references, he gave the names of Oscar Forel, director of Lucia's former sanatorium, Prangins, and Dr. Loy, the director of the sanatorium in Montreux where he had at one time hoped to place her.[50]

At the end of October, after six weeks of waiting, Joyce learned to his astonishment that Haldenwang had ignored his wishes and had instead applied on the Joyces' behalf for an entrance permit to Geneva. Then he learned that the lawyer had reapplied for entrance to Zurich. Though Joyce presumed this would once again fail,[51] someone had arranged to enhance Joyce's portfolio of references. Perhaps Joyce did it, or perhaps Carola Giedion-Welcker or Paul Ruggiero. We don't know any longer whom to credit. But Robert Faesi and Theodor Spörri stepped forward, as did the mayor of the city of Zurich, Dr. Emil Klöti; the director of the University of Zurich Clinic, Professor Löffler; the rector of the University of Zurich, Ernst Howald; and Professor Heinrich Straumann of the university and the Swiss Society of Authors.[52]

Joyce was next required to submit a declaration of his financial means, which might have been a reasonable request in other circumstances, but he had no way of knowing the size of his estate, scattered as his resources were in places with which he could not correspond. Even travel back and forth to Vichy, only twenty kilometers away, was impossible for him. The bus lines had stopped running, and private cars were forbidden. In a telephone call to the Swiss Legation at Vichy, he was told how to have his deposition notarized in Saint-Gérand-le-Puy, and he mailed it to Paul Ruggiero. Now the Brauchbars failed in their financial backing, and another series of letters was required before a 20,000-franc guarantee, shared equally by the Brauchbars and the Giedions, was secured.

As he waited painstakingly for these requirements to be fulfilled, Joyce could see that one bureaucracy was working against another bureaucracy. The delay imposed upon the family by the Swiss recalcitrance in approving their entrance application had flown in the face of the French readiness to let them leave. On 19 November Joyce told Paul Ruggiero that their French exit permits would expire in eight days' time. They had spent six weeks in service to what Joyce called the gods of "complications and misunderstandings and delays and contradictions."[53] He would try, he said dubiously, to extend their exit permits for a few more days. Their visas to Switzerland (with the exception of Giorgio's) were finally issued on 29 November 1940.

In the interim, he tried to coax forward the plans for Lucia. As far back as 28 September, Joyce had realized he might better manage Lucia's transportation from Zurich. At Saint-Gérand-le-Puy, he could not find a simple train schedule for his immediate family, much less negotiate the numerous changes that would be required for Lucia's journey from Pornichet to Corcelles. New regulations meant that he could no longer travel outside the village without special permission, and he still had no access to his money. Nonetheless, on 22 November, he wrote to Gustav Zumsteg that he had, against all odds, managed to find an escort for Lucia. Would Zumsteg, on one of his ordinary business trips to Paris, consider making a payment to Dr. Delmas on Joyce's behalf? He estimated that "several thousand" francs were involved. This seemed to Joyce to be one of the final pieces required in what he could now see as the "whole Odyssey" of his year since leaving Paris. It had required the fortitude, patience, and wiliness of a classical hero to manage the bureaucracies of "Geneva, Lausanne, Zurich and Berne leaving out Lyons and Vichy."[54]

Good man that he was, Gustav Zumsteg agreed to pay Lucia's fees for Joyce. On 13 December, he told Joyce he had seen Dr. Delmas and given him a check for 5,500 francs. The balance owing, he continued, was 20,873.85 francs, calculating in the 3,000-franc deposit dated 18 November 1939.[55] Joyce had not paid his daughter's board for over a year.

We can see from this circumstance that Lucia was in the hands of a doctor/administrator of extraordinary compassion. Zumsteg had apparently explained to Delmas the reason for Joyce's seeming neglect of his financial obligations and had persuaded him that the debt could be paid only by helping the Joyces gain access to their resources in Switzerland. "I have been able to put you and your daughter's health once more into rapport," he wrote.[56] Amazingly, the way now seemed clear for Lucia to leave France more or less in tandem with her family.

But Joyce's trials as a father were not yet over. Giorgio's lack of an exit permit (he was now considered "mobilizable" for the British military) was solved through another act of human compassion—this time from a petty official at the sous-préfet of Allier at Lapalisse. This young man counted the four passports and the three *permis de sortie* that Giorgio held in his hands, immediately saw the problem that was implied by them, and took all four passports to be stamped by an unsuspecting superior.[57] But just at the moment when suitcases could be closed and timetables considered, the whole painstaking and intricately wrought plan collapsed. The German authorities in France revoked Lucia's exit permit.

On 26 November, Joyce received a letter from Sean Murphy, minister plenipotentiary of the Irish legation in Vichy.

I was both surprised and disappointed to receive a note (of which I enclose a copy herewith) from the German Embassy through Count O'Kelly, to the effect that your daughter's journey to Switzerland cannot take place. I do not know why this decision has been reached unless it is because, as it may be possible to infer from the note, she is the holder of a British passport. I had gathered, as I told you at the time from the informal talk which I had with a member of the Embassy during my visit to Paris in August last that her journey would not give rise to any difficulty, in spite of her holding a British passport. I may add, however, that there is no doubt that since the month of September, the German authorities have become more strict in regard to the travelling of foreigners.[58]

This letter hit Joyce like a bomb. He succumbed to what must have seemed like a cosmic perversion—he considered giving up the whole trip—but within a day he had rallied. Like Odysseus when, in sight of Ithaca, the winds blew him back to sea, Joyce had no alternative except to persevere. His family's hand-to-mouth, begging-and-borrowing existence had to stop. To Carola Giedion-Welcker he wrote that he did not love Switzerland but that he had to gain access at least to the interest, if not the principal, of his British resources. To stay in Saint-Gérand-le-Puy was to become more and more powerless. There was no information, no means of travel, and soon, he feared, even the British dole that had sustained them would be withdrawn.

The battle for Lucia was resumed. Joyce would try to surmount the artificial, sectarian bureaucracies created by war. He telephoned Sean Murphy and asked him for a letter of introduction to the head of the League of Nations in Geneva. On 2 December, Murphy sent Joyce a brief note to carry with him into Switzerland: "To Sean Lester, Esq., Acting Secretary-General, League of Nations, Geneva. Dear Sean, This note will introduce to you Mr. James Joyce who is leaving France for Switzerland and intends, if possible, to bring his daughter there from the clinic in which she is at present a patient in the occupied zone. I would be much obliged if you would be so good as to assist him in any way possible."[59] To Carola Giedion-Welcker, Joyce listed his final resources in this moment of German betrayal. Besides the League of Nations and the International Red Cross, he listed "also Count O'Kelly, chargé d'affaires of Ireland in Paris whom I know; there is also Dr. Patrick O'Brien of the Rockefeller Foundation . . . who could also intervene."[60]

At three in the morning of 14 December, Nora, Giorgio, Stephen, and Joyce boarded the train to Geneva. There, according to the memory of Giorgio Joyce, they spent two days, while Joyce presumably tried to see Sean Lester at the League of Nations.[61] It is not clear whether Joyce had an actual meeting with Lester or whether their initial contact had to be made by mail, but we do know that Lester interceded on behalf of Lucia. Then the Joyces went on to Lausanne so that Joyce could go in person to ask Dr. Tschantz-Chevalier, director of the Pré Carré *maison de santé* in Vallorbe, to continue to hold a place open for Lucia. With this accomplished, the family finally left for Zurich. But Joyce clearly intended to return to Lausanne, for on 17 December, just before he boarded the train, he sent Edmond Jaloux a note saying that he expected to be in Lausanne again soon, "for I want to transfer my daughter to Corcelles."[62]

Once settled in the Hotel Pension Delphin in Zurich, Joyce wrote again to Sean Lester, and then apparently duplicated his effort. On 28 December, Lester replied, "Thank you for your further letter and enclosures. You had, however, with your first letter already sent me copies of the letter from Mr. Murphy and of the communication from the German Embassy, and I in turn had fully explained the matter to our charge d'affaires in Berlin, and had sent him a copy of the German note, as that in particular should be useful to him in his inquiries. I shall let you know immediately I hear from him."[63]

Joyce never heard anything; he never went anywhere. Within two weeks, on 13 January 1941, he died of peritonitis from a duodenal ulcer, and with him died the desire, the patience, and the intellectual acuity to save what was left of Lucia's life. On his last Christmas Day, which the Joyces spent with the Giedion family in Doldertal, outside Zurich, Joyce sang and listened with pleasure to a record of John McCormack singing "O Moon of My Delight."[64] "You remember Essie in our Luna's Convent?" (*FW* 27.14–15). At Yuletide, in the season of light that symbolized his daughter's clandestine and most powerful role in the life of her father, we can imagine Joyce's inward eye turned to the absent one, the child of great price, his "weird, haughty Niluna" (*FW* 627.29–30). Lucia.

IV. ABANDONING LUCIA

Within weeks of Joyce's death, the intricate structure of planning for Lucia's release from occupied France ceased altogether. The letter writing, the financial improvisations, the plans for trains and nurses crossing enemy borders, the silent, persistent conquest of bureaucratic requirements following on hostile troop movements, the acceptance of setback, the refusal of defeat—the thousand tangible ways that Joyce transmuted love into practice—were efforts made neither by Lucia's mother nor by her brother. On 17 February 1941, Giorgio wrote to Maria Jolas, "I hope Dr. Delmas has not put Lucia in the street as needless to say I cannot pay him nor can I communicate with him."[65] Few words could have better displayed the alien nature of Giorgio's birthright. Heir to neither his father's passion nor his compassion, unable to imagine the magnitude of another human being's fear or loneliness, unwilling to value the singular nature of his sister's bright, misplaced, and mistimed originality, he abandoned Lucia. In one sentence he dismantled the fragile lines of communion that had bound her to life and to the hope of human understanding.

v. "he's watching us all the time"

Lucia passed the remainder of World War II in the *zone rouge*, in Dr. Delmas's clinic in Pornichet. How Delmas managed to keep his patients from the fate of the many handicapped people who died at the hands of Nazi eugenicists is a secret that went to the grave with him and with the other administrators of the various *maisons de santé* of occupied France. Perhaps the war's extremity and territorial violence created other priorities for the Germans. In August 1940 Hitler began the Battle of Britain; at the beginning of September began the remorseless bombing of London; on 8 October 1940, his troops entered Romania; in March 1941 they invaded Yugoslavia and Greece. Perhaps we can explain Lucia's survival by the inherent unwieldiness of bureaucracies or by the lack in France of an administrative structure for "liquidating" the handicapped.

What explains the last-minute cancellation of her exit visa from France? There is no answer to this question, although several administrative changes within occupied France might have had an indirect bearing on her case. On 27 September 1940, Hitler instituted a formal ordinance against all French Jews. Perhaps Lucia, like her father, had been mistakenly identified as Jewish. On 5 October, the German police arrested three hundred Communist protesters; and during November in Paris, on the Champs-Elysées, French students increasingly protested the occupation. These protests could have evoked tighter restrictions on the movements of private citizens within German-held territory. Perhaps she was held back simply because she had a British passport at a time of war between Germany and Great Britain. The answers to all these questions are shrouded by a silence as resonant and as deep as that which surrounded Lucia after January 1941.

Although Giorgio eventually wrote to her, Lucia learned of her father's death accidentally by reading about it in a newspaper. In England Harriet Weaver heard the news in a radio broadcast.[66] By means of these haphazard public communications, the two women, once so disastrously paired as personal companions, were again brought together under the wings of Harriet Weaver's generous spirit. According to Joyce's will, Miss Weaver was to become the executrix of his literary estate. The war itself determined that Nora, executrix of the remainder of the estate, could not travel to England to prove the will, and the public trustee whom Joyce had appointed as an alternate declined the role. In this way, Miss Weaver and her lawyer, Fred Monro, were named administrators of Joyce's financial affairs. Thus it was Harriet Weaver, and not any member of the Joyce family, who assured that Lucia's fees at the Delmas clinic were paid both during and after the war.

Harriet Weaver's commitment to Lucia followed the same ethical standards that had determined her earlier ill-fated interventions. While Joyce's will was tied up in court or in disputes with the Bank of England—as it was in one way or another until 1947—no money could be drawn from the estate. So Harriet sent her own money both to Nora and Giorgio in Switzerland and to Lucia in France. Whatever battles with the Exchange Control Authorities needed to be fought, Miss Weaver did not fail to assure that Lucia had a minimum standard of decency and care while nations outside the walls that enclosed her continued the mass hysteria of war.

Beyond this, there was very little Harriet Weaver could do. Nothing could hide Giorgio and Nora's desertion of Lucia. Years passed with no visitors and no letters. We are left to imagine the effects of such sustained isolation and restraint upon Lucia's personality. We are also left to imagine the tidal wave of undirected anger that can accrue from such profound disregard. Lucia never again experienced anything but incarceration, and she never ceased to lobby for her own release. She wanted to go to Paris, to Switzerland, to Galway, to London. More than three decades later, just a few years before she died, Lucia would still be begging her cousin, Bozena Berta, to come and fetch her.[67]

Nino Frank, who went to visit her after the liberation of France in 1945, noted that Lucia had transferred her faint hope for freedom to the possibility of returning to Eileen Schaurek's apartment in Dublin. She had also transmuted the most significant relationship of her life into an uncanny image that conflated fact and fiction, life and death. To Frank, whom she at first failed to recognize, Lucia repeated three or four times that her father was now under the earth and that he was "watching us all the time." "Cet imbécile," she remarked, "qu'est ce qu'il fait sous la terre? Quand est ce qu'il se décide à sortir? Il vous regarde tout le temps." ("That imbecile. What is he doing under the earth? When will he decide to leave? He's watching you all the time.")[68] In the imagination of his daughter, death had transfigured Joyce into the giant sleeping under the earth at the Hill of Howth, or into a version of Tim Finnegan who refused to die, and the proof was in his acquisitive eyes. Even in death, Joyce retained one salient trait in the mind of the young woman whose life had provided so many of the rich and complicated preconditions of his art. He continued to keep her under surveillance.

One can imagine the importance of this fantasy in Lucia's life, for in effect she had no other family. Even after the end of the war neither Nora nor Giorgio made any effort to see Lucia. They did not return to Paris until late 1948 and 1949, and even then the purpose of their journey was to sell manuscripts, books, and papers and not to see a daughter or sister.[69] They had left Lucia alone for more than ten years. Giorgio went out to Ivry, spent an hour with his sister, and was so unsettled by her condition, according to Maria Jolas, that he decided Nora should not even see her. He also wanted to hide the broken, unkempt condition of the hospital, which had not been able to clear the rubble from the bombardments it had suffered during the war. In a letter to Harriet Weaver, Maria Jolas tried to disguise this as kindness: "It is so many years since [Nora] saw her that it hardly seems necessary now."[70]

Nothing had changed. Like the figures of some ancient tragedy, the players moved into their old accustomed and self-justifying roles. Maria Jolas played amateur psychologist, never doubting the correctness of her assessments. Having claimed that an old mother did not need to see her only daughter, she undertook to *talk to* Nora *about* Lucia, as if this were an adequate replacement for whatever broken fragment of a relationship might be rediscovered between them. She still considered Giorgio, an able-bodied man who never worked, who drank, and who seemed without direction in life, to be "of excellent counsel."[71] Giorgio, now alcoholic, tried to hide his belligerence, smarting, it would seem, because so much of Joyce's royalties went to Lucia's care. This was a faulty resentment at best, since Joyce's will specified explicitly that each child would receive a half share of his estate, no more, no less, this half share continuing down through any of their own children.[72] Nora acquiesced in the arrangements made by the son, who was now her most prized companion.

Lucia was excluded. She might as well have been under the care of the geneticists whose views of racial purity had just propelled the world beyond the pale of human civility. Occasionally she erupted into violence, but no one thought about the causes of such colossal rage.

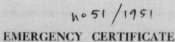

no 51/1951

EMERGENCY CERTIFICATE

THIS IS TO CERTIFY THAT—

..... Miss Lucia Joyce

has stated to me that ~~he~~ (she) is a

* .... BRITISH SUBJECT

and that I ~~have~~ no reason to doubt his (her) statement. AND CITIZEN

This Certificate is valid only for the journey

†to ... the United Kingdom ....

.. ..

‡leaving ... within one week ....

‡for ....,

and must be surrendered to the Immigration Officer

at the place of arrival.§

(Signed) .... amayan
British Pro-Consul
British Vice-Consul.

(Date) .... 13 MAR 1951

..... Lucia Joyce
(Signature of Bearer.)

Summary of the statements made by the holder in proof of his (her) British nationality :—

Holds Paris passport no 24838 issued on 5.2.1932.
Born at Trieste on 26th July 1907 ....

* Insert status.
‡ If the certificate is issue
vessel, date of sailing, &c., is r
traveller on arrival, that the
embarkation, and attested by
§ The possession of this c
immigration regulation in for
when required

Insert British territory of destination.
at an ..... post where the information as to the name of
..... in order to avoid possible inconvenience to the
..... ould be added by the British Consular Officer at the port of

..... does not exempt the holder from compliance with any
..... tination or from the necessity of obtaining a visa

2156 36808 F.O.P. (4)

13 MAR 51
CONSULAR
SERVICE

Exit permit for Lucia Joyce, 1951. (Courtesy of Special Collections, University College London)

15

KILLING TIME

NORTHAMPTON 1951-82

In 1951 Dr. Delmas died. As Harriet Weaver brooded about this development, wondering if the clinic at Ivry was keeping Lucia for primarily financial reasons, Maria Jolas went out to see Dr. Delmas's successors. To them Lucia seemed unchanged: she would experience long periods of quietness and then have unexpected and violent rages. If she broke anything or attacked anyone, she was placed in a straitjacket—by now the *camisole de force* was as familiar to her as a slip or stockings. It was their judgment that these alternations of mood were associated with a hormone imbalance that would not diminish until she ceased to menstruate. As part of a reorganization plan, the doctors at Ivry wanted to move some of their long-term patients—Lucia among them—to the French provinces.

Looking at the configuration of the Joyce family from across the channel, Harriet Weaver weighed the pros and cons of this move. By this time, Nora Joyce, still in Zurich, was mortally ill. She had spent the last several years badly crippled from arthritis. Giorgio, never far from her side, considered that the cortisone given as part of her treatment was hastening her end.[1] His mother's suffering had propelled him, for the time being, to stop drinking, but he wanted nothing more to do with his sister. Whatever the troubled secrets of their youth together—the experiences that Hélène Vanel had described as living "through many strange adventures which . . . were often with her brother"[2] and which had led Joyce to describe the relationship of brother and sister as an "out of the ordinary love"[3]—Giorgio wanted no part of them. He seemed comfortable only with Lucia's silence.

Nonetheless Miss Weaver consulted Giorgio about her next move, and she enlisted Maria Jolas's help. She recognized the sad truth that she herself, at seventy-five, was Lucia's closest friend and most frequent visitor. For this reason, she wanted Lucia to be closer rather than farther away. If a move was necessary for Lucia, could it not be to St. Andrew's Hospital in Northampton, where Lucia had been in 1935 and 1936? With the help of Dr. Macdonald, who remembered Lucia from her protoformotherapy days, this change of residence was arranged. Maria Jolas, stepping once again into her role as Sister of Mercy, came to escort Lucia from Paris to the Ruislip airfield, near London, where Dr. Macdonald met them and then drove Lucia the hundred miles to Northampton. She traveled with an identity card, some money (7,900 French francs), an emergency card that carried the address of Sylvia Beach's sister, and a package of Lucky Strikes that Jolas had bought for her. From this day, 15 March 1951, until her death on 12 December 1982, St. Andrew's Hospital was Lucia's substitute for home. At her death, those meager possessions (except the cigarettes) were deposited at the library of the University of London.

Of the many photographs taken of Lucia, the one accompanying the 1951 identity certificate is by far the most disturbing. Taken at a three-quarter angle, it shows the profile of a thin, forty-four-year-old woman with a gaze of searing intensity. She has strong cheekbones and a well-defined neck. Her hair is wavy, blunt cut, rather short, maybe gray. She does not meet the camera's eye. Stripped of the delicacy of childhood, the exoticism of dance, and the flaccid weight of old age—the poses in which we most frequently see Lucia—the photograph refuses our estrangement. This could easily be someone we know.

In a few years, phenothiazine drugs were discovered, and they, like the routines of St. Andrew's, contributed to the gray tedium of Lucia's days. For a number of years she was transferred to a Ladies' House in north Wales, but she basically lived at St. Andrew's Hospital for the remaining thirty years of her life. Less than a month after her arrival there,

Harriet Weaver told Lucia of her mother's death, on 10 April 1951. Miss Weaver observed Lucia's birthdays, arranged spending money and a clothing allowance, and saw to it that royalties from Joyce's books were invested so that she could continue to live with the small decencies that St. Andrew's allowed. When her own health began to fail, she arranged for Lucia's guardianship to be assumed by her godchild, Jane Lidderdale. Giorgio visited Lucia in England only once, in 1967, when he and his new wife, Asta Jahnke-Osterwalder, a German ophthalmologist, were returning from a Joyce conference in Dublin. They stayed long enough to complain about Lucia's duties in the routine of the hospital, not understanding their therapeutic purpose.[4] Various Joyce scholars and relatives visited her; people wrote letters. Alexander Calder and Samuel Beckett both remained loyal friends in their own ways.

II. FREEING LUCIA?

In 1959, just before publication of his biography of James Joyce, Richard Ellmann wrote to Maria Jolas to tell her that Frances Steloff, who was giving him a book party at her bookshop in New York, was "full of a notion of getting Lucia out of Saint Andrew's and giving her a job at the Gotham Book Mart. I gather she tried to discuss this with you and that you were, perhaps fortunately, out of town."[5] He wrote confidently about Lucia as an "incurable" person, which elicited from Jolas the comment that Frances Steloff was herself "[b]orderline."[6]

Nothing came of this proposal, but Steloff was the first person, aside from James Joyce himself, to question the inevitability of Lucia's incarceration and to raise, if only implicitly, the question of her leaving Northampton to live a more normal life. Sometimes Lucia seemed to want ecstasy—when she said she wanted to become a mountaineer who could scale great peaks. Sometimes she wanted simple and quiet pleasures: a house with a garden, a dog, a chance to be around children instead of cooped up with sick women. Always she wanted close personal companionship, and she had an undying preoccupation with marriage partners.[7]

Frances Steloff's gesture toward giving Lucia a place in the world showed not only that she saw her as a complete and sentient being but that she recognized the effectiveness of the newly developed psychotropic drugs. If Lucia could be made tranquil by them, Steloff seemed to say, why not let her be tranquil while shelving books in an environment like Shakespeare and Company, where, in the company of Sylvia Beach and the once loved Myrsine Moschos, she had grown to maturity in Paris?

We do not know who scotched the movement to free Lucia Joyce in 1959. As Lucia's guardian, Harriet Weaver would have been the person to make the decision, but there is no record of her discussing this with Frances Steloff. Judging from her actions, she seemed inclined simply to let Lucia's quiet life continue without disruption. By this time, as she could see, Lucia had become intimate with another inmate, Toria Thursby, the daughter of a Norfolk clergyman, and the grinding loneliness of her first years in England seemed somewhat diminished. A woman of extraordinary goodwill, Miss Weaver may have hoped that the ordinary things that could be given to Lucia—a new dress, new shoes, teas in shops, magazines to read, sheet music for the piano— would suffice. Jane Lidderdale was of even greater generosity of spirit: she set about a program to teach Lucia that she was a person valuable in her own right. Harriet Weaver had to examine her conscience and ask herself if she truly enjoyed Lucia's company, but Jane Lidderdale was able to say, simply and directly, "I loved her."[8]

III. A SACRIFICE FOR A BOOK

Dominique Maroger, Lucia's girlhood friend, had a different reading of Lucia's circumstances at St. Andrew's. She was approached in 1980 by Jacques Aubert and Fritz Senn, who were editing a special edition of *L'Herne*. They hoped to include new biographical material on the Joyces and asked Maroger to write a memoir about Lucia. She agreed and wrote to Richard Ellmann, asking whether he could provide her with the dates of Lucia's dance instruction, and she arranged to visit Lucia.[9] On 23 March 1980, in the company of Jane Lidderdale, she went to St. Andrew's to take tea with Lucia and to reminisce about their common girlhood in Paris.

Almost fifty years stood between that afternoon in the hospital and the time when Lucia had been a funny Charlie Chaplin mimic and a member of Les Six de rythme et couleur. Not knowing the generally accepted story of Lucia's past—the thousand small events, nuances of speech, and improvised decisions that eventually coalesce, creating both a direction and a rationale for a life—she was angry about what she saw. She took the whole sweep of years, went from then to now, and made another story that went right to the bone. Lucia was to her a medicated shadow, forced into submission by institutional needs, and forced into the institution as a sacrifice for a book.

Maroger listened to Lucia's evaluation of her own circumstances: "Here one is not permitted to be happy. Because of jealousy." "Here, the people don't understand me." "I mangle the language because I never have anyone to talk to."[10] Maroger thought of the halls of St. Andrew's as the portals to the Heart of Darkness. Like Marlowe in the office of the Belgian shipping company in Joseph Conrad's novel, she noticed the guarded doors, the knitting women, the unspoken horrors. The center of her reverie became the elevator, whose doors Lucia hated: "That horrible gate, I never want to see it!" Jane Lidderdale joked quietly that Lucia would jump into the elevator as soon as anyone's back was turned, but Maroger saw it as

> the gate to the prison that separates one from liberty. In its vicinity one is always under surveillance. There is a reason the exterior grills are wide open, for the patients must never be allowed to feel deprived of liberty. . . . One woman knits; the others are mute, staring forward, the gaze blank. . . . At a sign, all the women get up and are swallowed up in the open mouth. One of them is curved from rheumatism. They return in concerted silence to the first floor. One kills time. . . . In that "medicalized" milieu, every effort of the spirit appears dangerous. One kills time, one doesn't live, and undoubtedly all the patients must be imbued with a spiritual numbness favorable to maintaining them in an institution. All creative ardor is banished.[11]

She noticed an incident with an attendant that she regarded as typical. Lucia spoke of her wish to cross the Irish Sea in a luxurious boat, to stay in a hotel, and to visit Galway. "The enchanting overseer, with her sweet smile and implacable authority, says definitively, 'Miss Joyce, why do you always talk about voyages at dinnertime? We can want that on another day.' Thus reduced to the condition of a dependent child, Lucia

was forced to swallow her desire." As Maroger understood it, this institutional reduction of life to bland, unthinking mediocrity was exactly
what Joyce and his daughter had fought against all their lives. It was the
implicit foe at the heart of modernism's battle for new, unfettered ways
of thinking and feeling, and insofar as Joyce had fought that battle in the
name of future generations, his daughter's presence at St. Andrew's was
a travesty of fate. Maroger's mind was filled with the dark ironies of Lucia's life. What had happened to Lucia's creativity? Where were the poems she had written in her youth among the surrealist poets of *L'Oeuf
dur*? Where was the novel she knew Lucia had worked on as a young
woman? Thrown out, she supposed.[12]

"Why not let her dance?" she asked, looking around her. Where once
Lucia had trained to be a Margaret Morris instructor, pioneering in the
psychological values to be gained from physical health, she might now, in
these altered circumstances, find relief from her anguish in a return to
those same exercises. Maroger thought the origin of Lucia's troubles lay
in that fateful turning away from dance, and she saw her redemption,
even as an old lady, in returning to it. Had Lucia continued dancing, she
might have become a teacher bringing succor to the handicapped instead
of becoming someone in need of rehabilitation herself. "The movement
created by Margaret Morris is well received in England," Maroger observed; "the instructors could give courses in the hospitals for the handicapped. They could not but benefit Lucia who once found [in rhythmic
movement] . . . the privileged moments of her youth."[13]

What had brought her friend to this dark impasse? Lucia saw herself
in battle against superior forces. "Dilly didn't have a chance. Me neither.
I never had a chance! I was cumbersome, in the way," she told Dominique,[14] revealing a habit of mind that she took for granted because it
had been true in her family. Art can provide the grounds for understanding life; art is itself a transposition of life, and history, whether fictional or not, repeats itself. Dilly was the younger sister of the fictional
Stephen Dedalus, her father's early representation of a young man standing on the brink of a career as a writer. Stephen, like her own father, was
well educated and well traveled, and his stay-at-home sister represented
her longing for these forbidden, masculine realms in the purchase of a
used French primer. "What did you buy that for? he asked. To learn
French? She nodded, reddening and closing tight her lips. Show no sur-

prise. Quite natural" (*U* 200.869–80). Transposing herself into Dedalus's younger sister, Lucia saw herself as part of a family that educated only sons and, if need be, only the oldest son, a circumstance that Virginia Woolf also observed in the middle classes of England and identified in *Three Guineas* as "Arthur's Education Fund."[15] Dominique Maroger represented a similar attention to limited resources within the Joyce family as "*Finnegans Wake*."

In her eyes, Joyce's admirers had believed that Lucia's lot in life was to be an insistent supporter of her father's work. Her role was to dedicate herself, not to art, but to him. "As in the legends of central Europe, a woman was put into a bridge during its construction in order to ensure its preservation," Maroger observed. "[Lucia's] life was a supporting sacrifice for a novel."[16]

Her explanatory scheme was a simple one: "Joyce was lacking the calm needed to finish *Finnegans Wake*. The constant scandals that his daughter fomented within the house rendered that task impossible. The novelist installed her straightway in London," in the homes of numerous friends, with Harriet Weaver, and finally with his family in Ireland. When she left the beaten path, becoming a fugitive, "in Paris the idea blossomed that she could be arrested and officially interned." Maroger's idea was that Lucia had repeatedly experienced this pattern of exclusion until she internalized a sense of being expendable and grew suicidal: "Lucia fell into decay, as she continues to do today: she is cruel to herself."[17]

Did Lucia find solace in knowing that she figured prominently in *Finnegans Wake*? Maroger thought that Lucia must take heart in recognizing that her father had been an artist who projected his mental landscape into the tangible world. In her father's interior life, more vivid to him than the actual world of human relationship, his daughter appeared in one guise after another. Maroger hoped this would leave Lucia with an irrevocable sense of her centrality in the mind and heart of her father. "But the book exists, full of songs, the rounds of young girls, images of the young Lucia, eternally the child whom the father portrayed in his memories and dreams."[18] Maroger hoped, without feeling convinced, that such a tribute would suffice.

But it wasn't that simple, as anyone who had lived through the long years of Lucia's adolescence and watched Joyce's continually modulating response to it could have told her. To travel in "the crushing wake of one's parents,"[19] as Maroger put it, was not the same rite of passage for Lucia as it had been for other women of her generation. For her "the wake" had been a large and terrible book as well as a time of coming after.

PART THREE

THE RESURRECTION DANCE

Lucia Joyce, Paris, 1928. Painting by Myron Nutting. (Courtesy of the Library of Special Collections, Northwestern University)

16

A FATHER'S SCRUTINY, LOVE, AND ATONEMENT

THE LAND OF IMAGINATION

I. A LETTER WRITTEN TO LUCIA

In 1983, shortly after Lucia's death, Kay Boyle received a letter from Jane Lidderdale asking her if she or any of her contemporaries had noticed signs in Lucia of what came to be called madness. Had they noticed anything before her parents had been forced to do so? Boyle remembered Lucia's intense and complicated feelings. On the one hand, she had resented her father, and on the other, she had defended him ardently as a writer whose talent was as great as Rabelais's. Lucia had had obsessive emotions but nothing that could be considered deranged. "What a book could be written," she mused, "about [Lucia's] anguish!"[1]

Boyle had known Lucia during Lucia's dancing years, when the attention paid to Joyce had made Lucia feel intensely competitive. Eileen Schaurek distinctly remembered her young niece's driving ambition to be noticed in the newspapers before her father was.[2] Although Lucia retained her ambitions for many years, they were eventually complicated by an unexpected seduction. Unlike her mother, she entered into the novelty of her father's mind, especially as she came to realize that she herself was a subject of considerable interest to him. She grew up in tandem with a book in which she figured, moving from the position of amanuensis—copying out the *Wake*'s foreign word forms, which were "cinese" to her, to understanding that her father transposed the events of her life into these same strange signs.³ By 1928 she even merited her own small pink note-book with a picture and her code name, Isabeale, on its cover.⁴

As her friend Dominique Maroger sensed, Lucia's influence upon the life of her father and upon both the form and the substance of *Finnegans Wake* was profound. In the 1930s in writing to Harriet Weaver, Joyce paused to acknowledge this state of affairs. "People are always talking about my effect upon Lucia," he wrote, but what about Lucia's effect upon him?⁵ He knew that his moods were affected by her; his anxieties were aroused by her; his insomnia was increased by her; his health fal-tered in relation to hers; and his mind was constantly interested in her and, later, was engaged by trying to find a way out of her unhappiness. Like Dedalus, the mythic figure who had once inspired the portrait of his youthful self, Joyce refused to become lost in the maze presented by the mental-health profession. He learned to recognize the ignorance of doctors and to rely on his own intelligence when he sensed that they had come to the limits of their own understanding. In the years of Lucia's darkest struggles, his heart went out to her, not only in guilt but also in constantly weighing the moral issues that arose in the treatment of sup-posed mental illness. No quarrel with the Church interfered with Joyce's amazing fortitude and the careful evolution of a code of ethics to deal with the crises that arose in his daughter's life. She evoked compassion beyond measure.

In the last years of Joyce's life in Paris, Louis Gillet saw this preoccu-pation in his friend, and he named the drama that he saw unfolding on a daily basis "the Passion of the Father":

> During his last years, it [the thought that he was the cause of her suffering "through all the abnormality that his genius possessed"] gave him no peace. The image of his suffering daughter tortured him. This was almost the only topic of our conversation. Sometimes I fancied hearing the complaint of King Lear carrying Cordelia in his arms. "Stabat mater" was written. The Middle Ages have multiplied the group of the *Pietà*. Few artists except Shakespeare and Balzac knew how to depict the Passion of the Father. Joyce did not write this passion; he lived it.⁶

Joyce sensed darkly that there was not only a personal relation be-tween himself and his child, but also a compelling relation between his work and his child. By this he did not mean simply that she influenced the subject and form of his writing, which she so manifestly did, but that the writing itself was somehow implicated in her illness. To Jacques Mercanton, with whom he talked frequently in Lausanne in 1938, he revealed himself obsessed with this enigma—unwilling to talk about Lucia but able to talk about little else.

> In that night wherein his spirit struggled, that "bewildering of the nicht," lay hidden the poignant reality of a face dearly loved. He gave me details about the mental disorder from which his daughter suffered, recounted a painful episode without pathos, in that sober and reserved manner he maintained even in moments of the most intimate sorrow. After a long silence, in a deep, low voice, beyond hope, his hand on a page of his manuscript: "Sometimes I tell myself that when I leave this dark night, she too will be cured."[7]

When Dominique Maroger put her mind to it, she saw traces of Lucia in *Finnegans Wake* in quite simple categories. For her, her friend remained in the book's lilting voices of children and in their games and dances. But as Lucia herself came to realize, as one and then another of her life experiences were transposed into fiction, Joyce's Wakean portrait of girlhood was simultaneously darker and more compassionate. While watching his daughter, Joyce had become attuned to the narcissism of adolescent women, to their gullibility, and to the ease with which they could be wounded. He was aware too of the power of young women, their attraction, their beauty, and their ability to create delight. At the same time he saw the passage between girlhood and maturity as fraught with dangers, many of them occasioned by the very modernist values he had helped to engender. That he should see this correlation is not surprising when we consider that what Joyce wrote about, casting radical innovation into the nets of language, Lucia inherited as a free-floating context for living. In this respect, she was like Nathaniel Hawthorne's Pearl, a kind of living Scarlet Letter, bearing in her very being the same extravagant characteristics of the "letter" itself. We can see in her character her father's literary defiance of authority, his antagonism or indifference to the expectations of audiences, his desire to escape conventional languages and to seek as-yet-undiscovered subjects for expression. And perhaps of most singular importance, she grew eventually into an awareness of the observer's role in both creating and curtailing the world of perception.

II. THE RAINBOW GIRL

Among Joyce's many projections of his daughter's experience into the Wakean world of dream, one of the chief ones was, predictably, the world of dance with its spectacle of the female body in motion.[8] Her father watched her intently, seeing Lucia's own dancing, which he thought good, and also the lithe bodies of her friends, all nubile women who, in the age of Isadora Duncan, ardently pursued expressive movement as a way to regenerate the life force itself. Her repertoire group, Les Six de rythme et couleur, seemed to inspire Joyce to invent his own troupe of Rainbow Girls—the young, heavenly dancers who entertained him in imagination and became the vehicle by which he could make explicit an analogy between language and body language, between words and dance. Both of them were wrested from a world of constant flux, whose evanescence became increasingly interesting to him. In imagination the rainbow dancers carried the letters of the alphabet as they moved, first this way and then that way, circling. RAINBOW reversed was WOB-NIAR, but the words always stayed within the surge of rhythm that could, as Joyce saw, characterize the performance of both language and dance. "We are strictly correct," Havelock Ellis had said, "when we regard not only life but the universe as a dance."[9] In Lucia rhythm, cadence, force, and the organization of nonverbal behavior into a calculus of meaning were displayed before the appreciative eyes of another artist who increasingly understood the deepest implications of his own work to be a "sounddance." "In the muddle is the sounddance" (*FW* 378.29). "What does it mean?" Lucia asked at one point in her life as she tried to puzzle out the invented words of her father's unprecedented creation. "It is pleasing to the ear," Joyce had replied, "just as your drawings are pleasing to the eye."[10] The *Wake* is a performance, a "little Negro dance," as he said to Jacques Mercanton in another context.[11] It is not about something else; it is that transient, constantly displaced, and forever disappearing thing itself. But you know that, Joyce seemed to say to Lucia. Think about what you already understand.

> So and so, toe by toe, to and fro they go round, for they are the ingelles, scattering nods as girls who may, for they are an angel's garland.

> Catchmire stockings, libertyed garters, shoddyshoes, quicked
> out with selver. Pennyfair caps on pinnyfore frocks and a ring on
> her fomefing finger. And they leap so looply, looply, as they link
> to light. And they look so loovely, loovelit, noosed in a nuptious
> night. Withasly glints in. Andecoy glants out. They ramp it a
> little, a lessle, a lissle. Then rompride round in rout.
>   Say them all but tell them apart, cadenzando coloratura! R is
> Rubretta and A is Arancia, Y is for Yilla and N for greeneriN. B
> is Boyblue with odalisque O while W waters the fleurettes of novembrance.
> Though they're all but merely a schoolgirl yet these
> way went they . . . [226.21–34]
>   . . . And these ways wend they. And those ways went they.
> Winnie, Olive and Beatrice, Nelly and Ida, Amy and Rue. Here
> they come back, all the gay pack, for they are the florals, from
> foncey and pansey to papavere's blush, foresake-me-nought,
> while there's leaf there's hope, with primtim's ruse and marrymay's
> blossom, all the flowers of the ancelles' garden. [227.13–18]

But even at its most celebratory, Wakean dance is not idealized
or flattened into graceful motion. Beauty is at any moment subject to
alteration. Art grows out of pain; perfection has its share of "vice."
Perfectly heavenly girls can shift into "anger," become "virid with
woad" (Dutch *woede*, "fury"). Their "complementary rages" (*FW* 227.21)
can rock the devil himself. These dark emotions seem, in fact, to in-
habit a Wakean kingdom of their own, to arise from a "treerack
monatan" and out of a "scout of ocean" (*FW* 227.20). They seem, that
is, to spring up from a deep source that is inseparable from the bright
colors of their final presentation. It is hard to imagine that the mountain is "fortuitously" the land of the sleeping giant or that the ocean
is "by chance" the final home of the "cold, mad, feary father" (*FW*
628.02) that draws the flowing Anna Livia from her riverbed to her final
destination.

> But vicereversing thereout from those palms of perfection to
> anger arbour, treerack monatan, scroucely out of scout of ocean,
> virid with woad, what tornaments of complementary rages rocked
> the divlun from his punchpoll to his tummy's shentre as he displaid
> all the oathword science of his visible disgrace. He was
> feeling so funny and floored for the cue, all over which girls as
> he don't know whose hue. [227.19–25]

By the fall of 1930, when Joyce first drafted these lines, and certainly by February 1933, when they appeared in *transition* 22, Les Six de rythme et couleur was, for Lucia, a thing of the past.[12] This is the reason, perhaps, for the fictional dancing group's home as a rainbow sublimated among the stars of heaven, and for the textual affiliation of movement not only with erotic energy but with wrath. The dancing body of the daughter had been expropriated by language by this time in personal history; the tangible, Dionysian project of a talented and original young woman had been judged, by those in her father's circle, to be of lesser importance than the Apollonian mind of the father. It is the reflection of dance rather than its practice that will endure in the Joyce household.

III. NUVOLETTA, A LASS

If Joyce captured the beauties and interest of dance as poignant moments of regret for what is past, other of Lucia's experiences were more immediately translated into fiction. We can see, for example, how Lucia's very real trauma of giving up dance immediately became the precondition of a funny little story about a cloud-girl that rains on the earth. On 19 October 1929, her father wrote to Harriet Weaver, describing her anguish as "a month of tears as she thinks that she has thrown away three or four years of hard work and is sacrificing a talent."[13] On *exactly the same day*, Joyce had marked as ready for press a proof for *Tales Told of Shem and Shaun* (*FW* 152.18–159.18). "*Bon à tirer*. 19.X.1929."[14] And there she was as "Nuvoletta, a lass" whose tears (because she was "struck on dancing") were so numerous that they turned a stream into a river which flowed on and on "as though her heart was brook" (*FW* 159.17):

> . . . reflected for the last time in her little long life
> and she made up all her myriads of drifting minds in one. She
> cancelled all her engauzements. She climbed over the bannistars;
> she gave a childy cloudy cry: \Nu_e! Nu_e!\ A lightdress fluttered.
> She was gone. And into the river that had been a stream (for a
> thousand of tears had gone eon her and come on her and she was
> stout and struck on dancing and her muddied name was Mississliffi)
> there fell a tear, a singult tear, the loveliest of all tears (I
> mean for those crylove fables fans who are 'keen' on the prettypretty

commonface sort of thing you meet by hopeharrods) for it
was a leaptear. But the river tripped on her by and by, lapping
as though her heart was brook: \Why, why, why! Weh, O weh!
I'se so silly to be flowing but I no canna stay!\ [159.06–18]

IV. ISSY AND THE COLLEGE SWANKIES

In these same years, Joyce watched Lucia's transition from delight-
ful, impish clown and mimic, proud owner of a private Napoleon Museum—"Willingdone Museyroom" (*FW* 8.10)—to curious but curiously
vulnerable young vamp, thrust by her brother's early affair with Helen
Fleischman into a world of easy sexual liaisons in which she had far less
experience than many of the other players. The scene was a rough one, in
ways that we can begin to measure simply by taking stock of the number
of young women who ended the sexual adventures of their Parisian
youth by recuperating in asylums of one sort or another. By the end of
Lucia's youth, Helen Fleischman was institutionalized, as was her good
friend Yva Fernandez. Kay Boyle, Emily Coleman, Zelda Fitzgerald,
and Nancy Cunard—just to name those in her immediate circle—spent
time in asylums as well. Even Marthe Fleischmann, the young woman
with whom Joyce had flirted in Zurich in 1918, ended up in a sanatorium after Joyce had his way with her.[15]

Joyce saw his daughter's sexual eagerness, her growing preoccupation
with her appearance, her anxious relationship with a mirror whose
"voice" rarely reassured her, and recognized the rich texture and revital-
ized possibilities of his old theme of the cracked looking glass of art. To
portray female adolescence in fiction was, for him, to enter a hall of mirrors, wherein one projected both a desirable and a desiring subject. To
create a portrait of a youthful girl was simultaneously to see her and
to see her preoccupation with being seen. His own daughter, along
with other famous prepubescent sisters—Alice Liddell, Isa Bowman,
"Peaches" Browning—provided the precondition of a text that also mirrored back the author's own libidinal interest in nubile girls. The
father/creator became a voyeur whose appreciation of the spectacle
presented by his child can in some way be considered a precipitating
factor in the crises of the girl's later life. She already had, even before tra-

ditional courtship began, a spectral suitor. We can trace this dynamic repeatedly in the *Wake*; its theme is as manifold and varied as the tributaries of a river. It never ceases to flow.

What Joyce saw broke his heart. He watched as Lucia turned from provocative pubescent girl—"dadad's lottiest daughterpearl" (*FW* 561.15), his "Lucylight," his "subtle and barbaric" madcap, high-stepping daughter—into someone who was "unmerried" (*FW* 226.18) and then ditched. In the text written in 1928[16] the narrator, who speaks in the voice of the father, merely issues warnings: "I'll have no college swankies . . . trespassing on your danger zone in the dancer years" (*FW* 438.32, 439.02–03). I don't want any college graduates messing around with you while you're still a dancer.

But within a few years, the father's voice, as it records far darker events, becomes simultaneously more acute and more obscure. The daughter's image is tarnished; she has no "lovelinoise awound her swan's"; that is, she has no hold on ("noise awound" or noose around) her swain. He's walked off leaving a young woman wounded ("awound"), in sorrow and in fear ("woefear").

> Poor Isa sits a glooming so gleaming in the gloaming; the tincelles
> a touch tarnished wind no lovelinoise awound her swan's.
> Hey, lass! Woefear gleam she so glooming, this pooripathete I
> solde? Her beauman's gone of a cool. Be good enough to symperise.
> [226.04–07]

At this point (these gloomy "gloaming" lines were first drafted somewhere around 1930, worked on in 1932, the year that Lucia and Alec Ponisovsky became engaged, and continually revised until 1938)[17] Joyce uses the voice speaking the text almost as if the daughter were in conversation with him. She is present as a model of and creator of the text and also as its recipient. He speaks in the mode of a parent trying to reassure a battered child that all will be well again: "She'll meet anew fiancy, tryst and trow" (*FW* 226.14). She'll meet a new fiancé, tried and true. She'll meet, rendezvous ("tryst"), and when she thinks ("trow": Old English, to think, to suppose), she'll realize that "Mammy was, Mimmy is, Minuscoline's to be" (*FW* 226.14–15). That is, she'll know that she's next in the line of human regeneration. It's her turn.

The line has all the resonance of Joyce's many narrative histories of the family. It harks back to *Ulysses* with its identification of the mother and daughter as "Molly. Milly. Same thing watered down" (*U* 6.87). It repeats the formulaic "Anna was; Livia is and Plurabelle's to be" (*FW* 215.24) but with a wrenching difference. For the last term is not, as our ears want to hear, "miniscule"—another smaller version of the first two terms, hence a baby—but a "minus" "coline," or lack of a colleen, lack of a third term, lack of a child. A child taken away.

Given this failed progression in "poor Isa's" line of progeny, the "quickdoctor" of the next page seems suspiciously like a "quack" doctor or an abortionist who "helts her skelts up the casuaway the flasht instinct she herds" (*FW* 227.05–06). That is, we can imagine her as herding or harvesting the fruit of a "flasht" (flashy, fast) moment of passion. The daughter turns, in these lines, from child to "bopeep" who has been left, like many other unfortunate girls, "trailing their teenes behind them" (*FW* 227.12–13).

Such lines are, at best, suggestive. As fiction they are indeterminate in meaning and yet multiple in possibility. But they were written during the years when a real child was enduring the multiple betrayals that most certainly left her in tears and might possibly have left her pregnant. The narrative does not let go of these subjects. They are insistent themes, even when obscured by the puzzling nature of their presentation. Section II, ii of an early draft of *Finnegans Wake*, for example, describes itself as a "parrotbook of Datars, foully traduced."[18] And in words added most probably in 1934,[19] it asks its readers to "Beware how in that hist subtaile of schlangder lies liaison to tease oreilles!" (*FW* 270.15–16). At the same time that his daughter, sent away for seven months, was trying to cope with the trauma of her own life experience, the father turned to writing—in a funny way that teases the ears (French *oreilles*)—a subtle history of slanderous pregnancy (German *Schlanger*; German *Schwanger*). Or in another reading of the same line, Joyce's story is about (sexual) liaisons with that womb (Latin *hist*) that lies below the "tail" ("subtaile").

The evidence that these themes originated in personal history is found primarily in the early drafts of *Finnegans Wake*, where Joyce tended to work more literally and where, in this case, he used the personal names of the betraying players. So we can imagine that "Alex" is

Alec Ponisovsky and "Hazel" is Hazel Guggenheim. As part of an alge-
bra lesson, the Wakean children learn that "Alex" was "stumped" and
went to "pilfer turnips."[20] The voice of the teacher then puts several
problems to the students. How many of this or that can be got for one
hundred guilders or for one hundred thousand? But the underlying
equation is really about love for money—that old question involved in
Giorgio's marriage to Helen Fleischman, which, it is implied, also accounts for Alec's new choice of (wealthy, leisured) partner. The young
student, who is a "merbaby," is "outsung with a whispered wilfulness
heard fore you could whistle an Ave from Hazelizod."[21] The schoolmas-
ter continues to address his student, reminding her that "Hazelizod . . .
speaks Cashmir," the language of money, "and you, allbeyon her intended, cannot her industand." The young student is then described as
"disengaged" with "any hellsent lovethieves or beauty burglars who have
scraped her acquaintance when Jollycomes out for it mashing home."[22]
No one needs to have the words "lovethieves" or "beauty burglars"
glossed. We know "woefear" poor Isa is gloomy.

The substance of what later came to be called Issy's Letter, which is
contained, appropriately for a dancer, in a "footnote," reinforces these
preoccupations. This time the voice of the daughter speaks about being
jilted by gilded youth and moneyed Jews ("gelded ewes jilting about")
(*FW* 279.10) and she alludes metaphorically to the unexpected results of
sex in terms of the plant world. Instead of bearing fruit, she speaks of
"the thrills and ills of laylock blossoms" ("Miss Laycock" is slang for
cunt), which she immediately identifies as "three's so much more plants
than chants for cecillies" (*FW* 279.11). The third term, "plants" (seeds
sown, taking root), is more than chance ("chants"). In fact, it is so much
more that the speaking girl admits that she feels suicidal: "I was thinking
fairly killing times of putting an end to myself and my malody"
(*FW* 279.11–13). She represents sexual knowledge as a kind of grammar—"We'll conjugate tomorrow at amare hour" (*FW* 279.18)—or as if
loving were part of a book: "Ay loved have I on my back spine" (*FW*
279.19). She insists that she knows "the ruelles [rules and *ruelles*: French
lanes or ways] of the rut" (*FW* 279.39); and once again through
metaphor, the speaker looks back on what were surely her salad days, although she "parses" the salad through its ingredients. There is "Olive
d'Oyly" (olive oil); "Winnie Carr" (vinegar); "saladmon" (salad, salmon);

"peeper coster" (pepper); and a "salt sailor" (salt cellar) (*FW* 279.31–33). The result for her, like Shakespeare's Ophelia who is similarly left in the lurch by Hamlet, is "rue." And she attempts, feebly, to rise above betrayal by claiming that she is "throne away on" her "intended" (*FW* 279.20).

One interesting aspect of this footnote—aside from its lamentable subject, where a girl contemplating matters of life and death must still speak from a marginal position—is the modulation of the voice narrating the letter. It moves from the daughter's lament (I was thinking of killing myself) to the voice of the father in address to the girl (O my young friend and ah, my sweet creature), and it does so without any grammatical markers. One voice simply bleeds into the other, alerting us to a remarkable identification of one perspective with the other. It is as if the father has "eaten" the words of the daughter, subsuming her in the very act that claims to represent her. But it also seems as if the daughter has "eaten" the words of the narrator, seeing herself through the perspective that he provides for her. This modest footnote lets us see an amazing symbiosis at work; it shows us a powerful mutual influence. We're in the hall of mirrors again. We are let in on the secret of the mutual watching that is going on, and we are seeing one speaking voice internalizing the words of the other. It exhibits a compassion so strong that the father-creator simply modulates back into his own, older sadder perspective as if it were still part of the letter Issy sent to him—which clearly it is not. "For tough troth (truth, marriage) is stronger than fortuitous fiction and it's the surplice money, oh my young friend and ah me sweet creature, what buys the bed while wits borrows the clothes."[23] When we cut to the quick, says this fatherly voice, which identifies itself as "well voiced in love's arsenal" (*FW* 438.22–23), people like Giorgio are gigolos, for wealth (surplus money) has bought Helen his company in bed, and it's about to buy Alec Ponisovsky for Hazel Guggenheim as well.[24] Lucia, the one among all of them who has the "wit" (the talent), will be left borrowing Helen's left-over clothes, which was, as we know from both their memoirs, what happened.

Written in 1934 with drafts (nine and ten) that were revised up until 1937,[25] these words sound remarkably like a conversation we can imagine Joyce having with Lucia in 1935. In that year, as he wrote to Paul Léon on 16 January, Lucia finally decided not to sue Alec Ponisovsky but said that she considered he deserved six years in prison for what he had done to her, and that she was feeling suicidal.[26]

These themes—betrayal, desertion, the consequences of unguarded sex—are returned to frequently in Book II of *Finnegans Wake* where, in the final published version, Alec's name is expunged, although he is still apparently referred to by nationality as a "Russky" (*FW* 253.03) without honor. "His part should say in honour bound," explains the narrator, "I will stick to you, by gum, no matter what . . . and in case of the event coming off beforehand even so you was to release me for the sake of the other cheap girl's baby's name" (*FW* 253.11–15). Any man with honor would have married you in these circumstances.

Eventually these complicated events, rendered under the protective cover of fiction in a kaleidoscopic invented language that reduces communication to a chain of tantalizing hints, are connected to dancing and to illness. Joyce knits these disparate areas of experience together through several madcap references to *Macbeth*: "For a burning would is come to dance inane. Glamours hath moidered's lieb and here-fore Coldours must leap no more. Lack breath must leap no more" (*FW* 250.16–18). Playing off of Shakespeare's lines "till Burnam Wood do come to Dunsinane" (*Macbeth* V.v.51–52) and "Glamis has murther'd sleepe and therefore Cawdor shall sleep no more" (*Macbeth* II.ii.54–55), Joyce transmutes a Renaissance tragedy of noble death and betrayal into another tragedy with more local color. Burning "would" (desire) has led to madness (inanity).[27] "Glamours" (glamour and love [French *l'amour*]) have murdered the body (German *Leib*) and confused (Gaelic *moider*) the whole issue of love (German *Liebe*). Consequently "Coldours" (a member of Les Six de rythme et couleur dance troupe) must stop danc-ing and leaping about. She no longer has the wind for it. We are back to Dominique Maroger's memory that "an accident of health" dictated that Lucia should leave the world of performance behind.

Joyce's text may or may not leave us with a way to date this tragedy when he refers to three doctors who concur "seven sincuries" (seven cen-turies, seven sin cures) later. They say that the date "4.32" (April 1932) "to be precise" was the time of "waterburies" (water babies and water burials or drowning):

O Shee who then (4.32 M.P., old time, to be precise, according to
all three doctors waterburies that was Mac Auliffe and poor MacBeth

and poor MacGhimley to the tickleticks, of the synchronisms,
all lauschening, a time also confirmed seven sincuries later by
the quatren medical johnny, poor old MacAdoo MacDollett, with
notary, whose presence was required by law of Devine Foresygth [290.05–10]

We can all do the arithmetic. Nine months would bring us to December 1932 or January 1933, the time when the Joyces called upon Dr. Henri Vignes, the Parisian gynecologist-obstetrician.

One secret abortion would explain "Sis her mystery of pain"[28] as well as the Wakean narrator's penchant for writing about children in mystical terms that were suggested to him by Swedenborg's *Spiritual Diary*, where angel children enter a heaven whose entrance is filled with flowers.[29] Joyce writes of a "floral's school" and then asks, "Who is Fleur? Where is Ange? Or Gardoun?" (*FW* 250.33, *FW* 252.31–32). They are angels in heaven imagined as a garden, and their voices, we can imagine, announce that they are the souls of unborn children. Their movement is a dance of death, and it is they who speak the Nightletter that closes the children's section of Joyce's "book of the dark" (*FW* 251.24). "With our best youlldied greedings to Pep and Memmy," they write, "and the old folkers below and beyant, wishing them all very merry Incarnations in this land of the livvey and plenty of preprosperousness through their coming new yonks from jake, jack and little sousoucie" (*FW* 308.22–29). Seen in the light of such personal but easily generalizable events, Joyce's final novel speaks in a "clearobscure" (*FW* 247.34) way. Not only does it mention the disruption of regeneration implied by an ethos of "shifting about of the lassies, the tug of love of their lads," but it also identifies the potential lives sacrificed to an imagined celestial "childergarten" (*FW* 253.25–26, 31–32). Their "youlldied greedings" ironically identify Joyce's text as a meditation on the greedy pleasures that drive such sacrificial deaths while at the same time making it into a narrative that commemorates the unborn as part of the real. They are "the babes that mean too" (*FW* 308.29). They are children who were intended (mean to). They are children who, even in their absence, have meaning on the earth (mean, too).

V. A FATHER'S FATHOMGLASSES

If any of these speculations are true, they make *Finnegans Wake* into one of the most amazing documents ever penned by human hand. The text would become, at least on one level, an elaborate coded history of an actual family whose vicissitudes reiterated a story as old as Sodom and Gomorrah. But it would still be a text that had a rhetorical place within that family as part of its way of communicating with itself and leaving records of the salient events of its life. The difficult subjects it tackles would explain, for example, why the narration so frequently teases us about its own status as a book of "hides and hints and misses in prints" (*FW* 20.10–11) as well as taunting us about what cannot be said outright: "I've a seeklet to sell thee" (*FW* 248.26). When are we confronted with a clue ("tip!") in the text? How do we recognize what's left out of it ("mummum!")? That Joyce was concerned with the process of inferring what is implied but left unspoken can be surmised from a letter to Harriet Weaver. On 22 November 1930, he wrote that the phrase "there's a hole in the ballad" identified a verse that had been forgotten or left out.[30] These lines appear in the *Wake* as "And quite as patently there is a hole in the ballet trough which the rest fell out . . . to explain why the residue is, was, or will not be" (*FW* 253.20–22). In these instances, Joyce calls our attention to absence as a powerful way of explaining things. That which did not come to pass, he seems to say, is a kind of knowledge that can define life as well as the more tangible markers by which we create our stories of origin and family direction.

Thus among the many ways of regarding it, we might think of *Finnegans Wake* as a letter written to Lucia, a message that affirms, albeit in a wild, difficult, and oddball way, the truth of her experience. It would be the final installment of a habit as long-lived as her life: we recall "C'era una volta, una bella bambina," the song of her Triestine childhood, and the poignancy of the "my blue-veined child" poem, "A Flower Given to My Daughter." What may be a riddle to us might have been a surreptitious message that she could and did decipher in personal terms. "Every letter is a hard but yours sure is the hardest crux ever," says one of the voices that close the book (*FW* 623.33). The *Wake* is figured as a problem and then imagined in its own reception. This is the hardest puzzle I've ever received. Persist in reading, replies a dialogic voice, and "you're on the map. Rased on traumscrapt" (*FW* 623.35). You can do it; you've been raised on dream language (German *Traum*). We know that Lucia read in this personal way at least part of the time. Many of the people who lived in close proximity to Joyce during the years in which he composed *Finnegans Wake* considered themselves to be the origin of specific parts of the text. Maria Jolas, for example, told Richard Ellmann that she was the source of some of the closing lines of the book: "Carry me along, taddy, like you done through the toy fair!" (*FW* 628.08–09).[31] Interestingly, Giorgio told Ellmann that he was the origin of the very same lines.[32] Helen Joyce considered that she was at least in part the model for Anna Livia Plurabelle, and she took it for granted that Giorgio was encoded in the text as Shaun.[33] It is not surprising, then, that Lucia should understand herself to be deeply implicated in her father's work. To her cousins Bozena Berta and Nora Schaurek, she said unequivocally that the parts about eyes, dancing, men, and madness were written about her. She carried some of the text around with her in Ireland; sections of it made her cry.[34]

But if Lucia was a subject in the *Wake*, she was also its companion. She had grown to maturity in its presence, and the fact of its existence, its need to be created and born, affected her life as well. In the same way that her father regarded his work as a child, she, as we have seen, regarded it as a rival sibling who nearly always won. She was out the door in the afternoon. On any particular day, she was of less importance than a book. This is the position that Joyce seems to have taken when she was young, and this is the position that various people in the Joyce circle continued to hold for the duration of Joyce's life.

In 1959, just before the publication of Richard Ellmann's biography of Joyce, Maria Jolas cautioned him to retain a clear focus in his writing. She thought the principles that should guide him were "a. Here is undoubtedly the greatest literary genius of the xx century; b. Writing a completely original, much-combated book . . . ; c. Struggling against poverty, half-blind, and the increasing madness of his daughter . . ."[35] These were, of course, really *her* principles: Joyce was a genius; Lucia was not one. When Ellmann wrote that Joyce considered Lucia a genius, she questioned his judgment. "Are you sure," she replied, "that Joyce said Lucia was a genius?"[36] The generous, well-meaning Paul Léon and Harriet Weaver seem to have been of a similar mind, as we can tell from their copious and candid correspondence. Lucia is in the way, they agreed; let's do anything to help Joyce finish writing his book.

But if Joyce had accorded himself this unthinking priority early in life, he seems to have left this position behind in ways that we have charted by noticing the works of art to which he turned for guidance in the 1930s. As we have seen, he returned especially to the writings of Ibsen and Tolstoy. Through them he was able to reevaluate the ethical dilemmas posed by the centrality accorded to his writing life. An old and weary Ibsen led him to see the dangers of using models, of taking the quick, living energy of young subjects as a precondition of art. In *When We Dead Awaken*, the character Irene speaks words that Joyce could imagine on the lips of Lucia: "I should have borne children into the world and not such children as are hidden away in grave-vaults."[37] What toll had Joyce's need to have Lucia "expose . . . [her]self wholly and unreservedly to [his] gaze"[38] taken in his daughter's life?

As Joyce pondered these issues, Tolstoy led him to other questions that we usually confront only at the point of death. In the character of Vasili Andreevich Brekhunov, Joyce was confronted with another aspect of his own, unthinking values and the troubles they seem to have generated in his own family. In rereading "Masters and Servants," we can picture him in self-judgment. Was he the kind of man who would sacrifice the lives of those in his household in the pursuit of personal gain, sending his "servants" out into the storms of life without adequate protection? Or was he the man who would spread his arms over the suffering form of Nikita, the servant, shielding him from the snowy extremities of life? By the mid-1930s, Louis Gillet knew Joyce as a father whose deepest characteristic was an outspread arm; he saw in his friend the patient forbearance of someone like Mary, the mother of Jesus.

But if Joyce lived this "passion," he also wrote about it. In this respect, we can regard *Finnegans Wake* as metafiction, a book that points within itself to its own methods of composition. Here we see Joyce reenact, repeatedly and with variation, the artist's voracious impulse to watch, coloring it, as Ibsen had done, with shame. Scrutiny is everywhere. The eyes of an unseen, watchful male are ubiquitous, described as "spyballs witness" (*FW* 247.21), as "synopticals" (sin opticals) (*FW* 394.05), as "staregaze[rs]" (*FW* 382.17), as "the macroscope telluspeep[ers]" (*FW* 275.L2), as an "eyetrompit" (*FW* 247.32). Fictional Wakean lives move forward "while his deepseepeepers gazed and sazed and daze crazemazed into her dullokbloon rodolling olosheen eyenbowls" (*FW* 389.26). The Wakean witness "knows for he's seen it in black and white through his eyetrompit trained upon jenny's and all that sort of thing which is dandymount to a clearobscure" (*FW* 247.32–34). He calls himself "Watchman Havelook seequeerscenes" (*FW* 556.23–24). It is not simply that vision is eroticized in the *Wake*, and that Eros creates its own fugitive intensities, but that no place in the *Wake*'s fictional rooms can escape this scrutiny. It becomes an imagined space that the narrator eventually calls a "PANOPTICAL PURVIEW OF POLITICAL PROGRESS AND THE FUTURE PRESENTATION OF THE PAST" (*FW* 272.R1). For the daughter figure in Joyce's imagination, associated as she is with all the qualities of light, there is no way to evade these predatory maneuvers. She understands these hungry eyes to be "commanding the approaches to my intimast innermost" (*FW* 248.31). No matter how she may retreat into the depth of herself, she experiences herself as followed by "fathomglasses to find out all the fathoms" (*FW* 386.16–17). Her own advice to herself about how to live is "Musforget there's an audience" (*FW* 147.01–02).

If Joyce's text presents us with the ubiquity of an artist's voyeurism, it also makes a stark calculation of harm, which is represented in the text, at least in part, through the self-consciousness of the daughter figure. As John Bishop puts it succinctly, "Issy never appears in unmediated singularity"[39] but always in "apparition with herself" (*FW* 528.25). That is, Joyce represents the mirror of art as a kind of vanity, as if the daughter had internalized the eyes of the father and begun to judge herself from his position. This is the condition that Irene, in *When We Dead Awaken*, describes when she tells Rubek, "I gave you my young living soul. And that gift left me empty within—soulless. . . . It was that I died of."[40]

Luce Irigaray, our contemporary, gives women a more general way to understand how inward life can be stolen when the voice in *Elemental Passions* asks, as if speaking for Lucia, "But am I not a reminder of what you buried in oblivion to build your world? Where am I? . . . There and not there. In the space of your dreams. And how can I return from that landscape which I do not know. From those surroundings which I cannot see. Where I take place only in you. And you fallen into the depth of me, into that dark abyss which you imagine me to be."[41]

Looked at in other contemporary terms, this intensified self-consciousness, this life lived in the awareness of scrutiny until that scrutiny is "swallowed," is what Louis Sass identifies as one of the primary characteristics of modernist art as well as what we have become accustomed to call "schizophrenia." This division or doubling, this hesitation and detachment, this self-alienation may have been embodied by Ibsen in the singular character of Irene, but Louis Sass points out the pervasiveness of these qualities in modern writing. In this one respect we might consider Lucia Joyce to have been a kind of living writing, enacting in her life a circumstance that Joyce eventually recognized and re-created in his fiction, and that his fiction can, at least in part, make intelligible.

Michel Foucault, writing in general terms about modern culture, speaks about this tendency for internal division by using architecture as a trope. One of his cultural projects was to "to grasp how 'the self is not merely given but is constituted in relationship to itself as subject' and to understand how 'the subject is objectified by a process of division either within himself or from others.' "[42] We come to know who we are by understanding how others see us. In his *Discipline and Punish*, Foucault explains this process by referring to the Panopticon. Jeremy Bentham conceived this form of architecture in 1791, and though it was originally designed for prison buildings, it can also be used to think about other kinds of institutions requiring observation or discipline, such as schools, hospitals, or military barracks:

> Its essential point was to effect a radical separation between observer and ob-
> served, and to keep the latter under constant surveillance. The Panopticon
> consists of two elements: a central observation tower and an encircling build-
> ing containing numerous small cells. Because of the thinness of the encircling
> building, each cell would be open on two sides with bars on the outer wall al-
> lowing light to flood the cell and bars on the inner wall exposing the occupant
> to the gaze of the watcher in the central tower. In this way, those in the cells
> would always be within sight of the implacable tower, which itself was dark-
> ened and fitted with narrow slits so that those within could peer out, without
> being seen.[43]

What effect would such an environment have upon those who were forced to conform to its demands, especially if such surveillance were unwelcome? Since the prisoner would never know when he or she was being watched, he or she could never cease to be vigilant. The self would have to observe the self. Sass points out, "paradoxically enough, this situation may even give rise to a sense of freedom in the prisoner—the freedom of a self bent on scrutinizing and subduing a 'lower' or more objectified part of its own being."[44]

This dualism—the prisoner being both observer and observed—has the further consequence that he or she "cannot truly identify with either of these polarized roles (that is, either with a bodily self-presence or with an observing consciousness). One cannot experience one's own body from within but only from without, from the imaginary position of an observer in a tower. And insofar as one identifies oneself with the mind, one will be identifying with a being whose essence is always elsewhere—an imagined, alien consciousness, perpetually watching from a remove." The situation is, Sass claims, a variant of the master/slave dialectic; and taken to an extreme, he also claims that it describes the lived experience of schizophrenics. "Each self—observer and observed—comes to be defined almost completely by a relationship whose essence is distance and difference; thus the prisoner's body would have to be experienced by the prisoner as a body-as-perceived, a body for the distant observer; while the observer's being would be reduced to a single function, the 'being-who-observes-me-from-afar.'"[45]

Think about Lucia again. On being told in 1941 that her father had died, her response was, "What is he doing under the earth? . . . He's watching you all the time."[46] Without hesitation she formulated the panoptical nature of her own experience. Even at Joyce's death she configured her life in relation to his as a being-who-is-perceived. If, as Foucault claims, the tendency toward self-policing in the face of surveillance is a characteristic of subjectivity within all modern states, what must it have been like to inherit Lucia's social estate? Every aspect of her experience routinely became a shred of evidence, a possible epiphany, a modulation of experience into her father's art. Her creativity, her passion, her vulnerabilities provided Joyce with the preconditions of his writing. The very existence of *Finnegans Wake* tells us of a frightening dynamic that occurred in the Joyce household, a dynamic by which Joyce, hidden behind the dark frames of his glasses, grew to be like a dark observation tower to which the light of Lucia's very being stood exposed. "Heliotrope." The wonted turning of the eyes to light, to "flesh light"

(*FW* 222.21), to "loovelit" (*FW* 226.27), to a young girl perceived to be a "sweetishsad lightandgayle" (sweet and sad, light and gayle [stormy]) (*FW* 360.02) person.[47]

If Joyce did not immediately see the consequences of a certain kind of fatherly neglect with regard to his children (his initial failure to consider the prosaic questions of schooling or vocation or housing or stability for them), then neither did he anticipate Lucia's response to the kind of overwrought artistic attention that eventually became her lot. We can imagine his dismay as he gradually became aware that scrutiny could elicit its own unwelcome responses. Before his very eyes (where else?) his child seemed to transform herself into "the dotter of her father's eyes": the daughter doted upon, but then the daughter who played the scenes that would evoke that doting. It was as if Lucia began to perform the events of her life in order to evoke a metamorphosis of herself into Joyce's text.

VI. "TELL HIM I AM A CROSSWORD PUZZLE"

Reconsider the chilling implications of the conversations Cary Baynes recorded during her months of companionship with Lucia in Zurich, when Lucia would ask very directly if Joyce needed new material for his book. "Tell him I am a crossword puzzle," she would say. "If he does not mind seeing a crossword puzzle, he is to come out."[48] These are the words of a collaborator, of someone psychically invested in a coded performance and confident that its code will be deciphered. Ink on the face. Wearing an evening dress in the day. Setting a room ablaze. If this is mad behavior, it is also purposeful behavior directed at an audience for whom it was intelligible. Her father, as Lucia realized, was wearing his "fathomglasses." There were two artists in this psychic space, and they were mutually enthralled.

Then remember Harriet Weaver's shock in London the following year when she realized that Lucia *liked* being thought of as a person who was mad.[49] Even Lucia's insane moments could be staged in some way or played for effect. There is drama in insanity; it is an interesting role. Lucia di Lammermoor, her namesake, even got to sing out her grief before an appreciative operatic audience.

Of all the friends of the Joyce family during the late 1920s and into the 1930s, Stuart Gilbert came the closest to formulating what he saw happening among them and how it seemed to change over time. At first he was confident that Lucia was a somewhat imperious bourgeois child. She appeared to be obscured by her father but happy and loquacious in his absence. "Several times, when I had persuaded her to come with me to the nearby bar *Chez Francis* (in the Place de l'Alma) for a cocktail," he remembered, "I was struck by the change in her manner when I switched the conversation over to ordinary topics and encouraged her to talk about herself. Her ambition was to strike out on her own."[50] But in later years, and especially in 1932, he sensed that Lucia had changed. He began to speculate that somehow, in performing a role, she had grown to be that role.[51] She had made herself into the creature of her own and her father's imagination.

In retrospect we can see the progression better than Gilbert did. *Finnegans Wake* had functioned first as a sibling in Lucia's life. She perceived it as taking Joyce's emotional resources away from her and as a show-off-brat type of kid who grabbed everyone's attention. Then it grew into a kind of seductive lover, soliciting her tender poses and psychic commitment. Finally it became a kind of child whose life she helped, through deliberate performances or through unconscious modeling, to bring into being. Through this liaison, she participated in the imaginative world of her father, but she did so at great cost to her own inner life. What did not change was her father's scrutiny. His vision was her constant companion. It led her to think of her father as a creative partner. It led him to see in her a "mirrorminded curiositease" (*FW* 570.24).

Certainly we can imagine the erotic dimension of their partnership, but to linger here—at the hoary head of incest for which there is no historical evidence—is to miss another dynamic for which there is ample confirmation. Joyce and Lucia were paired by temperament, by intuitive understanding, and by the imperatives of art. This was so extreme that Beckett, in reflecting on his own attempted liaison with her, understood that he (and for all he knew, other suitors) were "in liu" men. That is, they were substitutes for a partnered identity already in place.

When, in future years, Jung would try to effect the psychological "transfer" of emotions that is at the heart of all successful therapeutic relations, Lucia became so terrified by the projected uncoupling with her father that she wrote a letter proclaiming her eternal allegiance. "Father, if ever I take a fancy to anybody I swear to you on the head of Jesus that it will not be because I am not fond of you. Do not forget that. I don't really know what I am writing Father. . . . Who knows what fate has in store for us? At any rate, in spite of the fact that life seems full of light this evening, here, if ever I should go away, it would be to a country which belongs in a way to you, isn't that true father?"[52]

Her words echo the language Joyce used to describe her situation in the psychological profile that he gave to the Burghölzli in 1934. As he understood it, her deepest desire was to prove that the bond between herself and her father was stronger than medical science.[53] Both of them knew what was up. Here was an enthralled existence. Here was a maiden in service to a liege lord, an Isolde who was breaking the story line and casting her lot with an aged King Mark instead of clasping the raptures promised by Tristan's youth.

VII. THE USES OF ENCHANTMENT

As shocked insight gradually replaced the unthinking assumptions of earlier adulthood, Joyce attempted not only to perform his guilt in *Finnegans Wake* but also to atone for it. He wanted to offer in dream and at the level of desire the reassurance that the waking world would not permit Lucia in fact. If fascination with a father's brilliance had kept a child in thrall to the composition of a book, then Joyce would make that book into the fullness of a dream come true. It would become a promise that, having loved a spectral lover, she could do it again in another, daylight kingdom. "Hence we've lived in two worlds," says one of the voices as it ambles on companionably at the end of Book IV (*FW* 619.11). Like Alice Liddell with her looking-glass world, Lucia, the "child of tree, like some losthappy leaf" (*FW* 556.19), was to have a spectral kingdom as well as the world of everyday life.

At the end of *Finnegans Wake*, in addressing a child imagined as a walking companion, a voice explains, "I will tell you all sorts of makeup things, strangerous. And show you to every simple storyplace we pass" (*FW* 625.05). The place for this journey is in the mind as it encounters the father's words: "That'll be some kingly work in progress" (*FW* 625.13). Through it the "mains of me draims" (the man of one's dreams) (*FW* 623.27) may come. "But it's by this route he'll come some morrow" (*FW* 625.14). Let imagination show you the way to fulfillment. In the land of dreams, no desire is beyond figuration; the blows dealt by reality can be redressed or, in the language of the *Wake*, "vicereversed." Love denied can be freely given, and even incest is not forbidden because, transcribed into written symbols, circumscribed by its transformation into the symbolic, it does no harm. It is part of a transfiguration that lets energy, love, and affirmation flow between one generation and another.

Read in the light of a father's terrible, pitying love for a lonely child whose hopes for herself refused to die, *Finnegans Wake*, especially at its endless end, is one of Western culture's most unsparing demonstrations of the uses of enchantment. For Joyce looked mercilessly at Lucia's dream of loving partnership and fashioned a book that would answer her dreams and that would, at the same time, point the way beyond fantasy to a waking world of adult emotional reality. "You know where I am bringing you? You remember?" the voice asks (*FW* 622.16–17). Into a story made powerful by my love for you.

It is a story of annunciation. At the end of *Finnegans Wake*, the father, figured as H.C.E., may wake, but it is important to notice that he is not the only figure undergoing transformation. The daughter, imaged as a Sleeping Beauty and later as a Cinderella, is also called to wakefulness. And indeed the rambling "plot" of the ending, insofar as it can be said to have a plot, is about getting a girl out of an enchanted forest and then about her finding herself awake and well. Like Snow White, the Wakean speaker's companion is under a spell that is described as a "prick of the spindle to me that gave me the keys to dream land" (*FW* 615.27–28). The spell in the real Lucia's life was cast not by pricked fingers but by an illness that seemed to call one to live in private, alienated dreams. As Joyce explained to Michael Healy in 1935, "In the form of mental or nervous malady she [Lucia] is subject to . . . the real trouble is not violence or incendiarism or hysterics or simulated suicide. These are hard to deal with but they prove that the person is still alive. The real danger is torpor. The patient falls asleep, so to speak, and prefers to live wholly in his or her inner world, losing more and more contact with the

outer world."[54] The language of the concluding pages of the *Wake* con-
flates these types of dreaming, making them both into a reverie that
threatens but then successfully evades total extinction. Disaster is averted
because the father/guide stands up, grows tall, and becomes a "here-
waker" (*FW* 619.12)—a her/here waker.

The dream world, or "wanterlond" (wonderland, or German *Wan-
derland*) (*FW* 618.22), is first viewed on a late-night hike through the
woods. The travelers get ready. They won't need their "laddy's lampern"
(Aladdin's lantern) (*FW* 621.05) or their "rucksunck[s]" (knapsacks)
(*FW* 621.07) because starlight will guide them. "Send Arctur guiddos" is
a prayer for Arcturus, in the constellation Boötes, to provide enough
light.[55] Amid chatter about delicious trout for "brookfisht" (breakfast),
the two start out. They have plenty of time. "Let's our journee sainto-
michael make it. Since the lausafire has lost and the book of the depth
is. Closed. Come!" (*FW* 621.01–03). Lucifer, author of the dark
underworld, has been defeated; come; let's make our way to the land of
blessings.

The child invites her companion to hold her hand at the same time
that she prides herself on her maturity. "Come, give me your great bears
paw," she says, as she imagines the admiration of "young chippies . . .
crying, me, grownup sister! Are me not truly?" (*FW* 621.20, 16). The two
begin to walk, going forward into an innocence that encompasses them
both. "The woods are fond always. As were we their babes in" (*FW*
619.23–24). They go past "goldylocks" (Goldilocks) (*FW* 615.23), "Peeter
the Picker" (Peter Piper) (*FW* 616.09), "goodiest shoeshoes" (Goody
Two Shoes) (*FW* 622.10), "possumbotts" (Puss and Boots) (*FW* 622.11),
"handsel for gertles" (Hansel and Gretel) (*FW* 618.03), "hampty
damp" (Humpty Dumpty) (*FW* 619.08–09), and "horner corner" (Little
Jack Horner) (*FW* 623.03). When the father/guide notices that the
girl is "about fetted up now with nonsery reams" (nursery rhymes)
(*FW* 619.17), he tells her that's "[e]nough of . . . old mutthergoosip"
(Mother Goose) (*FW* 623.03) and takes her further into the magical mystery tour.

"Olobobo!" (O look, Babbo!) (*FW* 622.23), she cries as she begins
to sight strange, imaginary beasts. They pass "foxy theagres," "the
moskers," and "the wald Unicorn Master" (foxy tigers, muskrats, and
the master of the wood, the unicorn) (*FW* 622.24–25). They see a stag, a

hart; they pass lords and ladies in hunting attire; but they are not harmed. "You came safe through" (*FW* 623.02–03). They consider calling on an old Lord—"what do you say?" (*FW* 623.04)—and then reject the idea because they would have to curtsey and take off their hats. The father/guide turns to the child so that she will not be disappointed. "I'll be your aural eyeness" (Royal Highness) (*FW* 623.18), he offers.

As the two walk, their surroundings grow into a recognizably Irish landscape. They pass townlands in Duleek Upper near Naul, Heathtown, Harbourstown, Fourknocks, Flemingstown, and Bodingtown.[56] They note this but continue their rapt conversation, "not a soul but ourselves" (*FW* 622.21). The nature of their mutual confession is utterly remarkable, for amid the gentle, teasing nonsense—which the father calls his "sillymottocraft" (*FW* 623.19)—they enter another kind of forbidden territory where love, longing, shame, and disappointment can be freely admitted. They walk right in. The child, who will undergo momentous transformations before the end of her journey, begins to court her own father: "A wee one woos" (*FW* 619.15). She takes on the trappings of adult womanhood, moving from a child in need of comfort in the night to a woman using a voice that can be easily, and often has been, mistaken for the voice of her own mother. She is still "leafy speafing" (Leafy speaking). But the woodland motif, the child as "leafy, your goolden"[57] (*FW* 619.29), could also be construed to be "Liffey," the sinuous, watery mother, whose characteristics she will have fully assumed by the end of the transformations her creator is able to imagine for her. She's in a liminal state, a child-woman. Gulliver and Alice had no more remarkable travels to make than this woodland child did. Like Daphne and other personifications of the ancient Greek imagination, and like all the souls of the dead at the Christian resurrection, she will find herself utterly changed.

Leafy's "wooing" is open; it is clandestine; it is childish; it is wise; and finally it will be "sad and weary." Her companion bestows a new name upon her: "Alma Luvia, Pollabella" (*FW* 619.16). It is a variation of her mother's designation as A.L.P., but now it is "All my love to you, beautiful, young girl" (French *poulet* chick, slang for young girl; Italian *bella* beautiful). Sometimes she is simply a girl, as when she reassures her father that she's up to their long walk. "But am good and rested. Taks to you, toddy, tan ye!" (*FW* 619.33). At other times she has to caution him not to walk so fast. "Not such big strides." But now her voice breaks into what culture usually forces us to repress, and she addresses her walking partner as "huddy foddy" (husband father) and identifies herself as his "elicitous bribe" (illicit bride) (*FW* 622.02–03).

He, for his part, is anxious in a way that the girl recognizes. "People think you missed the scaffold," she tells him, but she is equally anxious to reassure him. "All men done something. Be the time they've come to the weight of old fletch" (*FW* 621.32). She also notices his self-consciousness about old age and reassures him on that front as well. "I'll close my eyes. So not to see." I'll pretend you're an innocent boy, a child standing beside a small, white horse. "The child we all love to place our hope in for ever" (*FW* 613.34–35). Leave your trouble behind, she advises. "We will take our walk before . . . they ring the earthly bells" (*FW* 621.33). Darkness will cover us; we're safe now. The girl in turn admits the brokenness of her own life and relates it directly to the dark attraction of her companion. "Sometime then, somewhere there, I wrote me hopes and buried the page when I heard Thy voice" (*FW* 624.03–04). The father comforts her: "my sweetthings, was they poorloves abandoned by wholawidey world?" (*FW* 625.24–25). My sweet thing did no one in the whole wide world return your love?

Then, with a knifelike, stark, swashbuckling compassion, he takes the child across the doorstep of desire. Instead of prevaricating or making facile, parental predictions, he gives her what she wants. The real Joyce, who would not go to Lucia when she wanted him to join her in Ireland, transforms himself in Wakean fancy into the dearly beloved. He becomes a companion who can stroll with her, sit on Irish mountains, view the horizon, and build a "bankaloan cottage" (even in wonderland there's not enough money). We will do this, he says, "when the moon of mourning is set and gone . . . Ourselves, oursouls alone. At the site of salvocean" (*FW* 623.27–28).

This is the nighttime world, a world of obscure but pressing desire that obeys no law and heeds no god. Like Alice in Wonderland, anything can happen. Generation and kinship can vanish, and the heart can grow warm. But it is also a world apart and a world at daybreak when the spell will be broken. And this really is the point. Having transformed himself into a savior-prince who sees the sleeping beauty whom others have abandoned, the father-guide is tired. He asks the child-woman to let him rest for a moment, and then cautions her: "don't speak, remember! Once it happened, so it may again. How glad you'll be I waked you! How well you'll feel! For ever after" (*FW* 625.28–29). This is the projected wish of *Finnegans Wake* insofar as it is imagined as a letter for a troubled child left in her father's wake. You were loved once, *as this book attests*. It can happen again.

While Joyce the father worried about Lucia, asking himself "what then will happen when and if she finally withdraws her regard from the lightning reverie of her clairvoyance and turns it upon that battered cabman's face, the world,"[58] Joyce the writer fashioned a parable about private redemption. "Hence we've lived in two worlds" (*FW* 619.11). One world, this land of books and fantasy, this place from which my voice now speaks, is a place where we have often met. In it you can rush into my arms; I can return your love in any form that imagination can take, but remember, we're in "Platonic garlens" (we're in the realm of the platonic) (*FW* 622.36). This is an affair of the mind and heart, undertaken while you seem "loosed in reflexes" (*FW* 623.01). But there is reason to wake. Love repeats itself; recirculation, if anything, increases its force.

"What'll you take to link to light?" (*FW* 623.14), the father asks at the end of the book, repeating the sequence of words that designated the daughter remembered in the glory of her dancing years: "And they leap so looply, looply, as they link to light" (*FW* 226.26–27). Joyce himself didn't know. He could only bear witness to the complexities of human desire and its persistence in the face of the bitterest realities.

The end of *Finnegans Wake* reconfigures that desire, mixing it with rueful memory and resentment. The voice that speaks of its journey through life, troped as the run of a river to the sea, is not so much resigned as confused and afraid of its own isolation. It alternately speaks of alienation from the Other and its wish to find safety in relationship. It speaks in contradiction to itself. It speaks in the midst of transformation and with a stunning confusion of identities. "But you're changing, acoolsha, you're changing from me, I can feel. Or is it me is? I'm getting mixed" (*FW* 626.35). Is this voice a mother addressing a husband who is chasing skirts? "Yes," it says, "you're changing, sonhusband, and you're turning, I can feel you, for a daughterwife from the hills" (*FW* 627.01). Is this the voice of aging womanhood, anticipating being replaced by the next generation, the girl to whom she will give birth? "And she is coming. Swimming in my hindmoist" (*FW* 627.01). Or is it the voice of that child, the "just a whisk brisk sly spry spink spank sprint of a thing" (*FW* 627.04)? Whoever it is, the voice returns to a child's grudging need to have past injustices righted by a powerful parent. Like Giorgio with his fancy clothes and chauffeured car, "the swankysuits was boosting always, sure him, he was like to me fad. But the swaggerest swell off Shakvulle Strutt" (*FW* 626.09–11). It re-creates a child's delighted memory of a father's make-believe: "And you were the pantymammy's Vulking Corsergoth . . . My lips went livid for from the joy of fear" (*FW* 626.28–30). It remembers a time when she "was the pet of everyone then. A princeable girl" (*FW* 626.27). And it holds on to the affection of a father imagined as lover: "you said you'd give me the keys of me heart. And we'd be married" (*FW* 626.31). We can't find a single, consistent category for this voice, nor should we expect to. One can no more dam up a river into distinctive parts than one can capture the movements of a fugitive daughter's dancing body.

VIII. SAD AND WEARY CHILDREN

The paradox at the end of Joyce's final work appears when the idea that informs *Finnegans Wake*, that of life as constant flux, is joined with the preoccupation of his earliest writing, that of stunted life as a form of paralysis. For in closing his career as a writer, Joyce revisits his own beginnings. Clive Hart and Kimberly Devlin have both noticed that Anna Livia's final rush into the arms of the sea repeats, with variation, the situation of Eveline, one of the lost daughters in Joyce's first book, *Dubliners*.[59] In that early story, a young woman must choose between her lover, Frank, who wants her to go with him to Buenos Aires, and staying at home, where her brutish, violent father expects her to take her dead mother's place as housekeeper and nurse to the younger children. The girl, like some terrified animal, cannot spring for her own freedom. She seems mesmerized by dust and captivated by the demands of the past, which is represented by the father's unthinking assumption that it is appropriate for her to sacrifice herself for him. At the edge of the sea Eveline watches as a boat carries her sailor lover away to distant shores that she will never see. Joyce takes his Wakean daughter to a similar threshold at land's end and confronts her with a similar problem of "claiming kin."

The Wakean hikers reach the sea. The wind rises and whips the child's cheeks. She exclaims, "Sea, Sea! Here, weir, reach, island, bridge. Where you meet I" (*FW* 626.06–07). Somewhere around here she will find her "treeness" slipping away until all that remains of "Leafy" is a watery current bearing a single leaf as a reminder of the past. She is now the Liffey, a river imagined at the point where it runs into the Irish Sea. Somewhere around here her big, striding, bear-pawed father will gather his forces and find himself metamorphosed into the great swell of the ocean, recognizing himself as Mananaan McLir, the ancient Irish god of the sea. Joyce will represent the meeting of the waters as a love affair of a singular kind. It will be a marriage of what is old and fearful. Leafy, now Liffey, is also imagined as "Saltarella come to her own" (*FW* 627.05–06). She is a salty version of Cinderella, the poor sister obscured by her wealthy, leisured siblings (the "swankysuits"). It is dawn; light is coming; a spell is lifting; and part of the new clarity riding on the wind is the perception that the father is neither horrible nor exalted but an ordinary, man-sized man. "I thought you were all glittering with the noblest carriage. You're only a bumpkin. I thought you the great in all things, in guilt and in glory" (*FW* 627.22–23).

With this insight comes a chilling reunion: "And it's old and old it's sad and old it's sad and weary I go back to you, my cold father, my cold mad father, my cold mad feary father, til the near sight of him . . . makes me . . . seasilt saltsick and I rush my only, into your arms" (*FW* 628.01–04). Where Eveline gave up love for a cheerless existence with a father who expropriated her youth and high spirits, Liffey runs with full force into the arms of her oceanic father. She is "seasilt saltsick"; he is mad, and yet he is her savior and the only one who recognizes her. Remember me, she cries before she begins her transfigured recirculation as the water that replenishes the earth. And his final gesture to her is to throw her the keys, which we know from previous pages are "the keys of me heart" (*FW* 626.30–31).

If at the end of *Finnegans Wake* Joyce gives us another story about a girl who cannot leave her father, he writes it in language that echoes a decisive moment of his own youth. In *A Portrait of the Artist as a Young Man*, the young artist, Stephen Dedalus, is invited by the Jesuits to join

their order. After he leaves the priest's office, he wanders to the ramshackle home of his parents, where he finds his younger brothers and sisters drinking tea out of glass jars and broken jampots. When he enters
the kitchen, he feels remorse. "All that had been denied them had been
freely given to him, the eldest: but the quiet glow of evening showed him
in their faces no sign of rancor" (*P* 163). The children begin to sing to
pass the cheerless time, and he listens to them before joining in. "He was
listening with pain of spirit to the overtone of weariness behind their
frail fresh innocent voices. Even before they set out on life's journey they
seemed weary already of the way" (*P* 163).

For Joyce the voices of children had always been sad and weary. Long
before Anna Livia began her own weary journey to the sea, their voices
had contained pain and thus made more of a claim on his heart than the
somber, orderly rituals of the religious life. "He smiled to think that it
was this disorder, the misrule and confusion of his father's house and the
stagnation of vegetable life, which was to win the day in his soul" (*P* 162).
Little could he have known the extent of the disorder to which he had
pledged himself. In 1916 weary childhood was a romantic construction
that he invented to separate himself from his brothers and sisters in order to claim the birthright of the eldest son without guilt. He imagined
"no rancor" in the hearts of those left behind.

But even in these early years the unmet desires of the others who had
been neglected haunted him, for they challenged the privilege that
society accords to genius. He represented them in the fictional Dilly
Dedalus's pitiful desire to learn French, and, significantly he represented
the pull of guilt and compassion in the language of the sea. "She will
drown me with her, eyes and hair. Lank coils of seaweed hair around
me, my heart, my soul. Salt green death" (*U* 10.875–77).

Many years later Joyce cast the culminating image of his writing career in terms of a similar salt green death, the embrace of fresh and salt
water signaling a mutual submersion, the drowning embrace that had
once been contemplated but evaded. And he pictured the young woman
who extended that embrace as seeking knowledge and understanding of
the world that excluded her with another primer. Leafy, before her
transfiguration into river goddess, admits that she is trying to understand
her father's letter, the hardest "crux" ever, by "scratching it and patching
at with a prompt from a primer. And what scrips of nutsnolleges I

pecked up me meself" (*FW* 623.31–33). When we contemplate these two images of primers in relation to our knowledge that on his Sunday visits to Lucia in her Ivry clinic, Joyce actually took a primer with him to teach her Latin, we have some idea of what his world had come to.[60] He finally understood the daughter's claim to cultural agency; he finally saw the ruin that can lie in the wake of genius.

Lucia Anna Joyce's life lay between one primer and the other. She was a flesh-and-blood child who made the outrageous claim that she, a girl, wanted to be an artist. It took every breath of Lucia's life to make the point. It took every breath of her father's life to get the story right. "Ho capito il latino" (I have understood your Latin), he was finally able to write in 1935. In 1941 he would leave her the keys to his battered heart. By that time they had both survived endless disruptions, public commotion, the loss of fortune, and innumerable unwelcome truths. We might even say that they had survived the birth of tragedy.

But in their mutual story we come, at last, to understand that beauty in some way survives the injury it sustains. It endures in human memory and in the impulse to record what seems unprecedented and sacred. By his unfaltering allegiance Joyce shows us that "the love of the beauty of the world . . . involves . . . the love of all the truly precious things that bad fortune can destroy."[61] Lucia, child of light, disdainful of convention, unsparing in judgment of the world, angry, enamored of the power of art, herself the "hardest crux ever," shows us what harsh integrity evoked that loyalty.

EPILOGUE
A DAUGHTER'S LEGACY

I. THE GENERATIONS OF LUCIA JOYCE

Lucia Joyce died on 12 December 1982 in Northampton, England. There is no evidence that she ever read *Finnegans Wake* after her father's death or thought of it as having a personal message encoded within it. She remembered being watched. When Bonnie Kime Scott came to visit her, Lucia told her that her youth had been spent with her father's note cards always close at hand.[1] It was her impression that whatever she said or did went into a book. But when Richard Ellmann asked her about the *Wake* in the 1960s, she replied, "I don't know I mean I do not understand much about Anna Livia Plurabelle."[2]

She died with fond and loving memories of every member of her family. In her will, she gave various small amounts to friends she had made at Northampton. She left another small amount to her aunt Florence. But like her father she named two family members as her principal heirs, and she indicated a line of succession. Her aunt Nelly was one beneficiary. Her brother Giorgio was the other. Should he predecease her, as he did, his share of both capital and income was to go first to his widow, Asta Jahnke-Osterwalder, and then to Lucia's nephew, Stephen Joyce.[3] Thus it was that part of Lucia's estate was left in the hands of the very person who later decided that her story should remain buried in the dark cellars of "family privacy." Unconcerned about what she could not imagine, she died with her status as the daughter of James Joyce as the final thought about her own identity. But if she died a Joyce, she rested alone. Lucia is buried in Northampton, so she does not lie next to her parents and brother at the Flutern Cemetery on the outskirts of Zurich.

But that was not the end. The book that you are reading now was born in the midst of many others. It is only the most curious and tenacious of numerous creative tributes to Lucia's life. For many years, artists have intuitively sensed that her experiences with Joyce must have been extraordinary. Like the sleeping giant in *Finnegans Wake*, who "Haveth Childers Everywhere," she has turned out to have imaginary children all over the globe.[4]

One of the first and most interesting of her "offspring" was another island dweller whose creative life took her far from home. In the early 1950s, a young American college graduate returned to her birthplace on the island of Hawaii. She was newly married and was bringing her husband home to meet her family. As they traveled in a small boat in those tropical waters, he read to her from *Finnegans Wake*. He was Joseph Campbell, the mythologist who would write one of the first books about Joyce's monumental and seemingly impenetrable masterpiece. She was Jean Erdman, a fledgling dancer and soon-to-be member of Martha Graham's dance troupe in New York City.

Once again history had paired a writer, a dancer, and *Finnegans Wake*. Out of this journey would grow a performance piece called *The Coach with the Six Insides*, which took years to germinate. Like Lucia, Jean Erdman had at first experienced the book as a rival. "Well," she recalled, "my husband . . . had been working on *Finnegans Wake* when we first were married. I swore I would never read the book! Because I was on one arm and *Finnegans Wake* was on the other arm, and he spent just as much time with *Finnegans Wake* as he did with me. It took me some years to get over that but I did. Time mellows everything, right?"[5]

By the 1960s, Erdman acknowledged that she too was haunted by the beauty and mystery of Joyce's text. Where her husband had turned his fascination into a reader's guide,[6] she decided to combine dance, music, theater, and mime to tell her own version of the story of the great sleeping giant Finn MacCool who rises from his grave under the Hill of Howth in Ireland. But in a distinctive swerve, Erdman asserted that the focus of Joyce's work was not Finn MacCool but Anna Livia Plurabelle.

"I began to work on the idea in 1953," she told Walter Sorell. At that time, it was a dance with Anna Livia as the central figure. "She fascinated me because, as Joyce conceived her, she meant many things on many levels, being symbolic of the energy, of the dynamism of life. She is the river of time, the need for everything and its opposite, the archetype of all women. . . . From the very beginning the whole thing 'came upon me' like something unavoidable. I had heard my husband recite from it, and I was caught up in the rhythm of its musical language."[7]

In one scene after another of Erdman's creation, Anna Livia the dancer transforms herself into a young woman, an old woman, a mature woman. She becomes a hen discovering a letter in a dump heap. She becomes the mother of Humpty Dumpty, a bride, a gad-about-town, a girl with a mirror, a cloud girl whose tears nourish the earth in a raindrop dance. She is the subject of gossip. "She's the center," Erdman reminds us. "H.C.E. is only the scenery."[8] In the case of her own work, she meant this literally. Her production uses the ribs of a sleeping giant as a backdrop. Erdman saw Anna Livia as the goddess who was both the inspiration of the artist and the subject of his quest. Giants may speak, Erdman warned, but "if you think the words alone are doing the trick, don't forget that the movement leads to it."[9]

She had a distinctive artistic vision for this imaginary coach ride through time. She knew what she was doing, and she knew it, at least in part, from a lifetime spent in collaboration with Joseph Campbell, the great theorist of the hero's journey. They worked within arm's reach of each other. They used their respective arts to approach answers to similarly profound questions. What are the great mythic structures that underlie the transformations of everyday life? How do we gain access to these archetypal experiences? What lies beyond the expressive capacity of language? In both posing and answering these questions, James Joyce was never far from either of their imaginations. The groundbreaking innovations of *Finnegans Wake* acted as a kind of guide. For them it was the great modernist text of transformation, which reached beyond its own instabilities to the primal experiences of being alive.

And for Erdman, fascination was grounded in the book's longing for and expression of experiences that defy language's signifying power. For her, creating *The Coach with the Six Insides* was a kind of return home. Joyce's verbal dance, so to speak, called forth her own dance. It was a

question of kinship, of like responding to like. The dance's "power as poetic image," she said, "lies in its capacity to inform whatever aspect of
humanity it presents with the secret rhythm of some other, hidden, forgotten, yet essential portion."[10]

She was extraordinarily articulate about what happens when dancers
enter the symbolic space of the stage and use their bodies in a "highly
inflected visual language of aesthetic devices."[11] "The dance," she explained, "becomes a direct image of something that was formerly invisible, though denoted or suggested by words. It is built upon the pulse and
dynamics of a generating force. That seed quality within all tales of renewal is the only protagonist here. The unfolding path of the rhythm
bringing the generating force to maturity is the only plot. The beholder
experiences an archetypal form and is assured by that of the knowledge
that the earth shall bear again and again—through the sequence of these
rhythmical-spatial-movement events."[12] In her eyes the dance amplified
spiritual life through its evocation of a Dionysian ecstatic agony. It acted
as a corrective to what she called "the cult of the self-defensive Ego." It
could lead people back to the "unnamed immensity" within them. It
could serve as a "mystery of transfiguration."[13]

Erdman had no idea that Lucia Joyce had been a dancer. She did not
know that Joyce's synesthesia had its roots long ago in the body of a
dancing child. In fact, when I told her about Lucia, she seemed quietly
stunned, bemused by a fact whose importance she had not yet absorbed.
What did this coincidence mean? She was not only the interpreter of an
amazing book, but in some mystic way was the current manifestation of
its inspiration. She and Campbell had been living out a creative partnership whose affinities with Joyce and Lucia were undeniable. She danced.
He watched her go into unnamed emotional "rooms" and then found
ways to express those feeling states in words.

There were also some undeniable differences between Lucia and
Joseph Campbell's irrepressible young wife. Erdman was well educated,
stunningly articulate, and she took the right to express her creativity for
granted. In *The Coach with the Six Insides* this assumption is expressed
simply but eloquently by Anna Livia treading boldly over the silent and
prone body of Finn MacCool. The masculine giant no longer overshad-
ows anyone. When Erdman chose her life's partner, she chose a man who
understood the nature of her calling. "My wife is a dancer," Campbell

had no hesitation in saying. "I know lots of . . . women who go into the arts, a world in which one participates not in competition with somebody else but in her own development. . . . An artist is not in the field to achieve, to realize, but to become fulfilled. It's a life-fulfilling, totally different structure."[14] The American 1960s, as Jean Erdman encountered them, openly offered young women what Lucia had been granted only when it was too late.

In the register of these differences lies the larger importance of Lucia Joyce's life. Her very failures were articulate. We could say that the commotion she brought into being because of them expressed what needed to be changed before women could fully enter into their inheritance as modernist daughters. Lucia didn't need books like *Ulysses* to become modern. She needed a new way to see the very contours of her existence. A generation later, on another continent, Jean Erdman could reap the benefits of Lucia's struggle. She could mime rage or dance out a woman's broken, incomplete self-knowledge or her tempestuous urges. Campbell could look at her and name her impersonation "Medusa." He did not hesitate to follow her into the dark, inchoate, but regenerative "rooms" of the psyche.

And, when we look back, neither did James Joyce. He went where Lucia led. The "rooms" of Lucia's inner life were apparently as wild and electrifying as they come. He recognized in his daughter's anguish the same qualities that Jean Erdman had in mind when she spoke of the dance's capacity to express the "unnamed immensity" of the soul. In that Joyce has left us a message in the conduct of his life as well as in the language of his books, it has to do with this private and intense journey to join his daughter. He did not consider "madness" to be alluring or romantic. He saw it as one of the possible voices of spiritual life, and he saw it as containing mysteries that far exceed the facile categories of diagnosticians. Science couldn't grasp Lucia. Art at least could gesture in her direction. When it did, it imagined her in ways that Jean Erdman seems intuitively to have understood when she called Anna Livia Plurabelle a river of life. Like the river Liffey in Ireland, it begins in a modest source, growing in power until its own force compels it to flow into the sea. "And it's old and old it's sad and old it's sad and weary I go back to you, my cold father" (*FW* 627:38–628:01), says the flowing river. This image of Anna Livia at the end of *Finnegans Wake* shows us what rush of untamed feeling can be born when contrary energies are joined as one. The experience is irresistible; it is beautiful and it is terrifying all at once. But its maddest wisdom may be what men and women everywhere can know: the arms of the sea are waiting. Love for a child is infinite.

Lucia Joyce, Paris, 1936. Photographer unknown. (Courtesy of Special Collections, University College London)

ACKNOWLEDGMENTS

NOTES

BIBLIOGRAPHY

INDEX

ACKNOWLEDGMENTS

It has taken many years to assemble the evidence of Lucia Joyce's life. Innumerable people have helped with advice, encouragement, suggestions for discovering new information, and simple, direct support for completing the project. I would like to thank the following people in particular. For their groundbreaking work in assembling the bones of the story and for their distinctive views of its meaning, the late Richard Ellmann and Brenda Maddox. For reading a very early version of the manuscript, for suggesting the importance of writing Lucia's biography, and for many years of friendship, Morris Beja. For encouraging me to think of this book as a complete and distinct project, Christine Froula. For his long-term interest and belief in this project, Zack Bowen; for equally long-term interest and support, Richard Pearce. For early research on Lucia's life and accomplishments and for the archives that document them, David Hayman, Ira Nadel, Bonnie Kime Scott, and Suzette Henke. For more recent scholarship, Marilyn Reizbaum, Catherine Driscoll, Finn Fordham, and Marian Eide. For provocative work on Issy in *Finnegans Wake*, Robert Polhemus, Cheryl Herr, Shari Benstock, and Kim Devlin. For help with Stuart Gilbert's memoirs, for his long-term support of this project, and for his friendship, Thomas Staley. For calling my attention to French essays about Lucia in Éditions de l'Herne, Jacques Aubert; for calling my attention to the memoir of Stella Steyn, Mia Lerman-Hayes;

for providing material from Carola Giedion-Welcker and for help, support, and friendship through many years, Fritz Senn, Ruth Frehner, Frances Ilmberger, Ursula Zeller, and Christine O'Neill of the Zurich James Joyce Foundation; for providing a Lucia Joyce photograph and other help and support, Ken Monaghan, Helen Monaghan, and Declan Meade of the James Joyce Centre, Dublin. For his work in compiling an invaluable James Joyce chronology, Rick Watson. For help with song lyrics and information about Albert Hubbell, Ruth Bauerle. For searching so diligently for Jeanne Wertenberg's photographs of Lucia, I wish to thank Marilyn Reizbaum; for finding extant copies of Jeanne Wertenberg's photographs of Lucia and for other help and personal support, Carol Kealiher of the *James Joyce Quarterly*. For insight into the fate of various Joyce letters and manuscripts, William Brockman. For California "Joyce friends" who have hovered beneficently for many years, Austin Briggs and Bunny Searle (honorary Californians), John Bishop, Vince Cheng (defected Californian), Colleen Jaurretche, Judith Harrington, Margot Norris, Karen Lawrence, Kim Devlin, Bonnie Scott (newly arrived), and members of the Berkeley *Finnegans Wake* Reading Group. For "Joyce friends" farther away but no less appreciated, Ellen Carol Jones, Brandy Kershner, Jolanta Wawrzycha, Susan Sutcliffe Brown, Mary Power, Christine van Boheemen-Saaf, Hedwig Schwall, Vicki Mahaffey, Vince Sherry, Jean Paul Rabate. For particular support in Ireland, David Norris, Anne Fogarty, Terry Dolan, and the late Gus Martin. For sharing her memories and for singing "You're the Cream in My Coffee" to me over the telephone, Lucia's cousin Bozena Berta Delimata. Jean Erdman not only re-created "The Coach with the Six Insides" at the 1985 James Joyce Conference in Philadelphia, she also granted me access to her papers and consented to generous interviews. Peter Jung in Zurich looked in his grandfather's attic for any saved notes about Lucia from the 1930s. Therapists at the Institute for Psychoanalytic Psychotherapies in Bryn Mawr, Pennsylvania, welcomed a stranger into their midst for Saturday seminars. At Stanford I would like to thank Eavan Boland for particular encouragement and the loan of her computer when I needed one, the Stanford Creative Writing Program for giving me a place to work, Terry Castle for support and friendship, and Andrea Lunsford, Arnold and Marvina Rampersad, Al and Barbara Gelpi, Alex Woloch, Brett Bourbon, and Linda Jo Bartholomew. For their support in the daily, kindly, and efficient running of the Stanford English Department, Dagmar

Logie and Alyce Boster. To everyone else in the Stanford English Department, thanks for welcoming me into the community. In Philadelphia, where this project began, I would like to express gratitude to my friend Ted Schorske for years of curiosity and interest as well as his assistance in translating from the French, garnering information about *Lucia di Lammermoor* and Santa Lucia, and insight into the meaning of a writing father's closed door. To Sandy S. H. Sparrow, Gail Caruso, Suzanne Young, Shannon Coulter, and Lisa Spilde, thanks for being there from the opening words of the first chapter.

In addition to the support of friends, this project has been sustained by grants, fellowships, and travel money from an extraordinary array of institutions. My greatest and oldest debt is to the Pew Fellowships in the Arts, whose gift to me really did effect a shift in artistic fortune, and in particular to Melissa Franklin, Stephen Urice, and the late Ella King Torrey. West Chester University, where I worked when I began this research, supported me for many summers and many trips with grants from the Office of the Dean of Arts and Sciences, faculty development awards, and summer research grants. While I was writing, I was fortunate to be affiliated with the Alice Paul Center for the Study of Women at the University of Pennsylvania and with the Centre for Cross-Cultural Research on Women at Oxford University, England. The Harry Ransom Humanities Research Center at the University of Texas at Austin offered me a research fellowship for biography; Northwestern University offered me the Segal Professorship in Irish Literature, a chair established in memory of Richard Ellmann.

The unusually fraught nature of the project of writing about Lucia Joyce's life required me to have legal advice about intellectual property rights, and I had the best. I wish especially to thank Jeff Seilbach at the Stanford Office of Risk Management; Edward Black at Ropes and Gray; Thomas W. Fenner, Senior University Counsel in the Office of the General Counsel at Stanford University; Lawrence Lessig and the Creative Commons in the Stanford Law School; and Leon Friedman at Farrar, Straus and Giroux. Robert Spoo, whose friendship over many years and whose expertise as both a Joyce scholar and a specialist in intellectual property rights law, has earned my unending loyalty and gratitude.

I would like to thank librarians, archivists, and academics at these institutions for their help: the Rondelle Collection at the Bibliothèque de l'Arsenal, Paris; the Bibliothèque de l'Opéra, Paris; the Eidgenössische

Technische Hochschule Bibliothek, Zurich; the Zentralbibliothek, Zurich; the Bodleian Library, University of Oxford, England; the Bodleian Law Library, University of Oxford, England; the British Library, London; Special Collections, University College Library, London; the National Library of Ireland, Dublin; Special Collections, Trinity College Library, Dublin; Special Collections, University College Library, Belfield, Dublin, Ireland; the Library of the Performing Arts, Lincoln Center, New York; the Berg Collection, the New York Public Library; the Smithsonian American Art Museum / National Portrait Gallery Library, the Smithsonian Institution, Washington, D.C.; The National Library of the History of Medicine, Bethesda, Maryland; the Annenberg Rare Book and Manuscript Library and the Van Pelt Library, the University of Pennsylvania, Philadelphia; the Poetry and Rare Book Collection, the State University of New York at Buffalo Library, Buffalo, New York; the Beinecke Rare Book and Manuscript Library, Yale University, New Haven, Connecticut; Department of Rare Books and Special Collections, Firestone Library, Princeton University, Princeton, New Jersey; the Rare and Manuscripts Collections, Carl A. Kroch Library, Cornell University; Special Collections, Morris Library, Southern Illinois University, Carbondale, Illinois; the Charles Deering McCormick Library of Special Collections, Northwestern University, Evanston, Illinois; Special Collections, the McFarlin Library, University of Tulsa, Tulsa, Oklahoma; the Harry Ransom Humanities Research Center at the University of Texas at Austin, Texas; the Cecil H. Green Library and the Lane Medical Library at Stanford University, Stanford, California.

My greatest thanks are reserved for three people: Tina Bennett, my agent at Janklow and Nesbit, whose vision of this project's potential actively shaped the story and whose loyalty, level-headedness, and good judgment never flagged even in trying circumstances, even in crisis; Elisabeth Sifton, my editor at Farrar, Straus and Giroux, who showed me the grit, talent, intelligence, and finesse that characterize great editing and whose fierceness was more than matched by fearlessness; and Rob Polhemus, who believed in me, supported me, and loved me right from the beginning. All the people who have accompanied me in bringing Lucia's life to light have had more than their share of moral courage, and my thanks, for even the smallest stretch of fellow traveling, is heartfelt.

NOTES

The following abbreviations and short titles are used:

CW
The Critical Writings of James Joyce, ed. Ellsworth Mason and Richard Ellmann (New York: Viking Press and London: Faber and Faber, 1959).

Ellmann
Richard Ellmann, *James Joyce: The New and Revised Edition* (New York: Oxford University Press, 1982).

FW
James Joyce, *Finnegans Wake* (New York: The Viking Press, 1966).

GJ
James Joyce, *Giacomo Joyce*, ed. Richard Ellmann (New York: The Viking Press, 1968).

JJQ
James Joyce Quarterly.

Knowlson
James Knowlson, *Damned to Fame: The Life of Samuel Beckett* (New York: Simon and Schuster, 1996).

Letters I, II, III
The Letters of James Joyce, vol. I, ed. Stuart Gilbert, 1957, new ed. 1966; vols. II and III, ed. Richard Ellmann, 1966 (New York: The Viking Press and London: Faber and Faber).

Lidderdale
Jane Lidderdale and Mary Nicholson, *Dear Miss Weaver: Harriet Shaw Weaver, 1876–1961* (London: Faber and Faber, 1970).

Maddox
Brenda Maddox, *Nora: The Real Life of Molly Bloom* (Boston: Houghton Mifflin, 1988).

P
James Joyce, *A Portrait of the Artist as a Young Man* (New York: The Viking Press, 1964).

SL
Selected Letters of James Joyce, ed. Richard Ellmann (New York: The Viking Press and London: Faber and Faber, 1975).

U
James Joyce, *Ulysses: The Corrected Text*, ed. Hans Walter Gabler with Wolfhard Steppe and Claus Melchior (New York: Random House, 1986).

Frequent correspondents are cited in the notes by initials:

BM	Brenda Maddox
CC	Constantine Curran
CG-W	Carola Giedion-Welcker
EP	Ezra Pound
GJ	Giorgio Joyce
HKJ	Helen Kastor Joyce (Helen Fleischman)
HSW	Harriet Shaw Weaver
JJ	James Joyce
JL	Jane Lidderdale
LJ	Lucia Joyce
MH	Michael Healy
MJ	Maria Jolas
MN	Myron Nutting
NBJ	Nora Barnacle Joyce
PL	Paul Léon
RE	Richard Ellmann
SB	Samuel Beckett
SG	Stuart Gilbert
SJ	Stanislaus Joyce

University libraries and special collections are noted by the name of the university, with these exceptions:

Beinecke	Beinecke Rare Book and Manuscript Library, Yale University
Berg	Henry W. and Albert A. Berg Collection at the New York Public Library
BL	British Library, London
HRC	Harry Ransom Humanities Research Center, University of Texas at Austin
HSW Papers	Harriet Shaw Weaver Papers, British Library, London
NLI	National Library of Ireland, Dublin
NYLPA	New York Library of the Performing Arts
Opéra	Bibliothèque de l'Opéra, Paris
PL Papers	Paul Léon Papers, National Library of Ireland, Dublin
RE Papers	Richard Ellmann Papers, McFarlin Library, University of Tulsa
Rondelle	Rondelle Collection of the Performing Arts, Bibliothèque de l'Arsenal, Paris
SB Papers	Sylvia Beach Papers, Department of Rare Books and Special Collections, Princeton University
SG Papers	Stuart Gilbert Papers, Harry Ransom Humanities Research Center, University of Texas at Austin
SIU	Special Collections Department, Morris Library, Southern Illinois University at Carbondale
TCD	Trinity College, Dublin
UCD	University College, Dublin
UCL	University College London

The major repositories of manuscripts consulted for this book are

For the performing arts: Bibliothèque de l'Arsenal, Paris; Bibliothèque de l'Opéra, Paris; Zentralbibliothek, Zurich; Hauptbibliothek, Zurich; Kunstgewerbe Museum, Zurich; The Henry W. and Albert A. Berg Collection at the New York Public Library; The New York Library of the Performing Arts; The San Francisco Library of the Performing Arts; The Archives of American Art at the Smithsonian Institution, Washington, D.C.

For the history of medicine: E.T.H. Bibliothek (Eidgenössische Technische Hochschule), Zurich; National Library of Medicine, Bethesda, Maryland; Lane Medical Library, Stanford University

For the family and friends of the Joyces: The National Library of Ireland, Dublin; Trinity College, Dublin, Rare Books and Manuscripts Collection; University College, Dublin, Rare Books and Manuscripts Collection; The British Library, Rare Books and Manuscripts Collection, London; University of London, Rare Books and Manuscripts Collection; Cornell University, Olin Library, Department of Rare Books, Ithaca, New York; The Harry Ransom Humanities Research Center, the University of Texas at Austin; The New York Public Library; Northwestern University Library, Charles Deering McCormick Library of Special Collections; Princeton University Library, Department of Rare Books and Special Collections; Southern Illinois University at Carbondale, Morris Library, Special Collections Department; University of Buffalo, Lockwood Memorial Library, Poetry and Rare Books Collection; University of Tulsa, McFarlin Library, Department of Special Collections; Yale University, Beinecke Rare Book and Manuscript Library

INTRODUCTION: What Happened to Lucia Joyce?

1. HKJ and MJ to Padraic and Mary Colum, 2 November 1932, in Mary Colum and Padraic Colum, *Our Friend James Joyce* (Garden City, N.Y.: Doubleday, 1958), 144.
2. Nino Frank, "The Shadow That Had Lost Its Man," *Portraits of the Artist in Exile: Recollections of James Joyce by Europeans*, ed. Willard Potts (Seattle: University of Washington Press, 1979), 90.
3. HSW to JJ, 17 February 1935, RE Papers.
4. Cary F. Baynes, "Notes on Lucia Joyce," RE Papers.
5. Helen Nutting, Paris diary, RE Papers.
6. Stuart Gilbert, Paris diary, 20 July 1932, SG Papers.
7. HSW to JJ, 18 March 1935, RE Papers.
8. Patrick Collins, quoted in Maddox, 310.
9. JJ to GJ, 13 August 1935, *Letters III*, 372.
10. Maria Jolas, interview by Richard Ellmann, 22 July 1953, RE Papers.
11. Nora and Giorgio Joyce, quoted in PL to HSW, 8 May 1936, in RE Papers.
12. Dr. Thérèse Bertrand-Fontaine, quoted in Colum and Colum, *Our Friend James Joyce*, 142.
13. Hans Wolfgang Maier, quoted in Ellmann, 677.
14. Henri Codet, quoted in Colum and Colum, *Our Friend James Joyce*, 139.
15. Admissions officer at Les Rives de Prangins, quoted in Ellmann, 665.

16. JJ to GJ, 9 September 1934, RE Papers.

17. Theodor Brunner, quoted in Baynes, "Notes on Lucia Joyce."

18. Hans Wolfgang Maier, quoted in Ellmann, 676.

19. Dr. Agadjanian, quoted in PL to HSW, 22 May 1936, RE Papers.

20. See Ellmann, 649.

21. David Hayman, "Shadow of His Mind: The Papers of Lucia Joyce," in *Joyce at Texas*, ed. Dave Oliphant and Thomas Zigal (Austin: Harry Ransom Humanities Research Center, 1983).

22. See Maddox.

23. Dante Alighieri, *The New Life*, trans. Dante Gabriel Rossetti (New York: National Alumni, 1907), 85.

24. James Joyce and Paul Léon, "Anamnese von Fräulein Lucia Joyce," RE Papers.

25. JJ to CG-W, 15 October 1937, RE Papers.

26. Eugen Bleuler, *Dementia Praecox or the Group of Schizophrenias*, trans. J. Zinkin (New York: International Universities Press, 1950), 277.

27. C. G. Jung, "Recent Thoughts on Schizophrenia," in *The Psychogenesis of Mental Disease*, trans. R. F. C. Hull (Princeton: Bollingen Series XX, 1960), 250.

28. JJ to GJ, 9 September 1934, RE Papers.

29. Ibid.

30. Charles de Saint-Cyr, *La Semaine à Paris*, 1928, Rondelle.

31. "On the Left Bank," *Paris Times*, 14 March 1928, Buffalo.

32. Kay Boyle to JL, 15 January 1983, RE Papers.

33. Kay Boyle to RE, 6 January 1983, RE Papers.

34. Adaline Glasheen, *Third Census of "Finnegans Wake"* (Berkeley: University of California Press, 1977), 149.

35. PL to HSW, 19 July 1935, PL Papers.

36. JJ to HSW, 1 May 1935, *Letters I*, 366.

37. PL to HSW, 19 July 1935, PL Papers.

38. Dominique Maroger, "Dernière rencontre avec Lucia," in *James Joyce*, ed. Jacques Aubert and Fritz Senn (Paris: Editions de l'Herne, 1985), 82.

39. Baynes, "Notes on Lucia Joyce."

40. Jacques Mercanton, "The Hours of James Joyce," in Potts, ed., *Portraits of the Artist in Exile*, 114.

41. MJ to RE, "Notes re RE biography of JJ," 26 September 1959, RE Papers.

42. For the relationship between Maria Jolas and Richard Ellmann that follows, I have studied the archives at Yale and the University of Tulsa. But I wish to acknowledge an excellent paper on this subject by William Brockman, first delivered at the James Joyce Symposium in Zurich in 1996. He kindly sent me a copy of it: "'Give us back them papers': Possession, Control and Availability of Joyce's Manuscripts and Letters."

43. MJ to RE, 10 September 1953, RE Papers.

44. MJ to RE, 11 December 1954, RE Papers.

45. MJ to RE, 20 January 1954, RE Papers.

46. We can infer that the Weaver letters in the "famous trunk" are the ones summarized in notes now in the Ellmann Papers in Tulsa in the Harriet Weaver file. When Maria Jolas was thinking of giving the trunk back to Giorgio, Ellmann told her he didn't need it any longer, as he had already taken copious notes. The docu-

ments in Tulsa are neither the originals nor Harriet Weaver's expurgated typescripts; they are dated summaries, which would accord with Ellmann's admission
that he had what he needed in note form.

47. MJ to RE, 11 February 1955, RE Papers.
48. RE to MJ, 16 February 1955, RE Papers.
49. Maria Jolas, "Notes on final days at Saint-Gérand-le-Puy," Box 41, File 917, Maria Jolas Papers, Beinecke.
50. RE to MJ, 22 June 1981, Maria Jolas Papers, Beinecke.
51. MJ to RE, 4 October 1953, RE Papers.
52. MJ to RE, 11 February 1955, RE Papers.
53. MJ to RE, 4 October 1957, RE Papers.
54. MJ to RE, 20 January 1959, RE Papers.
55. Ibid.
56. MJ to RE, 16 May 1964, RE Papers.
57. MJ to RE, n.d., RE Papers.
58. MJ to RE, 22 October 1961, RE Papers.
59. Maria Jolas, interviews by Richard Ellmann, June and July 1954, RE Papers.
60. MJ to RE, 22 October 1961, RE Papers.
61. RE to MJ, 14 October 1961, RE Papers.
62. Lidderdale, 448n; and Lucia Joyce Papers, HRC.
63. MJ to RE, "Notes re RE biography of JJ," 26 September 1959, RE Papers.
64. For an excellent discussion of Ellmann's dependence on Stanislaus Joyce, see Joseph Kelly, "Ellmann's Joyce," in *Our Joyce: From Outcast to Icon* (Austin: University of Texas Press, 1998), 141–79.
65. Ellsworth Mason, "Ellmann's Road to Xanadu," in *Essays for Richard Ellmann: Omnium Gatherum*, ed. Susan Dick et al. (Montreal: McGill–Queen's University Press, 1989), 10.
66. Marvin Magalaner and Richard M. Kain, *Joyce: The Man, the Work, the Reputation* (New York: New York University Press, 1956), 90.
67. Ellmann, 663.
68. Gilbert agreed to this project for the benefit of Lucia and Giorgio. See SG to Patricia Hutchins, 29 November 1952: "The book of letters on which I'm working is, as I think you know, being published for the financial benefit of Lucia and Giorgio and is almost a 'labour of love' as far as I'm concerned." SG Papers.
69. Stuart Gilbert, "Introduction," *Letters I*, 34.
70. HSW to SG, 4 January 1954, SG Papers.
71. Stuart Gilbert, "A Note on the Editing," *Letters I*, 40.
72. Patricia Hutchins to SG, 8 August 1949, SG Papers.
73. HSW to SG, 1 September 1954, SG Papers.
74. HSW to SG, 17 November 1949, SG Papers.
75. Gilbert, "Introduction," *Letters I*, 32.
76. Gilbert, "A Note on the Editing," *Letters I*, 40.
77. Lidderdale, 404.
78. Ibid., 420.
79. HSW to SG, 18 November 1954, SG Papers.
80. Jane Lidderdale, interviews by Brenda Maddox, 22 June 1987 and 1 January 1988, in Maddox, 438.

81. Richard Ellmann, "Preface," *Letters II*, xxix.

82. Ibid., xxviii.

83. Harriet Weaver, quoted in Maddox, 438.

84. Harriet Weaver file, RE Papers.

85. Mary Reynolds, "Joyce and Miss Weaver," *JJQ* 19:4 (1982): 377.

86. Lidderdale, 454.

87. Reynolds, "Joyce and Miss Weaver," 394.

88. Ibid., 375.

89. Lucie Noël, *James Joyce and Paul L. Léon: The Story of a Friendship* (New York: The Gotham Book Mart, 1948), 36–37.

90. Ibid., 39–40.

91. Lidderdale, 411.

92. Ibid., 417.

93. Noël, *Joyce and Léon*, 36–37.

94. Patricia Donlon, *The James Joyce–Paul Léon Papers in the National Library of Ireland: A Catalogue*, comp. Catherine Fahy (Dublin: National Library of Ireland, 1992), v.

95. HSW to RE, 20 February 1958, RE Papers.

96. The dates of the missing letters are 2 October 1934; 4 April 1935; 19 July 1935; 8 May 1936; 22 May 1936; 22 August 1936; 3 November 1936; 4 August 1937; 7 October 1937; 18 December 1937; 16 December 1938; 20 December 1939. The dates of the letters in the Léon Papers are 12 July 1936; 18 November 1936; 18 August 1938; 14 February 1939.

97. Lidderdale, 343.

98. MJ to RE, 11 December 1954, RE Papers.

99. Maddox, 398.

100. RE to MJ, 10 December 1984, Maria Jolas Papers, Beinecke: "You will be interested to know that by a settlement reached last week, Stephen gets the famous trunk—though his step-brother Hans will first remove from it anything to do with his mother. As I recall there was nothing about Asta [Giorgio's second wife] there. I think the settlement reached was quite amicable and should make Stephen less touchy about his role."

101. Caryn James, "The Fate of Joyce Family Letters Causes Angry Literary Debate," *New York Times*, 15 August 1988, C11–12.

102. Friedrich Nietzsche, *Thus Spoke Zarathustra*, trans. R. J. Hollingdale (New York: Penguin Books, 1961), 132.

103. Mrs. Hester Hawkes to Carol Loeb Shloss, 3 May 1996.

1. THE CURTAIN OPENS: Trieste 1907–15

1. Eileen Schaurek, interview by Richard Ellmann, n.d., RE Papers. Joyce wrote this while they lived on the Via Vincenza Scussa, when Lucia was about two and a half.

2. Peter Hartshorn, *James Joyce and Trieste* (Westport, Conn.: Greenwood Press, 1997), 53.

3. JJ to SJ, 12 July 1905, *Letters II*, 95.

4. Margaret Joyce to JJ, 10 October 1907, Cornell, Scholes 710.

5. Dante Alighieri, *The New Life*, trans. Dante Gabriel Rossetti (New York: The National Alumni, 1907), 85.

6. Maddox, 82.

7. Martin Gilbert, *A History of the Twentieth Century* (London: HarperCollins, 1997), 143–57.

8. Hartshorn, *James Joyce and Trieste*, 49.

9. Josephine Murray to JJ, 29 July 1907, Cornell, Scholes 922.

10. JJ to SJ, 28 December 1904, *Letters II*, 75.

11. JJ to SJ, 28 February 1905, *Letters II*, 83.

12. Bozena Berta Delimata, interview by Richard Ellmann, 27 June 1953, RE Papers.

13. JJ to SJ, 2 or 3 May 1905, *Letters II*, 89.

14. JJ to SJ, 12 July 1905, *Letters II*, 93.

15. Ibid., 94–95.

16. Ibid., 96.

17. JJ to SJ, 18 September 1905, *Letters II*, 107.

18. JJ to SJ, 29 July 1905, *Letters II*, 101.

19. SJ to JJ, 31 July 1905, *Letters II*, 102.

20. John Wyse Jackson with Peter Costello, "Joyce Family Tree," in *John Stanislaus Joyce* (London: Fourth Estate, 1997), n.p.

21. High Court, Document 1942J, no. 456.

22. JJ to SJ, 19 August 1906, *Letters II*, 152.

23. JJ to SJ, 10 January 1907, *Letters II*, 206.

24. Josephine Murray to SJ, 6 June 1906, *Letters II*, 138–39.

25. JJ to Josephine Murray, 4 December 1905, *Letters II*, 128.

26. Alessandro Francini Bruni, "Joyce Stripped Naked in the Piazza," in *Portraits of the Artist in Exile*, ed. Willard Potts (Seattle: University of Washington Press, 1979), 32.

27. Herbert Gorman, *James Joyce* (New York: Farrar and Rinehart, 1939), 159.

28. Ellmann, 224–25.

29. JJ to SJ, 19 January 1905, *Letters II*, 78.

30. Maddox, 74.

31. JJ to SJ, 7 December 1906, *Letters II*, 202.

32. JJ to SJ, 10 January 1907, *Letters II*, 206.

33. JJ to SJ, 13 November 1906, *Letters II*, 192.

34. JJ to SJ, 6 February 1907, *Letters II*, 206.

35. Helen Kastor Joyce, "A Portrait of the Artist by His Daughter-in-Law," unpublished typescript, HRC.

36. Mary Colum and Padraic Colum, *Our Friend James Joyce* (Garden City, N.Y.: Doubleday, 1958), 147.

37. Ellmann, 204.

38. JJ to SJ, ?1 March 1907, *Letters II*, 219–20.

39. SJ to John Stanislaus Joyce, unsent, in Ellmann, 262.

40. Ellmann claims that Joyce's address between 7 March and November 1907 was Via San Nicolo 32 (*Letters II*, lvii). Hartshorn, basing his story on the "Stanislaus Joyce diary," RE Papers, Box 143, writes that in August 1907, "Matters worsened when Joyce was given one week's notice to vacate the Via Nuova apartment.... On August 18, Joyce and his family moved to an apartment at Via San Caterina 1"

(52–53). Richard B. Watson shows Joyce's address in March 1907 to be c/o Stanislaus at Via San Nicolo 32; on 24 September to be Via San Nicolo 33; and on 2 December to be Via San Caterina 1. See Richard B. Watson with Randolph Lewis, *The Joyce Calendar: A Chronological Listing of Published and Ungathered Correspondence by James Joyce* (Austin: Harry Ransom Humanities Research Center, 1994), 14. My best judgment is that the Joyces lived with Stanislaus until September 1907, at which point it looks as if they moved next door.

41. Ellmann, 262.

42. Hartshorn, *James Joyce and Trieste*, 49–50.

43. Ellmann, 296.

44. *P*, 481.

45. Ibid.

46. Thomas Staley, "James Joyce in Trieste." *Georgia Review* 16:4 (winter 1962): 449.

47. Lucia Joyce, "My Life," unpublished typescript, HRC.

48. In 1907, the year of Lucia's birth, Joyce purchased Edward Mott Woolley's *The Art of Selling Goods* (Chicago: American Business Man, 1907). The appropriateness of the author's name to the project of Donegal tweeds could not have escaped him. See Richard Ellmann, "Appendix: Joyce's Library in 1920," in Richard Ellmann, *The Consciousness of Joyce* (London: Faber and Faber, 1977), 113.

49. JJ to NBJ, 7 August 1909, *Letters II*, 233.

50. JJ to NBJ, 31 August 1909, *Letters II*, 242.

51. JJ to NBJ, 24 December 1909, *Letters II*, 281.

52. Watson, *Joyce Calendar*, 20.

53. Alice Curtayne, "Portrait of the Artist as Brother: Interview with James Joyce's Sister," *Critic* 21 (1963): 43.

54. Arthur Power, *Conversations with James Joyce*, ed. Clive Hart (Dublin: Millington, 1974), 70–71.

55. JJ to Eileen Joyce, 30 May 1912, *Letters II*, 295.

56. Eileen Schaurek, "Pappy Never Spoke of Jim's Books," in *James Joyce: Interviews and Recollections*, ed. E. H. Mikhail (New York: St. Martin's Press, 1990), 63.

57. Eva Joyce to SJ, 12 May 1912, Cornell, Scholes, 653.

58. Curtayne, "Portrait of the Artist as Brother," 63.

59. Ibid., 66.

60. Francini Bruni, "Joyce Stripped Naked in the Piazza," 20.

61. JJ to NBJ, ?25 October 1909, *Letters II*, 254.

62. LJ to JL, 19 March 1974, Lucia Joyce Papers, UCL.

63. Lucia Joyce, "The Real Life of James Joyce," unpublished typescript, HRC.

64. Ellmann, "Appendix: Joyce's Library in 1920," 97–134.

65. Bozena Berta Delimata, "Reminiscences of a Joyce Niece," ed. Virginia Moseley, *JJQ* 19:1 (fall 1982): 47.

66. Francini Bruni, "Recollections of Joyce," in Potts, ed., *Portraits of the Artist in Exile*, 41.

67. James Joyce, *Poems and Shorter Writings*, eds. Richard Ellmann, A. Walton Litz, and John Whittier-Ferguson (London: Faber and Faber, 1991), 114.

68. Francini Bruni, "Joyce Stripped Naked in the Piazza," 57, 45.

69. Delimata, "Reminiscences," 48.

70. Lucia Joyce, "Real Life of James Joyce."

71. Antonio Fonda Savio and Letizia Fonda Savio, "James Joyce: Two Reminiscences," in Potts, ed., *Portraits of the Artist in Exile*, 49.

72. Mario Nordo, "My First English Teacher," in Potts, ed., *Portraits of the Artist in Exile*, 58.

73. Nora Franca Poliaghi, "James Joyce: An Occasion of Remembrance," in Potts, ed., *Portraits of the Artist in Exile*, 59.

74. Lucia Joyce, "Real Life of James Joyce."

75. Ellmann, 322.

76. Lucia Joyce, "Real Life of James Joyce."

77. Maddox, 118.

78. Schaurek, "Pappy Never Spoke of Jim's Books," 64.

79. Delimata, "Reminiscences," 47.

80. *P*, 7.

81. Curtayne, "Portrait of the Artist as Brother," 46.

82. Ellmann, "Appendix: Joyce's Library in 1920," 97–134.

83. Bjørnstjerne Bjørnson, *The Fisher Lassie* (New York: Macmillan, 1891), 22–23.

84. Ibid., 32.

85. Ibid.

86. Ibid., 162.

87. Ibid., 166.

88. Ibid., 174.

89. Ibid., 184.

90. I wish to thank Ellen Handler Spitz, whose *Inside Picture Books* (New Haven: Yale University Press, 1999) led me to imagine Joyce as a father who read to his children.

91. Ellmann, 312.

92. Helen Kastor Joyce, "A Portrait of the Artist," HRC.

93. Ellmann, 412.

94. Curtayne, "Portrait of the Artist as Brother," 65.

95. Ellmann, 323.

96. NBJ to JJ, 11 July 1912, *Letters II*, 296.

97. NBJ to Eileen Joyce, 14 August 1912, *Letters II*, 302.

98. JJ to NBJ, [21 August 1912], *Letters II*, 308.

99. Maddox, 115.

100. Ibid.

101. Ellmann, 316.

102. Richard Ellmann, "Introduction" to *GJ*, ix.

103. *GJ*, 3.

104. James Joyce, "A Flower Given to My Daughter," in *Poems and Shorter Writings*, 53.

105. See "Notes" in James Joyce, *Poems and Shorter Writings*, 255.

106. James Joyce, "Simples," in *The Essential James Joyce*, ed. Harry Levin (London: Granada, 1977), 455.

107. *P*, 223.

108. JJ to CC, 10 August 1935, *Letters I*, 379.

2. THE THEATER OF WAR: Zurich 1915–19

1. Ellmann, 385.

2. Felix Béran to Herbert Gorman, 12 February 1931, quoted in Maddox, 141–42.

3. They went from 7 Reinhardstrasse to 10 Kreuzstrasse to 54 Seefeldstrasse.

4. Lucia Joyce, "My Life," unpublished typescript, HRC.

5. Ibid.

6. Lucia Joyce, "The Real Life of James Joyce," unpublished typescript, HRC.

7. Ibid.

8. Marilyn Reizbaum, "Swiss Customs," *JJQ* 27:2 (winter 1990): 213; Lucia Joyce, "My Life."

9. Lucia Joyce, "My Life."

10. Ellmann, 390.

11. Ibid., 390–92.

12. Ibid., 405–6.

13. Ibid., 422.

14. JJ to EP, 24 July 1917, quoted in Ellmann, 416.

15. EP to Jenny Serruys, 20 July 1920, *Letters III*, 9.

16. Lucia Joyce, "Real Life of James Joyce."

17. Frank Budgen, *James Joyce and the Making of "Ulysses"* (Bloomington: University of Indiana Press, 1960), 38.

18. Claud W. Sykes, interview by Richard Ellmann, 1954, RE Papers.

19. Georges Borach, "Conversations with Joyce," trans. Joseph Prescott, *College English* 15 (March 1954): 3227.

20. NBJ to JJ, 15 [August] 1917, Cornell, Scholes, 761.

21. Lucia Joyce, "Real Life of James Joyce."

22. NBJ to JJ, ?4 August 1917, *Letters II*, 401.

23. NBJ to JJ, ?11 August 1917, Cornell, Scholes, 758.

24. Lucia Joyce, "My Life."

25. NBJ to JJ, 15 [August] 1917, *Letters II*, 404.

26. Ellmann, 445.

27. Ibid., 418–19.

28. Lucia Joyce, "My Life."

29. Lucia Joyce, quoted in Dominique Maroger, "Dernière rencontre avec Lucia," in *James Joyce*, ed. Jacques Aubert and Fritz Senn (Paris: Editions de l'Herne, 1985), 77.

30. Lucia Joyce, "Real Life of James Joyce."

31. Lucia Joyce, "My Life"; Claud Sykes to Herbert Gorman, 31 May 1931, reply to questionnaire, 4, SIU.

32. JJ to Claud Sykes, ?23 September 1917, *Letters II*, 416.

33. Ellmann, 421.

34. JJ, *GJ* in *Poems and Shorter Writings*, ed. Richard Ellmann, A. Walton Litz, and John Whittier-Ferguson (London: Faber and Faber, 1991), 231.

35. Ellmann, 473.

36. JJ to Frank Budgen, 3 January 1920, *Letters I*, 134.

3. MOVING INTO ADOLESCENCE: Paris 1920–24

1. Lucia Joyce, quoted in Mary Colum and Padraic Colum, *Our Friend James Joyce* (Garden City, N.Y.: Doubleday, 1958), 137.
2. Sylvia Beach, *Ulysses in Paris* (New York: Harcourt Brace, 1956), 17.
3. MN to RE, 26 February 1954, RE Papers.
4. Helen Nutting, Paris diary, RE Papers.
5. Myron Nutting, *An Artist's Life and Travels* (Oral History Program, University of California, Los Angeles, 1972), 2: 432.
6. Ellmann, 486.
7. Ludmila Bloch-Savitsky to EP, 9 July 1920, Buffalo.
8. Myron Nutting, unpublished memoir, 1954, RE Papers.
9. JJ to John Quinn, 17 November 1920, quoted in Myron Schwartzman, "Quinnigan's Quake: John Quinn's Letters to James Joyce 1916 to 1920," *Bulletin of Research in the Humanities* 81:1 (summer 1978): 192.
10. JJ to SJ, 29 August 1920, *Letters III*, 17.
11. Ibid.
12. JJ to John Rodker, 9 December 1920; JJ to EP, 12 December 1920, *Letters III*, 132.
13. JJ to EP, 12 December 1920, *Letters III*, 133.
14. MN to RE, 16 April 1955, RE Papers.
15. Helen Nutting, Paris diary, RE Papers.
16. Ibid.
17. MN to RE, 23 January 1955, RE Papers.
18. William Bird, interview by Richard Ellmann, 2 August 1953, RE Papers.
19. André Levinson, *André Levinson on Dance: Writings from Paris in the Twenties*, ed. Joan Acocella and Lynn Garafola (Middletown, Conn.: Wesleyan University Press, 1991), 27.
20. Ellmann, 649.
21. Myron Nutting, unpublished memoir of Lucia, RE Papers.
22. Ibid.
23. Lucia Joyce, "My Life," unpublished typescript, HRC.
24. Myron Nutting, unpublished memoir.
25. Ibid.
26. This is the first placard in Charlie Chaplin's silent movie *The Kid*.
27. JJ to Valery Larbaud, ? February 1924, *Letters III*, 88.
28. Kenneth Lynn, *Charlie Chaplin and His Times* (New York: Simon and Schuster, 1997), 261.
29. Lucia Joyce, "Charlie et les gosses," *Le Disque vert* 3:4–5 (1924): 678; my translation.
30. Quoted in Bonnie Kime Scott, *Joyce and Feminism* (Bloomington: Indiana University Press, 1984), 76.
31. Djuna Barnes, "James Joyce," *Vanity Fair* 18 (April 1922): 65; quoted in Ellmann, 524.
32. Ellmann, 503.
33. Jacques Benoîst-Mechin, interview by Richard Ellmann, 1956, RE Papers.
34. August Suter, "Reminiscences," *JJQ* 7:3 (1972): 191.
35. James Joyce, quoted in Julia Kristeva, "Joyce 'The Gracehoper,' or the Return of

Orpheus," in *James Joyce: The Augmented Ninth*, ed. Bernard Benstock (Syracuse, N.Y.: Syracuse University Press, 1988), 179.

36. Ellmann, 506.

37. Lucia Joyce, "My Life."

38. JJ to Valery Larbaud, n.d. (summer 1921), quoted in Ellmann, 516, and *Letters I*, 169.

39. Helen Kastor Joyce, "We Meet," photostat of unpublished typescript, RE Papers.

40. Ira Wile, *The Sex Life of the Unmarried Adult* (New York: The Vanguard Press, 1931), 291.

41. Peggy Guggenheim, *Out of This Century: Confessions of an Art Addict* (New York: The Dial Press, 1946), 29.

42. Ibid., 30.

43. Ibid., 33.

44. JJ to NBJ, n.d., in Ellmann, 534.

45. Maddox, 195.

46. JJ to NBJ, n.d., in Ellmann, 534.

47. Dominique Maroger, "Lucia et la danse," in *James Joyce*, ed. Jacques Aubert and Fritz Senn (Paris: Editions de l'Herne, 1985); my translation.

48. JJ to Josephine Murray, 23 October 1922, *Letters I*, 191.

49. Helen Nutting, Paris diary, Myron C. Nutting and Muriel Tyler Nutting Papers, Archives of American Art, Smithsonian Institution, Washington, D.C.

4. THE ART OF DANCING: Paris 1924–28

1. There is no record of how Lucia first met Duncan, but an educated guess would place them together at Nathalie Barney's where, throughout the 1920s, the young girls who studied with him danced, long-haired and barefooted, in the back garden. It is also possible that she saw notices of him during her trip to Nice, where Duncan spent his summers for many years.

2. Helen Kastor Joyce, "Notes re mistakes in RE's 1959 JJ biography," unpublished typescript, RE Papers.

3. Adela Roatcap, *Raymond Duncan: Printer, Expatriate, Eccentric Artist* (San Francisco: Book Club of California, 1991), 12.

4. Lillian Loewenthal, *The Search for Isadora: The Legend and Legacy of Isadora Duncan* (Pennington, N.J.: Princeton Book Co., 1993), 175.

5. Roatcap, *Raymond Duncan*, 12.

6. Lois Rather, *Lovely Isadora* (Oakland, Calif.: Rather Press, 1976), 27.

7. Robert McAlmon and Kay Boyle, *Being Geniuses Together, 1920–1930* (Garden City, N.Y.: Doubleday, 1968).

8. Grace Pastor, "A Remarkable Family," *Physical Culture* (April 1910): 81.

9. Loewenthal, *Search for Isadora*, 174.

10. *Chicago Examiner*, 9 January 1912. All headlines are from the clippings collection, NYLPA.

11. Oscar Wolfe, "Raymond Duncan: The Executive," *Dance Magazine* (February 1930), n.p.

12. Loewenthal, *Search for Isadora*, 171.

13. Isadora Duncan, *My Life* (London: Victor Gollancz, 1928), 21.

14. Kay Boyle, *My Next Bride* (New York: Viking, 1986), 38.

15. McAlmon and Boyle, *Being Geniuses Together*, 116.

16. Raymond Duncan, *The Left Bank Revisited*, clipping file, Rondelle.

17. Martin Green, *Mountain of Truth: The Counterculture Begins, Ascona, 1900–1920* (Hanover, N.H.: University Press of New England, 1986), 136.

18. Loewenthal, *Search for Isadora*, 173. The sources of Duncan's movement strategies were archaeology and the sensibility of his young Greek wife, Penelope. He seems not to have been concerned with understanding the origins or purposes of these dances but only to pull them into contemporary relevance. His Hellenism seems, then, to have had a twofold purpose: to take his students out of the formations of familiar discourse, indicating in the simplicity and comfort of their tunics both a rejection (they would not be confined by the strictures of bourgeois attire) and an affiliation (classical Greece would become the symbolic locus of a new health and freedom). Reference to antiquity would identify a crude genealogy, a search for origins that modern life both deterred and obscured. Duncan's motives seem akin to Nietzsche's in that he wanted to trace the history of the present in order to undermine the self-evidence of the present to itself. In fact, we could claim that he served as an example of what Nietzsche called "the new philosophers"—people who "have found their task, their hard, unwanted, unavoidable task, but finally the greatness of their task, in being the bad conscience of their age." See Michael Mahon, *Foucault's Nietzschean Genealogy: Truth, Power and the Subject* (Albany: State University of New York Press, 1992), 86–87.

19. In this double focus, Duncan bridged the distinction that Nietzsche made between the *orchesis* and the *choros*, between the dance of individual rapture and the ceremonial ring dance—the "ecstatic dance in which a community expressed itself as a chorus of satyrs, a communal half-conscious quasi-mind below the level of individual thought, expressing in its ecstasy the community's will to overcome the agony of universal death." See Francis Edward Sparshott, *Off the Ground: First Steps to a Philosophical Consideration of the Dance* (Princeton, N.J.: Princeton University Press, 1988), 68.

20. Boyle, *My Next Bride*, 40.

21. JJ to HSW, 15 February 1928, *Letters III*, 171.

22. Raymond Duncan, *Echoes from the Studio of Raymond Duncan* (Paris: Akademia Raymond Duncan, 1930).

23. Raymond Duncan, *Exangelos: New–Paris–York* (Paris: Akademia Raymond Duncan, February 1932).

24. Ibid.

25. Ibid.

26. Hugo Ball, *Die Flucht aus der Zeit* (Munich: Duncker und Humblot, 1927), 41; my translation.

27. Helen Kastor Joyce, "We Meet," photostat of unpublished typescript, RE Papers.

28. Sylvia Beach, *Shakespeare and Company* (New York: Harcourt Brace, 1959), 69.

29. Myron Nutting, "Paris diary, 1924–25," Myron C. Nutting and Muriel Tyler Nutting Papers, Archives of American Art, Smithsonian Institution, Washington, D.C.

30. Ibid.

31. André Levinson, "Argentina," in *André Levinson on Dance: Writings from Paris in the Twenties*, ed. Joan Acocella and Lynn Garafola (Middletown, Conn.: Wesleyan University Press, 1991), 96–97.

32. Lucia Joyce, "The Real Life of James Joyce," unpublished typescript, HRC.

33. Beach, *Shakespeare and Company*, 49–50; and Lucia Joyce, "My Life," unpublished typescript, HRC.

34. Raffaella Benini to RE, 19 May 1985, RE Papers.

35. Jean-Michel Place, "Introduction," *L'Oeuf dur* (Paris: Editions Jean-Michel Place, 1975), n.p.

36. Dominique Maroger claimed that Lucia also used a nom de plume for her early published writing. See "Lucia et la danse," in *James Joyce*, ed. Jacques Aubert and Fritz Senn (Paris: Editions de l'Herne, 1985).

37. Place, "Introduction."

38. Emile Fernandez, "Epithélium," *L'Oeuf dur* 9 (April 1922), n.p.; my translation.

39. André Breton, "What Is Surrealism?" in *Selected Writings*, trans. John Ashbery (New York: Monad Press for Anchor Foundation, 1978), 36.

40. See André Breton, *Manifestos of Surrealism*, trans. Richard Seaver and Helen R. Lane (Ann Arbor: University of Michigan Press, 1969; first published by Paris: Sagittaire, 1924); and Louis Aragon, *Une Vague de rêves* (Paris: Commerce, 1924).

41. Louis Aragon, in Jacqueline Chenieux-Gendron, *Surrealism*, trans. Vivian Folkenflik (New York: Columbia University Press, 1990), 52.

42. Ibid., 22.

43. Kay Boyle to RE, 6 January 1983, RE Papers.

44. See Dominique Maroger, "Lucia et la danse" and "Dernière rencontre avec Lucia," in Aubert and Senn, eds., *James Joyce*, 81. "The poems have disappeared, probably thrown on the dustbin during the liquidation of the apartments in Paris and Zurich. Nora was never interested. The doctors in Jung's entourage who read them did not attach importance to the fact that they were generated among others of the surrealists"; my translation.

45. I am grateful to David Hayman and Ira Nadel for information about the Fernandez ancestry, the result of a personal interview with Emile Fernandez's daughter Raffaelle Benini Fernandez. Their essay, "Joyce and the Family of Emile and Yva Fernandez: Solving a Minor Mystery," can be found in *JJQ* 25:1 (fall 1987): 49–57.

46. Lucia Joyce, "Real Life of James Joyce."

47. Raffaelle Benini to RE, 19 May 1985, RE Papers.

48. Ibid.

49. Darius Milhaud, *My Happy Life* (London: Marion Boyers, 1995), 264.

50. Lucia Joyce, "My Life."

51. Samuel Beckett, interview by Richard Ellmann, 28 July 1953, RE Papers.

52. Adèle Fernandez to RE, n.d., unpublished letter, RE Papers.

53. William Bird, interview by Richard Ellmann, 2 August 1953, RE Papers.

54. See Maroger, "Lucia et la danse," 71: "Not only had she read far more of Joyce's books than Nora had, but she also knew his thoughts intuitively: she was the daughter of the spirit, the *anima*, of James Joyce"; my translation.

55. Beach, *Shakespeare and Company*, 184.

56. JJ to HSW, 23 October 1923, *Letters I*, 206; JJ to HSW, 2 November 1923, *Letters III*, 82.

57. JJ to HSW, 23 November 1925, *Letters III*, 134.

58. JJ to HSW, 9 October 1923, *Letters I*, 205.

59. JJ to HSW, 6 April 1924, *Letters III*, 93.

60. Maroger, "Lucia et la danse," 73.

61. Lucia Joyce, "My Life."

62. Myron Nutting, "Paris diary, 1924–25."

63. Helen Nutting, Paris diary, RE Papers.

64. JJ to Robert McAlmon, n.d. (early 1924), *Letters I*, 209.

65. JJ to HSW, n.d. (June 1924), *Letters I*, 216.

66. At the Trocadéro, the programs consisted of Beethoven, Wagner, Schubert, Chopin, Tchaikovsky, and Franck (March–April). At the Théâtre des Champs-Elysées, the programs included a Chopin festival and works by Liszt, Brahms, Wagner, and Berlioz (May–June). Again at the Trocadéro, with four of the Isadorables, she performed an all-Wagner program (November–December). During 25–31 January she and the four Isadorables completed the yearlong festival. See Loewenthal, *Search for Isadora*, 198.

67. Lucia's pin-up collection, now housed at the University of Buffalo, Lockwood Memorial Library, the Poetry and Rare Book Collection, includes pictures of Clothide and Alexandre Sakharoff, Anna Pavlova, Felia Doubrovska and Serge Lifar, Constantin Tcherkass, Alexandra Danilova, and Léonide Massine.

68. André Levinson, "The Girls," in *André Levinson on Dance*, 89; Lucia Joyce, "Note to Zdenka Podhajsky," Buffalo.

69. Hayman and Nadel, "Joyce and the Family of Emile and Yva Fernandez," 55.

70. Sparshott, *Off the Ground*, 7.

71. André Levinson, "The Spirit of Classical Dance," in *André Levinson on Dance*, 42–43.

72. Ibid., 80.

73. Ibid., 81.

74. Ibid., 4.

75. Ibid., 90.

76. Ibid.

77. Green, *Mountain of Truth*, 110.

78. Naima Prevots, *The Mary Wigman Book: Her Writings*, ed. and trans. Walter Sorell (Middletown, Conn.: Wesleyan University Press, 1975), 52; see also Sparshott, *Off the Ground*, 74.

79. Green, *Mountain of Truth*, 123.

80. Ibid., 108.

81. Ibid., 96.

82. Ibid., 222.

5. LEAPING WITH THE RAINBOW GIRLS: Nice 1928

1. André Levinson, "Articles sur la danse" (scrapbook), vol. 1, n.p., Bibliothèque de l'Arsenal.

2. Dominique Maroger, "Lucia et la danse," in *James Joyce*, ed. Jacques Aubert and Fritz Senn (Paris: Editions de l'Herne, 1985), 69; my translation.

3. Ibid.

4. Ibid., 74.

5. *Margaret Morris Dancing: A Book of Pictures by Fred Daniels, with an Introduction*

and Outline of Her Methods by Margaret Morris (London: Kegan Paul, Trench and Trubner, 1928), 26.

6. Ibid.

7. Ibid., 29.

8. Ibid., 35, 42.

9. Ibid., 44.

10. Ibid., 45–46.

11. Ibid., 46.

12. Ibid.

13. "Leur grande originalité est dans leur existence privée. Elles sont huit ou dix jeunes filles—peut-être seize et davantage—qui retirées pendant de longs mois, dans un coin sauvage des Alpes-Maritimes, consacrent leur existence à la danse." *Petit Journal* (February 1927), Rondelle.

14. See JJ to HSW, 22 September 1932: "We are all here. Lucia and the nurse came over from Vence today." *Letters III*, 259.

15. "Telle est, a quelques kilomètres d'Antibes, la vallée du Loup. Une rivière encadrée de grands arbres, un air de fraîcheur, un pays ombreux, touffu et verdoyant. . . . Si, de là, nous poursuivons vers l'intérieur, nous arrivons dans une région de collines gris clair, très différentes de tout ce que nous avons coutumé de voir en Provence. Le feuillage des oliviers s'accorde avec ce ton de boue sèche. Dans l'étendue des vignes, les files longues et basses de ceps sont tendues maintenant de pourpre violette. Partout dans les jardins le pêcher et l'oranger abondent. . . . J'en connais une ou un manuscrit s'achève en ce moment. Un vestibule laisse voir le départ d'un escalier de bois. Une salle, dont la cheminée est fort belle, a son plafond soutenu par des solives en saillie, brunes et crevassées. Les fenêtres ouvrent sur un abîme d'or, de vert clair et de ciel." Henri Bidou, "Les Danseuses de Saint-Paul," *Temps* 21 (October 1931); translation by Theodor Schorske.

16. Hélène Vanel, "Le Mouvement," *Cahiers rythme et couleur* 3 (May 1926): 91. Part of Lucia's training was to create rhythm and color in drawings, which she kept in notebooks. The drawings, which include images of tropical landscapes with palm trees, were evidently handed in to Hutton and Vanel, who annotated them: "Lucia design on [dance notation]" on the back and responded to their quality with comments like "couleurs d'une belle qualité—un certain lyrisme dans les formes."

17. Ibid.

18. The Lizard-on-the-Wall, "The Three Dancers," *Cahiers rythme et couleur* 2 (November 1925): 57.

19. Ibid.

20. Hélène Vanel, "La Danseuse artiste et éducatrice," *Cahiers rythme et couleur* 2 (November 1925): 34.

21. Ibid.

22. Ibid.

23. Ibid., 35.

24. Ibid.

25. Ibid., 36–37.

26. Ibid.

27. The performances for which playbills have survived are Théâtre des Champs-Elysées: 20 November 1926, and 18 December 1926; Ancien Théâtre du Marais:

21 December 1926; Théâtre du Vieux-Colombier: 19 February 1927, and 9 April 1927; Empire Théâtre: 12 August 1927. From newspaper reviews in Rondelle, we know that the group performed regularly through 1930.

28. Darius Milhaud, *My Happy Life* (London: Marion Boyers, 1995), 82.

29. Ibid., 84.

30. "Un groupement de jeunes artistes de la classe qu'elle a formée en Provence. Pendant deux ans, elles ont travaillé avec acharnement sur les collines qui avoisinent— la 'cité' de Saint-Paul, bien connue des peintres et leurs efforts ont été fort appréciés par l'élite artistique du Midi de la France et de la Suisse." *Petit Journal* (February 1927), Rondelle.

31. Ibid.

32. "Se conjuguent parfaitement: celli-ci, surtout d'attitudes, celle-là plus danseuse, toutes deux sensibles aux plus tenues variations de la musique et brodant sur la mélodie des arabesques fines et spontanées, lesquels n'en détournent ni le sens profond, ni la résonance intérieure,"clipping file, Rondelle; my translation.

33. André Levinson, "Bagatelles laborieuses," February 1930, clipping file, Rondelle.

34. Lucia shared this prejudice, for among her memorabilia is a page cut from the *Dancing Times*, a picture of "the Scala Girls," with the annotation "Tedesco's IDEAL?!" Buffalo. Jean Tedesco was then the director of the Théâtre du Vieux-Colombier.

35. Levinson, "Bagatelles."

36. The Lizard-on-the-Wall, "Three Dancers," 59.

37. Lucia's first stage appearance was with Margaret Morris in March 1926.

38. Hélène Vanel, "Souvenirs de Lucia Joyce," in Aubert and Senn, eds., *James Joyce*, 83–84.

39. In Ellmann, 581.

40. Vanel, "Souvenirs de Lucia Joyce," 85.

41. JJ to HSW, 5 March 1926, *Letters III*, 138.

42. JJ to HSW, 18 March 1926, *Letters I*, 240.

43. Maroger, "Lucia et la danse," 70.

6. CHOOSING PARTNERS: Paris and Salzburg 1928

1. Richard Ellmann, in an effort to locate the Joyces within a larger framework of the arts, tells us mistakenly that in 1923 Joyce took his whole family to see a performance of George Antheil's *Ballet Mechanique* [*sic*] and that they were all present at the Ballet suédois on 4 October 1923, "[w]hen the composer played his *Sonata* [*sic*] *Sauvage*, *Airplane Sonata*, and *Mechanisms*" (Ellmann, 557). Antheil's music for *Ballet Mécanique*, a ballet not of dancers but of "percussion in pictures," was not even begun until July 1924. See Hugh Ford, *Four Lives in Paris* (San Francisco: North Point Press, 1987), 30. It was not performed, even in private, until September 1924, and the public had to wait until 1925 to see it. For the project, Antheil had worked with Fernand Léger, who frequently did work for the Ballet suédois. But even this circumstance, which might seem to connect the collaboration with dance, is misleading; Léger, in this instance, was not choreographing but was instead making a film "using static objects repeated and reflected in mirrors and special lenses . . . that would create a moving and separating effect and like music, a definite

rhythm" (30). And according to Rolf de Mare, director of the Ballet suédois, who wrote the first full-length book on it, George Antheil did not compose any of his troupe's dance music; nor did it perform on 4 October 1923. See his "Tableau des représentations," in *Les Ballets suédois dans l'art contemporain* (Paris: Editions du Trianon, 1931).

2. *Archives internationales de la danse* 1 (1933): n.p.

3. Playbill, Théâtre du Vieux-Colombier, 19 February 1927, Rondelle.

4. In Sally Banes, "An Introduction to the 'Ballets Suédois,'" *Ballet Review* 7:2–3 (1978–79): 29.

5. Pierre Tugal, quoted in De Mare, *Les Ballets suédois dans l'art contemporain*, 30.

6. Banes, "Introduction to the 'Ballets Suédois,'" 29.

7. Victor Seroff, 23 September 1920, clipping file, Rondelle.

8. "Dances arranged by Harley Quinn" (*FW* 221.25).

9. "A czardanser indeed! Dervilish glad too" (*FW* 513.17).

10. "Les frontières entre les arts, les époques et les pays." See Ingrid-Marie Kessler, "Les Ballets suédois et les poètes français," *La Recherche en danse* 2:83: 79; my translation.

11. *New York News*, 26 November 1923.

12. *New York American*, 26 November 1923.

13. Banes, "Introduction to the 'Ballets Suédois,'" 45.

14. Ibid., 39.

15. Paul Claudel, *Claudel on the Theatre*, ed. Jacques Petit and Jean-Pierre Kempf, trans. Christine Trollope (Coral Gables, Fla.: University of Miami Press, 1972), 45–47.

16. Richard Brender, "Reinventing Africa in Their Own Image: The Ballets Suédois' 'Ballet nègre,' *La Création du monde*," *Dance Chronicle* 9:1 (1986): 125.

17. In Jay Bochner, *Blaise Cendrars: Discovery and Re-creation* (Toronto: University of Toronto Press, 1978), 67.

18. In Brender, "Reinventing Africa in Their Own Image," 124.

19. Fanoudh-Siefer, quoted in Brender, "Reinventing Africa in Their Own Image," 123.

20. Blaise Cendrars, "Hommage à Jean Borlin," in De Mare, *Les Ballets suédois dans l'art contemporain*, 176–77.

21. Brender argues that the Ballet suédois distinguished itself from other Western re-creations of the primitive by its insistence that African religious ritual be taken as seriously as the story of Adam and Eve, and by its posing of the modern artist, like his African precursor, as an integral part of the life of the community. The social structure of the tribe, he suggests, is "analogized to that of 'the new humanity.'" According to him, the troupe was neither presenting Africa in the stereotypes of Western colonialism—as bestial or senselessly passionate or childlike—nor appropriating another culture for use solely for avant-garde purposes, nor making a claim for universal similarity between the traditional and the new. It was, rather, re-creating the collective spectacle of the artist embraced by his society and thus replicating a folk wisdom made manifest first to Africa but in this performance finally understood on the Western stage. Whether we agree with Brender's formulation or not, rhythmic structure was clearly at the heart of the ballet's meaning for the dancers, for those who worked with them, and for those who watched its performance. See Brender, "Reinventing Africa in Their Own Image," 131–33.

22. If Julia Kristeva imagines literature to be rhythm made intelligible by syntax, then we can claim that dance turns the moving body into the generator of that syntax, translating an unfettered, irreducible energy into another kind of intelligible script. See *Revolution in Poetic Language*, ed. Margaret Waller (New York: Columbia University Press, 1984), 26.

23. In Roger Shattuck, *The Banquet Years: The Origins of the Avant-Garde in France, 1885–World War I* (New York: Vintage Books, 1968), 51.

24. JJ to HSW, 24 November 1926, *Letters III*, 146.

25. Hélène Vanel, "Souvenirs de Lucia Joyce," in *James Joyce*, ed. Jacques Aubert and Fritz Senn (Paris: Editions de l'Herne, 1985), 84.

26. Ibid., 85.

27. Ibid., 84.

28. JJ to HSW, 14 September 1927, *Letters I*, 259.

29. JJ to HSW, 8 October 1927, *Letters III*, 163.

30. Helen Nutting, Paris diary, RE Papers.

31. "Représentation unique," Programme: Comédie des Champs-Elysées, 18 February 1928, Opéra.

32. Helen Nutting, Paris diary, RE Papers.

33. Brender, "Reinventing Africa in Their Own Image," 120.

34. "On the Left Bank," *Paris Times* 1371 (14 March 1928).

35. Bozena Berta Delimata, "Reminiscences of a Joyce Niece," ed. Virginia Moseley, *JJQ* 19:1 (fall 1982): 50.

36. André Levinson, "The Spirit of Classical Dance," in *André Levinson on Dance: Writings from Paris in the Twenties*, ed. Joan Acocella and Lynn Garafola (Middletown, Conn.: Wesleyan University Press, 1991), 42.

37. Arthur Power, *Conversations with James Joyce*, ed. Clive Hart (Dublin: Millington, 1974), 95.

38. In Ellmann, 564.

39. Samuel Beckett, "Dante . . . Bruno, Vico . . . Joyce," in Beckett et al., *Our Exagmination Round His Factification for Incamination of "Work in Progress"* (London: Faber and Faber, 1972), 14.

40. Delimata, "Reminiscences," 50.

41. Eileen Schaurek, interview by Richard Ellmann, n.d., RE Papers.

42. Dominique Maroger, "Dernière rencontre avec Lucia," in Aubert and Senn, eds., *James Joyce*, 77.

43. "The Past of the Futurist: Zdenka Podhajsky's Dance of Life," newspaper clippings, RE Papers.

44. Ibid.

45. Schaurek interview.

46. Robert McAlmon and Kay Boyle, *Being Geniuses Together, 1920–1930* (Garden City, N.Y.: Doubleday, 1968), 354.

47. Ibid., 334.

48. Ibid., 353.

49. Maddox's statement, "In 1928 . . . Lucia was twenty-one and went with her dance group to the Isadora Duncan school near Salzburg" (232), is wrong. She went alone to the Elizabeth Duncan School. The contact was made through Raymond Duncan and not through her affiliation with Les Six de rythme et couleur. Isadora Duncan was already dead; she died on 14 September 1927.

50. Irma Duncan, *Duncan Dancer* (New York: Books for Libraries, 1980), 51.

51. Victor Seroff, *The Real Isadora* (New York: The Dial Press, 1971), 158.

52. Max Merz, "Die Ziele und die Organisation der Elizabeth Duncan-Schule," in *Elizabeth Duncan-Schule: Marienhöhe/Darmstadt* (Jena, Germany: Eugen Diederichs, 1912), 11; my translation.

53. Ibid., 12.

54. Ibid., 15.

55. A. Mallwitz, "The Physical Education of Girls in Light of the Physical Culture Movement," in *Elizabeth Duncan-Schule,* 19; my translation.

56. Ibid., 20.

57. Ibid., 21.

58. Seroff, *Real Isadora*, 158.

59. Ibid., 161.

60. Irma Duncan, *Duncan Dancer*, 112.

61. McAlmon and Boyle, *Being Geniuses Together*, 112.

62. Lucia Joyce, "The Real Life of James Joyce," unpublished manuscript, HRC.

63. Ibid.

64. JJ to HSW, 19 October 1929, *Letters III*, 283.

65. Maddox, 249.

7. STUMBLING AND RECOVERY: Paris 1928–31

1. Ellmann, 606–7; Maddox, 243–46.

2. Helen Kastor Joyce, "A Portrait of the Artist by His Daughter-in-Law," unpublished typescript, HRC.

3. HKJ to RE, 23 October 1959, RE Papers.

4. Ibid.

5. See note 30 below.

6. MN to RE, 9 April 1955, RE Papers.

7. Nino Frank, interview by Richard Ellmann, 20 August 1953, RE Papers.

8. Giorgio Joyce, interview by Richard Ellmann, 9 August 1953, RE Papers.

9. Helen Kastor Joyce, "A Portrait of the Artist."

10. Cited in Maddox, 230.

11. Helen Kastor Joyce, "A Portrait of the Artist."

12. Ibid.

13. Helen Kastor Joyce, "We Meet," photostat of unpublished typescript, RE Papers.

14. Maddox, however, states as fact that Helen seduced Giorgio (225); and "For Joyce, his son's sexual initiation by a Jewish beauty must have been deeply distressing" (232). Ellmann had a copy of Helen's unpublished memoir but apparently did not use it because he could not substantiate its claims. In 1955 he began an extensive correspondence with Myron Nutting, hoping that Nutting would either know of the alleged affair with Lillian Wallace or be able to lead him to the truth. On 30 January 1955, after Nutting had written a brief biographical note about Lillian, Ellmann wrote, "You have given me considerable help with the Wallaces about whom I had no information." Nutting evidently remained preoccupied with the Wallaces, for on 16 April 1955, he wrote again to Ellmann, with several paragraphs about how he, Richard Wallace, and Joseph Collins had met in the ambulance

corps and how their friendship had continued through their years together in Paris (1920–29). Using information that Nutting had given him about Lillian's maiden name and family background, Ellmann finally succeeded in finding her. On 9 December 1955, Nutting wrote, "I was delighted that you located Lillian Wallace. I got a wonderful letter from her." Three years later, Ellmann, Nutting, and Lillian Wallace were all still in correspondence with one another, but Nutting never suspected that she had a secret; Ellmann never told him what he was searching for, and Lillian never divulged the truth, if there was truth to be revealed. RE Papers.

15. Helen Kastor Joyce, "We Meet."

16. MN to RE, 23 January 1955, and 16 April 1955, RE Papers.

17. Helen Kastor Joyce, "We Meet."

18. Ibid.

19. Lucia Joyce, "My Life," unpublished manuscript, HRC.

20. Lucia Joyce, quoted in Maddox, 256. Maria Jolas had a similar assessment: "He was practically—I don't like to use the word 'gigolo'—but he was absolutely at the beck and call of this spoiled, attractive, rich woman"; quoted in Maddox, 256.

21. Adie Nelson and Barrie Robinson, *Gigolos and Madames Bountiful: Illusions of Gender, Power, and Intimacy* (Toronto: University of Toronto Press, 1994), 52–53.

22. Jean Marèze, *L'Apprenti gigolo* (Paris: J. Ferenczi, 1926), 13; my translation.

23. Ellmann, 600.

24. Stuart Gilbert, Paris diary, 8 December 1930, SG Papers.

25. William Bird to RE, 24 October 1955, RE Papers.

26. Lucia Joyce, "My Life."

27. André Breton, "Second Manifesto," in *Investigating Sex: Surrealist Research 1928–1932*, ed. José Pierre, trans. Malcolm Imrie (London, New York: Verso Press, 1992), 192, 21.

28. D. H. Lawrence, "A Propos of Lady Chatterley's Lover," in *Lady Chatterley's Lover (The Complete and Unexpurgated 1928 Orioli Edition)* (London: Bantam Books, 1968), 332.

29. Gilbert, Paris diary, 9 July 1932, SG Papers.

30. "Ihren Bruder habe sie ausserordentlich geliebt." James Joyce and Paul Léon, "Anamnese von Fräulein Lucia Joyce," RE Papers; my translation.

31. JJ to HSW, 24 June 1924, *Letters I*, 216.

32. In David Hayman, *A First-Draft Version of "Finnegans Wake"* (Austin: University of Texas Press, 1963), 225.

33. Ibid., 226. Hayman uses the following editorial conventions: "All of Joyce's additions are in italics; Joyce's cancellations are crossed out; Joyce's substitutions are in bold face" ("Reader's Key," 44).

34. Helen Nutting, Paris diary, RE Papers. This diary fragment is dated 1928, but it is not possible to verify if Patrick Tuohy was in Paris in 1928. It may be that this is a description of an earlier year between 1924 and 1927, when Tuohy was working on Joyce's portrait.

35. JJ to HSW, 15 February 1928, *Letters III*, 171.

36. "Le Championnat d'amateurs de danse rythmique," clipping file, Rondelle; my translation.

37. *Chronique parisien*, clipping file, Rondelle.

38. Ibid.

39. JJ to HSW, 28 May 1929, *Letters I*, 280.

40. Samuel Beckett, interview by Richard Ellmann, 28 July 1953, RE Papers.

41. *La Semaine à Paris*, clipping file, Rondelle; my translation.

42. Dominique Maroger, "Lucia et la danse," in *James Joyce*, ed. Jacques Aubert and Fritz Senn (Paris: Editions de l'Herne, 1985), 71.

43. Beckett interview.

44. Stuart Gilbert, *Reflections on James Joyce: Stuart Gilbert's Paris Journal*, ed. Thomas F. Staley and Randolph Lewis (Austin: University of Texas Press, 1993), 11.

45. Stuart Gilbert, "Introduction," *Letters I*, 34.

46. JJ to HSW, 26 April 1929, *Letters III*, 189n.

47. Ellmann, 614.

48. Helen Kastor Joyce, "Luncheon at Café Léopold," photostat of unpublished typescript, RE Papers.

49. Maroger, "Lucia et la danse," 71.

50. Ellmann, 616.

51. Gilbert, *Reflections on James Joyce*, 13.

52. Maroger, "Lucia et la danse," 71.

53. At the end of *Oedipus at Colonus*, as Oedipus lies dying, he refuses to pass his estate to his daughters. Instead he selects a surrogate son in Theseus, saying to Antigone and Ismene, "never ask to see what law forbids . . . Now go quickly. Only the appointed one, Theseus, let him stand behind me: He alone must see this mystery." See *Daughters and Fathers*, ed. Lynda Boose and Betty S. Flowers (Baltimore: The Johns Hopkins University Press, 1989), 42.

54. Victor Seroff, 23 September 1920, clipping file, Rondelle.

55. Maroger, "Lucia et la danse," 71.

56. André Levinson, "The Spirit of Classical Dance," in *André Levinson on Dance: Writings from Paris in the Twenties*, ed. Joan Acocella and Lynn Garafola (Middletown, Conn.: Wesleyan University Press, 1991), 45–46.

57. Ibid., 47–48.

58. Zelda began working with Egorova in 1927 and continued to do so until 1930, when she had a breakdown. She recuperated at Les Rives de Prangins in Nyon, Switzerland, where Lucia also spent time in 1934.

59. Zelda Fitzgerald, *Save Me the Waltz*, in *The Collected Writings of Zelda Fitzgerald*, ed. Matthew Bruccoli (New York: Charles Scribner's Sons, 1991), 116–17.

60. JJ to HSW, 19 October 1929, *Letters I*, 285.

61. Fitzgerald, *Save Me the Waltz*, 138.

62. Ibid., 151.

63. Fitzgerald, *Collected Writings*, 448.

64. Helen Kastor Joyce, "Notes re mistakes in RE's 1959 JJ biography," RE Papers.

65. Eileen Schaurek, interview by Richard Ellmann, n.d., RE Papers.

66. Maroger, "Lucia et la danse," 72.

67. Ibid., 67.

68. JJ to HSW, 22 November 1929, *Letters I*, 287.

69. Maddox, 249.

70. Margaret Morris, *My Life in Movement* (London: Owen, 1969), 65.

71. Ibid., 64.

72. Ibid., 69.

73. Ibid., 64, 67, 69.

74. Maroger, "Lucia et la danse," 68.

75. Ibid.

76. For an elaboration of similar ideas see Peggy Phelan, "Dance and the History of Hysteria," in Corporealities: Dancing, Knowledge, Culture and Power, ed. Susan Leigh Foster (New York: Routledge, 1996), 90–99: "Anna O.'s conversations with Breuer are not so much a performance in which her body finds words, but rather they are performances in which her body finds time, and more particularly, finds its past. Passing into language, the somatic symptom passes into the past. To put it in a slightly different key: If we think of psychoanalysis as a mode of psychic choreography, we can see the symptom as the body's psychic movement. Psychoanalysis and choreography are two different modes of performing the body's movement" (96).

77. Maroger, "Lucia et la danse," 73.

78. SB Papers.

79. JJ to HSW, 11 March 1931, Letters III, 303.

80. Ellmann, 663.

8. STEPPING OUT: Paris 1931–32

1. Stuart Gilbert, Paris diary, 6 May 1932, SG Papers.

2. Ibid., 5 and 8 December 1930.

3. Ibid., 29 January 1930.

4. Ibid., 31 January 1930.

5. Ibid., 6 May 1932.

6. For an excellent discussion of the ways in which categories about female adolescence have shaped various images of Lucia, see Catherine Driscoll, Appendix: Lucia Anna Joyce, Ph.D. diss.; and Catherine Driscoll, Girls (New York: Columbia University Press, 2002).

7. For a more extended discussion of this adolescent phenomenon—a female child's tendency to impose restrictions on herself at the period when she becomes aware of her sexual identity—see Carol Gilligan, In a Different Voice (Cambridge: Harvard University Press, 1982). Lucia's place in Joyce's imaginative economy made distinctive demands on her that cannot be fully explained with Gilligan's paradigm.

8. Samuel Beckett, interview by Richard Ellmann, 28 July 1953, RE Papers.

9. Knowlson, 105.

10. Samuel Beckett, "Dante . . . Bruno, Vico . . . Joyce," in Beckett et al., Our Exagmination Round His Factification for Incamination of "Work in Progress" (London: Faber and Faber, 1972), 17.

11. See Deirdre Bair, Samuel Beckett (New York: Harcourt Brace Jovanovich, 1978); Ellmann; and Maddox.

12. Samuel Beckett, Dream of Fair to Middling Women (London: Calder Publications, 1993), 150.

13. Knowlson, 110.

14. Beckett, Dream of Fair to Middling Women, 43.

15. Ibid., 40.

16. Maroger, "Dernière rencontre avec Lucia," in James Joyce, ed. Jacques Aubert and Fritz Senn (Paris: Editions de l'Herne, 1985), 77.

17. Beckett, *Dream of Fair to Middling Women*, 49.

18. Knowlson, 146.

19. Ibid., 104.

20. Beckett, *Dream of Fair to Middling Women*, 23–24.

21. Ibid., 18.

22. Ibid., 19.

23. Knowlson, 148.

24. Beckett, *Dream of Fair to Middling Women*, 34.

25. Ibid., 37, 36.

26. Ibid., 36.

27. Knowlson, 149.

28. Terance Killeen, "Play It Again Sam!" *Irish Times*, 5 November 1992.

29. Knowlson, 148.

30. James Knowlson makes the connection with Lucia through Dante's *Divina Commedia*, a book that Beckett gave to Lucia and that was annotated with his remark that one of the "très donne benedette" (three blessed women) comes from Syracuse. Knowlson, 149.

31. Lucia mentioned this as a book she read in her youth in her 1958 "The Real Life of James Joyce," unpublished typescript, HRC.

32. Beckett, *Dream of Fair to Middling Women*, 118.

33. Beckett interview, 28 July 1953. Brenda Maddox understands this behavior to be a symptom of schizophrenia. For a ballerina who was entreated by her dance mistress, Madame Egorova, to remain lean and sinewy, vomiting after meals might better be considered bulimia; to me the problem seems to be more directly about weight and the perceived beauty of a lean appearance.

34. Beckett, *Dream of Fair to Middling Women*, 50.

35. Knowlson, 149 n33, 646.

36. Beckett, *Dream of Fair to Middling Women*, 121.

37. Ibid., 33.

38. Scattered throughout Beckett's text are many other veiled allusions to *Finnegans Wake*: the description of anatomy as geometry (35); an allusion to the children's lesson in the *Wake* II, ii (293ff); the beautiful hen (35), an allusion to Belinda Doran, the hen who finds the buried letter in the *Wake* I (13ff); and an imitation of Joyce's hundred-letter "thunderwords" on (239): "Himmisacrakruzidirkenjesusmaria-undjosefundblutigeskreuz! All in one word. The things people come out with sometimes!" Throughout Beckett's *Dream* are portmanteau words from at least three languages that also suggest covert references to Joyce's writing.

39. Beckett, *Dream of Fair to Middling Women*, 116.

40. Ibid., 50.

41. Ibid., 46.

42. Ibid., 34.

43. Ibid., 50.

44. Gilbert, Paris diary, 6 May 1932, SG Papers.

45. Beckett, *Dream of Fair to Middling Women*, 48, 34. In reading this section of the novel, I am reminded of Peggy Guggenheim's description of a similar time in her own life: "At this time, I was worried about my virginity. I was twenty-three and I found it burdensome. All my boyfriends were disposed to marry me, but

they were so respectable they would not rape me. I had a collection of photographs of frescos I had seen at Pompeii. They depicted people making love in various positions, and of course I was very curious and wanted to try them out myself. It soon occurred to me that I could make use of Florenz [Laurence Vail] for this purpose. . . . I went home and dined with my mother and a friend gloating over my secret and wondering what they would think of it if they knew." *Out of This Century: Confessions of an Art Addict* (New York: The Dial Press, 1946), 25–26.

46. At another point in the text, the narrator refers to the Syra-Cusa's "Bilitis breasts." One wonders if Beckett in some way sensed or even knew that Lucia had lesbian tendencies. *Dream of Fair to Middling Women*, 33, 50, 116.

47. Ibid., 120.

48. Ibid., 137.

49. Ibid., 121.

50. Ibid., 120.

51. Ibid., 49. James Knowlson identifies the character Lucien as based on Jean Beaufret, Beckett's philosophy student at the Ecole normale (150), and adds in a footnote that Georges Belmont, a friend of both, concurs (646 n42). My own vote for Lucien would be Thomas MacGreevy. See Maddox: "When Lucia accused all the men around her of seducing her, [Joyce] responded by banning them all from the house, even the pious MacGreevy" (285). Regardless, the text reveals that the Syra-Cusa's desire for sexual experience is (at least in imagination) turned into a game of sexual bandying. If such sexual trading occurred among the men in Beckett's circle, it would explain Lucia's distress when she finally understood the nature of the game. In other words, she might have been upset about something real, and not hallucinating, as other writers have implied.

52. Beckett, *Dream of Fair to Middling Women*, 116, 117.

53. Ibid., 121. See also SB to Thomas MacGreevy, 1 October 1932, Rare Book and Manuscript Collection, TCD: "What I mean is I don't love her nor scape of land sea or sky nor our Savior particularly. I haven't signed any contract either. I couldn't quite bring it off. . . . I just feel fervent/ardent in a vague, general way."

54. Gilbert, Paris diary, 24 May 1932, HRC.

55. Peggy Guggenheim, quoted in Jacqueline Weld, *Peggy: The Wayward Guggenheim* (New York: E. P. Dutton, 1986), 83.

56. Guggenheim, *Out of This Century*, 118.

57. See Jacques Lacan, "Joyce le symptôme I," in *Joyce avec Lacan*, ed. Jacques Aubert (Paris: Navarin Editeur, 1987), 21–29. Lacan posited that Lucia "fragilized" herself to avoid incest.

58. Maroger, "Dernière rencontre avec Lucia," 77.

59. Ibid., 76.

60. Maroger, "Lucia et la danse," in Aubert and Senn, eds., *James Joyce*, 67.

61. Beckett, *Dream of Fair to Middling Women*, 49.

62. Ibid.

63. See Bair, *Samuel Beckett*, 101; Ellmann, 648–50; Maddox, 253–54.

64. See Issy's footnote in *Finnegans Wake*, II, ii, 271.

65. Beckett, *Dream of Fair to Middling Women*, 137.

66. Ibid., 50.

67. Ibid., 125.

68. Ibid., 50.

69. Guggenheim, *Out of This Century*, 205.

70. Maddox, 254.

71. Knowlson, 134.

72. Ibid., 179.

73. SB to Thomas MacGreevy, 10 March 1935, in Knowlson, 179.

74. Guggenheim, *Out of This Century*, 194.

75. Kay Boyle to RE, 29 January 1983, RE Papers. In August 1982, Boyle and Beckett met once again in Paris, and Boyle remembered that they seemed to pick up where they had left off fifty years ago. He wanted to talk about the plot of a Machiavelli play he had seen the night before they met, while she made clear, "It was only Lucia I wanted to talk about, and madness, which I had never believed in until he made it clear."

76. Helen Kastor Joyce, "Notes re mistakes in RE 1959 JJ biography," RE Papers.

77. Stella Steyn had been urged by Patrick Tuohy, then the art master of the School of Art in Dublin, to study French painting in Paris. When her mother consented to take her there, Tuohy gave the Steyns a letter of introduction to the Joyces. Stella Steyn, "A Retrospective View with an Autobiographical Memoir," in *Catalogue*, ed. S. B. Kennedy (Dublin: Gorry Gallery, 1995), 12. I wish to thank Mia Lerman-Hayes for calling my attention to this memoir.

78. Ibid., 13–14.

79. Ibid., 15, 8.

80. Ibid., 16.

81. Ibid., 17.

82. Ibid., 16–17.

83. Cary F. Baynes, "Notes on Lucia Joyce in Zurich, 1934," RE Papers.

84. Ibid.

85. Alexander Calder, Paris address book, Archives of American Art, Smithsonian Institution.

86. Albert Hubbell to RE, August 1981, RE Papers.

87. "Waldo Peirce to Betty Lockett Spender," *Bangor Daily News*, n.d. (1936); Waldo Peirce Papers, Archives of American Art, Smithsonian Institution.

88. Ibid.

89. Ibid.

90. Ibid.

91. Alexander Calder, *Calder: An Autobiography with Pictures* (New York: Pantheon Books, 1966), 92.

92. Steyn, "Retrospective View," 17.

93. Hubbell to RE, August 1981, RE Papers.

94. Lucia Joyce, "My Life," unpublished typescript, HRC.

95. See especially *Josephine Baker*, 1926, wire; *Acrobats*, 1928, wire; *Josephine Baker*, 1927, iron wire; *Action Toys*, brochure, 1926; *Dancer*, 1929, wire; *Grand Ecart*, 1929, wire.

96. See Alexander Calder to George Thomas, 29 June 1932: "I had another exposition in Paris last February. This time abstract sculptures which moved—so swaying when touched or blown and others propelled by small electric motors. I had some

15 individual motors so it was really quite a show," Alexander Calder Papers, Archives of American Art, Smithsonian Institution.

97. Calder, *Autobiography*, 91.

98. Joan M. Marter, *Alexander Calder* (Cambridge, England: Cambridge University Press, 1991), 45.

99. Calder, *Autobiography*; Marter, *Alexander Calder*, 63–64.

100. Calder, *Autobiography*; *Calder's Circus*, ed. Jean Lipman with Nancy Foote (New York: E. P. Dutton, 1972), 165.

101. Lipman, ed., *Calder's Circus*, 165.

102. Calder, *Autobiography*, 91.

103. Ibid., 95.

104. Ibid., 112.

105. Lucia Joyce, "My Life."

106. Hubbell to RE, August 1981.

107. Calder, *Autobiography*, 101, 112.

108. Calder returned home in December 1930.

109. Hubbell to RE, August 1981.

110. Ibid.

111. Beckett, *Dream of Fair to Middling Women*, 19.

112. Hubbell to RE, August 1981.

113. Ibid.

114. Ibid.

115. Baynes, "Notes on Lucia."

116. Léon held degrees in literature and law, was an editor of a law review, and had published *Lettres de Nicolas II et de sa mère* (1928) and *Benjamin Constant* (1930). Lucie Léon was a writer for the Paris *Herald Tribune*.

117. Stuart Gilbert, *Reflections on James Joyce: Stuart Gilbert's Paris Journal*, ed. Thomas F. Staley and Randolph Lewis (Austin: University of Texas Press, 1993), 46.

118. Ibid., 26.

119. Nino Frank described Liam O'Flaherty in this way: "In the course of one of these soirées I came upon a strapping fellow with a brick-red face and green eyes. He was the heaviest drinker of all and had an air of a tough boxer and a brutal laugh that did not harmonize at all with the tone of the party; however, the Joyces were attentive to him, and he inspired me with a lively enough curiosity that several days later we met for a drink. It was Liam O'Flaherty, a book of whose had just appeared in French (*The Informer*)." "The Shadow That Had Lost Its Man," in *Portraits of the Artist in Exile: Recollections of James Joyce by Europeans*, ed. Willard Potts (Seattle: University of Washington Press, 1979), 89–90.

120. Zdenka Podhajsky, interview by Richard Ellmann, n.d., RE Papers.

121. Maria Jolas, interview by Richard Ellmann, 22 July 1953, RE Papers. See also Gilbert, *Reflections on James Joyce*, 20. By "dope" Jolas may also have referred to Veronal, a barbiturate that was prescribed for nervousness and insomnia. See pages 340–42.

122. Mary Colum and Padraic Colum, *Our Friend James Joyce* (Garden City, N.Y.: Doubleday, 1958), 136–37.

123. Helen Kastor Joyce, "A Portrait of the Artist by His Daughter-in-Law," unpublished typescript, HRC.

124. Bozena Berta Delimata, interview by Richard Ellmann, 27 June 1953, RE Papers.

125. JJ to HSW, 11 March 1931, *Letters III*, 303.

126. For a fuller discussion of the terms and consequences of Joyce's will, see Carol Shloss, "Joyce's Will," *Novel: a forum on fiction* 6:24 (fall 1994). Joyce left no real property to Lucia.

127. Lidderdale, 449; Maddox, 265.

128. Bozena Berta Delimata, autobiographical typescript, n.d., RE Papers.

129. Maddox, 271.

130. JJ to Padraic Colum, 18 July 1931, *Letters III*, 221; Maddox, 272.

131. GJ to JJ, 18 August 1931, RE Papers.

132. LJ to Zdenka Podhajsky, 22 August 1931, RE Papers.

133. JJ to HSW, 27 September 1931, *Letters I*, 306.

134. JJ to HSW, 7 December 1931, *Letters I*, 308.

135. JJ to HSW, 21 November 1931, *Letters III*, 234.

136. Lucia Joyce, "My Life."

137. *Ulysses, by James Joyce; with an introduction by Stuart Gilbert and illustrations by Henri Matisse* (New York: The Limited Editions Club, 1935). Fifteen hundred copies.

138. The composers were E. J. Moeran, Arnold Bax, Albert Roussel, Herbert Hughes, John Ireland, Roger Sessions, Arthur Bliss, Herbert Howells, George Antheil, Eduardo Carducci, Eugene Goossens, C. W. Orr, and Bernard van Dieren.

139. Steyn, "Retrospective View," 17.

140. JJ to HSW, 17 April 1931, *Letters III*, 217.

141. Maroger, "Lucia et la danse," 73.

142. LJ to Zdenka Podhajsky, 1 December 1931, RE Papers.

143. JJ to HSW, 21 November 1931, *Letters III*, 234; JJ to HSW, 7 December 1931, *Letters I*, 308.

144. JJ to HSW, 21 November 1931, *Letters III*, 234; JJ to HSW, 27 November 1931, *Letters III*, 235.

145. JJ to HSW, 28 January 1932, *Letters I*, 313.

146. Maroger, "Lucia et la danse," 72.

9. LASHING OUT: Paris and Feldkirch 1932

1. Ellmann, 648.

2. Knowlson, 133.

3. He did write it between January and July 1932.

4. James Joyce, "Ecce Puer," 15 February 1932. Original manuscript in the possession of Robert N. Kastor.

5. Mary Colum and Padraic Colum, *Our Friend James Joyce* (Garden City, N.Y.: Doubleday, 1958), 136.

6. Helen Kastor Joyce, "A Portrait of the Artist by His Daughter-in-Law," unpublished typescript, HRC; Colum and Colum, *Our Friend James Joyce*, 136.

7. James Joyce and Paul Léon, "Anamnese von Fräulein Lucia Joyce," RE Papers.

8. George S. Hellman, *The Story of the Seligmans* (New York: 1945), 173.

9. Peggy Guggenheim, *Out of This Century: Confessions of an Art Addict* (New York: The Dial Press, 1946), 29.

10. Hazel Guggenheim, quoted in *Peggy Guggenheim and Her Friends*, ed. Virginia M. Dortch (Milan: Berenice, 1994), 33.

11. Ibid., 34.

12. Jacqueline Weld, *Peggy: The Wayward Guggenheim* (New York: E. P. Dutton, 1986), 66.

13. Dortch, ed., *Peggy Guggenheim and Her Friends*, 72.

14. Helen Kastor Joyce, "Notes re mistakes in RE's 1959 JJ biography," RE Papers.

15. Joyce and Léon, "Anamnese von Fräulein Lucia Joyce."

16. Stuart Gilbert, Paris diary, 9 July 1932, SG Papers; and Ellmann, 650. Maddox disputes this date, claiming the engagement took place in May, but Lucie Léon, Stuart Gilbert, and Mary Colum's memoirs all place the engagement in March, before the Joyces returned to England. See Maddox, 428, n4.

17. Lucie Léon, interview by Richard Ellmann, 1954, RE Papers.

18. Helen Kastor Joyce, "A Portrait of the Artist."

19. Giorgio Joyce, interview by Richard Ellmann, 9 August 1953, RE Papers.

20. Gilbert, Paris diary, 24 May 1932, SG Papers.

21. Lucia Joyce, "My Life," unpublished typescript, HRC.

22. See Gilbert, Paris diary, 9 July 1932, SG Papers: "She stayed with the Cs about ten days. Meanwhile she worried the maid by her curious questions. 'Have you had a lover? Do you think every girl should marry?'"

23. Bozena Berta Delimata, interview by Richard Ellmann, n.d., RE Papers.

24. Colum and Colum, *Our Friend James Joyce*, 140.

25. Gilbert, Paris diary, 3 May 1932, SG Papers.

26. Colum and Colum, *Our Friend James Joyce*, 137.

27. Stuart Gilbert, *Reflections on James Joyce: Stuart Gilbert's Paris Journal*, ed. Thomas F. Staley and Randolph Lewis (Austin: University of Texas Press, 1993), 46.

28. Gilbert, Paris diary, 6 May 1932, SG Papers.

29. Ibid., 24 May 1932 and 18 June 1932, SG Papers.

30. Colum and Colum, *Our Friend James Joyce*, 136–39.

31. Ibid., 140.

32. Ibid., 140–41. "The whole scene was something to throw Lucia off her balance. Every time I think of it I am indignant. Why did my husband have to be so authoritarian?"

33. Ibid., 139.

34. Of this episode, Richard Ellmann writes, "the doctor . . . could do little except to conclude that Lucia was more deranged than anyone had admitted," Ellmann, 651. Yet his source is Mary Colum.

35. Ibid., 140.

36. Ibid., 139.

37. Ibid., 142.

38. Ibid., 141.

39. Friedrich Nietzsche, *Thus Spoke Zarathustra*, trans. R. J. Hollingdale (New York: Penguin Books, 1961), 132.

40. JJ to HSW, 22 September 1934, *Letters I*, 346.

41. See, for example, Martin Green's quotation from *The Birth of Tragedy* in *Mountain of Truth: The Counterculture Begins, Ascona, 1900–1920* (Hanover, N.H.: University Press of New England, 1986), 102: " 'The original image of the Dionysian is the bearded satyr; in him existence expresses itself more truly, really, fully than in the man of culture . . . and in the festivals of this satyrlike Dionysiac man, Nature

mourns her dismembering into individuals. . . . He is no longer artist but artwork.' It is clear from photographs of the dancers in Monte Verità that Laban cast himself as that bearded Dionysiac satyr, with the troupe of bacchantes around him." See Isadora Duncan, *My Life* (London: Victor Gollancz, 1928) for her discussion of the importance of Nietzsche's philosophy in her development as a dancer. See also Dominique Maroger's description of a Margaret Morris dance performance in 1931: "Margaret Morris danced with delight, near a circle of similarly clad children. Their frolicking . . . achieved the spontaneity of some bacchanal figured on a Grecian vase. Presently a thickset faun himself began to bound, legs and body flexing, soon he darted forth, defiantly taking leave of gravity." "Lucia et la danse," in *James Joyce*, ed. Jacques Aubert and Fritz Senn (Paris: Editions de l'Herne, 1985), 68. See also the dances of Lucia's own repertoire with Les Six de rythme et couleur: *Faunesque*, *Les Vignes sauvages*, and *Panthère verte*.

42. Friedrich Nietzsche, *The Birth of Tragedy*, trans. Walter Kaufmann (New York: Vintage, 1967), 59.
43. Ibid., 97.
44. Ibid., 51.
45. Ibid., 56.
46. Ibid.
47. Ibid., 109.
48. Ibid., 110.
49. Ibid., 130, 140, 126, 139.
50. Ibid., 109.
51. Ibid., 124.
52. *P*, 197.
53. Ibid., 246.
54. Ibid., 139.
55. Green, *Mountain of Truth*, 102.
56. Nietzsche, *Birth of Tragedy*, 24.
57. *P*, 169.
58. Louis A. Sass, *Madness and Modernism: Insanity in the Light of Modern Art, Literature, and Thought* (New York: Basic Books, 1992), 40.
59. Maddox, 310.
60. Nietzsche, *Birth of Tragedy*, 34.
61. Ibid., 108.
62. Ibid., 144, 23.
63. See JJ to HSW, 17 April 1932, BL; Maddox, 287.
64. Eugen Bleuler, *Textbook of Psychiatry*, trans. A. A. Brill (New York: Macmillan, 1924), 277.
65. Eugen Bleuler, "On the Psychogenesis of Mental Disease," in *Textbook of Psychiatry*, 237.
66. "Aufenthalts-Bewilligung für Auslander Fräulein Lucia Joyce. Wohnhaft im Sanatorium Dr. Brunner. 1 Reisepass dat. v. 5 Feb. 1932 gültig bis 5 Feb. 1937 für Aufenthalt in der Gemeinde Küsnacht bewilligt bis 31 März 1935," PL Papers.
67. See discussion of Theodor Brunner's sanatorium on pages 276–77.
68. Martha Noel Evans, *Fits and Starts: A Genealogy of Hysteria in Modern France* (Ithaca, N.Y.: Cornell University Press, 1991), 41.

69. JJ to GJ, 13 August 1935, *Letters III*, 372n; also Maddox, 293.

70. Evans, *Fits and Starts*, 23.

71. Robert Castel, *The Regulation of Madness: The Origins of Incarceration in France*, trans. W. D. Hall (Berkeley: University of California Press, 1998), 246. Article 14 of the Law of 1838 Concerning the Insane spelled it out: "Even before the doctors have declared a cure to have been effected, every person placed in an institution for the insane shall likewise cease to be detained therein as soon as his discharge shall have been requested by one of the persons designated hereafter. . . . Nevertheless, if the institution doctor is of the opinion that the mental state of the patient might compromise public order or the safety of persons, notice of this shall be given to the mayor, who may immediately order a temporary postponement of the discharge. . . . With respect to persons whose placement is voluntary and in the case where their mental state might compromise public order and the safety of persons, the prefect may . . . grant a special order, so as to prevent such persons being discharged from the institution without his authorization, unless it is in order to be placed in another institution."

72. Ibid., 208.

73. Ellmann, 664. Hebephrenia, named after the Greek goddess of youth, Hebe, is a disorder characterized by regressive behavior. Maillard had only one publication to his credit: *Les Merveilles de l'autosuggestion: Conferences d'enseignement faites à l'Institute Coué de Paris* (Paris: Editions Oliven, 1924).

74. JJ to HSW, 11 November 1932, BL.

75. Henri Codet, *Psychiatrie* (Paris: Librairie Octave Doin, 1926), 50.

76. He is most remembered for his work with hysteria, but even in 1935 it was clear that he diluted Freudian ideas by amalgamating them with French clinical practices and by continuing to ignore etiological questions. In "Le Probleme actuel de l'hysterie" ("The Current Problem of Hysteria"), Codet identified hysteria as the disorder "one dares not name," giving us some understanding of the reason Lucia, despite the theatrical nature of her temper, was never diagnosed as hysterical. It was a tainted category that threatened to damage the reputations of those who dealt with it. In the years between the two world wars, French psychiatrists were faced with military casualties of battle who called into question the supposedly sexual and effeminate domain of the disease. Shell-shocked soldiers exhibiting the same symptoms as unruly women patients shook the theoretical base of the diagnosis, as did the symptoms of the epidemics of influenza and encephalitis lethargica that raged in Europe between 1917 and 1927. If delirium, hallucinations, agitation, and abnormal movements of the body could be characteristic of male responses to trauma or of viral damage to the nervous system, then the neat distinction between genders and between physical and mental diseases previously insisted on by psychiatrists became suspect. Increasingly French neurologists claimed mental illness as the territory of medical rather than psychological practice, and they would challenge the scientific credentials of those who practiced psychiatry without a thorough grounding in physiology.

77. Codet, *Psychiatrie*, 3–7.

78. Ellmann, 691.

79. Codet, *Psychiatrie*, 6.

80. Ibid., 9.

81. Ibid., 112.

82. Ibid., 113.

83. JJ to HSW, 6 August 1932, *Letters III*, 254.

84. JJ to SB, 26 September 1932, in Noel Riley Fitch, *Sylvia Beach and the Lost Generation: A History of Literary Paris in the Twenties and Thirties* (New York: W. W. Norton, 1983).

85. Gilbert, Paris diary, 28 July 1932, SG Papers.

86. Gilbert, Paris diary, 20 July 1932, SG Papers.

87. Codet, *Psychiatrie*, 118.

88. Maria Jolas Papers, Beinecke.

89. LJ to Zdenka Podhajsky, 21 July 1932, RE Papers.

90. LJ to Mathilde Wönecke, 8 August 1932, HSW Papers, BL; my translation from the original French.

91. *P*, 169.

92. "figures grimaçantes, des masques agrandis de personnes étranges." LJ to Wönecke, 8 August 1932.

93. In the Joyces' time, the type of printing needed could be done only in Paris and in Paris by only two or three firms. See JJ to Frank Vigors Morley at Faber and Faber, 10 November 1932, *Letters III*, 266. This book and *A Chaucer A.B.C.* were printed by Editions Vendôme/Imprimerie Vendôme Lecram-Servant. See PL Papers.

94. In October 1932, when ten copies of the books were shipped to England, the silk casings allowed New Haven customs officials to seize the books and ask for a high luxury tax (£4) on each one. See JJ to SG, 17 October 1932, quoted in Gilbert, *Reflections on James Joyce*, 79.

95. JJ to PL, 12 July 1932, PL Papers.

96. JJ to HSW, 6 August 1932, *Letters III*, 254.

97. JJ to HSW, 25 November 1932, RE Papers.

98. JJ to Robert McAlmon, August 1932?, *Letters III*, 252.

99. JJ to SJ, 22 September 1932, *Letters III*, 260.

100. PL Papers.

101. JJ to Padraic Colum, 2 October 1932, in Colum and Colum, *Our Friend James Joyce*, 142.

102. JJ to HSW, 6 August 1932, *Letters III*, 254, n1.

103. Codet, *Psychiatrie*, 118.

104. Ibid., 119.

105. JJ to John Sullivan, 25 August 1932, *Letters III*, 256.

106. JJ to HSW, 18 January 1933, *Letters I*, 332.

107. Louis Gillet, "The Living Joyce," in *Portraits of the Artist in Exile: Recollections of James Joyce by Europeans*, ed. Willard Potts (Seattle: University of Washington Press, 1979), 165.

108. Quoted in JJ to Frank Budgen, 17 June 1932, *Letters I*, 319; my translation.

109. JJ to HSW, 11 November 1932, *Letters III*, 326–27.

110. See Fritz Vanderpyl, *Exposition les jeunes graveurs contemporains: Galerie Marcel Guiot du 12–29 June 1929* (Paris: La Galerie, 1929).

111. PL to Carolus Verhulst, 17 February 1933, PL Papers. Fritz Vanderpyl's publications included *De Giotto à Puvis de Chavannes* (1913), *Mon chant de guerre* (1917),

Voyages (1920), *Exposition les jeunes graveurs contemporains* (1929), *Peintres de mon époque* (1931), *L'Art sans patrie* (1942).

112. Carolus Verhulst to JJ, 28 December 1932, PL Papers.

113. PL to John Holroyd-Reece, 28 December 1932, PL Papers.

114. Gilbert, Paris diary, 5 November 1932, HRC.

115. *Paris midi*, n.d.; *Herald Paris Sunday*, 31 July 1932; *Daily Telegraph*, 27 September 1932; *New York Herald*, 19 September 1932, Rondelle.

116. JJ to HSW, 25 November 1932, RE Papers.

117. Arthur Power, *Conversations with James Joyce*, ed. Clive Hart (Dublin: Millington, 1974), 31; PL to Frank Budgen, 7 May 1933, *Letters III*, 280.

118. PL to B. W. Huebsch, 18 February 1933, PL Papers.

119. PL to Ralph Pinker, 20 March 1933, PL Papers.

120. Ellmann mistakenly reported that the first edition was in 1934.

121. Nino Frank, "The Shadow That Had Lost Its Man," in Potts, ed., *Portraits of the Artist in Exile*, 90.

122. 8 January 1934, PL Papers.

123. John Holroyd-Reece to JJ, 12 July 1934, PL Papers.

124. JJ to John Holroyd-Reece, 4 August 1934, PL Papers.

125. The lettrines were not returned until 8 September 1934. See JJ to Frank Budgen, 8 September 1934, *Letters III*, 325.

126. The colophon of *A Chaucer A.B.C.* reads: "Of this, the original edition . . . 300 copies have been printed . . . numbered 1–300." Paperbound in light blue-gray; printed in deep blue; light blue paper over boards folder; silver paper shellback; printed silver paper label on spine; light blue and silver paper over boards slipcase. Year 1936.

127. Ellmann, 663.

128. Elaine Scarry, *The Body in Pain: The Making and Unmaking of the World* (New York: Oxford University Press, 1985), 280.

129. Ibid., 290.

130. Ibid.

131. Jack Kahane to PL, 13 December 1932, PL Papers.

132. JJ to HSW, 9 June 1936, *Letters III*, 385.

133. The colophon reads: "This book comprises the opening and closing pages of part II, section II of *Work in Progress*. The illuminated capital letter at the beginning is the work of Lucia Joyce, the author's daughter. Edition limited to 176 numbered copies."

134. "Wildering of the nicht" (*FW* 244.33); Jacques Mercanton, "The Hours of James Joyce," in Potts, ed., *Portraits of the Artist in Exile*, 214.

135. JJ to HSW, 25 November 1932, *Letters I*, 327.

136. Arthur Power was of the opinion that "If Joyce had listened to Nora instead of Maria Jolas, he would not have died so young." Arthur Power, interview by Brenda Maddox, 19 January 1984. Maddox concurs: "The ulcer had gone untreated for seven years as Joyce, in other ways so resistant to Freudian theories, had accepted the reassurances of Maria Jolas and Dr. Fontaine that his pains were psychosomatic, caused by 'nerves'" (343).

137. JJ to HSW, 18 January 1933, *Letters I*, 232.

138. Gilbert, Paris diary, 5 November 1932, SG Papers.

139. Herbert R. Lottman, "One of the Quiet Ones [Maria Jolas]," *New York Times Book Review*, 22 March 1970, 5.

140. Ibid., 6.

141. Gilbert, Paris diary, 19 August 1932, SG Papers.

142. Maria Jolas, interview by Richard Ellmann, 22 July 1953, RE Papers.

143. JJ to Padraic Colum, 2 November 1932, in Colum and Colum, *Our Friend James Joyce*, 144.

144. Ibid.

145. *P*, 171–72.

146. *P*, 238.

147. PL to HSW, 23 March 1933, PL Papers.

148. PL to HSW, 18 January 1933, *Letters III*, 275.

149. PL to HSW, 23 September 1933, *Letters III*, 287.

150. PL to HSW, 24 April 1933, *Letters III*, 278.

151. Joyce took out a lease on 7 rue Edmond Valentin in July 1934 but didn't move into it until February 1935. JJ to CC, 29 July 1934, *Letters III*, 345; and JJ to GJ, 5 February 1935, *Letters III*, 357.

152. JJ to SJ, 8 December 1933, *Letters III*, 293.

153. Ibid., 294.

154. Ellmann, 667.

155. Financial records, PL Papers.

156. Dominique Maroger, "Lucia et la danse," in Aubert and Senn, eds., *James Joyce*, 67.

157. Dominique Maroger, "Dernière rencontre avec Lucia," in Aubert and Senn, eds., *James Joyce*, 77.

158. A letter from George Borach, who lived in Zurich, to Paul Léon, 29 June 1932, had already recommended Dr. Hans W. Maier for Lucia. In the same letter Borach advised Léon that he knew of no sanatorium where the sisters did not wear uniforms. PL Papers.

10. PLAYING WITH FIRE: Zurich and Geneva 1933–35

1. When Ellmann annotated Joyce's letters about the decision to send Lucia to the Burghölzli, he claimed, "Apparently Professor Maier, of Burghölzli, had a private clinic adjacent to the public asylum," *Letters III*, 325n. But this was not correct. As director of the Burghölzli, Maier had spent the years 1929–34 overseeing a major renovation of the clinic buildings. He had increased the number of beds for patients by five hundred and the number of rooms for personnel by two hundred. The kitchen, washhouse, laboratories, and lecture halls had been rebuilt, and the entire interior of the main structure, including gardens and courtyards, had been made "friendly and modern." See Christian Arnold, *Der Psychiater Hans Wolfgang Maier* (Zurich: Juris Druck und Verlag Dietiko, 1992), 30; my translation.

2. Ellmann, 677.

3. Oscar Forel, Raymond Mallet, Otto Naegeli, C. G. Jung, and Theodor Brunner had all been trained by Bleuler.

4. Arnold, *Der Psychiater Hans Wolfgang Maier*, 15.

5. Ibid., 12–13.

6. Eugen Bleuler, *Dementia Praecox or the Group of Schizophrenias*, trans. J. Zinkin (New York: International Universities Press, 1950), 297.

7. John G. Howells, ed., *The Concept of Schizophrenia: Historical Perspectives* (Washington, D.C.: American Psychiatric Press, 1991), 77.

8. Bleuler, *Dementia Praecox*, 288.

9. Ibid., 272–73.

10. JJ to HSW, 9 June 1936, *Letters III*, 386.

11. Bleuler, *Dementia Praecox*, 277.

12. In Howells, ed., *Concept of Schizophrenia*, 64.

13. Bleuler, *Dementia Praecox*, 63.

14. Ibid., 296.

15. Ibid.

16. Ibid., 298–302.

17. Ibid., 327.

18. Ibid., 331–32.

19. Ibid., 328–29.

20. Lucia Joyce, "My Dreams," unpublished manuscript, HRC.

21. August Forel, *Die Sexuelle Frage* (Zurich: Rascher Verlag, 1942).

22. Financial records, with dates, PL Papers.

23. Ellmann, 665.

24. Ibid., 679.

25. Financial records, PL Papers.

26. PL to HSW, 2 October 1934, RE Papers.

27. By 1932, 717 men and women had taken the qualifying examination. With a retention rate of 80 percent they could claim that by then almost one quarter of the employees were holders of a diploma. Les Rives de Prangins fared particularly well, perhaps because Dr. Forel trained his own personnel on the premises. Prangins was eighth out of twenty-nine Swiss establishments in number of professional staff. It had hired between thirty and thirty-nine staff members from this pool of workers and could point with satisfaction to the fact that sixty-seven percent of its staff had professional training.

28. Oscar Forel and Walter Morgenthaler, *Die Pflege der Gemüts- und Geisteskranken* (Bern: Hans Huber, 1926), 201.

29. Ibid., 203.

30. Ibid.

31. Ellmann, 691.

32. Forel and Morgenthaler, *Pflege*, 242.

33. PL to HSW, 23 September 1933, *Letters III*, 287.

34. Maddox, 300.

35. Ellmann, 679.

36. Ibid. One of Lucia's contemporaries, Emily Colemen, wrote a memoir, *The Shutter of Snow* (New York: Virago Press, 1981), about her stay in an American asylum in the mid-1920s. Like Lucia, her first and most powerful impulse was to escape: "She tore from her tender skin the rough nightgown. She jumped out from the bed into the warm and heavy hall. She stampeded the big door that led outside. I will go out of here, why am I here? She pounded with her fists on the door. It has come, the hour has come. We are to be free. A voice shouted break it down, break it down. All the beds in the back began to shout. Godwin rushed to hold her wrists to twist them. She shook her off like autumn leaves. Godwin rattled and fell away. She struck Godwin in the face and looked savagely about for more resistance. The door

broke from the other side and she was surrounded. They twisted both her wrists and she was calm. It was the first pain she had had. She had thought pain was gone with the rest. My husband, she cried to Miss Sheehan, why can't I see him? She was being wound up like a French doll. She could not move. If she moved a finger two of them began to twist her wrists. The others wound the strips of cloth together. Miss Sheehan, how can you betray me like this? When it was done they carried her like a stone Pharaoh to her bed. She was put into bed with the blankets and over that the canvas sheet was pulled. It was very strong and thick with a hole for the head. But I can't sleep on my back" (7).

37. "Aus dem Bericht der Anstalt Les Rives de Prangins," RE Papers.

38. PL to HSW, 11 March 1934, PL Papers.

39. Ibid.

40. JJ to LJ, 15 June 1934, *Letters I*, 342.

41. JJ to CG-W, 2 September 1934, *Letters III*, 323.

42. JJ to CG-W, 2 September 1934, *Letters III*, 323; see also JJ to GJ, 9 September 1934, RE Papers.

43. "Aus dem Bericht der Anstalt Les Rives de Prangins," RE Papers.

44. James Joyce and Paul Léon, "Anamnese von Fräulein Lucia Joyce," RE Papers.

45. "Beobachtungen im Burghölzli vom 28 bis 29 September 1934," RE Papers.

46. Otto Naegeli, *Unfallsneurosen* (Leipzig: Verlag von Georg Thieme, 1923), 57.

47. Financial records, PL Papers.

48. JJ to GJ, 9 September 1934, RE Papers.

49. Cary F. Baynes, "Notes on Lucia Joyce in Zurich, 1934," 12 November 1934, RE Papers.

50. Ibid.

51. See Kathleen Ferris, *James Joyce and the Burden of Disease* (Lexington: University Press of Kentucky, 1995).

52. Baynes, "Notes on Lucia," 9 November 1934.

53. "As a matter of fact she has had blood taken from her of course in the tests that Naegeli made." Baynes, "Notes on Lucia," 12 November 1934.

54. In a letter to Harriet Weaver on 21 October 1934, Joyce mentioned that Dr. Brunner did not show Dr. Naegeli's opinion of the case to Lucia "as it would upset her." In another letter to Giorgio and Helen on 15 January 1935, he told them not to worry about the blood anomaly: "Dr. Naegeli says it will recede of itself. It is most unusual but neither dangerous nor symptomatic." *Letters I*, 350, 357.

55. Baynes, "Notes on Lucia," 15 December 1934.

56. John Kerr, *A Most Dangerous Method: The Story of Jung, Freud and Sabina Spielrein* (New York: Alfred A. Knopf, 1993), 34.

57. H. Girsberger, *Who's Who in Switzerland* (Zurich: Central European Times Publishing, 1952), 72.

58. Ellmann, 676. Maria Jolas seems to have been the family friend who first suggested Jung as a doctor for Lucia. One can well understand her hope for such a therapeutic intervention, for her husband, Eugene, had not only translated some of Jung's work into English but published "Psychology and Poetry" in the June 1930 issue of *transition: an international quarterly for creative experiment*. Jolas was in the vanguard of those interested in the newest ways of understanding modern culture. He was like Hans Prinzhorn, whose book about the configurations of art and the irra-

tional, *Das Bildnerei der Geisteskranken* (*The Artistry of the Mentally Ill*), had been published in 1922. Jolas was interested in the similarities that could be noted among the works of children, primitive peoples, mentally ill people, and the great artists of Europe. The 1920s were characterized by such books: see also Ewald Volhard, *Literaturwissenschaft und Psychoanalyse* as well as Hugo Bieber, *Dictung und Psychoanalyse*, both published in 1928. But where Prinzhorn's book excited great interest among the surrealists (Sophie Taeuber wrote to Hans Arp in 1922 telling him he must find it immediately), we can imagine no such enthusiasm on Joyce's part with regard to Jung's view of the arts.

59. William Walcott, "Carl Jung and James Joyce: A Narrative of Three Encounters," *Psychological Perspectives* 1:1 (spring 1970): 22–23.

60. *Neue Schweizer Rundschau* 1, 1928.

61. C. G. Jung, "*Ulysses*: A Monologue," in *The Spirit in Man, Art and Literature* (London: Routledge and Kegan Paul, 1971), 112–14.

62. Ibid., 112n, 115, 117.

63. CG-W to C. G. Jung, October 1934, Zurich James Joyce Foundation.

64. Jung, "*Ulysses*: A Monologue," 113–14.

65. Ibid.

66. Ibid.

67. Ellmann, 676.

68. Baynes, "Notes on Lucia," 20 November 1934.

69. William McGuire and R. F. C. Hull, eds., *C. G. Jung Speaking: Interviews and Encounters* (Princeton, N.J.: Princeton University Press, 1977), 78.

70. Ibid.

71. See Maggy Anthony, *The Valkyries: The Women around Jung* (Longmead, England: Element Books, 1990), 2.

72. Quoted in Patricia Hutchins, *James Joyce's World* (London: Methuen, 1957), 184–85.

73. These notes were sent to Richard Ellmann by Ximena de Angulo Roelli, the daughter of Cary F. Baynes, on 27 July 1981, with a small personal note about her mother and the comment, "I had thought that she had written up these notes on her contacts with Lucia for Jung's benefit, but on reading through it seems obvious that it was a memorandum for her own use, and that she reported to him directly." Ellmann obviously could not have used this material in his 1959 biography of Joyce, but he does allude to it in his notes to the 1982 revision.

74. Strong and Mann are both mentioned in Baynes's "Notes on Lucia."

75. This hostility continued even in Zurich. See Baynes, "Notes on Lucia," 19 November 1934. Joyce reported to Baynes that Lucia had "behaved abominably to her mother, made fun of everything she said, sneered at her."

76. Cary F. Baynes, "Introduction" to *Contributions to Analytical Psychology*, trans. H. G. Baynes and Cary F. Baynes (New York: Harcourt, Brace, 1928), xiv.

77. Ximena de Angulo Roelli to RE, 27 July 1981, RE Papers.

78. Baynes, "Introduction" to *Contributions to Analytical Psychology*, xv.

79. Ibid.

80. Ibid., xvi.

81. Baynes's notes begin on 29 October 1934; they allude to having seen Lucia "a month or five weeks ago." They end on 15 December 1934—a period of approximately three and a half months.

82. Baynes, "Notes on Lucia," 29 October 1934.

83. Ibid.

84. The six characteristics that follow constitute Bleuler's list of the forms of resistance characteristic of schizophrenia found in Jung's essay, "Bleuler's Theory of Schizophrenic Negativism," in *The Psychogenesis of Mental Disease*, trans. R. F. C. Hull (1911; reprint, Princeton, N.J.: Princeton University Press, 1972).

85. Baynes, "Notes on Lucia," 8 November 1934.

86. Ibid., 29 October 1934.

87. Five years after her work with Lucia, Baynes's husband, H. G. Baynes, published *Mythology of the Soul: A Research into the Unconscious from Schizophrenic Dreams and Drawings* (London: Rider, 1939). It is possible that Cary Baynes's notes about Lucia in some way contributed to this inquiry into the role of creativity in recovery from schizophrenia.

88. Joyce and Léon, "Anamnese von Fräulein Lucia Joyce."

89. Baynes, "Notes on Lucia," 15 December 1934.

90. Baynes, "Notes on Lucia," 20 November 1934.

91. Ibid.

92. Joyce and Léon, "Anamnese von Fräulein Lucia Joyce."

93. JJ to HSW, 21 December 1934, BL.

94. Baynes, "Notes on Lucia," 15 December 1934.

95. Ibid.

96. Jung, "*Ulysses*: A Monologue," 122, 114, 116.

97. Baynes, "Notes on Lucia," 20 November 1934.

98. Ibid.

99. Baynes, "Notes on Lucia," 30 October 1934.

100. In McGuire, *Jung Speaking*, 50.

101. Ibid., 51.

102. "The decisive part of the work is achieved by creating in the patient's relation to the doctor in the 'transference'—new editions of the old conflicts; in these the patient would like to behave in the same way as he did in the past. . . . In place of the patient's true illness there appears the artificially constructed transference illness, in place of the various unreal objects of his libido there appears a single, and once more imaginary, object in the person of the doctor." Sigmund Freud, *Introductory Lectures on Psychoanalysis*, trans. and ed. James Strachey (New York: W. W. Norton, 1977), 455.

103. C. G. Jung, "Psychology of the Transference," in *The Practice of Psychotherapy: Essays on the Psychology of the Transference and Other Subjects*, trans. R. F. C. Hull (New York: Pantheon Books, 1954), 172.

104. C. G. Jung, "Some Psychical Consequences of the Anatomical Distinction between the Sexes," in *The Practice of Psychotherapy*, 673. See also Robert M. Polhemus, "The Lot Complex: Rereading the End of *Finnegans Wake* and Rewriting Incest," in *Rereading Text/Rethinking Critical Presuppositions*, ed. Shlomith Rimmon-Kenan, Leona Toker, and Shuli Barzilai (New York: Peter Lang, 1996).

105. JJ to GJ, 29 October 1934, *Letters III*, 326–27.

106. JJ to HSW, 17 December 1934, *Letters I*, 353.

107. JJ to HSW, 21 October 1934, *Letters I*, 349.

108. LJ to JJ, October 1934, RE Papers. Original in Italian, translated at Jung's request.

109. Peter Jung (grandson), conversation with the author, Zurich, March 1992.

110. Jung, "Schizophrenia," in *The Psychogenesis of Mental Disease*, 260.
111. Ibid.
112. Jung, "Psychology of the Transference," 198.
113. Baynes, "Notes on Lucia," 20 November 1934.
114. Jung, "Psychology of the Transference," 198.
115. Jung, "Appendix," in *The Practice of Psychotherapy*, 328.
116. HSW to PL, 20 December 1934, PL Papers.
117. JJ to GJ, 5 February 1935, *Letters I*, 356–57.
118. Jung, "Anima and Animus," in *Alchemical Studies*, translated by R. F. C. Hull. (Princeton, N.J.: Princeton University Press, 1961), 85, 84.
119. Jung, "The Shadow and the Syzygy," in *Alchemical Studies*, 168.
120. "No one can get around the fact that by taking up a masculine profession, studying, and working like a man, woman is doing something not wholly in accord with, if not directly injurious to her feminine nature." Also, "It is a woman's outstanding characteristic that she can do anything for the love of a man. But these women who achieve something important for the love of doing a thing are exceptional because this really does not agree with their nature. Love for a thing is a man's prerogative." C. G. Jung, "Women in Europe," in *The Collected Works of C. G. Jung*, ed. Herbert Gerhard, Michael Fordham, and Read Adler (Princeton, N.J.: Bollingen Series XX, 1953–83), vol. 10. See also Anthony, *Valkyries*.
121. Baynes, "Notes on Lucia," 20 November 1934.
122. Ellmann, 677.
123. LJ to JJ, October 1934, RE Papers.
124. Baynes, "Notes on Lucia," 12 November 1934.

11. LOCKING UP DANCERS: London 1935

1. JJ to GJ and HKJ, 28 December 1934, *Letters I*, 354.
2. Peter F. Ostwald, *Vaslav Nijinsky: A Leap into Madness* (New York: Carol Publishing Group, 1991).
3. HSW to PL, 11 November 1934, PL Papers.
4. Romola Nijinsky, *Nijinsky* (New York: Simon and Schuster, 1934), 428–30.
5. Ibid., 432.
6. HSW to PL, 6 and 11 November 1934, PL Papers. Lucia's supposed clairvoyance has been a subject of considerable interest. Joyce and Nora's biographers use Joyce's faith in Lucia's extraordinary powers as an example of his misplaced credulity. Alison Leslie Gold, author of *The Clairvoyant: The Imagined Life of Lucia Joyce* (New York: Hyperion Books, 1992), uses Lucia's ability to "see" in an extraordinary way as a founding metaphor for her life. The truth is that clairvoyance was a subject of general interest to those in Jungian circles in Zurich in these years. Jung was, at the time, giving a series of seven lectures on clairvoyance at the Eidgenössische Technische Hochschule in Zurich. Focused on Justinus's famous *Clairvoyante of Prevorst*, the lectures were accompanied by numerous diagrams about the psychological nature of clairvoyance. If Lucia and the Joyces became interested in or influenced by clairvoyance, they were likely responding to what was in the forefront of many Jungian imaginations between 1933 and 1941. See Barbara Hannah, *Jung: His Life and Work* (New York: G. P. Putnam, 1976).
7. JJ to HSW, 9 June 1936, *Letters III*, 385.

8. Jung, "Schizophrenia," in *The Psychogenesis of Mental Disease*, trans. R. F. C. Hull (1911; reprint, Princeton, N.J.: Princeton University Press, 1972), 265.

9. Cary F. Baynes, "Notes on Lucia Joyce in Zurich, 1934," 20 November 1934, RE Papers.

10. Ibid.

11. Jung, "Schizophrenia," 267.

12. Maddox, 283.

13. Jung, "Schizophrenia," 256.

14. Joyce located this nurse "through Giorgio's aviator friend," Walter Aekermann. JJ to PL, 15 January 1935, PL Papers.

15. JJ to PL, 16 January 1935, PL Papers.

16. Lidderdale, 338.

17. The only independent evidence we have of syphilis as a real possibility is a cryptic letter dated 7 October 1937, in the Ponisovsky section of the PL Papers in Dublin. Here we learn that Ponisovsky was worried about an illness that he forbade his friends to talk about lest his father find out: "Dear Paul . . . I *think* Alec must *have forbidden* him to tell any of us anything. . . . He had been and was very angry, especially he doesn't want his father to know anything about his illness. *Please* make quite sure from Macgreevy (?) whether there are any new *developments*, whether he *is* conferring with *Fuller* and *whether Valmont is the best*. . . . *Don't fail* to let me know. *Please. Urgent.* H."

18. Baynes, "Notes on Lucia," 20 November 1934.

19. JJ to PL, 16 January 1935, PL Papers.

20. "Sie sei überhaupt von Männern schlechtbehandelt worden." James Joyce and Paul Léon, "Anamnese von Fräulein Lucia Joyce," RE Papers.

21. This is contrary to the accounts given by Ellmann and Maddox, which tell the story of a marriage seemingly arranged, in the French manner, by adults to a man whom Lucia barely knew. See Ellmann, 649–50; and Maddox, 284.

22. "Als er 1932 wieder auftauchte, machte er ihr einen Heiratsantrag, worauf sie zum ersten Mal psychotisch wurde." Joyce and Léon, "Anamnese von Fräulein Lucia Joyce."

23. This was most probably Mathilde Wönecke, the nurse who had accompanied her to Feldkirch, when the two young women stayed with Maria Jolas. Lucia's relationship with Sylvia Beach's assistant Myrsine Moschos also had sexual overtones, and we know that the two young women slept together at the Joyces' apartment when Moschos took over as Lucia's companion. See JJ to HSW, 18 January 1933, RE Papers.

24. On 31 January, Eileen Schaurek arrived in Paris, not in Zurich, as Ellmann states. Paul Léon was asked to meet her at Amiens Station. Joyce, Nora, and Lucia arrived back in Paris on 1 February 1935. Telegrams, PL Papers.

25. HSW to PL, 5 October 1934, PL Papers.

26. HSW to PL, 20 December 1934, PL Papers.

27. PL to HSW, 6 February 1935, PL Papers.

28. Ibid.

29. "Harriet certainly lacked the experience to distinguish between merriment and alcoholism, and probably thought the party drunker than it really was." "Bryher . . . has confirmed that everyone was dismayed by 'Josephine's stiff and utter dis-

approval of the misdirected joke.'" Ezra Pound, c. 1924, quoted in Lidderdale, 247.

30. Lidderdale, 39–44.

31. Ibid., 340.

32. JJ to GJ and HKJ, 19 February 1935, *Letters III*, 340, 344. See also HSW to PL, 25 February 1935: "Mr. Joyce's sister also wrote daily till she left London. Mr. Joyce asked her not to telephone directly to his own flat but to Léon's at 8 p.m. but this is a difficult time as Lucia would be in the room." *The James Joyce–Paul Léon Papers in the National Library of Ireland: A Catalogue*, comp. Catherine Fahy (Dublin: NLI, 1992), description of letter which is itself missing, 51.

33. HSW to JJ, 19 and 22 February 1935, RE Papers.

34. See Ellmann, 681. Lidderdale (487–88) took her account of this visit from Ellmann. Maddox took her story from Lidderdale: "Many of the details of Lucia's visit to London and Ireland come from this biography of HSW" (430). The opening of the Paul Léon Papers in Dublin lets us clarify this recirculation of misinformation to some extent.

35. HSW to JJ, 17 February 1935, Richard Ellmann's notes and summaries of letters, RE Papers.

36. Harriet Weaver enclosed Dr. Joly's report. It has been taken out of the PL Papers, as were most of Miss Weaver's daily letters to Joyce and all Lucia's own letters to her father.

37. HSW to JJ, 18 March 1935, Richard Ellmann's notes and summaries of letters, RE Papers.

38. This and the following details are assembled from letters 27 February to 2 March 1935, PL Papers.

39. HSW to JJ, 27 February 1935 (11:37 a.m.), PL Papers. HSW to PL, telegram 28 February 1935, PL Papers.

40. Ellmann, 681.

41. Lidderdale, 341.

42. Maddox, 305.

43. HSW to JJ, 4 March 1935, PL Papers.

44. HSW to JJ, 27 February 1935, PL Papers.

45. HSW to JJ, 4 March 1935, PL Papers.

46. Ellmann, 681.

47. HSW to JJ, 2 March 1935, PL Papers.

48. HSW to JJ, 7 March 1935, PL Papers.

49. LJ to HSW, 13 March 1935, UCL.

50. HSW to PL, 9 March 1935, PL Papers.

51. Bozena Berta Delimata, interview by Richard Ellmann, 27 June 1953, RE Papers.

52. HSW to JJ, 15 April 1935, PL Papers.

53. HSW to JJ, 4 March 1935, PL Papers.

54. For an excellent discussion of this subject, noticing the dates of the deletions and speculating about the subjects discussed in them, see Mary Reynolds, "Joyce and Miss Weaver," *JJQ* 10:4 (1982): 373–403.

55. JJ to HSW, 7 April 1935, HSW Papers.

56. Kay Redfield Jamison, *An Unquiet Mind: A Memoir of Moods and Madness* (New York: Alfred A. Knopf, 1995), 19.

57. During this time Joyce sent Lucia a copy of Dante's *Vita Nuova*. Ellmann, 681.

58. JJ to HSW, 7 April 1935, *Letters I*, 361.

59. HSW to JJ, 15 April 1935, PL Papers.

60. JJ to HSW, 7 April 1935, *Letters I*, 361.

61. PL to HSW, 28 March 1935, in Lidderdale, 343.

62. JJ to MH, 28 June 1935, *Letters I*, 373.

63. JJ to MH, 15 June 1935, *Letters III*, 362.

64. JJ to HSW, 1 May 1935, *Letters I*, 366.

65. Carola Giedion-Welcker, "Meetings with Joyce," in *Portraits of the Artist in Exile: Recollections of James Joyce by Europeans*, ed. Willard Potts (Seattle: University of Washington Press, 1979), 254–55.

66. PL to HSW, 19 July 1935, PL Papers.

67. James Joyce, "Ibsen's New Drama," in *CW*, 41.

68. Ibid., 42.

69. Ibid.

70. Franz Wedekind, *Spring Awakening*, trans. Edward Bond (London: Eyre Methuen, 1980), 24.

71. Henrik Ibsen, *The Wild Duck*, in *Three Plays* (New York: The Heritage Press, 1965), 152.

72. Gerhart Hauptmann, *Hannele's Ascension*, in *Three Plays*, trans. Horst Frenz and Miles Waggoner (Prospect Heights, Ill.: Waveland Press, 1977), 138–39.

73. Joyce, "Ibsen's New Drama," 371.

74. JJ to Henrik Ibsen, March 1901, *Letters I*, 52.

75. PL to HSW, 19 July 1935, PL Papers.

76. Ibid.

77. Ibid.

78. Ibsen's *When We Dead Awaken*, quoted in Joyce, "Ibsen's New Drama," 54.

79. Henrik Ibsen, *When We Dead Awaken*, in *The Oxford Ibsen* (Oxford: Oxford University Press, 1977), 8: 257.

80. Joyce, "Ibsen's New Drama," 66.

81. Ibid., 65.

82. *P*, 169.

83. Joyce, "Ibsen's New Drama," 65.

84. Ibid., 54.

85. Ibid.

86. Ibid., 57.

87. Ibsen, *When We Dead Awaken*, 8: 279.

88. Ibid., 8: 280.

89. JJ to HSW, 1 May 1935, *Letters I*, 365.

90. Ibsen, *When We Dead Awaken*, 8: 279.

91. HSW to PL, 5 April 1935, PL Papers.

92. Maria Jolas, quoted in Ellmann, 684.

93. PL to HSW, 19 July 1935, PL Papers.

94. Ibsen, *When We Dead Awaken*, 8: 297.

95. PL to HSW, 11 April 1935, PL Papers.

96. JJ to HSW, 1 May 1925, *Letters I*, 366.

12. ACTING ON HER FATHER'S BEHALF: Dublin and Bray 1935

1. Eileen Schaurek to JJ, 20 March 1935, PL Papers.
2. *U*, 1.181–82.
3. William Fitzpatrick, *Memories of Father Healy of Little Bray* (London: Macmillan, 1899), 28, 63–64.
4. Bozena Berta Delimata, autobiographical typescript, n.d., RE Papers.
5. Ibid.
6. Lucia Joyce, quoted in JJ to GJ, 10 April 1935, *Letters III*, 353.
7. Arthur Flynn, *History of Bray* (Dublin: The Mercier Press, 1986), 74.
8. JJ to CC, 15 May 1935, *Letters I*, 369.
9. Niall Rudd, *Pale Green, Light Orange: A Portrait of Bourgeois Ireland, 1930–1950* (Dublin: The Lilliput Press, 1994), 2.
10. Ibid., 28, 36.
11. Ibid.
12. Delimata, autobiographical typescript.
13. James Joyce, "Ibsen's New Drama," in *CW*, 66.
14. Rudd, *Pale Green, Light Orange*, 42.
15. Ibid., 50–57.
16. Bozena Berta Delimata, interview by Richard Ellmann, 27 June 1953, RE Papers.
17. Patrick Collins, quoted in Maddox, 310.
18. SG Papers.
19. JJ to LJ, 15 May 1935, *Letters I*, 369.
20. JJ to LJ, 27 April 1935, *Letters I*, 364.
21. JJ to LJ, 7 April 1935, *Letters III*, 353.
22. Ibid.
23. PL to HSW, 11 April 1935, PL Papers.
24. CC to PL, 7 May 1935, PL Papers.
25. "The Joyces," *New Yorker* (12 January 1935): 12–13.
26. Susanna Kaysen, *Girl, Interrupted* (New York: Random House, 1994), 153.
27. It was Stuart Gilbert's opinion, however, that Helen Fleischman got Lucia to end her engagement. Stuart Gilbert, Paris diary, 18 June 1932, SG Papers.
28. Giorgio's opinion can be inferred from Joyce's repeated reminders to his son to remember that "severe seclusion" was a "calamitous failure." See JJ to GJ, 16 July 1935, *Letters III*, 370; see also JJ to GJ, 14 August 1935, *Letters III*, 372.
29. JJ to GJ, 17 June 1935, *Letters I*, 371.
30. JJ to LJ, 27 April 1935, *Letters I*, 362.
31. Leo Tolstoy, "How Much Land Does a Man Need?" *Russian Stories and Legends* (New York: Pantheon Books, 1967), 48.
32. Ibid.
33. Ibid., 66.
34. Leo Tolstoy, "Masters and Servants," in *Russian Stories and Legends*, 192.
35. Ibid., 221.
36. PL to HSW, 19 July 1935, PL Papers.
37. Delimata interview.
38. Ibid.
39. JJ to GJ, n.d. (July 1935), *Letters I*, 375.

40. JJ to LJ, 15 May 1935, *Letters I*, 369.

41. JJ to LJ, 15 May 1935, *Letters III*, 356.

42. Delimata interview.

43. Joyce also suffered from the unanticipated effects of Veronal, which Léon's doctor "attributed chiefly to my abuse of somniferents. (I had even gone so far as to take 6 of these before going to bed to insure sleep). Then when going to Rouen I all of a sudden cut them out all together, which he said was a good intention with a bad effect, for the change around was altogether too sudden total abolition to which the system had become accustomed for nearly 12 months." See Ellmann's transcription of JJ to HSW, 18 January 1933, RE Papers.

44. K. M. Julien, "Sedative-Hypnotic Compounds: Drugs That Depress the Central Nervous System," in *A Primer of Drug Action* (San Francisco: W. H. Freeman, 1975), 41.

45. Ibid., 39.

46. Ibid., 40.

47. Ibid., 48.

48. JJ to CC, 10 August 1935, *Letters I*, 378.

49. Delimata interview.

50. Ibid.

51. Ibid.

52. Delimata, autobiographical typescript.

53. Isadora Duncan, *My Life* (London: Victor Gollancz, 1928), 215.

54. Delimata, autobiographical typescript.

55. Ibid.

56. Bozena Berta Delimata, "Reminiscences of a Joyce Niece," ed. Virginia Moseley, *JJQ* 19:1 (fall 1982): 55.

57. Delimata file, RE Papers.

58. Ibid.

59. JJ to LJ, n.d. (May 1935), *Letters I*, 367.

60. Raymond Duncan, *Exangelos: New–Paris–York* (Paris: Akademia Raymond Duncan, February 1932).

61. JJ to MH, ?15 June 1935, *Letters III*, 362.

62. JJ to MH, 28 June 1935, *Letters I*, 373.

63. *P*, 252.

64. JJ to LJ, 22 May 1935, *Letters I*, 368.

65. JJ to LJ, n.d. (August 1935), *Letters I*, 377.

66. Lucia Joyce, "Charlie et les gosses," *Le Disque vert* 3: 4–5 (1924): 677.

67. JJ to GJ, 10 July 1935, *Letters III*, 368.

68. *P*, 203.

69. Quoted in Maddox, 311.

70. JJ to GJ, n.d. (July 1935), *Letters I*, 275.

71. Delimata interview.

72. JJ to GJ, 16 July 1935, *Letters III*, 369.

73. Ellmann, 535.

74. Virginia Woolf, *Mrs. Dalloway* (New York: Harcourt Brace Jovanovich, 1925), 99–100.

75. JJ to GJ, 16 July 1935, *Letters III*, 369.

76. JJ to GJ, 13 August 1935, *Letters III*, 372.

77. PL to CC, 17 July 1935, PL Papers.

78. H. R. C. Rutherford, "Certificate about LJ's health," 19 May 1936, PL Papers.

79. H. R. C. Rutherford to CC, 13 May 1936, PL Papers.

80. PL to HSW, 19 July 1935, PL Papers.

81. "Latin me that, my trinity scholard" (*FW* 404.06).

82. JJ to GJ, 16 July 1935, *Letters III*, 370.

83. PL to HSW, 19 July 1935, PL Papers.

84. *U*, 10.875–77.

13. FALLING APART: England and Paris 1935–38

1. HSW to PL, 17 July 1935, PL Papers; and HSW to JJ, 2 September 1935, RE typescript of original letter, RE Papers.

2. JJ to LJ, n.d. (August 1935), *Letters I*, 377.

3. PL to HSW, 19 July 1935, PL Papers.

4. JJ to LJ, n.d. (July or August 1935), *Letters I*, 377–78.

5. JJ to CC, 31 July 1935, *Letters I*, 378.

6. JJ to CC, 10 August 1935, *Letters I*, 379.

7. Naum Efimowitsch Ischlondsky, *Physiologische Grundlagen [Neuropsyche und Hirnrinde] der Tiefen-Psychologie unter besonderer Berücksichtigung der Psychoanalyse: Ein Handbuch* (1930). Ischlondsky's other books include *Artificial Rejuvination [sic] and Voluntary Change of Sex according to Prof. Steinach* (1926); *Der bedingte Reflex und seine Bedeutung in der Biologie, Medizin, Psychologie und Pädagogik: Ein Handbuch der experimentellen Reflexologie* (1930); *Sécrétion interne et régénérescence* (1933); *Protoformotherapy in Treatment and Prevention: Fifteen Years of Research* (London: Henry Kimpton, 1937); and *Brain and Behavior: Induction as a Fundamental Mechanism of Neuropsychic Activity: An Experimental and Clinical Study* (1949).

8. See Ischlondsky, *Protoformotherapy*.

9. Charles Edouard Brown-Sequard (1817–94) was elected to the Royal Society of London in 1860 and to the American Academy of Arts and Sciences in 1867. In 1878 he became professor of medicine at the Collège de France, a position that followed many other appointments in both England and the United States. In 1881 Cambridge gave him an honorary L.L.D., and he later received the Baly Medal of the Royal College of Physicians of London. See Victor Cornelius Medvei, *A History of Endocrinology* (Lancaster: MTP Press, 1982), 291.

10. Ibid., 289.

11. Merrily Borell, quoted in Medvei, *History of Endocrinology*, 290.

12. A term coined by the English physiologist Edward Sharpey-Schafer, the endocrinologist who helped to discover the properties of adrenaline and insulin.

13. Medvei, *History of Endocrinology*, 303.

14. Joyce owned these books. They can be found in the PL Papers.

15. Medvei, *History of Endocrinology*, 391.

16. Ibid.

17. Ibid., 418–19.

18. William Sargant and Eliot Slater, *An Introduction to Physical Methods of Treatment in Psychiatry* (Baltimore: Williams and Wilkins, 1944), 3.

19. Ibid., 1.

20. JJ to LJ, n.d. (July 1935), *Letters I*, 377.

21. Ischlondsky, *Protoformotherapy*, 75.

22. Ibid., 78.

23. HSW to PL, 8 March 1935, PL Papers.

24. JJ to LJ, 15 September 1935, *Letters I*, 382.

25. Lidderdale, 351.

26. Ibid.

27. JJ to LJ, 14 September 1935, *Letters I*, 382.

28. HSW to PL, 29 October 1935, PL Papers.

29. HSW to JJ, 5 December 1935, PL Papers.

30. Lidderdale, 353.

31. HSW to JJ, 16 October 1935, PL Papers.

32. JJ to LJ, 17 October 1935, *Letters III*, 377.

33. Lidderdale, 354.

34. Tina Bennett, communication to author, October 2000.

35. JJ to HSW, 11 October 1935, *Letters I*, 385.

36. Hermione Lee, *Virginia Woolf* (New York: Alfred A. Knopf, 1997), 195.

37. JJ to HSW, 7 April 1935, *Letters I*, 362.

38. HSW to PL, 29 January 1936, PL Papers.

39. JJ to LJ, 9 December 1935, quoted in Lidderdale, 355.

40. PL to HSW, 5 February 1936, PL Papers.

41. HSW to PL, 29 January 1936, PL Papers.

42. W. G. Macdonald to HSW, 7 February 1936, RE Papers.

43. Maria Jolas, interview by Richard Ellmann, 22 July 1953, RE Papers.

44. JJ to LJ, 23 October 1935, *Letters III*, 378.

45. Jolas interview.

46. HSW to PL, 22 March 1936, in *The James Joyce–Paul Léon Papers in the National Library of Ireland: A Catalogue*, comp. Catherine Fahy (Dublin: National Library of Ireland, 1992), 61.

47. JJ to HSW, 9 June 1936, RE Papers.

48. Lucia Joyce file, RE Papers.

49. PL to HSW, 8 May 1936, RE Papers.

50. PL to HSW, 22 May 1936, RE Papers.

51. Cyclothymia was a term coined by Dr. Karl Kahlbaum (1828–99), who taught at the University of Königsberg and later worked at a private asylum in Görlitz, in East Prussia. He was following the medical model suggested by the new understanding of syphilis and tuberculosis as diseases caused by infection. Emil Kraepelin, the great classifier of psychiatry, knew of Kahlbaum's work and incorporated some of it into his nosology. See Peter Ostwald, *Vaslav Nijinsky: A Leap into Madness* (New York: Carol Publishing Group, 1991), 206.

52. JJ to HSW, 9 June 1936, RE Papers.

53. PL to HSW, 22 August 1936, RE Papers.

54. Eileen Schaurek, notes in Eileen Schaurek file, RE Papers.

55. PL to HSW, 8 May 1936, RE Papers.

56. PL Papers.

57. JJ to CG-W, 15 October 1937, RE Papers.

58. Helen Kastor Joyce, "A Portrait of the Artist by His Daughter-in-Law," unpublished typescript, HRC.

59. *U*, 3.13–15.

60. George Belmont, interview by Brenda Maddox, 22 October 1984, in Maddox, 32.

61. Knowlson, 544, 429–33.

62. JJ to Adolph Kastor, 30 August 1937, *Letters III*, 405.

63. JJ to Wilhelm Herz, 30 August 1937, *Letters III*, 406.

64. Peter F. Ostwald, *Vaslav Nijinsky*, 202.

65. Ibid., 296.

66. Ibid., 309.

67. Dr. Hans W. Maier, "Evaluation of Helen Fleischman Joyce," Maria Jolas Papers, Beinecke.

68. Adolph Kastor to HKJ, 7 April 1939, Maria Jolas Papers, Beinecke.

69. Hans W. Maier, "L'Etate physique; l'Etate psychique; Prognotique," Maria Jolas Papers, Beinecke.

70. It is important to keep this actual medical judgment in mind when reading Joyce's 1940 letters that state that Helen was interned with a "provisional certificate of lunacy" and that "the damage done cannot be remedied." See JJ to CC, 11 February 1940, *Letters III*, 465; and JJ to Mrs. Victor Sax, 23 April 1940, *Letters III*, 477. Maier's diagnosis lets us see the subjective, amateur psychologizing that was later taken as fact. It is also important that Helen had not been considered too sick to help Joyce correct page proofs of *Finnegans Wake* in 1938 and 1939, too sick to accompany Giorgio in quest of new singing venues, or too sick for Joyce and Nora to consider accepting her offer of asylum in the farmhouse in Beynes when invading Nazi troops made Paris unsafe in the spring of 1940. See JJ to PL, 24 September 1939, PL Papers.

71. Maria Jolas interview.

72. RE to MJ, 16 December 1954, RE Papers.

73. Peggy Guggenheim, *Out of This Century: Confessions of an Art Addict* (New York: The Dial Press, 1946), 196.

74. Ibid., 242.

75. Jacqueline Weld, *Peggy: The Wayward Guggenheim* (New York: E. P. Dutton, 1986), 191.

76. JJ to HKJ, 6 April 1938, *Letters III*, 419.

77. Nino Frank, interview by Richard Ellmann, 20 August 1953, RE Papers.

78. Dr. Thérèse Bertrand-Fontaine, interview by Richard Ellmann, n.d., RE Papers.

79. Helen Kastor Joyce, "Anniversary, February 2, 1939," unpublished typescript, RE Papers.

80. Guggenheim, *Out of This Century*, 240.

81. Helen Kastor Joyce, files in the Maria Jolas Papers, Beinecke.

82. In the first edition of *Out of This Century*, Guggenheim changed Beckett's name to Oblomov, Giorgio's name to Anthony, and referred to Helen in this section simply as Anthony's wife. In other parts of the book, Helen is referred to by her real name.

83. Ibid., 240.

84. Ibid.

85. JJ to Jacques Mercanton, 9 January 1940, *SL*, 402.

86. Maria Jolas Papers, Beinecke.

87. Ellmann, 728.
88. Guggenheim, *Out of This Century*, 240.
89. Ibid., 243.

14. FACING DANGER: Occupied France 1939–45

1. JJ to PL, 19 February 1938, PL Papers.
2. JJ to Daniel Brody, 5 October 1938, *Letters III*, 432.
3. C. G. Jung, 1953, in Ellmann, 691.
4. By February 1940 Joyce thought that the ending of the *Wake* not only characterized Lucia but prophesied Helen Joyce's nervous breakdown. He remembered that Helen had read the closing passage to the guests assembled at his 2 February birthday party in 1939, and then remarked, "Alas if you ever read them you will see that they were unconsciously prophetical!" JJ to CC, 11 February 1940, *Letters I*, 408.
5. JJ to PL, 23 August 1939, PL Papers.
6. JJ to GJ, 5 September 1939, in Ellmann, 727.
7. JJ to SG, 6 September 1939, *Letters I*, 407.
8. Lucia Joyce, "My Life," unpublished typescript, HRC.
9. JJ to PL, 11, 24, 25 September 1939, PL Papers.
10. JJ to PL, 28 September 1939, PL Papers.
11. JJ to PL, 5 October 1939, PL Papers.
12. PL to HSW, 11 October 1939, RE Papers.
13. PL to JJ, 6 October 1939, PL Papers.
14. PL to JJ, 19 November 1939, PL Papers.
15. Ellmann, 732.
16. JJ to Nino Frank, 18 April 1940, *Letters III*, 476.
17. JJ to HSW, 22 March 1940, *Letters I*, 411.
18. JJ to Mrs. Victor Sax, 20 April 1940, *Letters III*, 477.
19. JJ to HSW, 18 June 1940, *Letters I*, 413.
20. Ian Ousby, *Occupation: The Ordeal of France, 1940–1944* (New York: St. Martin's Press, 1998), 43.
21. Ibid., 45.
22. Ibid., 102–3.
23. JJ to Nino Frank, 5 August 1940 and 9 April 1940, *Letters III*, 480 and 474.
24. Ellmann, 731.
25. Henry Friedlander, *The Origins of Nazi Genocide: From Euthanasia to the Final Solution* (Chapel Hill: University of North Carolina Press, 1995), 17.
26. Ibid., 15.
27. Ibid.
28. Ibid., 16.
29. Ibid., 17.
30. Ibid., 26.
31. Ibid.
32. Ibid., 67.
33. There were initially four euthanasia institutions. During January 1940, one was opened at Grafeneck; Brandenburg was opened in February, Hartheim in May, and Sonnenstein in June. In the first half of the year, 8,765 persons were gassed in

these institutions, three-quarters of them in May and June, a time when world attention was focused on the Wehrmacht's invasion of France. By the end of 1940 a total of 26,459 patients had been killed, and in the first eight months of 1941 an additional 35,049 were "disinfected." These figures are given by the accounting section of T4's head office. See *Encyclopedia of the Holocaust*, ed. Robert Rozett and Schmuel Spector (New York: Facts on File, 2000), 452.

34. Friedlander, *Origins of Nazi Genocide*, 67, 68, 73, 85.

35. Rozette and Spector, eds., *Encyclopedia of the Holocaust*, 453.

36. Ibid.

37. Ousby, *Occupation*, 69.

38. JJ to Jacques Mercanton, 14 September 1940, *Letters III*, 485.

39. JJ to Bennett Cerf, 5 August 1940, *Letters I*, 415.

40. Leigh W. Hunt to JJ, 24 September 1940, Maria Jolas Papers, Beinecke.

41. JJ to CG-W, 28 July 1940, *Letters III*, 414.

42. JJ to Paul Ruggiero, 4 August 1940, *Letters III*, 414.

43. JJ to CG-W, 14 September 1940, *Letters III*, 486.

44. JJ to Jacques Mercanton, 13 August 1940, *Letters III*, 482.

45. Lucia Joyce, "My Life."

46. JJ to Jacques Mercanton, 14 September 1940, *Letters III*, 486.

47. Ibid.

48. JJ to Gustav Zumsteg, 16 September 1940, *Letters III*, 487.

49. JJ to CG-W, 18 September 1940, *Letters III*, 488.

50. JJ to Jacques Mercanton, 29 October 1940, *Letters III*, 491.

51. JJ to Gustav Zumsteg, 31 October 1940, *Letters III*, 494.

52. Ellmann, 736–37.

53. JJ to CG-W, 20 November 1940, *Letters III*, 499.

54. JJ to Gustav Zumsteg, 22 November 1940, *Letters III*, 500.

55. Gustav Zumsteg to JJ, 13 December 1940, Maria Jolas Papers, Beinecke.

56. Ibid.

57. Ellmann, 738.

58. Sean Murphy to JJ, 26 November 1940, Maria Jolas Papers, Beinecke.

59. Sean Murphy to Sean Lester, 2 December 1940, Maria Jolas Papers, Beinecke.

60. JJ to CG-W, 28 November 1940, *Letters III*, 503.

61. Giorgio Joyce, interview by Richard Ellmann, 9 August 1953, Zurich, RE Papers.

62. JJ to Edmond Jaloux, 17 December 1940, *Letters I*, 506.

63. Sean Lester to JJ, 28 December 1940, Maria Jolas Papers, Beinecke.

64. Ellmann, 740.

65. GJ to MJ, 17 February 1941, Maria Jolas Papers, Beinecke.

66. Lidderdale, 379.

67. LJ to Bozena Berta Delimata, 7 May 1973, HRC.

68. Nino Frank, interview by Richard Ellmann, 20 August 1953, RE Papers.

69. Maddox, 367.

70. MJ to HSW, 5 January 1949, HSW Papers.

71. Ibid.

72. High Court of Justice, Chancery Division, Document 1942J no. 456.

15. KILLING TIME: Northampton 1951–82

1. Maddox, 371.
2. Hélène Vanel, "Souvenirs de Lucia Joyce," in *James Joyce*, ed. Jacques Aubert and Fritz Senn (Paris: Editions de l'Herne, 1985), 84.
3. James Joyce and Paul Léon, "Anamnese von Fräulein Lucia Joyce," RE Papers.
4. Brenda Maddox, "Epilogue," unpublished manuscript, private possession.
5. RE to MJ, 28 September 1959, Maria Jolas Papers, Beinecke.
6. MJ to RE, 22 October 1961, RE Papers.
7. Lucia Joyce, "My Life," unpublished typescript, HRC.
8. Jane Lidderdale, quoted in Maddox, "Epilogue."
9. Dominique Maroger to RE, RE Papers.
10. Dominique Maroger, "Dernière rencontre avec Lucia," in Aubert and Senn, eds., *James Joyce*, 81.
11. Ibid., 80, 78; my translation.
12. Ibid., 81.
13. Ibid., 78.
14. Ibid., 80.
15. Virginia Woolf, *Three Guineas* (New York: Harcourt Brace Jovanovich, 1966), 7.
16. Maroger, "Dernière rencontre avec Lucia," 82.
17. Ibid.
18. Ibid.
19. Ibid.

16. A FATHER'S SCRUTINY, LOVE, AND ATONEMENT: The Land of Imagination

1. Kay Boyle to JL, 15 January 1983, RE Papers.
2. Eileen Schaurek file, RE Papers.
3. JJ to HSW, 23 November 1925, *Letters III*, 134.
4. David Hayman, ed., *A First-Draft Version of "Finnegans Wake"* (Austin: University of Texas Press, 1963), 321.
5. JJ to HSW, May 1935, *Letters I*, 367.
6. Louis Gillet, "The Living Joyce," in *Portraits of the Artist in Exile: Recollections of James Joyce by Europeans*, ed. Willard Potts (Seattle: University of Washington Press, 1979), 192.
7. Jacques Mercanton, "The Hours of James Joyce," in Potts, ed., *Portraits of the Artist in Exile*, 114.
8. What follows is not intended to be exhaustive. One could make the case that Lucia's biography to the age of thirty-one is refracted in *Finnegans Wake*. Here I want to use only a few selected examples to demonstrate the transpositions of life into art.
9. Havelock Ellis, *The Dance of Life* (Boston: Houghton Mifflin, 1923), xi.
10. JJ to LJ, 1 June 1934, *Letters I*, 341; and Ellmann, 703.
11. Mercanton, "Hours of James Joyce," 227.
12. Hayman, *First-Draft Version*, 304–6.
13. JJ to HSW, 19 October 1929, *Letters I*, 285.
14. Hanley Collection, University of Texas at Austin. David Hayman mistakenly reads Joyce's handwriting as "19.V. 1929." See Hayman, *First-Draft Version*, 299.

15. JJ to Frank Budgen, 11 June 1919, *SL*, 238–39.

16. *FW* III, ii (429–73), Draft 9 dated by printer 21.4.28, transition 13 proofs, Hayman, *First-Draft Version*, 321.

17. Hayman, *First-Draft Version*, 304.

18. Ibid., 150.

19. Ibid., 309.

20. Ibid., 153.

21. Ibid.

22. Ibid., 154.

23. Ibid., 158.

24. If this passage describes an actual state of affairs, where the young men in the Joyce circle gravitated toward women with money, it would explain Lucia's desire in 1932 to have a "dot" or marriage portion.

25. Hayman, *First-Draft Version*, 308–9.

26. JJ to PL, 16 January 1935, PL Papers.

27. Hazel is not far from this scene of madness. She appears in *FW* 250.22 as "a fork of hazel o'er the field."

28. Hayman, *First-Draft Version*, 144.

29. Roland McHugh, *Annotations to "Finnegans Wake,"* rev. ed. (Baltimore: The Johns Hopkins University Press, 1991), 250.

30. JJ to HSW, 22 November 1930, *Letters I*, 295.

31. Maria Jolas, interview by Richard Ellmann, 22 July 1953, RE Papers.

32. Giorgio Joyce, interview by Richard Ellmann, 9 August 1953, RE Papers.

33. Helen Kastor Joyce, "A Portrait of the Artist by His Daughter-in-Law," unpublished typescript, HRC.

34. Bozena Berta Delimata, interview by Richard Ellmann, 27 June 1953, RE Papers.

35. MJ to RE, 20 January 1959, RE Papers.

36. MJ to RE, 26 January 1959, "Notes re page 857 of [his] JJ biography," RE Papers.

37. Henrik Ibsen, *When We Dead Awaken*, in *The Oxford Ibsen* (Oxford: Oxford University Press, 1977), 8: 280.

38. Ibid., 8: 54.

39. John Bishop, *Joyce's Book of the Dark: "Finnegans Wake"* (Madison: University of Wisconsin Press, 1986), 242.

40. Ibsen, *When We Dead Awaken*, 8: 55.

41. Luce Irigaray, *Elemental Passions*, trans. Joanne Collie and Judith Still (New York: Routledge, 1992), 36.

42. Michel Foucault, *Discipline and Punish: The Birth of the Prison*, trans. Alan Sheridan (New York: Vintage Books, 1979) cited in Louis A. Sass, *Madness and Modernism: Insanity in the Light of Modern Art, Literature, and Thought* (New York: Basic Books, 1992), 251.

43. Ibid.

44. Ibid.

45. Ibid., 253.

46. Nino Frank, interview by Richard Ellmann, 20 August 1953, RE Papers; and Ellmann, 755.

47. For more detailed speculations about Joyce's transpositions of Lucia's experience into notebooks and then into the text of the *Wake*, see David Hayman, "I Think Her Pretty: Reflections of the Familiar in Joyce's Notebook VI.B.5," *Joyce Studies*

Annual (Austin: University of Texas Press, 1990), 43–60. See also David Hayman, *The "Wake" in Transit* (Ithaca, N.Y.: Cornell University Press, 1990).

48. Cary F. Baynes, "Notes on Lucia Joyce in Zurich, 1934," included in letter from Ximena de Angulo Roelli to RE, 27 July 1981, RE Papers.

49. HSW to JJ, 18 March 1935, RE Papers.

50. Stuart Gilbert, "Introduction," *Letters I*, 33.

51. Stuart Gilbert, Paris diary, 20 July 1932, HRC.

52. LJ to JJ, 10 July 1936, RE Papers; and Ellmann, 676.

53. James Joyce and Paul Léon, "Anamnese von Fräulein Lucia Joyce," RE Papers.

54. JJ to MH, 15 June 1935, *Letters III*, 362.

55. McHugh, *Annotations to "Finnegans Wake,"* 621.

56. Ibid., 622.

57. The sentiment in this section of the *Wake* seems to echo Gerard Manley Hopkins's poem that begins, "Margaret, are you grieving / Over Goldengrove unleaving," a poem about a child's reluctance to leave innocence behind to enter into the "fallen" world of adult sexuality.

58. JJ to CC, 10 August 1935, *Letters I*, 379.

59. Clive Hart, *Structure and Motif in "Finnegans Wake"* (Evanston, Ill.: Northwestern University Press, 1962); and Kimberly Devlin, *Wandering and Return in "Finnegans Wake"* (Princeton, N.J.: Princeton University Press, 1991).

60. Helen Kastor Joyce, "Anniversary, February 2, 1939," photostat of unpublished typescript, RE Papers.

61. Simone Weil, *Waiting for God*, cited in Elaine Scarry, *On Beauty and Being Just* (Princeton, N.J.: Princeton University Press, 1999), 8.

EPILOGUE: A Daughter's Legacy

1. Bonnie Kime Scott, conversation with the author, International James Joyce Symposium, Goldsmith College, London, 2000.

2. Lucia Joyce, "The Real Life of James Joyce," unpublished manuscript, HRC.

3. Probate Certificate no. 331 and Will of Lucia Anna Joyce, Family Division of High Court of Justice, Somerset House, London.

4. Here is a partial list of the fictional accounts of Lucia's life:

> Beckett, Samuel. *Dream of Fair to Middling Women*. London: Calder Publications, 1993.
>
> Gold, Alison Leslie. *The Clairvoyant: The Imagined Life of Lucia Joyce*. New York: Hyperion Books, 1992.
>
> Hall, Frances Benn. "Lucia." In *Ezra's Noh for Willie and Other Plays*. Lenox, Mass.: Mountain Press, 1996.
>
> Houser, Aimee. "Lucia's Commitment: A Poem Based on Brenda Maddox's *Nora*." *James Joyce Literary Supplement* (spring 1997).
>
> Kaufman, Lynne. *Speaking in Tongues*. A play, performed April–May 1991 at the North Coast Repertory Theatre, San Diego, Calif.
>
> Lombardi, Chris. *blue: season*. Unpublished novel. See also "Notes from a *blue: season*." Talk given at the 1993 California Joyce Conference, University of California, Irvine.
>
> Mabou Mines. *Cara Lucia*. Weaving sound, music, imaginary and original writing with documentary materials. New York, N.Y.

Murphy, Caitlin. *An Imagined Dialogue between Lucia Joyce and Suzanne Deschevaux-Dumesnil*. Undergraduate diss., University of Toronto.

Nigro, Don. *Lucia Mad*. A play, performed October 2000 at the Eastport Arts Center, Eastport, Me.

Oates, Joyce Carol. "Daisy." In *Major American Short Stories*. Edited by A. Walton Litz. New York: Oxford University Press, 1980.

Pig Iron Theatre Company. *James Joyce Is Dead and Paris Is Burning: A Lucia Joyce Cabaret*. Performed April 2003 at Christ Church, Philadelphia.

Weiss, Hedy. *dreaming lucia*. A play, performed April 1995 at the Athenaeum Theatre, Chicago, Ill.

The works of three generations of Joyce scholars are listed in the Bibliography.

5. Jean Erdman, quoted in Joseph Campbell, *The Hero's Journey: Joseph Campbell on His Life and Work*, ed. Phil Cousineau (Boston: Element, 1999).

6. Joseph Campbell and Morton Robinson, *A Skeleton Key to "Finnegans Wake"* (New York: The Viking Press, 1972).

7. Walter Sorell, "Coach to Spoleto: Jean Erdman Discusses Her Variation on James Joyce's *Finnegans Wake*," *Dance Magazine* (May 1963): 35.

8. Jean Erdman, "A Viewer's Guide to *The Coach with the Six Insides*," Dance Archives, NYLPA.

9. Sorell, "Coach to Spoleto," 63.

10. Walter Sorell, ed., *The Dance Has Many Faces* (New York: Columbia University Press, 1966), 212.

11. Ibid., 199.

12. Ibid., 200.

13. Ibid., 204.

14. Campbell, *Hero's Journey*, 94.

BIBLIOGRAPHY

Abbott, Berenice. *Photographs*. Washington, D.C.: Smithsonian Institution Press, 1990.

Achille-Delmas, François. *La Pratique psychiatrique*. Paris: Ballere, 1919.

———. *La Personnalité humaine, son analyse*. Paris: Flammarion, 1922.

———. *Psychologie pathologique du suicide*. Paris: Librairie Félix Alcan, 1932.

———. "Le Traitement individuel des psychopathies dans les maisons de santés." In *Voir congres international des sanatoria et maisons de santés privées*. Paris, 1937.

Amouroux, Henri. *Le Peuple du désastre: 1939–1940*. Vol. 1 of *La grande histoire des Français sous l'occupation*. Paris: Editions Robert Laffont, 1999.

Antheil, George. *Bad Boy of Music*. Garden City, N.Y.: Covici Friede, 1930.

———. "James Joyce." In *James Joyce: Interviews and Recollections*. Edited by E. H. Mikhail. New York: St. Martin's Press, 1990.

Anthony, Maggy. *The Valkyries: The Women Around Jung*. Longmead, England: Element Books, 1990.

Arieti, Silvestro. *Interpretation of Schizophrenia*. New York: Basic Books, 1974.

Arnold, Christian. *Der Psychiater Hans Wolfgang Maier*. Zurich: Juris Druck und Verlag Dietiko, 1992.

Artaud, Antonin. *Selected Writings*. Edited by Susan Sontag. New York: Farrar, Straus and Giroux, 1976.

Aubert, Jacques. *Joyce avec Lacan*. Paris: Navarin Editeur, 1987.

Aubert, Jacques, and Fritz Senn, eds. *James Joyce*. Paris: Editions de l'Herne, 1985.

Bair, Deirdre. *Samuel Beckett*. New York: Harcourt Brace Jovanovich, 1978.

Ball, Hugo. *Die Flucht aus der Zeit*. Munich: Duncker und Humblot, 1927.

———. *Damals in Zurich: Briefe aus den Jahren 1915–17*. Zurich: Verlag der Arche, 1978.

Bancroft, Mary. "Jung and His Circle." *Psychological Perspectives* 6 (1975): 114–27.

Banes, Sally. "An Introduction to the 'Ballets Suédois.'" *Ballet Review* 7:2–3 (1978–79): 28–59.

————. *Writing Dancing in the Age of Postmodernism*. Middletown, Conn.: Wesleyan University Press, 1994.

Banta, Melissa, and Oscar A. Silverman, eds. *James Joyce's Letters to Sylvia Beach, 1921–1940*. Bloomington: Indiana University Press, 1987.

Barber, Theodore. "Four Interpretations of Mevlevi Dervish Dance, 1920–1929." *Dance Chronicle* 9: 3 (1986): 328–35.

Barnes, Djuna. "James Joyce." *Vanity Fair* 18 (April 1922).

Barthes, Roland. *Image, Music, Text*. New York: Hill and Wang, 1977.

Baudot, Francois. *Elsa Schiaparelli*. London: Thames and Hudson, 1997.

Baudouin, Charles. "From Charles Baudouin's Journal: 1934." In *C. G. Jung Speaking: Interviews and Encounters*. Edited by William McGuire and R. F. C. Hull. Princeton, N.J.: Princeton University Press, 1977.

Bauerle, Ruth, ed. *The James Joyce Songbook*. New York: Garland, 1981.

Baynes, Cary F. Translator's Preface to *The Secret of the Golden Flower: A Chinese Book of Life*. New York: Harcourt, Brace, 1932.

————. "Notes on Lucia Joyce in Zurich, 1934." Richard Ellmann Papers, Special Collection, McFarlin Library, University of Tulsa, Oklahoma.

————. Translator's Preface to *The I Ching, or Book of Changes*. Translated by Cary F. Baynes. New York: Pantheon Books, 1955.

Baynes, H. G. *Mythology of the Soul: A Research into the Unconscious from Schizophrenic Dreams and Drawings*. London: Rider, 1939.

Beach, Sylvia. *Ulysses in Paris*. New York: Harcourt Brace, 1956.

————. *Shakespeare and Company*. New York: Harcourt Brace, 1959.

Beaumont, Cyril W. *The History of Harlequin*. New York: B. Blom, 1967.

Beckett, Samuel. *Dream of Fair to Middling Women*. London: Calder Publications, 1993.

————. "Letters to Thomas MacGreevy." Rare Books and Manuscripts, Trinity College, Dublin.

Beckett, Samuel, et al. *Our Exagmination Round His Factification for Incamination of "Work in Progress."* London: Faber and Faber, 1972.

Beja, Morris. *James Joyce: A Literary Life*. Basingstoke, England: Macmillan, 1992.

Benco, Silvio. "James Joyce in Trieste." In *Portraits of the Artist in Exile: Recollections of James Joyce by Europeans*. Edited by Willard Potts. Seattle: University of Washington Press, 1979.

Benstock, Shari. "The Genuine Christine: Psychodynamics of Issy." In *Women in Joyce*. Edited by Suzette Henke and Elaine Unkeless. Urbana: University of Illinois Press, 1982.

————. *Textualizing the Feminine: On the Limits of Genre*. Norman: University of Oklahoma Press, 1991.

Berger, Hélène. "Portrait de sa femme par l'artiste." *Lettres nouvelles* (March–April 1966): 44–67.

Berman, Louis. *The Glands Regulating Personality*. New York: Macmillan, 1922.

Bersot, H. *Statistique des examens du personnel des asiles suisses d'aliénés de 1927 à 1932*. Bern: Editions Hans Huber, 1933.

Bidou, Henri. "Les Danseuses de Saint-Paul." *Temps*, 21 October 1931.

Bidwell, Bruce, and Linda Heffer. *The Joycean Way: A Topographical Guide to "Dubliners" and "A Portrait of the Artist as a Young Man."* Baltimore: The Johns Hopkins University Press, 1981.

Bishop, John. *Joyce's Book of the Dark: "Finnegans Wake."* Madison: University of Wisconsin Press, 1986.

Bishop, Paul. *The Dionysian Self: Carl Gustav Jung's Reception of Friedrich Nietzsche.* Berlin: Walter de Gruyter, 1995.

Bjørnson, Bjørnstjerne. *The Fisher Lassie.* New York: Macmillan, 1891.

Black, Donald W., and Todd J. Boffeli. "Simple Schizophrenia: Past, Present and Future." *American Journal of Psychiatry* 146:10 (October 1989): 1267–73.

Bleuler, Eugen. *Textbook of Psychiatry.* Translated by A. A. Brill. New York: Macmillan, 1924.

———. *Dementia Praecox or the Group of Schizophrenias.* Translated by J. Zinkin. New York: International Universities Press, 1950.

———. *Autistic Undisciplined Thinking in Medicine and How to Overcome It.* Translated by Ernest Harms. Darien, Conn.: Hafner Publications, 1970.

Bleuler, Manfred, ed. *Beiträge zur Schizophrenielehre der Zürcher Psychiatrischen Universitätsklinik Burghölzli, 1902–1971.* Darmstadt: Wissenschaftliche Buchgesellschaft, 1979.

———. "On Schizophrenic Psychoses." *American Journal of Psychiatry* 136:11 (November 1979): 1403–09.

Blondel, Eric. *Nietzsche, the Body and Culture.* Translated by Sean Hand. Stanford: Stanford University Press, 1991.

Bochner, Jay. *Blaise Cendrars: Discovery and Re-creation.* Toronto: University of Toronto Press, 1978.

Boose, Linda, and Betty S. Flowers, eds. *Daughters and Fathers.* Baltimore: The Johns Hopkins University Press, 1989.

Borach, Georges. "Conversations with Joyce." Translated by Joseph Prescott. *College English* 15 (March 1954): 3227.

Bowen, Zack. *Padraic Colum: A Biographical-Critical Introduction.* Carbondale: Southern Illinois Press, 1970.

Boyle, Kay. Letters to Richard Ellmann. Richard Ellmann Papers, Special Collections, McFarlin Library, University of Tulsa, Oklahoma.

———. *Life Being the Best and Other Stories.* New York: New Directions, 1930.

———. *My Next Bride.* New York: Viking, 1986.

Brender, Richard. "Reinventing Africa in Their Own Image: The Ballets Suédois' 'Ballet nègre,' *La Création du monde.*" *Dance Chronicle* 9:1 (1986): 119–47.

Breton, André. *Manifestos of Surrealism.* Translated by Richard Seaver and Helen R. Lane. Ann Arbor: University of Michigan Press, 1969.

———. "What Is Surrealism?" *Selected Writings.* Translated by John Ashbery. New York: Monad Press for Anchor Foundation, 1978.

Brockman, William S. "'Give us back them papers': Possession, Control and Availability of Joyce's Manuscripts and Letters." Paper presented at the International James Joyce Symposium, Zurich, 1996.

Brown, John. *Valery Larbaud.* Boston: Twayne, 1981.

Bryher. *The Heart of Artemis: A Writer's Memoirs.* London: Collins, 1963.

Budgen, Frank. *Further Recollections of James Joyce.* London: The Shenval Press, 1955.

———. *James Joyce and the Making of "Ulysses."* Bloomington: University of Indiana Press, 1960.

———. *Myselves When Young.* New York: Oxford University Press, 1970.

Burrin, Philippe. *France under the Germans: Collaboration and Compromise*. Translated by Janet Lloyd. New York: The New Press, 1993.

Busfield, Joan. *Managing Madness: Changing Ideas and Practice*. London: Hutchinson, 1986.

Cahiers rythme et couleur: prose, poèmes, croquis, annales, photographies, 2 and 3 (November 1925 and May 1926).

Calder, Alexander. Alexander Calder Papers. Archives of American Art, Smithsonian Institution, Washington, D.C.

———. *Calder: An Autobiography with Pictures*. New York: Pantheon Books, 1966.

Campbell, Joseph. *An Open Life: Joseph Campbell in Conversation with Michael Toms*. Edited by John M. Maher and Dennie Briggs. Burdett, N.Y.: Larson Publications, 1988.

———. *The Hero's Journey: Joseph Campbell on His Life and Work*. Edited by Phil Cousineau. Boston: Element, 1999.

Campbell, Joseph, and Morton Robinson. *A Skeleton Key to "Finnegans Wake."* New York: The Viking Press, 1972.

Campbell, Sandra. "Mrs. Joyce of Zurich." *Harper's Bazaar*, October 1952.

Card, James. *Seductive Cinema: The Art of Silent Film*. New York: Alfred A. Knopf, 1994.

Castel, Robert. *The Regulation of Madness: The Origins of Incarceration in France*. Translated by W. D. Hall. Berkeley: University of California Press, 1998.

Cendrars, Blaise. "Homage à Jean Borlin." In Rolf De Mare, *Les Ballets suédois dans l'art contemporain*. Paris: Editions du Trianon, 1931.

Chenieux-Gendron, Jacqueline. *Surrealism*. Translated by Vivian Folkenflik. New York: Columbia University Press, 1990.

Chisholm, Anne. *Nancy Cunard*. New York: Alfred A. Knopf, 1979.

Cixous, Hélène. *The Exile of James Joyce*. Translated by. S. A. J. Purcell. New York: David Lewis, 1972.

Claudel, Paul. "Les Ballets suédois." *Archives internationales de la danse* 1 (1933): 102–8.

———. *Claudel on the Theatre*. Edited by Jacques Petit and Jean-Pierre Kempf. Translated by Christine Trollope. Coral Gables, Fla.: University of Miami Press, 1972.

Codet, Henri. *Psychiatrie*. Paris: Librairie Octave Doin, 1926.

Coleman, Emily. *The Shutter of Snow*. New York: Virago Press, 1981. Originally published in 1930.

Colum, Mary. *Life and the Dream*. Garden City, N.Y.: Doubleday, 1947.

Colum, Mary, and Padraic Colum. *Our Friend James Joyce*. Garden City, N.Y.: Doubleday, 1958.

Connolly, Thomas, ed. *The Personal Library of James Joyce*. Buffalo, N.Y.: University of Buffalo Monographs in English 6, 1955.

———. *James Joyce's "Scribbledehobble."* Evanston, Ill.: Northwestern University Press, 1961.

Copeland, Roger, and Marshall Cohen, eds. *What Is Dance?* New York: Oxford University Press, 1983.

Copley, Antony. *Sexual Moralities in France, 1780–1980*. New York: Routledge, 1989.

Costello, Peter. *James Joyce*. Dublin: Gill and Macmillan, 1980.

Costigan, Giovanni. *A History of Modern Ireland*. New York: Pegasus, 1969.

Craig, Gordon. *Gordon Craig on Movement and Dance*. Edited by Arnold Rood. New York: Dance Horizons, 1977.

Crise, Stelio.—*And Trieste Ah Trieste*. Milan: All'Insegna del Pesce d'Oro, 1971.

Cronin, Anthony. "Letter: Beckett and Joyces Remained Friends." *Observer*, 8 September 1996, 2.

Crosby, Caresse. "At a Party with James Joyce." In *The Passionate Years*. New York: Dial Press, 1953.

Crosby, Harry. *Shadows of the Sun: The Diaries of Harry Crosby*. Edited by Edward Germain. Santa Barbara, Calif.: Black Sparrow Press, 1977.

Cunard, Nancy. "On James Joyce—For Professor Ellmann." In *Joyce at Texas*. Edited by Dave Oliphant and Thomas Zigal. Austin, Tex.: Harry Ransom Humanities Research Center, 1983.

Curran, Constantine P. *James Joyce Remembered*. London: Oxford University Press, 1968.

Curtayne, Alice. "Portrait of the Artist as Brother: Interview with James Joyce's Sister." *Critic* 21 (1963): 43–47.

Daniels, Fred. *Margaret Morris Dancing: A Book of Pictures by Fred Daniels, with an Introduction and Outline of Her Methods by Margaret Morris*. London: Kegan Paul, Trench and Trubner, 1928.

Dante Alighieri. *The New Life (La Vita Nuova)*. Translated by Dante Gabriel Rossetti. New York: The National Alumni, 1907.

Davies, Stan Gebler. *James Joyce: A Portrait of the Artist*. New York: Stein and Day, 1975.

Dawson, Hugh J. "Thomas MacGreevy and Joyce." *James Joyce Quarterly* 25:3 (spring 1988): 305–21.

De Mare, Rolf. *Les Ballets suédois dans l'art contemporain*. Paris: Editions du Trianon, 1931.

De Tuoni, Dario. "James Joyce nella Vecchia Trieste." *Fiera Letteraria* 16:9 (26 February 1961): 5.

———. *Ricordi di James Joyce a Trieste*. Milan: All'Insegna del Pesce d'Oro, 1966.

Deleuze, Giles, and Felix Guattari. *Anti-Oedipus: Capitalism and Schizophrenia*. Minneapolis: University of Minnesota Press, 1983.

———. *A Thousand Plateaus: Capitalism and Schizophrenia*. Minneapolis: University of Minnesota Press, 1987.

Delimata, Bozena Berta. Interviews. Richard Ellmann Papers, Special Collections, McFarlin Library, University of Tulsa, Oklahoma.

———."Reminiscences of a Joyce Niece." Edited by Virginia Moseley. *James Joyce Quarterly* 19:1 (fall 1982): 45–62.

Desmond, Jane C., ed. *Meaning in Motion*. Durham, N.C.: Duke University Press, 1997.

Devlin, Kimberly. *Wandering and Return in "Finnegans Wake."* Princeton, N.J.: Princeton University Press, 1992.

Dillon, Eilis. "The Innocent Muse: An Interview with Maria Jolas." *James Joyce Quarterly* 20:1 (fall 1983): 33–66.

Divoire, Fernand. *Découvertes sur la danse*. Paris, 1924.

Donizetti. *Lucia di Lammermoor*. New York: Fred Rullman, n.d.

Donlon, Patricia. "Introduction." *The James Joyce–Paul Léon Papers in the National Library of Ireland*. Compiled by Catherine Fahy. Dublin: National Library of Ireland, 1992.

Donovan, Katie. "Legacy of the Artist as an 'Anti-Christ': Joyce's Fame—and Infamy—Proved a Heavy Burden for His Family. His Nephew, Ken Monaghan, Talks to Katie Donovan." *Irish Times*, 16 June 1995, 13.

Dortch, Virginia M., ed. *Peggy Guggenheim and Her Friends*. Milan: Berenice, 1994.

Driscoll, Catherine. *Girls*. New York: Columbia University Press, 2002.

Duncan, Anna. "Elizabeth Duncan Schule." *Ballet Review* 3:1 (October 1969): 25.

Duncan, Doree, Carol Pratl, and Cynthia Splatt. *Life into Art: Isadora Duncan and Her World*. Foreword by Agnes de Mille. Text by Cynthia Splatt. New York: W. W. Norton, 1993.

Duncan, Irma. *Duncan Dancer*. New York: Books for Libraries, 1980.

Duncan, Isadora. "The Dance as a Philosophy." *New York Times*, 16 February 1896.

———. "The Dance in Relation to Tragedy." *Theatre Arts* (October 1927).

———. *My Life*. London: Victor Gollancz, 1928.

———. *Isadora Speaks*. Edited by Franklin Rosemont. San Francisco: City Lights, 1981.

Duncan, Raymond. Raymond Duncan Papers, 1948–68. The Hoover Institution, Stanford University Libraries, California.

———. *La Danse et la gymnastique*. Paris: Akademia Raymond Duncan, 1914.

———. *La Musique et l'harmonie*. Paris: Akademia Raymond Duncan, 1914.

———. *Echoes from the Studio of Raymond Duncan*. Paris: Akademia Raymond Duncan, 1930.

———. *Exangelos: New–Paris–York*. Paris: Akademia Raymond Duncan, February 1932.

———. "The Left Bank Revisited." Clipping file. Rondelle Collection, Bibliothèque de l'Arsenal, Paris.

———. *Pages from My Press*. Paris: Akademia Raymond Duncan, 1948.

Edwards, Rem, ed. *Psychiatry and Ethics: Insanity, Rational Autonomy, and Mental Health Care*. Buffalo, N.Y.: Prometheus Books, 1982.

Egerton, Diane. "Shadow or Substance: Lucia Joyce's Illumination of Her Father's Manuscripts." *Devil's Artisan* 23 (1988): 15–22.

Elizabeth Duncan Gesellschaft. *Elizabeth Duncan Schule: Schloss Klessheim, Salzburg*. Vienna: Elizabeth Duncan Gesellschaft, 1928.

Ellis, Havelock. *The Dance of Life*. Boston: Houghton Mifflin, 1923.

Ellmann, Richard. *James Joyce*. New York: Oxford University Press, 1959; rev. ed., 1982.

———, ed. *Letters of James Joyce*. Vols. 2 and 3. New York: The Viking Press, 1966.

———, ed. *Selected Letters of James Joyce*. New York: The Viking Press, 1975.

———. *The Consciousness of Joyce*. London: Faber and Faber, 1977.

Ellmann, Richard, and Ellsworth Mason, eds. *The Critical Writings of James Joyce*. New York: The Viking Press, 1959.

Encyclopedia of the Holocaust. Edited by Robert Rozette and Schmuel Spector. New York: Facts on File, 2000.

Erdman, Jean. "The Meaning of Movement as Human Expression and as an Artistic Communication." Paper presented at the third annual conference of the American Dance Therapy Association, Madison, Wis., 1968.

———. *What Is Modern Dance?* New York: Lawrence R. Maxwell, 1954.

Esslin, Martin. *Antonin Artaud*. New York: Penguin Books, 1976.

Evans, Martha Noel. *Fits and Starts: A Genealogy of Hysteria in Modern France*. Ithaca, N.Y.: Cornell University Press, 1991.

Faerber, Thomas, and Markus Luchsinger. *Joyce in Zürich*. Zürich: Unionsverlag, 1988.

Fahy, Catherine, comp. *The James Joyce–Paul Léon Papers in the National Library of Ireland: A Catalogue*. Dublin: National Library of Ireland, 1992.

Ferris, Kathleen. *James Joyce and the Burden of Disease*. Lexington: University Press of Kentucky, 1995.

Fitch, Noel Riley. *Sylvia Beach and the Lost Generation: A History of Literary Paris in the Twenties and Thirties*. New York: W. W. Norton, 1983.

Fitzgerald, Zelda. *Save Me the Waltz*. In *The Collected Writings of Zelda Fitzgerald*. Edited by Matthew Bruccoli. New York: Charles Scribner's Sons, 1991.

Fitzpatrick, William. *Memories of Father Healy of Little Bray*. London: Macmillan, 1899.

Flanner, Janet. *Paris Was Yesterday, 1925–1939*. New York: The Viking Press, 1972.

Flynn, Arthur. *History of Bray*. Dublin: The Mercier Press, 1986.

Ford, Hugh. *Four Lives in Paris*. San Francisco: North Point Press, 1987.

Ford, Jane. "The Father, Daughter, Suitor Triangle in Shakespeare, Dickens, James, Conrad and Joyce." *Dissertation Abstracts International* 36:7 (1976).

———. "Why Is Milly in Mullingar?" *James Joyce Quarterly* 14:4 (summer 1977): 436–39.

———. *Patriarchy and Incest from Shakespeare to Joyce*. Gainesville: University of Florida Press, 1998.

Fordham, Finn. *"Finnegans Wake" and the Dance*. Ph.D. diss., University College London, 1996.

Forel, August. *Die Sexuelle Frage*. Zürich: Rascher Verlag, 1942.

Forel, Oscar, and Walter Morganthaler. *Die Pflege der Gemüts- und Geisteskranken*. Bern: Medizinischer Verlag Hans Huber, 1926. Translated into French as *Le Traitement des malades nerveux et mentaux*. Hans Huber, 1933.

Foster, R. F. *Modern Ireland: 1600–1972*. London: Allen Lane, 1988.

Foster, Susan Leigh, ed. *Choreographing History*. Bloomington: Indiana University Press, 1995.

———, ed. *Corporealities: Dancing, Knowledge, Culture and Power*. New York: Routledge, 1996.

Foucault, Michel. *Madness and Civilization: A History of Insanity in the Age of Reason*. Translated by Richard Howard. New York: Vintage, 1965.

———. *Discipline and Punish: The Birth of the Prison*. Translated by Alan Sheridan. New York: Vintage Books, 1979.

Fraleigh, Sondra Horton. *Dance and the Lived Body*. Pittsburgh: University of Pittsburgh Press, 1987.

Francini Bruni, Alessandro. "Joyce Stripped Naked in the Piazza." In *Portraits of the Artist in Exile: Recollections of James Joyce by Europeans*. Edited by Willard Potts. Seattle: University of Washington Press, 1979.

Frank, Nino. "Souvenirs sur James Joyce." *La Table ronde* [Paris] 23 (November 1949): 1671–93.

———. "The Shadow That Had Lost Its Man." In *Portraits of the Artist in Exile: Recollections of James Joyce by Europeans*. Edited by Willard Potts. Seattle: University of Washington Press, 1979.

Franko, Mark. *Dancing Modernism/Performing Politics*. Bloomington: Indiana University Press, 1995.

French, Marilyn. *The Book as World*. Cambridge, Mass.: Harvard University Press, 1976.

Freud, Sigmund. *Introductory Lectures on Psychoanalysis*. Translated and edited by James Strachey. New York: W. W. Norton, 1977.

Freund, Gisele. *Three Days with Joyce*. New York: Persea, 1985.

Friedlander, Henry. *The Origins of Nazi Genocide: From Euthanasia to the Final Solution.* Chapel Hill: University of North Carolina Press, 1995.

Friedman, Susan Stanford, ed. *Joyce: The Return of the Repressed.* Ithaca, N.Y.: Cornell University Press, 1993.

Froula, Christine. "The Daughter's Seduction: Sexual Violence and Literary History." *Signs* 11:4 (summer 1986): 621–44.

Gardiner, Juliet. *The New Woman.* London: Collins and Brown, 1993.

Garvin, John. *James Joyce's Disunited Kingdom and the Irish Dimension.* Dublin: Gill and Macmillan, 1976.

Georgiadis, Sokratis. *Sigfried Giedion: An Intellectual Biography.* Translated by Colin Hall. Edinburgh: Edinburgh University Press, 1993.

Gere, Charlotte. *Marie Laurencin.* London: Academy Editions, 1977.

Gibbon, Luke. *Transformations in Irish Culture.* Cork: Cork University Press, 1996.

Giedion-Welcker, Carola. Unpublished letter to Carl Gustav Jung, October 1930. Zürich James Joyce Foundation, Zürich.

———. *In Memoriam James Joyce.* Zürich: Fretz and Wasmuth, 1941.

———. "Les Derniers mois de la vie de James Joyce." *Le Figaro Litteraire,* 28 May 1949.

———. *James Joyce in Zurich.* Dublin, 1949.

———. *Schriften 1926–71: Stationen zu einem Zeitbild.* Koln: M. DuMont Schaubert, 1973.

———. "Meetings with Joyce." In *Portraits of the Artist in Exile: Recollections of James Joyce by Europeans.* Edited by Willard Potts. Seattle: University of Washington Press, 1979.

Gilbert, Martin. *A History of the Twentieth Century.* London: HarperCollins, 1997.

Gilbert, Sandra. "Life's Empty Pack: Notes toward a Literary Daughteronomy." *Critical Inquiry* 11:3 (spring 1985): 355–84.

Gilbert, Stuart. Stuart Gilbert Papers. Harry Ransom Humanities Research Center, University of Texas at Austin.

———. *James Joyce's "Ulysses."* New York: Alfred A. Knopf, 1931.

———. *Reflections on James Joyce: Stuart Gilbert's Paris Journal.* Edited by Thomas F. Staley and Randolph Lewis. Austin: University of Texas Press, 1993.

Gillespie, Michael Patrick. *Inverted Volumes Improperly Arranged.* Ann Arbor, Mich.: UMI Research Press, 1983.

Gillet, Louis. *Claybook for James Joyce.* Translated by George Markow-Totevy. New York: Abelard-Schuman, 1958.

———. "Farewell to Joyce." In *Portraits of the Artist in Exile: Recollections of James Joyce by Europeans.* Edited by Willard Potts. Seattle: University of Washington Press, 1979.

———. "The Living Joyce." In *Portraits of the Artist in Exile: Recollections of James Joyce by Europeans.* Edited by Willard Potts. Seattle: University of Washington Press, 1979.

Gilman, Sander. *Disease and Representation: Images of Illness from Madness to AIDS.* Ithaca, N.Y.: Cornell University Press, 1988.

Girsberger, H. *Who's Who in Switzerland.* Zurich: Central European Times Publishing, 1952.

Glasheen, Adaline. "*Finnegans Wake* and the Girls from Boston, Mass." *Hudson Review* 8 (spring 1954).

————. "Les Vignes sauvages." *A Wake Newslitter: Studies in James Joyce's "Finnegans Wake"* 13 (1976): 55.0049–6847.

————. *Third Census of "Finnegans Wake."* Berkeley: University of California Press, 1977.

Godfrey, John. "Joyce Without Joy: Play about the Famous Writer's Daughter Ends without an Explanation." *Los Angeles Times*, 22 April 1991, F1.

Goellner, Ellen W., and Jacqueline Shea Murphy. *Bodies of the Text: Dance as Theory, Literature as Dance.* New Brunswick, N.J.: Rutgers University Press, 1994.

Goffman, Erving. *Stigma: Notes on the Management of Spoiled Identity.* Englewood Cliffs, N.J.: Prentice-Hall, 1963.

Gold, Alison Leslie. *The Clairvoyant: The Imagined Life of Lucia Joyce.* New York: Hyperion Books, 1992.

Goldberg, Marianne. "She Who Is Possessed No Longer Exists Outside." *Women and Performance: A Journal* 3:5 (1986): 17–27.

Golding, Louis. *James Joyce.* London: Thornton Butterworth, 1933.

Goldman, Arnold. "Stanislaus, James and the Politics of Family." In *Atte del Third International James Joyce Symposium, 1977.* Edited by Nini Rocco-Bergera. Trieste: Università degli Studi Facultà di Magistero, 1974.

Goldstein, Jan Ellen. *Console and Classify: The French Psychiatric Profession in the Nineteenth Century.* Cambridge, England: Cambridge University Press, 1987.

Goodman, H. Maurice. *Basic Medical Endocrinology.* New York: Raven Press, 1994.

Gordon, John. "Notes on Issy." Colchester, Essex, England: Wake Newslitter Press, 1982.

Gorman, Herbert. *James Joyce: His First Forty Years.* New York: B.W. Huebsch, 1924.

————. *James Joyce.* New York: Farrar and Rinehart, 1939.

Gotkin, Janet. *Too Much Anger, Too Many Tears: A Personal Triumph over Psychiatry.* New York: Random House, 1977.

Green, Martin. *Mountain of Truth: The Counterculture Begins, Ascona, 1900–1920.* Hanover, N.H.: University Press of New England, 1986.

Groden, Michael, ed. *The James Joyce Archive. "Finnegans Wake": Book II, Chapter 2. A Facsimile of Drafts, Typescripts, and Proofs.* Preface by David Hayman. Arranged by Danis Rose. New York: Garland, 1978.

Groden, Michael, et al., eds. *The James Joyce Archive.* 63 vols. New York: Garland, 1977–79.

Grosz, Elizabeth. *Volatile Bodies: Toward a Corporeal Feminism.* Bloomington: Indiana University Press, 1994.

Groult, Flora. *Marie Laurencin.* Paris: Mercure de France, 1987.

Guggenheim, Peggy. *Out of This Century: Confessions of an Art Addict.* New York: The Dial Press, 1946.

Gutman, Israel, ed. "Euthanasia Program." In vol. 2 of *Encyclopedia of the Holocaust.* New York: Macmillan, 1990.

————, ed. "Final Solution." In vol. 2 of *Encyclopedia of the Holocaust.* New York: Macmillan, 1990.

Hachey, Thomas, Joseph Hernon Jr., and Lawrence McCaffrey. *The Irish Experience.* Englewood Cliffs, N.J.: Prentice-Hall, 1989.

Hannah, Barbara. *Jung: His Life and Work.* New York: G. P. Putnam, 1976.

Hart, Clive. *Structure and Motif in "Finnegans Wake."* Evanston, Ill.: Northwestern University Press, 1962.

Hartshorn, Peter. *James Joyce and Trieste*. Westport, Conn.: Greenwood Press, 1997.

Hauptmann, Gerhart. *Hannele's Ascension*. In *Three Plays*. Translated by Horst Frenz and Miles Waggoner. Prospect Heights, Ill.: Waveland Press, 1977.

———. *Before Sunrise*. Edited by Jill Perkins. Translated by James Joyce. San Marino, Calif.: Henry E. Huntington Library, 1978.

Hayman, David, ed. *A First-Draft Version of "Finnegans Wake."* Austin: University of Texas Press, 1963.

———. "Shadow of His Mind: The Papers of Lucia Joyce." In *Joyce at Texas*. Edited by Dave Oliphant and Thomas Zigal. Austin, Tex.: Harry Ransom Humanities Research Center, 1983.

———. "I Think Her Pretty: Reflections of the Familiar in Joyce's Notebook VI. B.5." In *Joyce Studies Annual*. Austin: University of Texas Press, 1990.

———. "Reading Joyce's Notebooks." In *"Finnegans Wake": 50 Years*. Edited by Geert Lernout. Amsterdam: Rodopi, 1990.

———. *The "Wake" in Transit*. Ithaca, N.Y.: Cornell University Press, 1990.

Hayman, David, and Ira Nadel. "Joyce and the Family of Emile and Yva Fernandez: Solving a Minor Mystery." *James Joyce Quarterly* 25:1 (fall 1987): 49–57.

Hellman, George S. *The Story of the Seligmans*. New York, 1945.

Henke, Suzette. *James Joyce and the Politics of Desire*. New York: Routledge, 1990.

Henke, Suzette, and Elaine Unkeless, eds. *Women in Joyce*. Urbana: University of Illinois Press, 1982.

Hering, Doris. "Jean Erdman Finds a New Approach to Dance." *Dance Magazine* (May 1950): 14–15, 36.

———. "Contemporary Dance, Inc. Presents *The Coach with the Six Insides*." *Dance Magazine* (May 1964): 72–73.

Herr, Cheryl. "Fathers, Daughters, Anxiety and Fiction." In *Discontented Discourses: Feminism/Textual Intervention/Psychoanalysis*. Edited by Marleen Barr and Richard Feldstein. Urbana: University of Illinois Press, 1989.

Hirsh, Marianne. *The Mother/Daughter Plot: Narrative, Psychoanalysis, Feminism*. Bloomington: Indiana University Press, 1989.

Historisch-Biographisches Lexikon der Schweitz. Neurenburg, 1924.

Hoch, A. "Review of Bleuler's Schizophrenia." *Review of Neurology and Psychiatry* 10 (1912): 259–78.

Hoenig, John. "Jaspers's View on Schizophrenia." In *The Concept of Schizophrenia: Historical Perspectives*. Edited by John G. Howells. Washington, D.C.: American Psychiatric Press, 1991.

Hofmann, Felix. *Das Burghölzli in der Vorstellung des Zürcher Volkes: Ergebnis einer Rundfrage*. Zürich: Juris, 1957.

Houser, Aimee. "Lucia's Commitment (A Poem Based on Brenda Maddox's *Nora*)." *James Joyce Literary Supplement* (spring 1997): 8–10.

Howard, Angela, ed. *Redefining the New Woman*. New York: Garland, 1997.

Howells, John G., ed. *The Concept of Schizophrenia: Historical Perspectives*. Washington, D.C.: American Psychiatric Press, 1991.

Hubbell, Albert. Letter to Richard Ellmann. Richard Ellmann Papers, Special Collections, McFarlin Library, University of Tulsa, Oklahoma.

Huddleston, Sisley. *Paris Salons, Cafés, Studios*. Philadelphia: Lippincott, 1928.

Hughes, Eileen Lanouette. "The Mystery Lady of *Giacomo Joyce*." *Life*, 19 February 1968.

Hutchins, Patricia. *James Joyce's World*. London: Methuen, 1957.

Hutton, Lois, and Hélène Vanel. *Cahiers rythme et couleur: Prose, poèmes, croquis, annales, photographies*. November 1925 and May 1926.

Ibsen, Henrik. *When We Dead Awaken*. In *The Oxford Ibsen*, vol. 8. Oxford: Oxford University Press, 1977.

———. *The Wild Duck*. In *Three Plays*. New York: The Heritage Press, 1965.

Irigaray, Luce. *Le Langage des déments*. The Hague: Mouton, 1973.

———. *Elemental Passions*. Translated by Joanne Collie and Judith Still. New York: Routledge, 1992.

Ischlondsky, Naum Efimowitsch. *Artificial Rejuvination [sic] and Voluntary Change of Sex according to Prof. Steinach*, 1926.

———. *Der bedingte Reflex und seine Bedeutung in der Biologie, Medizin, Psychologie und Pädagogik: Ein Handbuch der experimentellen Reflexologie*. Berlin: Urban und Schwartzberg, 1930.

———. *Physiologische Grundlagen der Tiefen-Psychologie unter besonderer Berücksichtigung der Psychoanalyse: Ein Handbuch*. Berlin, 1930.

———. *Protoformotherapy in Treatment and Prevention: Fifteen Years of Research*. London: Henry Kimpton, 1937.

———. *Brain and Behavior: Induction as a Fundamental Mechanism of Neuropsychic Activity: An Experimental and Clinical Study*. St. Louis: Mosby, 1949.

Issacharoff, Michael, and Robin F. Jones. *Performing Texts*. Philadelphia: University of Pennsylvania Press, 1988.

Jackson, John Wyse, with Peter Costello. *John Stanislaus Joyce*. London: Fourth Estate, 1997.

Jamison, Kay Redfield. *An Unquiet Mind: A Memoir of Moods and Madness*. New York: Alfred A. Knopf, 1995.

Jaspers, Karl. *General Psychopathology*. Translated by J. Hoenig and M. W. Hamilton. Chicago: University of Chicago Press, 1963.

"Jean Borlin." Clipping file, Library of the Performing Arts, Lincoln Center, New York.

"Jean Borlin." Clipping file, Rondelle Collection, Bibliothèque de l'Arsenal, Paris.

Jeschke, Claudia. *Tanzschriften: Ihre Geschichte und Methode*. Bad Reichenhalle: Comes Verlag, 1983.

Jolas, Maria. "The Joyce I Knew and the Women around Him." In *The Crane Bag Book of Irish Studies, 1977–1981*. Dublin: Blackwater Press, 1982.

Jolas, Maria, and Eugene Jolas. Papers. Letters, manuscripts, and photographs of Joyce family. Beinecke Rare Book and Manuscript Library, Yale University.

Jones, Kathleen. *Asylums and After: A Revised History of the Mental Health Services: From the Early Eighteenth Century to the 1990s*. London: The Athlone Press, 1993.

Jowitt, Deborah. *Time and the Dancing Image*. Berkeley: University of California Press, 1988.

Joyce, Helen Kastor. "A Portrait of the Artist by His Daughter-in-Law." Unpublished typescript. Harry Ransom Humanities Research Center, University of Texas at Austin.

———. "We Meet"; "Luncheon at Cafe Leopold"; "Anniversary, February 2, 1939." Unpublished typescripts. Richard Ellmann Papers, Special Collections, McFarlin Library, University of Tulsa, Oklahoma.

Joyce, James. *The Joyce Book*. Edited by Herbert Hughes. London: Sylvan Press and H. Milford, Oxford University Press, 1933.

———. *Pomes Penyeach*. London: Faber and Faber, 1933.

————. *The Mime of Mick, Nick and the Maggies*. The Hague: Servire Press, 1934.

————. *Ulysses* by James Joyce, with an introduction by Stuart Gilbert and illustrations by Henri Matisse. New York: The Limited Editions Club, 1935.

————. *The Critical Writings of James Joyce*. Edited by Richard Ellmann and Ellsworth Mason. New York: The Viking Press, 1959.

————. *A Portrait of the Artist as a Young Man*. New York: The Viking Press, 1964.

————. *Finnegans Wake*. New York: The Viking Press, 1966.

————. *Letters of James Joyce*. Vol. 1. Edited by Stuart Gilbert. New York: The Viking Press, 1966.

————. *Letters of James Joyce*. Vols. 2 and 3. Edited by Richard Ellmann. New York: The Viking Press, 1966.

————. *Giacomo Joyce*. Edited by Richard Ellmann. New York: The Viking Press, 1968.

————. *Selected Letters of James Joyce*. Edited by Richard Ellmann. New York: The Viking Press, 1975.

————. *Chamber Music, Pomes Penyeach and Occasional Verse: A Facsimile of Manuscripts, Typescripts and Proofs*. Edited by A. Walton Litz. New York: Garland, 1978.

————. *Ulysses: The Corrected Text*. Edited by Hans Walter Gabler with Wolfhard Steppe and Claus Melchior. New York: Random House, 1986.

————. *Poems and Shorter Writings*. Edited by Richard Ellmann, A. Walton Litz, and John Whittier-Ferguson. London: Faber and Faber, 1991.

————. *Reflections of Ireland*. Edited by Bernard McCabe and Alain Le Garsmeur. Boston: Little, Brown, 1993.

Joyce, Lucia. "Charlie et les gosses." *Le Disque vert* 3:4–5 (1924): 676–78.

————. "My Dreams." Unpublished manuscript. Harry Ransom Humanities Research Center, University of Texas at Austin.

————. "My Life by Lucia Joyce." Unpublished manuscript. Harry Ransom Humanities Research Center, University of Texas at Austin.

————. "The Real Life of James Joyce Told by Lucia Joyce." Unpublished manuscript. Harry Ransom Humanities Research Center, University of Texas at Austin.

————. Letters. Unpublished manuscripts. Harry Ransom Humanities Research Center, University of Texas at Austin.

Joyce, Stanislaus. "James Joyce: A Memoir." *Hudson Review* 2:4 (1949–50): 485.

————. *Recollections of James Joyce by His Brother*. New York: The James Joyce Society, 1950.

————. *My Brother's Keeper: James Joyce's Early Years*. Edited by Richard Ellmann. New York: The Viking Press, 1958.

"The Joyces." *New Yorker*, 12 January 1935.

Julien, Robert M. "Sedative-Hypnotic Compounds: Drugs That Depress the Central Nervous System." In *A Primer of Drug Action*. San Francisco: W. H. Freeman, 1975.

Jung, Carl Gustav. *Contributions to Analytical Psychology*. Translated by H. G. Baynes and Cary F. Baynes. New York: Harcourt Brace, 1928.

————. *Two Essays on Analytical Psychology*. Translated by H. G. Baynes and Cary F. Baynes. London: Bailliere, Tindall and Cox, 1928.

————. "Zur Gegenwartigen Lage der Psychotherapie." *Zentralblatt für Psychotherapie und ihre Grenzgebiete* 7 (1934): 1–16.

————. *The Practice of Psychotherapy: Essays on the Psychology of the Transference and Other Subjects.* Translated by R. F. C. Hull. New York: Pantheon Books, 1954.

————. *Aion: Researches into the Phenomenology of the Self.* Translated by R. F. C. Hull. New York: Pantheon Books, 1959.

————. "Concerning the Archetypes, with Special Reference to the Anima Concept." In *The Archetypes and the Collective Unconscious.* Translated by R. F. C. Hull. Princeton, N.J.: Princeton University Press, 1959.

————. "Psychology and Literature." In *The Spirit of Man, Art and Literature.* Princeton, N.J.: Princeton University Press, 1966. Originally translated by Eugene Jolas as "Psychology and Poetry" and published in *transition: an international quarterly for creative experiment*, 19–20 (June 1930).

————. *The Collected Works of C. G. Jung.* Edited by Herbert Gerhard, Michael Fordham, and Read Adler. Princeton, N.J.: Bollingen Series XX, 1953–83.

————. "*Ulysses*: A Monologue." In *The Spirit in Man, Art and Literature.* London: Routledge and Kegan Paul, 1971.

————. "The Apollonian and the Dionysian." In *Psychological Types.* Translated by H. G. Baynes. Princeton, N.J.: Princeton University Press, 1971.

————. "Critical Survey of Theoretical Views on the Psychology of Dementia Praecox." In *The Psychogenesis of Mental Disease.* Translated by R. F. C. Hull. Princeton, N.J.: Princeton University Press, 1972.

————. *Nietzsche's Zarathustra: Notes of the Seminar Given in 1934–1939.* Vols. 1–2. Edited by James L. Jarrett. Princeton, N.J.: Princeton University Press, 1988.

Kain, Richard M. "An Interview with Carola Giedion-Welcker and Maria Jolas." *James Joyce Quarterly* 11:2 (winter 1974): 94–122.

Kalman, Maira. *Calder's Circus.* New York: Whitney Museum of American Art, 1991.

Kaplan, Bert, ed. *The Inner World of Mental Illness: A Series of First Person Accounts of What It Was Like.* Reading, Mass.: Addison-Wesley, 1964.

Kaysen, Susanna. *Girl, Interrupted.* New York: Random House, 1994.

Kelly, Joseph. *Our Joyce: From Outcast to Icon.* Austin: University of Texas Press, 1998.

Keogh, Dermot. *Ireland and Europe, 1919–1948.* Dublin: Gill and Macmillan, 1988.

————. *Twentieth-Century Ireland: Nation and State.* Dublin: Gill and Macmillan, 1994.

Kerr, John. *A Most Dangerous Method: The Story of Jung, Freud and Sabina Spielrein.* New York: Alfred A. Knopf, 1993.

Kershner, Brandon, and Ellie Ragland-Sullivan. "More French Connections." *James Joyce Quarterly* 26:1 (fall 1988): 115–27.

Kessler, Ingrid-Marie. "Les Ballets suédois et les poètes français." *La Recherche en danse* 2:83: 79–85.

Khouri, Philippe. "Continuum Versus Dichotomy in Theories of Schizophrenia." *Schizophrenia Bulletin* 3:2 (1977): 262–67.

Killeen, Terance. *Irish Times*, 5 November 1992.

Kipling, Rudyard. *The Light That Failed.* New York: Charles Scribner's Sons, 1899.

Kirsch, Hildegaard. "Crossing the Ocean: Memoirs of Jung." *Psychological Perspectives* 6 (1975): 128–34.

Knowlson, James. *Damned to Fame: The Life of Samuel Beckett.* New York: Simon and Schuster, 1996.

Kraepelin, Emil. *Clinical Psychiatry: A Textbook for Students and Physicians.* Edited and translated by A. R. Diefendorf. New York: Macmillan, 1923.

———. *Dementia Praecox and Paraphrenia*. Translated by R. M. Barclay. Huntington, N.Y.: Krieger Publishing, 1971.

Kristeva, Julia. *The Revolution in Poetic Language*. Translated by Margaret Waller. New York: Columbia University Press, 1984.

———. "Joyce 'The Gracehoper' or the Return of Orpheus." In *James Joyce: The Augmented Ninth*. Edited by Bernard Benstock. Syracuse, N.Y.: Syracuse University Press, 1988.

Kuberski, Philip. "The Joycean Gaze: Lucia in the I of the Father." *SubStance: A Review of Theory and Literary Criticism* 14:1 (1985): 49–66.

L'Oeuf dur. Paris, Editions Jean-Michel Place, 1975.

Laban, Rudolf. *Choreutics*. London: MacDonald and Evans, 1966.

Lacan, Jacques. *Speech and Language in Psychoanalysis*. Translated by Anthony Wilden. Baltimore: The Johns Hopkins University Press, 1968.

———. *Ecrits: A Selection*. New York: W. W. Norton, 1977.

———. "Joyce le symptôme I." In *Joyce avec Lacan*. Edited by Jacques Aubert. Paris: Navarin Editeur, 1987, 21–29.

Lanoux, Armand. *Paris 1925*. Paris: Bernard Grasset, 1975.

Lawrence, D. H. *Lady Chatterley's Lover (The Complete and Unexpurgated 1928 Orioli Edition)*. London: Bantam Books, 1968.

"La lecture à fait de la fille du poète James Joyce, une danseuse . . . et la danse l'incita à la peinture." *Paris Midi*, 4 October 1932.

Lee, Hermione, *Virginia Woolf*. New York: Alfred A. Knopf, 1997.

Léon, Paul. Papers. Unpublished letters and documents. National Library of Ireland, Dublin.

Levinson, André. "Bagatelles laborieuses." February 1930. Clipping file, Rondelle Collection, Bibliothèque de l'Arsenal, Paris.

———. *André Levinson on Dance: Writings from Paris in the Twenties*. Edited by Joan Acocella and Lynn Garafola. Middletown, Conn.: Wesleyan University Press, 1991.

Lewis, Nolan Don Carpentier. *Research in Dementia Praecox (Past Attainments, Present Trends and Future Possibilities)*. New York: National Committee for Mental Hygiene, 1936.

Lidderdale, Jane, and Mary Nicholson. *Dear Miss Weaver: Harriet Shaw Weaver, 1876–1961*. London: Faber and Faber, 1970.

Linehan, Fergus. "It's an Accident I'm His Grandson." *Irish Times*, special supplement, 2 February 1982.

Lipman, Jean, ed., with Nancy Foote. *Calder's Circus*. New York: E. P. Dutton, 1972.

Loewenberg, Peter. "A Creative Epoch in Modern Science: Psychiatry at the Burghölzli, 1902–1912." *American College of Psychoanalysis Newsletter* 16 (1985): 1–2.

Loewenthal, Lillian. *The Search for Isadora: The Legend and Legacy of Isadora Duncan*. Pennington, N.J.: Princeton Book Company, 1993.

Lottman, Herbert R. "One of the Quiet Ones [Maria Jolas]." *New York Times Book Review*, 22 March 1970, 5, 28, 29.

"Lubov Egorova." Clipping file, Rondelle Collection, Bibliothèque de l'Arsenal, Paris.

"Lubov Nikolaevna Egorova." Clipping file, Library of the Performing Arts, Lincoln Center, New York.

Luchsinger, Thomas Faerber Markus. *Joyce in Zürich*. Zürich: Unionsverlag, 1988.

Lucia di Lammermoor. Playbill. Opera Company of Philadelphia, 1996–97.

Lund, Stephen, comp. *James Joyce: Letters, Manuscripts, and Photographs at Southern Illinois University*. Troy, N.Y.: Whitston Publishing, 1983.

Lynn, Kenneth. *Charlie Chaplin and His Times*. New York: Simon and Schuster, 1997.

Lyons, J. B. *James Joyce and Medicine*. Dublin: Dolmen Press, 1973.

———. *Thrust Syphilis Down to Hell and Other Rejoyceana*. Dublin: Glendale Press, 1988.

MacGreevy, Thomas. "James Joyce." *Times Literary Supplement*, 25 January 1941, 43, 45.

———. "Paradise Lost." Unpublished memoir written after Joyce's death. Rare Books and Manuscripts, Trinity College, Dublin.

Macherey, Pierre. *A Theory of Literary Production*. Translated by Geoffrey Wall. New York: Routledge, 1978.

Maddox, Brenda. *Nora: The Real Life of Molly Bloom*. Boston: Houghton Mifflin, 1988.

———. "Messing with History: *Clairvoyant: The Imagined Life of Lucia Joyce*." *Los Angeles Times*, 9 August 1992.

———. "Epilogue." Unpublished manuscript. Private possession.

Magalaner, Marvin, and Richard M. Kane. *Joyce: The Man, the Work, the Reputation*. New York: New York University Press, 1956.

Mahaffey, Vicki. "Giacomo Joyce." In *A Companion to Joyce Studies*. Edited by Zack Bowen and James C. Carens. Westport, Conn.: Greenwood Press, 1984.

Mahon, Michael. *Foucault's Nietzschean Genealogy: Truth, Power and the Subject*. Albany: State University of New York Press, 1992.

Maier, Hans Wolfgang. *Cocaine Addiction*. Translated by O. J. Kalant. Toronto: Addiction Research Foundation, 1987. Originally published Leipzig: Verlag von Georg Thieme, 1926.

Maillard, Gaston. *Les Merveilles de l'autosuggestion: Conferences d'enseignement faites à l'Institute Coué de Paris*. Paris: Editions Oliven, 1924.

Maletic, Vera. *Body-Space-Expression: The Development of Rudolf Laban's Movement and Dance Concepts*. Berlin: Mouton de Gruyter, 1987.

Mallet, Raymond. *Les Délirants*. Paris, 1930.

———. *La Démence*. Paris: Librairie Armand Colin, 1935.

———. *Le Mongolisme: Liste d'etablissements pour déficients mentaux*. Paris: Baillière, 1967.

Mallwitz, A. "The Physical Education of Girls in Light of the Physical Culture Movement." In *Elizabeth Duncan-Schule: Marienhöhe/Darmstadt*. Jena, Germany: Eugen Diederichs, 1912.

Manning, Susan. *Ecstasy and the Demon: Feminism and Nationalism in the Dances of Mary Wigman*. Berkeley: University of California Press, 1993.

Manzoni, Alessandro. *The Betrothed: A Tale of XVII Milan*. Translated by Archibald Colquhoun. London: J. M. Dent and Son, 1951.

Marchesseau, Daniel. *Marie Laurencin*. Tokyo: Curieux-Do, 1982.

———. *The Intimate World of Alexander Calder*. Translated by Eleanor Levieux and Barbara Shuey. New York: Harry N. Abrams, 1989.

———. *Marie Laurencin: Cent œuvres des collections du musée Marie Laurencin au Japon*. Martigny, Suisse: Fondation Pierre Gianadda, 1994.

Marèze, Jean. *L'Apprenti gigolo*. Paris: J. Ferenczi, 1926.

Maroger, Dominique. "Dernière rencontre avec Lucia." In *James Joyce*. Edited by Jacques Aubert and Fritz Senn. Paris: Editions de l'Herne, 1985.

————. "Lucia et la danse." In *James Joyce*. Edited by Jacques Aubert and Fritz Senn. Paris: Editions de l'Herne, 1985.

Marter, Joan M. *Alexander Calder*. Cambridge, England: Cambridge University Press, 1991.

Martin, Marianne W. "The Ballet *Parade*: A Dialogue between Cubism and Futurism."

Mason, Ellsworth. "Ellmann's Road to Xanadu." In *Essays for Richard Ellmann: Omnium Gatherum*. Edited by Susan Dick et al. Montreal: McGill–Queens University Press, 1989.

Massomi, Brian. *A User's Guide to Capitalism and Schizophrenia: Deviations from Deleuze and Guattari*. Cambridge, Mass.: MIT Press, 1992.

McAlmon, Robert, and Kay Boyle. *Being Geniuses Together, 1920–1930*. Garden City, N.Y.: Doubleday, 1968.

McCarthy, Jack. *Joyce's Dublin: A Walking Guide to "Ulysses."* Dublin: Wolfhound Press, 1986.

McCarthy, Michael. *Priests and People in Ireland*. Dublin: Hodges, Figgis, 1902.

McDonagh, Don. "Jean Erdman's 'Coach with the Six Insides.' " In *The Complete Guide to Modern Dance*. Garden City, N.Y.: Doubleday, 1976.

McDougall, Richard. *The Very Rich Hours of Adrienne Monnier*. London: Millington, 1976.

McFee, Graham. *Understanding Dance*. London: Routledge, 1992.

McGarry, Patsy. "Schizophrenia Ireland's 'Lucia Day' Highlights Joyce and Family's Tragedy to Heighten Awareness of Mental Illness." *Irish Times,* 27 July 1998, 4.

McGrory, Kathleen, ed. "Interview with Carola Giedion-Welcker, 15 June 1973, Burlington Hotel, Dublin." In Kathleen McGrory and John Unterecker, *Yeats, Joyce, Beckett*. Lewisburg, Pa.: Bucknell University Press, 1976.

McGuire, William, and R. F. C. Hull, eds. *C. G. Jung Speaking: Encounters and Interviews*. Princeton: Princeton University Press, 1977.

McHugh, Roland. *The Sigla of "Finnegans Wake."* London: Edward Arnold, 1976.

————. *Annotations to "Finnegans Wake."* Revised edition. Baltimore: The Johns Hopkins University Press, 1991.

Medvei, Victor Cornelius. *A History of Endocrinology*. Lancaster [England]; Boston: MTP Press, 1982.

Melchiori, Giorgio. *Joyce in Rome*. Rome: Bulzoni, 1984.

Melman, Billie. *Women and the Popular Imagination in the Twenties: Flappers and Nymphs*. London: Macmillan, 1988.

Mercanton, Jacques. *Les Heures de James Joyce*. Lausanne: Editions l'Age d'homme, 1967.

————. "The Hours of James Joyce." In *Portraits of the Artist in Exile: Recollections of James Joyce by Europeans*. Edited by Willard Potts. Seattle: University of Washington Press, 1979.

Merz, Max. "Die Ziele und die Organisation der Elizabeth Duncan-Schule." *Elizabeth Duncan-Schule: Marienhöhe/Darmstadt*. Jena, Germany: Eugen Diederichs, 1912.

Michaut, Pierre. "Notes on Some Paris Schools." *Dancing Times,* June 1945.

Mikhail, E. H., ed. *James Joyce: Interviews and Recollections*. New York: St. Martin's Press, 1990.

Milhaud, Darius. *Notes Without Music*. New York: Alfred A. Knopf, 1953.

————. *My Happy Life*. London: Marion Boyers, 1995.

"Les Mimo-danses de Lois Hutton et Hélène Vanel." 18 February 1930. Clipping file, Rondelle Collection, Bibliothèque de l'Arsenal, Paris.

Monro, Eleanor. *Memoirs of a Modernist's Daughter.* New York: The Viking Press, 1988.

Morris, Margaret. *Margaret Morris Dancing: A Book of Pictures by Fred Daniels, with an Introduction and Outline of Her Methods by Margaret Morris.* London: Kegan Paul, Trench and Trubner, 1928.

———. *The Notation of Movement.* London: Kegan Paul, Trench and Trubner, 1928.

———. *Basic Physical Training.* London: Heinemann, 1937.

———. *My Life in Movement.* London: Owen, 1969.

———. *Creation in Dance and Life.* London: Owen, 1972.

Muller, Hedwig. *Mary Wigman: Leben und Werk der Grossen Tänzerin.* Weinheim und Berlin: Quadriga, 1986.

Mundy, Liza. "The Wars of the Joyces: Burning Letters and Dueling Texts." *Washington Post*, 10 July 1988, F1.

Murphy, Hayden. "Sad Story of James Joyce's 'Sex-Starved' Daughter, Lucia." Glasgow *Herald*, 16 March 1994, 14.

Murphy, Henry. "Comparative Incidence of Schizophrenia in Rural Ireland." In *Comparative Psychiatry: The International and Intercultural Distribution of Mental Illness.* Berlin: Springer, 1982.

Nadel, Ira B. "Lucia Joyce: Archival Material at the James Joyce Centre, University College London." *James Joyce Quarterly* 22: 4 (summer 1985): 397–404.

Nadel, Ira B., and David Hayman. "Joyce and the Family of Emile and Yva Fernandez: Solving a Minor Mystery." *James Joyce Quarterly* 25: 1 (fall 1987): 49–57.

Naegeli, Otto. *Behandlung und Heilung von Nervenleiden und Nervenschmerzen durch Handgriffe, für Ärzte und Laien gemeinverständlich dargestellt.* Jena, Germany, 1899.

———. *Neurosen.* Leipzig: Verlag von Georg Thieme, 1923.

———. *Unfallsneurosen.* Leipzig: Verlag von Georg Thieme, 1923.

———. *Blutkrankheiten und Blutdiagnostik.* Berlin, 1931.

Nathanson, Constance. *Dangerous Passage: The Social Control of Sexuality in Women's Adolescence.* Philadelphia: Temple University Press, 1991.

Nelson, Adie, and Barrie Robinson. *Gigolos and Madames Bountiful: Illusions of Gender, Power, and Intimacy.* Toronto: University of Toronto Press, 1994.

Niero, Antonio. *Saint Lucy: Virgin and Martyr.* Translated by Edwin Mitchell. Venice: Stamperia di Venezia, 1962.

Nietzsche, Friedrich. *Thus Spoke Zarathustra.* Translated by R. J. Hollingdale. New York: Penguin Books, 1961.

———. *The Birth of Tragedy.* Translated by Walter Kaufmann. New York: Vintage, 1967.

Nijinsky, Romola. *Nijinsky.* New York: Simon and Schuster, 1934.

Nijinsky, Vaslav. *The Diary of Vaslav Nijinsky.* Edited by Romola Nijinsky. New York: Simon and Schuster, 1936.

Noël, Lucie. *James Joyce and Paul L. Léon: The Story of a Friendship.* New York: The Gotham Book Mart, 1948.

Norris, Margot. *The Decentered Universe of "Finnegans Wake."* Baltimore: The Johns Hopkins University Press, 1976.

———. "Anna Livia Plurabelle: The Dream Woman." In *Women in Joyce.* Edited by Suzette Henke and Elaine Unkeless. Urbana: University of Illinois Press, 1982.

North, Carol S. "Diagnostic Discrepancy in Personal Accounts of Patients with Schizophrenia." In *Multiple Personalities, Multiple Disorders: Psychiatric Classification and*

Media Influence. Edited by Carol S. North, Jo-Ellyn M. Ryall, Daniel A. Ricci, and Richard D. Wetzel. New York: Oxford University Press, 1993.

Nutting, Helen. Paris diary. Myron C. Nutting and Muriel Tyler Nutting Papers. Archives of American Art, Smithsonian Institution, Washington, D.C.

Nutting, Myron. "Paris diary, 1924–25." Myron C. Nutting and Murial Tyler Nutting Papers. Archives of American Art, Smithsonian Institution, Washington, D.C.

———. *An Artist's Life and Travels*. 4 vols. Oral History Program, University of California, Los Angeles, 1972.

Nutting, Myron, and Helen Nutting. Papers. Charles Deering McCormick Library of Special Collections, Northwestern University, Evanston, Ill.

O'Brien, David. *Privacy, Law and Public Policy*. New York: Praeger, 1979.

O'Brien, Edna. *James and Nora: Portrait of Joyce's Marriage*. Northridge, Calif.: Lord John Press, 1981.

———. *James Joyce*. New York: The Viking Press, 1999.

O'Neill, John. *The Communicative Body: Studies in Communicative Philosophy, Politics, and Sociology*. Evanston, Ill.: Northwestern University Press, 1989.

Oates, Joyce Carol. "Daisy." In *Major American Short Stories*. Edited by A. Walton Litz. New York: Oxford University Press, 1980.

Odem, Mary. *Delinquent Daughters: Protecting and Policing Adolescent Female Sexuality in the United States, 1895–1920*. Chapel Hill: University of North Carolina Press, 1995.

Oliphant, Dave, and Thomas Zigal, eds. *Joyce at Texas: Essays on the James Joyce Materials at the Humanities Research Center*. Austin: Harry Ransom Humanities Research Center, 1983.

"On the Left Bank: Lucia Joyce." *Paris Times*, 14 March 1928.

Orage, A. R. *Friedrich Nietzsche: The Dionysian Spirit of the Age*. London: Foulis, 1906.

Ostwald, Peter F. *Vaslav Nijinsky: A Leap into Madness*. New York: Carol Publishing Group, 1991.

Ousby, Ian. *Occupation: The Ordeal of France, 1940–1944*. New York: St. Martin's Press, 1998.

Parrinder, Patrick. *James Joyce*. Cambridge University Press, 1984.

Pastor, Grace. "A Remarkable Family." *Physical Culture* (April 1910): 81.

Pauck, Wilhelm, and Marion Pauck. *Paul Tillich: His Life and Thought*. New York: Harper and Row, 1976.

Peirce, Waldo. Waldo Peirce Papers. Archives of American Art, Smithsonian Institution, Washington, D.C.

Peters, C. P. "Concepts of Schizophrenia after Kraepelin and Bleuler." In *The Concept of Schizophrenia: Historical Perspectives*. Edited by John G. Howells. Washington, D.C.: American Psychiatric Press, 1991.

Peters, U. H. "The German Classical Concept of Schizophrenia." In *The Concept of Schizophrenia: Historical Perspectives*. Edited by John G. Howells. Washington, D.C.: American Psychiatric Press, 1991.

Pierre, José. *Marie Laurencin*. Paris: Editions Aimery Somogy, 1988.

———, ed. *Investigating Sex: Surrealist Research 1928–1932*. Translated by Malcolm Imrie. New York: Verso Press, 1992.

Place, Jean-Michel. "Introduction." *L'Oeuf dur*. Paris: Editions Jean-Michel Place, 1975.

Polhemus, Robert M. "Dantellising Peaches and Miching Daddy, the Gushy Old Goof:

The Browning Case and *Finnegans Wake.*" *Joyce Studies Annual.* Austin: University of Texas Press, 1994.

———. "The Lot Complex: Rereading the End of *Finnegans Wake* and Rewriting Incest." In *Rereading Texts/Rethinking Critical Presuppositions.* Edited by Shlomith Rimmon-Kenan, Leona Toker, and Shuli Barzilai. New York: Peter Lang, 1996.

Potts, Willard, ed. *Portraits of the Artist in Exile: Recollections of James Joyce by Europeans.* Seattle: University of Washington Press, 1979.

———. "Joyce's Notes on the Gorman Biography." *icarbS* 4:2 (spring–summer 1981): 83–99.

Power, Arthur. Untitled essay. In *The Joyce We Knew.* Edited by Ulick O'Connor. Cork: Mercier, 1967.

———. *Conversations with James Joyce.* Edited by Clive Hart. Dublin: Millington, 1974.

Prevots, Naima. *The Mary Wigman Book: Her Writings.* Edited and translated by Walter Sorell. Middletown, Conn.: Wesleyan University Press, 1975.

Prince, Morton. *The Dissociation of a Personality.* New York: Longmans Green, 1913.

———. *Psychotherapy and Multiple Personality: Selected Essays.* Edited by Nathan G. Hale. Cambridge, Mass.: Harvard University Press, 1975.

———. *The Dissociation of a Personality: The Hunt for the Real Miss Beauchamp.* Edited by Charles Rycroft. New York: Oxford University Press, 1978.

Prinzhorn, Hans. *Artistry of the Mentally Ill: A Contribution to the Psychology and Psychopathology of Configuration.* Translated by Eric von Brockdorff. Berlin: Springer Verlag, 1972. Originally published 1922.

———. *Krisis der Psychoanalyse.* Leipzig: Der Neue Geist Verlag, 1928.

Probate Certificate no. 331 and Will of Lucia Anna Joyce; Family Division of High Court of Justice, Somerset House, London.

Probate Certificate no. 456 and Will of James Joyce, High Court Document 1942J.

Rabate, Jean Michel. "'Alphybettyformed Verbage': The Shapes of Sounds and Letters in *Finnegans Wake.*" *Word and Image* 2:3 (July–September 1986): 237–42.

Ragland-Sullivan, Ellie. "Lacan's Seminars on James Joyce: Writing as Symptom and Singular Solution." In *Compromise Formations: Current Directions in Psychoanalytic Criticism.* Edited by Vera J. Camden. Kent, Oh.: Kent State University Press, 1988.

Rather, Lois. *Lovely Isadora.* Oakland, Calif.: Rather Press, 1976.

Reavey, George. Papers. Harry Ransom Humanities Research Center, University of Texas at Austin.

Reizbaum, Marilyn. "Swiss Customs: Zurich's Sources for Joyce's Judaica." *James Joyce Quarterly* 27:2 (winter 1990): 203–18.

Renaud [Pseud.]. "Le Championnat d'amateurs de danse rythmique." *Chronique parisienne*, 1929. Clipping file, Rondelle Collection, Bibliothèque de l'Arsenal, Paris.

Reynolds, Mary T. "Joyce and Miss Weaver." *James Joyce Quarterly* 19:4 (1984): 373–403.

Rings, Werner. *Life with the Enemy: Collaboration and Resistance in Hitler's Europe, 1939–1945.* Translated by J. Maxwell Brownjohn. Garden City, N.Y.: Doubleday, 1982.

Ripa, Yannick. *Women and Madness: The Incarceration of Women in Nineteenth-Century France.* Translated by Catherine du Peloux Menage. Cambridge, Mass.: Polity Press, 1990.

Roatcap, Adela. *Raymond Duncan: Printer, Expatriate, Eccentric Artist.* San Francisco: Book Club of California, 1991.

Rome, Howard P. "The Classifications of Schizophrenia: A Historical Review." *Psychiatric Annals* 9:1 (January 1979): 12–31.

Rose, Nikolas. *Governing the Soul.* London: Routledge, 1990.

Rosenberg, Morris. *The Unread Mind: Unraveling the Mystery of Madness.* New York: Lexington Books, 1992.

Rosenthal, David. "Eugen Bleuler's Thoughts and Views about Heredity in Schizophrenia." *Schizophrenia Bulletin* 4:4 (1978): 476–77.

Rosenzweig, Saul. "The Identity and Idiodynamics of the Multiple Personality 'Sally Beauchamp': A Confirmatory Supplement." *American Psychologist* 45:1 (January 1988): 45–48.

Rudd, Niall. *Pale Green, Light Orange: A Portrait of Bourgeois Ireland, 1930–1950.* Dublin: The Lilliput Press, 1994.

Ruggiero, Paul. "James Joyce's Last Days in Zurich." In *Portraits of the Artist in Exile: Recollections of James Joyce by Europeans.* Edited by Willard Potts. Seattle: University of Washington Press, 1979.

Sargant, William, and Eliot Slater. *An Introduction to Physical Methods of Treatment in Psychiatry.* Baltimore: Williams and Wilkins, 1944.

Sass, Louis A. *Madness and Modernism: Insanity in the Light of Modern Art, Literature, and Thought.* New York: Basic Books, 1992.

Sax, D. "Lucy, Martyr (A.D. 304)." In *Relics and Shrines.* London: Allen and Unwin, 1985.

Scarry, Elaine. *The Body in Pain: The Making and Unmaking of the World.* New York: Oxford University Press, 1985.

———. *On Beauty and Being Just.* Princeton, N.J.: Princeton University Press, 1999.

Schaurek, Eileen Joyce. "'Pappy Never Spoke of Jim's Books.' Interview by Alice Curtayne." In *James Joyce: Interviews and Recollections.* Edited by E. H. Mikhail. New York: St. Martin's Press, 1990.

Scheper-Hughes, Nancy. *Saints, Scholars and Schizophrenics: Mental Illness in Rural Ireland.* Berkeley: University of California Press, 1979.

Schiaparelli, E. *Shocking Life.* New York: E. P. Dutton, 1954.

Scholes, Robert E., comp. *The Cornell Joyce Collection: A Catalogue.* Ithaca, N.Y.: Cornell University Press, 1961.

Schreber, Daniel Paul. *Memoirs of My Nervous Illness.* Edited by Richard Feldstein. Carbondale: University of Illinois Press, 1989.

Schwartzman, Myron. "Quinnigan's Quake: John Quinn's Letters to James Joyce, 1916 to 1920." *Bulletin of Research in the Humanities* 81:1 (summer 1978).

Scott, Bonnie Kime. *Joyce and Feminism.* Bloomington: Indiana University Press, 1984.

Scott, Sir Walter. *The Bride of Lammermoor.* New York: E. P. Dutton, 1979.

Sechehaye, Marguerite. *Reality Lost and Regained: Autobiography of a Schizophrenic Girl.* Translated by Grace Rubin-Rabson. New York: Grune and Stratton, 1951.

Seroff, Victor. *The Real Isadora.* New York: The Dial Press, 1971.

Sheets-Johnstone, M., ed. *Illuminating Dance: Philosophical Explorations.* Lewisburg, Pa.: Bucknell University Press, 1984.

Shloss, Carol. "Joyce's Will." *Novel: a forum on fiction* 6:24 (spring 1996).

———. "Milly, Molly, and the Mullingar Photo Shop: Developing Negatives in 'Calypso.'" In *"Ulysses"—En-Gendered Perspectives: Eighteen New Essays on the Episodes.* Edited by Kimberly J. Devlin and Marilyn Reizbaum. Columbia: University of South Carolina Press, 1999.

Slocum, John J., and Herbert Cahoon. *A Bibliography of James Joyce*. New Haven: Yale University Press, 1953.

Smoller, Sanford J. *Adrift Among Geniuses: Robert McAlmon: Writer and Publisher of the Twenties*. University Park: Pennsylvania State University Press, 1974.

Sorell, Walter. "Coach to Spoleto: Jean Erdman Discusses Her Variation on James Joyce's *Finnegans Wake*." *Dance Magazine* (May 1963): 35, 63.

———., ed. *The Dance Has Many Faces*. New York: Columbia University Press, 1966.

———. *Mary Wigman: Ein Vermächtnis*. Wilhelmshaven: Florian Noetzel, 1986.

Soupault, Philippe. "James Joyce." In *Portraits of the Artist in Exile: Recollections of James Joyce by Europeans*. Edited by Willard Potts. Seattle: University of Washington Press, 1979.

———. *Terpsichore*. Paris: Papiers, 1986.

Sparshott, Francis Edward. *Off the Ground: First Steps to a Philosophical Consideration of the Dance*. Princeton, N.J.: Princeton University Press, 1988.

Spector, Irwin. *Rhythm and Life: The Work of Jaques-Dalcroze*. Stuyvesant, N.Y.: Pendragon Press, 1990.

Spielberg, Peter, comp. *James Joyce's Manuscripts and Letters at the University of Buffalo: A Catalogue*. Buffalo, N.Y.: University of Buffalo Press, 1962.

Staley, Thomas. "James Joyce in Trieste." *Georgia Review* 16:4 (winter 1962): 446–49.

Stallybrass, Peter, and Allon White. *The Politics and Poetics of Transgression*. Ithaca, N.Y.: Cornell University Press, 1986.

Stauth, Georg, and Bryan S. Turner. *Nietzsche's Dance: Resentment, Reciprocity and Resistance in Social Life*. Oxford: Basil Blackwell, 1988.

Steyn, Stella. "A Retrospective View with an Autobiographical Memoir." In *Catalogue*. Edited by S. B. Kennedy. Dublin: Gorry Gallery, 1995.

"The Story of Adolph Kastor." In *Camillus*. New York: Camillus Cutlery Co., 1951.

Suleiman, Susan Rubin. *Subversive Intent: Gender, Politics and the Avant-Garde*. Cambridge, Mass.: Harvard University Press, 1990.

———. "(Re) Writing the Body: The Politics and Poetics of Female Eroticism." In *The Female Body in Western Culture*. Cambridge, Mass.: Harvard University Press, 1991.

Sullivan, Ellie Ragland. "Lacan's Seminars on Joyce." In *Compromise Formations: Current Directions in Psychoanalytic Criticism*. Edited by Vera Camden. Kent, Oh.: Kent State University Press, 1989.

Sullivan, Ellie Ragland, and R. B. Kershner. "More French Connections." *James Joyce Quarterly* 26:1 (fall 1988): 115–27.

Sullivan, Kevin. *Joyce Among the Jesuits*. New York: Columbia University Press, 1958.

Svevo, Livia Veneziani. *Memoir of Italo Svevo*. Translated by Isabel Quigly. London: Libris, 1989.

Szasz, Thomas. *The Myth of Mental Illness: Foundations of a Theory of Personal Conduct*. New York: Harper and Row, 1974.

Tacou-Rumney, Laurence. *Peggy Guggenheim: A Collector's Album*. Translated by Ralph Runney. Paris: Flammarion, 1996.

Taylor, Robert. "Dreaming Up the Life of Joyce's Daughter." *Boston Globe*, 16 June 1992, 63.

Teddy. "Rythme et couleur." *Petit Journal*. February 1927. Clipping file, Rondelle Collection, Bibliothèque de l'Arsenal, Paris.

Teichman, Jenny. *Illegitimacy: A Philosophical Examination*. Oxford, England: Basil Blackwell, 1982.

Thomson, Virgil. "Antheil, Joyce, and Pound." In *Virgil Thomson*. New York: Alfred A. Knopf, 1966.

Tillich, Paul. "Das Dämonische, ein Beitrag zur Sinndeutung der Geschichte." In *The Interpretation of History*. Translated by N. Z. Rasetzki. New York: Charles Scribner's Sons, 1936.

————. "Tanz und Religion." In *Impressionen und Reflexionen*. Stuttgart: Evangelisches Verlagswerk, 1972.

Tolstoy, Leo. *Russian Stories and Legends*. New York: Pantheon Books, 1967.

Tugal, Pierre. "Lubov Egorova: A Witness of a Glorious Past." *Dancing Times* 50:1 (June 1952): 527–28.

Tymoczko, Maria. *The Irish Ulysses*. Berkeley: University of California Press, 1994.

Tysdahl, B. J. *Joyce and Ibsen: A Study in Literary Influence*. Oslo: Norwegian Universities Press, 1968.

Valente, Joseph. "Beyond Truth and Freedom: The New Faith of Joyce and Nietzsche." *James Joyce Quarterly* 25:1 (fall 1987): 87–104.

Vanel, Hélène. "Souvenirs de Lucia Joyce." In *James Joyce*. Edited by Jacques Aubert and Fritz Senn. Paris: Editions de l'Herne, 1985.

Vignes, Henri. *Physiologie obstétricale, normale et pathologique*. Paris: Masson, 1923.

————. *Physiologie gynécologique et médecine des femmes*. Paris: Masson, 1929.

————. *La Durée de la grossesse et ses anomalies*. Paris: Libraires de l'Académie de médecine, 1933.

————. *Les Prématurés*. Paris: Masson, 1933.

————. *Maladies des femmes enceintes*. Paris: Masson, 1935.

————. *Périodes de fécondité et périodes de stérilité chez la femme*. Paris: Masson, 1938.

————. *Hygiène de la grossesse*. Paris: Masson, 1942.

————. *Eclampsie et eclampsisme: Maladies des femmes enceintes*. Paris: Masson, 1948.

————. *Le Sport chez la femme*. Paris: Masson, 1949.

————. *Les Douleurs de l'accouchement*. Paris, 1951.

Wagner, Richard. *Tristan und Isolde*. Stuttgart: Philipp Reclam, 1981.

Walcott, William. "Carl Jung and James Joyce: A Narrative of Three Encounters." *Psychological Perspectives* 1:1 (spring 1970): 21–31.

Warner, Richard. *Recovery from Schizophrenia: Psychiatry and Political Economy*. London: Routledge, 1994.

Watson, Richard B., and Randolph Lewis, comps. "The Joyce Calendar: A Chronological Listing of Unpublished and Ungathered Letters by James Joyce." In *Joyce Studies Annual*. Austin: University of Texas Press, 1992.

Watson, Richard B., with Randolph Lewis. *The Joyce Calendar: A Chronological Listing of Published and Ungathered Correspondence by James Joyce*. Austin, Tex.: Harry Ransom Humanities Research Center, 1994.

Wedekind, Franz. *Spring Awakening*. Translated by Edward Bond. London: Eyre Methuen, 1980.

————. *Diary of an Erotic Life*. Edited by Gerhard Hay. Translated by W. E. Yuill. Oxford, England: Basil Blackwell, 1990.

Weiss, Hedy. "*Lucia* Examines Love, Madness in the Joyces." *Chicago Sun-Times*, 13 March 1995, 35.

Welbourn, Richard. *History of Endocrine Surgery*. New York: Praeger, 1990.

Weld, Jacqueline. *Peggy: The Wayward Guggenheim*. New York: E. P. Dutton, 1986.

Wigman, Mary. Mary Wigman Papers. Archiv der Akademie der Künste, Berlin.

———. *The Language of Dance*. Translated by Walter Sorell. Middletown, Conn.: Wesleyan University Press, 1966.

Wile, Ira. *The Sex Life of the Unmarried Adult*. New York: The Vanguard Press, 1931.

Wolfe, Oscar. "Raymond Duncan: The Executive." *Dance Magazine* 30 (February 1930): n.p.

Wood, Mary E. *The Writing on the Wall: Women's Autobiography and the Asylum*. Champaign: University of Illinois Press, 1994.

Woolf, Virginia. *Mrs. Dalloway*. New York: Harcourt Brace Jovanovich, 1925.

———. *Three Guineas*. New York: Harcourt Brace Jovanovich, 1966.

———. *To the Lighthouse*. New York: Harcourt Brace Jovanovich, 1981.

Young, Julian. *Nietzsche's Philosophy of Art*. Cambridge, England: Cambridge University Press, 1992.

Zobli-Gerhardt, Maria. "Lucia: Die Tochter von Dichters." *Zürcher Tages Anzeiger*, 14 December 1982.

INDEX

Page numbers in *italics* refer to illustrations.

PERMISSIONS ACKNOWLEDGMENTS

Grateful acknowledgment is made to the following for permission to reprint previously published and unpublished material: for the Estate of Cary F. Baynes, Ximena de Angulo Roelli; for Samuel Beckett, *Dream of Fair to Middling Women*, Rights and Permissions, Calder Publications; for Kay Boyle, *My Next Bride*, *Being Geniuses Together*, and correspondence with Richard Ellmann, the Watkins / Loomis Agency; for the Estate of Padraic Colum, Maire O'Sullivan; for excerpts from "Reminiscences of a Joyce Niece" and interviews with Richard Ellmann, Bozena Berta Delimata; for Richard Ellmann Properties, Lucy Ellmann; for Zelda Fitzgerald, *Save Me the Waltz*, Rights and Permissions, Simon & Schuster; for Stuart Gilbert's Paris diary entries, James Emmons and the Harry Ransom Humanities Research Center at the University of Texas at Austin; for Stuart Gilbert, *Reflections on James Joyce: Stuart Gilbert's Paris Journal*, Rights and Permissions, University of Texas Press; for quotations from letters from Carola Giedion-Welcker to C. G. Jung, Professor Doktor Andres Giedion; for the Estate of Lucia Joyce, Edward Gretton, acting on behalf of the Estate of Jane Lidderdale; for the Estate of Carl Gustav Jung, Niedieck Linder AG, Zurich, Switzerland, acting in the name and on behalf of the Estate of C. G. Jung; for the Estate of Maria Jolas, Betsy Jolas; for James Knowlson, *Damned to Fame: The Life of Samuel Beckett*, James Knowlson; for the Estate of Paul Léon, Alexis Léon; for excerpts from André Levinson, *André Levinson on Dance: Writings from Paris in the Twenties*, Rights and Permissions, Wesleyan University Press; for Brenda Maddox, *Nora: The Real Life of Molly Bloom*, Brenda Maddox; for Niall Rudd, *Pale Green, Light Orange: A Portrait of Bourgeois Ireland, 1930–1950*, Anthony Farrell for the Lilliput Press of Dublin, Ireland; for Stella Steyn, "A Retrospective View with an Autobiographical Memoir," Thérèse Gorry for the Gorry Gallery, Dublin; for the Estate of Harriet Weaver, Edward Gretton for the Estate of Jane Lidderdale.

A NOTE ON THE AUTHOR

Carol Loeb Shloss teaches English at Stanford University. She has written extensively on Joyce and other modernists and is the author of three other books, including a study of Flannery O'Connor. She lives in Palo Alto, California.